Information Management:
Technologies and Methodologies

Information Management:
Technologies and Methodologies

Edited by Iker Morris

CLANRYE
INTERNATIONAL
www.clanryeinternational.com

Clanrye International,
750 Third Avenue, 9th Floor,
New York, NY 10017, USA

ISBN: 978-1-63240-615-6

Cataloging-in-Publication Data

Information management : technologies and methodologies / edited by Iker Morris.
    p. cm.
Includes bibliographical references and index.
ISBN 978-1-63240-615-6
1. Information resources management. 2. Information technology--Management.
3. Information storage and retrieval systems--Management. 4. Management information systems. I. Morris, Iker.
T58.64 .I54 2017
658.403 8--dc23

For information on all Clanrye International publications
visit our website at www.clanryeinternational.com

Printed in the United States of America.

Contents

Preface

Information management encompasses all the aspects of information acquiring, storage and retrieval that is significant to an organization. This book on information management takes into account the main pillars of this field which are data, systems, information technology and data-related processes. Information systems are capable of high speed computing and allow for organizations to take knowledgeable decisions. This book is compiled in such a manner, that it will provide in-depth knowledge about the theory and practice of information management. A number of latest researches have been included to keep the readers up-to-date with the global concepts in this area of study. This book is an essential guide for both academicians and those who wish to pursue this discipline further.

This book unites the global concepts and researches in an organized manner for a comprehensive understanding of the subject. It is a ripe text for all researchers, students, scientists or anyone else who is interested in acquiring a better knowledge of this dynamic field.

I extend my sincere thanks to the contributors for such eloquent research chapters. Finally, I thank my family for being a source of support and help.

Editor

The architecture of information in organisations

Author:
Tiko Iyamu[1]

Affiliation:
[1]Department of Informatics, Tshwane University of Technology, South Africa

Correspondence to:
Tiko Iyamu

Email:
Connectvilla@yahoo.com

Postal address:
PO Box 4155, Cape Town 8000

Over the last two decades competition amongst organisations including financial institutions has increased tremendously. The value of information is critical to competition in different organisations. In addition, the management of cost of delivery and cohesiveness of information flow and use in the organisations continue a challenge to information technology (IT). In an attempt to address these challenges, many organisations sought various solutions, including enterprise information architecture (EIA). The EIA is intended to address the needs of the organisation for competitive advantage.

This research article focused on the role of principles in the development and implementation of EIA. The article aimed to investigate how EIA could be best leveraged, exploited, or otherwise used to provide business value. The research brings about a fresh perspective and new methodological principles required in architecting the enterprise information.

Introduction

Enterprise information architecture (EIA) is one of the domains of enterprise architecture (EA). Other domains of EA include business, technical, infrastructure, application and service oriented architecture (The Open Group Architecture Forum [TOGAF]; Spewak 1992; Cook 1996; Zachman 1987). The different domains of EA are inter-related and depend on each other. This article focuses on the EIA, specifically, how principles are applied in the design, development and implementation of the domain. The EIA enables the management of change in information exchange, service and its strategic use in the organisation. According to Watson (2000), information architecture describes the structure of a system; categorises artefacts of the organisational systems; defines flow, value chain, usage and management. The EIA provides the framework (Burke 2007) for planning and implementing rich, standards-based, digital information infrastructure with well-integrated services and activities. The EIA is intended to provide categorisation, classification and definition of information required to perform the organisation's processes and activities, periodically. This argument is supported by other works including Yan and Bitmead (2003) and Oki *et al.* (1993). The EIA is also intended to manage and share information, and to ensure that the business is supported by applications and data as required by the organisation (Rafidah *et al.* 2007). The categorisation, classification and common definition of business information needs, and their associated functions, facilitates the system role definition and the modelling of optimal information flows. Furthermore, common terminology enables the consistent use of semantics of meaning across information systems and the entire organisation. This could be facilitated through the concept of reuse and mediation of local variations to a common ground. This ultimately helps the organisation to meet business objectives and goals by providing employees, stakeholders, partners and customers with improved access to quality information. This is carried out through the design, development and implementation stages as defined by the principles of the EIA.

Iyamu (2009) defined principles as 'guiding statements of position which communicate the fundamental elements, truths, rules, or qualities that must be exhibited by the organisation'. For the purposes of this article, this definition is adopted in the context of the EIA. The primary aim of the principles is to enforce and enable the organisation to take an incremental and iterative approach in transitioning to formal modelling. Dong and Agogino (2001) argued that principles influence immediate and consistent decision making in the organisation. The processes of design, development and implementation of the EIA is a challenge (Armour, Faisler & Bitner 2007), hence the formulation of principles.

The formulation of the EAI principles is guided by structured format. The format describes the attributes (such as name and rationale) of each principle. This is to ensure validity, completeness, comparability, relevance and consistency to the principle. Many formats and templates for formulating principles exist. According to Burke (2007), a principle constitutes name, statement, rationale and implication.

An obligatory passage point (OPP) could be adopted in the development and implementation of the EIA. OPP could help enforce the evaluation criteria discretely and comprehensively. OPP acts as a compulsory set of rules and regulations within a legal entity. Iyamu and Dewald (2010) refer to an OPP as a situation that forces actors (employees) to satisfy the interests that have been attributed to them by the focal actor (employer). The focal actor defines the OPP through which other actors must pass and by which the focal actor becomes indispensable. The principles of the EIA, could as such, be defined as the OPP through the implementation of individual performance contracts in which agreed upon tasks are carried out.

The research adopted the qualitative case study and interpretive approaches. A semi-structured interview method was applied in the collection of data. The data analysis and findings are presented in sections 3 and 4 respectively.

Research approach

A qualitative approach has been adopted in many studies such as Orlikowski and Baroudi (1991) in information systems primarily because of its suitability from a social perspective. Qualitative research was more suitable for this type of study as it allowed for the clarification from respondents to the research questions. Clarifications could instantly be sought to enrich the data. The qualitative research approach has been argued to be a very useful method in conducting complex research (Myers 1997). The approach is employed to help close interaction with interviewees and develop deeper understanding of the EIA situation in the organisation.

The author applied the case study method because it allows an in-depth exploration of the complex issues involved in this research (Yin 2003). Data sources included semi-structured interviews and documentation from the organisation where the research was conducted. The number of interviewees was based on saturation, implying a point where no new information was forthcoming during the interview process. The interviews were labelled CS01–CS09, to avoid disclosing the identities of the interviewees. The respondents were selected from various levels of the organisational structure within the Business and IT departments of the organisation. This was a key factor in achieving a true reflection of the design, development and implementation of EIA in the organisation.

The organisation researched in this study is a government institution. The organisation was reconstituted in 1994 immediately after the political shift in South Africa. At the time of the study the organisation had about 8000 employees of which 600 were contract workers at both senior and junior levels. The organisation was selected on the basis that it provided a good example of critical information in its processes and activities. The organisation also provided some evidence of information architecture design, development and implementation. The interviewees were selected from different units in both the business and IT departments. The selection of interviewees was based on their years of service in the organisation and knowledge of the EIA. This was to ensure that the interviewee had enough understanding of the environment and the use of information. A total of 17 employees were interviewed. The interviewees included directors (2), IT architects (4), business analysts (2), project managers (2), IT managers (3), business managers (2) and a database administrator.

The author formulated interview questions, which were intended to understand how the EIA was currently designed, developed and implemented and its impact on the organisation. The questions included:

- What are the factors influencing the development and implementation of the information architecture in the organisation?
- How is information architecture designed, developed and implemented in the organisation?
- What are some of the contributions of the information architecture in the organisation?
- What are some of the challenges of the information architecture in the organisation?

This article focuses on the principles that enforce the requirements, design, development and implementation of the EIA in the organisation. In such a context, an interpretive research approach (Walsham 2006) was appropriate in order to understand the adaptation and influences from the perspective of a sociotechnical context within the organisation.

Data analysis

For interpretation purposes the unit-based approach was used for the data analysis. This is primarily because it allows for analysis of a unit-by-unit basis in the study. The data collected from the case study was analysed at two levels, namely, macro and micro interconnected levels. The macro level (executive level) addresses the importance of information architecture to the organisations as well as the relationship between technical and nontechnical actors in the design, development and implementation of information architecture in the organisation. At the micro level (middle management and lower level), the impact of principles on the design, development and implementation of information architecture in the organisations was analysed. The remainder of this section presents and discusses the analysis of the data.

Information architecture provided a standard based design, development and implementation methodology that assisted IT to respond to the rapid changes in the processes of the organisation's business in the shortest time possible. Through principles, the EIA was used to achieve the translation of functional requirements to the selection of services, standards, components, configurations, phasing and the acquisition of products. In the organisation, an EIA approach was well received and appreciated more than other disciplines such as project management and systems analysis. Project management and systems analysis based approaches have been widely adopted over the last three decades in trying to solve the same problems, yet many of the challenges remain. Hence, there is a need to explore other approaches such as the EIA.

The EIA was used to provide an initial classification and definition of the information required to perform the goals and functions of the organisation. A framework was employed to manage and share information, and to ensure that the business was supported by applications that provided the needed data. Classification and common definition of business information needs and their associated functions were guided by the EIA principles. It facilitated system role definition and the modelling of the optimal information flow. In addition, the EIA was adopted to provide common terminology, which was intended to enable consistent semantic meaning across information systems and organisations by facilitating concept reuse and mediation of local variations to a common ground. This ultimately, was to help the organisation to meet its objectives and provide stakeholders with improved access to quality information. The majority of the interviewees agreed that this was the case and it was emphasised by one of the employees of the organisation:

'I would consider it to be a success due to the recognition it receives from across the organisation as bringing about important input in the information sharing, security and technology acquisition process of the organisation. However this success can be better measured by use of a capability maturity model.'

(Interviewee; CS04)

The organisation adopted a model as recommended by TOGAF for the creation of principles. The model illustrated in Box 1 was used in creating principles, which extend beyond organisational boundaries to external sources and targets including other government institutions. This was understood to enable rapid business decision-making and information sharing within the organisation, with suppliers, partners and customers.

The principles were intended to provide guidelines and rationales for constant examination and evaluation of information in the areas such as design, accessibility, security, use and maintenance. Some employees affirmed that the principles as applied guided the development and implementation of the information architecture in the organisation. Generally, the principles were derived from the vision of the organisation and an intensive discussion (in the form of a workshop) with senior IT and business

BOX 1: Format for creating principles.

Name: A name that majority can relate to, and reflects the intention and essence of the objective of the organisation. It is recommended to avoid ambiguous wording.

Statement: This is to communicate the fundamental rule as set by the organisation. The statement must be clear and unambiguous.

Rationale: Primarily to highlight the potential benefits for the organisation in adhering to the principle.

Implications: Highlight the potential implications on the business and information technology for executing the principles. This includes impact and consequences of adopting the principle.

management. They were later validated within the structures of the organisations. The principles were viewed as a starting point for subsequent decisions that affected the EIA in the organisation.

In the organisation, the EIA encouraged decision makers to explore externalisation, optimise information value chains, plan application portfolios, increase the velocity of information across the organisation and further evolved the enterprise architecture.

The EIA was treated as a business-strategy-driven set of artefacts that describes and model the information value network (e.g. information flows, business events and linkages) of the organisation. The EIA was sponsored and endorsed by senior management in IT and business departments. It extended beyond the organisational boundaries to external sources. In addition, it was targeted to enable rapid business decision-making and information sharing. The EIA included rationale and implications such as:

- a catalogue of authentic sources of information (e.g. public and private company databases, information regarding foreign offices and news media)
- classes of relevant business information and their value to the government and the organisation in particular
- information governance processes that supported policy development and information management principles and practices, which were intended to address security access, privacy, confidentiality, information quality, integrity, authenticity, archival cycles, business continuity planning, and ownership of information and processes
- information management deliverables that address roles, responsibilities and organisational structure for managing information content and delivery (e.g. information management and ownership).

The design, development and implementation of EIA aimed to establish the value and importance of using information effectively across the various units of the organisation, as well as the need to achieve collaborative excellence with external partners and customers (citizenry). The EIA approach was employed to gain consensus between the senior and middle management levels in the organisation, within the rationale and implications of the associated principles. Some of the elements considered include:

- strategic versus nonstrategic information, especially in terms of security
- the use and definition of common terms (e.g. service, consumption, citizens, etc.)
- who had the information and in what form and capacity
- who owns and manages information and how it should be leveraged
- who will be responsible for the cost of developing IT systems that will create and deliver information to the users and clients in the organisation and outside the organisation
- what metrics will be used to measure information sharing success (e.g. security, intelligence, revenue increase, cost decrease and reduced service delivery times).

An employee who thought otherwise stated as follows:

'The effective management and exploitation of information through IT is one key to business success, and the indispensable means to achieving the goals and objectives of the organisation is supposed to address this need by providing a strategic context for the evolution of the IT system in response to the constantly changing needs of the environment.'

(Interviewee; CS03)

The EIA was required to encourage decision makers both in the business and within IT to explore externalisation, optimisation of information value chains. This includes planning of application portfolios and incremental use of the velocity of information across the organisation in an iteration process. As a result, the development of the EIA conveys a logical sequence, which was based on relationships and dependencies of the elements within the scope, rather than a linear sequence of events. The rationale for the logical sequence in developing the EIA was as follows:

- as the model was essentially business-driven, the enterprise business architecture (EBA) had to first model the impact of business visioning on the operations of the business
- because the EIA focuses on how information could best be leveraged, exploited, or otherwise be used to provide business value, it was dependent on a certain amount of EBA modelling to determine how and where the business could derive its value
- the approach to enterprise technical architecture (ETA) depended on the business strategies and business information requirements, so this dependency placed it logically after EBA and EIA.

The focus of the study was on the EIA. However, without some analysis on other related domains, there would have been some disconnect in terms of the analysis as well as the findings leading to the results of the study.

In the organisation a four-domain approach as illustrated in Figure 1 was adopted. The arrows in Figure 1 illustrate the function of EBA that led to the development and implementation of EIA. In terms of the ETA and the other architecture disciplines, EBA, EIA, and EAA were also interdependent as they each evolved and new opportunities and requirements were identified.

In the organisation, the EIA was designed to depend on the EBA. As such, it was difficult to embark on the development of the EIA without first establishing the EBA. The EBA defines the real time information that passes between the key processes and the integration requirements. This was enabled by the underlying application and technical architectures across the units of the organisation.

The EBA was used to express the organisation's key business strategies and tactics, and their impact and interaction with business functions, processes and activities. Typically, it consisted of the current-state and future-state models of the functions, processes and information value chains of the organisation. The EBA led to the development of the EIA,

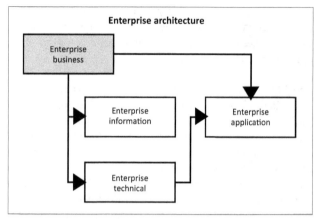

FIGURE 1: Relationship of enterprise application domains.

ETA and the enterprise application architecture (EAA). It defined the business design for sustainability and objectivity; those were the principles for its design. Hence, the EBA was intended to establish the foundations and details in the development of the EIA.

The development of the EIA began with the establishment of an overall information ecology in the organisation. Primarily it was intended to address the value proposition of the information and the processes and activities of the organisation.

Application portfolio decision-making was guided by the principles of both EBA and the EIA. This was used to identify the needed functionality and opportunities for reuse, also used to conceptualise the ETA architecture principles. The principles influenced the selection, design and implementation of software packages, application components and business objects.

Information architecture was intended to address the policy, governance and information products necessary for information sharing across the organisation, external partners and clients. This includes information management deliverables that address information management roles and responsibilities, information quality and integrity, data definition standards, data stewardship and ownership, and information security access. These objectives were within the scope of formulated principles. The principles were based on the vision of the organisation including the strategies of each of the units in the organisation.

Not all types of principles were necessarily identified in earlier paths through to the model. The basis for many principles was best practice-approaches that have consistently been demonstrated by diverse organisations to achieve similar results. Therefore, the degree to which the organisation could establish principles in the EIA was dependent on its process and capability to identify and apply best practice in each area.

The results from the analysis are articulated and presented in the next section.

Results

The focus is on how the EIA was designed, developed and implemented through a set of principles. The principles of the EIA provided guidance to the designers, developers and implementers of the EIA. The principles for each of the components of information architecture were derived from the organisation's vision and requirements. For each principle there was rationale that was documented along with other elements such as the statements of intent, repercussion for the intent and allocation of accountability.

Design principles

The EIA provided fundamental principles that assisted the organisation in achieving successful information. The factors included external partners and clients; a shared vision, change, evolutionary planning, classification and declassification, citizen empowerment, collaboration, problem coping, analysis, and restructuring organisational norms. These factors supported the implementation of processes and functions. Principles, which included interactive and interwoven, were formulated in order to achieve the objectives of the organisation. It began with the design principles.

The design principles guided the boundaries and limitations including the rationale and implication of the EIA in the organisation. It was based on both the short and long-term strategic intentions of the organisation. Table 1 depicts the guiding phenomena within which the design principles were formulated. The organisation customised the TOGAF format by adding the 'Ownership' column.

Some of the principles that were formulated and enforced as obligatory passage point (OPP) are as follows:

- information must be valued as an asset, leveraged across the information value chain to enhance competitive advantage and accelerate decision making in the organisation
- information must be shared to maximise the effectiveness of decision making throughout the organisation and to external partners, for citizens and other government departments
- the information value chain must continuously be identified and exploited within the organisation and the country in general
- the security of the categories of information must take priority above all requirements within the organisation and shared service with other organisations
- accessibility of information must be reviewed as frequently as possible
- data and information management must be unified across the organisation

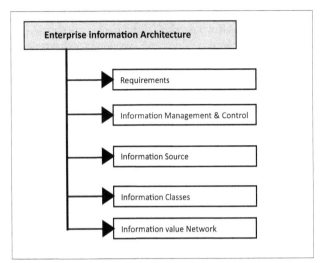

FIGURE 2: Enterprise information architecture design components.

- the organisation's data must be managed throughout its lifecycle by the appointment of data stewards and the definition and implementation of data management roles
- the interfaces across separate logical boundaries must be message-based and extend across the value-chain to employees, partners and customers
- the organisation's data must have accessible metadata which describes the definition, security classification, function class, ownership and stewardship
- leverage the business intelligence environment to accelerate decision-making and reduce development complexity.

Until the design is developed and implemented, it remains theoretical as to which adds no actual value to the organisation. This makes the next section, development principles, very critical.

Development principles

The aims and objectives of the EIA in the organisation included the reduction of integration complexity, control of duplication and replication, validation and correction at source, standards for information accessing and data isolation.

Based on these aims and objectives, the EIA was designed to address them in five categories as depicted in Figure 2.

As revealed in this study, each of these categories is explained in the following section (illustrated in Figure 2).

Requirements for information architecture

The principles to develop and implement an EIA were derived from the requirements and vision of the organisation.

TABLE 1: Design principles.

Design principles	Statement	Rationale	Implication	Ownership
Description	Indicate its identity, which it could be associated with.	Justification, expression of the value to the organisation.	For each principle, there must be an adopted standard, sometimes derived from best practices.	Each principle is allocation to individual or unit for execution and monitoring purposes.

The principles were formulated to legalise the scope and boundaries of each of the technical and nontechnical artefacts. In addition, the intended deliverables were also formulated to address roles, responsibilities and organisational structure for managing information content, including storage dissemination and delivery.

Information management and controls

The management and control of information required principles to ensure boundary and consistency across the organisation. The 'Management and Control' are statements of governance, monitoring, effectiveness and efficiency of information use, storage and ownership in the organisation. The principles were intended to address security access, privacy, confidentiality, quality, integrity, authenticity, archival cycles, business resumption planning, and ownership of information in the organisation.

Information sources

Within set principles, a catalogue of authentic information sources, such as the organisations' own databases, commercial databases, news media and government gazettes were used to establish the origins of authentic information on, about and for the organisation. It also formed the basis of input for the next step (information classes – as discussed later in the article), which obtained classes of relevant information and established their value to the organisation.

Information classes

There was a need for the classification of information in the organisation, primarily because it was the organisation's core business. The intention was to improve on information accessibility and manageability. This helped the stakeholders, including architects to understand the value of each category. Based on the requirements, information was classified according to the following criteria:

- functions (operational, managerial and strategic)
- business operations concerned with the operational (transactional) processing within the administration
- business management concerned with measurement (keeping score) and management of the administration
- business strategic in terms of planning for the future and identifying competitive opportunities.

Information value network

The information value network was one of the focal components of the principles of EIA in the organisation. An objective of the EIA was to define the sources of high-velocity information and ensure its availability and usage by the key business processes, enabled by the underlying EAA and ETA. High-velocity information was shared within the information value network of customers, suppliers, and partners in near real time, at both the transactional and decision support levels. This was to maximise operational effectiveness, efficiency, service delivery and high performance and competitive advantage.

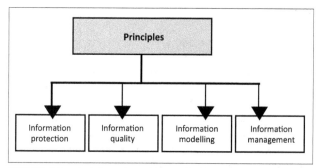

FIGURE 3: Enterprise information architecture implementation principles.

The value of information could be determined by different means, typically, the competitive advantage gained by the use of the information product. There where essentially three dimentions of information value, namely, (1) velocity, (2) density and (3) reach. Moving along one or more of these dimensions could have increased the value of information in the organisation.

Methods and tools such as 'information value network analysis' were used to diagnose problems or uncover opportunities to leverage information technology to create high value, low cost linkages with external parties and across the lines of business (LOB). The information value network describes the linkages in the network and the value of information across the business value chain. Seeing as information was an artefact of business processes, it surrounded and supported the physical value chain.

Principles were formulated to address the components of the EIA. Table 1 is an example of a template, which was used to record the design principles. This template could be populated and used to support strategic analysis over time.

The implementation of the entire design is summarised in four areas and enforced through a set of principles.

Implementation principles

The final phase of the EIA as a project was a gap analysis. This was conducted across all the categorised areas to determine corrective action, develop prioritised migration plans and finally draw up an implementation plan. The implementation enables the organisation to change current state to future state, as was defined during the project.

The primary and key components were implemented with the principles of the EIA and illustrated in Figure 3.

Information protection

Information shared across the organisation was regarded as corporate information and therefore demarcated to be managed accordingly. As revealed in the study, information accessibility and protection were a high priority in the organisation. Principles were therefore formulated to address ownership, security and accessibility classification, privacy, archival and recovery. This was intended to ensure the continuity of processes and activities in the organisation.

Information quality

The quality of information was based on business requirements. The quality of information was also principled to be governed in accordance to the requirements and vision of the organisation. The principles concentrated on the metadata, integrity, authenticity, classification and criticality of the organisation's information.

Information modelling

The principle stated '... an information model represents information in an understandable simplified format'. Information was to be modelled according to the principles of the EIA and the application development guidelines of the organisation.

Information management

The information management principles defined the roles, responsibilities and organisational structure required to implement the architecture of information in the organisation. It also defined, *inter alia*, the role that users play as custodians of information, the role of the IT department, and the roles of the Information Architect in ensuring that this principle was understood, adhered to, and effectively applied. There was an emphasis on the information architects as the domain owner.

Migration planning principles

The architects and other stakeholders in the organisation acknowledged positioning strategy and movement from one architectural phase to another as a very complex issue. It was much more complex than simply bringing in a new vendor or independent consultant to provide theoretical underpinning and advisory guidance.

One of the key decision processes involved with architectural planning was the need to have a future target. Shorter-term goals could then be defined as stepping-stones to the strategic goal. The problem here, again, was that historically, information technologists have not been very accurate in predicting product directions and timing. The migration principles were formulated based on the context of the organisation. During the implementation, gaps were identified and analysed for possible opportunities and solutions.

Measurement and validation

The principles of measurement and validation were an integral component of the overall EIA in the organisation. They were a set of obligations for the management,

BOX 2: Architecture conformance checklist of principles.

> 1. Organisation planning: The component ensures the alignment of requirements and vision with the information architecture. It specifies the core information areas, dependencies, implication, rationale and ownership.
>
> 2. Business analysis: It ensures that the business analysis addresses the business model including the impacts, duplications and change management. It ensures that the business information conform guidance such as protection, ownership, accessibility and classification as defined in the Information Management Principles.
>
> 3. Systems analysis: The systems analysis component covers the systems model. It ensures conformance to modelling guidelines, quality in terms metadata, integrity, authenticity and classification as defined by the respective principles.
>
> 4. Systems design: This ensures the adherence information architecture principles and information policies, standards, management roles and responsibilities.

administration, practices of information storage and usage in the organisation. The measures included a conformance checklist, the iterative process and domain architect who oversee the processes and activities within the scope of the EIA.

There were four main components, namely (1) Enterprise Planning, (2) Business Analysis, (3) Systems Analysis and (4) Systems Design, which constituted the Information architecture conformance checklist in the organisations. These components were a defined set of principles, within the organisational meaning and value, as described in Box 2.

Gap analysis

The gap analysis assessed the current state of the information architecture against the desired state as reflected by the drivers (business requirements). This assessment was an iterative and ongoing process and was reflected by a conformance checklist and an accompanying action plan as depicted in Box 2. These assessments were to be stored and managed within the agreed principles. Table 2 provides an example of the gap analysis.

There were a large number of constraints that had to be overcome to achieve full implementation of the EIA. As revealed in the study, some of these constraints include:

- the inherited technological environment that existed at the initiation of the process
- new technologies constantly emerging that must be accommodated
- immediate concerns such as providing information technology support for a new headquarters building
- the fact that any information systems architecture is always in transition and is ever changing and evolving.

Findings

From the results and analysis of the data, five factors were found to be key in the approach to deploying EIA through principles. The factors are presented as follows.

TABLE 2: Gap analysis.

Gap analysis.	Requirement (future state)	Action plan	Deliverables	Roles and responsibility
Description	Eradicate uncontrolled data duplication and redundancy	Project to be initiated	Project scope and migration plan	Project manager information architect

The criticality of principles

Within the domains of EA, fundamental principles were provided to assist in achieving change. This includes developing a shared vision, evolutionary planning, and provision for innovations, empowerment and regular training of employees, analysis, and restructuring organisational norms to support implementation and ongoing learning and processes of EA. These principles must be interactive and are interwoven throughout the process of Enterprise Architecture. According to one of the senior managers:

'The principle that we formulate help us to be consistent [sic], in fact it leads to the development and deployment of consistent, multiple software- and technology-based changes in the business, and amalgamation of both the IT and the business.'

(Interviewee; CS01)

Iterative process

Within the scope of the EIA, principles were articulated to address the information aims and objectives of the organisation in an iterative process. Some of the primary objectives included encouraging decision makers to:

- explore external trading and partnerships
- optimisation of information value chains
- plan application architectures and systems portfolio
- increase information velocity across the organisation.

Through the iterative approach, EIA was intended to identify the information flows for optimisation (increased velocity, density and reach) as well as the information entities. This was to define and consistently use information across the value chain. The intention was to increase the value of information across the organisation and the external transactions.

Thus, the EIA defined the sources of information and ensured the availability and usage of this information by the key business processes, and enabled the underlying application and technical architectures. Similar to the EBA domain, it was expected to provide guidance for business operations impacted by particular business strategies. The EIA was also expected to provide guidance concerning the organisation information assets to knowledge workers, information processors, IT application developers, infrastructure managers, and executives.

Information architect

Within the boundaries of set principles, the information architect's focus was on the construction of information models to meet business requirements and engineering 'out' gaps where business-critical, high-velocity information was not reaching customers, suppliers, and partners. The EIA models provided guidance concerning the organisation's information assets to knowledge workers, information processors, IT application developers, infrastructure managers, and the executives. However, there was a serious concern in terms of the availability of skilled information architects. The head of the architecture team explained:

'One of the primary objectives is to reduce cost. It could be used to achieve significant organisational advantage over competitors in a competitive marketplace. If we have qualified architects, we are expected to put in place process effectiveness and efficiencies arising from the eliminations of non-value adding and redundant tasks, streamlined information flow, systems placement, and business restructuring.'

(Interviewee; CS06)

Ownership

Data, storage, process, infrastructure and collaboration, were the principles of information architecture, which were allocated to individuals and units in the IT department. Through the irreversible nature of the OPP, the formulated principles were enforced. Primarily, it gave power to those people whom the design, development and implementation tasks were allocated. The OPP made each principle in all units irreversible by individuals or groups, irrespective of their positions in the organisation.

Stock of knowledge

The stock of knowledge was not necessarily as valuable as it was difficult to translate its value to usefulness in some cases and units in the organisation.

The role of the EIA was often misunderstood. It was difficult to differentiate between business analyst and information architects. As a result, the allocation of task, roles and responsibilities became a challenge to manage.

Conclusion

Enterprise information architecture (EIA) offers tangible benefits to the enterprise and those responsible for evolving the enterprise through its principles. The primary purpose of the principles is to *inform, guide,* and *constrain* decisions for the enterprise, especially those related to information flow. The true challenge of enterprise engineering is to maintain the information as a primary authoritative resource for enterprise IT planning. This goal is met via enforced EIA principles, which add value and utility of the information to the Enterprise Architecture.

The benefits as emphasised are of paramount importance to business and IT managers in organisations as well as in the academic domain. The study contributes to the body of knowledge through its empirical evidence. In addition, the findings open opportunity to researchers for further research areas, such as social construction of information, semiotics integration of information architecture into business strategy and the ontology of information architecture.

Applying EIA objectives through its principles within the context of a specific business enterprise enables an organisation to create a joint business and IT planning and execution processes. The integration of business and IT planning could result in faster time to market, increase customer intimacy, and improve operational efficiency through the set principles.

References

Armour, F., Kaisler, S. & Bitner, J., 2007, 'Enterprise Architecture: Challenges and Implementations', in *Proceedings of the 40th International Conference on System Sciences*, Maui, Hawaii, January 3–6, 2007, pp. 217–217.

Burke, B., 2007, 'The Role of Enterprise Architecture in Technology Research', in *Gartner Inc.*, viewed 14 April 2008, from http://www.gartner.com/technology/research.jsp

Cook, M.A., 1996, *Building Enterprise Information Architectures: Reengineering Information systems*, Prentice-Hall, New York.

Dong, A. & Agogino, M., 2001, 'Design Principles for the Information Architecture of a SMET Education Digital Library', in *Proceedings of the ACM+IEEE Joint Conference on Digital Libraries*, Virginia, USA, June 24–28, 2010, pp. 314–321.

Iyamu, T., 2009, 'Strategic Approach used for the Implementation of Enterprise Architecture: A Case of Two Organisations in South Africa', in *Proceedings of the International conference on Informatics and Semiotics in Organisations*, Beijing, China, April 11–12, 2009, pp. 100–108. doi:10.4018/jantti.2010071601

Iyamu, T. & Dewald, R., 2010, 'The use of Structuration and Actor Network Theory for analysis: A Case Study of a Financial Institution in South Africa', *International Journal of Actor-Network Theory and Technological Innovation* 2(1), 1–26.

Myers, M.D., 1997, 'Qualitative Research in Information Systems', *MIS Quarterly* 21(2), 241–242. doi:10.2307/249422

Oki, B.M., Pflugl, M., Siegel, A. & Skeen, D., 1993, 'The Information Bus: An Architecture for Extensible Distributed Systems', *ACM SIGCOMM Computer Communication Review* 27(5), 58–68.

Orlikowski, W. & Baroudi, J. J., 1991, 'Studying Information Technology in Organizations: Research Approaches and Assumptions', *Information Systems Research* 2(1), 1–31. doi:10.1287/isre.2.1.1

Rafidah Abd.Razak, A.F, Dahalin, M.Z., Dahari, R., Kamaruddin, S.S. & Abdullah, S., 2007, 'Enterprise Information Architecture (EIA): Assessment of Current Practices in Malaysian Organizations', in *Proceedings of the 40th Hawaii International Conference on System Sciences*, Maui. Hawaii, January 3–6, 2007, pp. 219–227, Maui, Hawaii.

Spewak, S.H., 1992, *Enterprise Architecture Planning: Developing a Blueprint for Data, Applications and Technology*, John Wiley & Sons Inc., New York.

The Open Group Forum (TOGAF), *What is Enterprise Architecture?*, viewed 28 November 2008, from http://www.realirm.com/enterprise-architecture

Walsham, G. (2006). Doing Interpretive Research. *European Journal of Information Systems* 15(3), 320–330. doi:10.1057/palgrave.ejis.3000589

Watson, R.W., 2000, 'An enterprise information architecture: A Case Study for Decentralized Organizations', in *Proceedings of the 33rd Hawaii International Conference on System Sciences*, Maui, Hawaii, January 4–7, 2000, pp. 1–10.

Yan, J. & Bitmead, R.R., 2003, 'Coordinated control and information architecture', in *Proceedings of the 42nd IEEE Conference on Decision and Control*, Maui, Hawaii, December, 2003, pp. 3919–3923.

Yin, R.K., 2003, *Case Study Research, Design and Methods*, Sage Publications, California.

Zachman, J.A., 1987, 'A framework for information systems architecture', *IBM Systems Journal* 26(3), 276–292. doi:10.1147/sj.263.0276

2

The Development of the IMIA Knowledge Base

Author:
Graham Wright[1]

Affiliation:
[1]Faculty of Health Sciences, Walter Sisulu University, South Africa

Correspondence to:
Graham Wright

Email:
profwright@gmail.com

Postal address:
PO Box 294, Bathurst 6166, South Africa

Background: The discipline of health or medical informatics is relatively new in that the literature has existed for only 40 years. The British Computer Society (BCS) health group was of the opinion that work should be undertaken to explore the scope of medical or health informatics. Once the mapping work was completed the International Medical Informatics Association (IMIA) expressed the wish to develop it further to define the knowledge base of the discipline and produce a comprehensive internationally applicable framework. This article will also highlight the move from the expert opinion of a small group to the analysis of publications to generalise and refine the initial findings, and illustrate the importance of triangulation.

Objectives: The aim of the project was to explore the theoretical constructs underpinning the discipline of health informatics and produce a cognitive map of the existing understanding of the discipline and develop the knowledge base of health informatics for the IMIA and the BCS.

Method: The five-phase project, described in this article, undertaken to define the discipline of health informatics used four forms of triangulation.

Results: The output from the project is a framework giving the 14 major headings (Subjects) and 245 elements, which together describe the current perception of the discipline of health informatics.

Conclusion: This article describes how each phase of the project was strengthened, through using triangulation within and between the different phases. This was done to ensure that the investigators could be confident in the confirmation and completeness of data, and assured of the validity and reliability of the final output of the 'IMIA Knowledge Base' that was endorsed by the IMIA Board in November 2009.

Background

The author undertook this research over a four-year period with a number of collaborators in five discrete phases, which utilised quantitative and qualitative approaches. The discipline of health or medical informatics is relatively new in that the literature has existed for only 40 years. The British Computer Society (BCS) health group was of the opinion that work should be undertaken to explore the scope of medical or health informatics. A qualitative approach was used to gather expert opinion and construct a cognitive map of the discipline of health informatics. Once the mapping work was completed the International Medical Informatics Association (IMIA) expressed a wish to develop it further to define the knowledge base of the discipline and produce a comprehensive internationally applicable framework. Various data extraction methods were then used to identify the most commonly used keywords in the health informatics published literature followed by a consensus method to produce a final framework and knowledge base. This mixed method approach was adopted as a pragmatic means to address the development of what the discipline considered the current knowledge base and thus a reflection of the thoughts and publications of the discipline. The work was overseen by an International Research Advisory Board and refereed by Professor Lorenzi on behalf of the IMIA Board and General Assembly.

Research problem

The discipline of health informatics had not been formally defined and many definitions of the discipline have emerged in the literature. Not only was there a lack of agreed definition in that the discipline was variously called: health informatics, medical informatics, clinical informatics and latterly bioinformatics, but the scope of the discipline had not been adequately defined. Some of the consequences included misunderstandings regarding standards and use of terminology, lack of consistency within educational curriculum and a lack of a framework for defining skills and workforce requirements.

Objectives

The aim of the project was to explore the theoretical constructs underpinning the discipline of health informatics and produce a cognitive map (Eden & Ackermann 2004) of the existing understanding of the discipline.

Subsequent aims of the project were to develop the knowledge base of health informatics, which was seen as central to the IMIA strategy (Murray 2008; Lorenzi 2007), and to undertake the task of exploring the current perceptions of the Health Informatics community as to the scope of the discipline.

Method

The project's international advisory board of health informatics experts provided advice on the methods that were used and facilitated access to source materials. The mixed methods used in the project were:

- a consensus conference using a cognitive mapping exercise
- workshops to verify international interpretation
- extraction of keywords from the entire published index papers on health informatics using computer software packages and techniques
- workshop to examine keywords and exclude terms
- voting in of keywords by international volunteers using a voting system based in an Excel spreadsheet.

The aim was to obtain different perspectives (data) on the issue of mapping the discipline of health informatics with the belief that the analysis would provide confidence and confirmation that the data was complete and the final outcomes from all the phases of the project were not just artefacts of one particular method of data collection or analysis. This process of data gathering and systematic analysis reflects the principles of grounded theory where the researcher begins with an area of study and allows the theory to emerge from the data. In this project the area of study was the discipline of health informatics and the knowledge base was derived from data systematically gathered and analysed through the research processes undertaken (Strauss & Corbin 1998).

Wolf (2010) in a recent article says the final consideration in using a mixed method approach is 'to consider thoroughly whether to engage in triangulation, and if doing so, to use tailor-made triangulation strategies fitted to the research questions and interests'.

The project undertaken to define the discipline of health informatics used all four forms of triangulation (Denzin 1970) and this article describes how each phase of the project triangulated with the other phases for confirmation and completeness of data, and validation and verification of the project outputs.

Triangulation is a strategy to 'overcome the intrinsic bias that comes from single methods, single observer and single theory studies' (Patton 1990). Its objective is the confirmation and completeness of data through cross checking data from several sources to seek out consistencies in the data (Begley 1996; O'Donoghue & Punch 2003). Many researchers also advocate triangulation as a means of resolving the quantitative and/or qualitative question through integrating the two approaches in one study and contributing to methodological rigor in order to validate the findings (Begley 1996; Cohen *et al.* 1994).

Denzin (1970) identified four forms of triangulation: data, investigator, theoretical and methodological. Data triangulation involves gathering data using different sampling strategies, so that segments of data are collected at various times, social situations and with different people. Investigator triangulation requires the use of more than one researcher in collecting and interpreting data. Using more than one theoretical position for data interpretation is called theoretical triangulation, whereas the most common form of triangulation, methodological triangulation, refers to the use of more than one method of data collection.

The ability to generalise findings to wider groups is one of the most common tests of validity for quantitative research. Triangulation is typically a strategy for improving the validity and reliability of research findings. Patton (2002:247) advocates the use of triangulation stating 'triangulation strengthens a study by combining methods'. However, the idea that triangulation is simply the combination of different methods of investigation is a restricted one, and researchers need to increase their use of the other less frequently employed forms of triangulation. When using triangulation of methods, researchers should also reflect on whether the use of within-method triangulation would be advantageous to their project. Within-method triangulation involves using dissimilar aspects of the same method in one study; for example, a questionnaire might contain two different scales to measure emotions. Between-method triangulation involves using different research methods, for example a questionnaire and observation to collect data (Bryman 2003; Begley 1996). Sequential use of quantitative and qualitative methods may also be more effective for some projects rather than simultaneous use, which do not permit the development and refinement of the methodologies. The deliberate use of multiple data sources and methods to cross-check and validate findings, should pervade all projects and lead to the objective of confirmation. Triangulation should be chosen intentionally, and a description of its rationale, planning and implementation is essential in project reports to give authority to triangulation and the project outcomes (Begley 1996).

The project explored the theoretical constructs underpinning the discipline of health informatics. The early project work was situated within a theoretical educational framework. Bloom's taxonomy affords a hierarchical scheme for categorising levels of complexity for objectives within educational settings (Bloom *et al.* 1984). It also overlays well against other academic levels, such as the progression from undergraduate to postgraduate levels (Furst 1981; Seddon 1978).

Bloom classified three domains of educational activity (Forehand 2005):

1. cognitive, describing knowledge and mental skills
2. affective, describing attitude, feelings and emotions
3. psychomotor, describing manual or physical skills.

Bloom identified six levels of educational objectives within the cognitive domain; from the lowest level, knowledge, through comprehension, application, analysis, synthesis and evaluation (Forehand 2005; Anderson *et al.* 2001). The first phase of the project was a mapping exercise that was based on these concepts.

The five phases of the project
Consensus conference

The 2005 Consensus conference was an intensive 24-hour workshop involving small group and plenary discussions, with participants and researchers in residence overnight. There were 24 invited participants drawn from a sample frame that had professions down one axis and organisations across the other. Organisations included health providers, family medicine, ASSIST the IT professions union, a number of United Kingdom (UK) health informatics groups and the IMIA; the world body for health and medical informatics. Most of the participants were from the UK whilst others came from Europe, Australia, South Africa and the USA. The conference aimed to capture all the elements of the discipline of health informatics and also the broad themes or subject areas into which these elements could be grouped. Within small groups, participants listed the main subject areas or themes from their own curricula, knowledge and experience. Then again within small groups they identified smaller elements of the subject areas. Finally, in a whole group activity, participants assigned each element to a subject area and a level from Bloom's cognitive domain (Forehand 2005) where possible. The discussions resulted in a first data set comprising 221 elements, grouped into 13 themes that varied in size, with the smallest containing six elements and the largest 37. It was recognised that the largest theme, the 'Toolkit', which consists of IT skills and knowledge of IT processes, would likely be divided following further discussions, which subsequently happened during a 24 hour workshop in Belfast.

This consensus conference therefore used group activities as its research methodology to produce lists of elements grouped into themes. There were six researchers involved in facilitating the group and plenary activities, thus adding investigator triangulation to reduce a single researcher bias.

Workshops to verify international interpretation

Workshops were conducted in 2005 at two major health informatics conferences, the European Federation for Medical Informatics (MIE 2005) in Geneva and the American Medical Informatics Association (AMIA 2005) in Washington DC. They were short workshops and hence only explored the overall concept and the clinical informatics theme. Participants commented that there were no major issues with either the methodology used in phase one or the initial outcomes that should modify the direction of the project. These workshops therefore used investigator triangulation in that three of the original six investigators were present at the European workshop and two at the American workshop. The investigators were therefore a subset of the original research team employing both data triangulation in that data was gathered using a different sampling strategy, in other words, those international conference participants who chose to attend the workshop and methodological triangulation as the method here was not to create themes and elements but rather take that data and refine it through smaller and shorter validation workshops. Another workshop to validate the outputs was held in Belfast in 2007 after the January 2007 workshop in London highlighted the size of the toolkit. This meeting focused on refining the technical and computing themes previously developed in phase one and successfully affirmed the two technical themes 'Computer Science for Health Informatics (ICT for Health) and Computer Systems Applications in Health (toolkit)'. Thus the large toolkit theme was logically separated and participants from computer science who had expressed concern that the single large theme did not reflect the computer science heading system were the main re-shapers of the two new themes. The resulting themes are:

- computer science for health informatics (ICT for Health)
- health and social care processes
- health (care) records
- health and social care industry
- health informatics standards
- knowledge domains and knowledge discovery
- legal and ethical
- people in organisations
- politics and policy
- technologies for health
- terminology, classification and grouping
- uses of clinical information
- using informatics to support clinical healthcare governance
- computer systems applications in health (Toolkit).

Extraction of keywords from the available published index papers on health informatics using computer software packages and techniques

Scopus is the largest abstract and citation database of research literature and quality web sources with smart tools to track, analyse and visualise research. A search of Scopus was undertaken using a set of keywords that are descriptors of Informatics. The project's International Advisory Board agreed that the following key words should be used:

- health informatics
- medical informatics
- clinical informatics
- nursing informatics
- pharmacy informatics
- dental informatics.

The keywords within each article of the Reference Manager 11 database were exported as a series of files and then imported one at a time to an Excel spreadsheet as in the raw data format the total number of keywords extracted exceeded the number of rows available in an Excel worksheet.

After processing the data to count the number of occurrences of each keyword a master list of some 10 000 different keywords were identified, many of which were just English terms rather than health informatics specific, for example the authors place of abode and conference venue or country of study. The use of keywords in many publications depends on author choice and often reflects the wish to have the article seen as being in a particular theme or subject area. This is particularly so with those conferences that identify themes for the submission of papers.

This activity produced a new set of data and so triangulated with phase one of the project that also produced raw data. In itself it was preparatory work for the next two phases of the project.

Workshop to examine and exclude keywords

The next phase of the project refined and reduced the raw data by removing keywords not directly associated with health informatics. The lists of keywords were given to information specialists, grouped into teams of three, at a workshop in London, UK in January 2007. The groups considered each word and excluded any that were not thought to be a health informatics term. Each word was tagged with the number of occurrences it had in the search. At the same time, keywords were assessed to see if they would fit into the existing cognitive map from the phase one workshop (Table 1).

The participants in the workshop reduced the list of 10 000 words to 444. The number of occurrences found in the literature search ranked each keyword on the spreadsheet and small focus groups excluded words unconnected with health informatics. The remaining 444 words appeared to be connected with areas of health informatics as opposed to being just English words and phrases used to describe the content of the papers.

Voting in of keywords by international volunteers using a voting system based in an Excel spreadsheet

An Excel spreadsheet was constructed with a list of the keywords from which participants were invited to chose (vote in) those that were associated with health informatics. The complete spreadsheet together with the instructions and examples of how to vote was emailed to the International Advisory Board, the IMIA working groups, the BCS specialist

groups, and the European Federation for Medical Informatics (EFMI) working groups.

The voting was conducted with all of the keywords listed on the spreadsheet and a choice box next to each. The 444 keywords were divided into groups and each group was given a range of letters, A to G, H to M, N to R, and S to Z. Participants were asked to complete the group that contained the initial letter of their surname. Thus, as an example, Heather Carter voted on the columns A to G and Peter Ross voted on columns N to R.

Participants voted for about 100 words in their group. They were asked to vote for the keywords they thought were health informatics terms and classify them according to which phase one theme they thought the keyword belonged with by putting the number of the theme next to the word on the spreadsheet. Keywords that were consistently chosen were added to the original phase one cognitive map. These final two phases used methodological triangulation to refine the data and match it with the output of the first two phases: the phase one workshop and the international interpretation workshops.

Results

The final spreadsheet, which forms the basis of the IMIA Knowledge Base, was constructed from the outcomes of the original phase one workshop, the subsequent phase to check international interpretation, a review and content analysis of the literature, and a two-phase refinement following the extraction of keywords from the entire electronic published papers on health informatics. The different phases to the project in all took:

- data from different sources (people and electronic papers) – data triangulation
- used different research methodologies (workshops, electronic searches, electronic analysis, electronic voting) – methodological triangulation
- information from different investigators (one primary investigator, with five secondary investigators) – investigator triangulation
- from different theoretical positions (grounded theory, educational theory) – theoretical triangulation.

Conclusion

Through using mixed modes of research within and between the different phases of the project the investigators and subsequently the IMIA Board and General Assembly can be confident in the confirmation and completeness of the data through cross confirmation and validation from more than one data source

TABLE 1: Illustrating how keywords fit into the 'theme' and 'element' framework and the number of occurrences of each keyword in the literature.

Theme	Uses of clinical information	Number of times tagged in search
Element	Data analysis and statistical presentation	-
Keyword	Automatic data processing	78
Keyword	Analysis	635

Triangulation strengthened the project and ensured the validity and reliability of the project outcomes. The endorsement of the 'IMIA Knowledge Base' took place at the IMIA Board and General Assembly meetings of IMIA in July 2010. The final report and spreadsheet are available on the IMIA website in the section on IMIA Endorsed Documents (Wright 2009).

The initial outputs from phase one have been used in a number of ways including to help formulate an undergraduate biomedical informatics degree programme (Pritchard-Copley et al. 2006) and as a framework to classify scientific papers for the European Federation for Medical Informatics (EFMI) conferences.

Acknowledgements

The author wishes to acknowledge the invaluable contributions of the CHIRAD health informatics team and in particular Dr Helen Betts and Dr Peter Murray, the BCS, the IMIA, and the many colleagues in the international health and medical informatics communities who contributed to the various stages of the project.

Author competing interests

I declare that I have no financial or personal relationship(s) which may have inappropriately influenced me in writing this paper.

References

Anderson, L., Krathwohl, D., Airasian, P., Cruikshank, K., Mayer, R., Pintrich, P., et al., 2001, A taxonomy for learning, teaching, and assessing: A revision of Bloom's taxonomy of educational objectives, abridged edn., p. 302, Longman, New York.

Begley, C., 1996, 'Using triangulation in nursing research', Journal of Advanced Nursing 24, 122–128. doi:10.1046/j.1365-2648.1996.15217.x, PMid:8807387

Bloom, B., Masia, B. & Krathwohl, D., 1984, Taxonomy of educational objectives, Longman, London.

Bryman, A., 2003, 'Triangulation', The Sage encyclopedia of social science research methods, Sage, Thousand Oaks, CA.

Cohen, L., Manion, L. & Morrison, K., 1994, Research methods in education, Routledge, London/New York.

Denzin, N., 1970, The research act in sociology: A theoretical introduction to sociological methods, Butterworths, London.

Eden, C. & Ackermann, F., 2004, 'Cognitive mapping expert views for policy analysis in the public sector', European Journal of Operational Research 152, 615–630. doi:10.1016/S0377-2217(03)00061-4

Forehand, M., 2005, Bloom's taxonomy: Original and revised. Emerging perspectives on learning, teaching, and technology, 1–9.

Furst, E., 1981, 'Bloom's taxonomy of educational objectives for the cognitive domain: Philosophical and educational issues', Review of educational research 51, 441. doi:10.2307/1170361, doi:10.3102/00346543051004441

Lorenzi, N., 2007, 'Towards IMIA 2015-the IMIA Strategic Plan', Yearbook of medical informatics, 1–5.

Murray, P., 2008, 'The IMIA strategic plan-towards IMIA 2015', Yearbook of medical informatics, 7–15.

O'Donoghue, T. & Punch, K., 2003, Qualitative educational research in action: Doing and reflecting, Routledge, Abingdon, Oxon, UK.

Patton, M., 2002, Qualitative research and evaluation methods, Sage, Newbury Park, CA.

Patton, M., 1990, Qualitative evaluation and research methods. 2nd edn., Sage, Newbury Park, CA.

Pritchard-Copley, A., De Lusignan, S., Rapley, A. & Robinson, J., 2006, 'Towards a benchmarking statement for biomedical informatics', Current Perspectives in Healthcare Computing 20–22.

Seddon, G., 1978, 'The properties of Bloom's taxonomy of educational objectives for the cognitive domain', Review of educational research 48, 303. doi:10.2307/1170087, doi:10.3102/00346543048002303

Strauss, A. & Corbin, J., 1998, Basics of qualitative research: Techniques and procedures for developing grounded theory, Sage Publications, Inc., Thousand Oaks, CA.

Wolf, F., 2010, 'Enlightened Eclecticism or Hazardous Hotchpotch? Mixed Methods and Triangulation Strategies in Comparative Public Policy Research', Journal of Mixed Methods Research 4, 144. doi:10.1177/1558689810364987

Wright, G., 2009, 'IMIA Knowledge Base' in Imia knowledge base final 09 (ed.), viewed 03 February 2011 from, http://imia.org/endorsed/IMIA_Knowledge_Base-final09.xls

3

Presenting a framework for knowledge management within a web-enabled Living Lab

Authors:
Lizette de Jager[1]
Albertus A.K. Buitendag[1]
Jacobus S. van der Walt[1]

Affiliations:
[1]Department of Computer Science, Tshwane University of Technology, South Africa

Correspondence to:
Lizette de Jager

Email:
dejagerL@tut.ac.za

Postal address:
Private Bag X680, Pretoria 0001, South Africa

Background: The background to this study showed that many communities, countries and continents are only now realising the importance of discovering innovative collaborative knowledge. Knowledge management (KM) enables organisations to retain tacit knowledge. It has many advantages, like competitiveness, retaining workers' knowledge as corporate assets and assigning value to it. The value of knowledge can never depreciate. It can only grow and become more and more valuable because new knowledge is added continuously to existing knowledge.

Objective: The objective of this study was to present a framework for KM processes and using social media tools in a Living Lab (LL) environment.

Methods: In order to find a way to help organisations to retain tacit knowledge, the researchers conducted in-depth research. They used case studies and Grounded Theory (GT) to explore KM, social media tools and technologies as well as the LL environment. They emailed an online questionnaire and followed it up telephonically. The study targeted academic, support and administrative staff in higher education institutions nationwide to establish their level of KM knowledge, understanding of concepts and levels of application.

Results: The researchers concluded that the participants did not know the term KM and therefore were not using KM. They only used information hubs, or general university systems, like Integrated Technology Software (ITS), to capture and store information. The researchers suggested including social media and managing them as tools to help CoPs to meet their knowledge requirements. Therefore, the researchers presented a framework that uses semantic technologies and the social media to address the problem.

Conclusion: The success of the LL approach in developing new web-enabled LLs allows organisations to amalgamate various networks. The social media help organisations to gather, classify and verify knowledge.

Introduction

This research is part of a study into the knowledge management practices of higher education institutions and how these institutions can improve their practices by applying various web technologies, like social media tools and the semantic web, in a Living Lab (LL) environment.

Background to the study

Recent research papers have pointed out the value of LLs as environments for collaborative innovation and discovering knowledge (Herselman, Marais & Pitse-Boshomane 2010; Herselman & Cunningham 2011). As part of ongoing research into agricultural knowledge-driven Communities of Practice (CoPs) in the Southern African context, Van der Walt et al. (2009:421–436) and Buitendag and Van der Walt (2009) presented a LL framework that uses web-based technologies as its basis. The LL framework (see Figure 1) uses an agricultural CoP as its basis. However, the same generic knowledge management practices apply in similar contexts and environments, like higher educational, medical and financial environments. Therefore, the researchers present the framework generically.

One of the main objectives of a LL is to use knowledge for further innovation. Knowledge by itself is useless unless one applies it in context. The general objective of a LL is to be a real life collaborative development platform.

Methodology

The methodology the researchers used in the study was a questionnaire and follow-up telephone calls to investigate the levels of understanding of knowledge management (KM) in higher education institutions nationwide.

In order to find a way for organisations to retain tacit knowledge, the researchers conducted in-depth research. They used case studies and Grounded Theory (GT) on KM practices and the use of social media tools and technologies in a LL environment.

Findings

The findings were similar across the board. Either the users did not know the term KM, or worked only with information hubs that used general university systems like the Integrated Technology Software (ITS) to store and capture information, leaving the general users of the system (often individuals) to apply decision making processes with little or no support.

The framework in Figure 1 highlights various research methodologies one could use as part of the knowledge discovery process that leads to innovative solutions and services. The knowledge discovery process, and other collaborative knowledge activities, could generate vast quantities of knowledge within the internal and external domains and make unique KM strategies necessary.

According to Van der Walt *et al.* (2009), the framework incorporates various 'factories' for accomplishing different tasks and objectives. They include:

- a social networking factory for profiling and registering community members
- a tools or product factory for creating tools and methodologies for the LL
- a service factory for establishing all the services the community needs, which may include physical and non-physical services like web services
- a knowledge factory that creates a dynamic set of knowledge objects that uses a Question and Answer Extrapolation Tool (QAET).

The QAET uses questions to create reusable knowledge objects. The primary purpose of the QAET is to manage user requests and to create knowledge objects that users store in the Knowledge Object Repository (KOR).

Essential elements of good knowledge management

Knowledge objects

Knowledge objects (KOs) are any artefacts that knowledge seekers could use to learn, or expand their current knowledge, about a topic. Merrill (2000) defines knowledge objects as sets of appropriate components of knowledge that users require for particular needs. The components of knowledge objects include various entities and properties of the entities as well as the various activities that one could associate with the processes of the entities to describe the knowledge they represent.

KOs can have a variety of formats, ranging from digital media to WEB 2.0 mashed objects. A Knowledge Object Repository

(KOR) stores and manages used KOs. A KOR is a semantic web cataloguing and tagging system. The researchers believe that introducing semantic tagging to applicable documents will help to overcome this problem. Tagging ontologies and techniques tag KO objects semantically. They store and manage the subsequent metadata as part of the semantic knowledge bases and KORs. Organisations, by themselves, cannot use corporate KM fully without using the correct tools to contribute, collaborate and integrate. The Internet provides social media tools for optimal KM functionality. Organisations should manage their knowledge assets so that they can achieve their objectives. This is the first and most important rule when organisations treat knowledge as assets.

Dieng (2002:14–17) emphasised that 'organizational memory aims to deliver the right knowledge to the right person at the right time in the right format to enable the right action'. To apply this concept, organisations must use the correct tools. The Internet provides all the necessary tools and using it makes such an operational platform possible. The Internet allows organisations to integrate knowledge and creates working systems within the cloud. Nabil (2010) defines cloud computing as 'clusters of distributed computers (largely vast data centres and server farms) which provide on-demand resources and services over a networked medium (usually the internet)'.

Doyle (2012) defines social media by stating that:

> social media includes the various online technology tools that enable people to communicate easily via the internet to share information and resources. Social media can include text, audio, video, images, podcasts, and other multimedia communications. (n.p)

Social networks are social media sites through which people connect to businesses or people with similar interests.

The intranet, Internet and Living Labs

An intranet can use internal corporate memory whereas external memory relies on extranets that connect companies and their selected partners. These partners can include customers, suppliers and subcontractors. A number of employees in organisations use the Internet to create and reuse corporate memories. Organisations can create corporate memories, allow them to evolve and then distribute or centralise them. Distributed corporate memories support cooperation and knowledge sharing between numerous people in organisations even if they are geographically dispersed.

Qualman (2010), from Socialnomics, found that over 50% of the world's population was under the age of 30 in 2009. Therefore, Qualman predicted that the social media were increasing because of the growth and addition of younger generations of users. In the United States of America (USA), 75% of the current generation uses social media. This figure used a 2010 Pew Research Center study on the millennial generation (Kern 2010) as its basis. Students make up a

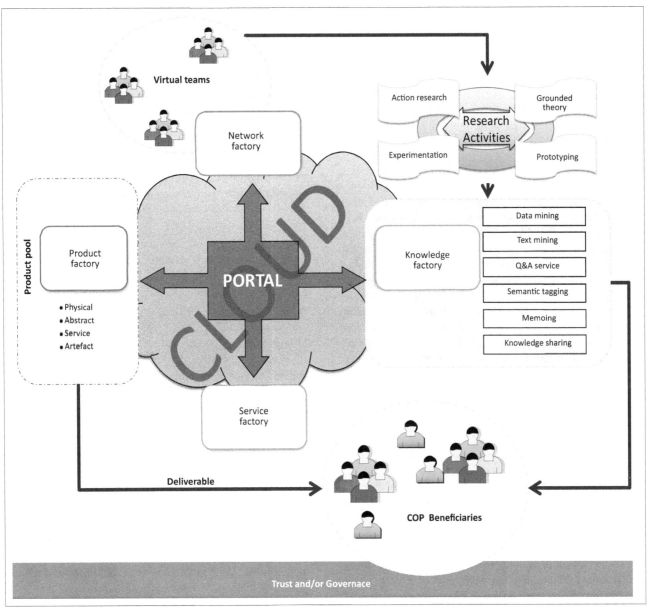

FIGURE 1: Web-enabled Living Lab Framework.

significant proportion of this population. Therefore, the social media is the perfect platform for higher education institutions to roll out KM.

The researchers believe that the social media allow LLs to work. Therefore, integration, collaboration and full participation can occur. LLs for KM allow end users to share and bank knowledge. LLs allow end users to see the bigger picture and provide insight into strategic and behavioural KM efforts. The KM drivers slot in perfectly with social media platforms and allow seamless operation in a LL.

Living Labs, thinking processes and knowledge management labs

The LL is just a tool organisations use within a cloud. However, they make integration, collaboration and optimisation possible. Pallot (2006) describes a Living Lab as

an 'innovation platform' that engages all stakeholders, like end users, researchers, industrialists and policy makers at an earlier stage of the innovation process.

In the knowledge economy, knowledge became the most valuable resource for maintaining competitiveness and advantage for people or organisations (Mukhlason, Mahmood, Arshad & Abidin 2009:335–339). The value of KM systems is the way organisations acquire knowledge and apply it after they have captured it. LLs also help organisations to transfer knowledge to various role players or groups.

The social media emphasise the principle of social networking (Wahlroos 2010:7–14). The researchers believe that the Web is the platform for the most creative minds in the world, where the concepts of open innovation and co-creation emerge. Bartl, Jawecki and Wiegandt (2010) explained that open innovation refers to opening the innovation process to improve the users' and other stakeholders' knowledge, creativity and skills. The idea of open innovation and co-creation are core activities and processes of a LL environment.

A LL turns environmental knowledge into assets and gives inherent value to the knowledge that organisations generate. From this perspective, knowledge, as an asset, also does not depreciate. Instead, it increases in value over the years because organisations can only build onto their existing assets. Knowledge cannot become outdated but organisations can improve it by adding newer knowledge. Generating knowledge and artefacts are core activities in a LL to stimulate innovation, amongst others, because it is the main reason that LLs exist. Without knowledge, there is no business and organisations will be unable to generate solutions. LL stakeholders learn to apply knowledge themselves. KM, generation and dissemination are the core of LL activities, as cooking is core to restaurants. Without food, there will be no restaurants. Simply put, without knowledge and sound KM, there will be no innovation and no LLs. Applying knowledge means turning knowledge into action. No knowledge becomes dormant, but organisations share it so that others can capture the newer knowledge on the shared aspect. Organisations constantly reintegrate and classify earlier KOs as parts of newer solutions. In turn, they speed up the process of acquiring knowledge.

KM involves connecting people with people and people with information. Technology can speed up strategic decision-making by making knowledge available through databases, intranets, virtual video conferencing, knowledge repositories and collaborative tools for sharing knowledge (Fotache 2002). Newman and Conrad (1999) stated that KM offers a framework for balancing the numerous approaches and technologies that add value and integrating them into seamless wholes. The primary focus of KM is to use information technology and tools, business processes, best practices and culture to develop and share knowledge in organisations as well as to connect those who hold the knowledge with those who need it (Anantatmula 2005:50–67). According to Zhao, Gütl and Chang (2008), the challenge of KM is to make the right knowledge available to the right people at the right time. KM connects people with people and people with information.

Thinking processes as parts of a Living Labs environment

The main objective of any community-orientated LL is to create prosperous communities. Research papers have identified many critical success factors for prosperous communities (cf. Lepik & Varblane 2010; Eskelinen 2010). The ones they mention most relate to trust, involving members in the innovation process, access to adequate knowledge about the problem environment, state of the art information communication technology (ICT) tools and methodologies as well as good governance. The purpose of a LL is to

support core research capabilities and shared understanding in order to learn and understand the thinking processes (Van der Walt & Thompson 2009).

Thinking is a process of working things out, knowing why and how things work or do not work. A LL is a thinking and rethinking support environment, connected to generic decision-making (intelligence, design, choice and implementation) and action research (sense, learn and act) processes. Simply put, a LL framework that uses thinking as its basis can function as a springboard for prosperous communities to build their entrepreneurial capacities and achieve sustainable continuous improvement (Aronson n.d.).

According to Aronson (n.d.), the LL approach uses systems thinking as its basis. This author continues to identify and describe a number of thinking paradigms. Amongst them are that systems thinking ensures collaborative, innovative, explorative, strategic and process thinking.

Multidisciplinary and collective intelligence thinking supports collaborative thinking. Performance, value chain and factory thinking support innovative thinking. Critical, Grounded Theory, action research and experimental research thinking support explorative thinking. Workflow, architectural, real time, risk, effectiveness, maturity and intelligent services thinking support process thinking.

Systems-thinking.org (2011) explains that systems thinking is a mindset for understanding how things work. It is a way of going beyond events, looking for patterns of behaviour or seeking underlying systemic interrelationships that are responsible for behavioural patterns and events. Systems thinking embodies a worldview. On the other hand, innovative thinking links to creative thinking and to solving problems. It generates new things or finds new ways to solve them. Explorative thinking stimulates innovation by finding patterns in data, events, design processes, research processes and decision-making. These patterns transform into knowledge and best practices in order to improve human cognition and derive fundamental insights into complex problems and systems. Analytical and critical thinking research processes support the process of discovering (Van der Walt &Thompson 2009).

Critical thinking is the means and ends of learning. Critical thinkers should:

- remain open to new ideas and think like scientists
- be sceptical about ways of doing things
- use and create their own information and reject information that is irrelevant and faulty
- state their own arguments
- come to their own conclusions
- listen to other people and tolerate their ways of thinking (Van der Walt &Thompson 2009).

Strategic thinking is a way of thinking about changes and preparing for them. It is a process of helping organisations to confront changes, analyse their effects and look for new opportunities (Thompson, Strickland & Gamble 2007).

Simply put, performance thinking helps organisations to achieve their strategic goals. Performance thinking is the process of assessing progress toward achieving predetermined goals. Performance management builds on that process and adds the relevant communication and action to the progress organisations make in achieving their predetermined goals (Wikipedia 2008).

The main purpose of performance thinking is to link performance objectives with organisational strategies to increase profit. A performance problem is any gap between desired and actual results. Performance improvement is any effort targeted at closing the gap between actual results and desired results (Van der Walt *et al.* 2009).

Process thinking focuses on identifying, understanding, designing and managing processes. Activities and related activities from workflows lead to the completion of work – objective integrated systems manage it. Workflow, architectural, real time, risk, effectiveness, maturity and intelligent services thinking support process thinking (Van der Walt *et al.* 2009).

It is clear that, in a LL environment, one needs to control the various thinking processes and to manage the subsequent processes in order to ensure that the various thinking processes result in manageable deliverables in the form of KO as well as other knowledge artefacts and solutions.

The social media and knowledge management

Organisations are becoming extremely interested in the benefits of applying Web 2.0 technologies to their work practices. They include social media tools like blogs, wikis, Really Simple Syndication (RSS) feeds, sharing content, tagging and social networking. Online or Web 2.0 communities are people who share a common purpose and organisations use them to improve their business (Leask 2009). Facebook, MySpace and Twitter are 'the big three' in social networking. The researchers believe that organisations should follow a targeted approach when using social media websites based on demographics.

These social spaces play significant roles as sources and enablers of the network and knowledge factories (see Figures 1 and 2). Tools, like blogging tools, social media tools and content sharing tools (such as Flickr and YouTube) are freely available and the only expenses they incur are Internet up-time and website maintenance. The tools have worldwide recognition and are the most popular Web 2.0 platforms because they are easy to use and support knowledge distribution between organisations and various

CoP members, both internally and externally. Community social websites intend to design a common platform for an intended purpose. It is also possible to customise websites in order to share and capture knowledge as well as to communicate with various audiences.

Organisations want to benefit by engaging with a large group of people who provide knowledge. Organisations can then use this knowledge to assist them with their strategies and to improve their products and services. The success of the social media depends on meeting the right online users in the right settings with the right messages. KM, according to Reichental, Gamliela and Ayalb (2007:1–22) is the identification, retention, effective use and retirement of institutional insight. However, it has been an elusive goal for most large organisations. The emergence and effect of the social media on organisations forces them to rethink KM and creates completely new challenges for them. Today, one can categorise some of the core issues with existing KM approaches as behavioural and technical in nature. In order for a KM system to have value, employees must contribute knowledge regularly. The researchers believe that a KM system that uses LL tools will achieve the best results. In a LL setting, organisations achieve optimisation by transferring knowledge between experts and knowledge seekers and vice versa. LLs improve collaboration between many entities. This ensures that they capture up to date knowledge and more thinking can go into a subject. Involving more experts leads to specialist knowledge in the KM system.

A KM system, which uses LL tools, is especially important for CoPs because many experts reside outside the geographical boundaries of the LL. Collaboration links with knowledge transfer and technologies. From the point of view of LL tools, large groups, internal and external to CoPs, can use many technologies in order to share and capture knowledge that is wider than the CoPs themselves are. In a LL, organisations capture data and information and then convert them into knowledge. The collaborative environment supports problem solving by applying the knowledge in the knowledge bank (Van der Walt *et al.* 2009).

The researchers constructed Figure 2. It is an adaptation from Melakoski (2007) and Roux, Buitendag and Van der Walt (2008) and shows some social media (Web 2.0) tools that one could use as part of the LL environment. It also highlights their strengths, weaknesses and possible relationships with generating knowledge.

The researchers do not suggest incorporating all possible social media tools in a LL environment. However, the focus of the LL should determine which tools are best suited for its purpose. The number of social tools it includes will have an effect on the KM strategies and approaches it will follow.

The researchers support the notions of Reichental *et al.* (2007) when they stated that:

it's likely that social-media-driven KM will require much less of the "management" component. Historically we've spent far too

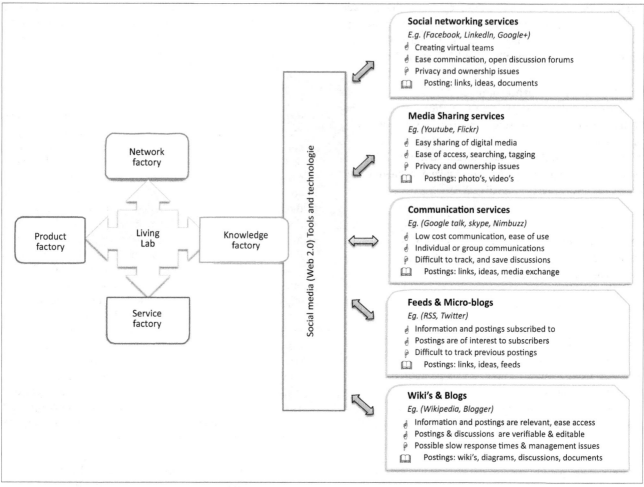

FIGURE 2: Examples of social media (Web 2.0) tools and technologies as part of a Living Lab.

much time cleaning up the data, validating, and categorizing it. In the future, more time will be spent analyzing newly created knowledge through social interactions. Smart analysis can result in new insight, and that has powerful value for organizations. (n.p.)

Some reasons why one should use social media are that one can use them for:

- research
- learning from others
- community building
- sharing expertise
- collaborating in real time.

The Digital Marketing Agency (2010) suggested that connected groups could learn from each other continuously. New ways of managing knowledge between projects and of collecting knowledge from employees who leave companies will reduce the loss of knowledge (Lietsala 2008; Otala 2008).

Grounded Theory and discovering knowledge

In collaborative organisational and research environments, the GT process could apply in virtual teams. Therefore, it has an effect on the validity of the knowledge because groups of experts and entities in the networked domain could validate

it. This process promotes the concept of 'e-collaboration'. Jones and Burger (2009) describe e-collaboration as a new approach to forming and maintaining cooperative enterprises that involve introducing electronic communication tools to facilitate collaboration.

The GT research methodology is one of the primary research activities in the LL domain for discovering knowledge. The GT method gives guidelines for collecting data, analysis and building inductive theory. Researchers collect data and conduct analyses in successive steps (Charmaz 2000). Interpreting the data they collect in one step helps them to focus on collecting the data in the next one. The researchers compared the data and found them to be consistent and parallel. They presented these findings quantitatively as percentage measurements and representations. Davidson (2002) defines and motivates the use of GT by explaining that:

GT is described as a research method in which the theory is developed from the data, instead of the other way around. In doing so makes it an inductive approach, meaning that it moves from the specific to the more general. The study method is fundamentally based on three elements: concepts, categories and propositions, initially called 'hypotheses'. Concepts are the key elements of analysis since the theory is developed from the data conceptualization instead of the actual data. (n.p.)

Muller (2010), at IBM Research, motivates using GT by stating that:

> The GT process is good for explorative research, which lead to the disciplined development of new and innovative ideas, and in developing a theory and structure in areas where there is no a prior guidance, whilst working with both qualitative and quantitative data. (n.p.)

Knowledge interchange and management processes

The network and knowledge factories are parts of the framework. They provide tools for communicating and disseminating information, called knowledge interchange (KI). The KM researchers, Groff and Jones (2003) and Malhotra (2000:5–16), identified the information technology (IT) capabilities that contribute positively to absorptive KM in organisations:

- knowledge acquisition capability, which is the IT ability to identify, obtain and maintain useful knowledge from several sources
- knowledge distribution capability: IT can distribute knowledge to knowledge consumers
- knowledge identification capability, which is the IT function of retrieving stored knowledge in knowledge repositories and of identifying the sources of expertise effectively
- knowledge upgrade capability: IT can upgrade knowledge effectively and discard irrelevant knowledge.

KI activities and processes correlate closely with KM processes and knowledge sharing (Hall & Paradice 2004). KI is the process of classifying, verifying and storing information and knowledge from various sources (like other users, experts and the semantic web) in a data store like a data mart, semantic knowledge base or digital library. In other words, KI activities refer to services the portal provides to facilitate the exchange of relevant information to groups in the portal with the same interests. The knowledge and information becomes available for future retrieval to help users or CoPs to solve their problems (Buitendag & van der Walt 2007).

Figure 3 shows the KI process, as part of the knowledge factory, in the LL framework. It emphasises that organisations receive continuous feedback, verify information and knowledge throughout the KI phases by using knowledge workers. As organisations complete adaptations and new classifications of current knowledge objects, they also keep the various knowledge factory data stores up to date.

One additional solution that organisations could use in conjunction with the standard KI practices is using tools and services. They allow users to combine lexical, structural and knowledge-based techniques to exploit or generate web documents (Martin & Eklund 2002:18–25). Organisations take advantage of the most popular Internet services. They include emails and the Web itself. They use the Web for distributing uniform information. Knowledge flow relies on populating knowledge elements on the Web. Users can access all types of knowledge, information and news archives over the Internet (Dieng 2002).

Other possible techniques and technologies for discovering knowledge, which use the various research activities (see Figure 1), include:

- data and text mining
- question and answer services
- semantic search techniques
- memorandums
- sharing knowledge via social web spaces like wikis and blogs.

The researchers argue that organisations should remember that several knowledge servers and services, in the form of web services, might cause problems in retrieving available knowledge if they have not arranged and managed the information and knowledge they have stored properly. Furthermore, using sophisticated IT does not always guarantee successful KM.

The role of knowledge is to enable users to choose rational actions so that they become vital components of competitiveness. Organisations should ensure that they receive important knowledge that many others can use and that these contributions improve their processes or outputs (Guo 2006). Organisations can use valuable knowledge to create differential advantage and it can affect their ability to stay ahead of their competitors. Stewart (1997:69) describes the data-to-wisdom hierarchy as, 'one man's knowledge is another man's data'.

In a LL, critical operational and strategic managers are often more concerned with generating reports because they support good decision-making. Therefore, the strategies of managers will determine what the IT system should be capable of and user input will define the system further according to their needs. Hijazi and Kelly (2003) make it clear that the IT infrastructure is essential to support the implementation of knowledge creation.

It is easy to find information with information visualisation software. It produces graphs that assist with identifying complex patterns and relationships in large databases (Zhu & Chert 2005:139–177). The visualisations may be one-, two- or three-dimensional. One can view related concepts together and colour becomes extremely meaningful. Börner, Chen and Boyack (2003:179–255) define this software as a way of analysing and transforming abstract data (document collections, descriptive words or phrases, journals, author citations or websites) into graphical maps. Reduced search time and discovering developments that might have passed by unnoticed are a huge advantage.

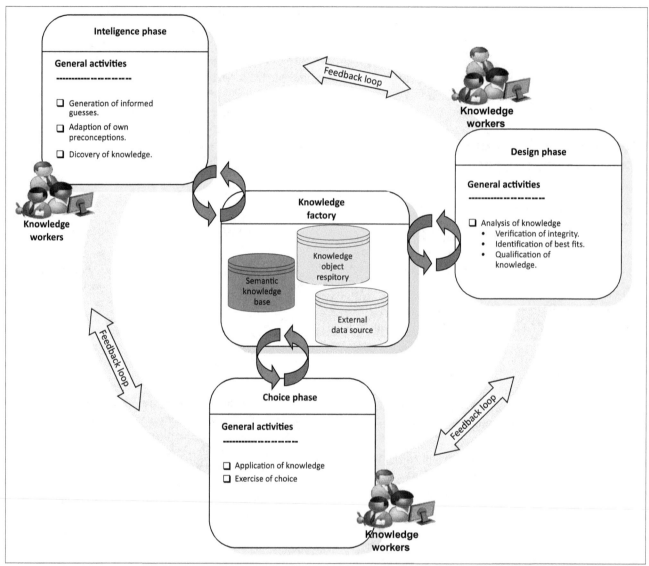

FIGURE 3: Knowledge interchange.

Guidelines for good knowledge management practices

According to David Skyrme Associates (2008), KM manages its related processes of creating, organising, disseminating and usage to meet the objectives of businesses. There are many KM practices and processes that organisations can apply in a LL environment. The table below, from David Skyrme Associates (2008), highlights some of these practices. They include general KM practices, creating and discovering knowledge, sharing knowledge and learning as well as organising and managing knowledge.

Applying current available technologies and services, like standard data and text mining tools, as well as social media technologies, could support many of the highlighted processes. Skyrme Associates (2008) highlighted them in Table 1.

Another good KM practice is to measure activities that focus on the specific KM practices that organisations apply in

their projects or processes to determine their effects. When organisations measure activity, they look at specific things to determine how often users access, contribute to, or use the knowledge resources and practices they have established (Mavodza 2010).

According to Gifford (2011), good KM practice integrates technology and people that a KM expert steers. This will ensure that everyone involved understands its value and will engage in the process.

It is important to ensure that people, processes and technologies align with KM goals and that organisations use best practice approaches in their KM programmes. This will help organisations to benefit from the skills that people acquire (Gilbert, Morse & Lee 2007). Guidelines for good KM practices include understanding KM, generating, acquiring, capturing, retaining, organising, disseminating and reusing knowledge. It also involves responding to the new knowledge (Mavodza 2010).

TABLE 1: Some knowledge management practices and processes.

Creating and dicovering	Creativity techniques
	Data mining
	Text mining
	Environmental scanning
	knowledge elicitation
	Business simulation
	Content analysis
Sharing and learning	Communities of practice
	Learning networks
	Sharing best practice
	After action reviews
	Structured diaolgue
	Share fairs
	Cross functional teams
	Decision diaries
Organising and managing	Knowledge centres
	Expertise profiling
	Knowledge mapping
	Information audits or inventory
	IRM (information or inventory)
	Measuring intellectual capital

Knowledge management, collaboration and the Internet

When organisations use the Internet as a social tool for KM, circulating information amongst people and groups as well as in organisations will improve – and innovation will flourish. Internet social tools allow people to access, share and reuse knowledge. The Internet offers remarkable possibilities to access information and knowledge.

The Hyper Text Transfer Protocol (HTTP), mark-up technologies like the Hyper Text Mark-up Language (HTML) and Extensible Mark-up Language (XML) are key technologies for exchanging information and knowledge. Resource Description Frameworks (RDFs) are the key technologies for presenting ontologies. XML and RDFs are two web technologies that allow for significant changes to information interchange worldwide. Many technologies, like the semantic web, have still to realise their potential. Intranets, which rely on Internet technologies, facilitate internal communication and information sharing in organisations. Multidimensional collective organisations, like LLs and multinational corporations, can benefit from the Internet and Intranet to gather, manage, distribute and share knowledge, internally as well as externally.

The roles of the Internet and the social media in creating the correct technological platforms for KM have wide recognition. Knowledge by itself has little value unless organisations can acquire, identify, apply, manipulate and store it for later use (Han & Anantatmula 2006). Technology can speed up strategic decisions by making knowledge available through databases, Intranets, virtual video conferencing, knowledge repositories and collaborative tools for sharing knowledge (Fotache 2000).

Correct technological platforms ensure that organisations capture, archive and group knowledge correctly. KM allows organisations to integrate and consolidate Intranet platforms. Organisations can benefit from KM by creating and maintaining relevant knowledge repositories, improving access to knowledge, improving the knowledge environment and valuing knowledge.

The researchers constructed Figure 4. It shows the role of the Internet and includes the cloud and Intranets in the LL as part of the knowledge factory. The knowledge factory allows for a general memory management cycle. The cycle and process conform to the practice that Davidson (2002) described.

Organisations must make human knowledge sources – like experts, normal end users and single workers from within the LL environment – explicit and available in their memories. Knowledge bases, also called corporate memory bases, store and manage the knowledge. These memory bases contain KORs, which refer to artefacts of knowledge that organisations can apply in LL domains and the semantic knowledge bases that include semantic references to external and internal data sources.

Knowledge objects or artefacts that organisations have referenced and catalogued in the KOR and used, as part of previous knowledge and information enquiries and searches, are available for subsequent searches. Therefore, subsequent searches could become faster because organisations can link previous knowledge to current needs.

External knowledge watchers and workers use external web sources and apply semantic tagging processes that use standard ontologies like the Dublin Core (DC) ontology (dublincore.org 2012) for metadata descriptions. Internal and external expert groups and developers develop, organise and maintain corporate memories. Experts validate knowledge elements before inserting them in the semantic knowledge base or knowledge object repository.

Normal users, which include knowledge seekers, must have easy access to the various memory elements and knowledge objects and they must be able to reuse these elements and objects in order to meet their knowledge requirements. Organisations supervise and manage their LL memory environments or knowledge bases in collaborative processes to ensure that they continually verify the various knowledge stores.

Collaboration software on the Internet

The rise of the Internet has helped to propel collaboration. Microsoft's SharePoint software (a new generation of Internet-inspired collaboration software) provides alerts, discussion boards, document libraries, categorisation, shared workspaces and the ability to pull in and display information from data sources outside of SharePoint itself, including the Internet (Wilson 2010), amongst others.

The social media improve organisations' KM by promoting ease of use, practical results and emotional gratification

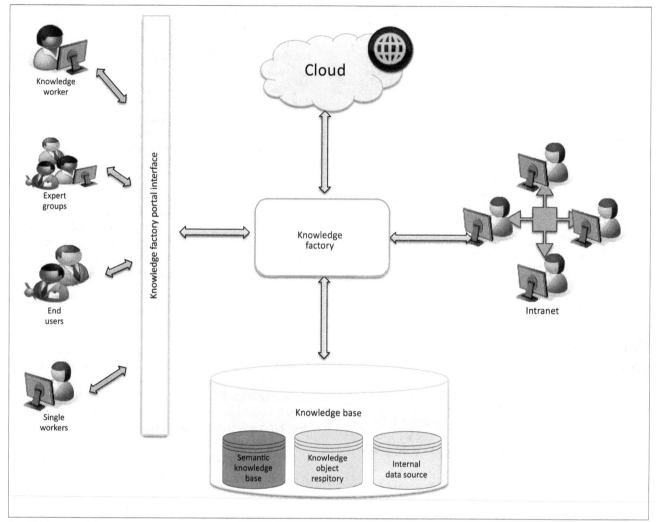

FIGURE 4: Position of the Internet and Intranet as knowledge sources in a Living Lab.

through collaboration systems. The social media make it easy for people to connect with other people, who have posted specific items, with a single click. The social media could improve organisations' collaborative performance without reengineering their current KM systems. For example, organisations can preserve how they store and structure information as well as integrations like workflows. Therefore, they can reduce migration costs.

The social media allow organisations to get connected and KM cannot survive without connecting to groups with the same areas of interest. Being connected is all about people, knowledge and opportunities. Srisawas and Rotchanakitumnuai (2011) emphasise that the quality of content on social network sites has major effects on sharing business knowledge and the subsequent value of customer relationships. However, the question of whether KM and collaboration have increased in proportion to the volume of information available, and whether this information would be useful if more people could get their hands on it, remains (Wilson 2010).

White's list of world populations (2010), which includes social media platforms according to country ratings, makes

for interesting reading. White lists Facebook as the third largest 'country' on the world map (it accounts for more than 7% of the world's population), beating the USA. White lists MySpace, Twitter and Orkut (as well as mobile platforms like Facebook mobile) all in the top 20. David Tice (2011), vice president and group accounts director of Knowledge Networks, said that the success of the social media lies in them being people-centred.

The Living Lab Knowledge Management framework

Figure 5 shows the LL framework the researchers developed from the exposition they have given. It incorporates the various technologies the researchers have described. Knowledge support is an activity rendered as part of the knowledge factory. Figure 5 shows that various users and tools, like Web 2.0, are all possible sources of data and knowledge. The knowledge factory consists of three key systems. They comprise various services its intended user community needs to meet its knowledge support needs and requirements. The services include a KM system, a learning system and a knowledge support service. The primary objective of a KM system is to ensure the validity of the

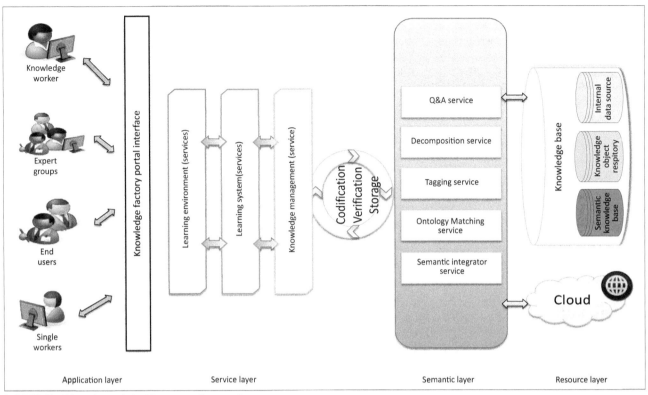

FIGURE 5: The Living Lab Knowledge Management Framework.

knowledge or solutions that users post. It uses the standard knowledge sharing practices that industry has adopted.

A learning system (LS) means implementing the Knowledge Support Portal (KSP). It comprises many sub-portals like a Question and Answer (Q&A) portlet. The learning system acts as the physical interface for acquiring and sharing knowledge. It also supports and enables collaboration between the various user groups. The knowledge support service orchestrates the process of acquiring information and knowledge and manages a possible reverse auction service for supplying knowledge.

The researchers' proposed framework for KM within a LL environment (see Figure 5) uses a layered approach. It highlights the position of the various knowledge factory systems and shows that KM activities are part of the services layer. The various services enable the processes Table 1 describes. They comply with the guidelines of Mavodza (2010:242, 313). The layered approach comprises an application layer, a services layer and a semantic layer.

The application layer provides the interface that allows different users to access the various tools and the LL environment. The services layer contains the various subsystems, as single or embedded tools to allow learning, and KI in various formats. Some activities that web services could provide include sharing and clustering knowledge, generating services, providing access to smart tools, automatic tracking and tracing knowledge objects, mobile

support and expert interlinking. The cloud, as web services, could render many of these services. The semantic layer provides the technical functionality and embedded process logic of the knowledge support and KI activities. The process of classifying the question domain, which is part of the semantic layer, is a stepwise one. It processes and disseminates questions that users post via the Q&A interface and the KI. The processes of the semantic layer follow.

They dissect and break down a posted question or request into common sentence units, like verbs, adjectives and nouns. The text mining service uses the sentence parts and performs an initial matching activity with earlier questions stored in the questions and answer repository. They apply and match similarities and artificial intelligence (AI) matching methods and return matching result-sets from the Q&A repository. They then analyse the returned result-set and original question further by using natural language processing tools and services. The ontology wrapping service uses service ontology for a Q&A web service based on OWL-S.

They write a knowledge object, that simple knowledge ontology describes, to the KOR, the repository stores, amongst others, and the metadata of stored artefacts in an external data warehouse. They also gather additional web sources using semantic processes from the Web itself. This may include links to other WEB 2.0 sites and extracting other potential KO metadata. The semantic extrapolation process generates tags that it compares to existing metadata by using semantic pattern clustering in the semantic knowledge repository. The repository matches existing classes, relations, axioms, functions and instances of earlier searches and results. The KOR contains metadata descriptions of KOs that apply to the current LL domain, whilst the semantic knowledge repository contains repository references and semantic knowledge from external domains.

The web service or semantic integrator incorporates web services with bus architecture. It uses the Web Services Description Language (WSDL) and Web Ontology Language (OWL) for retrieving and discovering possible data sources that are not part of the current Semantic Knowledge Repository (SKR). It applies this process to external web content and to external domain knowledge bases. Various knowledge officers then evaluate the results retrieved from external sources, as part of the knowledge-seeking process, as part of the research process. They tag the subsequent new knowledge or discoveries, describe them semantically and store them as part of the KOR for future use.

Conclusion

In today's knowledge-driven economy, companies and teams, which include CoPs, must work smarter and not harder. Now that open source technologies are gaining momentum (based on open standards), companies and organisations must, more than ever before, tap into existing technologies to avoid reinventing the wheel. Therefore, the researchers suggest that CoPs incorporate current successful technologies, which are freely available, to create valuable products, services and knowledge systems.

The social media changed the existing KM paradigm completely. Currently, the social media take knowledge and make it highly iterative. In the old world order, organisations usually created and stored knowledge as a point in time. This often meant it was difficult to access it. Now, cooperation, sharing knowledge and interactivity between people in different physical locations has never been as easy. The researchers are convinced that knowledge support services (like a semantic Q&A service) as parts of the KM framework, will become key deliverables in developing any information-driven portal that will become part of a LL.

From a South African perspective, these services can play critical roles in limiting and overcoming obstacles like information poverty and knowledge deprivation. The objectives, uses and advantages of knowledge support services are not limited to higher education environments. They apply to knowledge- or information-driven environments, like agricultural and medical ones. The researchers believe that semantic-based web service technologies satisfy the requirements, and improve the interoperability, of distributed service component integration.

Acknowledgements

Competing interests

The authors declare that they have no financial or personal relationship(s) that may have inappropriately influenced them when they wrote this paper.

Authors' contributions

L.D. (Tshwane University of Technology) was the research coordinator. She conducted the research interviews, initiated the investigation into the knowledge management practices of higher education institutions and reported on some of the findings.

A.A.K.B. (Tshwane University of Technology) presented the conceptual and design contributions to the design of the layered KM framework, which incorporates semantic technologies and the use and description of the knowledge objects. A.A.K.B. (Tshwane University of Technology) was responsible for the diagrams.

J.S.V. provided conceptual input and initially designed the generic LL framework, which incorporates the various thinking frameworks, the researchers used as part of this study.

L.D. (Tshwane University of Technology) and A.A.K.B. (Tshwane University of Technology) wrote the manuscript.

References

Anantatmula, V., 2005, 'Outcomes of Knowledge Management Initiatives', *International Journal of Knowledge Management* 1(2), 50–67. http://dx.doi.org/10.4018/jkm.2005040105

Aronson, D., n.d., Targeting Innovation, *Using systems thinking to increase the benefits of innovation efforts*. A version of this article appeared in R&D Innovator (now Innovative Leader), vol. 6(2).

Bartl, M., Jawecki, G. & Wiegandt, P., 2010, *Co-Creation in New Product Development: Conceptual Framework and Application in the Automotive Industry*, viewed 21 May 2011, from http://www.radma.ltd.uk/conference2010/papers_abstracts/Bartl,%20Jawecki%20and%20Wiegandt.pdf

Börner, K., Chen, C. & Boyack, K.W., 2003, 'Visualizing knowledge domains', in B. Cronin (ed.), *Annual review of information science and technology*, vol. 37, pp. 179–255, Information today Inc., Medford.

Buitendag, A.A.K. & Van der Walt, J.S., 2007, *A Question and answer knowledge-sharing system to support emergent farmers in Southern Africa*, viewed 20 May 2011, from http://www.efita.net/apps/accesbase

Buitendag, A.A.K. & Van der Walt, J.S., 2009, 'Knowledge support in a living lab environment though the utilization of Web 2.0 and Web 3.0 technologies', *Proceedings of the 11th Annual Conference On World Wide Web Applications*, viewed 16 May 2011, from http://www.zaw3.co.za

Charmaz, K., 2000, 'Grounded Theory: Objectivist and Constructivist Methods', in N. Denzin & Lincoln, Y. (eds.), *The Handbook of Qualitative Research*, vol. 2, pp. 509–535, Sage Publications, New York.

David Skyrme Associates, 2008, *Resources – KM basics*, viewed 20 May 2011, from http://www.skyrme.com/resource/kmbasics.htm

Davidson, A.L., 2002, *Grounded Theory – Defined*, viewed 09 January 2009, from http://www.essortment.com/all/groundedtheory_rmnf.htm

Dieng, R., 2002, 'Corporate KM through Intranet and Internet', *Web Technologies, ERCIM News* 41(3), pp. 14–17.

Digital Marketing Agency, 2010, *4THWeb*, viewed 05 May 2011, from http://4thweb.com/social-media-2010-numbers

Doyle, A., 2012, *Social Media – Social Media Definition*, viewed 14 January 2012, from http://jobsearch.about.com/od/networking/g/socialmedia.htm

DublinCore.org., 2012, *The Dublin Core Metadata Initiative*, viewed 03 February 2012, from http://dublincore.org/

Eskelinen, J., 2010, 'HELSINKI Living Lab (Volume 2) Convergence of Users, Developers', *Utilizers and Enablers*, viewed 02 February 2011, from http://www.forumvirium.fi/en/project-areas/innovation-communities/helsinki-living-lab

Fotache, D. (ed.), 2002, *Groupware –Methods, techniques and technologies for working groups*, Polirom Publishing House, Bucharest.

Gifford, A., 2011, 'Member of Melbourne KMLF', *What constitutes good KM practice?*, viewed 20 May 2011, from http://www.meetup.com/Melbourne-MLF/members/13875699

Gilbert, P., Morse, R. & Lee, M., 2007, *Enhancing IT support with KM. Governance and Service Management*, CA Technologies, New York.

Groff, T.R. & Jones, T.P., 2003, *Introduction to KM in Business*, Butterworth-Heinemann, Philadelphia.

Guo, Z. & Sheffield, J., 2006, 'Habermasian Inquiring System: Towards a General Framework for Knowledge Management Research', *proceedings of the 39th Annual Hawaii International Conference on System Sciences*, Hyatt regency Kauai, Poipu, Hawaii, January 04–07, 2006, 10 pages, IEEE Computer Society Press, viewed n.d., from http://csdl2.computer.org/comp/proceedings/hicss/2006/2507/07/250770162c.pdf

Hall, D.J. & Paradice, D., 2004, *Philosophical foundations for a learning-oriented knowledge management system for decision support*, viewed 28 February 2009, from http://www.sciencedirect.com

Han, B. & Anantatmula, V., 2006, 'KM in IT organization for employee's perspective', *HICSS proceedings of the 39th Annual Hawaii International Conference on System Sciences* – Hyatt regency Kauai, Poipu, Hawaii, January 04–07, 2006, vol. 07, IEEE Computer Society Washington, DC.

Herselman, M.E., Marais, M.A. & Pitse-Boshomane, M.M., 2010, 'Applying living lab methodology to enhance skills in innovation', *Proceedings of the eSkills Summit 2010*, Cape Town, July 26–28 July, p. 7

Herselman, M. & Cunningham, P., 2011, *Supporting the Evolution of Sustainable Living Labs and Living Labs Networks in Africa*, vol. 1(8)a, IIMC International Information Management Corporation Ltd, Dublin.

Hijazi, S. & Kelly, L., 2003, 'Knowledge creation in Higher Education Institutions: a conceptual model', *proceedings of the 2003 ASCUE Conference*, Myrtle Beach, South Carolina, June 08–12, 2003, viewed 02 April 2011, from www.ascue.org

Jones, D.M. & Burger, A., 2009, 'Generic materials property data storage and retrieval for the semiconducting materials knowledge base', *Proc. of SPIE*, vol. 7449 74491R-10, viewed 20 May 2011, from http://144.206.159.178/FT/CONF/16436607/16436642.pdf

Kern, R., 2010, '5 Social Media Tools for College Students', *US News and World Report: Knowledge Sharing Network: Gradeguru.com*, viewed 13 May 2011, from http://www.usnews.com/education/articles/2010/05/12/5-social-media-tools-for-college-students

Leask, M., 2009, *Web 2.0 and knowledge management for local government in England – A model for the public sector*, Brunel University London, viewed 01 May 2011, from http://bura.brunel.ac.uk/handle/2438/3559

Lietsala, K., 2008, 'How I became a commidity', *Interaktiivinen Tekniikka Koulutuksessa conference proceedings 2008*, Aulanko, Hämeenlinna, April 16–18, 2008, viewed 13 August 2011 from http://citeseerx.ist.psu.edu/showciting?cid=10027364

Lepik, A. & Varblane, U., 2010, 'How to speak the same language with European Innovation-policy in terms of living labs?' *Discussions on Estonian economic policy Summaries*, pp. 215– 232, viewed 02 February 2010, from http://www.mattimar.ee/publikatsioonid/majanduspoliitika/2010/2010.pdf#page=215

Malhotra, Y., 2000, 'Knowledge Management for E-Business Performance: Advancing Information Strategy to Internet Time', *Information Strategy: The Executive's Journal* 16(4), 5–16.

Martin, P. & Eklund, P.W., 2002, 'Knowledge retrieval and the World Wide Web', *IEEE Intelligent Systems* 15(3), 18–25. http://dx.doi.org/10.1109/5254.846281

Mavodza, J., 2010, 'KM practices and the role of an academic library in a changing information environment', D.Litt et Phil. thesis, Dept. Information Science, University of South Africa, South Africa.

Melakoski, C., 2007, 'Crave, but scared', *The Finnish content production sector views on participation in the economy, and social media*, Tampere University of Applied Sciences publication, Tampere.

Merrill, M.D., 2000, *Knowledge Objects*, viewed 05 June 2011, from http://mdavidmerrill.com/Papers/KnowledgeObjects.PDF

Mukhlason, A.L., Mahmood, A.K., Arshad, N.I. & Abidin, A.I.Z., 2009, 'SWA-KMDLS: An enhanced e-Learning Management System using semantic web and KM technology', *Innovations in Information Technology (IIT)*, pp. 335–339.

Muller, M., 2010, 'Grounded Theory Methods', *Human-Computer Interaction Consortium*, Winter Park, Colorado, February 24–28, 2010, viewed 15 September 2010, from www.slideshare.net/traincroft/grounded-theory-method-hcic-2010-muller

Nabil, S., 2010, Cloud computing for education: A new dawn? *International Journal of Information Management* 30(2), 109–116. http://dx.doi.org/10.1016/j.ijinfomgt.2009.09.004

Newman, B. & Conrad, K.W., 1999, A framework for characterizing KM methods, Course notes distributed in the unit, EMGT 298.T1, Practices and Technologies in support of The Introduction to Knowledge Management, George Washington University, Washington.

Otala, L., 2008, *Human capital management a competitive advantage*, WSOY, viewed 07 May 2011, from http://lib.tkk.fi/Dipl/2008/urn012879.pdf

Pallot, M., 2006, *Living Labs*, viewed 10 July 2009, from www.ami-communities.eu

Qualman, E., 2010, Socialnomics, *World of mouth*, viewed 03 May 2011, from http://www.socialnomics.net/2010/04/13/over-50-of-the-worlds-population-is-under-30-social-media-on-the-rise

Reichental, Y., Gamliela, T. & Ayalb, N., 2007, 'Intergenerational Educational Encounters: Part 1', *A model of knowledge* 33(1), 1–22.

Roux, L., Buitendag, A.A.K. & Van der Walt, J.S., 2008, 'Investigating Web 2.0 as a platform for a collaborative Living Lab environment', *conference proceedings of the 10th Annual Conference on World Wide Web applications*, Cape Town, South Africa, September 03–05, 2008, viewed 19 May 2011, from http://www.zaw3.co.za

Srisawas, S. & Rotchanakitumnuai S., 2011, 'Social Network Management Enhances Customer Relationship', *World Academy of Science, Engineering and Technology* 77, viewed 21 May 2011, from http://www.waset.org/journals/waset/v77/v77-111.pdf

Stewart, T.A., 1997, *Intellectual capital: the new wealth of organizations*, Nicholas Brealey, London.

Systems-Thinking.org., 2011, *Systems Thinking: An Operational Perspective of the Universe*, viewed 21 May 2011, from http://www.systems-thinking.org/systhink/systhink.htm

Tice, D., 2011, 'Report: OTT Video Viewing Up by One Third in 2011', in *Telecompetitor*, viewed n.d., from http://www.telecompetitor.com/report-ott-video-viewing-up-by-one-third-in-2011/

Thompson, A.A., Strickland, A.J. & Gamble, J.E., 2007, *Crafting and Executing Strategy*, 15th edn., McGraw- Hill, New York.

Van der Walt, J.S., Buitendag, A.K.K., Zaaiman, J.J. & Van Vuuren J.J., 2009, 'Community living lab as a collaborative innovation environment' *Issues in Informing Science and Information Technology* 6, 421–436.

Van der Walt, J.S. & Thompson, W.J. , 2009, 'Virtual Living Lab. Quality Assurance of meat e-markets for Emergent Farmers in South Africa', *Proceedings of the 11th annual conference On world wide web applications*, Port Elizabeth, South Africa, September, 2–4, 2009, viewed 21 May 2011, from www.zaw3.co.za/index.php/ZA-WWW/2009/paper/view/132/12

Wahlroos, J.K., 2010, 'Social media as a form of organizational knowledge sharing. A case study on employee participation at Wärtsilä', MA thesis, Dept. Social Studies, University of Helsinki, Finland

White, D.S., 2010, *Global population and Social Media*, viewed 17 May 2011, from http://dstevenwhite.com/2010/09/11/global-population-and-social-media-2010/

Wikipedia, 2008, *Performance Management*, viewed 12 April 2011, from http://en.wikipedia.org/wiki/Performance-management

Wilson, D.J., 2010, *System and method for user driven interactive application integration*, International Business Machines Corporation, Armonk, New York.

Zhao, C., Gütl, C. & Chang, E., 2008, 'How modern technology in KM can support Higher Educational Institutions in modern learning settings', in *conference proceedings of the 11th International Conference on Interactive Computer Aided Learning*, Villach, Austria, September 24–26, 2008, n.p.

Zhu, B. & Chert, H., 2005, 'Information visualization', in B. Cronin (ed.), *Annual review of Information science and technology*, vol. 39, pp.139–177.

4

Challenges of Executive Information Systems in listed Johannesburg Stock Exchange companies

Authors:
Elmarie Papageorgiou[1]
Herman de Bruyn[2]

Affiliations:
[1]School of Accountancy, University of the Witwatersrand, South Africa

[2]Department of Business Management, University of Johannesburg, South Africa

Correspondence to:
Elmarie Papageorgiou

Email:
Elmarie.Papageorgiou@wits.ac.za

Postal address:
Private Bag 3, Wits 2050, South Africa

Background: The widespread use of Executive Information Systems (EISs) as a management information tool was noted in listed Johannesburg Stock Exchange (JSE) companies. The digital business environment exposed executives to so much data that data need to be converted into useful information that is organised and summarised.

Objectives: The purpose of this study is to establish and to determine the existence, and to what extent EISs exist in all levels of management and to identify the challenges companies experienced in listed JSE companies. Therefore the problem exists that EIS-users at all levels of management are unaware of the challenges of EISs and that EISs can be used as a tool to analyse their businesses' performance and competitiveness.

Method: A mixed method was used; both quantitative and qualitative in nature. Questionnaires were sent to 334 listed JSE companies and 13 interviews were conducted with users of EISs in all levels of management.

Results: The results of the study demonstrate that the majority of respondents of the questionnaire have an EIS or plan to implement an EIS. The results further revealed the respondents' positive attitude towards EISs as it is an excellent management information tool that adds strategic value to their business, that is critical for real-time decision-making, solves problems and creates a competitive edge. From the results it is evident that there is a need for an EIS to be 'everybody's information system'. The results of the interviews demonstrate that an EIS is a seamless reliable system necessary for proper timeous decision-making. The respondents to the questionnaire and the interviewees indicated that they understood the value of EISs as a useful part of their company.

Conclusion: The study adds value to the awareness and understanding of EISs that creates a business environment in which business and management can enhance sustainability and strategic competitiveness.

Introduction and background

Executive Information Systems (EISs) were originally developed solely for executives' use in businesses in the late 1980s (Martin, Dehayes, Hoffer & Perkins 2005:223) and caused many problems with regard to data disparity between the layers of the business. Traditionally it was the responsibility of lower management levels to deal with internal data and to know what was reported to the top executive level, but nowadays the base has been broadened to encompass all levels of management.

Nichols (1990:17) concluded that '… greater use would be in the designing of information systems for decision-making in the whole business' and that '… general functions of information systems are to determine user needs'. But Friend (1992:328) was the first to suggest a name change that an EIS ought to be '… everybody's information system …' as an EIS is defined as '… an information system for executives …' only. Wheeler, Chang and Thomas (1993:182) experience an EIS differently: '… an EIS failed as a system for senior executives, since it was almost certainly not appropriate for them in the first place'. However, the EIS did supply lower level staff with vital corporate information. Ikart (2005:78) suggests that there is a higher degree of EISs usage by middle managers than top-level managers. Businesses are therefore faced with an even bigger challenge: the emergence of EISs in all levels of the business.

Definitions of an EIS vary and 20 different studies (Arnott, Jirachiefpattana & O'Donnell 2007:2078; Averweg & Roldán 2006:626; Bajwa, Rai & Brennan 1998:31; Bergeron, Raymond, Rivard & Gara 1995:131; Boci, Chaffey, Greasley & Hickie 2003:257; Byrd & Marshall 1996:449; Elam & Leidner 1995:89; Frolick & Robichaux 1995:157; Khan 1996:16; Martin, Dehayes, Hoffer &

Perkins 2005:223; Nord & Nord 1995:96; Olson & Courtney 1992:217; Pijpers, Bemelmans, Heemstra & Van Montfort 2001:960; Rainer & Watson 1995:147; Remenyi 1991:48; Salmeron 2002:111; Sterrenberg 1990:32; Turban, Mclean & Wetherbe 1996:42; Xu & Kaye 2002:81; Young & Watson 1995:153) were investigated to define an EIS. The different definitions of an EIS of the 20 studies were compared and evaluated amongst each other. Most of the studies included the internal and external environment, explained the kind of information to be used, to make decisions, to solve problems and included executives and top management as the main users; however, only a few of the studies mentioned how to display the information to users. For the purpose of this study an EIS can be defined as a computerised system that provides executives, top management and other senior managers with access to internal and external information; in short, information that is relevant, accurate, timely and up-to-date in order to make decisions, solve problems, determine critical success factors and satisfy information needs. These interest groups are primarily interested in summarised data that has been transformed into meaningful information, through the use of graphs, reports and on-line screens.

EISs function effectively in dynamic business conditions and are used in the most intensely competitive environment of businesses. Executives need to develop skills to respond to and to understand how to interact with the global environment that will eventually increase the value of the business and the value of the shareholder.

Purpose of the study and research question

The purpose of the study was to establish and to determine the existence and to what extent EISs exists in all levels of management and to identify the challenges companies experienced in listed JSE companies. This is demonstrated by an elucidation of business concepts for understanding an EIS and major challenges of EISs in listed JSE companies. The research question is to establish what the existence of EISs is to create awareness amongst EIS-users in understanding the challenges presented by EISs in listed JSE companies to compete successfully in a global environment.

Literature study

The literature study investigates the business concepts for understanding EISs and the challenges presented by EISs in listed JSE companies.

Business concepts for understanding Executive Information Systems

The challenges presented by an EIS are discussed and examined in the context of three business concepts, namely:

1. information
2. decision-making
3. the business environment.

Information

According to Hall (2007:21), '... the value of information to a user is determined by its reliability'. When all attributes and qualities are consistently present, information has reliability and adds value to the user. Unreliable information and information with no value may lead to wrong decisions, affect the performance of the business and may ultimately threaten the survival of the business. Meyer (2005) argues that information comes in many different forms and businesses need to investigate how to deal with relevant and discarded information: archive it or delete it. Another type of information that is highly significant and useful for executives is soft information, such as rumours, ideas, opinions and explanations, (Byrd & Marshall 1996:456) that is less structured than hard information, such as numbers, graphs and tables, and is often more difficult to store and retrieve in a computerised system. According to Boone and Kurtz (2006:490), '... information is the final frontier of organisations seeking to gain an edge over their competitors ...' and therefore management needs information and technology to manage their businesses successfully. Information systems assist the business to organise the overwhelming flood of information in a logical and accessible manner. Users need to be exposed to information to establish a connection between the business and the environment (Correia & Wilson 1997).

According to Boone and Kurtz (2006:490), you can give people responsibility and authority, but without any information they are helpless. For any information to be efficient and effective, and to add value and knowledge to the business, the information needs to be controlled and managed in the business. An information overflow can provide too much data for management to absorb and thus become irrelevant for decision-making. Paradoxically, too little information may also jeopardise the ability of management to make decisions. Information not only provides top management with direct access to information, but is also accessed or is filtered through to lower levels of management. Lower levels of staff are not always able to recognise the importance of information and in some cases pass the information on without interpreting its relevance and/or without consolidating and understanding the potential of the information. According to Martin, Dehayes, Hoffer and Perkins (1994:38), most successful EISs '... are available in consistent detail to all levels ...' in businesses and are still valid today; according to Averweg and Roldán (2006:632), 'the most important EIS groups are top functional managers and middle managers'. Therefore the value of information is also increased '... by providing rapid access to critical information' (Arnott et al. 2007:2078) to senior and middle management. Bocij et al. (2003:5) supplies several definitions of information that provide information in systems:

- data that have been processed that is meaningful
- data that have been processed for a certain purpose
- data that have been interpreted and understood by the recipient.

Bocij et al. (2003:37) define a system as '... a collection of interrelated components that work together towards a collective goal'. In all businesses the primary goal is to make a profit or to improve the quality of a product or a service. All systems in a business context receive inputs that need to be transformed into outputs.

Decision-making

Management is a series of decision-making processes. According to Averweg and Roldán (2006:625), an '... EIS is a computer-based technology designed in response to the specific needs of executives and for making both strategic and tactical decisions'. Therefore strategic and significant decisions need to be made quickly and accurately in a short period of time in order to solve problems effectively and efficiently. Mintzberg (1975:56) includes the information role as one of the managerial roles that incorporate monitoring, filtering and disseminating of information as a universal part of management and is still true today, according to Averweg and Roldán (2006:631), who state that 'one of the capabilities of an EIS is the filtering, organisation and consolidation of multiple data sources'.

Lessing and Scheepers (2004:23) state that communicating information to decision-makers is the most important function of the business. On the other hand Mintzberg and Waters (1990:4) argue that the concept of decision-making has outlived its usefulness and there are situations where actions are taken by management without decisions being made. Over the past few years several businesses confirmed the value of 'gut' feeling when management decisions are optimally made and realistic decision-making is based on existing data, which can be solved by the application of computer technology (Van Zyl 2010:12). According to Naicker (2010:21), decisions are based on the information available to users. Sourcing relevant and accurate information ensures that the decision making process encompasses all the aspects of the business and future trends. Averweg and Roldán (2006:626) stated that definitions of an EIS varied between different studies but all identify the need for information that supports decisions about the business as the most important reason for the existence of an EIS.

Business environment

Wessels (2008:148) states that advances in information technology have been identified as a key driver that affects the business environment. According to Typanski (1999:32), if an information environment is to be truly effective '... its resources must be managed so that they are in synch ...' with the overall business goals and strategies. The business is influenced by certain elements that affect the way in which it operates and is surrounded by the business environment. A new concept added to the business environment is the influence of e-business that involves the increasing efficiency of information flow, both within the business and with external sources. E-business supports business processes and is continually updating the external environment in order for managers to extract information in real-time to make decisions and solve problems. According to Averweg and Roldán (2006:632), an 'EIS is going through a major change to take advantage of Web-based technologies in order to satisfy information needs of an increasing group of users'.

Challenges of an Executive Information System

The challenges of an EIS may influence the implementation of an EIS in a business; 14 challenges of an EIS are identified in Figure 1 and are discussed in the next section. In context with the different challenges the 'input of data', streams of raw facts representing events occurring in the business before they have been organised and arranged into a form people can understand them, to be converted into 'output of information', data that have been shaped into a form that is meaningful and useful to human beings, in a business environment making decisions to provide feedback on a regular basis to solve problems. Persons at all levels need to feel that they have a role to play in the achievement of strategy and need feedback on their progress (Meyer 2011:50). One area, managing the everyday budget expenses of management, yields really fast benefits from real-time systems as the information needs to be fast, relevant, real-time, accessible and easy to understand (Phillips 2011:37).

Global environment

A global environmental analysis in which the EIS operate is conducted in such a way that it influences the way in which the business attains their overall goals (Bocij et al. 2003:519). Lessing and Scheepers (2004:14) define the environment as '... people and organisations'. Braman (1989:239) defines information in context with the global environment, as '... information that is not just affected by its environment, but is itself a factor affecting other elements in the environment'. Palvia, Kumar, Kumar and Hendon (1996:177) argue that businesses need to incorporate a global and international dimension in the design of EISs in global businesses in a global environment in order to conduct business and compete globally. Prokesch (2000:69) believes that all businesses are battling it out in the global information environment and facing common challenges like using knowledge more effectively than their competitors do.

Strategy of the business

Globalisation has forced South African businesses that wish to survive or to perform in a global environment, to consider a management information system as a strategic management information tool to achieve objectives within a specified time period (Nieman & Bennett 2002:376). Strategy development is strongly influenced by the environment the business operates in (Bocij et al. 2003:519). A combination of strategy and management processes is delivered through an EIS, which raises the standard of management performance for executives, management and users to ensure sustainability and strategic competitiveness for the business. 'Executing strategy successfully requires making tough, often uncomfortable choices based on simple logic and clear principles' (Simons 2010:100) as the road to success is to engage in emerging data and eventually in action plans. Porter (1996:64) states that the '... essence of strategy is in the activities – choosing to perform activities differently

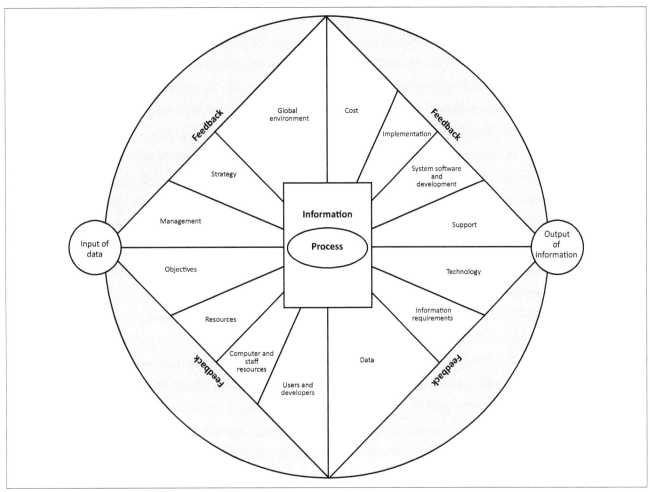

Source: Adapted from Boddy, D., Boonstra, A. & Kennedy, G., 2005, *Managing information systems: An organisational perspective*, 2nd edn., Pearson, Harlow, UK.

FIGURE 1: Challenges in an Executive Information System in context.

or to perform different activities than rivals'. In one of the studies, Pitts and Lei (2003:7) define strategy as '… referring to the ideas, plan, and support that firms employ to compete successfully against their rivals'.

Businesses need to know how to compete and to build a competitive advantage over their competitors. There is tension between an internal and external focus; on the one hand the focus is on external strategy in terms of positioning the business in its environment. On the other hand, the focus is on the extent to which it is able to be dependent on the internal capabilities and strategies of the business (Meyer 2011:51). Pitts and Lei (2003:7) argue that '… strategy is designed to help firms achieve competitive advantage'. To strategically position the business to be competitive is often not obvious nor an easy task and to position the business correctly requires creativity and insight by management. According to Burgelman and Doz (2004:118), new positions become available because of change; for example, new customers, distribution channels and new techniques.

Management of the business

Burgelman and Doz (2004:1181) state that the unique role of top management is the task of '… developing a strategy-making process that can balance the challenges associated with exploiting existing and new opportunities simultaneously'. Senior management owns a fiduciary responsibility to their stakeholders to ensure the business delivers value to its shareholders, the owners of the business (Pitts & Lei 2003:21). Management and senior executives need to be motivated and committed to influence their employees and to develop strategies that add value to the business and remain competitive in the industry (Stephenson 1986:33). If management do not commit and dedicate themselves, the result is poor management and a lack of control and direction. Voogt (2010:28) states that the role of the Chief Information Officer (CIO) has changed dramatically over the past few years. This as a result of the fact that the skills of the Chief Financial Officer (CFO) addressing IT risk strategically and understanding the impact of IT across all business functions will be invaluable in addressing IT governance.

Objectives of the business

Hall (2007:16) suggests three fundamental objectives that are common to all information systems. They are:

- to support the responsibility function of management
- to support management decision-making
- to support the business's day-to-day activities.

Objectives or goals are set during the design phase of a new system and stipulate what the system is responsible for, and how the system will contribute in assisting users to perform their tasks. The performance of the business (system) is measured by comparing it to the objectives of the business (Bocij *et al.* 2003:38). In the South African environment with diverse cultures, languages, religions, races and social backgrounds, personal objectives that may vary from person to person and this may cause conflict and rivalry amongst groups. Managers need to assist employees to solve any conflicts and personal problems in order to help attain the goals and objectives of the employees, which, in turn, will help to attain the goals and objectives of the business, and thus assuring the success of the business.

Combining data of multiple resources: Internal and external

According to Boone and Kurtz (2006:492), businesses can create their own databases of multiple resources to serve as an input in their information system. Averweg and Roldán (2006:631) stated that there are different types of sources of information that support an EIS, internal and external: corporate databases; operational databases; individuals; external databases; reports; the Internet; intranet and extranet. Watson, Watson, Singh and Holmes (1995:174) state that the top five motivating factors to develop an EIS are internal by nature. The five motivating factors in their rank order are as follows:

1. provide easier, faster access to information
2. improve the efficiency and effectives of senior executives
3. monitor organisational performance
4. improve communication
5. extract and integrate data from incompatible sources.

They continue by stating that the two factors relating to external environment are the '… competitive information …' and being able to '… monitor the external environment' (Watson *et al.* 1995:174).

Computer and staff resources

Watson *et al.* (1995:174) state that resource requirements are initiated and developed by teams with technical and business skills. The choice of software depends on the type of business and the availability of experienced and committed staff to make the correct choices to suit the needs of their business. Volonino, Watson and Robinson (1995:106) state that a common technology infrastructure drives the EIS and is achieved by customising interfaces and system capabilities. Salmeron (2003:35) argues that in order to develop staff in a business, certain computer, human and information technology resources are required.

Variety, complexity and defining of information requirements

Watson *et al.* (1995:173) state that EISs spread, evolve and '… over time, additional users are given access to the system and capabilities are put in place'. Information requirements change as the information technology and global environment change, therefore the variety of information to choose from becomes more complex and copious. Information is complex in the sense that there are so many sources with different versions of data available, that management must implement criteria that defend against the increasing risk from using unreliable sources (Lessing & Scheepers 2004:184). Frolick and Robichaux (1995:168) conclude that '… executive information requirements are dynamic, in many, perhaps most …' businesses. They also suggest that successful EIS information requires a thorough examination of the business's input from executives. According to Cheung and Babin (2006:1590), executive users become more computer literate, request more sophisticated information technology support and in many cases take charge of the system development process.

Controversy between users and developers

Young and Watson (1995:162) suggest that technical staff must be proficient to update EISs, as they change frequently. According to Frolick and Robichaux (1995:168), '… EIS developers must build and maintain a model of executives' information requirements'. There must be a mutual understanding between the specifications and requirements of executives and EIS users in order for developers to interpret the specifications and requirements correctly.

Data

Information systems need to provide instantaneous and controlled information for multi-user access to common corporate data files on a need-to-know basis (Cash, Mcfarlan & Mckenney 1992:126). Data is categorised as hard or soft, and internal or external. In contradiction, adhocracy leaders tend to avoid precise data and are more interested in opinions, explanations, written data and verbal stimuli (Byrd & Marshall 1996:456). The daunting task of management is to coordinate all the data and use well-chosen tools and procedures to ensure effective information systems.

Technology

'All innovation is now driven by technology in some way' and it is happening much faster (Cramm 2011:124). According to Nord and Nord (1995:102), '… as commercial EIS software improves, top executives must utilise the software technology for strategic decision-making and managing daily business activities in order to be competitive'. Therefore software technology changes constantly and management needs to keep up with the latest technology in order to be competitive. McLeod and Jones (1992:67) state that the use of technology improves the quality of information as computes have the potential to play an important role in the executive's information system. Klenke (1993:214) argues that existing and emerging technologies provide leadership opportunities for IS professionals to expand their role from technical managers to strategic leaders.

Support

EISs and information systems need technical and information support. Grindley (1991:3) describes the duties and responsibilities of developers and technical staff as follows: '... we control the computer. After all, we write the programs. But, once they're up and running we seem to lose the control we thought we had'. Clark (1994:33) states that IS managers are reluctant or unable to employ people to define and develop a variety of specialised systems in a diverse business environment. Watson (1992:242) stresses that '... good EIS support staff is critical'.

Development

Watson *et al.* (1995:175) state that '... developing an EIS may require an organisation to enhance its overall computing environment'. Watson *et al.* (1995:176) argue that there is no generally accepted EIS development life cycle and no agreement by businesses on the sequencing of activities in the life cycle. Byrd and Marshall (1996:462) contend that Chief Executive Officers (CEOs) do not have a great amount of time to devote to the development of systems such as EISs. Singh, Watson and Watson (2002:80) also conclude that the executive time needed to spend time with analysts is a scarce resource as executives get involved in what information is most important for them, how the information can be enhanced, how it should be displayed and how frequent it should be updated (Singh *et al.* 2002:80).

Implementation

Studies in the implementation of information systems vary whilst many businesses transform business operations successfully and enhancing business performance, to businesses that fail to meet the specified requirements. Boddy *et al.* (2005:223) state that businesses that operate in a volatile environment motivate competing businesses to implement new processes. People need to change the way they work and be willing to make significant technical and organisational changes.

Cost

Watson *et al.* (1995:175) state that '... EISs tend to be expensive' as 19% of the business's EIS are built in-house compared to 60% of businesses that rely exclusively on off-the-shelf software. Money is mostly wasted on market research, personnel cost and seeking suitable EIS software to implement. On the other hand many advantages of implementing EISs relating to cost are put forward such as low marketing and advertising cost, lower communication cost and lower printing and stationery cost.

Research design and methodology

The research study used a mixed method design that is quantitative and qualitative in nature. Questionnaires and interviews were used to collect data. The exploration proceeded in three stages: firstly, questionnaires were used to determine the status quo and the existence of EISs in businesses; secondly, interviews with management were conducted with businesses that have an EIS and plan to implement an EIS and thirdly, interviews with EIS-users in all levels of management were conducted. In stage one, the questionnaires were distributed via e-mail to all the

listed JSE companies for the attention of executives and top management as per the Questionnaire Annexure (added as a supplementary file), a total of 334 listed JSE companies at the time of the study. In stage two, seven respondents from the questionnaire were selected to participate in the interview process to collect in-depth information regarding their company's EISs status. The questions and results are reflected as per the Interviews Annexure in Group A and Group B (added as a supplementary file). In stage three, one company was selected from stage two (companies with an EIS) that consists of EIS-users in different levels of management. Six interviews were conducted from the different management levels of the company as per the Interviews Annexure in Group C (added as a supplementary file). Questions asked in the interviews varied from structured questions to open-ended questions. The results collected from the interviews were documented and analysed as per the Interviews Annexure (added as a supplementary file); in addition, the background and general observations from the interviews of all the companies per group were analysed and explained.

Findings

The findings from each of these three stages made a contribution to the study. For the purpose of this study the emphasis was on companies with EISs and companies that plan to implement EISs. Findings on companies with no EIS were analysed but not disclosed in this article.

Quantitative results: Questionnaires

The survey data from the questionnaires provided useful insight into listed JSE companies who have already implemented EISs and for those who plan to implement EISs. The data confirmed, as per Table 1, that there is a growing interest in EISs. Of the 65 companies that responded, (a response rate of 19.5%) 38.5% companies have currently implemented EISs and 20% of the remaining companies plan to implement EISs. Companies responded as followed:

- Group 1 – Twenty-five companies with EISs
- Group 2 – Twenty-seven companies with no EISs
- Group 3 – Thirteen companies plan to implement EISs.

Of the 13 respondents who planned to implement an EIS in the future (in Table 2), 38.5% of respondents planned to implement an EIS within one to two years, whilst both groups of 23.1% of the respondents planned to implement an EIS in 1 to 6 months and 6 to 12 months respectively. One respondent indicated that they wanted to implement an EIS in under 1 month.

Fifty two percent (52.1%) of the respondent's software formed part of the standard package, which included EIS.

Table 4 indicates that the number of users that access EISs is higher for larger companies.

Purposes for using Executive Information Systems

Respondents could select more than one purpose for using EISs. Potentially an EIS fulfils a wide range of purposes but as per Table 5 only the main purposes were listed.

The respondents could select more than one person as main users of EISs as per Table 6.

There was definitely a significant relationship evident between decision-making and problem solving in Table 6 versus quality and integrity of information in Table 7.

Decision-making and problem solving scored the highest as the most important purposes of EISs as per Table 5 and therefore executives rated the quality (35.4%) and integrity (32.3%) of information as the most important criteria for the success of EISs. There is definitely a significant relationship visible between the challenges of EISs and the criteria for success of EISs regarding the decision-making and problem solving versus quality and integrity of information. The third most important criterion for the success of EISs is user-friendliness (24.6%), followed by quick response time (23.1%).

The criterion 'cost' was not a major factor for the success of EISs and the criterion 'interest of staff' was not even considered important by respondents. Surprisingly the criterion 'better communication amongst management' (15.4%) was added as a last criterion to test the diversity of staff in current South African companies as well as the relationship of information technology developers versus users.

Qualitative results: Interviews

Seven executives from the respondents of the questionnaire were interviewed to determine how EISs or other information systems were used by executives and management and how the systems influenced the decision making process as per Group A and B. Six EIS-users were interviewed, as per Group C, in all levels of management. Interviews were conducted as follows:

1. Group A: Companies with EISs – Interviews with management of five companies.
2. Group B: Companies who plan to implement EISs – Interviews with management of two companies.
3. Group C: Company with an EIS with extended availability to all levels of management – Interviews with six EIS-users.

Companies with Executive Information Systems: Results of Group A

A successful EIS provides the executive with the necessary real-time information that is needed in decision-making and solving problems under time pressure. An EIS is a trusted source of information to be used as a management information tool for the companies. Companies had different software options for their EISs, the stand-alone off the shelf package was the most popular; EISs have been used for five years plus. The number of users accessing EISs varied from 26 to over 500 users. The accountant was the most prolific user. The three most ranked motivation factors were: to improve the effectiveness and efficiency of executives, to provide easier and faster access to information, and finally, to interface with other software. The five top-ranked purposes of EISs were:

TABLE 1: Existence of Executive Information Systems (EISs) in Johannesburg Stock Exchange companies.

Companies with an EIS	Frequency	Valid %
Yes	25	38.5
Yes, plan to implement an EIS	13	20.0
No	27	41.5
Total	65	100

TABLE 2: Implementation time of Executive Information Systems (EISs) in the near future.

Implementation time of an EIS	Frequency	Valid %
Less than 1 month	1	7.7
1–6 months	3	23.1
6–12 months	3	23.1
1–2 years	5	38.5
3–4 years	1	7.7
Total	13	100

TABLE 3: Software for existing Executive Information Systems (EISs).

Software for existing EISs	Frequency	Valid %
Part of the standard package which included an EIS	13	52
Hiring of external consultants to develop an EIS	4	16
Stand-alone off the shelf package	3	12
Own developed software	2	8
Other	3	12
Total	25	100

TABLE 4: Number of users accessing the complete Executive Information Systems (EISs).

Number of users accessing the complete EISs	Frequency	Valid %
26–50	7	28
51–75	5	20
76–100	2	8
101–200	3	12
201–500	2	8
501+	6	24
Total	25	100

TABLE 5: Purposes for using Executive Information Systems (EISs).

Purposes for using EISs	Marked	
	Count	%
Decision-making	24	36.9
Problem solving	15	23.1
Quick reference	8	12.3
Scheduling	6	9.2
Electronic mail	6	9.2
Other	3	4.6
Total	65	100

TABLE 6: Main users of Executive Information Systems (EISs).

Main users of EISs	Marked	
	Count	%
Executive	22	33.8
Chief Executive Officer	17	26.2
Accountant	15	23.1
Manager	13	20.0
Management Information Services	10	15.4
Other	3	4.6
Total	80	123

TABLE 7: Criteria for the success of Executive Information Systems (EISs).

Criteria for the success of EISs	Marked	
	Count	%
Quality of information	23	35.4
Integrity of information	21	32.3
User-friendly	16	24.6
Quick response time	15	23.1
Decision-making	13	20.0
Regularly updated	13	20.0
Management involvement	12	18.5
Better communication amongst management	10	15.4
Cost	9	13.8
Other	1	1.5

1. trend analysis
2. drill down facility
3. critical success factors
4. exception reporting
5. quick and immediate access.

The following five factors of EISs were the most crucial to add strategic value within companies:

1. quality of information
2. response time
3. availability of regularly required information
4. availability of market indicators
5. viruses.

Companies identified the following areas to improve EISs:

- to handle volume of data faster
- accessing relevant information
- automated systems.

The EIS, the Internet and e-mail were the most popular media executives used to source information. All companies confirmed that EISs assisted in decision-making.

Companies planning to implement Executive Information Systems: Results of Group B

One company planned to implement an EIS over a six-month period as phase one and the other company had already implemented an EIS in six of its 13 operations. Both companies felt that the EIS would:

- improve the immediate availability of information and the drill down to transaction level
- provide a system that is user-friendly
- decrease the working days substantially to produce consolidated Group results
- increase the strategic value for decision making and immediate problem solving.

The EIS is supported and empowered by the Chief Executive Officers (CEOs), Financial Directors (FDs) and Company Secretary (CS). Both the interviewees seek quicker, better and more efficient ways to do their day-to-day activities and produce timeous reports. Both companies use software that is part of a standard package. The implementation of an EIS is seen as being able to enhance the communication capabilities and improve the existing database of the company.

Company with an Executive Information Systems with extended availability to all levels of management: Results of Group C

All staff at all levels use the EIS on a daily basis, except for Junior Management staff who use the EIS monthly. The EIS enhances the positions of all staff members to add strategic value to the company by making decisions and solving problems much quicker, by identifying which business unit is performing or not, by extracting relevant trend analysis, by reducing the amount of paper-based reports, by managing the business effectively and by allowing quick and immediate access to up-to-date information. Different kinds of information are extracted from the EIS and vary from each management level. All the staff, at all levels of management, agreed that the EIS supports their day-to-day activities. Extracted information from the EIS is used differently in each category and varied from, amongst others:

- reporting to the Executive Committee and the Board
- running and managing the business
- answering queries
- confirming data and/or information
- making decisions
- sharing information and planning for future developments.

All staff members confirmed that there were areas to improve their EIS; for example, to be able to slice and dice information, to create a 'what if' analysis, to provide timeous provision of results, to improve the accuracy of information, to view a single customer, to centralise data, to navigate data, and to locate data logically.

Limitations of the study

The most crucial part of the empirical study was that questionnaires were limited to the top management and executives.

The following issues had an impact on the response rate of the questionnaires:

- Executives were out of office for a long period of time and reminders were sent out more than once.
- The mailing list with e-mail addresses was obtained from McGregor BFA. A few e-mail addresses were not included; therefore e-mail addresses were obtained from websites and telephonically. The Internet only provides general contact information e-mail addresses and not the e-mail addresses of CEOs, FDs, Managing Directors (MDs), directors and executives; therefore questionnaires were only e-mailed to the general information contact e-mailed addresses. Recipients of these e-mails were asked to forward the questionnaires to the addressed CEOs, FDs, MDs, directors or executives as per the mailing list.
- Nonrespondents that had no websites were contacted telephonically, but in some cases the telephone numbers were incorrect.
- Some listed JSE companies obtained from McGregor BFA were delisted or suspended.
- Some addressees e-mailed the sender directly without completing the questionnaire.

- Some listed JSE companies were contacted telephonically and phone calls were forwarded to the personal assistants (PAs) of the CEOs, FDs, MDs, directors or executives as they informed the author that their superiors do not participate in surveys or were unable to complete the survey as a result of time constrictions.
- A few JSE companies were not in the position to disclose the name or e-mail address of the CEOs, FDs, MDs, directors and executives telephonically.
- The McGregor mailing list did not include the most recent executives, as the annual reports of firms were only made available after the firm's financial year-end. Executives listed in the annual report at year-end already left the firm although the information needed by McGregor for their mailing list was obtained from the annual reports.

In addition, the research is limited to listed JSE companies in South Africa. The results are therefore only applicable to South Africa, but can be applied to other businesses that are not listed in South Africa.

Conclusion

From the findings of the study it was evident that companies view an EIS as an excellent management information tool which makes use of standard tools and built-in features that is critical for real-time decision-making, solving problems, creating a competitive edge and adding strategic value to companies. The speed of the decision-making process definitely increases the rapidity of problem identification since EISs are used by executives, top management and managers. Companies all confirmed that EISs could be of assistance in the decision-making process. The main reasons motivating companies to plan implementing an EIS include the following:

- major expansions in the company
- to improve the immediate availability of information
- a drill down facility to transaction level
- user-friendliness
- to decrease working days substantially to produce consolidated group results
- quicker and better ways to improve their daily routine and/or reduce or eliminate paper-based reports.

Companies confirmed that using an EIS as a management information tool, added value to their business, which contributed to the objectives of the study to understand the challenges presented by EISs in listed JSE companies.

Recommendations for future research

The research provides guidance for future research, as this study was to establish the existence of and challenges implicit in EISs in listed JSE companies. Furthermore the study also intended to explore the reasons why listed JSE companies do not have an EIS. Several respondents to the questionnaires and interviewees requested a report on the outcome of the results. As users need systems as an on-going process that provide access to diverse types of information there is therefore a need for continued research in the area of future EIS implementations and to document successful EIS development.

References

Arnott, D., Jirachiefpattana, W. & O'Donnell, P., 2007, 'Executive information systems development in an emerging economy', *Decision Support Systems* 42(4), 2078–2084. doi:10.1016/j.dss.2004.11.010

Averweg, U.R. & Roldán, J.L., 2006, 'Executive information system implementation in organisations in South Africa and Spain: A comparative analysis', *Computer Standards & Interfaces* 58(6), 625–634. doi:10.1016/j.csi.2005.06.001

Bajwa, D.S., Rai, A. & Brennan, I., 1998, 'Key antecedents of executive information system success: A path analytic approach', *Decision Support Systems* 22(1), 31–43. doi:10.1016/S0167-9236(97)00032-8

Bergeron, F., Raymond, L., Rivard, S. & Gara, M-F., 1995, 'Determinants of EIS use: Testing a behavioural model', *Decision Support Systems* 14(2), 131–146. doi:10.1016/0167-9236(94)00007-F

Bocij, P., Chaffey, D., Greasley, A. & Hickie, S., 2003, *Business information systems: Technology, development and management for the e-business*, 2nd edn., Prentice-Hall, Harlow, UK.

Boddy, D., Boonstra, A. & Kennedy, G., 2005, *Managing information systems: An organisational perspective*, 2nd edn., Pearson, Harlow, UK.

Boone, L.E. & Kurtz, D.L., 2006, *Contemporary Business 2006*, Thomson, Mason, USA.

Braman, S., 1989, 'Defining information: an approach for policymakers', *Telecommunications* 13, 233–242. doi:10.1016/0308-5961(89)90006-2

Burgelman, R.A., Christensen, C.M. & Wheelwright, S.C., 2004, *Strategic Management of technology and innovation*, McGraw-Hill, Singapore.

Burgelman, R.A. & Doz, L.D., 2004, 'The power of strategic integration' in R.A. Burgelman, C.M. Christensen & S.C. Wheelwright (eds.), *Strategic management of technology and innovation*, pp. 1174–1181, McGraw-Hill, Singapore.

Byrd, T.A. & Marshall, T., 1996, 'Corporate culture, related chief executive officer traits, and the development of executive information systems', *Computers in Human Behaviour* 12(3), 449–464. doi:10.1016/0747-5632(96)00018-0

Cash, J.I., Mcfarlan, F.W. & Mckenney, J.I., 1992, 'Corporate information systems management', 3rd edn., Irwin, IL.

Cheung, W. & Babin, G., 2006, 'A metadatabase-enabled executive information system (Part A): A flexible and adaptable architecture', *Decision and Support Systems* 42, 1589–1598. doi:10.1016/j.dss.2006.01.005

Clark, T.D. Jr, 1994, 'Corporate systems management' in R.D. Galliers & B.S.H. Baker (eds.), *Strategic Information Management*, pp. 29–51, Butterworths-Heinemann, Oxford, UK.

Correia, Z. & Wilson, T.D., 1997, 'Scanning the business environment for information: a grounded theory approach', *Information Research* 2(4), viewed 27 June 2006, from http://www.informationr.net/ir/2-4/paper21.html

Cramm, S., 2010, 'Helping Businesses help themselves', *Harvard Business Review* November, 124.

Elam, J.J. & Leidner, D.G., 1995, 'EIS adoption, use, and impact: the executive perspective', *Decision Support Systems* 14(2), 89–103. doi:10.1016/0167-9236(94)00004-C

Frolick, M.N. & Robichaux, B.P., 1995, 'EIS information requirements determination: Using a group support system to enhance the strategic business objectives method', *Decision Support Systems* 14(2), 157–170.

Friend, D., 1992, 'EIS and the collapse of the information pyramid' in H.J. Watson, R.K. Rainer & G. Houdeshel, *Executive Information Systems: Emergence, Development, Impact*, pp. 327–335 Wiley, New York.

Frolick, M.N. & Robichaux, B.P., 1995, 'EIS information requirements determination: Using a group support system to enhance the strategic business objectives method', *Decision Support Systems* 14(2), 157–170. doi:10.1016/0167-9236(94)00009-H

Grindley, K., 1991, *Managing IT and board level*, Pitman, London, UK.

Hall, J.A., 2007, *Accounting Information Systems*, 5th edn., Thomson, Mason, USA.

Ikart, E.M., 2005, 'Executive information systems and the top-officers' roles: An exploratory study of user-behaviour model and lessons learnt', *Australian Journal of Information Systems* 13(1), 78–100.

Khan, S.J., 1996, 'The benefits and capabilities of executive information systems', MBA dissertation, University of the Witwatersrand, Johannesburg, South Africa.

Klenke, K., 1993, *SIGCPR Annual conference, changing roles of information systems professionals: From technical managers to strategic leaders*, ACM, New York.

Lessing, N. & Scheepers, C., 2004, *Information is a management issue*, 9th edn., CSIC Publishers, Johannesburg.

Martin, E.W., Dehayes, D., Hoffer, J.A. & Perkins, W.C., 2005, *Managing information technology*, 5th edn., Pearson, Upper Saddle River, NJ.

Martin, E.W., Dehayes, D., Hoffer, J.A. & Perkins, W.C., 1994, *Managing information technology: What managers need to know*, 2nd edn., Macmillan, New York.

Mcleod, R. Jr & Jones, J.W., 1992, 'Making executives information systems more effective', in H.J. Watson, R.K. Rainer & G. Houdeshel, *Executive Information Systems: Emergence, Development, Impact*, pp. 53–69, Wiley, New York.

Meyer, H.W.J., 2005, 'The nature of information, and the effective use of information in rural development', *Information Research* 10(2), 214–225.

Meyer, T., 2011, 'The art of strategy what CEOs need to know', *Accountancy SA,* December 2010 – January 2011, 50–51.

Mintzberg, H. & Waters, J.S., 1990, 'Studying deciding: An exchange of views between Mintzberg and Waters, Pettigrew, and Butler', *Organizational Studies* 11(1), 1–16. doi:10.1177/017084069001100101

Mintzberg, H., 1975, 'The managers' job: Folklore and fact', *Harvard Business Review,* July–August, 49–61.

Naicker, D., 2010, 'CFO Responsibilities in an emerging market', *Accountancy SA,* September, 21.

Nichols, G.E., 1990, 'On the nature of Management Information' in R. Galliers, *Information Analysis,* pp. 7–17, Addison-Westley, Sydney.

Nieman, G. & Bennett, A., 2002, *Business management,* Van Schaik, Pretoria.

Nord, J.H. & Nord, G.D., 1995, 'Executive information systems: A Study and comparative analysis', *Information & Management* 29(2), 95–106. doi:10.1016/0378-7206(95)00013-M

Olson, D.L. & Courtney, J.F., 1992, *Decision support models and expert systems,* Macmillan, New York.

Palvia, P., Kumar, A., Kuma, N. & Hendon, R., 1996, 'Information requirements of a global EIS: An exploratory macro assessment', *Decision Support Systems* 16(2), 169–179. doi:10.1016/0167-9236(95)00005-4

Phillips, K., 2011, 'To Liberate Accountants first empowers the business', *Accountancy SA,* December 2010 – January 2011, 37.

Pitts, A. & Lei, D., 2003, *Strategic Management: Building and sustaining competitive advantage,* Thomson, Canada.

Pijpers, G.G.M., Bemelmans, T.M.A., Heemstra, F.J. & Van Montfort, K.A.G.M., 2001, 'Senior executive' use of information technology', *Information and Software Technology* 43(15), 959–971. doi:10.1016/S0950-5849(01)00197-5

Porter, M., 1996, 'What is strategy?', *Harvard Business Review,* November–December, 61–78.

Prokesch, S.E., 2000, *Harvard Business Review: Interviews with CEOs: Unleashing the power of learning,* 5th edn., Harvard Business School, Boston, MA.

Rainer, R.K. & Watson, H.J., 1995, 'What does it take for successful executive information system?', *Decision Support Systems* 14(2), 147–156. doi:10.1016/0167-9236(94)00008-G

Remenyi, D.S.J., 1991, *Introduction strategic information systems planning,* NCC Blackwell, Oxford, UK.

Salmeron, J.L., 2002, 'EIS date: findings from an evolutionary study', *The Journal of Systems and Software* 64(2), 111–114. doi:10.1016/S0164-1212(02)00030-4

Salmeron, J.L., 2003, 'EIS success: keys and difficulties in major companies', *Technovation* 23(1), 35–38. doi:10.1016/S0166-4972(01)00076-1

Simons, R., 2010, 'Stress-Test your strategy', *Harvard Business Review,* November, 92–100.

Singh, S.K., Watson, H.J. & Watson, R.T., 2002, 'EIS support for the strategic management process', *Decision Support Systems* 33(1), 71–85. doi:10.1016/S0167-9236(01)00129-4

Stephenson, B.Y., 1986, 'Information: A strategic business weapon: DSS-86 Transactions', *Sixth international conference on Decision Support Systems,* edited by J. Fedorowicz, College on Information Systems, Washington, DC.

Sterrenberg, G.K., 1990, 'The structure of executive information systems', MBA dissertation, University of the Witwatersrand, Johannesburg, South Africa.

Turban E, Mclean, E. & Wetherbe, J., 1996, *Information technology for management,* Wiley, Toronto.

Typanski, R.E., 1999, 'Creating an effective information environment', *Information Systems Management* 16(2), 32–39. doi:10.1201/1078/43188.16.2.19990301/31174.6

Van Zyl, J., 2010, 'More than a gut feeling', *Finweek,* 11 November 2010, 12.

Volonino, L., Watson, H.J. & Robinson, S., 1995, 'Using EIS to respond to dynamic business conditions', *Decision Support Systems* 14(2), 105–116. doi:10.1016/0167-9236(94)00005-D

Voogt, T., 2010, 'IT Governance Dear CFO what should we do?', *Accountancy SA,* October, 28–30.

Watson, H.J., Watson, R.T., Singh, S. & Holmes, D., 1995, 'Development practices for executive information systems: Findings of a field study', *Decision Support Systems* 14(2), 171–184. doi:10.1016/0167-9236(94)00010-P

Watson, H.J., 1992, 'Avoiding hidden EIS pitfalls a case study: What you see isn't always what you get', in H.J. Watson, R.K. Rainer & G. Houdeshel, *Executive Information Systems: Emergence, Development, Impact,* pp. 237–244, Wiley, New York.

Wessels, P.L., 2008, 'The identification and discussion of strategies for implementing an IT skills framework in the education of professional accountants', *SA Journal of Accounting Research* 22(1), 147–172.

Wheeler, F.P., Chang, S.H. & Thomas, R.J., 1993, 'Moving from EIS to everyone's information system: Lessons from a case study', *Journal of Information Technology* 8, 177–183. doi:10.1057/jit.1993.24

Xu, X.M. & Kaye, G.R., 2002, 'Knowledge workers for information support: Executives' perceptions and problems', *Information Systems Management* 19(1), 81–90. doi:10.1201/1078/43199.19.1.20020101/31480.11

Young, D. & Watson, H.J., 1995, 'Determinants of EIS acceptance', *Information & Management* 29(3), 153–164. doi:10.1016/0378-7206(95)00011-K

5

Fusing website usability and search engine optimisation

Authors:
Eugene B. Visser[1]
Melius Weideman[2]

Affiliations:
[1]Purple Cow Communications, Cape Town, South Africa

[2]Website Attributes Research Centre, Cape Peninsula University of Technology, South Africa

Correspondence to:
Melius Weideman

Email:
weidemanm@cput.ac.za

Postal address:
PO Box 3109, Tyger Valley 7536, South Africa

Background: Most websites, especially those with a commercial orientation, need a high ranking on a search engine for one or more keywords or phrases. The search engine optimisation process attempts to achieve this. Furthermore, website users expect easy navigation, interaction and transactional ability. The application of website usability principles attempts to achieve this. Ideally, designers should achieve both goals when they design websites.

Objectives: This research intended to establish a relationship between search engine optimisation and website usability in order to guide the industry. The authors found a discrepancy between the perceived roles of search engines and website usability.

Method: The authors designed three test websites. Each had different combinations of usability, visibility and other attributes. They recorded and analysed the conversions and financial spending on these experimental websites. Finally, they designed a model that fuses search engine optimisation and website usability.

Results: Initially, it seemed that website usability and search engine optimisation complemented each other. However, some contradictions between the two, based on content, keywords and their presentation, emerged. Industry experts do not acknowledge these contradictions, although they agree on the existence of the individual elements. The new model highlights the complementary and contradictory aspects.

Conclusion: The authors found no evidence of any previous empirical experimental results that could confirm or refute the role of the model. In the fast-paced world of competition between commercial websites, this adds value and originality to the websites of organisations whose websites play important roles.

Introduction

Background to the study

Small and medium-sized enterprises (SMEs) make up approximately 95% to 98% of all businesses in most countries. They provide many work opportunities and are essential for any country's economic growth (Samujh 2011). Information technology (IT) is also a main driver of economies. It facilitates the growth of SMEs through expansion into new markets, overcoming obstacles, allowing for quicker responses to changes in consumer patterns and allowing SMEs to compete internationally (Thurasamy et al. 2009). Internet-based technology is a significant part of IT and is an investment that drives innovation (Oliveira & Martins 2010).

In order for SMEs to sustain financial growth, they must adopt marketing systems that facilitate the buyers' and the sellers' decision-making processes (Layton 2011). In recent years, many SMEs have adapted to e-marketing. This allows dynamic business growth and changes the shape and nature of business by overcoming threats and creating new business opportunities (El-Gohary 2010). Because of e-business, e-marketing, e-commerce and internet user activity, SMEs often use websites to present and market products and/or services because the internet is rapidly becoming a communication, commerce and marketing medium that is changing business globally (Canavan, Henchion & O'Reilly 2007; Küster & Vila 2011; Visser 2007).

After 1993, the release date of Archie Like Indexing for the WEB (ALIWEB), search engine development progressed rapidly. This occurred in the methods developers used to index information on the internet and the methods they used to provide searchers with the most relevant information available in the shortest time possible, given the search query.

The process of search engine optimisation (SEO) aims to improve the visibility of web pages to search engine crawlers. Today, SEO is an online marketing channel. SEO addresses design, architecture and content to allow for the better ranking of selected keywords. The results searchers receive are the search engine result pages (SERPs). They fall into two sections: organic (that occupies the primary real estate of the SERPs) and pay per click (PPC) that occupies the right-hand sides and sometimes the tops of the SERPs). Today, three major search engines dominate the market: Google, Bing and Yahoo! Of these, Google is by far the most popular (Carpineto *et al.* 2009). Currently, these three combined command over 95% of the world market in core searches per month (Adamo 2013).

In order to satisfy searchers' needs best, engines must extract and present the indexed information, which is most relevant to the searchers' queries, to the searchers for scrutiny. However, this is a complicated process because of the sheer volume of information available on the internet. Search engines must index this using search engine crawler programs and rank it appropriately using organic ranking algorithms.

The inner algorithmic workings of search engines are essential because searchers are often more interested in the quality of the search results than their quantity (Yang, Yang & Yuan 2007). Research has shown that, on average, searchers view no more than three SERPs for any particular search query. In fact, the closer any particular web page ranks to the first position on the first SERP, the higher the chances are for searchers to view that particular web page (Weideman 2009).

The research problem of this paper is that of the reduced productivity that results from the lack of guidance on the synergy between applying SEO and the usability of websites. The goal of this paper was to determine whether there is a relationship between search engine optimisation and website usability. If there is, this paper wants to determine this relationship. A model embodies this goal, which will be useful to industry and academe alike.

Literature review

Soon after search engines became popular, it emerged that people discovered between 42% and 86% of all websites through search engines (Thurow 2003). More recently, it emerged that almost 85% of all e-commerce began with queries submitted to search engines (Murphy & Kielgast 2008). These statistics make e-marketing a crucial component from a business perspective. Engines keep organic ranking algorithms confidential in order to avoid abuse (Jerkovic 2010).

An in-depth look at the literature on the search engine optimisation, website usability and spamdexing is necessary at this stage.

Search engine optimisation

SEO is the process of altering websites. It emphasises semantically themed keywords for search engines in order to improve website rankings. This, in turn improves websites' chances of being found in SERPs (Weideman 2009).

The head Google spam engineer has indicated that the Google organic ranking algorithm consists of approximately 200 elements. This suggests that Google considers 200 on- and off-page elements, which determine the relevancy of the search results presented in the SERPs (Cutts 2010). Many industry experts speculate what these elements are, along with the weight assigned to each element based on results when they conduct their own experiments. Several authors list a number of elements that would improve organic rankings (Google 2011d; Moz 2013; Sullivan 2011; Sullivan 2012).

The methodology uses understanding search queries from the searchers' perspectives as its basis. Search engines can attempt to determine the context of search queries, based on past searches, although this may seem almost impossible. Search engines do this by analysing the estimated time searchers spend on websites before returning to the search engines in order to submit refined queries and discussions on social networks that provide integrated and associated search engine results (Google 2011c; Rayson 2013). The foundation of the methodology uses the fact that search engines have interpretations of current indexed information as its basis. Therefore, search engines may actually be able to interpret the current indexed information better by associating search queries to the indexed content using searcher behaviour patterns. By monitoring ever-changing searcher behaviour patterns, search engines could constantly reorganise search results according to relevance (Google 2009; Sullivan 2009).

Google (along with other search engines) allows users (anonymous or identified) to share data with Google. Searchers conduct approximately 400 million searches every day on the Google search engine (Google 2011a; Enge *et al.* 2010). The vast amount of interpreted data search engines extract anonymously could give them enough information to make an appropriate interpretation of searched queries. Google's predictive search functionality is only one example of how Google uses searcher behaviour patterns based on popularity (see Figure 1).

Search engines also depend on editorial judgement, or link popularity, to interpret and determine the relevance of the

FIGURE 1: Google's predictive search functionality.

indexed information better. Search engines would perceive a link from a credible website as a good quality link. Therefore, they would apply a positive 'vote' to the website at which the link is directed. Consequently, search engines can only perceive credible websites if the links they obtain come from other credible websites. This suggests that the quality of links they obtain is more important than the quantity of links. Furthermore, they need to associate the content on the website from which the link originated, and the content on the destination website of the same link, in some way from a thematic perspective. The anchor text (keywords the actual link uses) is also important and ideally should align with the destination web page's semantic themes and targeted keywords if search engines are to regard the link as worthy (Thurow 2008).

Search engines do yield relevant results. However, non-relevant results still appear in SERPs more often than not. In a perfect world, SEO marketers could assist search engines by ensuring that search engines apply only white hat SEO tactics to particular websites, thus 'cleaning' up the internet and reducing spamdexing. Unfortunately, as long as they can earn money through spamdexing, search engines will have to generate new ideas and organic ranking algorithm updates in order to discourage black hat SEO tactics. Eventually, this should reduce spamdexing.

Researchers have conducted new research recently. It involved university institutional repositories and using metadata to optimise them for search engine crawler visits. One study focused specifically on Google Scholar™. The researchers found that, if they changed the metadata in these repositories from Dublin Core to Google Scholar's own prescriptions, indexing rose significantly (Arlitsch & O'Brien 2012).

SEO is an online marketing strategy. The basis of the SEO strategy is to address website design, architecture and content so that search engine spiders can make appropriate interpretations in terms of the themed keywords and rank websites accordingly. Strictly speaking, the goal of SEO is to satisfy search engine spiders and organic ranking algorithms by aligning the targeted themed web page content with the semantically interpreted keywords when considering search queries.

Spamdexing

The basis of the search engine revenue model is PPC advertising. However, the search functionality is available at all times and is free for public use. Search engine success still depends on providing relevant results to searchers in the shortest time possible as non-relevant and/or slow results may deter searchers from using particular search engines. Therefore, non-relevant results could have a direct effect on search engines' revenue.

Because of the direct association between search engine rankings and searchers' behaviour when viewing SERPs, it

becomes clear that website owners may attempt to manipulate search engine rankings to increase their businesses' exposure. Spamdexing (also known as search engine spam) refers to websites that attempt to deceive search engines, whereby the results they provide to searchers are not relevant when one considers their search queries (Weideman 2009). Search engines regard this behaviour as unscrupulous and unsolicited.

As a result, major search engines use engineers who focus only on eliminating spamdexing. However, search engines do not publish their preventative spamdexing rules. Instead, they publish their (mostly vague) best practice guidelines. They do this to protect their organic ranking algorithms because are part of the foundation of their revenue models (Enge *et al.* 2010). At the same time, some search engines regularly adapt their algorithms to detect and flag websites that contain attempts at spamdexing. In Google's case, some of these updates (termed Panda and Penguin) often have dramatic effects on a small percentage of search results (Cooper 2013; Quinton 2012). The industry watches these changes closely. They normally cause a spurt of activity because commercial concerns could experience decreases in revenue if their websites drop in position on the ranking lists.

Spamdexing can occur on two levels: content manipulation and link structure manipulation. Content manipulation is restricted to on-page factors – elements over which only website authors have control. In earlier days, search engines depended primarily on what search engine spiders could see during indexing. This allowed website authors to manipulate web page structure so that search engine spiders could not see some content and only visitors could – and vice versa. Furthermore, it often included targeted keywords and/or repeated them a number of times on a particular web page (keyword stuffing), whereby the web page content would not make contextual sense to visitors. However, search engine spiders would prioritise the keywords irrespective of the website's semantic theme for ranking purposes (Wu & Davison 2006). This is becoming less of a problem today because search engines' algorithms now depend more on link popularity. Conversely, this discloses the opportunity to link structure manipulation. Because of the importance of link popularity, in terms of organic ranking algorithms, one should note that link popularity manipulation is more difficult to detect than is content manipulation.

In the past, black hat SEO marketers sometimes sold apparently undetectable spam methods. However, Google engineers have indicated that one can detect spamdexing (Cutts 2007). This is an interesting statement given the recent findings of spamdexing in the Google SERPs because of link manipulation. The JC Penney fiasco provided more than enough evidence to indicate that one can regard Google's best practice guidelines for link schemes as nothing more than interesting reading (Google 2011b). An article, which the *New York Times* published, discovered that JC Penney (a department store chain) obtained over 2000 links, mostly from non-related websites. They varied from nuclear engineering and property portholes to casino-focused websites, all with the appropriate JC Penney themed anchor text (see Segal 2011). Although the JC Penney website seemed to have participated in search engine prohibited link schemes, the website still maintained high rankings for a number of targeted terms in Google SERPs. This discovery convinced SEO marketers that link farms and off-topic website linking schemes still have positive ranking effects, despite Google best practice guidelines. The recent Google organic ranking algorithm update 'Panda' (as a direct result of the JC Penney fiasco) is another attempt to fight spamdexing and enforce prohibited link schemes.

Spamdexing is increasing significantly, simply because black hat SEO marketers can make money from it. Unfortunately, it is difficult to measure search quality because search result quality is relative to searchers' perspectives of their search queries. Ultimately, automated algorithmic solutions may not be the best way to solve the spamdexing problem. The different search engines may actually have to collaborate in order to find an effective solution. However, it is interesting to note that the Google search engine may be responsible, to some extent, for a number of spamdexing websites. Personally owned websites, as opposed to SERPs, display Google AdSense™ ads (which is part of PPC advertising). Websites that contain AdSense™ ads are, in some circumstances, created with the sole purpose of obtaining visitors who could click on any of the displayed AdSense™ ads. With every click on any of the AdSense™ ads, Google earns money, as does the author of the website that displays the AdSense™ ads. Therefore, certain search engines might first have to look at their revenue models and their functionality before addressing the spamdexing problem successfully (Cutts 2011).

Website usability

Visitors to a website usually have specific questions about a particular problem or need (Eisenberg *et al.* 2008). Although one may perceive search engines as facilitators, they must still address searchers' needs in terms of finding the appropriate website associated with the search queries. Searchers have come to understand that search engines attempt to provide the most relevant results first. This implies that, if they do not obtain the 'correct' result within the first three SERPs, the remaining results will probably also be irrelevant. Because search engines do not always comprehend search queries from the searchers' perspectives fully – often resulting in non-relevant and/or spamdexing results – searchers must frequently alter their search queries to clarify the information they need.

Figure 2 illustrates a typical searcher's process for finding information.

Searchers seldom leave search engines if they do not meet the searchers' information needs. The reason for this is that search engines are the facilitators and because there are not many alternatives (in layout and/or functionality) that can

guarantee that they will meet the information needs. On the other hand, visitors treat websites differently.

One can categorise the intentions and motivations for visiting websites as:

- exploration
- information
- entertainment
- shopping.

Whatever reasons visitors have for visiting websites, developers create websites for information, opinion, marketing and/or for financial gain in one way or another. Website usability (WU) addresses the functional application of information about visitors' ability to interact successfully with that information. Therefore, the goal is to remove any obstacles that could impede visitors' experiences when interacting with websites (Eisenberg *et al.* 2008).

Website usability defines the quality of the visitors' experiences because it addresses mechanical and persuasive usability problems (Visser & Weideman 2011a; Visser & Weideman 2011b). Website usability statistics have shown that there is only a 12% probability that visitors will revisit a particular website. This shows that, once a website has lost a visitor because of the lack of WU, the visitor is usually lost for good (Nielsen & Loranger 2006). Therefore, one should see WU as important (if not more important) than SEO, which, in turn, emphasises the importance of fusing SEO and WU.

Although developers ultimately create websites for visitors, the visitors may initially not be aware of the websites' existence. Searchers are never fully aware of all the websites on the internet relevant to particular search queries. Therefore, search engines that will provide searchers with

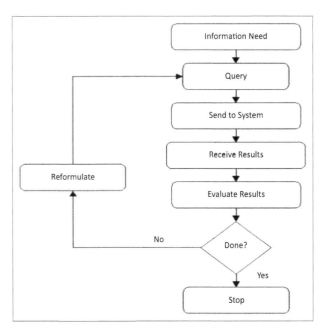

Source: Baeza-Yates, R. & Ribeiro-Neto, B., 1999, *Modern information retrieval*, Addison-Wesley, Harley

FIGURE 2: Standard information access process.

the most relevant results using organic ranking algorithms' interpretations are necessary. Although designers create these search engine results dynamically, the results are still subjective. They depend on the organic ranking algorithms that often provide irrelevant and/or spam results.

In addition, the SERPs may not have listed the ideal website results (or listed them very low down), because those websites were not visible to the search engine spiders (or did not satisfy the organic ranking algorithms appropriately). Search engine spiders and organic ranking algorithms depend on a number of pre-programmed rules that correspond with the conceptual models of the internet. This shows that, if search engine spiders have not crawled and indexed a website, that website cannot possibly rank in the SERPs. Furthermore, if the organic ranking algorithms do not interpret the web page appropriately, then that web page may not rank at all for the targeted keywords.

In summary, website authors must regard the search engine optimisation guidelines (SEO elements) as priorities whilst designing and developing websites if search engines are to crawl, index and rank websites for targeted keywords.

One should not interpret WU as the usefulness of websites from personal angles. Instead, one should regard WU as a task-orientated function from anonymous, yet personal perspectives. It is important for visitors to know, exactly and intuitively, how to accomplish specific tasks on any particular website. Therefore, WU addresses the effectiveness, efficiency, learnability, memorability, error recovery and satisfaction of websites (Thurow & Musica 2009). Although artificial intelligence or algorithms do not govern it, WU has a number of attributes that one could apply to particular websites in order to improve interaction. All websites are different. However, the fundamental attributes remain the same in terms of how visitors interpret web pages. The actual design of websites is a crucial component of WU, and, by using graphic and textual signals, visitors should, at any point, be able to identify the current location, as well as the process involved in order to reach the desired destination whilst considering their objectives.

SEO is an essential component, as is WU, of successful websites. Therefore, SEO and WU will form the foundation for successful websites. However, spamdexing is also an essential component because developers must apply SEO so that search engines ideally never perceive business websites as spam. In addition, information-seeking platforms are changing. This will have an effect on WU if websites do not change to accommodate platform-specific devices appropriately (Nicholas *et al.* 2013). One can view successful SEO as the card to draw visitors to websites (via SERPs), whilst usability is the glue that keeps visitors interacting with websites. When combined correctly, the two will convert searchers to users to buyers – an action often called conversion.

Research method and design

The effect of SEO on websites depends largely on a simultaneous combination and deployment of all SEO elements. On the other hand, WU addresses the functional application of information to visitors.

The authors used a pre-test and post-test quantitative methodological design. They analysed the on-page SEO elements, which conflict with WU attributes, by using three websites that offer identical services. The authors analysed:

- **The control website (CW):** The CW (which a business with minimal knowledge of SEO and WU created) has existed since 2006 (http://www.copywriters.co.za). It consists of 34 pages and 17 114 words of content. Because of the domain age, search engines had already successfully crawled and indexed the website. In addition, the website had generated a number of existing inlinks from several sources on the world wide web. However, for the purpose of this experiment, the authors excluded the referrer and direct traffic sources from the traffic-source data collection. One should note that the authors made no changes to the CW during the experiment.
- **The experimental website (EW):** The authors created the EW with WU in mind. However, they deliberately ignored all SEO elements with minimal content (http://www.copywriters.co.za/ppc/). They isolated it from all forms of website traffic other than that PPC generated. They obtained user feedback by measuring the number of conversions the website obtained. One should also note that they made no changes to the EW during the experiment.
- **Experimental website 2 (EW2):** The authors created EW2 with SEO in mind. However, they deliberately ignored all WU attributes. They launched the newly formed http://www.translation-copywriters.co.za website on 01 July 2010. It had no existing in-links, 29 web pages and 48 923 words of content. They also excluded referrer and direct traffic from the traffic-source data collection on this website. Organic and PPC traffic were the primary traffic sources. The first search engine crawled and indexed this website on 08 July 2010. During the next four months, the authors made systematic SEO changes to the website and recorded the primary experiment ranking measurements on 08 November 2010. These changes appear below.
  - On 08 August 2010, the authors added 8077 words. They also optimised the metadata. This included headings and the anchor text in terms of the keywords.
  - On 08 September 2010, the authors added 5362 words. They also optimised the metadata. This included headings and the anchor text in terms of the keywords (similar to the changes the authors made in the previous month).
  - On 08 October 2010, the authors added 5726 words. They applied theming and internal linking to emphasise contextual phrasing and semantically related keywords.

- On 08 November 2010, the authors added 3080 words. They increased keyword density, frequency and proximity using the benchmarks they obtained for high-ranking competitors on the same-targeted keywords.

The primary experiment focused on monitoring 130 specific keywords and their rankings on the three major search engines (Google, Yahoo! and Bing). The intention was to compare the control website's rankings with those that Experimental Website Two generated in order to determine whether applying SEO elements to a particular website had a direct effect on improved website ranking for targeted keywords. An extract of this keyword or phrase list follows.

Ad jingles; advertising and editorial writing; advertising copy; industry specific articles copywriting; informative media writing; internet copywriting; jingle writing; strategic business copywriting; strategic copywriting; technical editing; translate English into Afrikaans.

The authors conducted three additional experiments:

- **Organic traffic:** The authors measured organic traffic for the CW and the EW2 daily on each domain. They grouped the results every month and interpreted them using a linear regression analysis. The objective was to determine whether the organic ranking improvements had a direct effect on increases in organic traffic.
- **Conversion (submitting a contact form):** To establish the effectiveness of WU, the authors conducted conversion testing using a PPC campaign that they applied to all three websites for 49 days, with a budget of R3000.00 each. They decided to use the Kruskal-Wallis test to inspect the difference between variables. The specific variables the authors examined were the *average time on site per visitor*, *the average page views per visit* and *the average number of conversions obtained per visitor*. The objective was to determine whether the WU attributes, which contradict SEO elements, are essential to implement in order to improve website conversions.
- **Interviews:** The authors conducted interviews with five randomly selected website users with a minimum of eight years of internet exposure in order to:
  1. Identify WU attributes that they might have overlooked.
  2. Consider human interaction compared to a focus on theory only.

Results

Through statistical analysis (using a univariate analysis of variance testing), the authors determined whether or not the web page to which a search was directed and the direction from which the search originated (global or local) has a significant effect on ranking positions. Although the results from the primary experiment, recorded on 08 November 2010, indicated that the search engine from which the search originated does not have a significant effect on rankings, the authors determined that, in all instances, the rankings for the EW2 were significantly better than those of the CW were.

This showed that applying SEO elements to a particular website had a direct effect on improved website rankings for targeted keywords.

The additional experiments the authors conducted revealed:

- **Organic traffic:** Using linear regression analysis, the authors determined that the coefficient for X showed that the traffic trend for the EW2 increased significantly over time. However, the coefficient for X on the Control Website indicated there was no significant trend for traffic over time. The authors determined that 51.4% of the variation in traffic to both websites was because of changes in time and alterations to the website. This showed that the organic ranking improvements had a direct effect on organic traffic increases.
- **Conversion:** The results the authors gleaned from the conversion analysis of all three websites on the three main variables (*average time on site per visitor, the average page views per visit* and *the average number of conversions obtained per visitor*) showed that there was a significant statistical difference between the CW, EW and EW2. The EW yielded the highest number of conversions. This shows that applying WU attributes is essential to improving website conversions.
- **Interviews:** The user feedback showed that WU attributes are important factors when visitors are deciding whether or not to interact with a website. The authors determined that participants perceived that some SEO elements were obstacles to WU. This confirmed the existence of SEO and WU contradictions. The participants agreed unanimously that the EW website was the one that provided the best user experience.

On the surface, it seems that SEO and WU complement each other (Visser & Weideman 2011b). However, one should note that SEO and WU contradict each other in some cases. Figure 3 presents the 'fused SEO and WU model' on the left (marked A). On the right, marked B, Figure 3 presents the key to interpreting the model. The model consists of three main sections: SEO, WU and additional considerations. The connecting red lines illustrate the contradictions between SEO and WU. The bottom of the Figure illustrates the fused SEO and WU solution.

Essentially, the contradictions between SEO and WU revolve around content, keywords and their presentation. Search engines are not human and, regardless of how advanced artificial intelligence may become, the probability of their completely simulating human behaviour is low. Essentially, search engine crawlers consider two components: the information actual web pages provide and other web pages that give opinions about the information on the web pages. The opinions of others could have an effect on the human decision-making process. However, reflecting on previous actions and human intuition defines the human decision-making process (Eisenberg *et al.* 2008; Pather & Remenyi 2005).

Furthermore, search engines also need to evaluate the competitive component for ranking priorities. This shows that

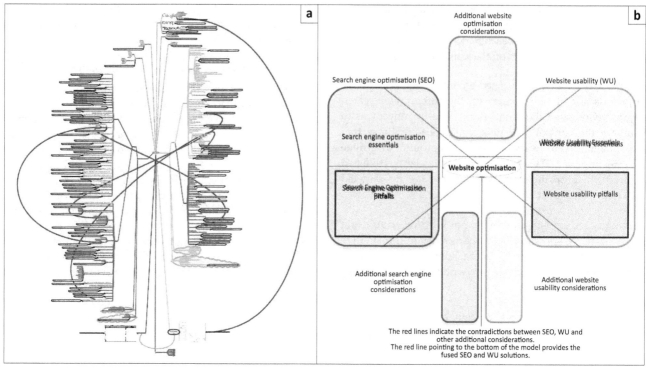

FIGURE 3: The fused search engine optimisation and website usability model (a) and the fused search engine optimisation and website usability model key and colour codes (b). (A scalable image of the model is available at http://www.eugene-visser.co.za)

it is important to understand what websites are about and whether website X will better satisfy visitors' needs compared to website Y. In order to achieve this, websites must emphasise the information they provide to search engines. This would lead to an enormous amount of content and keyword or phrase semantic emphasis. Conversely, visitors are not interested in an overwhelming amount of content. This could entice visitors to leave websites out of frustration.

Other contradictions revolve around how search engines have attempted to simulate visitors' interpretations of websites by evaluating their behaviour patterns. Search engines assume that, if a visitor visits a single web page on any particular website and leaves shortly afterwards, the web page did not satisfy the visitor's needs. This are 'bounces' and have negative connotations. The contradiction exists with landing pages and conversion optimisation, where search engines optimise web pages to provide all the necessary information and functionality to satisfy visitors' needs best given their objectives.

Ironically, industry experts do not acknowledge any contradictions. However, in both SEO (Thurow & Musica 2009) and WU (Nielsen & Loranger 2006:16), experts indicate that there are elements and attributes, which occur during website optimisation, that do not consider competitors. When scrutinising the SEO elements and WU attributes, which the industry experts define, the model reveals the contradictions (see Figure 3).

Developers could resolve the identified contradictions in the website architecture whilst developing websites. The solution uses SEO methodology, whereby developers categorise

websites into themes, thus isolating each category within the website for emphasis (to address the competitive component).

Ideally, each category should consist of a number of content heavy web pages based on semantically targeted keywords or phrases (in order to address search engine phrase indexing). Therefore, the internal linking structure within each category needs to emphasise the primary category web page (landing page) by linking the actual semantically-related keywords or phrases in content web pages to the landing page (in order to address semantic-related keyword emphasis). Editorial judgement (inbound links) should target the appropriate semantic phrase content pages. This, in turn, will emphasise the landing pages. The high authority (good quality) websites relevant to the category should link directly to the landing page. Therefore, primary navigation should consist of the landing pages (which should be the actual product or service pages). Ideally, developers should optimise landing pages in order to optimise conversion. This will provide all the necessary information and functionality to allow visitors to convert on the landing pages.

Applying this architectural methodology (along with all other SEO elements) should address the SEO requirements of websites.

Discussion and conclusions

The SEO methodology prioritised the landing pages during search engine ranking. This indicates that visitors will arrive on the appropriate category web page, which should align with the visitors' search queries (in order to address the visitors' particular needs). Here, the primary navigation and using the breadcrumbs would already have addressed the WU in terms of current location and desired destination.

Optimising the landing pages for conversion will reduce unnecessary clicks and visitor frustration. Reducing web page content is a major challenge. However, developers can reduce content through the functionality of expendables. Developers should only apply this solution where appropriate and with caution. The functionality entices website interaction, allowing visitors to request additional information on the same web page without impeding interaction and/or visitor experience.

Although a few search engines use this technology, developers must implement it correctly to ensure that crawlers will crawl and index the content of entire web pages.

In conclusion, a listing in the top position on SERPs is not enough. In addition to the web page result description being enticing enough to convince searchers to click on the results (assuming that the search results align with the search queries), it is essential that searchers engage with websites in terms of their objectives (Thurow 2008; Visser & Weideman 2011b).

Finally, unforeseen contradictions may still surface during website development, even when one considers the identified SEO elements, WU attributes and the suggested website architecture.

The authors created the model in Figure 3 to provide a website optimisation guide for any business. It will address SEO and WU simultaneously. This model is the major contribution this research has produced to knowledge.

The reality is that each website is unique and its developer must optimise it with critical considerations of its business objectives.

Acknowledgements

Competing interests

The authors declare that they have no financial or personal relationship(s) that may have inappropriately influenced them when they wrote this article.

Authors' contributions

E.B.V. (Purple Cow Communications) was the doctoral student, was responsible for the experimental and project design and producing the first draft of the manuscript. E.B.V. also effected ongoing changes and improvements and also created and managed the test and result websites. M.W. (Cape Peninsula University of Technology) initiated this research, was the only supervisor, contributed ideas on an ongoing basis to the design and experimentation, selected the journal, did the proofreading and layout and handled all editorial matters. Both authors made conceptual contributions to this research, participated in the writing and approval of this research project.

References

Adamo, S., 2013, 'comScore releases August 2013 U.S. Search Engine Rankings', in *comScore*, viewed 16 October 2013, from http://www.comscore.com/Insights/Press_Releases/2013/9/comScore_Releases_August_2013_U.S._Search_Engine_Rankings

Arlitsch, K. & O'Brien, P.S., 2012, 'Invisible institutional repositories: Addressing the low indexing ratios of IRs in Google Scholar', *Library Hi Tech* 30(1), 60–81. http://dx.doi.org/10.1108/07378831211213210

Baeza-Yates, R. & Ribeiro-Neto, B., 1999, *Modern information retrieval*, Addison-Wesley, Harley.

Canavan, O., Henchion, M. & O'Reilly, S., 2007, 'The use of the Internet as a marketing channel for Irish speciality food', *International Journal of Retail & Distribution Management* 35(2), 178–195. http://dx.doi.org/10.1108/09590550710728110

Carpineto, C., Osiński, S., Romano, G. & Weiss, D., 2009, 'A survey of web clustering engines', *ACM Computing Surveys* 41(3), 17.1–17.38.

Cooper, L., 2013, 'Aiming high', *Marketing Week* 41(3), 39–41.

Cutts, M., 2007, 'Undetectable spam', in *Matt Cutts: Gadgets, Google, and SEO*, viewed 01 May 2013, from http://www.mattcutts.com/blog/undetectable-spam/

Cutts, M., 2010, 'Google incorporating site speed in search rankings', in *Matt Cutts: Gadgets, Google, and SEO*, viewed 01 February 2013, from http://www.mattcutts.com/blog/site-speed/

Cutts, M., 2011, 'My thoughts on this week's debate', n *Matt Cutts: Gadgets, Google, and SEO*, viewed 26 January 2013, from http://www.mattcutts.com/blog/google-bing/

Eisenberg, B., Quarto-von Tivadar, J., Davis, L.T. & Crosby, B., 2008, *Always be testing: the complete guide to Google website optimizer*, Sybex, Indianapolis.

El-Gohary, H., 2010, 'E-Marketing – A literature review from a small business perspective', *International Journal of Business and Social Science* 1(1), 214–244.

Enge, E., Spencer, S., Fishkin, R. & Stricchiola, J.C., 2010, *The art of SEO – Mastering search engine optimization*, O'Reilly Media Inc., Sebastopol.

Google, 2009, *Personalized search for everyone*, viewed 25 August 2013, from http://googleblog.blogspot.com/2009/12/personalized-search-for-everyone.html

Google, 2011a, *Frequently asked questions for the Google analytics data sharing options*, viewed 29 November 2012, from http://www.google.com/support/analytics/bin/answer.py?answer=87515

Google, 2011b, *Link schemes*, viewed 27 January 2013, from http://www.google.com/support/webmasters/bin/answer.py?answer=66356

Google, 2011c, *High-quality sites algorithm goes global, incorporates user feedback*, viewed 25 August 2013, from http://googlewebmastercentral.blogspot.com/2011/04/high-quality-sites-algorithm-goes.html

Google, 2011d, *More guidance on building high-quality sites*, viewed 25 August 2013, from http://googlewebmastercentral.blogspot.com/2011/05/more-guidance-on-building-high-quality.html

Jerkovic, J.I., 2010, *SEO warrior*, O'Reilly Media Inc., Sebastopol.

Küster, I. & Vila, N., 2011, 'Successful SME web design through consumer focus groups', *International Journal of Quality & Reliability Management* 28(2), 132–154. http://dx.doi.org/10.1108/02656711111101728

Layton, R.A., 2011, 'Towards a theory of marketing systems', *European Journal of Marketing* 45(1/2), 259–276. http://dx.doi.org/10.1108/03090561111095694

Moz, 2013, *Google algorithm change history*, viewed available 25 August 2013, from http://moz.com/google-algorithm-change

Murphy, H.C. & Kielgast, C.D., 2008, 'Do small and medium-sized hotels exploit search engine marketing?', *International Journal of Contemporary Hospitality Management* 20(1), 90–97. http://dx.doi.org/10.1108/09596110810848604

Nielsen, J. & Loranger, H., 2006, *Prioritizing web usability*, New Riders Press, Berkeley.

Nicholas, D., Clark, D., Rowlands, I. & Jamali, H.R., 2013, 'Information on the Go: A case study of Europeana mobile users', *Journal of the American Society for Information Science and Technology* 64(7), 1311–1322. http://dx.doi.org/10.1002/asi.22838

Oliveira, T. & Martins, M.F., 2010, 'Understanding e-business adoption across industries in European countries', *Industrial Management & Data Systems* 110(9), 1337–1354. http://dx.doi.org/10.1108/02635571011087428

Pather, S. & Remenyi, D., 2005, 'Some of the philosophical issues underpinning research in information systems – From positivism to critical realism', *South African Computer Journal* 35, 76–83.

Quinton, B.D., 2012, 'Google's Penguin update: Unhappy feat for marketers?', *Chief Marketer* 3(10), 8.

Rayson, S., 2013, *10 Ways Google+ will improve your SEO*, in *socialmediatoday*, viewed 25 August 2013, from http://socialmediatoday.com/node/1600736

Samujh, H., 2011, 'Micro-businesses need support: survival precedes sustainability', *Corporate Governance* 11(1), 15–28. http://dx.doi.org/10.1108/14720701111108817

Segal, D., 2011, 'The dirty little secrets of search', in *The New York Times*, viewed 02 February 2013, from http://www.nytimes.com/2011/02/13/business/13search.html

Sullivan, D., 2009, *Google now personalizes everyone's search result*, in *Search Engine Land*, viewed 25 August 2013, from http://searchengineland.com/google-now-personalizes-everyones-search-results-31195

Sullivan, D., 2011, *Why Google Panda is more a ranking factor than algorithm update*, in *Search Engine Land*, viewed 25 August 2013, from http://searchengineland.com/why-google-panda-is-more-a-ranking-factor-than-algorithm-update-82564

Sullivan, D., 2012, *Google Penguim update recovery tips & advice*, in *Search Engine Land*, viewed 25 August 2013, from http://searchengineland.com/penguin-update-recovery-tips-advice-119650

Thurasamy, R., Mohamad, O., Omar, A. & Marimuthu, M., 2009, 'Technology adoption among small and medium enterprises (SME's): A research agenda', *World Academy of Science, Engineering and Technology* 53, 943–946.

Thurow, S., 2003, *Search engine visibility*, New Riders Press, Indianapolis.

Thurow, S., 2008, *Search engine visibility*, 2nd edn., New Riders Press, Indianapolis. PMCid:PMC2613660

Thurow, S. & Musica, N., 2009, *When search meets web usability*, New Riders Press, Berkeley. PMCid:PMC2676734

Visser, E.B., 2007, 'Search engine optimisation elements' effect on website visibility: The Western Cape real estate SMME sector', unpublished MTech thesis, Cape Peninsula University of Technology.

Visser, E.B. & Weideman, M., 2011a, An empirical study on website usability elements and how they affect search engine optimisation, *SA Journal of Information Management* 13(1), Art. #428, 9 pages. http://dx.doi.org/10.4102/sajim.v13i1.428

Visser, E.B. & Weideman, M., 2011b,' Search engine optimisation versus Website usability – Conflicting requirements?', *Information Research* 16(3), paper 493.

Weideman, M., 2009, *Website visibility: The theory and practice of improving ranking*, Chandos Publishers, Oxford. http://dx.doi.org/10.1533/9781780631790

Wu, B. & Davison, B.D., 2006, Detecting semantic cloaking on the Web, in *Proceedings of the International World Wide Web Conference Committee (IW3C2)*, Edinburgh, Scotland, 23–26.

Yang, C., Yang, K. & Yuan, H., 2007, 'Improving the search process through ontology-based adaptive semantic search', *The Electronic Library* 25(2), 234–248. http://dx.doi.org/10.1108/02640470710741359

6

Pathways for retaining human capital in academic departments of a South African university

Authors:
Luyanda Dube[1]
Patrick Ngulube[2]

Affiliations:
[1]Department of Information Science, University of South Africa, South Africa

[2]Department of Interdisciplinary Research and Postgraduate Studies, University of South Africa, South Africa

Correspondence to:
Patrick Ngulube

Email:
ngulup@unisa.ac.za

Postal address:
PO Box 392, Pretoria 0003, South Africa

Background: The article underscores the process of knowledge retention for academics in select academic departments in the College of Human Sciences (CHS) at the University of South Africa (UNISA). The knowledge economy is ubiquitous and necessitates that organisations foster innovation and improve efficiency, effectiveness, competitiveness and productivity through knowledge retention. In an academic setting, which is the focus of this article, the situation is no different because there seems to be an accord worldwide that the quality of higher education largely depends on the qualifications of staff and professorial capability in quality research, instruction and doctoral level certification. By implication, it is critical that the retention of knowledge should be prioritised to ensure the curtailment of the impact of knowledge attrition.

Objective: The study intends to profile knowledge assets in CHS, determine retention strategies and offer suggestions about regenerating knowledge retention initiatives.

Research methodology: A quantitative approach, more specifically the informetrics technique of data mining, was adopted to profile academics in CHS at UNISA.

Results: The results confirm the assertion that there is a discrepancy between senior academics who are probably due to leave the university in the next few years, and entrants who will replace them. The issue is worsened by the lack of an institutional framework to guide, standardise, strengthen or prioritise the process of knowledge retention.

Conclusion: The study recommends the prioritisation, formalisation and institutionalisation of knowledge retention through the implementation of a broad range of knowledge retention strategies.

Introduction

Literature has revealed that in the knowledge-driven economy, knowledge is regarded as a strategic, valuable and competitive asset that enables organisations to foster innovation and improve efficiency, effectiveness, productivity and competitiveness (Alstete 2003; Desouza & Awazu 2004; Drucker 2001; Hira 2011; Horwitz, Heng & Quazi 2003). This is based on the notion that knowledge is deemed to be central not only to power, but also to wealth. Knowledge is embodied in a person or carried, created, augmented, improved, applied, taught and passed on, used or misused by a person; which means that the person is at the centre (Castro 2008; Choo & Bontis 2002; Drucker 2001; Nelson & McCann 2010). Unlike during the industrial age where physicality was of primary importance, in the knowledge economy it is the brains rather than the brawn of the workforce that will add value to intelligent organisations or learning organisations (Alvin Toffler, cited in Desouza & Awazu 2004). Thus, it is knowledge, the intellectual capital of astute workers, which is the fundamental resource for economic development.

The inherent value of knowledge means that the leverage of knowledge assets is imperative. Obviously, if those who possess this powerful resource leave the organisation, they take away the knowledge, skills and experience accumulated over a period of years on the job (Hira 2011; Horwitz *et al.* 2003; Knoco Ltd n.d.; Madsen, Mosakowski & Zahher 2003; Malthora 2003; Ramlall 2003; Smith 2007; Tettey 2006). Clearly, knowledge attrition encompasses loss of skills, experience, knowledge, corporate memory and, more importantly, the loss of strategic competitive advantage (Castro 2008; Choo & Bontis 2002; Drucker 2001; Nelson & McCann 2010; Smith 2007). Thus, if critical knowledge is not retained, organisations will have to continually reinvent the wheel. As indicated in the literature, this will result in wastage of resources, which organisations cannot afford in this era of economic turmoil and global competition. Given the value of knowledge, organisations undoubtedly need to have strategies to capture, retain and manage knowledge before it is lost.

Needless to say, knowledge retention is critical to organisational success, but not all knowledge in an organisation is worth retaining. Knowledge that warrants retention is that which is valuable in terms of affording competitive advantage due to its rarity, relevance, heterogeneity or non-substitutability (Ramlall 2003; Smith 2007; Tettey 2006). It is critical knowledge, often embodied in experience, skills, knowledge and capabilities of individuals and groups, that is worth retaining (Seidman & McCauley, cited in Martins 2010). These individuals are employees with exceptional capabilities that are critical for the development of organisational competence (Castro 2008; Choo & Bontis 2002). Such employees have a high degree of expertise, education or experience in the execution of their jobs (Davenport & Prusak 2000; Hira 2011). Drucker (2001) refers to these employees as 'knowledge workers' or 'golden workers'. Clearly, the tacit knowledge possessed by these individuals is invaluable and irreplaceable; hence, it should be retained to avoid knowledge gaps that will have a strategic impact on the achievement of organisational goals (Castro 2008; Choo & Bontis 2002).

Knowledge retention is a multifaceted component of an organisation's human resource strategies to retain expert and critical knowledge (Frank, Finnegan & Taylor 2004; Martins 2010). Knowledge retention begins with the hiring of people with the right skill sets, mindsets and experience; it also entails the deliberate and persistent retention of these employees so that competitors cannot get hold of them (Castro 2008; Choo & Bontis 2002; Frank et al. 2004). Embedded in knowledge retention is the identification of risks that could lead to knowledge loss (Nelson & McCann 2010; Ramlall 2003; Smith 2007; Tettey 2006, 2010). As indicated in the literature, knowledge retention is also a cost-cutting strategy, considering that knowledge is a valuable asset that has to be managed strategically to maintain competitive advantage (Madsen et al. 2003; Malthora 2003; Nelson & McCann 2010; Tettey 2006, 2010).

Due to recent trends in the world of work, knowledge retention has been lauded as a useful strategy to mitigate turnover challenges that threaten organisational survival and growth. The latest trends include 'war for talent' (Axelrod, Handfield-Jones & Welsh, cited in Oosthuizen & Nieber 2010), which is based on the heightened appreciation for the value of knowledge and increased mobility of employees with critical knowledge as they are hunted by many organisations (Lom 2012; MacGregor 2008; Martins 2010; Thomas 2009; Wamundila & Ngulube 2011). It is imperative for organisations to face this reality as it threatens stability and growth. Thus, it becomes critical that organisations should manage turnover challenges deliberately and purposefully through appropriate retention strategies that are capable of strengthening intellectual capital renewal and mitigating knowledge attrition or 'organisational forgetting' (Castro 2008; DeLong 2004; Malthora 2003; Nelson & McCann 2010). Therefore, organisations need to figure out beforehand which knowledge, if lost, could undermine the organisational strategy (DeLong 2004) and whose knowledge might be at risk of being lost (Martins 2010). This is critical because there is evidence according to Castro (2008), Choo and Bontis (2002) and DeLong (2004) that organisations cannot compete effectively in the knowledge economy unless they are serious about knowledge retention.

Knowledge retention in academe: Challenges and prospects

Badat (2010) affirms that the South African academic workforce exhibits complexity because it was racialised and gendered, which bestowed South African universities with a predominantly White male academic workforce. In the first decade since democracy (1994–2004) most professors and associate professors in South African universities, who constitute most highly qualified, experienced and productive researchers and are experts in their chosen disciplines, are older workers above the age of 50. Unfortunately, as observed by Badat (2010) and Van der Walt (2010), the trend seems to be ongoing. For instance, there is evidence that even after 2004 the most highly qualified, experienced and top-rated researchers are largely White, older men, although in the past few years there has been a slow progression of African scholars entering the professoriate bracket.

Some of the pronouncements that were linked to the transformation of the higher education landscape had adverse effects for the retention of academic human capital. After 1994 the retirement age for academic employees was reduced by most South African universities from 65 to 60. In view of skewed representation of human capital in academe as presented in the foregoing arguments, it is disheartening to note that on the basis of the current retirement age most senior academics are due to retire in the next five to ten years. As a form of intervention, the Minister of Higher Education articulated that it was counter-productive to let university professors and lecturers retire at 60, when they could still help train desperately needed skilled professionals. In response to the situation, most universities reverted back to 65 as the retirement age for academic employees.

Action to retain knowledge in academe is needed if universities are to serve humanity in the wake of an ageing workforce. For instance, Professor Saleem Badat, vice-chancellor of Rhodes University, warned that '[w]ithout action, South Africa's efforts to transform the social composition of its scholarly workforce will be undermined, academic quality will be debilitated along with the capacity to produce high quality graduates and knowledge, and their ability of universities to contribute to development and democracy through a new generation of outstanding scholars committed to critical and independent scholarship and social justice will be hampered'. In the case of Senegal, Lom (2012) observed that Senegal's premier Université Cheikh Anta Diop (UCAD) in Dakar was set to lose 60% to 70% of academics by 2015 as a result of large-scale retirements.

It is undeniable that senior academics fit into the category of golden workers. This is because they bear the responsibility that entails increasing the research output by not only supervising postgraduate students but also publishing in accredited journals. Supervision and publishing are both critical elements that determine the ranking of the institution as well as its standing and visibility in the national and international academic milieu. Needless to say, several factors contribute to the ranking process, which is multifaceted and complex. However, what cannot be denied is the importance of the right skill levels, unique capabilities, knowledge and experience that can only be acquired over time. This highlights a challenge wherein experienced academics will be exiting the system without an equivalent entry rate by young researchers. This discrepancy creates a void or imbalance in scholarly and academic productivity and growth.

However, the fact of the matter is that it is not only through the retirement conduit that knowledge assets are lost. There other suppositions or causal factors that lead to the growing number of senior academics retiring and exiting the workforce and the shrinking pool of qualified younger academics. These include such risk factors as staff turnover (resignations), downsising, retrenchment, emigration, employment equity, mergers, acquisitions, globalisation, uncompetitive remuneration packages, onerous working conditions and the notion of advancing equity versus realising academic excellence (Habib & Morrow 2006; Lom 2012; MacGregor 2008; Martins 2010; Notshulwana 2011; Tettey 2006, 2010; Wamundila & Ngulube 2011). It becomes very clear in the literature that South African academics are inadequately remunerated relative to occupations in the public sector (state, public enterprises and science councils) and private sector that require similar levels of qualifications and expertise. To the detriment of universities, the economy and society at large, the remuneration differences between universities and the public and private sectors also discourages potential academics (postgraduate students) to replace at an equivalent pace the void that will be left by the exiting professoriate (Habib & Morrow 2006; Notshulwana 2011).

Clearly, these differences cause academics to be relatively mobile and to be continuously drawn to administrative portfolios and management positions within universities; some focus on commissioned research, some divert to consultancy work and some move to the public and private sectors. Unfortunately, as Ntuli (2007) cautions, job hopping usually exerts pressure on organisations' stability and sustainability. The costs of replacing employees refer to separation or severance pay, recruiting replacements, developing their skills and experience and factoring in a loss of productivity (Ntuli 2007).

It is worth noting that universities generally face challenges from different fronts that impact negatively or positively on their financial standing, which has a direct impact on academic excellence. For instance, challenges that universities are likely to face include (but are not limited to) competition for students, financial constraints, political interference, academic credibility, low throughput rates, low research output, meeting institutional, local, national and international imperatives and market expectations. As one can deduce, most of these are worsened by the lack of intellectual capital and academic capabilities that are critical competencies for academic and research excellence, innovation and leadership.

As indicated earlier, it is undisputed that the greatest deterrence to knowledge attrition is a robust knowledge management initiative that will enable existing information to circulate efficiently, thereby reducing the impact of attrition on organisational knowledge. In view of the preceding statement, the problem facing academe is how to retain knowledge vital to academic success, efficiency and sustainability whilst also mitigating the decline of the country's scholarly profile and infrastructure in the coming decades.

Establishing a strategy to cope with knowledge attrition may save academic institutions millions, if not billions, of rands every year. It is critical that universities should save money whenever possible to ensure sustainability in an era characterised by national and global economic volatility. It is clear that knowledge retention strategies may enable organisations to manage critical intellectual assets by determining risk and thereby creating a provision whereby the exiting of experienced scholars and the entry of new scholars are systematically balanced with each other. Through knowledge retention strategies, critical knowledge may be transferred to new entrants to ensure that they establish and develop confidence and academic credibility in academic circles. The value of this initiative is multifaceted: it will contribute to personal and professional growth but, of more importance, it will also contribute to organisation effectiveness, efficiency, growth, sustainability, resilience and competitive advantage.

Research questions

It is an undisputed fact that employee turnover is a considerable university problem. Knowledge management, with its focus on retaining and transferring knowledge, holds the promise of solutions to resolve the problem of knowledge attrition. The critical question posed by Alstete (2003) and Desouza and Awazu (2004) is that in the knowledge economy do universities have a rudimentary understanding of the necessity and imperative to retain tacit knowledge? Based on this notion, this article intends to give a profile of knowledge assets and identify retention practices and strategies that are in place in the College of Human Sciences (CHS) at the University of South Africa (UNISA). The following are the research questions that informed this study:

- What is the nature and range in terms of intergeneration and interracial actualities of knowledge assets in the College of Human Sciences?
- What strategies does the College of Human Sciences use to retain knowledge assets?
- How can the College regenerate knowledge retention initiatives?

Research methodology

The study adopted a quantitative approach, more specifically the informetrics technique of data mining, to profile academics in CHS at UNISA. This study employed data mining techniques as outlined in Onyancha (2010) to extract data from the Institutional Information and Analysis Portal maintained by the Department of Information and Strategic Analysis (DISA) at UNISA. The Department of Information and Strategic Analysis uses Higher Education Data Analyzer (HEDA) software to provide automated, accurate and up-to-date web-based information. The study is based on 2011 data. The study utilised an analytical and descriptive method to present the data from the institutional management system as well as related documents.

Findings

This section presents and discusses the findings of the study.

Academic staff profile in the College of Human Sciences

The object of the article was to profile knowledge assets in CHS according to nature and range by analytically looking at the intergeneration, interracial and gender actualities. As indicated earlier, knowledge assets are designated as the highly qualified, experienced and productive researchers, who are mostly professoriate. These are the people whom the university should target and prioritise as most of them are likely to exit in the next few years. However, providing data on all academic levels, including lower categories, was deemed necessary to give a broader picture of the academic staff profile in CHS. Providing concrete data will build a case for knowledge retention in the college which could necessitate the prioritisation of the retention of critical knowledge. Figure 1 gives a synopsis of the staff profile according to different academic levels or categories.

The structure in Figure 1 shows that the total numbers of permanent academic staff members in CHS is 472. From this number the highest percentage were at lecturer level (117; 25%), followed by professors (111; 24%), associate professors (90; 19%), senior lecturers (80; 17%) and lastly junior lecturers (74; 16%). The implications of this distribution will only be evident when dynamics of age, gender and race are factored in. If, for instance, the average age of the professoriate is, as alleged in the literature, in the bracket above 50, this would be a cause for concern. At this stage it might be reasonable not to pre-empt this issue since it will be interrogated in the sections below.

Table 1 reports the following.

Professors

Professors constitute the second largest group (111 or 24%) after senior lecturers (117). The age distribution in this category is an issue that should concern the college. Considering that the retirement age at UNISA stands at 60 (14%) of academics in this category are likely to retire in the next few years, with the exception of those who were in the employ of UNISA before the retirement age was adjusted from 65 to 60. Notably, there are a number of academics (4%) who are above the 60 years bracket and who can be accorded the extension of contracts in particular cases. This is

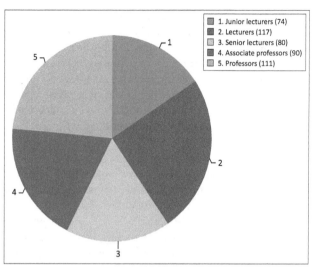

FIGURE 1: Levels or categories of academic staff.

TABLE 1: Profile of academics in the College of Human Sciences.

Category	Age	%
Professors†	30–39 = 7	1
	40–49 = 20	4
	50–59 = 66	14
	60–69 = 18	4
Total	111	24
Associate professors‡	30–39 = 9	2
	40–49 = 31	7
	50–59 = 15	3
	60–69 = 35	7
Total	90	19
Senior lecturers§	30–39 = 6	1
	40–49 = 21	4
	50–59 = 34	7
	60–69 = 19	4
Total	79	17
Lecturers and junior lecturers¶	20–29 = 21	4
	30–39 = 55	12
	40–49 = 63	13
	50–59 = 41	9
	60–69 = 11	2
Total	191	40

†, youngest and oldest 32 ≤ 65.
‡, youngest and oldest 33 ≤ 63.
§, youngest and oldest 33 ≤ 63.
¶, youngest and oldest 24 ≤ 64.

a short-term solution; the risk or the threat needs long-lasting solutions to ensure continuity and growth in academic excellence, innovation and leadership.

The reality of the situation is that about 18% of college staff members, who are mostly renowned scholars and rated researchers (golden workers), are due to retire soon. These are attributes that add value not only to the department but also to the college and the university at large. Only 5% of college professors are under 50 years old. It is commendable though that only 1% of academics in the professoriate category are between 30 and 39 years old. Given the regular mobility of academics as discussed previously in this article, the retention of younger academics might be a risk that the college as well as the university would like to consider seriously since it cannot be guaranteed.

Associate professors

Associate professors constitute 19% of the total academics in the college. In this category, the 60–69 age bracket (7%) poses a threat or a risk to attrition of academic intellectual capital. As indicated earlier these are people who were appointed before the implementation of the new retirement age. Clearly, since there are people over 65 the likelihood is the extension of contractual agreements. Nevertheless, that is a short-term solution as these people will still retire soon. However, it is promising that below the age of 50 there are about 9% of academics who are likely to be here longer to further the goals of the college and the university.

Senior lecturers

Senior lecturers are in the middle of the academic ladder, positioned between the professoriate and lower academic levels. Evidently, 11% of college staff in this category are between the ages of 50 and 69. This is a cause for concern considering that about 4% are already beyond the current retirement age. Looking at the two senior levels discussed above, this category is by implication under tremendous pressure to progress and fill in the ranks in the professoriate categories. Although upward mobility may have its challenges, the college and the university might consider implementing strategies to regenerate this group to enhance upward mobility. However, cognisance should be taken of the fact that it is not merely about numbers moving up. In essence it is about academic and scholarly competencies embodied in integrity, professionalism and excellence.

Lecturers and junior lecturers

Lecturers constitute 25% and junior lecturers 16% of academics in CHS. As indicated in Table 1, about 11% in these categories are between the ages of 50 and 69. However, a reasonable 29% of college academics in this category are between the ages of 20 and 49. Related to this is the number of honours or master's graduates who can be attracted to academe by narrowing remuneration differentials between academe and the private and public sectors. This could actually be regarded as an encouraging element for the college, because these are future professors who need to be leveraged, developed and nurtured properly through progressive retention strategies.

Gender differentiation in the college

It has emerged in the literature that White men dominate the ranks, especially in the category of the professoriate. After 1994 the transformation of the higher education landscape introduced initiatives to redress these imbalances.

The numbers from Figure 2 show that at the number of male professors and associate professors exceeds that of their female counterparts. In the category of professors 67% are male and 33% female, and for associate professors 53% are male and 47% female. In lower academic categories there are more female than male academics. This translates into the following numbers of female academics in the different categories: senior lecturers 56%, lecturers 63% and junior lecturers 62%. Evidently, the gender discrepancy is slightly

narrower or marginal at associate professor and senior lecturer levels. Considering the gender representation in academe, the data confirms the assertion mentioned earlier by several authors that men dominate in the ranks of the professoriate and women are still more dominant in lower ranks. Based on institutional imperatives towards gender representation or empowerment, the college might consider strengthening initiatives to advance the cause of female academics. The causes and implications of this matter are beyond the parameters of this study.

Differentiation according to racial ranges

As indicated earlier the higher education landscape was racialised and politicised. This section presents differentiations according to racial ranges. To summarise, the study confirms the pronouncements made earlier in this article that White academics dominate in numbers in the professoriate. For professors, 76% are White, 17% are African, 4% are Indian and 4% mixed race. There are 51% White associate professors, 41% are African, 4% are Indian and 3% are mixed race. For senior lecturers 54% are African, 44% are White, 8% are mixed race and 1% are Indian. At lecturer and junior lecturer levels 51% are African, whilst 39% are White, 5% Indian and 4% mixed race. Notably, at professoriate level there is a huge discrepancy between

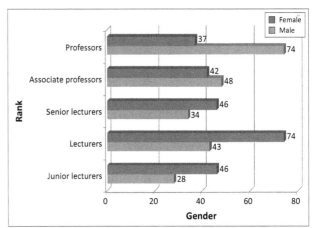

FIGURE 2: Female versus male academics.

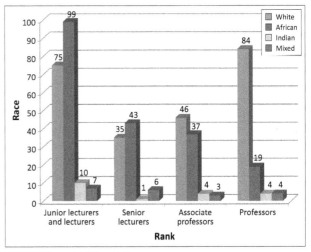

FIGURE 3: The racial differentiation.

the different racial groups. At associate professor level the discrepancy is marginal between African and White professor and it widens between them and Indian and mixed race professors. At senior lecturer level African lecturers are in the majority, followed by White, mixed race and Indian lecturers. At lecturer and junior lecturer levels African lecturers are in the majority, followed by White, Indian and mixed race lecturers respectively. It should be cautioned that in terms of knowledge retention the racial representation might have negative implications. Several studies reveal that racial ranges or diversity can have negative undertones for knowledge flows and transfer. Given that knowledge retention includes the systematic transference of knowledge from golden workers to other employees, if it is not properly managed to lessen the impact of racial differentiations, it might not succeed irrespective of its noble intentions.

Knowledge retention in the College of Human Sciences: How can it be regenerated?

Organisations differ from one another in terms of strategic focus, how pressing the nature of the knowledge retention problem is and the fact that there clearly is no 'one-size-fits-all' solution when it comes to knowledge retention (DeLong & Davenport 2003). Knowledge retention partly involves the transfer and sharing of knowledge, skills and competencies. Studies by Finestone and Snyman (2005) indicate that cultural, racial, ethnic and national differentiations are rampant in South African organisations. These breed a lot of mistrust, resentment, competitiveness and a lack of collective goals. As indicated earlier, for knowledge sharing to flourish, the environment has to be enabling, and other enhancers and possible inhibitors have to be identified and managed to maximise or cancel out their impact. Based on the preceding discourse this section examines knowledge retention strategies in CHS and suggests how these could be regenerated. The strategies presented are distilled from the researchers' experience as academics at UNISA.

Institutional knowledge retention framework

The University of South Africa does not have a specific knowledge retention policy. Some knowledge retention issues are integrated in various human resource policies such as the Policy for the Integrated Performance Management System (IPMS). This policy is aimed at recruiting, developing and retaining employees with the requisite mindsets, knowledge and skills to achieve the university's Agenda for Transformation (UNISA 2008). The policy generally provides an overview of IPMS-related issues and does not provided succinct information about the management of knowledge assets. Due to the lack of guiding frameworks or canons on knowledge retention the practice remains uncoordinated and haphazard. This results in an institutional culture that does not enhance knowledge sharing. It perpetuates a culture that is still leaning towards recognising and rewarding individual excellence. Without the provision of an enabling culture as well as the alignment of institutional systems and policies, it will be difficult for UNISA as an institution to negate

the effects of knowledge attrition. The institution needs a succinct knowledge retention strategy that will be responsive to the institutional needs and culture. A knowledge retention strategy will also enable the institution to retain critical intellectual capital.

Talent management

As indicated by Wellins, Smith and Erker (2006), organisations need to realise that their financial value often depends upon the quality of the talent. The term talent usually refers to a blend of skills, knowledge, cognitive ability, values and preferences that give individuals the highest levels of potential (Jeffrey 2011). Because there is no universal definition of the term talent, it is important that each organisation should define the term according to local realities. Despite issues with the definition of the term, there is a unanimous sense that talent is a critical resource that organisations should prioritise. Jeffrey (2011) reiterates the fact that due to the economic downturn organisations need to invest in people in order to maximise innovation and the capability to meet challenges of the future. The University of South Africa (UNISA) has a diverse workforce with unique combinations, backgrounds, skills and experience. In order to manage and maximise diversity, it has introduced talent management programmes in the past few years. These programmes, amongst other things, include formalised mentorship programmes. Given the value of knowledge, it is critical that the university harnesses knowledge retention through what Wellins et al. (2006) refer to as the ability to effectively hire, retain, deploy and engage talent for competitive advantage. To be effective, UNISA needs not only to invest in talent management but also to align remuneration and other institutional systems and processes with the crux of talent management. Failure to invest in people (talent) could lead to the loss of critical skills and of the richness of future talent (Jeffrey 2011). Ideally, the decision to invest in the institutional talent has to be preceded by a knowledge audit that will map out knowledge assets at risk as well as gaps in the depth and breadth of organisational knowledge. Clearly, without this exercise the institution will not have a clear picture of the nature and extent of knowledge threats and gaps.

Mentorship programmes

In the College of Humanities, senior academics are expected to mentor young academics and those on probation. The object of these mentorship programmes is to familiarise new entrants with the systems, processes and practices of UNISA as an open distance learning (ODL) institution. Mentorship programmes are still in their infancy; one can deduce that they are still piloted as there no clear guidelines informing them. From the foregoing arguments it can be deduced that the existing mentorship programmes might not be adequate for knowledge retention due to their intention, focus and time span, the pairing of mentors and mentees and the lack of monitoring mechanisms and a guiding framework. To enhance knowledge retention through mentorship programmes UNISA needs to have a clear regulatory framework with clear guidelines, targets and evaluation mechanisms.

Career conversations

In the college, there are career conversations between academics to a limited extent. These are in the form of workshops, meetings, seminars and conferences. These career conversations are usually at departmental, interdepartmental, institutional and inter-institutional levels. If these could be deepened and purposefully driven by leveraging knowledge assets, they might maximise the transfer and retention of critical academic knowledge, skills and competencies. In line with the university prescripts, career conversations could lead to collaborative projects and initiatives.

Exit interviews

It is the norm at UNISA, as in many other organisations, that when employees leave they partake in an exit interview. Once again these interviews are not driven by knowledge retention goals. They are more focused on identifying causal factors for high turnover, which may be useful for determining turnover trends. For knowledge retention purposes, exit interviews need to ensure that critical tacit knowledge is leveraged, harvested and retained through personification or codification approaches. Ideally, institutions should not wait until knowledge assets threaten to leave or exit. Instead of being reactive, institutions should be proactive through human resources and other appropriate strategies. These include purposeful recruitment and hiring based on identified risks and threats that are likely to impact on critical knowledge assets. If the process is strategically and deliberately managed, institutions can avert knowledge attrition and maintain competitive advantage.

Career development

The university champions the provision of opportunities for personal as well as professional development. Comparatively speaking, UNISA as an institution has progressive and fair opportunities for growth and upward mobility. For instance, there are deliberate and conscious efforts to empower those who were previously marginalised, through skills development funding, ad hominem promotions, research awards, National Research Funding grants, support for conference, workshop or seminar attendance, leave opportunities, salary adjustments based on performance management systems, and many others forms of recognition. Despite these provisions, it is evident that upward mobility for academics is still fairly limited. Mostly, previously disadvantaged people, that is, Black people and women, are confined to the lower academic categories: senior lecturer, lecturer and junior lecturer. Quite evident is the fact is that there is a bottleneck that impedes passage on the trajectory between lectureship and professorship. Given that UNISA provides an open trajectory for upward mobility, there is a need to determine why racial and gender discrepancies are still rampant in the academic profile. Further studies could determine causal factors obstructing academic upward mobility in CHS. Without concrete evidence of the causal factors one can only speculate about what challenges potential candidates face. For example, promotion to professorship is based on research output. This might be a challenge due to a myriad of factors, including:

1. The heavy teaching loads for those in lower level categories compared to higher categories.
2. The lack of research skills resulting from a system of education that did not enhance a strong research ethos or champion the inculcation of research. For example, in most universities research is not embedded in the undergraduate or even postgraduate curriculum. A master's degree by coursework is a case in point.
3. The effects of socialisation wherein most previously marginalised people have not broken the mould to step into the arena of academic scholarship.
4. The consequences of individual as opposed to collective performance. Currently, the reward system is aligned towards individual excellence. Although there is a drive towards developmental or collective initiatives, this has not been factored into reward institutional systems.

Conclusions and recommendations

The University of South Africa runs the risk of letting knowledge walk out of its door as 14% of the academics at professorship level may retire in the next few years and 18% of other college staff members, who are mostly renowned scholars and top-rated researchers, are due to retire soon. Most of them are White men. Strategies to capture and retain their knowledge should be formulated so that it is passed to academics in all categories and both gender groups. In conclusion, there are many uncoordinated initiatives that need to be streamlined and enhanced before knowledge retention is a reality in the institution. In order to manage talent, the university needs to audit its knowledge assets, identify risk areas and put plans in place to mitigate those risks. It needs to align institutional systems and policies with collective performance principles rather than individual performance. Finally, there is a need for the development of an institutional knowledge retention framework that will facilitate the implementation of talent management and mentorship programmes, career conversations, career development initiatives and exit interviews as formal and effective strategies to engender the retention of human capital in the College of Humanities at UNISA.

Acknowledgements

Competing interest

The authors declare that they have no financial or personal relationship(s) that may have inappropriately influenced them in writing this article.

Authors' contributions

L.D. (University of South Africa) and P.N (University of South Africa) made equal contributions to the writing of this article.

References

Alstete, J., 2003, *Trends on corporate knowledge asset protection*, viewed 17 February 2011, from http://www.tlainc.com/articl147.htm

Badat, S., 2010, *The challenges of transformation in higher education and training institutions in South Africa*, viewed 11 February 2011, from http://www.dbsa.org/pdf

Castro, M.L., 2008, 'The relationship between organisational climate and employee satisfaction in a South African information and technology organisation', MA dissertation, Department of Psychology, University of South Africa.

Choo, C.W. & Bontis, N., 2002, 'Knowledge, intellectual capital, and strategy: Themes and tensions', in C.W Choo & N. Bontis (eds.), *The strategic management of intellectual capital and organizational knowledge*, pp. 3–22, Oxford University Press, Oxford.

Davenport, T.H. & Prusak, L., 2000, *Working knowledge: How organizations manage what they know*, Harvard Business School Press, Boston.

DeLong, D.W., 2004, *Lost knowledge: Confronting the threat of an aging workforce*, Oxford University Press, Oxford. http://dx.doi.org/10.1093/acprof:oso/9780195170979.001.0001

DeLong, D.W. & Davenport, T., 2003, 'Better practices for retaining organizational knowledge: Lessons from the leading edge', *Employment Relations Today* 30(3), 51–63. http://dx.doi.org/10.1002/ert.10098

Desouza, K.C. & Awazu, Y., 2004, 'Securing knowledge assets: How safe is your knowledge?', viewed 11 November 2010, from http://www.entrepreneur.com/tradejournals/article/120354108.html

Drucker, P.F., 2001, *The essential Drucker*, Harper Collins, New York.

Finestone, N. & Snyman, R., 2005, 'Corporate South Africa: Making multicultural knowledge sharing work', *Journal of Knowledge Management* 9(3), 128–141. http://dx.doi.org/10.1108/13673270510602827

Frank, D.F., Finnegan, R.P. & Taylor, C.R., 2004, 'The race for talent: Retaining and engaging workers in the 21st century', *Human Resource Planning*, September, 12–25.

Habib, A. & Morrow, S., 2006, 'Research, research productivity and the state in South Africa', *Transformation* 62, 9–29. http://dx.doi.org/10.1353/trn.2007.0006

Hira, F., 2011, 'Does employee retention affect organizational competence?', *Industrial Engineering Letters* 1(1), 24–39.

Horwitz, F.M., Heng, C.T. & Quazi, H.A., 2003, 'Finders, keepers? Attracting, motivating and retaining knowledge workers', *Human Resource Management Journal* 13(4), 23–44. http://dx.doi.org/10.1111/j.1748-8583.2003.tb00103.x

Jeffrey, B., 2011, 'Practitioner guide: how to create a talent management strategy that reflects diversity', viewed 21 November 2011, from http://www.civilservice.gov.uk/wp-content/uploads/2011/09/Talent-Strategies-Practitioner-Guide_tcm6-35853.pdf

Knoco Ltd. n.d., *When experts depart: Addressing the risk of knowledge loss*, viewed 11 November 2010, from http://www.knoco.com

Lom, M.M., 2012, 'Looming problem of ageing academics threatens top university', *University World News*, Global edition, 01 July (Issue 228), viewed 11 November 2010, from http://www.universityworldnews.com/article.php?story=20120630122709196

MacGregor, K., 2008, 'South Africa: Challenges of equity, ageing, expansion', *University World News*, Global edition, 14 December (Issue 57), viewed 15 November 2011, from http://www.universityworldnews.com/article.php?story=20081214092139847

Madsen, T.L., Mosakowski, E. & Zahher, S., 2003, 'Knowledge retention and personnel mobility: The non-disruptive effects of inflows experience', *Organisation Science* 14(2), 173–191. http://dx.doi.org/10.1287/orsc.14.2.173.14997

Malthora Y., 2003, *Measuring knowledge assets of a nation: Knowledge systems for development*, viewed 21 November 2010, from http://km.brint.com

Martins, E.C., 2010, 'Identifying organisational behavioural factors that influence knowledge retention', DPhil thesis, Dept. Information Science, University of South Africa, viewed 11 November 2011, from http://uir.UNISA.ac.za/bitstream/handle/10500/4753/pdf

Nelson, K. & McCann, J.E., 2010, 'Designing for knowledge worker retention and organization performance', *Journal of Management and Marketing Research* 1, 1–18, viewed 11 November 2010, from http://www.aabri.com/manuscripts/09272.pdf

Notshulwana, V., 2011, 'Expanding opportunity through international equity', *Africa Insight* 41(2), 142–159.

Ntuli, D., 2007, 'Companies will shell out to retain skills in 2007', *Sunday Times: Business Times: Careers,* 14 January, p. 1.

Onyancha, O.B., 2010, 'Profiling students using an institutional information portal: a descriptive study of the Bachelor of Arts degree students, University of South Africa', *South African Journal of Libraries and Information Science* 76(2), 153–167. http://dx.doi.org/10.7553/76-2-78

Oosthuizen, P. & Nieber, H. 2010. 'The status of talent management in the South African consulting civil engineering industry in 2008: a survey', *Journal of the South African Institution of Civil Engineering* 52(2), 41–47.

Ramlall, S., 2003, 'Managing employee retention as a strategy for increasing organizational competitiveness', *Applied HRM Research* 8(2), 63–72.

Smith, L.D., 2007, 'Standard process for knowledge retention', viewed 11 November 2010, from http://www.levidsmith.com/articles/ie591_research_article.pdf

Tettey, W.J., 2006, *Staff retention in African universities: Elements of a sustainable strategy*, viewed 11 November 2010, from http://siteresources.worldbank.org/INTAFRREGTOPTEIA/Resources/Academic_Staff_Retention_Final_2_06.pdf

Tettey, W.J., 2010, *Challenges of developing and retaining the next generation of academics: Deficits in academic staff capacity at African universities*, viewed 11 November 2010, from http://www.foundation-partnership.org/pubs/pdf/tettey_deficits.pdf

Thomas, A., 2009, 'Knowledge retention strategies', viewed 11 November 2010, from http://pmtips.net/knowledge-retention-strategies/

University of South Africa (UNISA), 2008, 'Integrated performance management system (IPMS) policy', viewed 11 November 2011, from http://www.unisa.ac.za/cmsys/staff/contents/departments/hr_policies/docs/IPMS_Council3Oct08.pdf

Van der Walt, R., 2010, *The contributions of the grey wave to organizations and societies*, viewed 11 November 2011, from http://www.workinfo.com/Articles/greywave.htm

Wamundila, S., & Ngulube, P., 2011, 'Enhancing knowledge retention in higher education: A case of the University of Zambia', *South African Journal of Information Management* 13(1), 9 pages. http://dx.doi.org/10.4102/sajim.v13i1.439

Wellins, R.S., Smith, A.B. & Erker, S., 2006, *White Paper – Nine best practices for effective talent management*, Development Dimensions International, Inc., viewed 5 November 2011, from http://www.ddiworld.com/DDIWorld/media/whitepapers/ninebestpracticetalentmanagement_wp_ddi.pdf

7

Critical success factors for business intelligence in the South African financial services sector

Authors:
Lionel Dawson[1]
Jean-Paul Van Belle[1]

Affiliations:
[1]Department of Information Systems, University of Cape Town, South Africa

Correspondence to:
Jean-Paul Van Belle

Email:
jean-paul.vanbelle@uct.ac.za

Postal address:
Private Bag, Rondebosch 7701, South Africa

Background: Business intelligence (BI) has become an important part of the solution to providing businesses with the vital decision-making information they need to ensure sustainability and to build shareholder value. Critical success factors (CSFs) provide insight into those factors that organisations need to address to improve new BI projects' chances of success.

Objectives: This research aimed to determine which CSFs are the most important in the financial services sector of South Africa.

Method: The authors used a Delphi-technique approach with key project stakeholders in three BI projects in different business units of a leading South African financial services group.

Results: Authors regarded CSF categories of 'committed management support and champion', 'business vision', 'user involvement' and 'data quality' as the most critical for BI success.

Conclusions: Researchers in the BI field should note that the ranking of CSFs in this study only correlate partially with those a European study uncovered. However, the five factors the authors postulated in their theoretical framework ranked in the seven highest CSFs. Therefore, they provide a very strong validation of the framework. Research in other industries and other emerging economies may discover similar differences and partial similarities. Of special interest would be the degree of correlation between this study and future, and similar emerging market studies. Practitioners, especially BI project managers, would do well to check that they address the CSFs the authors uncovered before undertaking BI projects.

Introduction

Business intelligence (BI) has become an important part of the solution to providing businesses with the vital decision-making information they need to ensure sustainability and to build shareholder value. Critical success factors (CSFs) provide insight into those factors that organisations need to address to improve new BI projects' chances of success.

This research aimed to determine which CSFs are the most important in the financial services sector of South Africa. The research used a Delphi-technique approach to key project stakeholders in three BI projects in different business units of a leading South African financial services group.

The findings show that the CSF categories of 'committed management support and champion', 'business vision', 'user involvement' and 'data quality' are the most important in the participating business units. The top CSFs align almost perfectly with the five factors hypothesised in the much more parsimonious theoretical framework. The CSF rankings also correlate partially with those a European study generated.

In today's ever-changing world of business, organisations need to be competitive and innovative in order to provide value to shareholders (Blenkhorn & Fleisher 2007). One way organisations can achieve this is to extract the maximum possible value from their internal data assets by using techniques like interactive graphical data analysis, data mining and predictive analytics. These techniques and tools are part of a discipline referred to as business intelligence (Hawking & Sellitto 2010).

However, the success BI implementations have achieved has varied across organisations and industries. Whilst each organisation and industry provides a specific context, researchers have identified a group of more generic factors critical to the success of BI projects. These factors, referred to as Critical Success Factors, cover a wide spectrum of influences like top manager support, market dynamics, data quality of the source systems and BI system usage (Adamala & Cidrin 2011). This research aimed to ascertain which CSFs organisations regard as the most critical in the South African financial services context.

Several recent studies have investigated the outcomes of organisational BI projects by using the CSF approach (Yeoh, Gao & Koronios 2007; Hawking & Sellitto 2010; Yeoh & Koronios 2010; Olbrich, Pöppelbuß & Niehaves 2012; Presthus, Ghinea & Utvik 2012).

Therefore, the research questions are:

- Which CSFs are the most critical in the South African financial services context?
- How do they compare against the actors hypothesised in the theoretical framework (see infra)?
- How do the CSF rankings correlate with those from a European study?

In line with the theoretical framework, the authors will rate CSFs in two contexts: project specific versus CSFs that are more general. They will compare the ratings for the individual projects to the overall general ratings to determine whether a generalisable set of CSFs applies across the projects. Because there seem to be no published studies on CSFs in BI implementations in South Africa, the authors hope that this research will be a platform for further research in this area.

Literature review

Defining business intelligence and its organisational benefits

Business intelligence is more than a collection of tools and techniques. It is a multi-dimensional concept 'concerned with the effective deployment of organisational practices, processes, and technology to create a knowledge base that supports the organization' (Olbrich, Pöppelbuß & Niehaves 2012:4149). Its main purpose is to 'identify information needs and process the data and information gathered into useful and valuable managerial knowledge and intelligence' (Pirttimäki 2007:4). Therefore, it subsumes more specific intelligence activities like competitive intelligence, customer intelligence, product intelligence and others. Successful BI implementations can provide decision makers with information that enables them to make operational, tactical or strategic decisions and to implement metrics-driven management (Pirrtimäki 2007). Metrics-driven management is an approach to ensuring that organisations achieve the organisational goals their business strategies define (Lutu & Meyer 2008).

The proper use of BI can have a material benefit on organisations' bottom line (Ranjan 2008). Research that has shown the importance of BI for information technology (IT) executives has substantiated this (Luftman & Ben-Zvi 2010). Gartner highlighted the importance of investing in BI in 2009 when Gartner predicted that 'BI system vendor revenue will reach $7.7 billion by 2012' (Hawking & Sellitto 2010). However, the demand for BI, analytics and performance management software resulted in revenue that exceeded the 2009 prediction, coming in at $12.2 billion in 2011. This was a 16.4% increase over the 2010 revenue of $10.5 billion (Gartner Research 2012).

Organisations do not always recognise the benefits of BI (O'Brien & Kok 2006). The literature review by Hawkins

(2010) validated this. Hawkins (2010) found that organisations do not realise the main driver of using BI, a higher quality of decisions. Business intelligence systems are complex entities and, with complexity, comes cost (Yeoh & Koronios 2010). Organisations need to manage, measure and justify expenditure to ensure that the information it yields meets the requirements they define (Lönnqvist & Pirttimäki 2006).

Critical success factors for business intelligence

Whilst organisations often see BI as a technology solution, many internal and external factors influence the outcome of BI investments. These include the quality of the data sources, the investment funding, the types of industries in which the organisations compete, the level of support from senior managers and the skills of the technical resources (Olbrich et al. 2012).

Depending on the industry and type of organisation, some factors will have a greater influence on the BI solution than others will. The challenge for organisations is to identify the factors that have the greatest influence on their BI system. An important criterion organisations should remember when they select the factors, is that they must have some effect on the factors for the duration of the project. The effect can be partial because they will set guidelines for how they expect to meet the target for a factor, whereas full control defines the expectations of what the target for the factor is precisely (Olbrich et al. 2012). By focusing on these factors, organisations will be able to provide the platform for increasing the potential success of the IT solutions.

Over the last five years, there have been several empirical studies on CSFs in BI (Yeoh et al. 2007; Hawking & Sellitto 2010; Yeoh & Koronios 2010; Olbrich et al. 2012; Presthus et al. 2012). In these studies, committed top manager support, source system data quality and user involvement emerged consistently as the most important CSFs.

Empirical business intelligence research in South Africa

A number of studies on BI in the private and public sector provide insights into the extent of South African BI use and its success. O'Brien and Kok (2006) conducted an early empirical study into the financial and other benefits of BI use in the large private telecommunications organisations using a combination of quantitative and qualitative methods. They found that even large businesses in this sector did not fully understand BI and its benefits or, where they did, they never used BI to its full potential. They also recommended that smaller businesses (fewer than 100 employees) should not consider BI because of its complexity. They emphasised that organisations must integrate BI processes and technologies to reap full BI benefits.

An empirical case study research project identified the importance of a value driven framework for BI (Smith & Crossland 2008). It showed that aligning BI strategy with organisational strategy and explicitly measuring business benefits using metrics are key to realising the value of BI.

Pellissier & Kruger (2011) conducted a more recent empirical study in the long-term insurance industry. However, they focused only on a sub-set of BI: the use of strategic intelligence. Their research also found a lack of awareness and under use of intelligence capabilities. They recommended the use of a strategic intelligence framework to drive the intelligence processes to manage the complexity and reap the full benefits of strategic intelligence that improved decision-making, competitive advantage and innovation.

Ponelis (2011) conducted an exploratory study into using BI in knowledge-based small, medium and micro-enterprises (SMMEs) located in Gauteng. The research findings identified a number of CSFs that the SMMEs were not meeting. All the SMMEs had standard operational payroll software. However, only one had bought the BI add-on module and even that SMME was not using the BI capability optimally. Therefore, these SMMEs were accumulating data but were not converting it into information through BI technology because the owners (top managers) did not see the benefits of BI. Where they did have BI technology installed, there was a lack of skills to take advantage of its functionality. Reluctance to use consultants because of the perceived lack of knowledge transfer further compounded the problems. Interestingly, the earlier study by O'Brien & Kock (2006) also uncovered most of these issues and largely confirmed the findings.

On the other hand, there have been several successful achievements in the rollout of BI in the public sector. Awards to the South African Revenue Service (SARS) and the City of Cape Town acknowledged these. The Western Cape Education Department (WECD) has achieved further successes (Lutu & Meyer 2008). Researchers have identified that BI has an important contributory role to play in addressing the current service delivery needs in the public sector through the performance management system (PMS) (Hartley & Seymour 2011). The public sector would achieve this through understanding where it needs investments most and by monitoring the consumption of state resources.

One can identify CSFs at a granular level, depending on the context of the subject matter. Hartley & Seymour (2011) have researched the factors that affect the adoption of BI technology in the public sector. The researchers used the Heeks Design-Reality Gap model, an information systems development model for developing countries, to assess seven factors.

The model works on the principle that the closer the design requirement is to the reality (as is), the smaller the gap to adoption will be and, therefore, the higher the level of success that organisations can achieve. The results of the study showed, that for the BI system to provide valuable information, the quality of the data at source is fundamental and reporting must be timely. The South African Revenue Service, whose knowledge of the taxpayer has resulted in its increased ability to collect taxes, has demonstrated this. Another outcome was that, to build the data source accurately, organisations must identify and monitor the key processes. The data produces information that can help to identify and monitor service delivery needs.

A study by Bijker (2010) noted the importance of taking an incremental approach to BI to deliver sustained value to organisations. One of the business units that participated in this research, and which has delivered incremental benefits over a four-year period, has reinforced this finding.

Theoretical framework

The authors' theoretical framework derives from empirically validated multi-stage model for Data Warehousing Success (Wixom & Watson 2001). Their model integrated a number of theoretical models. However, it draws most on the information systems (IS) success model of DeLone & McLean (1992) by explaining the perceived overall success (net benefits) of a data-warehousing project in terms of both data and system quality. Three types of implementation successes explained these in turn: organisational, project and technical. Seven key implementation factors, in turn, explain implementation success: manager support, champion, resources, user participation, team skills, source systems and development technology.

However, the focus of this research is on measuring the *contextual* variables (the non-project specific organisational implementation factors). Therefore, the authors excluded team skills, source systems and development technology as factors. The focus was also on organisational and project implementation success, not technical success, because too many organisations easily consider BI projects 'technical successes' but do not use them. Therefore, only the top part of the Wixom-Watson model applies (see Figure 1 and Figure 2).

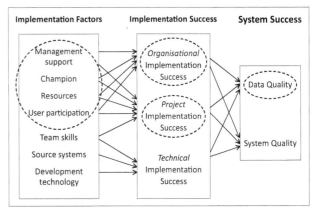

Source: Wixom, B.H. & Watson, J., 2001, 'An Empirical Investigation of the Factors Affecting Data Warehousing Success', *MIS Quarterly* 25(1), 1-24. http://dx.doi.org/10.2307/3250957

FIGURE 1: Wixom-Watson model for data warehousing success.

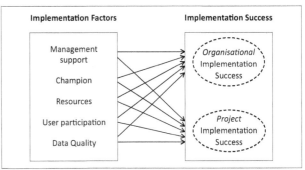

FIGURE 2: Proposed business intelligence project success model.

However, unlike in data warehousing, where data quality is an outcome of successful projects, one should see BI data quality as an(other) antecedent of successful BI projects because they rely on the quality of the data in the warehouse. Therefore, the modified BI organisational success model, based on the Wixom-Watson model, uses this construct as an independent factor.

Research methodology

Research objective and hypotheses

The main objective of this research is to determine the key CSFs that information technology (IT) and business experts, who worked in a South African financial services company and in different BI projects, identified.

A secondary objective is to test the extent to which these CSFs are generalisable. Therefore, the participants should rate the CSFs hypothesised in the theoretical research model relatively highly. How well the CSFs align between business and IT experts, between project-specific and general CSFs as well as with those CSFs highlighted in prior BI research literature has highlighted should also reflect this.

To provide a baseline for the second objective, the authors chose the Olbrich et al. (2012) study from Europe. It uses a comprehensive list of factors in three rounds of a Delphi study and covers three dimensions of interest: importance, variability and controllability. Therefore, the authors can convert the secondary research objective into the hypotheses below:

> **Hypothesis 1:** the participants should rate the CSFs hypothesised in the theoretical research model highly.

> **Hypothesis 2:** the relative importance of project-specific CSFs will align with the general BI CSF ratings.

> **Hypothesis 3:** the relative importance of CSFs, as the South African participants rated them, will align with those of the European study. (Olbrich et al. 2012)

Sample

The authors approached a number of business units of a major South African financial services organisation to participate in this research. They selected three business units that covered a cross section of BI projects: a very large strategic project, a small strategic project and a medium-sized operational project. They regarded each business unit as a separate case study. The three business units that participated in the research cover the affluent and short-term insurance segments of the market. Each business unit then recommended people to participate in the research.

The authors held separate presentation sessions at each business unit to explain the purpose and objectives of the research and the benefit to the business units to the employees who participated. This was to ensure a high participation rate. The participants were from IT and business. Thirty-one participants received the initial email in the first round and 26 responded. This is a response rate of 84% and represented high quality stakeholders (Table 1). The authors regarded the sample size of 26 as sufficient to obtain results of material value (Yeoh & Koronios 2010).

The authors achieved good response rates for both iterations of the data they collected (see Table 2a and Table 2b).

Instrument design

The instrument the authors used was a macro-free Microsoft Excel® 2010 spreadsheet. They distributed it to all participants via email. Apart from the initial instructions, it also provided space for the participants to note their top five CSFs before they viewed the list the authors provided.

The authors used the Olbrich et al. (2012) list of 25 factors for their initial list of CSF factors. They dropped five factors because they were not relevant for a single sector, single organisation study. They adapted five CSFs for this research. Because this research focused on business units, 'corporate strategy' became 'business unit strategy' and 'influence of IT on corporate strategy' became 'influence of IT on business unit strategy'. They felt that the CSFs' 'sophistication of IT infrastructure' and 'sophistication of competitors' BI technology' were not clear. Therefore, they changed these CSFs to 'technologically advanced IT infrastructure' and 'capability of competitors' BI technology' respectively. Because the

TABLE 1: Summary of the participants (N = 26).

Participants	Number	%
Information or Business intelligence managers	4	15.4%
Business intelligence professionals	2	7.7%
Project managers	2	7.7%
Other Information technology staff	6	23.1%
Executives	2	7.7%
Middle management users	7	26.9%
Analysts (like actuarial analysts)	3	11.5%

TABLE 2a: Summary of response rates by business unit and background (round 1).

Response round	Participants	Number of participants contacted	Number of responses received	Response rate
Round 1	Business unit 1, 2 and 3	17, 9 and 5	12, 9 and 5	71%, 100% and 100%
	IT versus business	13 and 18	13 and 13	100% and 72%
Total	-	31	26	84%

IT, information technology.

TABLE 2b: Summary of response rates by business unit and background (round 2).

Response round	Participants	Number of participants contacted	Number of responses received	Response rate
Round 2	Business unit 1, 2 and 3	12, 9 and 5	11, 6 and 3	92%, 67% and 60%
	IT versus business	13 and 13	10 and 10	77% and 77%
Total	-	26	20	77%

IT, information technology.

description of 'Data sources' in the original study emphasised data quality, they renamed it 'Data quality' for this study.

The authors added four additional factors for the study. They regarded 'business champion' (a high-level champion from business) as separate from 'top management support' because they considered a business champion as much closer and involved with the project than the top managers were.

A 'business case', which defines the high-level scope and benefits, sets the framework of business expectations and the business sponsor, or champion, drives it for the project. 'Data classification' defines common meanings for concepts across the organisation or divisions. Because the BI system depends on data from the source systems, the degree to which data entities have the same meaning across the systems can affect the BI solution.

Adopting new BI initiatives vs. keeping the business going by doing upgrades in a maintenance ('business as usual') mode demonstrates the 'organisational culture' towards BI.

This resulted in a final list of 23 CSFs for the first round. In the second round, the authors added another CSF ('user involvement'), because of participant input (see below).

A further unique improvement to the instrument is that, instead of merely providing a graded Likert scale (like from 'very important' to 'not important'), the authors provided a detailed descriptive label for each of the five levels of importance. In addition, they asked participants to rate all CSFs *twice*: once for the respondents' business unit's specific BI project and once for the participant's perception of BI projects in general.

In the second Delphi round, the authors also asked the respondents to rate perceived variability and controllability of the most important CSFs.

Delphi methodology overview

A popular approach to investigating the general CSFs in BI has been to use the Delphi method to collect information (Yeoh *et al.* 2007; Yeoh & Koronios 2010; Olbrich *et al.* 2012). Delphi is a 'technique to apply expert input in a systematic manner using a series of questionnaires with controlled opinion feedback' (Linstone & Turoff 2011:1712).

The motivation for using the Delphi method in those studies was that it:

> has proven to be valuable in surfacing new issues and moving participants toward consensus. It is considered to be well suited to situations in which subjective and complex judgments are of interest, as opposed to precise quantitative results. (Olbrich *et al.* 2012:4151)

One can condense the perceptions of a disparate group into a collective view to reach consensus (Skulmoski, Hartman & Krahn 2007). However, Linstone & Turoff (2011) challenge this. They note that consensus can be an outcome, but is not essential. Untapped value also lies in analysing where the feedback diverges.

When one decides on the number or rounds of sampling, the target should be to achieve consistent and stable feedback. Therefore, researchers should be flexible and finish the sampling once they feel they have achieved this (Linstone & Turoff 2011). In the Olbrich *et al.* (2012) study (that targeted consensus), researchers felt that they had achieved moderate consensus after round 2, but continued with a third round of sampling. This resulted in the participation rate dropping from 27 to 13. They concluded that the participants might have been satisfied with their feedback from round two. With regard to the number of participants, two studies by Yeoh, Gao and Koronios (2007) and Yeoh & Koronios (2010) used a small sample of 10 to 15 participants, based on research by Adler and Ziglio (1996). They found that one could obtain satisfactory results from such small sample sizes.

Description of the three business intelligence project case studies

Business unit one: strategic predictive analytics dashboard. Business unit one regards its BI solution as very strategic to the success of the business unit. Before the implementation of the system, the business unit experienced 'Excel hell' because it was using hundreds of spreadsheets to provide information to managers. This resulted in several sources of the truth.

The main driver for the project was to drive profitability and growth. Over a four-year period, the unit implemented the system in phases. The backend source systems range from mainframe to enterprise resource planning (ERP) systems. The unit used extract, transform and load (ETL) programs to populate the enterprise data warehouse with the backend system data. Some data transformation occurs at this stage.

The unit performs data processing using data cubes and other techniques to analyse data. It also uses predictive analytics software as part of the data analysis. A dashboard provides the data to the users using QlikView. This enabled users to drill down in the specific data they require. The plan was to roll out the system over time to approximately 200 users. Positive feedback has resulted in a very significant increase in requests to use the system. There are now over 670 active users on the system. The unit now presents a single version of the data. With the data now being easily accessible to the user, this system has also provided productivity improvements.

Business unit two: an operational key performance indicators reporting system. Business unit two implemented an operational BI system. This was in response to an operational efficiency drive in their back-office processing department. A consultant recommended a variety of key performance indicators (KPIs) for measurement.

The unit extended the back-office system to capture the additional information it required and established a data warehouse. It created an ETL program to extract the information for the data warehouse for online analytical processing (OLAP). The project took about one year because other projects had higher priorities for resources.

The outcome was a variety of reports that covered the workflow of the back-office agents. The unit delivered these reports in Microsoft Excel® format. Some of the reports were complex and used cross-tabbed functionality. The unit regarded the system a success because it did not need to fill a number of vacancies. The solution has subsequently needed minimal maintenance.

Business unit three: a drill-down reporting system. Business unit 3 implemented a BI solution to increase the level of reporting. The unit previously reported using Excel 'manually'. Because of the volume of transactions, the unit was reporting only on transactions over a certain threshold and mainly at branches.

However, there were differences in opinion between the branches as to what they needed to report. The unit loaded data from five backend systems using an ETL process into their multidimensional database management system, Essbase. During this process, data transformation occurred.

The unit performed analyses of the data and initially produced a number of reports. From the reports, the unit identified a number of oversights in the manual reporting. It requested further reports. This significantly increased the coverage and granularity of the reporting.

Because the business unit is small, no business analyst was involved in the project. This resulted in issues between what the business expected and what IT thought they wanted. The project also had data quality issues that only emerged in production.

Notwithstanding these shortcomings, executive managers saw the value in the solution and have embarked on further BI projects.

Data analysis and findings

Critical success factors the participants identified

In the first round, participants provided what they thought their top five CSFs were *before* viewing and rating them on the list the researchers provided. The participants provided 109 unique CSFs.

The authors analysed the data and could generally match them with, or map them to, items already in the researcher-provided list (see Table 3).

However, seven respondents thought that the new factor of 'user experience' was an important CSF. Because this represented more than a quarter of the respondents, the authors regarded it as significant enough to add it as a new CSF in the second round.

In both Delphi rounds, participants rated each of the CSFs the authors provided using a detailed descriptive importance rating. Few participants changed their ratings in the second round. Therefore, one can assume that the participants reached a sufficient degree of consensus after only two rounds.

TABLE 3: Participants' free text feedback on what they considered their top five critical success factors ($N = 26$).

Critical success factors used in survey	Number of matches
User Involvement	14
Business Case	10
Data Quality	10
Top Management Support	10
Business Champion	4
Business Unit Strategy	4
Financial Resources	3
Literacy	4
Data Classifications	1
Time Restrictions	1
User Experience (not in survey)	7
Out of scope for research	19
Other BI project activities	22

Figure 3 gives the ratings of the second round for the general CSFs (not project specific). One can use several criteria to rank the CSFs given their importance scores. Figure 3 ranks CSFs using the 'Very Important' scores as the primary sorting key and, within that, 'Decidedly Important' as a secondary criterion. This order aligns quite well ($r = .965$) with a weighted average score based on the traditional 'equidistant' Likert weights except that, in the latter case, business unit strategy and technical capability rank markedly higher.

In both cases, the top three CSFs (with equal averages) are data quality. It influences business unit strategy and the business case for the BI project. Other critical CSFs the authors identified in the study are: having a business champion, user involvement, technical capability, top manager support and IT influence on the business unit strategy.

These factors and their relative importance align well with the European study (see Hypothesis 3 below). Most surprisingly, the empirical findings align almost perfectly with the theoretical framework.

Hypothesis 1: Alignment between theoretical framework and general Critical Success Factors

Theoretical framework postulates these key implementation factors: manager support, champion, resources, user participation and data quality. If the theoretical framework is valid and the empirical findings from the survey are generisable, then the participants should rank these implementation factors highly amongst all the CSFs.

One should note that, in this survey, the authors split 'resources' into two composite factors: financial resources versus technical resources and capabilities. If one takes a high ranking of either of the two resource types as valid, then it is extremely satisfying to find that the respondents *ranked the five key implementation factors in the theoretical framework within the top seven general BI CSFs.*

This finding is statistically highly significant. One calculates the *p*-value using the probability of finding five specific values out of 23 in a set of (in this case, the top) seven factors. This follows a hypergeometric distribution HyperGeomDist [the

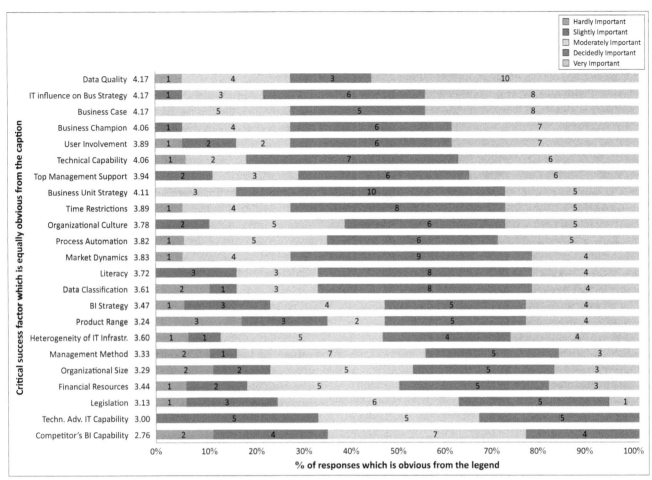

FIGURE 3: Importance ratings for each Critical Success Factor (round 2) by average and detailed breakdown.

number of required values ('successes') in sample = 5, sample size = 7, number of allowed values ('successes') in population 5, population size = 23] = .000624. Because one allows for either of two different possible resource types, but excludes the double counting of the cases where one includes both resource types in the top 7, p = 2×.000624–.000069=.001179 (that is, statistically highly significant). Therefore, one must support the hypothesis that the findings conform strongly to the theoretical framework.

Hypothesis 2: Alignment between project specific and general critical success factors

The projects involved in the research covered two types of BI projects: strategic and operational.

The business units were at very different stages in their BI maturity. This made the study more challenging.

Business unit one had completed many iterations of a BI program over a period of four years. There had been significant success, which the increase in user demand and pervasiveness within the business unit measured. Business unit two had completed their first project using a data warehouse. The backend data source was the operational system for their back office. Even though the managers saw the implementation as a success, they always regarded it as a once-off project and

undertook no subsequent major BI initiatives. The executive sponsor of business unit three regarded the unit to be at a very early stage of experience with their implementation of BI solutions. Most likely the consumers of this research will also be at different stages in their BI maturity. Therefore, one can regard the cross section of selected business units as representative of the wider market.

The challenge, with such a diversity of BI implementation experiences, is to be able to draw generalisable conclusions. The first test was to compare the project-specific ratings of each business unit with the overall general rating of the three business units. The authors chose this comparison to determine how the rating specific to each project would correlate with ratings based on all the participants' general experience of BI. The authors made the comparison using Spearman's ranking correlation and Pearson's correlation. The project specific ratings for the three business units correlated with the mean overall general ratings for both rounds.

As the authors expected, business unit one obtained the highest correlation. The other two business units also had strong correlations for both rounds. Business unit three, as the authors expected, had the lowest correlation. Therefore, this supports Hypothesis 1. A cautionary note is that, because business units one and two made up 81% of the sample, it can introduce bias and result in an inflated correlation.

The surprisingly high correlations prompted the question at the interviews of whether the project specific ratings had materially influenced the general ratings. Two of the interviewees representing business units two and three believed there was bias for their business unit's feedback when completing the survey. According to interviewee 3: 'the project is almost all that you know, I think our people would definitely lean back to the project'. Interviewee 4 said: 'I think there would be in any case because each project has its own specific requirements; the general would be an average across many projects'.

Based on the feedback from interviewee 3 and interview 4, one can deduce that, for the business participants, there was to some degree a bias in the general ratings based on their experience of their specific project used in this research.

Hypothesis 2$_{sub}$: Alignment of project specific critical success factors between projects

Because of the diversity in the project type and the business units' BI maturity, the authors drew a comparison between projects to determine the degree of commonality in the ratings across the projects.

In the literature the authors reviewed, they posited that the CSFs applied generally across industries and types of projects. The Olbrich et al. (2012) study made no distinction between the types of BI projects, attempted to include a wide as possible spectrum of industries, and limited the number of participants per industry. Other researchers (Presthus et al. 2012; Yeoh & Koronios 2010) identified similar factors that contributed to BI implementation success in different industries.

The authors had mixed findings. The only correlation they found was between business units one and two for both the project and general ratings. There were no significant correlations with business unit three. One could attribute this to the unit's lack of experience in BI.

The authors undertook further investigation into these finding at the interviews. Interviewee 1 and interviewee 2 believed that there should be a standard generic list applicable to any type of BI project, irrespective of its industry. According to one of the interviewees:

'I think in BI there are certain things that you can use in a generic way or generic approach and I think key success factors are definitely one of those'. (Interviewee 1)

Interviewee 1 also mentioned that, in addition to the generic factors, one could add others:

'I do think that yes your generic list could probably cover about 80%' and 'Yes they will start listing their own key success factors from experience gained so there's a difference between the theory and the actual experience'. (Interviewee 1)

When the authors asked interviewee 2 whether they would use a subset of the factors from the study for the next project, the response was:

'No, I wouldn't even take a subset of this, I mean most of these things are actually absolutely spot on, a lot of the stuff is very important'. (Interviewee 2)

These views contradicted those of interviewee 3 and interviewee 4. Their view was that there would be project influences on which factors would be important. Interviewee 3 noted: 'for me the critical success factors of a BI project would differ between a small and a large' business unit. When the authors asked interviewee 4 to comment on the differences in the top ten factors highlighted between the business units, interviewee 4 responded that: 'I would say their results indicate why I expect a difference between the organisations depending on their specific needs'.

The authors' findings correlated with a study on CSFs by Olszak and Ziemba (2012). It dealt with Small and Medium-sized Enterprises (SMEs) in Upper Silesia, Poland. They found that, whilst most of the CSFs they identified aligned with those of other researchers, there were notable differences like budget, available skills and well-defined user expectation.

Differences in views between information technology and business experts

The authors drew further comparisons between the absolute ratings by the IT and business participants from each of the business units. This was to ascertain whether there was a difference in their views about the importance of the different factors. They drew the comparisons from both views and compared the IT ratings of the top ten CSFs to the business ratings on the same CSFs. They then drew the same comparisons for the top ten business CSFs.

The authors excluded business unit three from this analysis because there were only five participants: two from IT and three from business.

For business unit one, the IT ratings saw the categories of 'committed management support and champion' ('business unit strategy', 'influence of IT on business unit strategy', 'top management support' and 'business champion') and 'business vision' ('business case' and 'BI strategy') make up the bulk of the top ten. The business participants' top ten was also heavily weighted towards the same two categories. Data quality was also in their top ten. There were six CSFs common to both sets of top ten ratings. An interesting view was that business saw the technical capability of IT to deliver the BI solution as their most important CSF.

The business participants from business unit one rated 'competitor's BI capability' in their top ten factors. Interviewee 1 noted that, as IT, 'we don't do much work around what the competitors are doing, these guys (business) need to tell us that' and:

'we don't see what the brokers are getting, so to me the competitors are not that important. What is important is that I understand how we can be better where business is comparing us to the competitors'. (Interviewee 1)

This is an example of where business and IT participants view some of the CSFs from a different perspective, resulting in different levels of importance.

For business unit two, there were seven CSFs common to both sets of top ten ratings. The average ratings between the two datasets were closer than for business unit one. They again placed clear importance on the 'committed management support and champion' category. Information technology and business both rated data quality as the top CSF. As interviewee 4 noted: 'data is a very high quality, very high importance to the customer, damage to the reputation would be very high'.

Business unit two also rated management methods high because the main aim of the BI system was to produce reports that show whether the business was meeting the efficiency metrics it specified. As interviewee 4 noted: 'The BI project was very much around the balance score card and the performance of the environment, so for this project those were rated really high'.

Consistent with the efficiency drive, it also rated process automation in the top set for both sets of participants.

Information technology also rated the literacy the users required as important. Moreover, according to one of the interviewees:

'The process automation and literacy, our users need to have a good understanding of the business to get through the requirements and our people also need a good understanding of the business in order to deliver value'. (Interviewee 4)

For business, articulating the vision was important with 'business case' and 'BI strategy' featuring in their top ten.

There is a clear similarity in the categories of CSFs that are important to both IT and business in both business units. They saw the roles the top managers played in supporting the project as influential in achieving the business goals for the system. Therefore, for a BI project's outcome to succeed, one should view it as a business project that extracts value from business data. The high importance both business and IT participants placed on CSFs in the 'committed management support and champion' and 'business vision' categories indicates the significant role non-technical CSFs play in the success of a BI implementation. This is consistent with the findings of Adamala and Cidrin (2011). Another study, by Yeoh *et al.* (2007) in the field of engineering asset management, also noted that, in industry, the top CSFs were weighted towards business skills and manager involvement.

Hypothesis 3: Comparison with Europe

The authors drew a comparison with the CSF importance rankings between round one of both studies, between round 2 of this study and round 3 of the European study (Olbrich *et al.* 2012). The sample demographics for the European study are unknown. However, the researchers indicate that they selected experts from practicing senior managers and project managers from different industries with an average BI experience of more than seven years. The expert profile should match that of the South African participants (see below), although this study occurred in the financial services industry. This may bias or limit the comparison.

Olbrich *et al.* 2012 based their first comparison on ratings and the second comparison on rankings. Because the authors of this article based all the South African results on ratings, they calculated the rankings for the second round using the mean ratings. They based their comparisons on the sixteen CSFs that were common to both studies for round one and the nineteen CSFs that were common to both studies for round two.

The statistical tests showed a good correlation between the two studies with a rank-correlation coefficient of .577 (statistically significant at $p = .01$).

However, whilst the South African study comprised IT and business participants, the European study comprised only IT participants who were senior managers and project managers. Therefore, the authors of this article refined

TABLE 4: Summary of hypothesis findings.

Hypothesis	Business Unit	Indicator	Delphi round 1		Delphi round 2	
			Correlation coefficient	*p*-value	Correlation coefficient	*p*-value
H₁ The five implementation factors hypothesised in the theoretical framework will be amongst the highly-ranked CSFs	*All*	Supported	NA	.0011	NA	.0011
H₂ The project specific ratings for Importance will align with general average ratings	1	Supported	.86592	.0000	.7906	.0000
	2	Supported	.6660	.0006	.6236	.0017
	3	Supported	.5721	.0050	.5293	.0106
H₂ₛᵤᵦ The project specific ratings for importance will align between projects	1 to 2	Supported	.6096	.0024	.4227	.0410
	1 to 3	Not supported	.4016	.0569	.3901	.0591
	2 to 3	Not supported	.3175	.1225	.3529	.0855
H₃ The generic ratings for importance of all South African participants will align with the European study	All	Supported	.5062	.0454	.5766	.0103
H₃ₐ The generic ratings for importance of the South African *IT* participants will align with the European study	All	Supported	.6391	.0077	.5792	.0099
H₃ᵦ The generic ratings for importance of the South African *business* participants will align with the European study	All	Not supported	.2511	.3483	.3540	.1178

H₁, Hypothesis 1; H₂, Hypothesis 2; H₃, Hypothesis 3; CSFs, critical success factors; IT, information technology; NA, Not applicable.

the analysis to distinguish whether there is a correlations between the European and the rankings of the South African IT (H_{3a}) and business participants (H_{3b}) respectively. Not surprisingly, the ratings of the IT participants showed a much stronger correlation (.579), with the p-value of .0099 being highly significant. The ratings of the business participants, on the other hand, showed only a weak, statistically non-significant correlation (.354, $p = .118$) between the datasets. This illustrates clearly how the criteria researchers use to select samples can influence research outcomes.

Summary of hypothesis testing

Based on the analysis of the quantitative and qualitative data, the outcomes of the hypotheses the authors tested are shown in Table 4 (previous page).

Variability and controllability of critical success factors

In the second round, the authors also asked the participants to rate the variability (Figure 4) and controllability (Figure 5) of the top ten rated factors from the South African BI in general context from round 1. The decision to include these dimensions was to add a more holistic and rounded narrative to the CSF.

An example is top manager support. The mean response showed that the participants in this study found that the variability ranged between 'consistent for the majority of the duration of the project' to being 'fairly consistent; variation starts to be noticed as hurdles are encountered on the project' (Figure 4). For controllability, the finding was in a similar range between 'BI management secures top management support on an ad-hoc basis' and 'Secures support on a regular basis' (Figure 5). This highlighted that some executives gave support when they had a 'need for specific information that they deem to be strategic' whilst others saw the overall importance of BI in their organisations.

Only seven factors for both dimensions occurred in both studies. As the European study used ranking for rounds two and three and this study used ratings, the authors of this article drew the comparison with round one of the European study. For neither of the two dimensions could they establish a statistically significant correlation. The respective correlation coefficients were .3055 for variability and .1868 for controllability.

When the authors examined the absolute values, they seemed to show that the South African participants perceive that there is less variability in their environments and that they have more control over the factors. This could be because there is bias in the sample because ten of the participants in round one come from business unit one, whose BI implementation has been very successful. Because the researchers conducted the European study in different industries, the authors believe that the European ratings for the variability and controllability dimensions may be a truer reflection of the reality organisations generally experience.

Conclusion

Business intelligence has become an important part of the solution to providing decision makers, at different levels of organisations, with the accurate, relevant and up-to-date information on which to base their decisions. However, BI solutions are generally challenging given their complexity, especially when they span several business units or information systems. To help deal with these challenges, organisations are looking toward best practices and research on increasing BI success. Critical success factors provide BI practitioners with insights into which factors organisations should address within the constraints of their projects in order to improve their chances of success.

The literature review provided a number of studies that researchers had conducted in different parts of the world (Olbrich et al. 2012; Yeoh et al. 2007). These studies provided insights into the CSFs that were key to enabling successful BI project implementation. A review of South African BI research did not reveal any research dedicated to CSFs in the BI domain. This presented an opportunity to add to the body of existing knowledge and provide findings that are relevant to the South African context.

The theoretical framework the authors used for the study followed the model of Wixom and Watson (2001) for their business warehouse project success. They modified it for the context of business intelligence as well as to focus on organisational and project implementation success instead of technical success (Figure 2).

The authors used a mixed-method approach of a survey and interviews. The survey followed the Delphi method approach with the participants primarily required to rate the CSFs for importance based on a Likert scale for their business unit's project and separately for the context of BI in general. The participants rated a subset of factors for variability and controllability. The interviews were semi-structured and asked open-ended questions. The authors asked follow-up questions when interesting points surfaced.

The study identified that the most important CSFs for the participating business units belonged to the categories of 'committed management support and champion', 'business vision', 'user involvement' and 'data quality'. The highest rated CSFs for the importance dimension for the BI in the general context were 'data quality', 'business case' and 'influence of IT on business unit strategy', whilst the highest rated in the project context were 'data quality', 'top management support' and 'business champion'.

These findings were almost a perfect validation of the theoretical framework, because all five factors the authors postulated for organisational and project implementation success feature amongst the seven most highly ranked CSFs ($p = .00125$).

The authors achieved a moderate correlation between the overall rating of this study for the BI in the general context

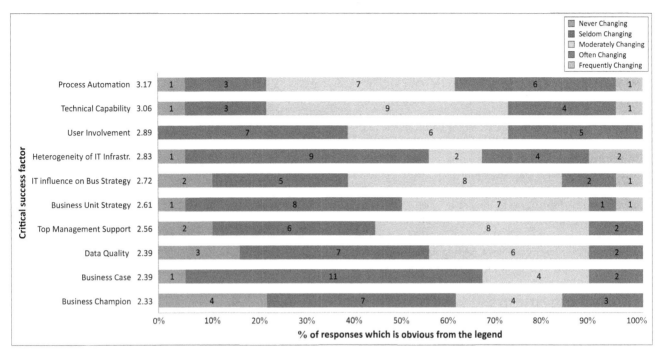

FIGURE 4: Perceived variability of top critical success factors.

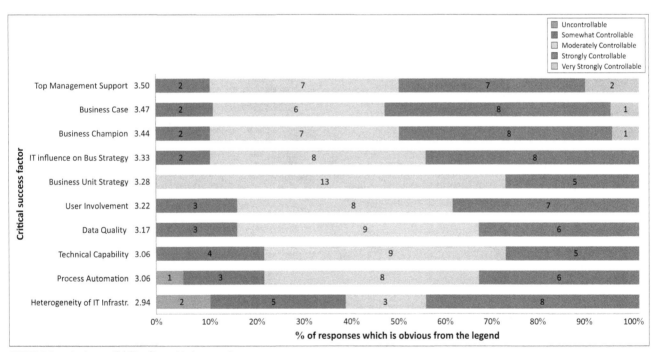

FIGURE 5: Perceived controllability of top critical success factors.

with the European study. There were minor but significant differences in the ratings the IT and the business experts gave. Participants also identified a few differences between project-specific and 'generic' BI CSFs.

The participating business units had achieved different levels of BI maturity. Project-to-project comparisons reflected this, where the ratings resulted in correlations between only two of the business units. This difference in the BI maturity of the business units is a natural expectation and adds value to the research for consumers. If the authors had selected only organisations with very mature BI approaches, it may have

limited the relevance for those starting with BI or those still developing their expertise.

Because one can assume that there will be varying levels of BI maturity in other financial organisations in South Africa, the authors expect that one can generalise their findings to other South African financial institutions. However, further research would need to be undertaken before one can generalise these results to other industries.

From a theoretical perspective, the authors' proposed theoretical framework fared very well. All five factors featured in the top seven CSFs the respondents identified. This means that the framework can provide a 'short-cut' summary of the key CSFs and validates the generalisability of the findings. However, future models may look at incorporating the other two key variables the authors uncovered: business case and IT influence on business unit strategy.

What did emerge from the interviews was that none of the projects had explicitly identified upfront the CSFs together with the relevant metrics they needed for their projects to succeed. However, the respondents did address some implicitly. Encouragingly, some interviewees noted that, now that they had had exposure to the list of CSFs, they would use it as a reference for future projects. Additional research could compare the outcomes of BI projects of organisations that do explicitly identify the key CSFs together with metrics upfront for their projects versus those that do not.

Acknowledgements

The authors hereby gratefully acknowledge the contribution of the participating staff and managers of the insurance company in which they undertook the research. The National Research Foundation (NRF) and the University of Cape Town (UCT) provided partial funding for the conference paper in which the authors presented their initial findings.

Competing interests

The authors declare that they have no financial or personal relationships that may have inappropriately influenced them when they wrote this article.

Authors' contributions

L.D. (University of Cape Town) collected the empirical data for this study as part of his Honours empirical research report under supervision of J-P.V.B. (University of Cape Town). J-P.V.B. (University of Cape Town) edited the original report substantially and added most of the theoretical background.

References

Adamala, S. & Cidrin, L., 2011, 'Key Success Factors in Business Intelligence', *Journal of Intelligence Studies in Business* 1, 107–127.

Adler, M. & Ziglio, E., 1996, *Gazing into the oracle: the Delphi method and its application to social policy and public health*, Jessica Kingsley Publishers, London.

Bijker, M., 2010, 'Understanding the Factors that Influence Pervasiveness of Business Intelligence in South Africa', Technical report, Dept. of Information Systems, University of Cape Town, Cape Town.

Blenkhorn, D.L. & Fleisher, C.S., 2007, 'Performance Assessment in Competitive Intelligence: An Exploration, Synthesis, and Research Agenda', *Journal of Competitive Intelligence and Management* 4(2), 4–21.

DeLone, W.H. & McLean E.R., 1992, 'Information systems success: the quest for the dependent variable', *Information Systems Research* 3(1), 60–95. http://dx.doi.org/10.1287/isre.3.1.60

Gartner Research — BI Revenue, 2012, 'Gartner Says Worldwide Business Intelligence, Analytics and Performance Management Software Market Surpassed the $12 Billion Mark in 2011', viewed 5 December 2012, from http://www.gartner.com/it/page.jsp?id=1971516

Hartley, K. & Seymour, L.F., 2011, 'Towards a framework for the adoption of business intelligence in public sector organisations: the case of South Africa', *SAICSIT Annual Research Conference*, Cape Town, South Africa, October 3–5, 2011, pp. 116–122.

Hawking, P. & Sellitto, C., 2010, 'Business Intelligence (BI) Critical Success Factors', *21st Australian Conference on Information Systems*, Brisbane, Australia, December 1–3, 2010, AIS Electronic Library.

Linstone, H.A. & Turoff, M., 2011, 'Delphi: A brief look backward and forward', *Technological Forecasting & Social Change* 78(9), 1712–1719. http://dx.doi.org/10.1016/j.techfore.2010.09.011

Lönnqvist, A. & Pirttimäki, V., 2006, 'The Measurement of Business Intelligence' *Information Systems Management* 23(1), 32–40. http://dx.doi.org/10.1201/1078.10580530/45769.23.1.20061201/91770.4

Luftman, J. & Ben-Zvi, T., 2010, 'Key Issues for IT Executives 2010: Judicious IT Investments Continue Post-Recession', *MIS Quarterly Executive* 9(4), 263–273.

Lutu, P.E. & Meyer, B., 2008, 'The successful adoption and usage of business intelligence in public sector organisations: an exploratory study in South Africa', *Proceeedings of IFIP WG 9.4-University of Pretoria Joint Workshop*, Pretoria, South Africa, September 23–24, 2008, pp. 164–173.

O'Brien, J. & Kok, J.A., 2006, 'Business Intelligence and the telecommunications industry: can business intelligence lead to higher profits?', *South African Journal of Information Management* 8(3), 1–16.

Olbrich, S., Pöppelbuß, J. & Niehaves, B., 2012, 'Critical Contextual Success Factors for Business Intelligence: A Delphi Study on Their Relevance, Variability, and Controllability', *45th Hawaii International Conference on System Sciences*, Hawaii, USA, January 4–7, 2012, pp. 4148–4157.

Olszak, C.M. & Ziemba, E., 2012, 'Critical Success Factors for Implementing Business Intelligence Systems in Small and Medium Enterprises on the Example of Upper Silesia, Poland', *Interdisciplinary Journal of Information, Knowledge, and Management* 7, 129–150.

Pellissier, R. & Kruger, J-P., 2011, 'Understanding the use of strategic intelligence as a strategic management tool in the long-term insurance industry in South Africa', *SA Journal of Information Management* 13(1), Art. #426, 13 pages. http://dx.doi.org/10.4102/sajim.v13i1.426

Pirttimäki, V.H., 2007, 'Conceptual analysis of business intelligence', *SA Journal of Information Management* 9(2), 17 pages.

Ponelis, S.R., 2011, 'An exploratory study of business intelligence in knowledge-based growth small, medium and micro-enterprises in South Africa', PhD thesis, Dept. of Information Technology, University of Pretoria, South Africa.

Presthus, W., Ghinea, G. & Utvik, K.-R., 2012, 'The More, the Merrier? The Interaction of Critical Success Factors in Business Intelligence Implementations', *International Journal of Business Intelligence Research* 3(2), 34–48. http://dx.doi.org/10.4018/jbir.2012040103

Ranjan, J., 2008, 'Business justification with business intelligence', *The Journal of Information and Knowledge Management Systems* 38(4), 461–475.

Skulmoski, G.J., Hartman, F.T. & Krahn, J., 2007, 'The Delphi Method for Graduate Research', *Journal of Information Technology Education* 6, 1–21.

Smith, D. & Crossland, M., 2008, 'Realizing the value of Business Intelligence', *Advances in Information Systems Research, Education and Practice, IFIP Vol. 274*, 163–174.

Wixom, B.H. & Watson, J., 2001, 'An Empirical Investigation of the Factors Affecting Data Warehousing Success', *MIS Quarterly* 25(1), 1–24. http://dx.doi.org/10.2307/3250957

Yeoh, W. & Koronios, A., 2010, 'Critical Success Factors for Business Intelligence Systems', *Journal of Computer Information Systems* 50(3), 23–32.

Yeoh, W., Gao, J. & Koronios, A., 2007, 'Towards a Critical Success Factor Framework for Implementing Business Intelligence Systems — A Delphi Study in Engineering Asset Management Organizations', *IFIP TC 8 WG 8.9 International Conference on Research and Practical Issues of Enterprise Information Systems*, Beijing, China, October 14–16, 2007, pp. 1353–1367.

8

Value of a mobile information system to improve quality of care by community health workers

Authors:
Mark Tomlinson[1]
Mary Jane Rotheram-Borus[2]
Tanya Doherty[3]
Dallas Swendeman[2]
Alexander C. Tsai[4,5]
Petrida Ijumba[3]
Ingrid le Roux[6]
Debra Jackson[3,7]
Jackie Stewart[1]
Andi Friedman[8]
Mark Colvin[9†]
Mickey Chopra[10]

Affiliations:
[1]Department of Psychology, University of Stellenbosch, South Africa

[2]Global Center for Children and Families, University of California, United States of America

[3]Health Systems Research Unit, Medical Research Council, South Africa

[4]Robert Wood Johnson Health and Society Scholars Program, Harvard University, United States of America

[5]Center for Global Health, Massachusetts General Hospital, United States of America

[6]Philani Nutrition and Development Project, Cape Town, South Africa

[7]School of Public Health, University of the Western Cape, South Africa

[8]Clyral, Durban, South Africa

[9]Maromi Health Research, South Africa

[10]UNICEF, New York, United States of America

Correspondence to:
Mark Tomlinson

Email:
markt@sun.ac.za

Background: We will be unable to achieve sustained impact on health outcomes with community health worker (CHW)-based interventions unless we bridge the gap between small scale efficacy studies and large scale interventions. Effective strategies to support the management of CHWs are central to bridging the gap. Mobile phones are broadly available, particularly in low and middle income countries (LAMIC), where the penetration rate approaches 100%.

Objectives: In this article, we describe how mobile phones and may be combined with mobile web-based technology to assist in the management of CHWs in two projects in South Africa.

Methods: This article is a descriptive study, drawing lessons from two randomised controlled trials outlining how a mobile phone information system can be utilised to enhance the quality of health interventions. We organised our comprehensive management and supervision system around a previously published management framework. The system is composed of mobile phones utilised by CHWs and a web-based interface utilised by CHW supervisors. Computerised algorithms were designed with intervention and assessment protocols to aid in the real-time supervision and management of CHWs.

Results: Community health workers used mobile phones to initiate intervention visits and trigger content to be delivered during the course of intervention visits. Supervisors used the web-based interface for real-time monitoring of the location, timing and content of intervention visits. Additional real-time support was provided through direct support calls in the event of crises in the field.

Conclusion: Mobile phone-based information system platforms offer significant opportunities to improve CHW-delivered interventions. The extent to which these efficiency gains can be translated into realised health gains for communities is yet to be tested.

Introduction

With the health budgets of more than 40 African nations spending less than $30 per person annually, it is critical that more cost-effective delivery strategies are identified for health care (Lewin *et al.* 2008). The personnel necessary for serving the health care needs for HIV-related diseases cannot feasibly be met until the year 2050 (Anyangwe & Mtonga 2007). Therefore, community health workers (CHWs) are increasingly identified as a potential vehicle for strengthening community based care; especially for maternal, newborn and child survival. Whilst successful CHW programs alone will not solve the maternal and child health crises facing many poor countries, they have the potential to make a large impact by significantly expanding access to healthcare (Haines *et al.* 2007).

Healthcare systems in many African and South Asian countries currently utilise CHWs in their programs as part of their plan to achieve the Millennium Development Goals and other human development priorities (Haines *et al.* 2007). It is estimated that there are more than 40 million CHWs around the world at present (Lewin *et al.* 2010). Several trials have shown the efficacy of CHWs in reducing morbidity and mortality amongst neonates and infants (Bang *et al.* 2005; Sazawal & Black 2003; Manandhar *et al.* 2004). However, most research evaluating the impact of CHW programs has been limited to small and short-term interventions in heavily resourced research settings (Haines *et al.* 2007). Larger scale CHW programs such as the national implementation of the Integrated Management of Childhood Illness strategy in Peru (Huicho

Postal address: Private Bag X1, Matieland, Stellenbosch 7602, South Africa

et al. 2005), and the national CHW program in Sri Lanka (Walt *et al.* 1989) have been hindered by barriers to effective scaling up. Large scale programs are frequently undermined by high attrition and low activity levels of CHWs, which are less likely in smaller scale initiatives where supervision is often more intense and consistent (Walt *et al.* 1989). Whilst the use of CHWs has achieved many successes (Baqui *et al.* 2008; Rahman *et al.* 2008), the system has also been characterised by a lack of consistent supervision and linkages to the health system (Walley *et al.* 2008; Haines *et al.* 2007).

We will be unable to achieve sustained impact utilising CHWs unless we can bridge the gap between small scale efficacy studies and large scale interventions. An important part of this process lies in building effective strategies to support the management and supervision of CHWs (Rowe *et al.* 2005). The performance of CHWs in achieving their health objectives is influenced by multiple factors, but it is widely accepted that effective management is of fundamental importance (Rowe *et al.* 2005; Gray & Ciroma 1988; Haines *et al.* 2007; Kelly *et al.* 2001; Walt *et al.* 1989). The difficulties in establishing an effective information system that provides managers with high quality and timely information about the activities and performance of a dispersed group of workers may be an important cause of the loss of quality in information and supervisory systems as programs scale up.

South Africa has over 60 000 CHWs most of whom are paid by national government but are employed, monitored, and evaluated by non-governmental organisations (NGOs). The National Department of Health in South Africa is currently implementing a Primary Health Care revitalisation strategy, where community-based outreach functions are being prioritised and funded based on a large extent Brazil's Family Health Program (Paim *et al.* 2011). Primary health care teams are currently being implemented in South Africa, and linked to a local health facility and staffed by community health workers and nurses (National Department of Health 2011). Central to this re-vitalisation process is improving the management of CHWs and a renewed commitment to the use of Information and Communication Technology and particularly mobile phones in this process (Leon & Schneider 2011).

The rapid technological innovation in the mHealth (which are interventions categorised under the rubric 'mobile health' or 'mHealth' are broadly defined as medical and public health practice supported by mobile devices (Van Heerden *et al.* 2012). The mHealth field has led to a proliferation of untested methods and small-scale projects. This has recently begun to change with studies showing the potential impacts of scaling up using mHealth innovations (Zurovac *et al.* 2011). The implementation of mobile phone information systems has the potential to provide practical and simple solutions to management difficulties at scale. With more than 5.3 billion mobile phones in use, there is an organically created information platform that can rapidly disseminate innovations in health care (Tomlinson *et al.* 2009). In this article, we draw on our experience over the last six years

to describe a system we developed and to suggest ways in which this information platform can be used to improve the supervision, management and quality of interventions provided by CHWs.

Methods

Management of community health care workers

CHWs are effective when there is an effective health system or NGO that provides supervision, supplies, monitoring and on-going training. However, organising these critical support activities at scale has proven very difficult. Our mobile information system was based on a previously published framework (Bosch-Capblanch & Garner 2008). Their model (see Figure 1) links health care worker performance including activities of the CHW (counseling, education), outputs (coverage) and outcomes (morbidity) with aspects of management such as comparing service delivered against norms, problem identification and examining data against expected outputs. This model is in line with the work of Rowe and colleagues who have outlined a number of typical reasons for the inadequacy of supervision of CHWs at scale (Rowe *et al.* 2010). These include poor co-ordination, inadequate management skills, problems related to decentralisation, increasing supervision workload, time required for supervision activities, lack of transportation, insufficient knowledge of how to plan visits and a lack of tools to assess supervision (Rowe *et al.* 2010).

Our mobile information system

In partnership with a private, South Africa-based digital company (Clyral) we have developed a comprehensive information and supervision system that combines mobile phones with a web-based information interface. Our primary

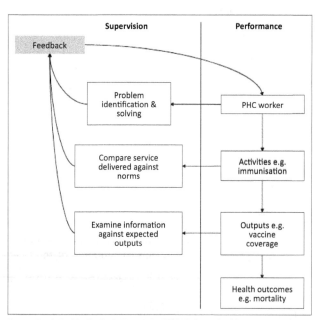

Source: Bosch-Capblanch, X. & Garner, P., 2008, 'Primary health care supervision in developing countries', *Tropical Medicine International Health* 13, 369–383. http://dx.doi.org/10.1111/j.1365-3156.2008.02012.x

FIGURE 1: The framework for supervision.

motivation was to develop a system of daily monitoring of CHW visits to aid in the supervision of a large cadre of CHWs. Specific focus areas (all of which are central to supervision [Rowe *et al.* 2010]) for the system were:

1. recruitment of study mothers, CHW assessment, and adaptive scheduling and visit planning
2. intervention delivery support, fidelity monitoring and individual case monitoring
3. caseload reporting and information management. (n.p.)

The system was designed to integrate all CHW activities into a web-based information narrative that is initiated the moment a participant is recruited; all intervention and data milestones are triggered automatically. Computerised algorithms have been designed to monitor and trigger the intervention and assessment protocols to aid in the real-time supervision and management of CHWs. These protocols include assessment of intervention fidelity, quality control, visit planning, and monitoring of CHW productivity. The web based information system was developed in partnership with a private digital company in South Africa, Clyral. Our system imposes few requirements with regards to the specific handset models to be used. The single requirement is that they need to be enabled for Java programming (Tomlinson *et al.* 2009). All of the CHWs were women with no previous administrative or data collection experience, but all had previous experience using basic mobile phone functions such as making calls and sending SMSs. Training CHWs in the use of the mobile phone application consisted of a one day training workshop, followed by several one hour refresher courses throughout the duration of the project. We also implemented weekly face-to-face group supervision, with individual supervision when necessary. Each CHW was supplied with her own project mobile phone.

Results

Recruitment, assessment, and adaptive scheduling and planning

We have been working with local CHWs in two projects in South Africa to explore how mobile-information-based supervision could be used to improve supervision and management of CHW's (see Box 1). In both projects, CHWs recruit expectant mothers in clusters through door-to-door home visits. The global positioning system (GPS) captures the geographical coordinates on the CHW's mobile phone for each household visited. As a CHW enters a household, the CHW begins monitoring the visit duration with a single click on the phone. Then, as she leaves the home at the end of the intervention visit, she repeats the click on the phone. The GPS- and time- stamping functions are built into each mobile phone, allowing the location and duration of the household visit to be assessed and transferred in real-time to the web-based information, supervision and management system. The GPS function reduces the possibility of falsifying data substantially, as the time between visits and the location of the visit is automatically recorded and transmitted to the CHW supervisors. Compared to systems implemented in prior studies, the lag time between protocol deviations (by

CHWs) and triggering of reactive monitoring (by supervisors) is thereby substantially reduced. Similar advantages exist for the assessment of interviewers and recruiters in research trials.

Once a woman is enrolled in the program, a short intake questionnaire is completed using the mobile phone. This information includes her personal details, selected health information, gestation and risk profiling. Once received by the central web based program, the system combines the woman's expected date of delivery with an algorithm for her health information to determine her relative level of risk. Based on the result, the system determines the quantity and scheduling of antenatal visits that she is required to receive from the CHW before her infant is born.

After the birth of each participant's child, the system schedules the quantity and timing of her postnatal visits. A woman who is assessed to be at high risk (e.g. if she gives birth to an infant of low birth weight) is assigned to receive more home visits than a woman who is considered low risk. At present, this process occurs through a manual case consultation process rather than occurring automatically according to an algorithm loaded on the mobile phone (but the system can be designed so that this process is automated). Once this decision has been made, the information system automatically schedules and follows up on these 'extra visits'.

For each visit that a participating mother is due to receive, a dated milestone is created on her participant page in the web-based information console (see Figure 2). The dated visit milestones for all mothers in the program filter through

---

BOX 1: Two case studies: Goodstart 3 and Philani Mentor Mothers Project.

Goodstart 3

The Goodstart 3 study is a cluster randomised controlled trial being implemented in Umlazi, a peri-urban settlement close to Durban in South Africa with a population of approximately 1 million. The 2010 antenatal HIV prevalence in this district was 41% (SANDOH 2010) and infant mortality is estimated to be 42 per 1000 live births (Day *et al.* 2011). Mobile phone connectivity in Umlazi is excellent. The goal of Goodstart 3 study is to develop, evaluate and cost an integrated and scalable home visit package delivered by CHW's targeting pregnant and postnatal women and their newborns to provide essential maternal or newborn care as well as interventions for Prevention of Mother to Child Transmission (PMTCT) of HIV. Umlazi has a mixture of formal and informal housing, and whilst it is a relatively well-resourced peri-urban area; it has a non-optimally functioning health system. South Africa is one of twelve countries worldwide where child mortality has increased since 1990 (Bradshaw *et al.* 2008). This is primarily related to the HIV epidemic, with more than half of child deaths attributed to HIV and AIDS (Liu *et al.* 2012). The evaluation trial consists of 30 randomised clusters (15 in each arm) of the population. Results from this study are forthcoming.

The Philani Mentor Mothers Project

The Philani Mentor Mothers Project) is a longitudinal, cluster-randomised controlled trial. The study was conducted in Khayelitsha, a peri-urban settlement of approximately one million people, on the outskirts on Cape Town, South Africa. Khayelitsha, like many South African township settings, has high levels of violence, with poor infrastructure, vast areas of informal houses (shacks), and high levels of unemployment (Nleya & Thompson 2009). Mobile phone connectivity in Khayelitsha is excellent. The project aims to evaluate the effectiveness of a home-based care intervention delivered by CHWs for preventing and managing illnesses related to HIV, TB, alcohol use and malnutrition in pregnant mothers and their infants. The study has 1200 mothers in 24 neighbourhood clusters, 12 of which are intervention neighbourhoods, and 12 of which are control neighbourhoods. A cohort of women from each neighbourhood is followed from pregnancy until their infants are 18 months old. The home visits are designed to be both supportive and educational in nature. They are intended to empower pregnant mothers to better protect the health of their families by accessing available clinic services, implementing preventive behaviours in daily life routines, and sustaining preventive behaviours over time. The home-based delivery strategy addresses the cluster of behaviours necessary to deal with chronic conditions simultaneously, as opposed to individually (Le Roux *et al.* 2013).

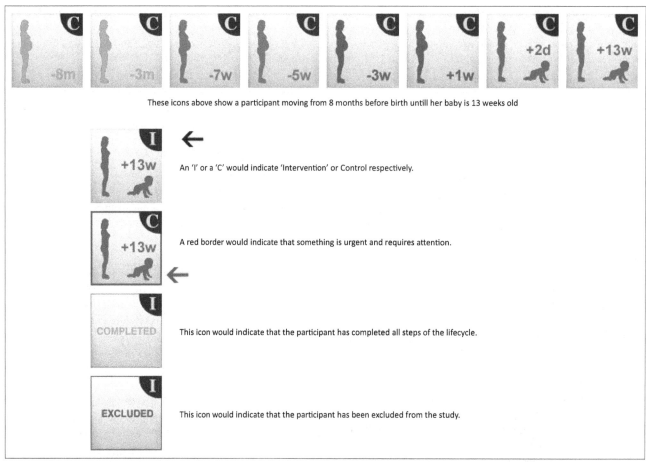

Source: Mobenzi Researcher n.d., *Philani Mentor Mothers Project*, viewed from http://www.mobenzi.com/researcher/Case-Studies/View/Philani-Mentor-Mothers-Project; Mobenzi Researcher n.d., *Good Start III (Saving Newborn Lives)*, viewed from http://www.mobenzi.com/researcher/Case-Studies/View/Good-Start-III-(Saving-Newborn-Lives)

FIGURE 2: The icons on web-console.

to a weekly timetable for each CHW. This timetable details which mothers she needs to visit that week (see Figure 3). At each visit, the CHW records the duration and content of the visit on her mobile phone, which ticks off each milestone in the participant's lifespan as completed. Once completed, the visit reminder is removed from the weekly timetable. As can be seen from Figure 3, before the birth of the infant the console simply reflects antenatal visits completed thus far. The postnatal visits are portrayed as to be completed. As soon as the woman gives birth, the birth date and time is entered into the mobile phone and transferred to the web-based system, which automatically schedules and triggers all postnatal visits. Simultaneously, the CHW and the CHW supervisor receive an SMS notification of the birth and the dates of all scheduled visits.

The GPS co-ordinates of each household could also be used in such a way that within each week, those mothers who live closest to each other are scheduled for appointments on the same day. This system could minimise the distance the CHW needs to travel each day and improve the efficiency of the time they spend in the field. Currently, the specific set ups used in our studies do not co-ordinate at this level of detail. However, the underlying computer code for the mobile information system has been structured so that significant

changes to its function and content can be made, depending on the particular requirements of the specific project. The GoodStart 3 study for instance is aimed at reducing neonatal mortality and improving levels of exclusive and appropriate feeding. As a result, visits are highly structured with a particular emphasis on visits occurring at particular times in the early neonatal period (e.g. 24 hours to 48 hours and 3 days to 4 days after birth) (see Figure 3). In the Philani study on the other hand, visits are less structured - in terms of both the day on which visits must take place and the time taken for each visit. To monitor both the date of visit and time spent (per visit and across time), we developed an interface that included a cumulative time counter (comparable to an egg timer) (see Figure 4). By tracking visit duration (and total time spent on the intervention), we are able to characterise the potentially dose-dependent response to the intervention, as well as calculate intervention delivery costs in a more precise way.

Intervention delivery support, fidelity monitoring and individual case monitoring

A significant difficulty when scaling up interventions is the issue of intervention fidelity and how to ensure quality control of intervention delivery. We developed a series of short questionnaires that were triggered on the mobile phones when the CHW entered the identification number

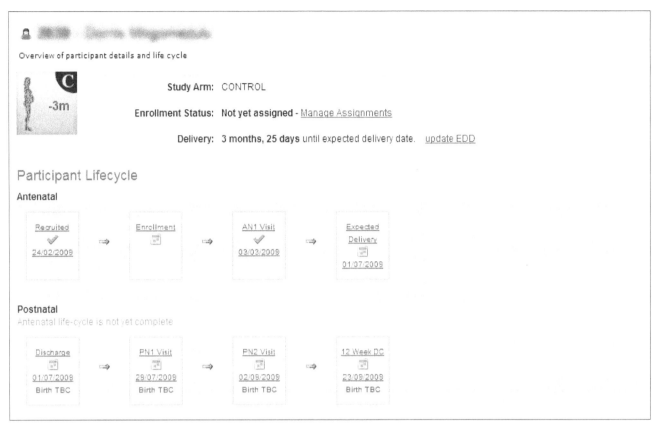

Source: Mobenzi Researcher n.d., *Philani Mentor Mothers Project*, viewed from http://www.mobenzi.com/researcher/Case-Studies/View/Philani-Mentor-Mothers-Project; Mobenzi Researcher n.d., *Good Start III (Saving Newborn Lives)*, viewed from http://www.mobenzi.com/researcher/Case-Studies/View/Good-Start-III-(Saving-Newborn-Lives)

FIGURE 3: The intervention schedule.

of the household being visited. This questionnaire serves as a reminder about the core intervention messages to be covered at that visit, a check on intervention fidelity that the topics were covered, and as the data source for the adaptive scheduling of follow up visits and intervention content. Antenatal questions include whether the woman has made a booking at the antenatal clinic; what her feeding plan is and whether she has been tested for HIV. Postnatal questions include questions about maternal and neonatal illness; whether the baby received AZT; whether the mother went to the clinic at six days post-birth; breast health; whether the infant has been tested for HIV; and if babies are HIV-positive, whether they are receiving cotrimoxazole.

To account for day-to-day participant availability, the system allows a CHW to suspend a visit based on the availability of the participant. If the CHW determines that she should return to complete a visit at some other time in the future, she can tick the appropriate box on the mobile phone. Her tick is immediately registered on the web based system. This is also the case for missed visits (participant not home when CHW arrives) or visits cut short for other reasons (e.g. an irritable infant). In this way, the system is able to monitor all aspects of the intervention such as CHW caseloads, clusters with higher levels of missed visits compared to other clusters; reasons for missed or suspended visits; and CHW performance in real time on a daily basis. The web-based management system (and mobile-phone connectivity) allows supervisors to (remotely) access the information console and monitor real-time information about each participating mother and child in the intervention program, as well as information on each CHW's activities and caseloads.

The console has a live report of all visits that have taken place, which can be filtered by date and by CHW, to establish how many visits are happening on any given day or week by any given CHW. The console also generates a 'visit-time' report (see Figure 5), with details for each participant in the intervention; not only how many visits they have had, but also the cumulative amount of time for all visits combined. In this way, one can easily identify outliers amongst participants or amongst CHWs. Based on these reports, together with the system flags that are generated, supervisors are able, in real time, to schedule a 'shadow' or 'spot' visit for the supervisor to conduct checks on the quality of home visits. In addition, visits are randomly generated and scheduled based on each weekly schedule for each CHW. These visits allow the supervisor to validate the observational reports of the CHW or identify households which should receive extra support.

The system can be used to optimise supervision at every level of the intervention program including:

- recruitment and scheduling of visits
- monitoring activity and progress of CHWs
- managing health information and emergencies
- accessing data such as date of visit to household and duration of visit

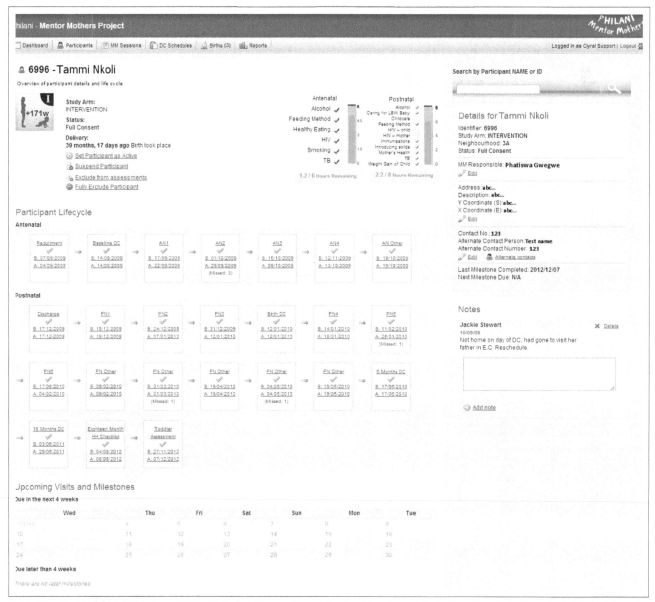

Source: Mobenzi Researcher n.d., *Philani Mentor Mothers Project*, viewed from http://www.mobenzi.com/researcher/Case-Studies/View/Philani-Mentor-Mothers-Project; Mobenzi Researcher n.d., *Good Start III (Saving Newborn Lives)*, viewed from http://www.mobenzi.com/researcher/Case-Studies/View/Good-Start-III-(Saving-Newborn-Lives)

FIGURE 4: The participant dashboard.

- provide knowledge of visit schedule
- pinpoint discrepancies and anomalies automatically with alerts sent to supervisors.

For instance, a visit of very short duration in the first 48 hours of birth will be flagged as problematic (given the detail required during the visit) and supervisors will be informed, [*and*] a spot or shadow visit automatically scheduled.

Caseload reporting

The console has a live report that allows managers access at any time to the current caseload of each CHW. This assists in the planning of staffing needs, as the system is able to send alerts when a CHW's caseload approaches its maximum threshold. The caseload report is able to differentiate between active and inactive cases for each CHW, allowing the report to give an accurate picture of each CHW's workload. When a

participating family has temporarily left the area or declines to receive visits for any period of time, their status in the system can be changed from active to inactive. The caseload reports details only of those families who are actively being visited by the CHW. Detailed information about the nature of each caseload is also summarised in the report. It is also possible to view the caseload filtered by any type of risk factor of interest, which is helpful in determining workloads when families or mothers meeting certain criteria qualify for extra intervention visits. The system also provides the data to aid the face-to-face supervision that takes place about particular cases and problem areas.

Future possibilities

In developing the two mobile systems, we have been conceptualising the future possibilities and applications that

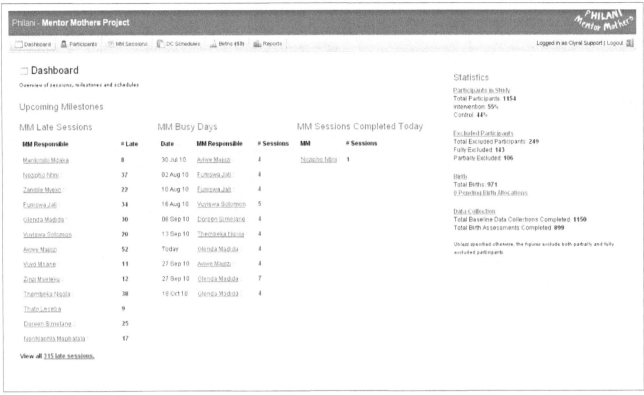

Source: Mobenzi Researcher n.d., *Philani Mentor Mothers Project*, viewed from http://www.mobenzi.com/researcher/Case-Studies/View/Philani-Mentor-Mothers-Project; Mobenzi Researcher n.d., *Good Start III (Saving Newborn Lives)*, viewed from http://www.mobenzi.com/researcher/Case-Studies/View/Good-Start-III-(Saving-Newborn-Lives)

FIGURE 5: The visit report.

might further aid information-gathering and management. Whilst we are not as yet utilising these applications, the technology is available to implement the following possibilities:

- We are presently developing a set of screening questions and pictures that can be used by CHWs to screen women for common mental and physical illnesses. Once again, it will take advantage of the ability of mobile technology to send information to a central database and receive specific information back in real time.

- We are in the process of refining the system to ensure that upon SMSing the unique household number, the database sends back a few of the key questions or points to be made for that particular visit, rather than general questions applicable to sessions, as is currently the case. This function will also allow the database to send back more specific individually tailored questions or advice. This will be achieved by developing algorithms that can be reliably applied in the field by persons with limited training. Currently we use the information gathered from the mobile system to fulfill this function during face-to-face supervision, rather than the tailored advice happening automatically via the mobile information system.

- Over time, we will refine this system so that the database sends back more specific individually tailored questions or advice. This will be achieved by developing algorithms that will analyse previously entered basic medical history (previous pregnancies, previous test results, etc.) to generate key messages. For instance, a mother who had a previous history of anaemia will be reminded of the importance taking iron supplements or getting her Hb (haemoglobin) checked again.

- In many countries, most births occur at home and the rapid and timely recognition of early neonatal illness is vital. We are planning (in the Philani study) to use mobile phones with an integrated camera for CHWs to take a photograph of the neonate if they are concerned about an infection or illness. This image can then be transferred in real time and assessed by a trained professional followed by an SMS sent back to the CHW to ensure that the appropriate action is taken or a referral is made.

- We have not been showing videos on the mobile phones, but we realise this feature is easily available to us in the future for two purposes: first, demonstration videos to support CHW message delivery or implementation of more complex intervention activities; and, second videos that CHWs show to mothers and families to supplement their verbal communication and paper-based materials.

- Mobile phones offer the promise of linking data from clinics or hospitals to CHWs. Current studies of loss to follow-up along the 'PMTCT cascade' are not based on linked data, only serial cross sections (Reithinger *et al.* 2007). Yet, as investments are made in health infrastructure, the types of information that need to be linked in integrated systems for health data are similar cross-nationally and regionally, including: tracking individuals or households' health visits over time, and anticipated, developmentally-linked or condition-linked milestones or check-lists. The functions in such a system are also similar, including: probing, monitoring, training, supporting and educating. These linking activities and functions require the same programed applications across many domains of health applications.

Ethical considerations

The type of data that is available on mobile phones is increasing steadily. Phones also allow data to be collected with a potentially lower respondent burden compared to previously developed platforms. CHWs utilising mobile phones to improve the quality of their work performance can be supported and monitored in ways not previously possible. The potential intrusiveness of this technology for both the CHW and the mother or family being supported and monitored is unlikely to be appreciated by either the CHW or the family. It is critical that we develop standards and strategies for protecting this information with multiple levels of access specified and with the potential opportunities and risks outlined to those from whom the data is being collected. An international set of standards for the protection of privacy and for confidentiality with these types of platforms is urgently needed. In addition, despite the high level of mobile penetration in Africa, many people consider themselves technologically challenged. In our experience with this mobile information system, training some CHWs on the system was easy whilst with others it was more challenging. However, these difficulties were resolved within a two-week period. Central to this was ensuring particularly tight monitoring during the early phase of implementation to ensure that difficulties were picked up and attended to early.

Limitations

Technology will not completely solve the human resource crises confronting healthcare systems globally, nor will it resolve all the complex issues involved in scaling up large scale interventions. It will also not replace the need for the 'human face' of support as well as supervision. There is a danger that this 'human face' might be forgotten given the ubiquity of mobile technology. In addition, many of the reasons for inadequate supervision at scale relate to problems such as poor motivation caused by low salaries, limited professional and career development for supervisors and lack of incentives (Rowe *et al.* 2010). There are problems that cannot be solved by technology or a mobile information and management system. These require another set of human resource skills and interventions as well as a shift in the professionalisation of community health work and supervision. In addition, many countries have policies that support the use of health care institutions rather than CHWs and the system that we have developed would have limited value in these contexts. Qualitative work exploring the interface between the 'human factors' and the new technologies being developed is vital. The field is currently expanding rapidly, and this fast iterative approach should not be lost, but a certain amount of caution is warranted. We need to ensure that time and money are not wasted on ineffective programs in the belief that 'technology' will solve all problems.

Conclusion

This article summarises our experience in two South African RCT's with a mobile information system for supervising a CHW-delivered, home-visit-based community health intervention for pregnant and postnatal women. Mobile phones offer unprecedented opportunities to improve the quality of care provided by CHWs. These devices could be used to dramatically speed up the process and ability of all countries and healthcare systems to meet their healthcare delivery goals. Yet, their potential has yet to be realised. Mobile technology has been widely used by private enterprises, which have made dramatic, rapid, and significant improvements and penetrated entire populations with exceptional speed. Health care, especially health interventions for LAMICs, has not had the technological expertise, the financial commitment, or the political will to implement these strategies broadly. The examples reported in this article represent the first steps in a process of continuous quality improvement, which must begin to keep pace with the possibilities offered by mobile technologies. The web-based mobile information system that we describe in this article has been developed on an open-source platform with no proprietary conditions attached. In addition, the Java's core code is available under open-source distribution terms. It is therefore available to researchers, government health planners or non-governmental and community based organisations to assist in improved management to aid scale up health interventions. The field and general approach is novel and there is a general lack of published literature describing mHealth system experiences with CHWs, particularly in the context of scaling up programs. This article provides evidence that such systems are feasible in aiding to train, sustain, and scale-up CHW programs with a high degree of fidelity and relatively limited in-person supervisory support (i.e. weekly meetings instead of supervisors accompanying CHW teams in the field).

Acknowledgements

The studies mentioned in this paper were funded by National Institute of Alcoholism and Alcohol Abuse (NIAAA) and Saving Newborn Lives. We acknowledge the support of the National Research Foundation (South Africa). Alexander Tsai acknowledges salary support from the Robert Wood Johnson Health and Society Scholars Program.

Competing interest

The authors declare that they have no financial or personal relationship(s) which may have inappropriately influenced them in writing this paper.

Authors' contributions

M.T. (Stellenbosch University), M.R.B. (University of California Los Angeles), I.L.R. (Philani Nutrition and Development Project), T.D. (Medical Research Council), D.J. (University of Western Cape) and M.C. (UNICEF) were the project leaders in both projects. M.T. (Stellenbosch

University), M.R.B. (University of California Los Angeles), I.L.R. (Philani Nutrition and Development Project), J.S. (Stellenbosch University), T.D. (Medical Research Council), D.J. (University of Western Cape), M.C. (UNICEF), P.I. (Medical Research Council), A.F. (Clyral), MColvin (Maromi Health Research) made conceptual contributions to the development of the system. M.T. wrote the first draft of the paper. M.T. (Stellenbosch University), M.R.B. (University of California Los Angeles), I.L.R. (Philani Nutrition and Development Project), D.S. (University of California Los Angeles), A.T. (Massachusetts General Hospital), J.S. (Stellenbosch University), T.D. (Medical Research Council), D.J. (University of Western Cape), M.C. (UNICEF), P.I. (Medical Research Council), A.F. (Clyral), M.C. (Maromi Health Research) contributed to writing the paper and approved the final version of the paper.

References

Bang, A., Reddy, H., Deshmukh, M., Baitule S. & Bang, R., 2005, 'Neonatal and infant mortality in the ten years (1993–2003) of the Gadchiroli field trial: Effect of home based neonatal care', *Journal of Perinatology* 25, 92–107. http://dx.doi.org/10.1038/sj.jp.7211268

Baqui, A.H., El-Arifeen, S., Darmstadt, G. L., Ahmed, S., Williams, E.K., Seraji, H.R., 2008, 'Effect of community-based newborn-care intervention package implemented through two service-delivery strategies in Sylhet district, Bangladesh: A cluster-randomised controlled trial', *Lancet* 371, 1936–1944. http://dx.doi.org/10.1016/S0140-6736(08)60835-1

Bradshaw D., Chopra M., Kerber K, Lawn J.E., Bamford L., Moodley, J. *et al.*, 2008, 'Every death counts: Use of mortality audit data for decision making to save the lives of mothers, babies, and children in South Africa', *Lancet* 371, 1294–1304. http://dx.doi.org/10.1016/S0140-6736(08)60564-4

Bosch-Capblanch, X. & Garner, P., 2008, 'Primary health care supervision in developing countries', *Tropical Medicine International Health* 13, 369–383. http://dx.doi.org/10.1111/j.1365-3156.2008.02012.x

Day, C., Gray, A. & Budgell, E. (eds.), 2011, 'South African Health Review', Health Systems Trust, Cape Town.

Gray, H. & Ciroma, J., 1988, 'Reducing attricion among village health workers in rural Nigeria', *Socio-economic Planning Sciences* 22, 39–43. http://dx.doi.org/10.1016/0038-0121(88)90033-X

Haines, A., Sanders, D., Lehmann, U., Rowe, A., Lawn, J., Jan, S. *et al.*, 2007, 'Achieving child survival goals: potential contribution of community health workers', *The Lancet* 369, 2121–2131. http://dx.doi.org/10.1016/S0140-6736(07)60325-0

Huicho, L., Dávila, M., Campos, M., Drasbek, C., Bryce, J. & Victora, C., 2005, 'Scaling up Integrated Management of Childhood Illness to the national level: Achievements and challenges in Peru', *Health Policy and Planning* 20, 14–24. http://dx.doi.org/10.1093/heapol/czi002, PMid:15689426

Kelly, J.M., Osama, B., Garg, R., Hamel, M., Lewis, J., Rowe, S. *et al.*, 2001, 'Community Health Worker Performance in the Management of Multiple Childhood Illnesses: Siaya District, Kenya, 1997–2001', *American Journal of Public Health* 91, 1617–1624. http://dx.doi.org/10.2105/AJPH.91.10.1617, PMid:11574324

Leon, N. & Schneider, H., 2011, 'A review of the role of mobile technology for monitoring and evaluation of community based health services (mHealth4CBS) (Draft report)', University of the Western Cape, Bellville.

Le Roux I.M., Tomlinson M., Harwood J.M., O'Connor M.J., Worthman C.M., Mbewu, N. *et al.*, 2013, 'Outcomes of home visits for pregnant township mothers and their infants in South Africa: A cluster randomised controlled trial', AIDS. http://dx.doi.org/10.1097/QAD.0b013e3283601b53

Liu L., Johnson H.L., Cousens S., Perin J., Scott S., Lawn, J.E. *et al.*, 2012, 'Global, regional, and national causes of child mortality: An updated systematic analysis for 2010 with time trends since 2000', *Lancet* 379, 2151–2161. http://dx.doi.org/10.1016/S0140-6736(12)60560-1

Manandhar, D., Osrin, D., Shrestha, B., Mesko, N., Morrison, J., Tumbahangphe, K.M. *et al.*, 2004, 'Effect of a participatory intervention with women's groups on birth outcomes in Nepal: Cluster-randomised controlled trial', *The Lancet* 364, 970–979. http://dx.doi.org/10.1016/S0140-6736(04)17021-9

Mobenzi Researcher n.d., *Good Start III* (*Saving Newborn Lives*), viewed from http://www.mobenzi.com/researcher/Case-Studies/View/Good-Start-III-(Saving-Newborn-Lives)

Mobenzi Researcher n.d., *Philani Mentor Mothers Project*, viewed from http://www.mobenzi.com/researcher/Case-Studies/View/Philani-Mentor-Mothers-Project

National Department of Health (NDOH), 2011, 'Primary Health Care re-engineering document', Government of South Africa, Pretoria.

Nleya, N. & Thompson, L. 2009, 'Survey Methodology in Violence-prone Khayelitsha, Cape Town, South Africa', *IDS Bulletin* 40, 50–57. http://dx.doi.org/10.1111/j.1759-5436.2009.00038.x

Paim, J., Travassos, C., Almeida, C., Bahia, L. & Macinko, J., 2011, 'The Brazilian health system: history, advances, and challenges', *Lancet* 377, 1778–1797. http://dx.doi.org/10.1016/S0140-6736(11)60054-8

Rahman, A., Malik, A., Sikander, S., Roberts, C. & Creed, F., 2008, 'Cognitive behaviour therapy-based intervention by community health workers for mothers with depression and their infants in rural Pakistan: A cluster-randomised controlled trial', *Lancet* 372, 902–909. http://dx.doi.org/10.1016/S0140-6736(08)61400-2

Reithinger, R., Megazzini, K., Durako, S.J., Harris, D.R. & Vermund, S.H., 2007, 'Monitoring and evaluation of programmes to prevent mother to child transmission of HIV in Africa', *BMJ* 334, 1143–1146. http://dx.doi.org/10.1136/bmj.39211.527488.94, PMid:17540943

Rowe, A.K., De Savigny, D., Lanata, C.F. & Victora, C.G., 2005, 'How can we achieve and maintain high-quality performance of health workers in low-resource settings?', *The Lancet* 366, 1026–1035. http://dx.doi.org/10.1016/S0140-6736(05)67028-6

Rowe, A.K., Onikpo, F., Lama, M. & Deming, M.S., 2010, 'The rise and fall of supervision in a project designed to strengthen supervision of Integrated Management of Childhood Illness in Benin', *Health Policy Plan* 25, 125–134. http://dx.doi.org/10.1093/heapol/czp054, PMid:19923206

South African National Department of Health (SANDOH), 2010, 'National Antenatal Sentinel HIV and Syphilis Prevalence Survey in South Africa, 2009', Pretoria.

Sazawal, S. & Black, R., 2003, 'Effect of pneumonia case management on mortality in neonates, infants and preschool children: A meta-analysis of community based trials', *The Lancet Infectious Diseases* 3, 547–556. http://dx.doi.org/10.1016/S1473-3099(03)00737-0

Tomlinson, M., Solomon, W., Singh, Y., Doherty, T., Chopra, M., Ijumba, P. *et al.*, 2009, 'The use of mobile phones as a data collection tool: A report from a household survey in South Africa', *BMC Medical Informatics Decisicion Making 9*, 51. http://dx.doi.org/10.1186/1472-6947-9-51, PMid:20030813

Walley, J., Lawn, J.E., Tinker, A., De Francisco, A., Chopra, M., Rudan, I. *et al.*, 2008, 'Primary health care: making Alma-Ata a reality', *Lancet* 372, 1001–1007. http://dx.doi.org/10.1016/S0140-6736(08)61409-9

Walt, G., Perera, M. & Heggenhougen, K., 1989, 'Are large scale volunteer community health worker programs feasible? The case of Sri Lanka', *Social Science and Medicine* 29, 599–608. http://dx.doi.org/10.1016/0277-9536(89)90179-2

Zurovac, D., Sudoi, R.K., Akhwale, W.S., Ndiritu, M., Hamer, D.H., Rowe, A.K. *et al.*, 2011, 'The effect of mobile phone text-message reminders on Kenyan health workers' adherence to malaria treatment guidelines: A cluster randomised trial', *Lancet* 378, 795–803. http://dx.doi.org/10.1016/S0140-6736(11)60783-6

9

Factors influencing e-collaboration for knowledge development and innovation

Authors:
Tendani J. Lavhengwa[1]
Jacobus S. van der Walt[1]
Eve M. Lavhengwa[2]

Affiliations:
[1]Department of Informatics, Tshwane University of Technology, South Africa

[2]Audit Services, Department of Minerals Resources, South Africa

Correspondence to:
Tendani Lavhengwa

Email:
usapfa@gmail.com

Postal address:
PO BOX 11271, Vorna Valley, 1686, South Africa

Background: Knowledge development and innovation are at the heart of the progress of academic and research institutions (ARIs) through individual and coordinated research projects. Collaboration initiatives remain a challenge for many researchers for a myriad of reasons which are further intensified by the many technology options that are available both freely and at varying prices. Although multiple theories were considered, the focus on electronic communication supported by the interest in how innovation is diffused and the richness of media motivated the focus on *diffusion of innovations* (DOI) and media richness theory (MRT).

Objectives: The objective was to develop a multi-dimensional matrix of e-collaboration factors for research institutions. This study investigated collaboration by ARIs while focusing on the supporting and enabling technologies.

Method: The grounded theory method (GTM) was adopted. E-collaboration literature was reviewed followed by data collection using observations, interviews and a blog. DOI and MRT were considered as theories that assist in the implementation of collaboration. A blog was developed as an e-collaboration platform to examine the emergent ideas and to collect data. Data was analysed through the coding method which led to the development of the multi-dimensional e-collaboration factors matrix.

Results: The findings reveal that e-collaboration has multiple factors that must be considered. Collaboration by participants was improved through knowledge development and innovation.

Conclusion: The multi-dimensional matrix of e-collaboration factors presented collaborators with a checklist that will enhance and improve their work. ARIs continue to collaborate at multiple levels depending on their needs and objectives.

Introduction

Collaboration, the development of knowledge and the improvement thereof for the sake of innovation are important for the research community. Because knowledge development is at the centre of research, academic and research institutions (ARIs) need to remain up to date with the changing electronic environment and requirements. Collaboration can entail one individual or one business, or it could entail multiple academics, institutions, nations or multinationals.

Soliman, Brown and Simoff (2005:372) assert that having a clearer understanding of what collaboration entails can help in with decision-making regarding future technology. The understanding of Soliman *et al.* (2005) of collaboration needs to be examined and relevant technologies must be identified for present and future use. This understanding will be improved by introducing a multi-dimensional matrix of e-collaboration factors.

Bettoni *et al.* (2011) observed that participative work is assumed to form part of academic activities. At times, this desire and need to work together is not natural; effort must be made and initiatives must be taken to make it possible. Anyangwe (2012) explain that higher-education institutions and further-education colleges must be prepared to share expertise. This statement is important since it joins ARIs to collaboration. When investigating the value of knowledge workers, Steyn and du Toit (2009:12) asserted that they were encouraged by participants' willingness to share their private knowledge stock and the willingness to using conversations as an approach to obtain the required knowledge. The motivation to focus on the use of electronic communication and blogs came from an investigation conducted by De Jager, Buitendag and Van der Walt (2012). De Jager *et al.*'s (2012) investigation was supported by the importance of discovering innovative collaborative knowledge. The need to share is thereby essential for various ARIs. There is also an inherent need to investigate supporting technology and derive improved levels of understanding.

De Jager *et al.* (2012) state that collaborative knowledge activities are necessary to generate vast quantities of knowledge within multiple domains. E-collaboration is considered as a contributor to knowledge development and innovation where similar challenges exist. This is more prevalent amongst ARIs where one of their core objectives is to conduct research. Understanding the factors that enable e-collaboration can assist in this challenge. The proposed matrix will also bridge the gap on the effective use of e-collaboration.

This article starts by discussing the literature related to driving forces, technology, e-collaboration concepts, knowledge development and ARIs. This is followed by examining the diffusion of innovation (DOI), media richness theory (MRT) and grounded theory method (GTM) as a grounding lens for analysis and discussion. The methodology adopted is GTM. The final outcome is to develop a multi-dimensional matrix of e-collaboration factors for research institutions.

The importance of driving forces and factors

Forces and factors are used interchangeably in this article. Driving forces or forces working towards achieving an objective are important. The focus is on driving forces for e-collaboration. The work of a number of authors work was reviewed to establish the driving forces as explained in the section below.

Caldwell (2009) listed five commonly used driving forces as follows: science and technology, economics, demographics, political and social. In support of driving forces, Bechina and Ndlela (2009) listed six factors that contribute to the effectiveness of knowledge management systems (KMS). These are leadership, training, clear business strategy, aligning business goal with technology, collaboration and adaptive culture.

Thomas (2013) asserts that collaboration works best for problems that have the following three characteristics measured as forces: There is no obvious solution, the problems lack structure, and the problems require collective volition.

These characteristics are significant since they also act as driving forces for individuals or groups to collaborate. It is also notable that the driving forces provide areas for further analysis.

Collaboration is, furthermore, listed as a driving force for KMS. The Canadian Health Services Research Foundation

(CHSRF) (2003a:1) explains that knowledge brokering is a process of bringing people together and building relationships to make knowledge transfer more effective.

This linking of people can feature researchers, decision makers, practitioners and policy makers. The ability to bring people together and facilitate their interaction is listed as one of the basic skills required by a knowledge broker (CHSRF 2003a:1). The CHSRF (2003b:6) further asserts that there can be no standard definition of knowledge brokering since the job differs from context to context and is seen as an unfolding journey. The need to manage knowledge is central to improving the collaboration, hence the introduction of knowledge brokers who bring together knowledge participants. Technology is another primary driving force which connects collaborators from widely differing geographical areas and which presents multiple opportunities to collaborate.

Technology in the world today

Tools and technology have become central in facilitating interaction and communication. Tools and technology are used as interchangeable concepts. The days of seeing technology as a 'nice to have' have long passed. We need to acknowledge that technology has become pervasive. It is therefore essential for organisations and ARIs to be able to evaluate technology. Table 1 below shows a list of technological tools that can be used for collaboration, grouped by authors.

It is notable from Table 1 below that there is technology that is commonly used for collaboration. Knowing these can make it easier to work together with other participants to improve collaboration on projects.

In a detailed review, Sahin (2006) confirms the relationship between computer knowledge and the adoption of innovation. This relationship is why it is important to select the best technology for collaboration. It is also noted that the present level of computer knowledge as well as elements for e-collaboration require further investigation.

E-collaboration and key elements

Today's communication features e-collaboration as an integral component since work is mostly shared over electronic media, more specifically the Internet. With this in mind, it is important to develop an understanding of the origin and key elements of e-collaboration. Kock (2005) describe e-collaboration as the interaction of individuals

TABLE 1: Technology used for collaboration.

Author(s) name	List of technological tools
Blau (2011)	Online discussion groups, integrated calendaring and collaborative authoring tools.
Gartner (2010)	Wikis, blogs, instant messaging, collaborative office and crowdsourcing.
Hudson (2011:3)	Group-decision support systems, audio-conferencing and Internet-based web conferencing.
Vignarajah (2010)	E-mail, blog, micro-blogging, MySpace, Facebook, Twitter, LinkedIn, Podcast, Wiki, YouTube, text-messaging, web conferencing, iPhone and iPad.
Hill (2005)	Blogs, chat, email, list serve, message boards, online conferencing and threaded discussion.
Crow (2002)	E-mail exchange, drawing viewing sites (intranet and web-based), workflow and groupware software, teleconferencing and videoconferencing, web-hosted meetings and computer-aided design (CAD).

engaged in a common task using electronic technology. Hudson (2011:3) presents a definition that encapsulates the objectives by denoting that collaboration occurs at any time where there are two or more people sharing complex information and knowledge building over the Internet.

Twinomurinzi (2007) explains that e-collaboration is the exchange of information, with the stakeholders playing a role in the outcome of the collaborative process. A more recent definition by Bettoni *et al.* (2011) described e-collaboration as a web-based group process of working, learning and sharing knowledge over distance in space and time.

Mindbuilt Technologies (2012) lists nine benefits of e-collaboration: increased efficiency, reduction in complexity, enhanced organisational intelligence, the development of stronger relationships, a reduction in travel costs, a reduction in long-distance phone calls, ease of installation and management, low overheads and a boost in employee morale.

The definitions and benefits listed above guided this article toward the proposed multi-dimensional matrix of e-collaboration factors.

Knowledge development related to innovation

E-collaboration is viewed as an improved mode of communication while using technology which varies from one interaction to another. Knowledge development and innovation can subsequently be listed as one of the outcomes of collaboration. The concepts contained in the preceding statement are discussed further in this section.

According to Rogers (2003), knowledge is the first step in the innovation-decision process. The other steps are persuasion, decision, implementation and confirmation. This endorses the relationship between knowledge and innovation. It also supports the idea that knowledge must precede innovation or be part thereof. Rogers (2003) further discusses the knowledge stage of the innovation-decision process which features three types of knowledge, namely awareness, how-to and principles. It is important to note that the 'how-to' knowledge can be associated with the selection of technology for use in an e-collaboration initiative.

Rogers (2003:12) describe innovation as an idea, practice or project that is perceived as new by an individual or other unit of adoption. This perception can be shared by one or many people and by one or many organisations or institutions. The definition of innovation is extensive and can also include products and processes for future implementation. From the above discussion, it follows that knowledge development and innovation can be linked to the improvement of e-collaboration. E-collaboration technology therefore assists in the development of knowledge and innovation. Because the focus is on ARIs, it is imperative to discuss their connection to collaboration.

Academic and research institutions as a platform for collaboration

The Academy of Science of South Africa (ASSAf) (2010) classified universities into three categories: university, comprehensive university and university of technology. Statutory research bodies and institutions that fund research are also included since they are involved in research and funding. A number of collaboration initiatives were noted between universities and other research institutions and amongst universities themselves:

1. A memorandum of understanding was signed between UNISA and Mogale City (UNISA web 2013).
2. Planning, Research and Management issues relating to Mogale City Parks Service/Business excellence which may include operational and scientific management of resources, internal and external customer needs/satisfaction, management of biodiversity areas. (n.p.)
3. Mintek collaborates with the faculty of science at UJ (UJ web 2013): 'Collaboration between Mintek which is an organisation that works with the government on mineral technologies'. This collaboration connected a university, government and Mintek.
4. TUT web (2013) states that there is collaboration between the university and the French South African Institute of Technology (F'SATI), supported by the statement: '... a national asset that contributes to the creation of knowledge and prosperity as well as the transfer of technology in the Southern African region'. UCT web (2013) describes the following: '... is an important step towards building drug discovery and development capabilities in Africa – and educating the next generation of drug-discovery scientists in Africa'.

The above sections were intended to illustrate and motivate the focus on ARIs and their collaborative relationships. The foundational theories for this study are discussed as a lens for analysis and further investigation.

Exploring theories related to e-collaboration

Theory is a good foundation for discussions on knowledge development and innovation. Theories are important in academia since they present underpinning arguments and researched views for further development. The section to follow discusses DOI, MRT and GTM.

Diffusion of innovation (DOI)

With e-collaboration being a form of innovation, we are discussing DOI elements related to the work by Rogers (2003). Rogers (2003:4) emphasises that DOI is a social process that is simultaneously a technical matter. One needs to understand the social surroundings and context in order to achieve a successful diffusion of innovation. Rogers (2003:5) further asserts that, in order to launch a self-gathering diffusion process, one must work with the correct participants from the start. This highlights the impact of that perceptions concerning DOI can have and how it needs to be managed. In order to improve and understand knowledge development for the sake of innovation, one needs to identify and influence the correct participants with whom to start. Rogers (2003:5) regarded diffusion as both the planned and spontaneous spread of new ideas and later listed the four elements of DOI. Table 2 lists these elements together with practical translations related to this investigation.

Media richness theory (MRT)

Daft and Lengel (1984) argued that MRT originates from information processing, developed by organisational scientists. Communication between people is affected by the fitness of the media and the characteristics of the communication task. Daft and Lengel (1984) further specified that MRT advances the notion that the richness or leanness of communication is an objective property of the communication media. These authors conclude by defining MRT as the ability to facilitate shared understanding within a time interval.

Miles (2014) asserts that people who use a communication channel most fit for their task will be more effective than people who use a communication channel that does not fit. This supports the importance of selecting the best-suited channel of communication for a collaboration experience.

Regarding media richness, Daft, Lengel and Trevino (1987) provided four criteria:

1. Capacity for immediate feedback: The medium facilitates quick convergence on a common interpretation.
2. Capacity to transmit multiple cues: An array of cues, including physical presence, voice inflections, body gestures, words, numbers and graphic symbols, facilitate interpretation and meaning rather than simply the transfer of information or data.
3. Language variety: Numbers and formulas provide greater precision, but natural language conveys a broader set of concepts.
4. Capacity of the medium to have a personal focus: This refers to either the conveyance of emotions and feelings or the ability of the medium tailored to the specific needs and perspectives of the receiver.

The criteria above were useful for determining the levels of media richness and also contribute towards measuring e-collaboration. Kock (2012) investigated media-richness and noted that it presents a partial confirmation that group members perceive e-collaboration as a relatively unnatural medium. The findings show that there is a perceived increase in the quality of outcomes in a group if the quality of member contribution increases. There is a higher departmental heterogeneity enabled by the low disruptiveness inherent in the e-collaboration medium used that is applicable to an asynchronous communication medium. The above theoretical work by Kock (2012) supports the argument that media richness makes a significant contribution to the improvement of communication.

In support of MRT, Dennis and Valacich (1999:5) describe media synchronicity as the extent to which individuals work together on the same activity at the same time. Multiple dimensions are presented: media characteristics, task, functions and communication processes.

Grounded theory method (GTM)

According to an early definition by Glaser and Strauss (1967), GTM refers to the discovery of theory from data systematically obtained and analysed in social research. Trochim (2000) further suggests that the research starts with generative questions since it is a complex iterative process. Strauss and Corbin (1990) described GTM as an approach where the data collection, analysis and theory stand in a reciprocal relationship with each other.

Research methodology and design

GTM was the approach selected for this study as described in the section on theory. The authors noted that the findings in each stage influence subsequent stages. The methodology adopted is as follows:

1. Literature and theoretical reviews were conducted on the key topics and subjects.
2. The notes from the primary data collected in the main study were reviewed. The data were collected through observations and interviews with information-rich participants, guided by the ideas below:

   - Purposive sampling was selected as suitable as described by Welman, Kruger and Mitchell (2010:63) as an approach which allows researchers to rely on their experience, ingenuity and/or previous research findings.
   - Patton (1990) asserts that information-rich cases are those from which one can learn a great deal about issues of central importance to the purpose of the research. From this term, purposeful sampling is introduced.
   - The observations were conducted by the researcher who was physically present at the selected ARIs.

TABLE 2: Diffusion of innovation elements and practical translations.

Element name	Description by Rogers (2003)	Practical translations related to this investigation
Innovation	'An idea, practice or project that is perceived as new by an individual or other unit of adoption'.	Working together while making use of technology such as e-collaboration.
Communication channels	'A process in which participants create and share information with one another in order to reach a mutual understanding'.	The different technological tools in place for collaboration to take place.
Time	'The impact and dimension of time on the diffusion'.	Time needs must be considered closely when addressing the diffusion of knowledge and innovation.
Social system	'A set of interrelated units engaged in joint problem solving to accomplish a common goal'.	These are the academic and research institutions involved in research. This social system can also feature independent researchers.

3. A blog was developed, based on the preceding phases and on those elements identified as significant and requiring further investigation.
4. An analysis of findings from multiple sources was done, using open coding described by McCallin, Nathanial and Scott (2011) as an activity that can take place while data are being collected.
5. A multi-dimensional matrix for e-collaboration factors was developed.
6. Discussions on the matrix factors and other related phenomenon began.

The methodology also used a blog for data collection and for further exploring the ideas. Lavhengwa and Van der Walt (2011) motivated the use of websites by asserting their value in being a platform for e-collaboration. One of the fundamentals identified is that Lavhengwa and Van der Walt (2011) argue that websites must be dynamic or interactive to improve research. Nardi, Schiano, Gumbrecht and Swartz (2004) asserts that blogs are a promising tool for knowledge management. Hill (2005) further supports blogs as a tool that enables collaborative learning over the Internet. Blogs were therefore selected for their collaborative qualities and their ability to work towards knowledge management and innovation. A blog was developed. Data was collected over a period of two years, and multiple findings emerged in support of and a focus on knowledge development and innovation. Below is a list of selected posts as questions that were used on the blog:

1. Mobile platforms and collaboration: How easy are these to identify, and how dominant are they as contributors towards e-collaboration?
2. What are the tools and technology for e-collaboration?
3. What drives and influences e-collaboration?

Table 3 shows the categories of participants for the research.

The non-blog data were collected through observation, e-mail, telephone and personal interviews conducted by the researcher. Observations allowed the data collection to take place while other researchers and academics were participating in academic activities. The significant level of interest can be noted from Table 3 by focusing on the numbers and the quality of the contributions which will be detailed in the findings section.

Findings and discussion

This section addresses the findings, followed by a discussion of each of the findings.

TABLE 3: Categories of respondents.

Category name	Units
Non-blog participants: (observation, emails, telephones and personal interviews)	31
Blog participants – page views	837†
Blog participants – published comments	73†

†, denotes that this is an on-going data collection and the number may have increased since they were last retrieved.

Empirical findings

The discussions that follow are related to the data collected from the participants as indicated in Table 3:

- Findings from non-blog participants: These were findings collected from 31 participants using multiple data-collection methods:
  - Mutual interest was found to be a motivator for collaboration.
  - Collaboration for learner support was listed as important for ARIs.
  - Collaboration agreements were noted as essential between the participants.
  - Geographical distances had previously limited and hindered opportunities for collaboration. This challenge has been addressed with the introduction of e-collaboration.
  - Technology bridged the physical and logical gap between collaborators through the introduction of virtual environments.
  - The knowledge economy is driven by electronic communication, thereby motivating an improvement in e-collaboration.
  - The following collaboration technology was identified as prevalent: blogs, collaborative authoring tools, e-mail, telephone, fax and the Internet.
  - Findings from the blog: These findings represent a list of the data collected from the e-collaboration blog:
  - Auditors share knowledge at conferences, both physically and online.
  - A number of auditors make use of templates from their companies for conducting audits. These can be in a word, excel or web-based solution with access control.
  - Internal auditors collaborate through audit tools such as TeaMate. This tool enables them to work together towards a common outcome. Reports are later generated from the multiple contributions made by the audit team.
  - Internal and external auditors collaborate at the start of an audit project. They later work together towards the end when they have to generate and distribute reports. This collaboration is done primarily through email. The review notes or comments or responses are shared amongst the auditors.
  - Audit findings are shared since they are the main deliverables or output for auditors.
  - Technology such as blogs is examples of e-collaboration.
  - Discussions are quite helpful, and we need to invite more people involved in e-learning, e-collaboration and related research projects.
  - Self-service kiosks are also used for e-collaboration.
  - Social media and mobile devices make it easy to e-collaborate.
  - E-collaboration facilitates the collaboration of researchers from disadvantaged parts of the world with affluent peers from well-resourced universities.
  - Eagerness to use technology: This means that the introduction of new technology determines the possibility of advanced e-collaboration.

What follows is a list of key discussion points from the findings. The Internet and blogs can be useful as a technology for knowledge development. The introduction of e-collaboration discussions motivated and improved knowledge-development opportunities. Innovation was the next achievement when collaborators started to discuss new ideas on how to solve their challenges. Creating platforms for working together improves knowledge development.

There were indications that geographical distances are no longer a limiting factor for collaboration when technology is introduced.

In the next section, the outcome of the multi-dimensional matric for e-collaboration factors is introduced with all the key elements.

A multi-dimensional matrix for e-collaboration factors

A matrix is denoted as a grid which presents arrangements containing elements that require focus. In describing media synchronicity, Dennis and Valacich (1999:5) present multiple dimensions which motivated the key elements of the matrix of e-collaboration factors. These are presented in Table 4 and discussed thereafter.

Generic driving factors: There are generic driving forces that must be addressed. The relevant ones for this investigation are people, economics, financial, political, leadership and training. These are factors that affect general initiatives. The other dimensions of the matrix for e-collaboration factors can also be featured in this section, but they are in separate sections with comprehensive details.

Environmental and virtual: This refers to the environment or setting where the e-collaboration takes place.
This collaboration can take many forms, from physical to logical and virtual work spaces. E-collaboration must not be geographically limited to a specific area.

According to Chetty and Mearns (2012), virtual environments present effective knowledge-management platforms through communities of practice. These virtual environments assist when the participants are in geographically dispersed areas.

Knowledge development and innovation: Knowledge development can be defined by the identified objectives and projects that are in focus at a particular time. Collaborators must identify knowledge areas of interest.

The relevant knowledge brokers must be identified and approached to participate and assist in the development of the initiative. Improvement in people's work and new ideas on how to gain advantage over their competitors can be featured in this section. Innovation will result as reviews and reflections are made concerning the knowledge that is being developed.

Theoretical dimensions

The sections below focus on each of the theoretical dimensions.

Diffusion of innovation: An understanding must be developed on how collaboration and the related technology are being adopted. Relevant updates must follow and ensure that this process is on-going. The collaborator must consider the four elements of DOI listed by Rogers (2003:5), being innovation, communication channels, time and the social system. The diffusion of e-collaboration must not be assumed but planned, monitored and updated as changes immerge over time.

Media richness: The richness of media presents both benefits and challenges. Rich e-collaboration media is good as it can lead to an improvement in the clarity of the interaction and messages. However, e-collaboration is considered a relatively unnatural medium of communication (Kock 2012). This problem needs to be addressed, and the related concerns must be understood by the participants. Media richness must be considered very carefully and will differ from case to case. Communication must be adjusted to meet the needs of the specific collaboration initiative.

Grounded theory method: There must be a reciprocal approach in developing an e-collaboration experience. The process must start with generative questions, as suggested by Trochim (2000), without any prescriptive outcomes.

Tools and technology

Tools and technology have an important role to play in all electronic interactions. The selection of these must be done with the involvement of all relevant participants.

Figure 1 represents a diagrammatic view of the multi-dimensional e-collaboration factors matrix.

The abovementioned multi-dimensional matrix of e-collaboration factors does not prescribe an application sequence. Each individual project must set an order that is relevant for it. The users can decide what is of importance to them and start with that dimension.

TABLE 4: Matrix of e-collaboration factors.

Dimensions	Key elements identifies
Generic driving factors	Economics, finance, leadership, people, political and training.
Environmental and virtual	No geographical limitation and online access available anywhere.
Knowledge development and innovation	Identify knowledge areas of interest, identify relevant knowledge brokers and innovation must be initiated and improved.
Theoretical dimensions	Communication channels, time, social system, type and clarity of media in use for collaborating. An iterative process must be followed.
Tools and technology	Email, blogs, teleconferencing, Internet, social-media networks and online discussion groups.

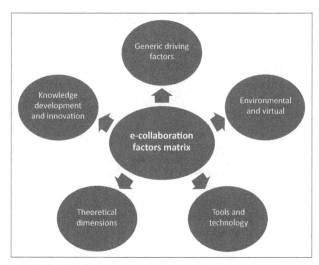

Source: Authors' own data.
FIGURE 1: Multi-dimensional matrix of e-collaboration factors.

The use and value of an e-collaboration matrix

This section initiates a discussion on the use of the matrix proposed. The primary purpose of the matrix is to assist in advancing a discussion on e-collaboration initiatives. The dimensions included are generic elements that would be adopted and addressed by collaborators. The matrix presents a high-level view of the focus of e-collaboration whilst focusing on research institutions. It is a guideline that can be applied, and it initiates a discussion for improved collaboration.

Conclusion and prospects

Work on e-collaboration was presented for knowledge development and innovation. The article concludes that there is more work that can be done towards understanding e-collaboration, knowledge development and innovation.

Whilst the article focuses on ARIs in order to identify the e-collaboration factors, other environments (business or government) can be investigated with varying results to update the e-collaboration matrix. The factors identified in the article are a starting point for further investigation. They are also generic enough as a useful guide to initiate other discussions and improvements. Further work can feature a number of ideas such as the following:

1. Consider other theories as a lens for further investigation
2. Knowledge brokering can be included as a dimension of the factors matrix with additional details also featured.
3. The matrix can be used in a team as a guide for improved knowledge development and innovation.
4. The intention of investigation is that collaboration teams must consider and address all the dimensions in the matrix.
5. The factors matrix can be extended by adding other dimensions specific to a geographical area or community for an improved level of specialised understanding.

The final conclusion is that collaboration should be reviewed and adapted as time progresses. The technology in use must also be revised with the changing needs whilst guided by the e-collaboration matrix.

Acknowledgements

Competing interests

The authors declare that they have no financial or personal relationship(s) which may have inappropriately influenced them in writing this article.

Authors' contributions

T.J.L. (Tshwane University of Technology) initiated the paper; allocated and co-ordinated all the roles for all authors; maintained and consolidated all contributions into the manuscript from start to finish. J.S.W. (Tshwane University of Technology) advised and supervised on all aspects of quality. E.L. (Department of Minerals Resources) contributed in the start-up discussions, assisted in language and logical advice to enhance the flow of the manuscript. E.L. also contributed in examining and grouping the empirical findings. The author further assessed the matrix developed.

References

Academy of Science of South Africa (ASSAF), 2010, 'The PhD study: An evidence-based study on how to meet the demands for high-level skills in an emerging economy', Academy of Science of South Africa, Pretoria, viewed 09 October 2010, from http://www.assaf.org.za/wp-content/uploads/2010/10/40696-Boldesign-PHD-small-optimised.pdf

Anyangwe, E., 2012, 'HE in FE: Top tips and resources to promote collaboration. Guardian Professional', viewed 29 February 2012, from http://www.guardian.co.uk/higher-education-network/blog/2012/feb/09/he-in-fe-colleges?INTCMP=ILCNETTXT3487

Bechina, A.A. & Ndlela, M.N., 2009, 'Success factors in implementing knowledge based systems', Electronic Journal of Knowledge Management 7(2), 211–218.

Bettoni, M., Bernhard, W., Eggs, C. & Schiller, G., 2011, 'Participative faculty devel opment with an online course in e-collaboration', 6th International Conference on e-Learning, Kelowna.

Blau, I., 2011, 'E-collaboration within, between, and without institutions: Towards better functioning of online groups through networks', International Journal of e-Collaboration, 7(4), 37–60. http://dx.doi.org/10.4018/jec.2011100102

Caldwell, R.L., 2009, 'A new framework for anticipating the future', viewed 30 June 2013, from http://cals.arizona.edu/~caldwell/docs/decision-framework-1-25-09.pdf

Canadian Health Services Research Foundation (CHSRF), 2003a, 'Preliminary report: The practice of knowledge brokering in Canada's health system', viewed 15 July 2013, from http://www.cfhi-fcass.ca/migrated/pdf/event_reports/brokers_final_e.pdf

Canadian Health Services Research Foundation (CHSRF), 2003b, 'CHSRF 2003 knowledge brokering workshop report', CHSRF knowledge brokering workshop, 02 October 2003, Montreal, viewed 15 July 2013, from http://www.chsrf.ca/migrated/pdf/event_reports/Montreal_Report_e.pdf

Chetty, L. & Mearns, M., 2012, 'Using communities of practice towards the next level of knowledge management maturity', SA Journal of Information Management 14(1), Art. #503, 9 pages. http://dx.doi.org/10.4102/sajim.v14i1.503

Crow, K., 2002, 'Collaboration: DRM associates', viewed 14 December 2012, from http://www.npd-solutions.com/collaboration.html

Daft, R.L. & Lengel, R.H., 1984, 'Information richness: A new approach to managerial behaviour and organization design', Research in Organizational Behavior 6, 191–233. http://dx.doi.org/10.2307/248682

Daft, R.L., Lengel, R.H. & Trevino, L.K., 1987, 'Message equivocality, media selection, and manager performance: Implications for information systems', Management Information Systems Quarterly 11, 355–368.

De Jager, L., Buitendag, A.A.K. & Van der Walt, J.S., 2012, 'Presenting a framework for knowledge management within a web-enabled living lab', SA Journal of Information Management 14(1), Art. #506, 13 pages. http://dx.doi.org/10.4102/sajim.v14i1.506

Dennis, A.R. & Valacich, J.S., 1999, 'Rethinking media richness: Towards a theory of media synchronicity', Proceedings of the 32nd Hawaii International Conference on System Sciences, 5–9 January, Hawaii.

Gartner, 2010, 'Gartner identifies the top 10 strategic technologies for 2011', Analysts examine latest industry trends during gartner symposium, ITxpo, Orlando, 17-21 October, viewed 09 May 2014, from http://www.gartner.com/it/page.jsp?id=1454221

Glaser, B.G. & Strauss, A.L., 1967, 'The discovery of grounded theory', Aldine Publications, New York.

Hill, C., 2005, 'Collaboration and e-learning', Interactive Technology in Education Conference 865, viewed 15 August 2014, from http://itec.sfsu.edu/wp/865wp/s05_865_hill_collaboration.pdf

Hudson, A., 2011, 'The eight essential ingredients of small group e-collaboration technology', viewed 01 May 2013, from http://www.grouputer.com/papers/8_essential_ingredients.pdf

Kock, N., 2005, 'What is e-collaboration', International Journal of E-collaboration 1(1), 1–7.

Kock, N., 2012, 'Unexpected outcomes of lean e-collaboration', viewed 25 February 2012, from www.cits.tamiu.edu/kockencycecollab/SampleManuscript2.doc

Lavhengwa, T.J. & Van der Walt, J.S., 2011, 'Websites: A platform for researchers and academic institutions to e-collaborate', Paper read at the 10th Annual Information & Knowledge Management Conference, 22–23 June 2011, Sandton, South Africa.

McCallin, A., Nathanial, A. & Scott, H., 2011, 'Grounded theory online supporting GT researchers: Getting started', viewed 29 September 2011, from http://www.groundedtheoryonline.com/getting-started.

Miles, J.A., 2014, 'Media richness theory: Management and organization theory', viewed 12 May 2014, from http://citeseerx.ist.psu.edu/viewdoc/download?doi=10.1.1.108.7118&rep=rep1&type=pdf

Mindbuilt Technologies, 2012, Why collaborate?, viewed 03 June 2012, from http://www.mindbuilt.com/ecs/reasons.php

Nardi, B., Schiano, D.J., Gumbrecht, M., Swartz, L. 2004, 'Why we blog', Communications of the Association for Computing Machinery 47(12), 41–46. http://dx.doi.org/10.1145/1035134.1035163

Patton, M., 1990, Qualitative evaluation and research methods, Sage, Beverly Hills.

Rogers, E.M., 2003, Diffusion of innovations, 5th edn., Free Press, New York.

Sahin, I., 2006, 'Detailed review of Rogers' diffusion of innovations theory and educational technology: Related studies based on Rogers' theory, The Turkish Online Journal of Educational Technology 5(2), 14–23.

Soliman, R., Braun, R. & Simoff, S., 2005, 'The essential ingredients of collaboration', Proceedings of the 2005 International Symposium on Collaborative technologies and Systems, p. 366, Saint Louis. http://dx.doi.org/10.1109/ISCST.2005.1553336

Steyn, P. & Du Toit, A., 2009, 'Maximising the value of knowledge workers', South African Journal of Information Management 11(1).

Strauss, A. & Corbin, J., 1990, Basics of qualitative research: Grounded theory procedures and techniques, Sage, London.

Thomas, R.J., 2013, 'The three essential ingredients of great collaborations', Harvard Business Review, viewed 12 May 2013, from http://blogs.hbr.org/cs/2011/06/the_three_essential_ingredient.html

Trochim, W., 2000, 'The research methods knowledge base', 2nd edn., Atomic Dog Publishing, Cincinnati.

Tshwane University of Technology (TUT web), 2013, 'TUT signs new agreement with French technology partner', viewed 30 June 2013, from http://www.tut.ac.za/News/Pages/TUTsignsnewagreementwithFrenchtechnologypartner.aspx

Twinomurinzi, H., 2007, 'E-collaboration for development innovations in rural communities: A South African experience', Proceedings of the 9th International Conference on Social Implications of Computers in Developing Countries, São Paulo, Brazil, 28–30 May.

University Of Cape Town (UCT web), 2013, 'Collaboration with pharmaceutical giant to foster drug development in Africa', UCT Monday Paper, 32(3), viewed 30 June 2013, from http://www.uct.ac.za/downloads/news.uct.ac.za/monpaper/mp32_03.pdf

University of Johannesburg (UJ web), 2013, 'Mintek – faculty of science collaboration', viewed 30 June 2013, from http://www.uj.ac.za/en/research/research information/strategic partnerships/national partnerships/pages/mintek-facultyofsciencecollaboration.aspx

University of South Africa (UNISA web), 2013, 'Collaborations', viewed 30 June 2013, from http://www.unisa.ac.za/Default.asp?Cmd=ViewContent&ContentID=19426

Vignarajah, A., 2010, 'Current trends in computer technology', Proceedings of the Global Business and Technology Association (GBATA), Twelfth Annual International Conference, pp. 911–915, Kruger National Park Vicinity, South Africa, 5-9 July.

Welman, J.C., Kruger, S.J. & Mitchell, B., 2010, Research methodology, 3rd edn., Oxford University Press, Cape Town.

10

Significant factors for enabling knowledge sharing between government agencies within South Africa

Authors:
Avain Mannie[1]
Herman J. van Niekerk[1,2]
Chris M. Adendorff[1]

Affiliations:
[1]Department of Business and Economics Science, Nelson Mandela Metropolitan University, Port Elizabeth, South Africa

[2]Suritec, Cape Town, South Africa

Correspondence to:
Avain Mannie

Email:
avain.mannie@gmail.com

Postal address:
1A Shirley Street, Newton Park, Port Elizabeth 6045, South Africa

Background: Globally, organisations have recognised the strategic importance of knowledge management (KM) and are increasingly focusing efforts on practices to foster the creation, sharing and integration of knowledge.

Objectives: This study aimed to validate the significant factors that influence the effectiveness of KM between government agencies in South Africa. The commonly identified pillars of KM in the extant literature served as a primary framework in establishing these factors.

Method: Data were gathered using an electronic survey made available to different national government agencies within the security cluster. Responses were analysed using structural equation modelling.

Main findings: Existing literature highlighted organisational culture, learning organisation, collaboration, subject matter experts and trust as being determinants for knowledge management. The first two were identified as the most significant factors for knowledge sharing to succeed.

Conclusion: Whilst there is universal consent as to the strategic importance of KM, actionable implementation of knowledge sharing initiatives appears to be lacking. This study emphasised the fact that leaders must instil a knowledge sharing culture either through employee performance contracts or methods such as the balanced score card. The study also showed that it is imperative for leaders to acknowledge that KM is a multi-faceted discipline that offers strategic advantages. Leaders of developing countries should note that they are on a developmental journey. This requires their organisations to be learning organisations, which necessitates a change in the organisational culture and knowledge interventions through their academies of learning.

Introduction

It is interesting to note that infamous United States of America gangster Al Capone (during the Prohibition period) was charged for tax evasion rather than the assumed illegal sale of alcohol. This point highlights the fact that a collective knowledge sharing effort between government agencies is key in finding alternate solutions for problem solving.

After further elaboration on the problem in this section, the commonly identified factors for knowledge sharing as per the global literature will be looked at. These factors are depicted in the theoretical model (see Figure 1), which is highlighted below. Thereafter, a brief discussion on the significant factors (independent variables) and dependant variable are elaborated upon. The research design and approach is then discussed, whilst the results and conclusion are finally conveyed.

The strategic importance of knowledge management (KM) has been widely acknowledged (Alavi and Leidner 1999; Bebensee, Helms & Spruit 2011; Cortes, Sa'ez & Ortega 2007; Ibrahim & Reed 2009). Whilst it is evident that knowledge management in the private sector has made tremendous inroads, the application of KM practices in the public sector has followed only in a limited fashion. The potential for KM in assisting the public sector is however widely encouraged and recognised (Cong & Pandya 2003; Durrant 2001; Salavati, Shafei & Shaghayegh 2010; Yuen 2007).

From a South African perspective, it is accepted that the country is an emerging democracy when compared to the global village. As a developing country, it has many challenges, including poverty eradication, skills shortages and high levels of crime. It has been found that, more often than not, knowledge is not effectively shared because organisations and business units tend to operate in silos (Rogers 2007). Ultimately, mandates of government organisations or business units are seldom achieved, resulting in non-service delivery to the citizens of the country. Organisations pursuing knowledge management in general, and knowledge sharing in particular, have traditionally focused on the information technology infrastructure (Davenport, Delong & Beers 1998). Whilst information technology is important to the overall knowledge management endeavour, a lack of attention to cultural factors has proven to be a roadblock to any sustainable success. The researchers have witnessed several deployments of information management and team collaboration solutions that have failed to meet their objective of facilitating consistent information and knowledge exchange. Whilst there may be many factors contributing to these deployment failures (for example insufficient training, application champions, communication or support), the organisations in question neglected to take into account the social and motivational drivers behind why an employee would share what they know regardless of what tool was available.

In this study the literature findings indicated that in attempting to resolve problems, and if used effectively, the discipline of knowledge management can be a critical tool in assisting government agencies to inculcate a knowledge sharing culture and, ultimately, achieve their mandates.

Problem statement and explanation

Indications are that knowledge sharing amongst South African government agencies is limited. In his address at the Knowledge Management conference at Stellenbosch Business School, former president Thabo Mbeki pointed out that the purpose of the conference was to discuss: 'the role of knowledge in the betterment of society' (see Mbeki 2012:4). This may be linked to the 'Batho Pele' principles, which aim to achieve overall service delivery. The problem may be stated succinctly as follows: There is insufficient and ineffective knowledge sharing between government agencies in South Africa in the pursuit of effective problem solving.

In 2007, Rogers interviewed renowned ichthyologist and environmental activist Professor Peter Britz on the subject of abalone poaching. In this interview, Professor Britz stated categorically that government agencies were not effectively working together towards resolving the problem (Rogers 2007). Britz's comment highlighted the lack of cooperation between and inefficiency of relevant government agencies. It is against this backdrop that the researchers proposed investigating the state of knowledge management in selected government agencies, thereby assisting to establish knowledge sharing practices within and between various government agencies. The opportunity in this instance (thinking back to the Capone case) is that if a culture of sharing is installed in the seemingly siloed mentality of government, then the KM discipline will be in action and problem solving will be greatly enhanced.

Previous research by McDermott and O'Dell (2005:84) and Yao, Kam and Chan (2007:65) highlighted numerous barriers to knowledge sharing, including aspects such as organisational culture and leadership. Other factors and barriers may also be prevalent, such as a lack of an appropriate information and communication technology (ICT) infrastructure, no knowledge sharing practices such as communities of practice and a lack of trust within organisations and even in government itself (Cloete 2007; Riege 2005; Yuen 2007). The theoretical model below is a reference for the commonly identified enablers for knowledge sharing as well as being a basis for the list of hypotheses.

The theoretical model and the factors influencing the perceived effectiveness of knowledge management

In this investigative theoretical model (see Figure 1), the dependent variable is the perceived effectiveness of knowledge sharing between South African government agencies. The intervening variables were initially knowledge management and a relatively new concept in military circles known as netcentricity. With regard to the independent variables, it is widely acknowledged by authors such as Bechina and Ndlela (2009) and Hsu (2006) that for knowledge management to succeed, certain 'enablers' – also known as pillars or crucial drivers – need to be present. In order to focus on the pillars of KM, the researchers used the adapted model of Stankosky's KM Pillars to Enterprise Learning (Cranfield &Taylor 2008). This theoretical model was amended during the research methodology phase and will be appropriately expanded upon. The theoretical model and the hypothesised interrelationships between the variables are outlined in Figure 1.

The objective of the study was primarily to investigate and test the impact of independent variables (identified in the literature) on the perceived effectiveness of knowledge management in government agencies. Furthermore, the study intended to investigate barriers influencing knowledge sharing. As such, a number of hypotheses were formulated to test these barriers:

- Hypothesis 1: There is a positive relationship between effective leadership and the perceived effectiveness of knowledge sharing.
- Hypothesis 2: There is a positive relationship between a collaborative organisational culture and the perceived effectiveness of knowledge sharing.
- Hypothesis 3: There is a positive relationship between ICT application and the perceived effectiveness of knowledge sharing.
- Hypothesis 4: There is a positive relationship between a continuously learning organisation and the perceived effectiveness of knowledge sharing.
- Hypothesis 5: There is a positive relationship between communities of practice and the perceived effectiveness of knowledge sharing.
- Hypothesis 6: There is a positive relationship between policy and legislation support and the perceived effectiveness of knowledge sharing.
- Hypothesis 7: There is a positive relationship between high levels of trust embedded in an organisation and the perceived effectiveness of knowledge sharing.

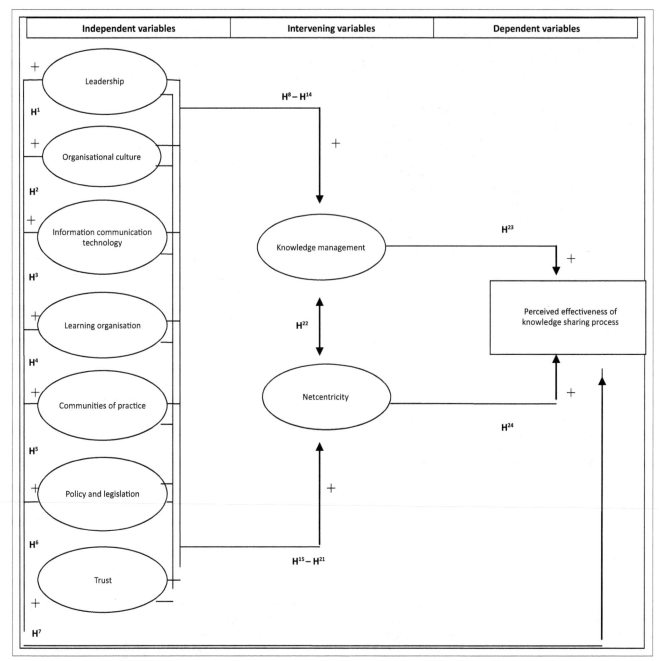

FIGURE 1: Theoretical model of perceived effectiveness on knowledge sharing.

Only the significant factors or independent variables (organisational culture and a learning organisation) identified through this study and the dependent variable (knowledge management) will be discussed next.

Organisational culture

In this article, organisational culture is defined as the perception of the character of an organisation by its employees. The individual perceptions combine to create the collective organisational culture. If the culture is collaborative, then knowledge sharing amongst employees should be occurring. However, a lack of important enablers such as rewards, or the presence of noticeable barriers, may inhibit a sharing culture (Riege 2005). As asserted by Riege (2005), it is thus critical to identify the barriers in order to remove them so

that knowledge sharing may become a common culture with the relevant organisation.

Kreitner, Kinicki and Buelens (1999:58) identified four functions of organisational culture: 'it gives members an organisational identity; it facilitates collective commitment; it promotes social system stability; and it shapes behaviour by assisting members to make sense of their surroundings'. If the leadership commits and drives a collaborative, learning culture, then employees at lower levels will acknowledge that their leaders indeed reward innovative and collaborative work behaviour. Conversely, if no reward systems are put in place, then the motivation to share will be inhibited (Riege 2005). This highlights the fact that variables such as leadership and organisational culture are interdependent.

Campbell (2009) pointed out that social factors, like trust and collaboration, also form part of the overall organisational culture. Thus, by focusing on developing organisational culture, these factors will improve. Similarly, by acknowledging an organisation as a learning organisation, subject matter experts are more likely to be recognised, empowered and used in order to share their knowledge with employees and thus the overall organisation. The point being driven by the researchers is that although social factors like collaboration and trust were not found to be significant, they are nevertheless important as they form part of the overall culture, which is found to be significant in this study.

The issue of trust can be widely accepted as being closely linked to organisational culture. Globally, trust in governments has come under scrutiny because of the corrupt practices of leaders. Increasingly, people are losing trust in governments and their leaders (Cloete 2007). With technology evolving at a rapid pace, an increasingly competitive global market and the need for quicker decision-making, organisations require external support in terms of technology and information sources (Foos, Schum & Rothenberg 2006). These types of interactions, however, usually require an element of trust (Paroutis & Al Saleh, 2009; Scarso & Bolisani 2011).

Learning organisation

For the purposes of this article, a learning organisation is one that promotes the exchange of information between employees and creates a more knowledgeable workforce. An organisation requires a particularly flexible organisational structure, in which people will accept and adapt to new ideas and changes through a shared vision (Schein 1996). This brings a new perspective and growing importance to organisational knowledge, and the learning organisation accepts the challenge of creating a culture of managing knowledge. Clearly, a learning organisation is also driven by its leadership and culture.

Goh (2002:23) viewed 'knowledge transfer' as a key dimension of a learning organisation and hence as a critical factor for knowledge management. One of the methods used for knowledge transfer by learning organisations is that of initiating communities of practice. Communities of practice are therefore viewed as 'actionable' means of creating a sharing culture whilst ensuring a sustainable platform with known knowledge workers and a suitable method for communicating, either in a virtual set-up or within an informal meeting strategy (Cross, Borgatti & Parker 2001). Kimble and Hildreth (2005:103) concurred, considering communities of practice as groups of people who are joined together 'with an internal motivation and common purpose'. Key to this group of people is the relationship that is built between the members. Ardichvili, Page and Wentling (2003:64), who focused more on virtual communities of practice, indicated that one of the critical success factors of this type of learning and sharing in an organisation is that there must be active participation. Ardichvili et al. (2003) also suggested that the group must have a common motive for actively communicating and sharing. Furthermore, these

authors viewed intrinsic motives to be of more influence than extrinsic motives such as monetary reward.

The dependent variable: Knowledge management

Knowledge management has emerged in the last decade as an important organisational concept and whilst definitions still differ on what KM is, consensus is emerging. In a study by Kippenberger (1998:14) involving nearly 40 respondents, the majority of respondents agreed that knowledge management is defined as 'the collection of processes that govern the creation, dissemination, and utilisation of knowledge to fulfil organisational objectives'. In terms of the global, strategic importance of knowledge management, a report from the Economic Intelligence Unit (2006:3), which assessed likely changes to the global economy between 2006 and 2020, stated that knowledge management as a discipline would be the major boardroom challenge. In fact, the report highlighted survey results in which knowledge management was rated the area that offered the greatest potential for productivity gains. Yuen (2007), in a global workshop held on managing knowledge to build trust in governments, highlighted the explosion of digital connectivity and further stated that most governments had accepted the use of information technology (IT) for knowledge and ultimate public sector reform. The strategic importance of the knowledge management discipline for governments and organisations has also been acknowledged by a number of subject matter experts, including Bebensee et al. (2011), Cheng, Ho and Lau (2009), Cortes et al. (2007), Ibrahim and Reid (2009), Jakubik (2007), Riege (2005) and Tiago, Tiago and Couto (2009).

Knowledge management, in its simplest sense, establishes the ways in which organisations create, retain and share knowledge. As knowledge management is a broad discipline (Dalkir 2005), the thinking is that if organisations embrace the discipline, then knowledge sharing methodologies and processes will have a platform to ensure the success of knowledge sharing.

The scope of this article is the public sector and, as acknowledged by various authors, knowledge management in government is relatively new (Cloete 2007; Cong & Pandya 2003; Gaffoor & Cloete 2010; Riege 2005). By implication, the successes of knowledge management in the private sector need to be practised in the public sector as well. This article therefore seeks to identify the level of understanding of knowledge management as well as the key factors that contribute to effective management of knowledge in those government agencies whose mandate and powers are to enforce laws for the betterment of society and the country as a whole.

The following section will expand on the research design and research objectives.

Research design
Research approach

Whilst government has many departments overlooking many sectors, this article focused on a particular sector:

the criminal sector. Departments tasked with resolving the problem of abalone poaching were selected, primarily due to the recent publicity in local newspapers, such as the *Eastern Cape Herald* (see Rogers 2007), which highlighted the problem of government agencies not operating collaboratively. The regional managers of the relevant agencies operating in the Eastern Cape were initially identified due to the researchers being based in the Eastern Cape. However, to ensure national benefit is obtained, the researchers further targeted the national counterparts via the regional managers, in order to adhere to government agency protocols.

Through the initial engagement, it became apparent that the relevant agencies required total anonymity due to the nature of criminal investigations. As such, it must be emphasised that the relevant government agencies shall not be named, especially with regard to the analysis and findings. Instead, specific government agencies will be referred to as Agency A, Agency B and so on, in order to respect the anonymity requested. For purposes of this study, a quantitative and positivist approach appeared to be the most appropriate. The rationale for selecting the positivist approach was primarily based on the following facts:

- The researchers were independent.
- A relatively large sample was used.
- Hypotheses were formulated in order to be tested.

Research method

For this research, a comprehensive questionnaire, covering the identified independent variables required for knowledge management, was made available electronically and in hard copy where required. In terms of the research participants, relevant employees, mainly within the audit and investigations units within the relevant government agencies, were identified as appropriate for this research. After obtaining approval from the selected agencies to conduct the research, probability sampling was used: all employees (mainly team members) were invited to participate in the research.

Research procedure

After obtaining permission to conduct the research, the questionnaire was made available to participants between April and July 2012 on the Nelson Mandela Metro University (NMMU) website. Participants were informed via a research engagement letter and the necessary Internet link was also communicated. The research objectives, instructions on how to complete the questionnaire and the fact that responses were to be held in strictest confidence were further highlighted in the formal communications.

In terms of the statistical analysis, the statistical technique of structural equation modelling was used in this study to assess hypothesised relationships in the theoretical model, in order to understand the state of knowledge sharing in and between government agencies in South Africa.

Results
Validation process

In order to assess the discriminant validity of the measuring instrument, exploratory factor analysis (EFA) using a maximum likelihood EFA was applied, such that latent constructs contained in the original variables could be identified. In order to determine how many factors to extract, a combination of several criteria, namely the Eigenvalues, the percentage of variance criterion, and the scree test criterion, was used (Hair *et al.* 1998:104). During this step, it was found that there was a lot of definitional overlap between constructs, which led the researchers to conclude that some of the variables measured the 'same thing'. Due to a lack of discriminant validity, the theoretical model had to be adapted. Emanating from this exploratory factor analysis, the model was split and grouped into three categories of outcome variables: organisation variables, intervening variables and interpersonal variables.

In order to assess the adequacy or the suitability of the respondent data for factor analysis, the software programme SPSS, which includes Bartlett's test of sphericity and the Kaiser-Meyer-Olkin (KMO) measure of sampling adequacy, was applied. According to Kaiser (1974), a KMO of 0.70 is considered 'middling', whereas values below 0.70 are considered 'mediocre', 'miserable' or 'unacceptable'. Consequently, for the purpose of this study, data with KMOs of more than 0.70 ($p < 0.05$) were considered factor-analysable. Eigenvalues are used to explain the variance captured by the factor. During a factor analysis, a number of values are generated. These values are the correlations between each variable and each factor, and are known as factor loadings. According to Hair *et al.* (2006:128), factor loadings of 0.30 and 0.40 are considered significant for sample sizes of 350 and 200 respectively. In this study, items that displayed no cross-loadings, that loaded to a significant extent on one factor only, and had factor loadings of 0.35 or higher were considered significant and regarded as evidence of discriminant validity.

In the EFA, the initial numbers of factors to be extracted were not specified. However, the Eigenvalues determined the number of factors to be used (highlighted in Table 1, Table 2 and Table 3). A process of deleting items that did not demonstrate sufficient discriminated validity ensued; the exploratory factor analysis was re-run until all the remaining items loaded to a significant extent ($p > 0.35$) with no cross-loadings (i.e. loaded on only one factor). The most interpretable factor structures are presented in the tables. All items with loadings of over 0.35 were deleted.

Although an Eigen value of greater than 1 is generally accepted, the value of 0.941 for factor 4 was deemed as acceptable in this instance as it was interpretable.

Table 1 indicates that a total of 18 organisational items were loaded on four factors, and explain a total of 62.1% of the variance in the data.

Table 2 indicates that a total of 15 items measuring the intervening variables were grouped into three factors, and explain a total of 57.6% of the variance in the data. Out of the three factors identified, the factor information sharing was removed due to poor construct validity.

Table 3 indicates that a total of 11 items measuring the interpersonal variables loaded on three factors, namely internal communities of practice, trust and external communities of practice, and explain a total of 63.3% of the variance in the data. Whilst two of the initial six items loaded onto trust, two of the remaining four (TRUST2 and TRUST6) loaded onto the communities of practice factors. With regard to both internal and external communities of practice factors, all of the seven items loaded, with the exception of COP1.

The variables (internal communities of practice and external communities of practice) combined such that they merged with the variable learning organisation. The initially identified independent variable of trust was deemed as the appropriate variable when all three factors merged.

The interpretation of the EFA indicates that the items and constructs (factors) remaining in the data demonstrate sufficient evidence of discriminated validity. The reliability of the research instrument will be discussed next.

Reliability of the research instrument

For this study, the software application IBM SPSS Version 19.0 for Windows® was used to measure the Cronbach alpha for each of the identified factors. A Cronbach alpha of greater than 0.70 was required in order to regard a score as reliable. A summary of the variables in terms of reliability is presented in Table 4.

As listed in Table 4, all variables were reliable (having Cronbach alpha values greater than 0.70). From the originally proposed independent variables of the proposed theoretical model, one (policy and legislation) was removed as it did not demonstrate sufficient discriminate validity during the initial data analysis process. A further five variables were removed from the model as the exploratory factor analysis conducted was unable to confirm adequate discriminant validity amongst all the latent variables. Noticeably, some items from the deleted variables did, however, load on other factors in the exploratory factor analysis. For instance, one item expected to measure the variable leadership (L6) loaded with items ICO3, CULT7 and LO7 to form a newly identified latent variable termed *subject matter expert*. The item (NETC10) loaded with other items NETC9, SUCC6, KNOW5 and KNOW6 to form a variable termed *collaboration*. In essence, although the above terms were removed via the exploratory factor analysis, they were instrumental in forming new variables.

The latent variable of knowledge sharing, which was first proposed as the dependent variable, loaded together with the initial intervening variable (knowledge management).

TABLE 1: Rotated factor loadings: Organisational variables.

Item	Factor 1: Learning Organisation (LO)	Factor 2: Netcentricity (NETC)	Factor 3: Subject matter expert (EXPERT)	Factor 4: Organisation culture (CULT)
LO4	.792	.064	-.032	.048
COP4	.745	.079	.035	.058
CULT5	.687	-.026	.041	-.059
ICO5	.566	-.196	.130	-.144
LO3	.501	-.069	.059	-.221
LEAD4	.451	-.030	.028	-.298
ICO3	.030	.730	.137	.054
LO2	-.037	.398	-.104	-.208
LO7	-.032	.009	.920	-.048
LEAD6	.264	.188	.415	.012
CULT7	.139	-.026	.360	-.278
CULT2	.030	.036	.052	-
CULT3	-.035	.164	.077	-
CULT4	-.003	-.073	.304	-
LEAD2	.309	.101	-.020	-
LEAD1	.277	.058	-.011	-
CULT1	.194	.077	-.049	-
CULT6	.272	.100	.183	-
Eigen value	8.319	1.454	1.069	0.941

LO, learning organisation; NETC, netcentricity; EXPERT, subject matter expert; CULT, organisational culture; COP, communities of practice; ICO, internal communities of practice; LEAD, leadership.

TABLE 2: Rotated factor loadings: Intervening variables.

Item	Factor 1: Knowledge management (KNOW)	Factor 2: Collaboration	Factor 3: Information sharing
SUCC1	.839	-.052	-.052
KNOW1	.797	-.022	-.040
SUCC2	.786	.052	-.080
KNOW2	.695	-.097	-.026
SUCC5	.674	.028	-.003
KNOW3	.653	.039	.070
KNOW4	.599	.061	.208
SUCC3	.504	.125	.145
NETC10	.007	.762	-.026
KNOW5	-.084	.752	.118
SUCC6	-.080	.692	-.048
KNOW6	.188	.548	-.089
NETC9	.020	.441	.066
SUCC4	.209	-.021	.723
NETC8	-.042	.015	.364
Eigen value	5.081	2.394	1.175

KNOW, knowledge management; SUCC, success of knowledge sharing; NETC, netcentricity.

TABLE 3: Rotated factor loadings: Interpersonal variables.

Item	Factor 1: Communities of practice (Internal) (COP)	Factor 2: Trust	Factor 3: Communities of practice (External) (COP)
COP3	.876	.043	.122
COP5	.703	-.043	-.068
COP4	.491	.135	-.169
TRUST6	.490	.032	-.150
TRUST4	.021	.831	.059
TRUST5	.049	.385	-.265
TRUST3	-.001	-.045	-.725
COP2	-.075	.111	-.656
COP6	.111	-.003	-.622
TRUST2	.218	.001	-.545
COP7	.345	.068	-.411
Eigen value	5.061	0.990	0.914

COP, communities of practice; TRUST, trust.

The analysis then combined the two variables (knowledge sharing and knowledge management), which subsequently reflected *knowledge management* as *the dominant* dependent variable. As such, both intervening variables (knowledge sharing and netcentricity) were removed due to poor discriminant validity. As a result of the factor analysis, the original theoretical model and the associated hypotheses formulated were revised.

Through this research, five primary determinants of perceived effectiveness of knowledge management for South African government agencies were examined.

The research has confirmed that the factors organisational culture and learning organisation have a significant impact on the effectiveness of knowledge management. The literature revealed that there are numerous factors impacting on organisational culture, hence the need to identify what these factors are and their levels of importance. In the study conducted, latent social factors like collaboration and trust were identified as factors that need to be looked at if a positive collaborative and trusting culture is the objective. It must be noted that understanding a culture and identifying the complex knowledge sharing processes is not an easy task. As such, more research needs to be done, especially within the public sector and in terms of understanding what employees want', what drives employees to hoard or share knowledge and what knowledge sharing methodology is best suited for the specific public organisations. One thing is certain: a collaborative effort involving all stakeholders is required in order to ensure the effective implementation of knowledge management in the public sector in South Africa. In support of the critical factors found pertinent in this study, the following model for knowledge management in the public sector is proposed.

Based on the current literature on KM and the significant factors identified in this study, the use of the knowledge tree model was seen as an ideal comparison between a tree and a typical organisation. A tree, similar to a learning organisation should grow continuously. Furthermore, trees, like organisations and governments, have various branches which requires nurturing – similar to learning in the organisational sense. The culture of an organisation, which cannot be simply interpreted or viewed at first glance, is like the underlying roots of a tree. The model above has at its centre (central strategy of an organisation) the core knowledge management discipline; the various branches of government have to collaboratively support and influence the direction of knowledge in order to grow and improve on service delivery and ultimate problem solving. Leadership and policy-making are important in understanding and investigating the 'factors beneath the surface' of the tree (organisation), in that they need to look 'beyond and beneath' in order to deal with organisational culture and learning issues, as issues of trust and subject matter experts are to be viewed as the roots 'below the surface'. A relatively young developing country like South Africa is to be viewed as a growing tree

TABLE 4: Summary of all variables in terms of reliability.

Variable	Eigen value	Cronbach alpha
Organisational culture	0.941	0.866
Learning organisation	8.319	0.860
Subject matter expert	1.069	0.708
Collaboration	2.394	0.771
Trust	0.990	0.771
Knowledge management	5.081	0.887

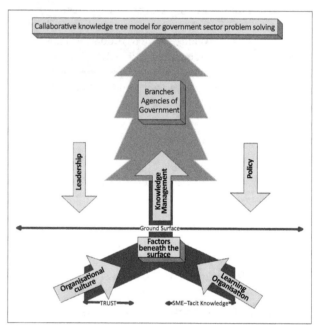

FIGURE 2: Collaborative knowledge tree model for public sector problem solving.

in this instance, which requires the caretakers (leaders) to ensure that the 'seeds and fertiliser' (organisational culture and learning) are firmly planted in order for the country to continuously grow and provide the fruits of success.

Conclusion

The study has confirmed and exposed the two significant factors, organisational culture and a learning organisation, for leaders to use in their pursuit of enabling the KM agenda in public sector organisations. Further research may look at amounts spent by government organisations on technology as opposed to people (learning, rewarding, incentivising, etc.). This, in turn, requires deeper research into the organisational culture and questions such as 'why' people share, and what the barriers to and enablers of effective sharing are.

Contrary to the question posed by Wilson (2002), knowledge management is not a fad but indeed a discipline that is continuously being embraced by visionary leaders. South African government departments currently face a serious challenge in terms of improving their service delivery commitments to the public. If knowledge management is correctly addressed and implemented, this will certainly enable these departments to meet their national obligation to service excellence.

Acknowledgements

Competing interest

The authors declare that they have no financial or personal relationship(s) that may have inappropriately influenced them in writing this article.

Authors' contributions

A.M. (Nelson Mandela Metropolitan University) was the lead researcher and H.J.v.N. (Nelson Mandela Metropolitan University) was the main promoter and responsible for advising on the relevant subject matter. C.M.A. (Nelson Mandela Metropolitan University) was the co-promoter, whose contributions were with regard to the structure and advice on the research process and analysis conducted.

References

Alavi, M. & Leidner, D., 1999, 'Knowledge management systems: Issues, challenges, and benefits', *Communications of AIS Journal* 1, 2–37.

Ardichvili, A., Page, V. & Wentling, T., 2003, 'Motivation and barriers to participation in virtual knowledge-sharing communities of practice', *Journal of Knowledge Management* 7(1), 64–77. http://dx.doi.org/10.1108/13673270310463626

Bebensee, T., Helms, R. & Spruit, M., 2011, 'Exploring web 2.0 applications as a mean of bolstering up knowledge management', *The Electronic Journal of Knowledge Management* 9(1), 1–9.

Bechina, A. & Ndlela, N., 2009, 'Success factors in implementing knowledge based systems', *Electronic Journal of Knowledge Management* 7(2), 211–218.

Campbell, M.J., 2009, 'Identification of organisational cultural factors that impact knowledge sharing', Capstone report presented to the Interdisciplinary Studies Program, Graduate School, University of Oregon.

Cheng, M., Ho, J. & Lau, P., 2009, 'Knowledge sharing in academic institutions: A study of multimedia university Malaysia', *Electronic Journal of Knowledge Management* 7(3), 313–324.

Cloete, F., 2007, 'Knowledge management and trust in government: Lessons from South Africa', paper presented at the 7th Global Forum on Re-inventing Government, Vienna, 26–29 June.

Cong, X. & Pandya, K., 2003, 'Issues of knowledge management in the public sector', *Electronic Journal of Knowledge Management* 1(2), 25–33.

Cortes, E., Sa'ez, P. & Ortega, E., 2007, 'Organizational structure features supporting knowledge management processes', *Journal of Knowledge Management* 11(4), 45–57. http://dx.doi.org/10.1108/13673270710762701

Cranfield, D.J. & Taylor, J., 2008, 'Knowledge management and higher education: A UK case study', *The Electronic Journal of Knowledge Management* 6(2), 85–100.

Cross, R., Borgatti, S.P. & Parker, A., 2001, 'Beyond answers: Dimensions of the advice network', *Social Networks* 23(3), 215–235. http://dx.doi.org/10.1016/S0378-8733(01)00041-7

Dalkir, K., 2005, *Knowledge Management in theory and practice*, Butterworth-Heinemann Publications, Burlington.

Davenport, T.H., DeLong, D.W. & Beers, M.C., 1998, 'Successful knowledge management projects', *Sloan Management Review*, 43–57.

Durrant, F., 2001, 'Knowledge management in the context of government', paper presented at a High Level Workshop on E-Government, Information and Communication Technologies in Public Sector Management, Caribbean Ministerial Consultation, Jamaica, 10–14 December.

Economic Intelligence Unit, 2006, *A report of the economic, industry and corporate trends for the year 2020*, viewed July 2009, from http://graphics.eiu.com/files/ad_pdfs/eiuForesight2020_WP.pdf

Foos, T., Schum, G. & Rothenberg, S., 2006, 'Tacit knowledge transfer and the knowledge disconnect', *Journal of Knowledge Management* 10(1), 6–18. http://dx.doi.org/10.1108/13673270610650067

Gaffoor, S. & Cloete, F., 2010, 'Knowledge management in local government: The case of Stellenbosch municipality', *South African Journal of Information Management* 12(1), Art. #422, 7 pages.

Goh, S.C., 2002, 'Managing effective knowledge transfer: An integrative framework and some practical implications', *Journal of Knowledge Management* 6(1), 23–30. http://dx.doi.org/10.1108/13673270210417664

Hair, J.F., Anderson, R.E., Tatham, R.L. & Black, W.C., 1998, *Multivariate data analysis*, 5th edn., Prentice Hall, Englewood Cliffs.

Hair, J.F., Black, W.C., Babin, J.B., Anderson, R.E. & Tatham, R.L., 2006, *Multivariate data analysis*, 6th edn., Prentice Hall, Upper Saddle River.

Hsu, I.C., 2006, 'Enhancing employee tendencies to share knowledge – Case studies of nine companies in Taiwan', *International Journal of Information Management* 26, 326–338. http://dx.doi.org/10.1016/j.ijinfomgt.2006.03.001

Ibrahim, F. & Reid, V., 2009, 'What is the value of knowledge management practices?', *Electronic Journal of Knowledge Management* 7(5), 567–574.

Jakubik, M., 2007, 'Exploring the knowledge landscape: Four emerging views of knowledge', *Journal of Knowledge Management* 11(4), 6–19. http://dx.doi.org/10.1108/13673270710762675

Kaiser, H.F., 1974, 'An index of factorial simplicity', *Psychometrika* 39, 31–36. http://dx.doi.org/10.1007/BF02291575

Kimble, C. & Hildreth, P., 2005, 'Dualities, distributed communities of practice and knowledge management', *Journal of Knowledge Management* 9(4), 102–113. http://dx.doi.org/10.1108/13673270510610369

Kippenberger, T., 1998, 'Knowledge management: The current state of play', *Management Research* 11, 14.

Kreitner, R., Kinicki, A. & Buelens, M., 1999, *Organizational behaviour*, 1st European edn., McGraw-Hill Publishing, Berkshire.

Mbeki, T., 2012, 'The democratisation of knowledge: The role of knowledge in the betterment of society', address at the knowledge management conference, in *Thabo Mbeki Foundation*, viewed 29 May 2012, from http://www.thabombekifoundation.org.za/pages/address-of-the-patron-of-the-tmf,-thabo-mbeki,-at-the-university-of-stellenbosch-business-school-knowledge-management-speec.aspx

McDermott, R. & O'Dell, C., 2005, 'Overcoming cultural barriers to sharing knowledge', *Journal of Knowledge Management* 5(1), 76–85. http://dx.doi.org/10.1108/13673270410567000

Paroutis, S. & Al Saleh, A., 2009, 'Determinants of knowledge sharing using web 2.0 Technologies', *Journal of Knowledge Management* 13(4), 52–63. http://dx.doi.org/10.1108/13673270910971824

Riege, A., 2005, 'Three-dozen knowledge-barriers managers must consider', *Journal of Knowledge Management* 9(3), 18–35. http://dx.doi.org/10.1108/13673270510602746

Rogers, G., 2007, 'Clamps on perlemoen poaching ineffectual', *Eastern Cape Herald*, 16 April, p. 1.

Salavati, A, Shafei, R. & Shaghayegh, E., 2010, 'A model for adoption of knowledge management in Iranian public organisations', *European Journal of Social Sciences* 17(1), 109–116.

Scarso, E. & Bolisani, E., 2011, 'Knowledge-based strategies for knowledge intensive business services: A multiple case-study of computer service companies', *Electronic Journal of Knowledge Management* 8(1), 151–160.

Schein, E.H., 1996, 'Three cultures of management: The key to organisational learning', *The Sloan Management Review* 38(1), in *harvardmacy.org*, viewed October 2010, from http://www.harvardmacy.org/Upload/pdf/Schein%20artilce.pdf

Tiago, F., Tiago, M.T.B. & Couto, J.P., 2009, 'Assessing the drivers of virtual knowledge management impact in European firms' performance: An exploratory analysis', *Electronic Journal of Knowledge Management* 7(2), 277–286.

Wilson, T.D., 2002, 'The nonsense of "knowledge management"', *Information Research* 8(1).

Yao, L., Kam, T. & Chan, S., 2007, 'Knowledge sharing in Asian public administration sector: The case of Hong Kong', *Journal of Enterprise Information Management* 20(1), 51–69.

Yuen, Y., 2007, 'Overview of knowledge management in the public sector', paper delivered at the 7th Global Forum on Reinventing Government: Building Trust in Government, Vienna, Austria, 26–29 June.

11

Using communities of practice towards the next level of knowledge-management maturity

Authors:
Lameshnee Chetty[1]
Martie Mearns[1]

Affiliations:
[1]Centre for Information and Knowledge Management, University of Johannesburg, South Africa

Correspondence to:
Martie Mearns

Email:
mearnsm@uj.ac.za

Postal address:
PO Box 524, Auckland Park 2006, South Africa

Background: Effective communities of practice undoubtedly impact organisations' knowledge management and contribute towards building a learning-organisation culture. Communities of practice represent an environment conducive to learning and for exchanging ideas, and they are a formal learning forum. However, the level of organisational learning to which communities of practice contribute is difficult to measure.

Objectives: The research was conducted to analyse the impact of communities of practice on building a learning organisation. The organisational system, culture and people offer the key towards leveraging knowledge as a strategic resource in a learning organisation. The awareness of the organisation concerning knowledge management was measured on a replicated knowledge-management maturity model.

Method: The organisational knowledge base was analysed prior to the implementation of the communities of practice and was compared to the situation three years later. The research was based on experiential learning cycles that consisted of five consequential but perpetual stages, namely reflect, plan, act, observe and reflect again.

Results: The results indicated that communities of practice were instrumental in leveraging the organisation to the next level in the knowledge-management maturity model. A collaboration framework was developed for each business unit to work towards a common goal by harnessing the knowledge that was shared.

Conclusion: Although a positive impact by communities of practice is visible, an instrument for the measurement of intellectual capital is necessary. It is recommended that the monetary value of knowledge as an asset is determined so that the value of the potential intellectual capital can be measured.

Introduction

Communities of practice (CoP) have become an imperative element in accumulating and maintaining an organisation's intellectual capital (IC) (Davel & Snyman 2005). Companies that adopt a strategic approach instead of an opportunistic approach to managing their IC have harnessed opportunities to improve their market position (Klein 1998:4, Kruger & Johnson 2011:269). Despite realising the importance of knowledge management, understanding how to manage knowledge is still not an easy task for many organisations (Arling & Chun 2011:231).

CoPs are strategic knowledge-management tool utilised in an effort to capture and share tacit knowledge (Wenger 2007). In essence, CoPs are proving to be a breakthrough for organisations to identify and manage their tacit intellectual assets so that these can become explicit sources to be utilised as IC. If CoPs are nurtured by management structures within organisations, they may be able to generate knowledge as one of their greatest assets (Pearlson & Saunders 2006:287). The sharing of information, thoughts and ideas based on a common goal in a CoP results in members of the community gaining more knowledge and raising each other's competence through sharing (Burke 2000:18). The advantage of a CoP is that members of that community in an organisation are peers and are alike for that reason, regardless of job titles and positions. This equality is the result of the relationship on which a CoP is based. Employees are therefore able to naturally share knowledge without trepidation or evaluation from other employees. Valuing the expertise and the sharing of knowledge is seen as one of the characteristics of a knowledge-based organisation. Where knowledge creation is at the centre of an organisation, the bridge between working and innovation is learning.

A learning organisation is an organisation that learns vigorously and collectively, continually transforming itself to more effectively manage knowledge and empower its people to learn (Gilley & Maycunich 2000:14). Learning organisations are continually expanding their capacity to create their own future (Aktarsha & Anisa 2011:27, Senge 1990:3). Such organisations are skilled at creating, acquiring and transferring knowledge and at modifying the organisation's behaviour to reflect new knowledge and insight (Garvin 1993:79, Smith 2011:7). Typical activities in a learning organisation are systematic problem solving, experimentation with new approaches, learning from own and others' experiences and transferring knowledge efficiently. The steps that are required to become a learning organisation include, firstly, the creation of an environment that is conducive to learning. Secondly, the exchange of ideas should be stimulated, and thirdly, learning forums should be created (Garvin 1993:91; Wilson 2011:111).

MultiChoice is an example of a learning organisation that favours the use of CoPs as a learning forum to exchange ideas and create a learning environment to ultimately capture and utilise intellectual assets. Using MultiChoice as a case in point, this article argues that CoPs can make a substantial contribution towards creating a learning-organisation culture. This argument is moulded around the main research problem that was investigated, namely: What contribution does CoPs make towards building a learning organisation such as MultiChoice. In order to measure whether MultiChoice has become a learning organisation, it is important to determine MultiChoice's level on the knowledge-management maturity model (Snyman & Kruger 2005:10). This will gauge the organisation's progress towards being in a position to identify IC as a true business asset.

IC is considered to be one of the main drivers of knowledge management. The objective of organisations should be to maximise IC by linking it to knowledge management. Zhou & Fink (2003:36) state that this objective can only be realised if knowledge processes are managed methodically and with intent. This article highlights the way in which MultiChoice has used a knowledge-management tool such as CoP in order to build more effective processes and capture tacit knowledge to ultimately derive organisational IC.

Defining the case study

MultiChoice was founded in 1986 as a subscription television service in South Africa and has as its mission the distribution of digital media entertainment, content and services to subscribers through multiple devices (MultiChoice 2010). MultiChoice is a knowledge-intensive company that, in 2006, has formally embraced knowledge management. The research for this article was conducted as a longitudinal study drawing on the findings of a 2006 baseline report (Hiscock 2006).

The position of knowledge management in MultiChoice prior to the introduction of CoP had been analysed in the 2006 baseline report conducted as a knowledge audit (Hiscock 2006). Key stakeholders were identified throughout the organisation. A combination of one-on-one interviews and focus groups were completed to identify the knowledge entities that existed within the organisation, the knowledge

flows between the entities and the resulting knowledge gaps that could then be identified. To ensure a good cross section of all levels throughout the organisation, 55 one-on-one interviews were conducted, and 139 participants were included in the focus-group discussions. The purpose of the baseline assessment was to determine the level of organisational learning in MultiChoice in an attempt to understand the (then) current knowledge-management processes of the organisation. It was furthermore necessary to identify and understand the key drivers of business value and to identify the areas of improvement and strategic gaps.

As a result of the baseline assessment, it was concluded that there is an indication of an awareness of knowledge management as an emerging business discipline. The awareness of the capability of knowledge management to improve MultiChoice's performance, however, remained low. Despite this low awareness, the overall interest in knowledge management was high. This was supported by the enthusiasm shown by interviewees in the baseline report requesting to be kept informed of follow-up knowledge-management activities.

The baseline assessment also highlighted and supported the fact that MultiChoice is familiar with many knowledge-management principles. In addition these knowledge-management principles are actively practiced. These include the need to focus on the consistent application and improved quality of knowledge-management principles across the company. This meant that MultiChoice had to establish a rigorous knowledge-management awareness campaign within the organisation.

The knowledge-management pyramid of excellence (Figure 1) was adopted as the agreed framework for knowledge-management implementation at MultiChoice. The framework represents a systematic approach to implementing and adopting six core knowledge-management principles.

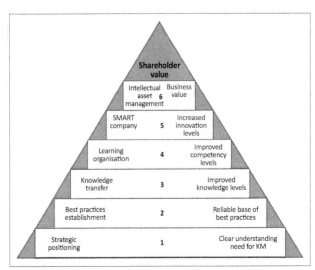

Source: Adapted from Hiscock, M., 2006, 'Knowledge management baseline assessment', Unpublished internal report for MultiChoice.

FIGURE 1: Pyramid of Excellence Framework and Maturity Model.

The six core knowledge management principles are strategic positioning, the establishment of best practices, knowledge transfer, learning organisation, becoming a specific measurable attainable realistic timely (SMART) company and intellectual-asset management. These have been combined with the knowledge-management maturity model that is discussed later and shown in Figure 4, Figure 5 and Figure 6. Considering the baseline report, the third level, namely knowledge transfer, showed that informal CoPs do exist, but they could be further optimised to focus on specific knowledge areas. It was also found that more CoPs could be developed.

An analysis of the critical success factors of CoPs in MultiChoice was conducted by Murphy (2008). Based on the baseline study of Hiscock (2006) and building on the work of Murphy (2008), a period of time had to elapse to assess the level of organisational learning that the formalised CoPs contributed. This article therefore reports on the results of the investigation into the current level of organisational learning that CoPs contribute to MultiChoice.

Research methods

In order to grasp the extent to which CoPs have impacted on MultiChoice, the methodology had to interpret factual reflections and opinions of the community members and organisation. The research methodology used for this study is primarily based on Participatory Action Research (PAR). PAR is a method of research where creating an optimistic social change is the principal driving force. Hughes and Seymour-Rolls (2000) contend that:

> PAR grew out of social and educational research [that] exists today as one of the few research methods which embrace principles of participation ... reflection ... empowerment and emancipation of groups seeking to improve their social situation. (p. 1)

The possibilities of using PAR in the information and knowledge-management sciences are vast and entirely appropriate. Firstly, a PAR project arises from the practitioners themselves, the practitioners being the participants who are chosen as the sample. The participants become the basis of the actionable change, and their qualitative feedback becomes the basis for the scientific research outcomes. Secondly, PAR is research focussing on developing new knowledge and theory (Hughes & Seymour-Rolls 2000, Genat 2009:102). Similarly CoPs are platforms used as change enablers whilst continuously gaining new knowledge by experiencing in practice or in action; this is not unlike the action-learning groups which are utilised for PAR. CoPs are therefore actually continuous, cyclic PAR projects. The research design is based on Kolb's Experiential Learning Cycle (Kolb & Yeganeh 2011:4), which applies the approach of participatory action research in the following stages:

- **Reflect 1:** The participants are engaged in a critical evaluation process regarding what is currently happening in the process that needs to be changed. The increased understanding which emerges from this first session of initial criticism is put to use in creating the later stages.

- **Plan**: Subsequent to the feedback that has emerged in the initial reflection stage, planning sessions then occur. The action points are distributed and allocated to participants.
- **Act**: This phase is putting the plan into action. This is where the changes are implemented as stipulated in the reflection and planning phase.
- **Observe**: Observations are made by the participants on the impact of their implementation plan. Observations are based on whether prior assumptions were correct, whether the team is working together and what impact the implementation has had on other people in the organisation.
- **Reflect 2**: This is the second reflection phase of the initial cycle. In this phase, observations are brought forward and discussed with all participants, and a new plan is suggested based on the new critics.

Focus groups (consisting of 10 members each) were applied to document the stages of the experiential learning cycle in the PAR approach. A purposive sample of two CoPs was drawn from a possible five CoPs, and these acted as the focus groups for the PAR sessions that were documented. The two CoPs that participated in the research were the project management (PM) CoP and the knowledge management (KM) CoP. The criteria were included as part of the sample stipulated that the CoPs should meet at least once in two months. The subject matter experts of the CoPs and the objective of the CoPs should be representative of each other, and the CoPs should consist of more than five people.

In addition to focus groups, a survey was also utilised to capture relevant information from an organisational perspective. Each of the 11 business divisions within MultiChoice has a knowledge champion, and each of the 11 knowledge champions was included in the survey. Questionnaires were administered to the 11 knowledge-management champions, which resulted in a 90.9% response rate. The survey aimed to achieve a holistic organisational view of the role of CoPs in MultiChoice. The total sample size for the data collection stage of this study was therefore 31 participants, two CoPs with 10 participants each and 11 knowledge champions.

Positioning knowledge management, intellectual capital and Communities of practice

In essence, knowledge management can be defined as a dynamic, multi-disciplined approach towards achieving organisational objectives by making the best, most efficient use of knowledge. Earl (2001:218) has identified three knowledge-management schools of thought: technocratic, economic and behavioural. The technocratic approach emphasises technology-based information-management applications, such as knowledge bases and organisational directories disclosing the repositories and custodians of knowledge. The economic approach focuses on the exploitation of knowledge as an asset. The behavioural approach, to which MultiChoice subscribes, focuses on business strategy and culture by facilitating knowledge exchange through communities and awareness (Earl 2001:218).

The technocratic approach is however not ignored at MultiChoice, but technology for knowledge sharing is seen from a supportive perspective whilst the economic slant of knowledge sharing is regarded as an outcome once knowledge maturity is reached. There is therefore a focus on the organisational system, culture and people as supported by Carrillo (2004), Currie and Kerrin (2004) and Hwang (2005). The people, culture and relationship of the organisation are therefore key to IC.

Intellectual capital consists of human capital, which encapsulates the knowledge and wisdom within the employees of an organisation; the structural capital that refers to the hardware, software and trademarks left behind in an organisation once the employees have vacated; and the relational capital referring to the relationships built up with the customers and stakeholders. IC is often inadequately identified and assessed because information is salvaged in a dissimilar fashion, and fiscal reporting patterns are frequently unsuccessful in recognising IC as an asset (Industry Canada 1999). Bontis (1998:65) views human capital as a source of innovation and strategic renewal, saying that the essence of human capital lies in the sheer intelligence and ingenuity of staff members. Using more of what people know requires minimising mindless tasks and bureaucracy. For Stevenson (1995), command and control theories of management are inappropriate if human capital is to be unleashed. Opportunities should be created for making private knowledge public and tacit knowledge explicit (Jeon, Kim & Koh 2011:12423). Informal as well as virtual networks, relationships, forums and CoPs are all important in harnessing what people know and leveraging it in an organisation. It can therefore be concluded that a CoP is a knowledge-management tool that can be utilised to harness IC that exists within an organisation's human capacity.

There have been various Intellectual Capital frameworks that have been developed by pioneers in the field, such as Sveiby's Model (1997), Sullivan's model (2000) and the Skandia Intellectual Capital Value Scheme developed by Edvinson (2002). The MultiChoice Intellectual Capital framework takes into account a number of factors from the abovementioned three models and is shown in Figure 2.

Taking the above framework into account, at MultiChoice, IC is captured using CoPs that reside on the Innovation and Knowledge Management levels.

According to Sandrock (2008:78), a community of practice has three dimensions:

1. the domain, which is the topic of interest on which the group wishes to collaborate
2. the members, the people that make up the community of practice where they trust each other's input and are willing to share and investigate new ideas and methodologies

Source: Authors' own data

FIGURE 2: MultiChoice's Intellectual Capital Framework.

3. the community work, where the sharing of best practices takes place, and members share experiences and are able to fulfil the objective of the community of practice.

It is important to note that the most important role within the above-mentioned dimensions is the responsibility of the CoP coordinator. This person works hand in hand with the CoP leader but has the additional task of making sure that the community meets on a regular basis, is constantly updated, the online community portal is up to date and relevant information and collaboration takes place in a structured and healthy manner.

Nickols (2003:4) specifies that there are two types of CoP, sponsored and self-organising. Both types of CoP are alike in their relations but are different in the way in which they are formed. Sponsored CoPs are initiated and planned by management, often a Chief Knowledge Officer. Once the CoP is aware of and participates in the knowledge sharing community, this type of CoP will develop into a self-organising CoP. Self-organising CoPs pursue the shared interests of the group members whilst being self-governed (Jeon, Kim & Koh 2011:12423). They are formed informally in an organisation by a group of colleagues who might share the same interest on a topic, industry or subject matter. This type of CoP adds value to an organisation by sharing lessons learnt, best practices and problem solving; in essence, they learn from one another. The two CoPs studied for this research are both sponsored CoPs, sponsored by MultiChoice's management.

Figure 3 demonstrates the cycle of learning that takes place amongst members of a CoP. Knowledge capital is created and utilised in an effort to perfect processes and skills. Knowledge capital is generated by documenting knowledge and validating the knowledge against employees' experiences and expertise, thus resulting in a continuous cycle of learning and adapting. Barab and Duffy (1998) call this cycle of continuous learning 'practice fields'. Knowledge capital is applied to problem solving, quality assurance and the leveraging of knowledge amongst employees. This knowledge capital is then taken back to working groups and teams to which each employee belongs in the organisation; then it is applied.

A direct link exists between learning in an organisation and innovation. The knowledge-management maturity model, according to Snyman and Kruger (2005:10), serves as a methodology through which one can decipher how far an organisation has evolved towards becoming a learning organisation. Gallagher and Hazlett (2000) state that maturity models are typically:

> incremental in nature and represent an attempt to interpret a succession of positions, phases or stages with regard to growth and maturity, all with the ultimate aim of improving processes and business performance. (p. 12)

This means that, in order for knowledge to be effectively managed towards a higher level of maturity, organisations must grow to such an extent that these organisations are capable of leveraging knowledge as a strategic resource. In addition, the use of knowledge management should be applied in a productive way and in doing so enhance the development of organisational competence and capabilities. Figure 4 demonstrates Snyman and Kruger's (2005:10) strategic knowledge-management maturity model.

The four-stage process depicted in Figure 4 includes initiate, be aware, manage and optimise. This reflects the dedication of knowledge management in identifying and relating knowledge-management issues to organisational growth and profitability. Klimko (2001:269) refers to maturity modelling as a developing process that depicts the growth of an entity over a period of time. This includes explicitly defining, managing, measuring and controlling the growth of an entity. The MultiChoice knowledge-management maturity model replicates Snyman and Kruger's (2005:10) maturity model in Figure 5.

When knowledge is not managed, it does not have the desired impact on the business. However, if business strategies reflect learning, knowledge excellence would have been reached.

Findings to plot the organisational learning maturity

The two CoPs that participated in the PAR approach showed valuable outputs from the reflection stages. The findings that emanated from the experiential learning cycles for the project management CoP showed the value of reflection, planning, acting and observation that took place. The first finding during the first experiential learning cycle for the project management CoP indicated that participation in the CoP needs to be encouraged. The development of an incentive programme was planned and activated by establishing an incentive scheme three months later. Members observed that the incentive scheme promised high rewards. This needed to be proven in a credible approach as participants did not believe that such incentives existed. During the second experiential learning cycle for the project management CoP, reflection on the first finding indicated that the usage of the CoP's virtual site and overall awareness of the project management CoP did not pick up after the incentive scheme was established. In order to deal with the credibility of the incentives, a plan

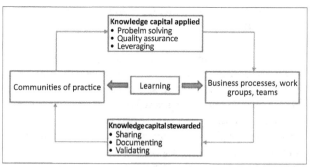

Source: Adapted from Wenger, E., 2007, *Communities of practise leaning as a social system*, viewed 14 June 2010, from http://www.co.i.l.com/coil/knowledge-garden/cop/lss.shtml

FIGURE 3: Multi-membership learning cycle of CoPs.

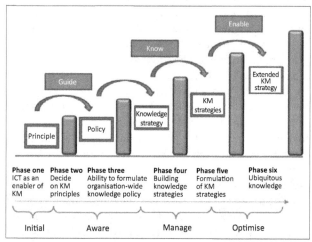

Source: Adapted from Snyman, M.M.M. & Kruger, C.J., 2005, 'Formulation of a Strategic Knowledge Management Maturity Model', *Journal of Knowledge Management* 8(1), 5–10 http://dx.doi.org/10.1108/13673270410523871

FIGURE 4: Strategic knowledge management maturity model.

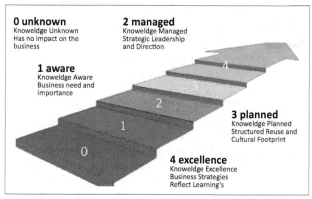

Source: Authors' own data

FIGURE 5: The MultiChoice Maturity Model.

was devised for using sponsors. Sponsors were responsible to present the CoP's strategic objectives and vision in alignment with the corporate strategy and to meet with the CoP to publicise the incentive. Further awareness campaigns were planned via MultiChoice's intranet. Controversy exists in the literature on the practice of incentives and reward systems for enhancing the quality of work. Some authors are of the opinion that incentives and rewards are counter-productive to establishing an organisational culture in which knowledge sharing is embedded (Gurteen 2010, Kohn 1999,

Pink 2010). Incentives and rewards are therefore aspects that require further investigation in the field of knowledge management. However, Stafford and Mearns (2009) reported on individuals and teams responding positively to public recognition within an organisation for contributions made to knowledge-sharing initiatives and activities.

The second finding during the first experiential learning cycle for the project management CoP indicated that there were various project managers from different business units working in silos, and the project management CoP wanted to act as a platform for them to collaborate. There were existing meetings to target the same objective, namely for project managers to work in synergy rather than in silos. Even though meetings were already scheduled with the same purpose as that of the project management CoP, the structure of the meetings did not follow a specific agenda and debates usually went around in circles. There was no facilitator that took responsibility for reaching any given objective. It was planned that the meetings would therefore be pulled in under the umbrella of the project management CoP in order to give it more structure and to achieve the expected outcomes. This reflection and plan still needs to be acted on for a second experiential learning cycle to commence.

The experiential learning cycle for the knowledge management CoP indicated that, in order to assist the organisation in learning and sharing best practices, in sharing expertise online and in encouraging innovation, a collaboration framework would have to be created. A collaboration framework (Figure 6) was planned along the

same principles as Kolb's Experiential Learning Cycle. Each stage in the collaboration framework would have a different focus area. In the 'learning' stage, preparing the organisation via learning courses, e-library and virtual counselling would be the primary focal area.

The 'act' stage would enable people to work effectively and efficiently towards a common goal. Participation would be enabled over time and space using a virtual platform. The three primary elements in the action phase were identified as communication, workplace and co-ordination. Communication is seen as the method by which messages are conveyed over a platform, such as text, voice and video chat, online conferencing, web casts, blog forum, RSS, podcasts and e-mail. Workplace signifies the working area shared between individuals, such as collaborative editing, self-organising knowledge lists of project documents and collaboration areas. Coordination is the management of project tools, to-do calendars and workshops. The three elements mentioned, communication, workplace and co-ordination, can be further re-used.

The reflection stage of the envisioned collaboration framework is seen as the documentation, sharing and re-use of experiences to improve the way in which CoP members work. The reflection stage would probably be most beneficially achieved by getting feedback on best practices, constructive criticism and ways of working. All three stages, namely learning, action and reflection, would be underpinned and supported by social networking elements, such as making expertise available online and through

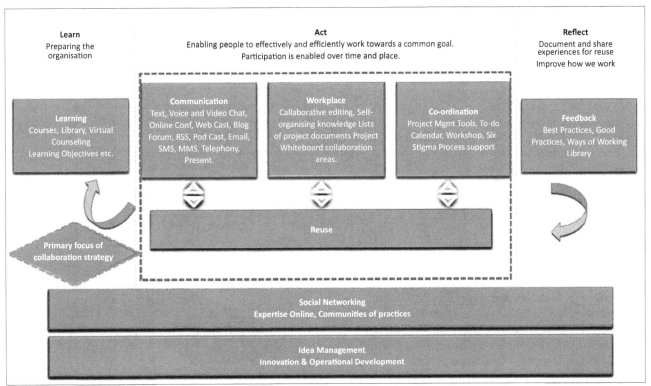

Source: Authors' own data

FIGURE 6: The MultiChoice Collaboration Framework.

virtual CoPs. The three stages would be further supported by idea management, which is continuous innovation and operational development working towards operational excellence. The members were of the opinion that building the collaboration platform would be less demanding. However, there was a perception that the content management and collaboration aspects will be more tedious efforts.

Due to the comprehensive nature of the plan that was designed to assist the organisation to learn and share, an entire experiential learning cycle has not yet been completed. The collaboration framework was being acted on at the time of the writing of this article. The virtual collaboration platform was initiated by the knowledge management CoP, and plans to pilot the framework and test the applicability was underway. Lessons learnt from the pilot test will be taken into account for the organisation-wide roll out.

The survey conducted with the 11 knowledge-management champions indicated that 9 respondents recognise knowledge management as a business tool and therefore acknowledge the significant contribution that knowledge management can make. Eight respondents were of the opinion that CoPs benefit the business and elaborated that CoPs added value to business processes and facilitated a culture of transparency. Eight respondents had one to two years of experience with CoPs, given the reality that CoPs only gained attention three years prior to the commencement of the research project. Considering that only two of the 11 knowledge champions that were interviewed did not recognise the importance of the contribution that CoPs and knowledge management made within the organisation begs the question whether these two knowledge champions adhered to the criteria that were used to select knowledge champions. When asking whether CoPs were established and managed more regularly on a face to face or a virtual basis, the results showed that the existing CoPs interact on a face to face level more regularly than a virtual level.

On an organisational level, the role of CoPs in MultiChoice is largely seen in a positive, and the perception exist that it is beneficial to the business processes. It is in the organisation's best interest to continuously monitor the attitudes and perceptions of employees regarding the use of CoPs to establish whether these continue to serve their purpose in knowledge sharing and the management of the organisation's intellectual assets.

Sandrock (2008:79) suggest that the following activities are conducted within a CoP to assist in building a learning organisation:

• **Assisting with knowledge mapping**: This is defined as networking and building on knowledge expertise within the organisation and accumulating this information in a database for future reference. The knowledge database for CoPs are not extensively utilised as the survey results indicates that 60% of the participants do not believe that there is a divisional platform to share information in MultiChoice. The development of the collaboration

platform, which is a result of the PAR group interaction, will be able to accomplish the CoPs goal of becoming learning organisations via knowledge mapping.

• **Process mapping**: Each division has a fundamental process that should be mapped in a CoP. It is clear from the PAR focus groups that members do believe that CoPs assist with validating and improving business processes. However the extent to which this is done has not been made explicit and further investigation is required.

• **Determining best practices**: What serves as a good practice in one business unit could potentially lead to a best practice for the rest of the organisation to implement. It is clear from the PAR focus groups held that the members do believe that best practices can materialise from CoPs. One such best practice is the development of the collaboration framework as suggested in the planning phase of the experiential learning cycle for the knowledge management CoPs.

• **Captured shared learning:** CoPs are good places to share experiences and lessons learnt. Results from the survey's responses to the question whether respondents view CoPs as adding value to the business indicated that, through lessons learnt, shared experiences and how work is done, there is a perception that CoPs are of value. Furthermore during the PAR group sessions, the project-management CoP indicated that the platform for project managers to collaborate serves as an effective tool to share lessons learnt. The knowledge-management CoP, had similar feedback to the effectiveness of collaboration platforms to capture lessons learnt.

The results of the 2006 baseline report indicated that MultiChoice implemented CoPs to overcome some of the perceived challenges. Challenges included employees expressing the need to share knowledge and experience, but they were of the opinion that they did not have the time to do that. Further challenges showed that information and knowledge need to be shared and communicated in a closer, innovative, collaborative environment, across departmental silos, and internal communication needs attention with the requirement for more innovative means of communication.

The results of the survey signified that CoPs are seen as valuable to the business. The transparency which is created

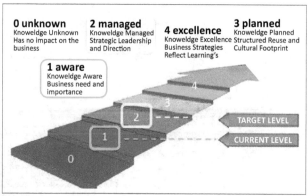

Source: Authors' own data

FIGURE 7: Maturity level of MultiChoice.

by CoPs lead to more learning across the organisation since business units work together rather than in silos. The problem of the retention of intellectual property and the overall threat of losing skills and knowledge to competitors and the market, both permanent and contract-based employees, are recognised. The results from the survey and focus group discussions indicated that MultiChoice has progressed one level on the knowledge-management maturity model and has entered level two (Figure 7).

This means that MultiChoice has grown from a level of being unaware, during the 2006 baseline study, to a level of having limited awareness of knowledge management. A level of awareness has been created, and the significance of knowledge management as a vital business tool has recently been realised. The next level of achievement for MultiChoice is to reach the 'knowledge managed' level as indicated in Figure 7. The typical activities in a learning organisation have become more prevalent in MultiChoice since the initial baseline study. The environment that has been created through CoPs to solve problems systematically and the experimentation with new approaches is another step for MultiChoice towards becoming a learning organisation.

An organisation needs to mature its knowledge capabilities and measure its knowledge assets if it is interested in determining its intellectual capital (Ngosi, Helfert & Braganza 2011:302). Kruger and Johnson (2011:270) see knowledge-management maturity not only in terms of growing capability, but they focus on the richness and consistency of execution in reaching an idealistic ultimate state of processes being defined, managed, measured and controlled.

Recommendations and conclusion

As would be expected, knowledge-management implementation at MultiChoice has been a relatively slow process, yet the next level in the knowledge management maturity model, namely knowledge managed through strategic leadership and direction, is within reach. The existence of CoPs played a significant role in stimulating the awareness that knowledge management plays a vital role in the business, bringing the organisation one step closer to becoming a true learning organisation. The use of participatory action research as a relevant methodology for knowledge-management research was also proven through CoPs acting as action learning groups in themselves that learn from experience and actions through the experiential learning cycle. In fact, the experiential learning cycle was adopted as a collaboration framework to encourage the online sharing of expertise and innovation. It is evident from the results that CoPs in MultiChoice have a significant role to play and will become increasingly valuable.

CoPs offer both virtual and face-to-face platforms where sharing and consequently learning takes place so that the bridge between working and innovation can be created. CoPs form powerful and collective knowledge-sharing opportunities, and the knowledge can be effectively managed, especially in a virtual environment. Thus, empowering people to learn can act as an impetus generating the drive towards becoming a learning organisation. CoPs are instrumental in creating, acquiring and transferring knowledge and in modifying the organisation's behaviour to reflect new knowledge and insight, thereby expanding its capacity to create its own future. The steps that are required to become a learning organisation are embedded in the very nature of CoPs in, firstly, being a platform that creates an environment that is conducive to learning. Secondly, the exchange of ideas is stimulated, seeing that it is the actual reason why CoPs are formed. Thirdly, with the sharing of ideas in CoPs, they become learning forums where new knowledge leads to innovation.

Lessons learnt from this research at MultiChoice include some findings that can be generalised. CoPs should be in a mature phase of the knowledge-management maturity model to be in a position to be measured fiscally. Fiscal proof indicating the monetary value of the IC encapsulated within the CoP exchanges of any organisation can only be established when the CoPs have progressed through a specific time frame. Three time frames within knowledge management have become apparent from this research. The first time frame is dependant on quantity in a process to get as much input from CoPs as possible. The second time frame is typified by quality, when the company is sifting through the numerous inputs gathered during the quantity phase so that valuable, reusable contributions can be extracted. The third time frame represents measurements, the process that takes the quality extracted from the quantity and measures the return on investment, therefore measuring reusable inputs. This remains a process that happens over time, and organisations need to assess their status within these time frames to establish their next step. The final finding that can be generalised from this research is that PAR as a research-design approach has been shown as a very valuable technique in the field of knowledge-management research.

The results of this research point toward the significant role that CoPs play in creating a learning organisation. However, the actual impact, especially how to establish the extent of value-added by CoPs, require further fiscal investigation to determine a monetary value. Fiscal value will be established when direct IC can be measured. In the words of Winston Churchill: 'However beautiful the strategy one must occasionally look at the results.' The monetary value of knowledge as an asset needs to be ascertained.

Acknowledgements

Competing interests

The authors declare that they have no financial or personal relationship(s) which may have inappropriately influenced them in writing this paper.

Authors' contributions

L.C. (University of Johannesburg) conducted the research as a postgraduate student under the supervision of

M.M. (University of Johannesburg). L.C. (University of Johannesburg) and M.M. (University of Johannesburg) jointly developed all data collection instruments.

L.C. (University of Johannesburg) collected the data and the work was written up as a research report by L.C. (University of Johannesburg).

The review of the report from which this article was extracted as well as the writing of the article was done by M.M. (University of Johannesburg) and L.C. (University of Johannesburg) reviewed and commented where necessary.

References

Aktharsha, U.S. & Anisa, H., 2011, 'Knowledge management systems and learning organisation: an empirical study in an engineering organisation', *The IUP journal of knowledge management* IX(2), 26–43.

Arling, P.A. & Chun, M.W.S., 2011, 'Facilitating new knowledge creation and obtaining KM maturity', *Journal of knowledge management*, 15(2), 231–250. http://dx.doi.org/10.1108/13673271111119673

Barab, S.A. & Duffy T., 1998, 'From practice fields to communities of practice', Centre for Research on Learning and Technology, Indiana University, Indiana.

Bontis, N., 1998, 'Intellectual capital: An explanatory study that develops measures and models', *Management Decision* 36(2), 63–76 http://dx.doi.org/10.1108/00251749810204142

Burke, M., 2000, 'Communities of practice', *Public roads* 63(6), 18–21.

Carrillo, P., 2004, 'Managing knowledge: Lessons from the oil and gas sector', *Construction Management and Economics* 22, 631–642. http://dx.doi.org/10.1080/0144619042000226289

Currie, G. & Kerrin, M., 2004, 'The limits of a technological fix to knowledge management', *Management Learning* 35(1), 9–29. http://dx.doi.org/10.1177/1350507604042281

Davel, R. & Snyman, M.M.M., 2005, 'Influence of Corporate Culture on the use of knowledge management techniques and technologies', *South African Journal of Information Management* (7)2, viewed 17 February 2011, from http://www.sajim.co.za

Earl, M., 2001, 'Knowledge management strategies: Toward a taxonomy', *Journal of Management Information Systems* 18(1), 215–233.

Edvinson, L., 2002, *Corporate longitude*, Prentice Hall, London.

Gallagher, S. & Hazlett, S.A., 2000, 'Using the Knowledge Management Maturity Model (KM3) as an evaluation tool', *Proceedings of the Conference on Knowledge Management Concepts and Controversies*, Coventry, UK, 10–11 February 2000.

Garvin, D.A., 1993, 'Building a learning organisation', *Harvard Business Review on Knowledge Management* 71(4), 78–91.

Gilley, J.W. & Maycunich, A., 2000, *Beyond the learning organisation*, Perseus books, Cambridge.

Genat, B., 2009, 'Building emergent situated knowledges in participatory action research', *Action Research* 7(1), 101–115. http://dx.doi.org/10.1177/1476750308099600

Gurteen, D., 2010, *Gurteen Knowledge Website*, viewed 17 February 2011, from http://www.gurteen.com

Hiscock, M., 2006, 'Knowledge management baseline assessment', Unpublished internal report for MultiChoice.

Hwang, Y., 2005, 'Investing enterprise systems adoption: Uncertainty avoidance, intrinsic motivation, and the technology acceptance model', *European Journal of Information Systems* 14, 150–161. http://dx.doi.org/10.1057/palgrave.ejis.3000532

Hughes, I. & Seymour-Rolls, K., 2000, 'Participatory action research: Getting the job done', *Action Research eReports 4*, viewed 17 February 2011, from http://www.fhs.usyd.edu.au/arrow/arer/004.htm

Industry Canada, 1999, 'Measuring and reporting intellectual capital', viewed 17 February 2011, from http://www.strategis.ic.gc/SSG/pi00009e.htm

Jeon, S., Kim, Y. & Koh, J., 2011, 'Individual, social, and organisational contexts for active sharing in communities of practice', *Expert Systems with Applications* 38, 12423–12431, http://dx.doi.org/10.1016/j.eswa.2011.04.023

Klein, D.A. (ed.), 1998, *The strategic management of intellectual capital*. Butterworth-Heinemann, Boston.

Klimko, G., 2001, 'Knowledge management and maturity models: Building common understanding', *Proceeding of the 2nd European Conference on Knowledge Management*, IEDC Bled School of Management, Bled, Slovenia, 08–09 November 2001.

Kohn, A., 1999, *Punished by rewards: The trouble with gold stars, incentive plans, A's, praise and other bribes*, Houghton Mifflin, New York.

Kolb, D.A., & Yeganeh, B., 2011, 'Deliberate experiential learning: Mastering the art from learning from experience', *ORBH Working paper case, Western Reserve University*, viewed 24 April 2012, from http://learningfromexperience.com/research-library/deliberate-experiential-learning/

Kruger, C.J. & Johnson, R.D., 2011, 'Is there a correlation between knowledge management maturity and organisational performance?', *The Journal of Information and Knowledge Management Systems* 41(3), 265–295.

MultiChoice, 2010, *About MultiChoice*, viewed 17 February 2011, from http://www.multichoice.co.za

Murphy, S., 2008, 'Critical success factors for communities of practice at MultiChoice', Masters dissertation, Gordon Institute of Business Science, University of Pretoria, South Africa.

Ngosi, T., Helfert, M. & Braganza, A., 2011, 'Increasing knowledge management maturity in organisations: A capabilities-driven model', *Proceedings of the 3rd European Conference on Intellectual Capital*, University of Nicosia, Cyprus, 18–19 April 2011.

Nickols, F., 2003, *Communities of practice: A start-up kit*, viewed 17 February, from http://www.nickols.us/CoPRoles.pdf

Pearlson, K. & Saunders, C., 2006, *Managing and using information systems*, John Wiley & Sons, New Jersey.

Pink, D.H., 2010, *Drive: The surprising truth about what motivates us*, Canongate, Edinburgh.

Sandrock, J., 2008, *The art of managing knowledge*, Corpnet, Johannesburg.

Senge, P., 1990, *The fifth discipline: The art and practice of the learning organisation*, Doubleday, New York.

Smith, P.A.C., 2011, 'Elements of organisational sustainability', *The Learning Organisation* 18(1), 5–9. http://dx.doi.org/10.1108/09696471111095957

Snyman, M.M.M. & Kruger, C.J., 2005, 'Formulation of a Strategic Knowledge Management Maturity Model', *Journal of Knowledge Management* 8(1), 5–10 http://dx.doi.org/10.1108/13673270410523871

Stafford, C. & Mearns, M., 2009, 'What happens when organisations embrace social networking? Knowledge sharing at a multinational business solutions corporation', *South African Journal of Information Management* 11(4), viewed 14 June 2010, from http://www.sajim.co.za

Stevenson, D., 1995, *Intellectual Capital and EA*, viewed 14 June 2010, from http://www.users.iafrica.com

Sullivan, P., 2000, *Profiting from intellectual capital: Extracting value from innovation*, Wiley, New York.

Sveiby, K.E., 1997, *The new organisational wealth*, Berett-koehler, San Francisco.

Wenger, E., 2007, *Communities of practise leaning as a social system*, viewed 14 June 2010, from http://www.co.i.l.com/coil/knowledge-garden/cop/lss.shtml

Wilson, P.N., 2011, 'Shared learning in and from transformational development programs', *Transformation: An International Journal of Holistic Mission Studies*, 28(2), 103–113.

Zhou, A.Z. & Fink, D., 2003, 'The intellectual capital web: A systematic linking of intellectual capital and knowledge management', *Journal of Intellectual Capital* 4(1), 34–38. http://dx.doi.org/10.1108/14691930310455379

12

The use of online technologies in the small church

Authors:
Joel Arthur[1]
Chris Rensleigh[1]

Affiliations:
[1]Department of
Information and Knowledge
Management, University of
Johannesburg, South Africa

Correspondence to:
Joel Arthur

Email:
jarthur@uj.ac.za

Postal address:
PO Box 524, Auckland Park
2006, South Africa

Background: The lack of consideration of the developmental opportunities that online technologies offer small churches in the 21st century forms the foundation of this research article. This article reports on a master's study which seeks to investigate whether small churches are aware of the opportunities generated by the use of online technologies.

Objectives: This study was done to identify the current online technology usage and seeks to create awareness as to how these technologies are impacting congregation members in the small church environment.

Method: A quantitative study was conducted in the form of a survey of four small churches in the Johannesburg metropolitan area to identify the current usage and the potential impact online technologies could have upon the small churches.

Results: The study indicated that online technologies have a large role to play in the development of small churches and have the ability to increase the involvement of members in church programmes.

Conclusion: It is clear that online technologies offer substantial benefits. Small churches should incorporate the opportunities associated with online technologies in their strategic plans.

Introduction

Pastor Warren at a church ministry conference:

> Every time there is an advance in technology, The Kingdom advances. ... Technology has a huge impact on our mission ... not the 'what' of our mission, but the 'how'. ... Technology is the frontline of evangelism. (Nicholau 2010)

Can small churches sit on the fence when it comes to employing the services of Web technology? The challenge that small churches face is to decide which direction will be taken when looking at Web technology. Marcotte (2010) and Larson (2000) confirm religious environments are not utilising the Web and Internet to their full potential. Partnership for 21st Century Skills (2009) affirm Wilson's (2000) stance that small organisations should seek to use technological advancements to assist the churches to move into the 21st century.

The dramatic increase in Internet access in recent years, due to the lower prices of processing power, is availing the Web to just about anyone (Niemand & Rensleigh 2003). Information Communication Technologies (ICT) bring people with common interests and ideas together via the Web without having them having to ever meet face to face (Niemand & Rensleigh 2003). Stephenson (2006) discusses the Web's influence on the church and further emphasises how the church should unleash its Internet ministry and seek to Web empower itself.

The inadequacy in understanding the developments and challenges online technologies place upon small churches in the 21st century defines the background to this research article, as it investigates the Internet and the Web and how it can influence the small church environment. Small churches have similar information needs to their larger counterparts; however, they find themselves in a disadvantaged information position in terms of their finances and expertise.

From the research done by Thumma and Travis (2007) it is evident that larger churches are utilising online technologies to a large extent; however, this is not the case for the smaller churches.

This article seeks to investigate this issue and give direction to small churches who find themselves vacillating on the pendulum of indecision when reviewing the use of online technologies in the church. Valdez (2012) identifies how these technologies impact the youth and modern society. Some of the findings from this study were presented at conferences (Arthur & Rensleigh 2012, 2013). The underlying purpose for this research was to identify the current and potential usage of the Internet and the Web within the small church environment. In addition, the study identified respondents' views on their current usage of the Web regarding content they access and would like to have access to and how a church Web presence would potentially influence the respondents' view of their future involvement in the church.

Defining the small church

Fish (2006) defines a small church as constituting a membership between 1 and 500 members; a medium church encompasses a membership of between 501 and 1000 members and a large church can be demarcated by a membership larger than 1000 members (see Figure 1).

The definition was created using the following three variables to classify the church size:

- The physical size of the church, taking into consideration the church building and structure. The capacity of the building, in most cases, defines how many people can attend a church service in one sitting. Thus, in some churches, because there are too many people attending the church, the need arises to organise a second or third service.
- Secondly, the number of full-time members plays a large role in the classification of the church size. It is safe to conclude that the larger the number of members in the church, the bigger the size of the church. The opposite is true as well: the smaller the number of members on the church register the smaller the church.
- The third variable is the financial income of the church, which in most churches is one of the most defining factors in the size of the church. The inconsistency that is found when linking the membership to the financial income of the church is that the size of the church membership does not necessarily indicate the financial income of the church.

The different church sizes have different needs, financially, strategically and in terms of information. Therefore, one needs to identify the various technologies that can assist in meeting these needs. Stamoulis (2010) indicates that an online presence is not always effective; however, there are ways in which creating a more effective site can aid an organisation in becoming more operative.

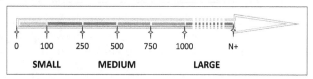

FIGURE 1: A generic congregation size scale.
Source: Adapted from Fish, T., 2006, *Church size*, viewed 30 October 2013, from http://www.timothyfish.net/Articles/Article.asp?ID=17

Defining online technologies

The Internet forms the foundation upon which systems such as the World Wide Web run (Haynal 2013). The World Wide Web consortium (W3C 2013) defines the World Wide Web or the Web as 'the universe of network-accessible information, an embodiment of human knowledge'. The Web creates an online environment where the church community can have access to valuable information such as the pastor's notes, calendar activities and weekly devotions, all of which encourage the members to be more involved within the church. Online technologies encourage the sharing of human knowledge and teaching of the biblical word.

These technologies give access to a variety of information resources. On the Web it is evident that there are many applications that people would find themselves making use of. These include email, blogs, forums, podcasts, polls, wikis and online social networks.

There are many online social networking websites that can be utilised. The responsibility of monitoring the church online community belongs to the moderators to help maintain an acceptable form of communication. It is essential that rules and regulations are formulated to assist in governing the communication inside the online community. One such example is 'the respect of others' which must be adhered to by all users. An effective method to restrict visitors from posting unsolicited content is to ensure that they first register on the church website by using a verifiable email address.

Emails, instant messaging (IM) and short messaging systems (SMS) are all part of the various forms of communication in the online environment. Whilst investigating different forms of communication and online technologies, it is imperative to take note of the use of mobile devices. Cellular devices allow people to have access to a mobile online environment.

Research approach and methodology

The research approach undertaken for this study is categorised under Pasteur's quadrant of Stokes's (1997) research classification quadrants. An in-depth literature review was used to introduce the theoretical foundation of the research problem. A quantitative research approach was used in the form of questionnaire survey, all taking place amongst the congregant members in small churches within the Johannesburg metropolitan area. Quantitative research was selected as it is able to address the research question more appropriately and it was able to address the resource constraints.

The literature study provided the background knowledge from which the questionnaire was developed. The questionnaire was used to assess the views, approaches and practices and usage of online technologies within the small church environment. Convenience sampling was used for this, surveying 150 respondents from four small churches within the southern suburbs of Johannesburg. Members from all age groups participated in the study.

Empirical findings

The questionnaire consisted of four sections: church biographical information, online activities, religious information requirements and church online community needs. Some of the responses are discussed below.

Section A: Church biographical information

Section A concentrates on the biographical information within the sample group. The distribution in the age category within the churches allowed for an inclusive view based on age groups. The largest grouping (27%) was that of the respondents under the age of 20, whilst the smallest portion (12%) of respondents can be classified as the young adults in the age bracket between 21 and 30 years of age (see Figure 2). It is important to understand the age distribution within the church and then seek to identify the online need that can be met.

The results of Question 2, which dealt with gender, revealed that 39% of the respondents were male and 61% female. Figure 3 shows a cross-tabulation between the questionnaire variables of age and gender. The survey indicated that there are more women than men in all the age categories with the exception of those above the age of 60. A clear curve shape is visible, identifying a good spread in the age distribution for both the women and the men who took part in the research.

When seeking to develop an online environment it is important to identify the target audience as well as who within the target audience will be making most use of the online technologies.

Section B: Online activities

This section of the questionnaire focused on aspects such as the respondents' choice of Web access.

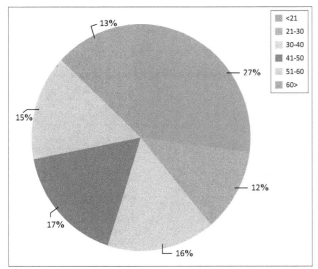

FIGURE 2: Age distribution of respondents.

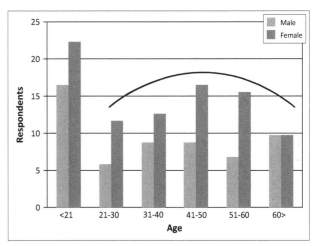

FIGURE 3: Cross-tabulation between age and gender.

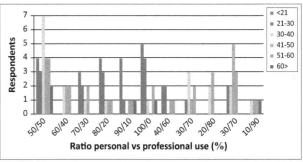

FIGURE 4: Web usage in terms of personal verses professional activities.

Figure 4 shows the respondents' use of the Internet and Web for their personal (e.g. interacting with friends) versus professional (business networking and transactions) interactions. It is clear that the younger respondents use the Web more for personal than professional use. The 31–50 year group on the other hand shows the direct opposite, with a propensity towards less personal and more professional use.

It is interesting to note that the highest peak is that of 50% personal versus 50% professional use in the age category of 31–40. This can be due to the fact that a large group of the working class falls into this age bracket; thus, they will be using the Web for business purposes as well for personal use. This can also be linked to those in the age bracket 41–50; however, this age group peaks at a point where the usage is primarily for professional (90%) rather than personal (10%) activities. As can be expected, the under 20 age group uses the Web more for personal rather than business use as the largest number of respondents use the Web (100%) for personal reasons. This is also noticeable in the age bracket 21–30 where the Web is used largely (100%) for personal rather than professional activities. An interesting point to note is that of those over the age of 60. Contrary to popular belief, this group of individuals is using technology and the Web for personal and professional use.

From Figure 5, a cross-tabulation between gender and the view of the Web, it is clear that the largest number of female

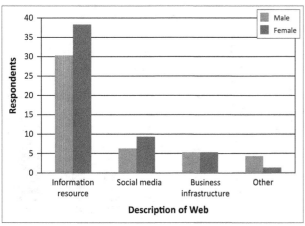

FIGURE 5: Cross-tabulation between gender and view of the Web.

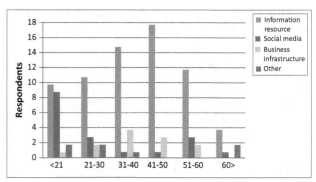

FIGURE 6: Cross-tabulation between age and view of the Web.

respondents indicated that they view the Web primarily as an information resource. There are an equal number of men and women who view the Web as a business infrastructure. It is important to note that a large portion of the respondents view the Web as an information resource. Churches seeking to utilise the online environment should enquire as to what information is seen to be valuable to the members, taking notice as to whom the information will impact the most.

Figure 6 is a cross-tabulation that identifies the different age groups' view of the Web as an information resource, social media portal or business infrastructure tool. This is interesting when seeking to identify ways to develop the Web technologies in the future. From the figure, the highest perception of the Web is as an information resource.

The age bracket 41–50 is the group with the most respondents who view the Web as an information resource. The only other high number of respondents is in the age group under the age of 21, who view the Web as a social media tool. From the results depicted, this age bracket would be ideal to develop an online social media group to keep them up to date with current and future happenings within the church.

Few respondents in the age categories of 21 to the oldest age group of 60 understand the Web as a social media tool. In terms of those who view the Web as a business infrastructure it makes sense that there is a rise from the younger age groups to the middle age groups and then a drop as respondents enter the age of retirement. The highest numbers of respondents who see the Web as a business infrastructure fall into the age bracket between 31 and 40. This makes sense due to people that age bracket being involved in the business environment at work. Due to many church members seeing the Web as an information resource first, it is ideal to first develop an online presence that will provide valuable information to its members before developing online social networks.

In Figure 7 is the cross-tabulation between age and the respondents' ability to adapt to new technology. As expected

the group under the age of 21 find it easy to adapt to, and develop skills when using, new technologies. The opposite is true for those over the age of 60, as they are hesitant to use new technology and seldom move away from their existing technology. In the age category 51–60 the highest number of respondents indicated that they convert gradually to new technology. In the age bracket 21–30 the highest number of respondents indicated they easily acquire the skills to use new equipment. The ability of the younger age groups to adapt to newer technologies is evident. This enforces the idea that as the church grows older, the current younger generations will be much more settled in an online friendly environment.

The cross-tabulation in Figure 8 depicts the respondents' gender compared to the age of their cellular devices. Eight men and 21 women do not own a cellular phone. The largest group, comprising 26 men and 26 women, have cellular phones that are no older than one year. When seeking to gather information in a push or pull manner, it can be best done via cellular devices (Fasolo et al. 2006). It is worth noting that most respondents have access to mobile technologies that allow them to access the Web.

In Figure 9 is a depiction of the cross-tabulation between age and respondents' willingness to access the church website from their cellular devices. In the age category under 21, 88%

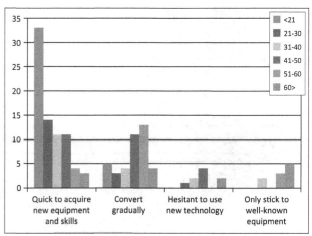

FIGURE 7: Age of respondents and ability to adapt to new technology.

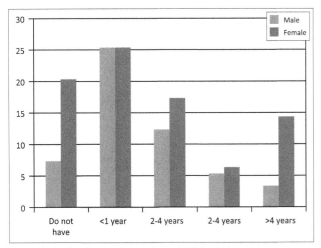

FIGURE 8: Gender of respondents and age of cellular devices.

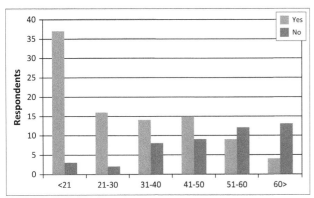

FIGURE 9: Age of respondents and willingness to access the church website via cellular devices.

of respondents indicated they indeed would use their cellular phones to access the church website and only 12% indicated they would not. In the age group 21–30, 86% respondents revealed they would use their cellular phones to access the church website whilst 14% indicated they would not. Only in the age categories over 50 did respondents indicate the opposite. Statistics reveal that 68% of respondents would prefer not to use their cellular phones to access the church website. These churches should seek to invest in developing a website that is designed to be operational on a cellular device. In all age categories, there were respondents who indicated they would use their cellular phones to access the church website.

To the question 'Do you think making use of online social networking can enhance your involvement in the church activities?', 62% of the respondents indicated 'Yes'. The respondents indicated their willingness to make use of their church's online presence, should it have one: 82% to download information, 74% to upload information onto the church website and 38% to utilise the social networking. In addition, 41% of the respondents would make use of other online tools such as Mxit and Blackberry messenger (BBM) applications to share information within the church (see Figure 10).

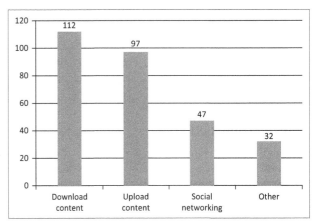

FIGURE 10: Utilisation of the church online presence.

It is worth taking note that the majority of the respondents indicated that the presence of such online technologies would enhance their involvement in the church, as it will help to keep them updated as to what is happening within the church. The correct use of online technologies in the small environment will have a positive impact on member participation.

Conclusion

Based on the research conducted for this study it is evident that these small churches currently do not effectively utilise online technologies. Their current usage of online technologies is minimal or none at all. The findings reveal that as the churches' timeline moves forward, they cannot afford not to use online technologies. The younger generations find technology to be a necessity and do not find it in any way difficult to use. Online technologies are an accepted part of the younger generational culture and so small churches need to identify the potential these technologies have currently and also will have in the future. The church leadership need to have foresight and look as to how they will best use online technology in the church.

It is evident that by using online technologies, an environment for people to stay up to date and informed of the happenings of the church will be created. In addition, it will improve the involvement of the congregation members in the church functions. When small churches look to increase involvement of church members, it is important that they find the best practices that work for the church and use the appropriate online technologies.

Online mobile technologies make people accessible any time of day, allowing the church to share and gather information at ease. These online mobile technologies are ideal when the church seeks to stay in touch with their congregation members.

In the future, churches need to identify the trends in terms of information needs and social media needs of the congregation members and to find ways to share appropriate information at convenient times with their members.

Acknowledgements

Competing interests

The authors declare that they have no financial or personal relationship(s) that may have inappropriately influenced them in writing this article.

Authors' contributions

J.A. (University of Johannesburg) and C.R. (University of Johannesburg) contributed equally to the writing of this article.

References

Arthur, J. & Rensleigh, C., 2012, 'Augmenting information dissemination in the small church environment via the Web and related technologies', paper presented at the 14th annual Conference on WWW Applications, Durban, South Africa, 07–09 November 2012.

Arthur, J. & Rensleigh, C., 2013, 'Internet and Web: The impact on the small church environment', paper presented at the 13th annual Information and Knowledge Management Conference, Johannesburg, South Africa, 02 December 2013.

Fasolo, E., Prehofer, C., Rossi, M., Wei, Q., Widmer, J., Zanella, A. *et al.*, 2006, 'Challenges and new approaches for efficient data gathering and dissemination in pervasive wireless via networks, in *InterSense '06: Proceedings of the first international conference on integrated internet ad hoc and sensor networks*, p. 25, viewed 11 June 2014, from http://icapeople.epfl.ch/widmer/files/Fasolo2006Inter Sense.pdf

Fish, T., 2006, *Church size*, viewed 30 October 2013, from http://www.timothyfish.net/Articles/Article.asp?ID=17

Haynal, R., 2013, *Internet: The big picture*, viewed 01 November 2013, from http://navigators.com/internet_achitecture.html

Larson, E., 2000, *Wired churches, wired temples: Taking congregations and missions into cyberspace*, viewed 15 December 2013, from http://www.pewinternet.org/report_display.asp?r=28

Marcotte, R.D., 2010, *Editorial New virtual frontiers: Religion and spirituality in cyberspace*, viewed 11 June 2014, from file:///C:/Users/jarthur/Downloads/10060-28717-1-PB.pdf

Nicholau, N.B., 2010, *Church management software*, viewed 15 July 2011, from http://www;mbsinc.com/articles/doc_view/162annual_church_a-donor_management_software_2011_article

Niemand, C. & Rensleigh, C., 2003, 'Convergence of on-line community technologies: Internet relay chat (IRC) and peer-to-peer (P2P) file sharing', *South African Journal of Information Management* 5(3), 11 pages.

Partnership for 21st Century Skills, 2009, *Professional development: A 21st century skills implementation guide*, viewed 11 June 2014, from http://www.p21.org/storage/documents/p21-stateimp_professional_development.pdf

Stamoulis, N., 2010, *Ways to compete online effectively*, viewed 30 October 2013, from http://www.searchengineoptimizationjournal.com/2011/03/14/compete-online/

Stephenson, M.M., 2006, *Web empower your church*, Adington Press, Nashville.

Stokes, D.E., 1997, *Pasteur's quadrant: basic science and technological innovation*, Brookings Institute Press, Washington, DC.

Thumma, S. & Travis, D., 2007, *Beyond megachurch myths*, Josey-Bass, San Francisco.

Valdez, A., 2012, *The disadvantages of modern technology among the youth*, viewed 30 October 2013, from http://www.ehow.com/ist_7229326_disadvantages-modern-technology-among-youth.html

W3C, 2013, *W3C*, viewed 30 October 2013, from http://www.w3.org/

Wilson, W.P., 2000, *The Internet church*, Word Pub, Nashville.

13

A knowledge sharing framework in the South African public sector

Author:
Peter L. Mkhize[1]

Affiliation:
[1]School of Computing,
University of South Africa,
South Africa

Correspondence to:
Peter Mkhize

Email:
mkhizpl@unisa.ac.za

Postal address:
PO Box 392, UNISA 0003,
Pretoria, South Africa

In the knowledge economy, organisations are shifting their investment focus to intellectual capital in order to sustain a competitive advantage in the global marketplace. Organisational survival is increasingly dependent on the organisation's ability to create and distribute knowledge that contributes to the improvement of performance. The purpose of this article is to evaluate individual knowledge-acquisition and sharing practices in the South African public sector. I applied the techniques of grounded theory analysis to extract themes from data that could provide insight into the knowledge sharing that takes place in the South African public sector. Findings revealed that the informal sharing of knowledge takes place in discussion forums within communities of practice through web-based, socially orientated platforms. These communities of practice are widespread throughout the public sector and are established with the purpose of soliciting expert knowledge from those who have been using open-source software successfully.

Introduction

Innovation and change in an organisation bring about a need to upskill employees in order to keep up with new organisational demands. In the knowledge economy, efficiency and effectiveness are dependent on the organisation's ability to adapt to rapid technological changes. According to Acton and Golden (2003), organisations need to focus on improving their knowledge-acquisition strategy because skills and knowledge become obsolete quickly.

Durst and Wilhelm (2012) assert that knowledge is increasingly becoming a crucial asset for organisations – unlike in the industrial age, where machinery was the most important asset. According to Pacharapha (2012), knowledge resides with individuals in the organisation and becomes an instrument for process improvement whereby processes become more efficient and effective. Knowledge kept in the individual's mind does not contribute to organisational success if it is not shared by other employees within the organisation. In this article, the researcher investigates some of the knowledge sharing practices in the South African public sector.

Problem statement

Existing skills-training mechanisms are either not used optimally or are failing altogether (Statistics South Africa 2010). Pacharapha (2012) suggests that some individuals in the workforce possess knowledge which could be useful in the improvement of service delivery. Skills transfer from the individuals who have such skills to other employees organisation-wide entails a challenge. Individuals' knowledge does not help the public sector because it could be lost if such individuals leave the organisation through death, retirement or resignation.

The diffusion of knowledge through social media is growing fast in South Africa and other African countries (World Wide Worx 2012). In South Africa, many people have widely adopted social media for social interaction. World Wide Worx (2014) reports show that social media and instant messaging usage has grown exponentially in South Africa, mentioning one of the fastest growing mobile applications such as WhatsApp. Its usage is expected to grow to 63% amongst adults within a year from the date of the report. Despite diffusion through social media, which enables instant collaboration at a minimal cost, social media are not used to facilitate knowledge sharing in the workplace. In this study, the researchers investigate the potential application of social media to share knowledge in the workplace with a specific focus on the biggest employer in the country – the public sector.

Knowledge sharing

According to Andreeva and Kianto (2012), organisations in the global knowledge economy depend on the ability to acquire and share knowledge in order to gain a competitive advantage. In an organisation, there could be individuals who possess valuable knowledge, but individual knowledge is not a competitive advantage for the organisation if it is not shared with other relevant stakeholders (Crane 2012). According to Alavi and Leidner (1999), knowledge sharing enables an entire organisation to gain competitive knowledge and improve its productivity.

Knowledge transfer takes place between individuals and teams (Durst & Wilhem 2012). It could be technical knowledge that is important for functional departments (Mueller 2012). It is imperative to note the fact that every bit of knowledge that could improve business performance is critical, whether it resides within individuals' minds or is shared by teams in departments (Schuima 2012).

Organisations that wish to facilitate knowledge sharing between individuals and teams must be cognisant of the type of knowledge involved. Polanyi (1966) distinguishes between two types of knowledge. The first type is tacit knowledge, characterised by difficulty to articulate and codify. Tacit knowledge is usually acquired through apprenticeship and extended time with experts. Moreover, this type of knowledge is key to the development of competitive advantage as competitors would usually struggle to cope (Nonaka, Von Krogh & Voelpel 2006). Conversely, explicit knowledge, Polanyi's second type of knowledge, is easy to codify and to express in an understandable format. According to Nonaka (1994), this type of knowledge can be expressed through traditional learning methods. It will then be useful to discuss knowledge conversion in the following section by discussing the manipulation of tacit and explicit knowledge.

Knowledge conversion

Nonaka (1994) proposed socialisation, externalisation, combination and internalisation (SECI) as modes of knowledge conversion. These modes are important for organisations that intend to extend their competitive advantage by ensuring that tacit knowledge in the minds of a few is shared within the organisation. Knowledge conversion is important to enable knowledge creation, sharing and retention, especially in the economic sectors that are experiencing a brain drain (Kraak 2004). It is then important to heed Jarrar's (2002) warning that intellectual capital is replacing finance, commodities and natural resources in order to keep up with the rapidly evolving global knowledge economy.

It is important to note that knowledge conversion is also critical as an enabler of dissemination of knowledge within the organisation in order to ensure that tacit knowledge, which resides in the minds of individual employees, can be transferred throughout the organisation (Nonaka & Takeuchi 1995). In line with the SECI modes of knowledge conversion, the public sector needs to create an environment that enables interplay between individuals in the organisations, sharing tacit knowledge through mechanisms such as observation and imitation (Lottering & Dick 2012). According to Martin and Martin (2011), sharing tacit knowledge requires a high level of socialisation that could also involve personal experience and close physical proximity while work is being

done. It may even imply building and managing emotional relationships.

Nonaka and Takeuchi (1995) also argue that tacit knowledge can be converted into explicit knowledge through iterative social interaction, and explicit knowledge can be transferred to others in the organisation through a social medium. Explicit knowledge is articulative and can be transferred by electronic media. Meetings and traditional workshops can be used to reconfigure and reconceptualise existing knowledge in the combination mode (Chatti 2012). Externalisation enables articulation of tacit knowledge to explicit knowledge through social interaction (Sowe, Stamelos & Angelis 2008) where individuals involved in the creation of knowledge have to spend extensive amounts of time engaging in mutual interaction (Silva *et al.* 2012). Internalisation, however, relates converting explicit knowledge into tacit knowledge (Wang, Yang & Chou 2008). According to Jeon, Kim and Koh (2011), knowledge sharing initiatives should be organised into communities of practice to create a space where individuals with common interests in the subject matter can interact.

Communities of practice

Balcaen and Hirtz (2007) argue that online-based knowledge sharing promotes critical thinking. Employees participating in online communities have the advantage of engaging the subject of interest critically, especially when they are encouraged to learn independently and work interdependently because they bound by a social contract. Kanuka and Garrison (2004) claim that collaborative, yet reflective, learning has a great potential for facilitating critical thinking, which, in turn, would enable a learning organisation to facilitate the transfer and creation of skills and knowledge. Critical thinking is encouraged within communities of practice as major players in the industry would be able to share insight with employees who also aspire to be experts in their field of interest (Balcaen & Hirtz 2007).

Within a community of practice, knowledge is socially constructed by the group of participants, who weigh each contribution in order to add value to the discussion (Salmon 2002). Each participant in the community of practice is free to make a contribution towards a solution to the problem or to a subject of concern amongst members of the community. Contributors to the discussion and debate become engaged in the debate until consensus is reached, and the agreed solution remains tentative until a better solution comes along (Wenger & Snyder 2000). The facilitator has to be there to ensure that the discussions are not diverted towards the wrong direction and to redirect the discussions, if necessary (Levinsen 2006). In order to realise the success of a community of practice, the sponsor of an online community takes into account participants' demographic characteristics such as culture and economic background. This provides insight into participants' inclinations and preferences so that they can customise knowledge sharing in order to achieve success. Knowledge of participants' demographics can help with initiating collaborative engagement where every member of the community can equally contribute.

Collaborative engagement

Zhu, Valke and Schellens (2009) argue that collaborative engagement is shaped and guided by the fundamentals of the social constructivist paradigm. In this paradigm, collaborative engagement enables the co-creation of knowledge by active participants as they explore the concept of interest (Glover, Hardaker & Xu 2004). Collaborative engagement is carried out through social interaction at group level, based on interdependence between members of the group (Doolan 2013). In the collaborative engagement process, it is imperative that collaborators understand the rules of engagement and the expected outcomes of the process (Bogenrieder & Van Baalen 2007).

According to Glover *et al.* (2004), collaborators are convened for a specific goal, which could be planned or unplanned. It is further mentioned that, in the collaboration process, multiple ideas are presented and explored to create a broader mental model of the concept. This is achieved through mutual engagement of the participant in a coordinated effort (Hudson 2003).

The coordinated effort to combine the knowledge and competencies of a group of people enables concept development. This happens on the condition that individuals in a group engage mutually to achieve a specific goal, and everyone is equally responsible for the activities of creating and sharing knowledge (Doolan 2011). All the participants should understand that they are responsible for the creation and dissemination of knowledge to the entire community of practice.

In an attempt to derive a solution, even partly, to the above research problem, I tried to gain insight from the literature into the importance of knowledge sharing. I also looked at models used to facilitate knowledge sharing within the organisation and between organisations. From the literature, I came to understand the role of collaboration in enabling knowledge sharing within communities of practice. In light of the fact that collaboration thrives on socially orientated media, I went on to conduct empirical research in order better to understand the environment in which public sector employees practise knowledge sharing. I also wanted better to understand the application of social media in facilitating knowledge sharing even if it is not formally institutionalised.

Research questions

In order to achieve the aim of this study, I used the following research questions to provide a guidepost for the subsequent research process:

- What are the key issues that have to be considered in the facilitation of knowledge sharing in the South African public sector?

- How is social media used in the public sector's knowledge sharing practice?
- How do these key constructs interrelate in the design of a knowledge sharing mechanism in the South African public sector?

Research methodology and data analysis

I chose a qualitative approach within the social constructivist paradigm so that I could gain in-depth understanding of the knowledge practice in the workplace. This is in line with the aim to co-create or co-develop a model with the research participants that could provide a solution to some aspects of the problem. Due to the scarcity of literature and theories that specifically address online knowledge sharing in the South African context, I applied the method of grounded theory analysis within a case-study design (Glaser & Strauss 1967).

The unit of analysis is service departments that are actively involved in knowledge sharing practices in the public sector. Even though knowledge sharing practices were not formally institutionalised at the time of collecting data, there were pockets of communities of practice that shared ideas informally, using social media platforms such as blogs and group tweets. A theoretical sample was used to ensure that each participant enrolled for this study has the knowledge required to answer research questions. This was achieved with the help of the gatekeeper who works in the public sector. Sampling also involved elements of the snowballing technique as participants identified each other and then referred the researcher to those they knew had the knowledge required to answer the research questions. A combination of theoretical and snowball sampling processes resulted in the enrolment of 11 participants from the Department of Public Administration. These participants are deployed as training agents in various service departments involved in software migration or are people who required specific knowledge training. Some of the interviews had more than one participant per session, which resulted in seven interview transcripts and policy documents that were used for analysis.

The concept of grounded theory and some of its techniques were used as a framework with which to conduct this research. According to Charmaz (2006), the principles of grounded theory are not prescriptive but provide guidelines for the detailed analysis of qualitative data and the generation of theory. In applying grounded theory, I conducted data collection and analysis concurrently because subsequent interview probing is dependent on the analysis results from the previous interview (Strauss & Corbin 1997).

I developed a case-study protocol, including an interview schedule based on the research questions of the study (Remenyi & Williams 1998). Questions in the interview schedule could be refined from one interview to another as I became more theoretically sensitive (McCallin 2003; McGhee, Marland & Atkinson 2007; Strauss & Corbin 1997). I then applied theoretical sampling to find prospective participants who were more likely to give further information or clarity to the questions which might not have been answered by the initial sample (McCallin 2003). All interviews were transcribed by a qualified transcriber and then uploaded into the qualitative data analysis software, ATLAS.ti.

The techniques of grounded theory analysis were applied by conducting open coding to identify codes as they emerged from data. Codes were extracted from each interview transcript, each representing an attached quotation. A bracketing technique was also used to suppress the researcher's preconceived ideas about the researched subject in the coding process (McGhee *et al.* 2007). Secondly, axial coding was performed in order to categorise emergent codes into families of codes in Atlas. Ti. I then formulated contextual relationships between codes using a relationship network. At this stage of the analysis, I conducted subsequent interviews with new categories in mind. This process was repeated until data saturation was reached. The final stage of analysis was selective coding, which enabled me to formulate conceptual relationship networks between code families in order to create a storyline.

In the discussion of the findings below, I present quotations from transcripts as evidence. In line with Creswell (2007), quotations are presented verbatim in order to honour participants' voices. Some of the quotations may contain grammar errors because they are presented as they were uttered by the participant. In addition to quotations that are used as evidence, I present relationship diagrams that represent a network of codes extracted during the open coding stage.

Discussion of findings

In this section, I present results of the grounded theory analysis by providing a code of networks, depicting relationships with a specific theme. The analysis entails direct quotation from the interview transcripts and the discussions. The networks were formed in the axial coding phase of the analysis. Every code in the network was linked to a quotation. The numbers in each code depict the groundedness of the code and the relationships with other codes in the hermeneutic unit.

Social technology infusion in the public sector

According to my observation, collaborative engagement in the public sector takes place in discussion forums which are based on social technology. In line with Rogers (1995), any technology-enabled initiatives should be introduced with technology-infusion concerns in mind.

Participant 1 revealed that most South African (SA) government departments are engulfed by infrastructural deficiencies. Thus, knowledge sharing practices should be designed to be carried out on a technology platform that is compatible and that could optimally exploit available computing resources. Participant 1 asserts that some departments are trying hard to ensure that the technology resources that are available are used to optimal levels.

> **P1:** 'They get a command they will do this, where you sit about 5 minutes for a screen in the Defence Force you will wait for that screen to come down but with the SAPS that's not the situation so that screen not up for your screen for 15 seconds, they say this useless go away and the same with other students outside your infrastructure is a key constraint'.

> **P6:** 'People resist certain technology because it brings in with it a new strange environment that is not even functioning properly. If you want to introduce people into something new entice them with something good, not too different to what they a familiar with'.

Participant 1 also asserted that infusing technology into the knowledge sharing process could be made easy by introducing

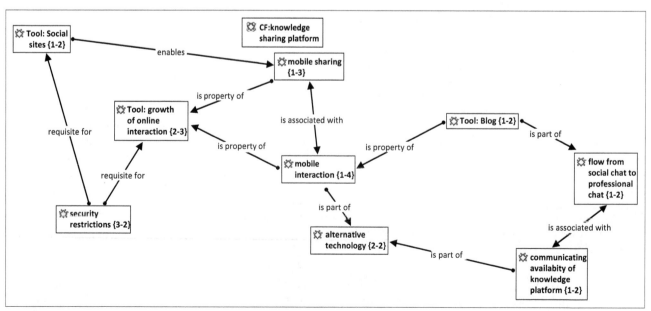

FIGURE 1: Knowledge sharing platform.

it as a social activity. This can be achieved by incorporating social computing concepts during the introduction of technology in the knowledge sharing process. Many social networks such as blogs, Wikis, Facebook and Twitter have gained popularity in many sectors, such as education, and in other private-sector workplaces (World Wide Worx 2012).

Participant 4 argued that social networks should be used as an introductory strategy in the public sector as many employees are already familiar with and using social networks. He also argued that people make meaningful contributions in the social space with respect to social issues. The same principle can be extrapolated to the knowledge sharing environment. Participant 4 also believed that social networks can be used for continuous learning in the workplace where employees can constantly explore new ideas.

> P4: 'It's not, you can pinpoint it down as one little tool, it's actually a migration from … networks where 1 person contributes to the content through technology making it available and interactive so that lots of people can contribute to that, people they create their own content and that what Web 2.0 … is, so with this collaboration thing each one of these tools wiki has got certain pros and cons and set application as blog and set applications as social networking so I think what we've seen in the market … it's got social networking, it's got micro blogging, it's got blogs, it's got Wikis, it's got RSSP's, it's got …, it's got everything, so but on the Internet you could get that is just a blogging tool, it's just wiki tool, … what's a business problem you want to solve, if you know what a problem is what a problem you want to solve …'

Social networks are important in facilitating an informal knowledge sharing process. Participant 2 suggested that some artificial intelligence should be built into knowledge sharing platforms such as Wiki and blogs to ensure that the correct content is directed to the appropriate employee.

Collaboration in a social space should not be confined to desktop-computer technology but should be extended to mobile technology and other forms of ICT. Therefore, content should be adaptive to different technology platforms such as cellular phones.

> P1: 'Adaptation, we need to … for instance basic one of the ideas being thrown around is M-learning in other words your Mobile Learning, given the fact that the reach of the cell phone is +-90% so if you were to adopt to innovate or use mobile as an alternative or an enhancement to e-learning, that will definitely make a big difference, but trying to get +80% of South Africa to be connected that is more like a dream'.

> P5: 'M-learning … packages that are out there you know about Blackberry and any other phone that is there but firstly the move will be how many people have cell phones in SA for instance, MTN for instance they will say we've got 17.1 million subscribers'.

According to all participants, South Africa is ready to adopt social computing in the workplace. Participants advise that knowledge sharing should be creative. In this process, one should remain aware of the characteristics of the SA workforce such as socio-economic diversity. Such awareness would help in determining the technological platform that can be used for knowledge sharing purposes, and such platform should be accessible to every employee.

Collaborative engagement

Collaboration is gaining popularity in both business and academic institutions where collaborators who share resources or work on the same project can exchange information and ideas in order to co-create solutions to eminent problems and to create knowledge. The sharing of information and ideas could be an interaction between individuals within a community of practice or with individuals from outside of the

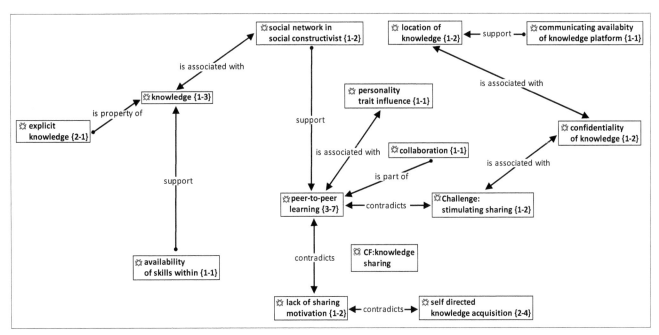

FIGURE 2: Network showing collaborative engagement in the South African public sector.

community (Mkhize, Huisman & Lubbe 2011). Figure 2 shows the network of codes that represent activities involved in the development of collaborative experience in the public sector. Some collaboration is informal and some is well-coordinated, depending on the objectives and resources available to community participants (Allan & Lawless 2005).

Membership of the collaborative forum was by invitation to the qualifying prospective participants, who are expected to make a meaningful contribution to the community. An administrator made a judgement decision about who qualifies to be a participant and then allowed them to join the group that discusses a specific topic regarding a new open-source platform.

> P4: 'You might be able to invite external people but then you would qualify them, so in that government-wide collaboration we on the administrator, so I set it up I need to say who's in and who's out and then they would do the same with that'.

The collaboration group sometimes invited subject experts from other collaboration forums by going out of the official government discussion group to find people who may make a major contribution in the current issues of concern. The administrator would even go to the extent of scouting on the social networks to find bloggers who might be experts on a specific subject:

> P4: 'Say I was a local developer in SA I would do 1 of 2 things. I would either see if there's existing forums linked in specific groups that are discussing that specific topic, it is possible that those groups won't be focused enough or there might … but you've got specific needs, what I'll do then is I'll create my own group I'll choose a certain media like I would say I'm going on Facebook or I'm going on this, I would find something that's more like a super cool kind of personalities that use that, … I would find something that is suited to my community, having more technical or whatever and then I would start extending that network … the thinkers in that area and I would extend an invite to that somebody that writing a blog that's … or start talking to that network and say who are the real experts in open source migration'.

Inviting renowned experts in a certain field allowed the administrator to create a ripple effect by attracting the experts' followers into their discussion forum. Although collaborating groups would need outside experts' contributions to the discussions and debates on issues of concern, it is still important to maintain confidentiality:

> P4: 'Think it's just about the confidentiality of the information, say you are in government you typically want to control whoever joins cause you might discuss strategies, communication strategies, things that you want to first vet with different stakeholders before you bring them to the public so in that case you will firstly have the private network'.

As a result, administrators have to be careful in their selection of new members and ensure that confidential information is not openly discussed in the forums. This is to avoid exposure of government's strategies and operational plans.

Participant 5 suggested that a collaborative forum should apply the same model as was applied by early collaborators

in government but now with the guidance of an expert to facilitate engagement and debate about topical issues in open-source migration. Through engagement, collaborators would be able to deduce meaning from or come to agreement about new solutions, which could be an extension of existing knowledge. In setting up collaboration, instructional designers can explore the application of technology in facilitating online collaboration. Participant 4 pointed out that Moodle is an effective and efficient collaborative tool for the SITA collaboration group: 'Within Moodle there are some kinds of collaboration or that kind of functionality that you can use and we kinda put them into our project'.

Moodle is an open-source application that can be acquired free of charge. This means easy access and affordability for collaborators. Besides, Moodle incorporates even extended pedagogical features that can be used for the administration and management of the knowledge exchange process.

Instructional designers are facing the task of converting pure collaborative activities into a knowledge transfer mechanism and enabling an environment where knowledge transfer practice can be modelled around the existing collaborative instructional strategy. In doing so, it can ease tensions between management and employees regarding the use of social networks in the office because a formalised collaborative instructional strategy could be institutionalised and then form part of the institutional policy.

Learning by discovery within a community

Some of the participants quoted in the discussion above also mentioned or implied communities of practice (CoP). Figure 3 shows the CoP theme: I shall discuss a concept that seems to be prominent in the transcripts and which is directly related to communities of practice, namely learning by discovery.

Learning by discovery in a community starts with the creation of the community where learners or employees who share common interests converge to discuss critical issues on a specific topic. Participant 4, who administrates the collaboration forum for government collaboration groups, suggested that collaboration should be designed for free social platforms such as Google or any other Web2.0 platform where an instructional designer can create a group that can share text or video files.

The collaborative forum is secured because of the security and confidentiality requirement. Some of the information shared is sensitive in nature, which means that high security measures should take priority over functionality. However, free social networks can be used where security is not a sensitive issue:

> P4: 'Start to building that functionality into the tool so whether you in the design of the course or whether you want employees to interact you need to build the social media the social learning at stake as facilitating the process of learning either by using that functionality in the application you use such as Google or just signing up to any free collaboration

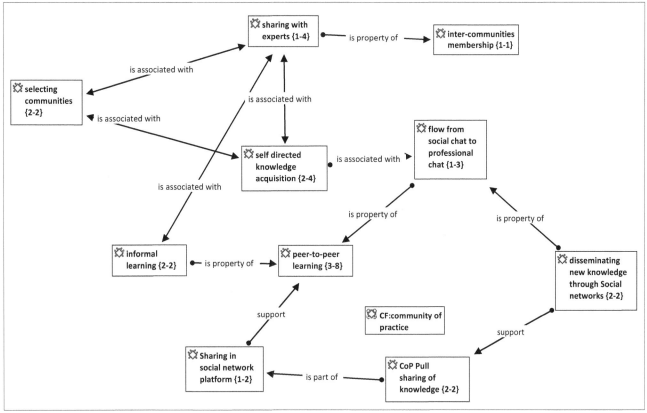

FIGURE 3: Network showing learning through discovery within communities.

tool, create a group then you collaborate so most of these tools they have a model where you can use those functionality for free and those functionalities you can connect with people … which is making sure that if you doing a course for the military then there's specific requirements around security confidentiality, so that's what SITA is doing in this project, we could use social networks or social tools that are on the Internet but because of that requirement we need to have something that can secure on our firewall and the access of control is very strict'.

Once the security requirements have been established in order to create parameters for membership in the collaboration forum, instructional designers have to consider an instructional strategy that is appropriate for the target audience. In line with the collaborative strategy for government's open-source training, a collaborative environment has to be created within a community of practice. Participant 5 thought that social networks represent the most effective platform for collaborative learning within a specialised group, called a community of practice. Interaction within the community can be standardised into specific time intervals, or openness and flexibility:

> **P5:** 'Community of practice would see people who share common interest in a particular field something, they will be able to seat and collaborate, discuss, move forward and look at the development, to me community those are groups … they seat every week or every month or people collaborate through that social platform they are all related and they'll say they also contribute to the management of knowledge and knowledge gathering that can be preserved'.

In these communities, members get to share their experiences and learn from those who have been through the learning curve. That way, members of the community would not have to repeat the same mistakes made by those who have become experts over the years. Less experienced collaborators in the community can learn best practices with regard to a specific trade from more experienced community members without going through trial and error. The sharing of information and knowledge enables all concerned to learn new skills to solve persisting problems:

> **P4:** 'Think the main thing about collaboration in government is the culture is pretty much … so everybody is busy with their own stuff, fighting their own battles and not knowing that another department has maybe kinda a step further in a particular area and they basically got a better solution, so collaboration for us is about creating the tool that can connect these people so that they can form groups, networks of interests and can become aware of other projects, other best practices, other people that have gone through the learning curve, that have got skills'.

A collaborative environment allows for the co-creation of knowledge, based on the collective and agreed interpretation of the studied phenomenon. As members of the community of practice engage one another in a collaborative environment, different forms of expertise interplay into the development of new models that emerge from the convergence of ideas. This is eminent where communities are interlinked in order to engage in issues of common interest, even though communicating individuals might belong to separate communities:

P4: 'Collaboration in terms of the different roles, to …, and that what's exciting us, getting together to work out a solution for the government we've had architects, we've had business analysts, we've had the now the content developers as where I'm coming from, we've got the technology architects for government and then we've got change managers who are also involved from beginning to end although they are observing what is coming up first more than anything'.

Members of SITA's collaboration group are not restricted to one community of practice: They can join multiple communities of practice. In that way, one can find communities of practice interlinked by dual membership. Those members with dual membership can source some input from peers of the other community where specialised expertise is required to solve a specialised problem – such as that of anti-corruption:

P2: 'More of the discussion forum and semi-informal course that is being run, the course is called anti-corruption, so it's just more of a discussion forum, we calling in experts from time to time to give more information on how to deal with corruption and so on'.

A collaborative environment encourages the exchange of ideas and knowledge amongst learners or employees within a community of practice. This enables learners or employees to learn through discovery. Participants in the knowledge exchange do not have to enrol for a formal classroom course and then expect the lecturer to present learning material to them while they become passive recipients of knowledge. Rather, they actively engage each other on important issues or concepts relating to the current situation, which makes it easier to find direct and relevant solutions.

Proposed framework

Figure 4 shows a proposed framework that could provide conceptual insight into the design and development of a knowledge sharing mechanism in the public sector. It also shows that the knowledge sharing process takes place within the social constructivist paradigm, which means that knowledge is created through social interaction, and everybody involved equally contributes to the creation of knowledge.

The creation and sharing of knowledge in the public sector is facilitated through collaborative engagement that takes place within communities of practice. Subjects of discussion are proposed to the communities, and members of the communities then apply collaborative strategies to openly discuss, analyse

and evaluate issues of interest to the community. The process enables learning through discovery as members discover new meanings to current problems. The definition of 'new meaning' is the product of social engagement between the novices and expert employees who openly share knowledge and ideas for the purpose of knowledge development and improving institutional performance.

Knowledge agents in the public sector are already operating within the social constructivist paradigm to allow for social engagement between all parties involved in the knowledge sharing process. They openly debate the extension of their current knowledge as new perspectives emerge from new employees, and both novices and experts learn from one another.

Contribution of the study

Through this study, I sought to make a theoretical and practical contribution to knowledge sharing practices. In order to eliminate skills challenges, organisations need to create an environment for the instant acquisition of skills. Otherwise, they would miss out on opportunities made possible by the rapidly changing business environment. The rapidity of change in the business environment could be attributed to rapidly changing technology and other factors beyond the control of organisational personnel. However, an organisation such as the public sector can cope with rapid change emanating from both the global and local business environment if personnel could acquire sets of skills required to face changes.

This study also contributes to knowledge practice in the SA public sector by explicating important factors that knowledge agents should take into account when facilitating knowledge sharing initiatives geared towards improved performance (Matlhape & Lessing 2002). Amongst other factors, social media could enable flexible learning, collaborative learning and just-in-time, just-in-context and lifelong learning. Social media could also enhance employees' access to knowledge in already flourishing and easy-to-use technology. This is important for both business practice and academia as the framework above could be applied to provide predictive and explanatory value to the theoretical development of knowledge sharing practices in the South African public sector as the biggest employer in the country. According to Acton and Golden (2003), employees should not dread a knowledge-acquisition initiative but, instead, jubilantly look forward to exciting engagement activities that are made possible by social media.

It is important to note that South Africa and Africa as a whole are said to be engulfed by a digital gap in terms of Internet access and computer literacy (Ziemba, Papaj & Zelazny 2013). However, the social media diffusion in South Africa proves that people do access the Internet and do use computers if they are motivated by social needs, which make a socially orientated platform more attractive as a knowledge sharing platform (Horton & Horton 2003; World Wide Worx 2012; World Wide Worx 2014).

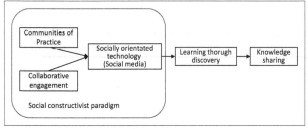

FIGURE 4: Conceptual framework for knowledge transfer in SA public sector.

Organisational leaders should start to recognise the impact of social networks, which forms the basis of socially orientated instructional technology as was evident in the London riot of October 2011 where the youth organised themselves, using social media, and brought London to a standstill (Baker 2011; Tonkin, Pfeiffer & Tourte 2012). Socially orientated instructional technology is as powerful in facilitating knowledge sharing in the workplace (World Wide Worx 2014).

Conclusion

This study set out to determine key concepts that have to be considered in the facilitation of a knowledge sharing mechanism in the public sector. The results of the case study revealed that public sector employees are engaging in not-yet institutionalised but effective knowledge sharing initiatives. Amongst the themes that emerged from a grounded theory analysis are the following: collaborative engagement, communities of practice, learning through discovery and the co-creation of meaning. Some of these themes are sub-themes embedded in the themes discussed above.

Despite the existence of comprehensive learning programmes, it is important to formulate guidelines for knowledge sharing that can be transferable to or adapted by different stakeholders in the public sector when knowledge transfer is needed. A limitation to this study is the fact that results cannot be generalised to the entire population because it was a qualitative study. However, the results are transferable to a similar environment (Denzin & Lincoln 2011).

Acknowledgements
Competing interests

The author declares that he has no financial or personal relationships which may have inappropriately influenced him in writing this article.

References

Acton, T. & Golden, W., 2003, 'Training the knowledge worker: A descriptive study of training practices in Irish software companies', *Journal of European Industrial Training* 27(2/3/4), 137–146.

Alavi, M. & Leidner, D.E., 1999, 'Knowledge management systems: Issues, challenges, and benefits', *Communications of Association of Information Systems* 1(7).

Allan, J. & Lawless, N., 2005, 'Learning through online collaboration by SME staff: A scoping investigation into likely team-role stressors', *Education + Training* 47(8/9), 653–664.

Andreeva, T. & Kianto, A., 2012, 'Does knowledge management really matter? Linking knowledge management practices, competitiveness and economic performance', *Journal of Knowledge Management* 16(4), 617–636. http://dx.doi.org/10.1108/13673271211246185

Baker, S.A., 2011, 'The mediated crowd: New social media and new forms of rioting', *Sociological Research Online* 16(4), 21. http://dx.doi.org/10.5153/sro.2553

Balcaen, P. & Hirtz, J., 2007, 'Developing critically thoughtful e-learning communities of practice', *proceedings of the 2nd International Conference on e-Learning*, 27–28 June 2007, University of British Columbia, Canada, p. 11.

Bogenrieder, I. & Van Baalen, P., 2007, 'Contested practice: Multiple inclusion in double-knit organizations', *Journal of Organizational Change Management* 20(4), 579–595. http://dx.doi.org/10.1108/09534810710760090

Charmaz, K., 2006, *Constructing grounded theory: A practical guide through qualitative analysis*, Sage Publications, Thousand Oaks.

Chatti, M.A., 2012, 'Knowledge management: A personal knowledge network perspective', *Journal of Knowledge Management* 16(5), 829–844. http://dx.doi.org/10.1108/13673271211262835

Crane, L., 2012, 'Trust me, I'm an expert: Identity construction and knowledge sharing', *Journal of Knowledge Management* 16(3), 448–460. http://dx.doi.org/10.1108/13673271211238760

Creswell, J.W., 2007, *Qualitative inquiry & research design: Choosing among five approaches*, Sage Publications, Thousand Oaks.

Denzin, N.K. & Lincoln, Y.S., 2011, *The SAGE handbook of qualitative research*, Sage Publications, Thousand Oaks.

Doolan, M.A., 2011, 'Developing a pedagogy: The role of the tutor in enabling student learning through the use of a wiki', *Cutting-edge Technologies in Higher Education* 1, 189–205. http://dx.doi.org/10.1108/S2044-9968(2011)0000001012

Doolan, M.A., 2013, 'A pedagogical framework for collaborative learning in a social blended e-Learning context', *Cutting-edge Technologies in Higher Education* 6, 261–285. http://dx.doi.org/10.1108/S2044-9968(2013)000006G012

Durst, S. & Wilhelm, S., 2012, 'Knowledge management and succession planning in SMEs', *Journal of Knowledge Management* 16(4) 637–646. http://dx.doi.org/10.1108/13673271211246194

Glaser, B.G. & Strauss, A.L., 1967, *The discovery of grounded theory: Strategies for qualitative research*, Aldine de Gruyter, Chicago.

Glover, I., Hardaker, G. & Xu, Z., 2004, 'Collaborative annotation system environment (CASE) for online learning', *Campus-Wide Information Systems* 21(2), 72–80. http://dx.doi.org/10.1108/10650740410529501

Horton, W. & Horton, K., 2003, *E-learning tools and technologies: A consumer's guide for trainers, teachers, educators, and instructional designers*, John Wiley & Sons, Chichester.

Hudson, B., 2003, 'Promoting collaboration in an international online learning community', *Industrial and Commercial Training* 35(3), 88–93. http://dx.doi.org/10.1108/00197850310470294

Jarrar, Y.F., 2002, 'Knowledge management: Learning for organisational experience', *Managerial Auditing Journal* 17(6) 322–328. http://dx.doi.org/10.1108/02686900210434104

Jeon, S., Kim, Y. & Koh, J., 2011, 'Individual, social, and organizational contexts for active knowledge sharing in communities of practice', *Expert Systems with Application* 38, 12423–12431.

Kanuka, H. & Garrison, D.R., 2004, 'Cognitive presence in online learning', *Journal of Computing in Higher Education* 15(2), 21–39. http://dx.doi.org/10.1007/BF02940928

Kraak, A., 2004, *An overview of South African human resources development*, Human Sciences Research Council Press, Cape Town.

Levinsen, K., 2006 'Collaborative on-line teaching: The inevitable path to deep learning and knowledge sharing', *Electronic journal of e-learning* 4(1), 41–48.

Lottering, F. & Dick, A.L., 2012, 'Integrating knowledge seeking into knowledge management models and frameworks', *South African Journal of Information Management* 14(1), 9. http://dx.doi.org/10.4102/sajim.v14i1.515

Martin, E.C. & Martin, N., 2011, 'The role of organisational factors in combating tacit knowledge loss in organisations', *Southern African Business Review* 15(1), 49–69.

Matlhape, M. & Lessing, N., 2002, 'Employees in total quality management', *Acta Commercii* 2, 21–34.

McCallin, A.M., 2003, 'Designing a grounded theory study: Some practicalities', *Nursing in critical care* 8(5), 203–208. http://dx.doi.org/10.1046/j.1362-1017.2003.00033.x

McGhee, G., Marland, G.R. & Atkinson, J., 2007, 'Grounded theory research: Literature reviewing and reflexivity', *Journal of advanced nursing* 60(3), 334–342. http://dx.doi.org/10.1111/j.1365-2648.2007.04436.x

Mkhize, P.L., Huisman, M. & Lubbe, S., 2011, 'Analysis of collaborative learning as prevalent instructional strategy of South African government elearning practices, *proceedings of the 10th European Conference on e-Learning*, University of Brighton, UK, November 10–11, 2011, pp. 492–501.

Mueller, J., 2012, 'Knowledge sharing between project teams and its cultural antecedents', *Journal of Knowledge Management* 16(3), 435–447. http://dx.doi.org/10.1108/13673271211238751

Nonaka, I., 1994, 'A dynamic theory of organizational knowledge creation', *Organizational Science* 5(1), 14–37. http://dx.doi.org/10.1287/orsc.5.1.14

Nonaka, I. & Takeuchi, H., 1995, *The knowledge-creating company: How Japanese companies create the dynamics of innovation*, Oxford University Press, New York.

Nonaka, I., Von Krogh, G. & Voelpel, S., 2006, 'Organizational knowledge creation theory: Evolutionary paths and future advances', *Organization Studies* 27, 1179. http://dx.doi.org/10.1177/0170840606066312

Pacharapha, T., 2012, 'Knowledge acquisition: The roles of perceived value of knowledge content and source', *Journal of Knowledge Management* 16(5), 724–739. http://dx.doi.org/10.1108/13673271211262772

Polanyi, M., 1966, *The tacit dimension*, Routledge and Kegan, London.

Remenyi, D. & Williams, B., 1998, *Doing research in business and management: An introduction to process and method*, Sage Publications, London. http://dx.doi.org/10.4135/9781446280416

Rogers, E.M., 1995, *Diffusion of innovation*, Free Press, New York.

Salmon, G., 2002, *E-tivities: The key to active online learning*, Routledge Falmer, London.

Schuima, G., 2012, 'Managing knowledge for business performance improvement', *Journal of Knowledge Management* 16(4), 515–522. http://dx.doi.org/10.1108/13673271211246103

Silva, L.C.S., Kovaleski, J.L., Gaia, S., De Matos, S.A. & De Francisco, A.C., 2012, 'The challenges faced by Brazil's public universities as a result of knowledge transfer barriers in building the technological innovation center', *African Journal of Business Management* 6(41), 10547–10557. http://dx.doi.org/10.5897/AJBM12.315

Sowe, S.K., Stamelos, I. & Angelis, L., 2008, 'Understanding knowledge sharing activities in free/open source software projects: An empirical study', *Journal of Systems and Software* 81, 431–446. http://dx.doi.org/10.1016/j.jss.2007.03.086

Statistics South Africa, 2010 'Quarterly labour force survey, quarter 1, 2010', Stats SA Library Cataloguing-in-Publication (CIP) Data.

Strauss, A.L. & Corbin, J.M., 1997, *Grounded theory in practice,* Sage Publications, Thousand Oaks.

Tonkin, H., Pfeiffer, H.D. & Tourte, G., 2012, 'Twitter, information sharing and London riots?', *Bulletin of the American Society for Information Science and Technology* 38(2), 49–57. http://dx.doi.org/10.1002/bult.2012.1720380212

Wang, C., Yang, H. & Chou, S.T., 2008, 'Using peer-to-peer technology for knowledge sharing in communities of practices', *Decision Support Systems* 45, 528–540. http://dx.doi.org/10.1016/j.dss.2007.06.012

Wenger, E. & Snyder, W., 2000, 'Communities of practice: The organizational frontier', *Harvard Business Review* 79(1), 139–145.

World Wide Worx, 2012, *Social media breaks barriers in SA,* viewed 25 November 2012, from http://www.worldwideworx.com/socialmedia2012/

World Wide Worx, 2014, *WhatsApp takes SA by storm*, viewed 10 March 2014, from http://www.worldwideworx.com/whatsapp/

Zhu, C., Valke, M. & Schellens, T., 2009, 'A cross-cultural study of online collaborative learning', *Multicultural Education & Technology Journal* 3(1), 33–46. http://dx.doi.org/10.1108/17504970910951138

Ziemba, E., Papaj, T., & Zelazny, R., 2013, 'New perspectives on information society: The maturity of research on a sustainable information society', *Online Journal of Applied Knowledge Management* 1(1), 52–71.

14

Knowledge creation and transfer amongst post-graduate students

Authors:
Kreeson Naicker[1]
Krishna K. Govender[1,2]
Karunagaran Naidoo[1]

Affiliations:
[1]School of Management, Information Technology & Governance, University of KwaZulu-Natal, South Africa

[2]Regenesys Business School, Johannesburg, South Africa

Correspondence to:
Krishna Govender

Email:
krishnag@regenesys.co.za

Postal address:
4 Pybus Road, Sandton 2146, South Africa

Background: The skill shortages, hyper-competitive economic environments and untapped economies have created a great deal of focus on knowledge. Thus, continuously creating and transferring knowledge is critical for every organisation.

Objectives: This article reports on an exploratory study undertaken to ascertain how knowledge is created and transferred amongst post-graduate (PG) students, using the knowledge (socialisation, externalisation, combination, internalisation [SECI]) spiral model.

Method: After reviewing relevant literature, a personally administered standardised questionnaire was used to collect data from a convenience sample of PG students in the School of Management, IT and Governance at the University of KwaZulu-Natal, South Africa. The data was analysed to determine if it fit the model based on the four modes of knowledge conversion.

Results: Although the School of Management, IT and Governance has mechanisms in place to facilitate knowledge creation and transfer, it nevertheless tends to focus on the four modes of knowledge conversion to varying degrees.

Conclusion: The study confirmed that PG students utilise the 'socialisation' and 'externalisation' modes of knowledge conversion comprehensively; 'internalisation' plays a significant role in their knowledge creation and transfer activities and whilst 'combination' is utilised to a lesser extent, it still plays a role in PG students' knowledge creation and transfer activities. PG students also have 'space' that allows them to bring hunches, thoughts, notions, intuition or tacit knowledge into reality. Trust and dedication are common amongst PG students. With socialisation and externalisation so high, PG students are aware of each other's capabilities and competencies, and trust each other enough to share knowledge.

Introduction

Information on demand is a powerful aspect of the mode in which academic organisations, teams and individuals operate. There is a constant need for academic organisations, teams and individuals to accelerate the communication of information and knowledge to each other and organisations outside the academic sphere (Nelson 2005). An individual is often afraid to share their knowledge and they have a tendency to guard their knowledge and selectively release it. This tendency is often cited as a core problem when working in a team and the cause of poor collaboration between team members (Gilmour 2003). In order to leverage on innovation as one of the most important sources of competitiveness and success, academics need to have access to and mobilise their knowledge resources (Voelpel, Von Pierer & Streb 2006).

Knowledge is generally separated into two types: explicit and tacit knowledge. Hautala (2011:605) explains that 'academic knowledge aims at creating or exploring the new' tacit and explicit elements, which together with theory and practice are used to form knowledge. Tacit knowledge is a personal, contextual and practical entity that is difficult to communicate (Polanyi 1966). For example, balancing a bicycle to ride it requires tacit knowledge that is not easy to explain to someone who has never actually ridden one. Similarly, understanding and conducting a research project as part of an academic field, research group and society also includes tacit knowledge (Hautala 2011:605).

Davenport and Prusak (1998:81) argue that codifying tacit knowledge is difficult, but that 'its substantial value makes it worth the effort'. Notwithstanding some of the challenges cited by the scholars and practitioners referenced above, the decision to focus only on tacit knowledge instead of knowledge in general can be justified by reasons that include, but are not limited to, its substantial volume and value to the organisation (Suppiah & Sandhu 2011). The ability to create, store, disseminate and utilise knowledge and expertise has become a primary way for organisations, teams and individuals to compete (Hayashi 2004). Amassing and synthesising specialised knowledge from multiple sources is a pivotal factor in resolving the technical and operational uncertainties that impede Nonaka and Takeuchi's (1995) knowledge (SECI) spiral theory.

In light of the above, this article focuses on determining which of the four modes of knowledge conversion assist post-graduate (PG) students to access information on demand.

It is widely accepted that there is difficulty in disseminating tacit knowledge, since tacit knowledge is personal and understandable by the possessor (Alavi & Leidner 2001; Nonaka & Takeuchi 1995; Polanyi 1966). Thus, this study also attempts to establish, through an assessment of the knowledge spiral, if extracting tacit knowledge or engaging with explicit knowledge is essential for a paradigm shift when transcending from the old self to the new self.

Literature review

The genesis of the knowledge (SECI) spiral process

Knowledge is sought and shared in a global arena, whether at a corporate or academic level (Hautala 2011). McKenzie and Van Winkelen (2011) argue that:

> sound decisions rely on having the right knowledge in the right place at the right time, to be able to act effectively. 'Right' knowledge may be different for every decision – some decisions require only surface knowledge, some require more investigation and an evidence base, some use tacit expertise, and others creative insight, intuition and judgment. (p. 403)

Rai (2011) believes that despite the subtle differences between the various knowledge definitions, scholars agree that effective and efficient knowledge management is central to organisational performance and success. In order to assess the capacity of an organisational system to generate new knowledge, the first step is to define knowledge and then how to determine if it is 'new' knowledge, as the aforementioned has a justified belief that increases an entity's capacity for effective action (Arling & Chun 2011).

The conversion of tacit knowledge into explicit knowledge helps knowledge to be crystallised and shared by others, which becomes the basis for the creation of new knowledge. The successful conversion of tacit knowledge into explicit knowledge depends on the sequential use of metaphor, analogy and models (Rai 2011). The materialisation of new knowledge always begins with the individual. A resourceful individual may become conscious of a position that has not been developed, which may lead to the growth or advancement of a product, service or theory. An individual's personal knowledge is transformed into organisational knowledge that is valuable to the company. Making personal knowledge available to others is the central activity of the knowledge-creating company. Nonaka and Konno (1998:26) argue that 'it takes place continuously and at all levels of the organisation', in that one's personal knowledge is transformed into organisational knowledge through the interactions between tacit knowledge and explicit knowledge.

Within several loops of interaction where community members share their experiences, ideals and ideas, new knowledge – individual as well as collective knowledge – emerges through this process (Renzl 2006). Oguz and Sengün (2011:446) argue that Nonaka and Takeuchi (1995) popularised tacit knowledge in the management literature. Using the example of the bread master, they promote the link between tacit and explicit knowledge. Their work legitimised the tacit-explicit dichotomy by viewing the two as separate spheres of knowledge. Even though they cite and use Polanyi (1966) approvingly, the ontological dimension of knowing remained inconspicuous. In their view, knowledge creation is the result of an interactive spiral between tacit and explicit knowledge. This rendition has been widely accepted in most of the following literature and has created the tendency to see tacit and explicit knowledge as substitutes (e.g. Nonaka & Takeuchi 1998). According to Nonaka and Takeuchi, there are four ways of converting between tacit and explicit knowledge; these are: socialisation (tacit to tacit), externalisation (tacit to explicit), combination (explicit to explicit) and internalisation (explicit to tacit).

Grant (2007) views tacit knowledge as the ability or skill of an individual to do something or to resolve a problem that is based, in part, on one's own experiences and learning, and probably not all of this knowledge can be shared between individuals. Capturing tacit knowledge is seen as the challenge to organisations that want to spread knowledge throughout the organisation or spur greater innovation. It is treated as a reserve deposited deep within the ground that needs to be detected and then pumped out (Mooradian 2005).

The aforementioned development led Nonaka and Takeuchi (1995), the pioneers of the knowledge spiral model, to believe that tacit and explicit are not totally separate but mutually complementary entities; this led them to further develop the notion that tacit and explicit knowledge interact with and interchange into each other in the creative activities of human beings. The interaction between tacit and explicit knowledge is known as knowledge conversion, which consists of four modes. Girard (2006) believes that the four modes of knowledge conversion need to operate in sync. The four modes of knowledge conversion consist of socialisation, externalisation, combination and internalisation, which are shown in Figure 1. It is important to stress that the success of each mode of knowledge conversion will depend on the leadership and culture of the organisation or team. After all, managing knowledge is all about creating a culture that will institutionalise trust and facilitate knowledge creation, transfer and storage (Kermally 2002). Socialisation helps to move knowledge in tacit form between individuals (in this instance post-graduate students), externalisation is the application of tacit insights on an outside entity, combination represents the act of synthesising explicit pieces of knowledge and finally internalisation is the process through which one increases one's knowledge by learning from external events (Desouza & Awazu 2006).

Knowledge (SECI) conversion refers to the four modes of knowledge creation identified by Nonaka and Takeuchi (1995): socialisation that transfers tacit knowledge, externalisation that converts tacit knowledge into explicit knowledge, combination that integrates explicit knowledge and internalisation that embodies new tacit knowledge (Choo & Drummond de Alvarenga Neto 2010). The knowledge conversion (SECI) process (Figure 2) is deemed to be the blueprint for the knowledge spiral model (Figure 2), where the interaction or dialogue between the modes plays an integral role in knowledge creation and transfer.

Arling and Chun (2011) and Perez-Araos *et al.* (2007), after an examination of Alavi and Leidner's (2001) and Nonaka and Takeuchi's (1995) research respectively, explain that socialisation is the process of converting one individual's tacit knowledge to another individual's tacit knowledge through interpersonal interaction. Tacit knowledge to tacit knowledge (socialisation) is a process of sharing experiences in a direct face-to-face approach to create tacit knowledge, often done through shared mental models, technical skills, observation, imitation and practice. Externalisation is the process of converting tacit knowledge to explicit knowledge. Tacit knowledge to explicit knowledge (externalisation) is a knowledge creation process where a part of tacit knowledge is articulated and turned somehow into explicit form, through analogies, concepts, hypothesis, models, reports, and so on. Combination is the process of creating new explicit knowledge by reconfiguring, re-categorising and re-conceptualising existing explicit knowledge. Explicit knowledge to explicit knowledge (combination) is a process of combining different bodies of explicit knowledge and internalisation is the process of converting explicit knowledge to tacit knowledge.

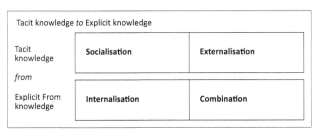

Source: Adapted from Nonaka, I. & Takeuchi, H., 1995, *The knowledge creating company*, Oxford University Press, New York

FIGURE 1: Four modes of knowledge conversion.

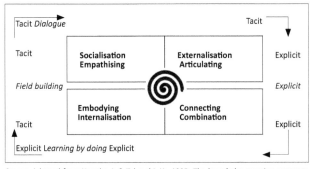

Source: Adapted from Nonaka, I. & Takeuchi, H., 1995, *The knowledge creating company*, Oxford University Press, New York

FIGURE 2: The knowledge spiral.

Explicit knowledge to tacit knowledge (internalisation) is a process of embodying explicit knowledge into tacit knowledge by experiencing knowledge through the explicit source (learning-by-doing approach).

Nonaka and Takeuchi's (1995) knowledge (SECI) spiral model is reliant on the interaction between the micro and macro environments, and changes occur at both the micro and the macro level; an individual (micro) influences and is influenced by the environment (macro) with which they interact (Little, Quintas & Ray 2002).

Against the brief literature review, this study explored knowledge creation and transfer amongst PG students at a research university.

Research methodology

An exploratory research design was employed based on Saunders *et al.*'s (2007:133) affirmation that 'an exploratory study is a valuable means of finding out what is happening; to seek new insights; to ask questions and to assess phenomena in a new light'. Furthermore, Sekaran (2003:119) argues that 'exploratory studies are undertaken to better comprehend the nature of the problem since few studies might have been conducted in that area'.

This study was quantitative in nature, since:

> quantitative methods require the use of standardized measures so that varying perspectives and experiences of people can be fitted into a limited number of predetermined response categories to which numbers are assigned. (Patton 2002:14)

Furthermore:

> the advantage of a quantitative approach is that it's possible to measure the reactions of many people to a limited set of questions, thus facilitating comparison and statistical aggregation of the data. This gives a broad, generalizable set of findings presented succinctly and parsimoniously. (Patton 2002:14)

A questionnaire was used, which comprised a five-point Likert scale that ranged from 1–5 (with 5 = strongly agree and 1 = strongly disagree). The responses were converted to frequencies and percentages, and the results were related to Nonaka and Takeuchi's (1995) knowledge (SECI) spiral model and interpreted accordingly.

As a first step in deciding on the sample, all PG students in the School of Management, Information Technology & Governance, at the University of KwaZulu-Natal constituted the target population. The reason for choosing this group of 'knowledge creators' was a matter of convenience, since a sample from this population would have been easily accessible, since they comprised individuals who were known to the primary researcher. According to McBurney and White (2007) the sampling frame is a population as it is defined for the purposes of selecting subjects for a study; in the context of this study, the *sampling frame* is all accessible post-graduate students in the School of Management, Information

Technology & Governance. The *sample size*, which required making some judgement about the number of participants needed for the study (Devlin 2006), was determined using a non-probability sampling technique, namely convenience sampling. The population of post-graduate students comprises 204 honours students and 132 master's and PhD students. The total number of post graduate students (336) was used in the calculation of the sample size. Using a confidence level of 95% with a confidence interval of 12 results in a sample size of 56 required whilst a confidence level of 95% with a confidence interval of 10 results in a sample size of 75. It was therefore decided to use a sample size within the range of 56 and 75. Approximately 60 students were targeted. The researcher collected 70 completed questionnaires.

Sekaran (2003) explains that for personally administered questionnaires:

> when a survey is confined to a local area, and the organisation is willing and able to assemble groups of employees to respond to the questionnaires at the workplace, a good way to collect data is to personally administer the questionnaires. The main advantage of this is that the researcher or a member of the research team can collect all the completed responses within a short period of time. Any doubts that the respondents might have or any question could be clarified on the spot. (p. 236)

Thus, the questionnaires were personally administered to the PG students.

The reliability of a measure, which indicates the 'extent to which it is without bias (error free) and hence ensures consistent measurement across the various items in the instrument' (Sekaran 2003:203), is reliant on the stability and consistency with which the instrument measures the concept, model or theory. The internal consistency of the measure was maintained as all the sections of the questionnaire focused on measuring if the adaptation of Nonaka and Takeuchi's (1995) knowledge (SECI) spiral model has an influence on the way knowledge is created and transferred by PG students.

Sekaran (2003) proposes that validity is concerned with the authenticity of the cause-and-effect relationships (internal validity), and their generalisability to the external environment (external validity). Although there are several ways of testing validity, this study focused on content validity which is the best test of validity for a questionnaire. Content validity ensures that the measure includes an adequate and representative set of items that tap the concept, theory or model. The questions based on Nonaka and Takeuchi's (1995) knowledge spiral is an adequate and representative set of items that tap into the way knowledge is created and transferred by PG students. The questions are dimensions and elements of Nonaka and Takeuchi's knowledge (SECI) spiral model. For completeness, see the questionnaire in Annexure 1.

Empirical findings

The majority (93%) of respondents were honours students. The remaining 7% were master's students and PhD students. A total of 380 questionnaires were administered.

The Likert scale that was used in the questionnaire had five categories. For the purpose of analysis, all 'strongly agree' and 'agree' responses were collapsed into one category, namely 'agree' because it can be seen from the results that even if 'neutral' is combined with 'disagree' and 'strongly disagree', the results would not be changed.

The use of socialisation

The first mode of the knowledge conversion process, *socialisation*, is determined by seven statements. Table 1 reflects the respondents' agreement or disagreement with each statement.

It is evident from the information in Table 1, that the overwhelming majority of respondents agreed with all seven statements, implying that the 'socialisation' mode was effective in knowledge creation and transfer amongst the PG students.

Use of combination

The third mode of the knowledge conversion process, *combination*, is determined by six statements in the questionnaire.

It is evident from Table 2, that since a two-thirds majority was not achieved for some statements pertaining to 'combination', the 'combination' mode is not predominantly used by the PG students. This confirms that transforming tacit knowledge to explicit knowledge is not a significant activity in the knowledge creation and transfer process.

TABLE 1: Respondents' use of socialisation.

Response	% Who agreed
'I will actively share my experience with others'	82.9
'In my academic team, my teammates and I will share life or work experience with each other'	84.3
'During group discussion, I try to find out others' opinions, thoughts and other information'	94.3
'During discussion, I will bring out some concepts, thoughts or ideas'	92.9
'I often encourage others to express their thoughts'	87.1
'Before group discussion, I will collect necessary information and show it to the group'	68.6
'I like to get to know the people with whom I will work before going into a project together'	75.7

Source: Developed by researchers from the research data

TABLE 2: Respondents' use of combination.

Response	% Who agreed
'During the discussion, I tend to organise ideas and make conclusions to facilitate the discussion'	74.3
'When coming across problems, I tend to use my experience to help solving problems'	84.3
'After every event, I have the habit of organising and making a summary of what happened'	58.6
'During discussion, I will organise everyone's thoughts in my mind'	61.4
'I like to collect new information and make a connection of new and old knowledge to work up new concepts'	77.1
'I like to organise ambiguous concepts into structure'	63.33

Source: Developed by researchers from the research data

The use of internalisation

Five statements (Table 3) served to ascertain information about the respondents' *internalisation* of information. From Table 3, it is evident that for the majority (four-fifths) of the statements that comprised 'internalisation,' the sample was in agreement, which implies that this mode is predominantly being used by the PG students in the School of Management, Information Technology & Governance, at the University of KwaZulu-Natal.

The use of externalisation

The second mode of the knowledge conversion process, externalisation, was determined by seven statements.

In order to ascertain whether the mode of 'externalisation' is predominantly used by the PG students, at least a two-thirds majority (66%) agreement (Table 4) with each of the seven statements is required. The study revealed that there was overwhelming agreement for each individual statement. Therefore, the 'externalisation' mode is effective and being frequently used by the PG students. This shows that PG students are able to articulate their tacit knowledge to explicit knowledge effectively, or that there are academic mechanisms in place to help post-graduate students transform their tacit knowledge into explicit knowledge.

Recommendations

More research should be carried out on how knowledge is created and transferred by PG and undergraduate students on a larger scale, since students are the individuals that directly deal with the generation, transfer and storage of knowledge in academic institutes. Both qualitative and quantitative research should be carried out in this area using a larger sample size, at least 1000 students, depending on the student population of the university. Future research in addition should concentrate on the conditions that drive the knowledge spiral process, the five-phase model of the organisational knowledge-creation process (in an academic context) and the factors that affect the knowledge spiral process and the individual modes of knowledge. Moreover, the researcher strongly believes that a study should be done to compare new joiners in corporate university graduate programs, post-graduate students and undergraduate students. A study of the influence of trust, communication, culture, organisational networks, technical infrastructure and other influences such as investment should be carried out, to determine their effects on knowledge creation and transfer in academic institutes. Future studies should also compare knowledge creation, transfer and storage in South African academic institutions with that of other American, European and Asian academic institutions; it should be country specific. This will help to gauge if there are any similarities or differences between academic institutions other than political, social and economic differences. This would also enable future researchers to observe the cultural differences between students or academic institutions.

Future studies on knowledge conversion activities in academic institutes should focus on the years of existence, number of students, faculty, schools and the academic year of the student. Furthermore, future research should determine if students in specific years of study and who have certain access to academic knowledge mechanisms are more adept at creating, transferring and storing knowledge. Finally, as the culture of the university could not be established with a single school or a few disciplines, the author strongly believes that multiple colleges should be surveyed to determine if a knowledge creating and transfer culture exists.

Conclusion

The aim of this study was to assess how knowledge is created and transferred amongst PG students, using Nonaka and Takeuchi's (1995) knowledge (SECI) spiral model. The study confirmed that PG students utilise the 'socialisation' and 'externalisation' modes of knowledge conversion comprehensively; 'internalisation' plays a significant role in their knowledge creation and transfer activities too, whilst 'combination' is less utilised but still plays a role in their knowledge creation and transfer activities. PG students have space that allows them to bring hunches, thoughts, notions, intuition or tacit knowledge into reality. Trust and dedication are common amongst post-graduate students. With the use of 'socialisation' and 'externalisation' so high, PG students are aware of each others' capabilities and competencies, and trust each other enough to share the knowledge.

As 'socialisation' and 'externalisation' received the majority of the positive responses, the activities associated with these

TABLE 3: Use of internalisation.

Response	% Who agreed
'After hearing a new idea or concept, I tend to compare it with my experience to help me comprehend the meaning'	78.6
'I understand others' thoughts better by repeating what they said and asking them "Is this what you mean?"'	78.6
'I will tell others what I think to make sure my understanding is the same as theirs'	84.3
'When I have finished saying something, I will ask the other person if it is necessary to repeat to make sure they understand exactly what I mean'.	60.0
When communicating with others, I will give others time to think about we discussed	77.1

Source: Developed by researchers from the research data

TABLE 4: Respondents' use of externalisation.

Response	% Who agreed
'When others can't understand me, I am usually able to give them examples to help explaining'	95.7
'Most of the time, I can transcribe some of the unorganised thoughts into concrete ideas'	68.6
'I can describe academic or technical terms with conversational language to help communicate in a group'	82.9
'I tend to use analogy when expressing abstract concepts'	84.3
'When I try to express abstract concepts, I tend to explain with examples'	94.3
'I will help others to clearly express what they have in mind by encouraging them to continue what they are saying'	87.1
'When others cannot express themselves clearly, I usually help them clarify their points'	75.7

Source: Developed by researchers from the research data

modes will illustrate the trusted source of information and knowledge. Therefore, brainstorming, informal meetings, discussions, dialogues, observation, mentoring, learning groups, as well as meetings, building hypotheses and models, pictures for communication, after-action reviews, workshops, master classes, assignment databases, best practice exchange, diagrams, illustrations, sketches, metaphors and analogies are the trusted sources of information and knowledge for post-graduate students at the School of Management, Information Technology & Governance, at the University of KwaZulu-Natal.

Acknowledgements

Competing interests

There are no financial or non-financial competing interests inherent in the publication of this article, other than the fact that it was extracted from the mini-dissertation of a master's student, whose study was co-supervised by the co-authors.

Authors' contributions

K. Naicker (University of KwaZulu-Natal) is the author of the mini-dissertation from which this article was extracted. However, the article was primarily written by the research supervisor K.K.G. (University of KwaZulu-Natal; Regenesys Business School) and formatted and edited by K. Naidoo (University of KwaZulu-Natal), the co-supervisor.

References

Alavi, M. & Leidner, D.E., 2001, 'Review: Knowledge management and knowledge management systems: Conceptual foundations and research issues', *MIS Quarterly* 25(1), 107–136.

Arling, P.A. & Chun, M.W.S., 2011, 'Facilitating new knowledge creation and obtaining KM maturity', *Journal of Knowledge Management* 15(2), 231–250. http://dx.doi.org/10.1108/13673271111119673

Choo, C.W. & Drummond de Alvarenga Neto, R.C., 2010, 'Beyond the ba: Managing enabling contexts in knowledge organisations', *Journal of Knowledge Management* 14(4), 592–610.

Davenport, T.H. & Prusak, L., 1998, *Working knowledge: How organisations manage what they know*, Harvard Business School Press, Boston.

Desouza, K.C. & Awazu, Y., 2006, 'Knowledge management at SME's: Five peculiarities', *Journal of Knowledge Management* 10(1), 32–43.

Devlin, A.S., 2006, *Research methods: Planning, conducting and presenting research*, Thomson Wadsworth, California.

Gilmour, D., 2003, 'How to fix knowledge management', *Harvard Business Review* 16, 31–38.

Girard, J.P., 2006, 'Where is the knowledge we have lost in managers?', *Journal of Knowledge Management* 10(6), 22–38.

Grant. K.A., 2007, 'Tacit knowledge revisited – We can still learn from Polanyi', *The Electronic Journal of Knowledge Management* 592, 173–180.

Hautala, J., 2011, 'Cognitive proximity in international research groups', *Journal of Knowledge Management* 15(4), 601–624. http://dx.doi.org/10.1108/13673271111151983

Hayashi. A.M., 2004, 'Building better teams', *Sloan Management Review*, Winter, 179–186.

Kermally, S., 2002, *Effective knowledge management*, John Wiley & Sons, Ltd., West Sussex.

Little, S. Quintas, P. & Ray, T., 2002, *Managing knowledge: An essential reader*, Sage Publications Ltd, London.

McBurney, D.H. & White, T.L., 2007, *Research methods*, Thomson Wadsworth, California.

McKenzie, J. & Van Winkelen, C., 2011, 'Developing organizational decision-making capability – A knowledge manager's guide', *Journal of Knowledge Management* 15(3), 403–421.

Mooradian, N., 2005, 'Tacit knowledge: Philosophic roots and role in KM', *Journal of Knowledge Management* 9(6), 104–113.

Nelson, R.R., 2005, 'Economic development from the perspective of evolutionary economic theory', *Oxford Development Studies* 36(1), 9–21.

Nonaka, I. & Konno, N., 1998, 'The concept of "ba": Building a foundation for knowledge creation', *California Management Review* 40, 40–54.

Nonaka, I. & Takeuchi, H., 1995, *The knowledge creating company*, Oxford University Press, New York.

Oguz, F. & Sengün, A.E., 2011. 'Mystery of the unknown: Revisiting tacit knowledge in the organizational literature', *Journal of Knowledge Management* 15(3), 445–461.

Patton, M.Q., 2002, *Qualitative research and evaluation methods*, Sage Publications, Inc., California.

Perez-Araos, A., Barber, K.D., Munive-Hernandez, J.E. & Eldridge, S., 2007, 'Designing a knowledge management tool to support knowledge sharing networks', *Journal of Manufacturing Technology Management* 18(2), 153–168.

Rai, R.K., 2011, 'Knowledge management and organizational culture: A theoretical integrative framework,' *Journal of Knowledge Management* 15(5), 779–801. http://dx.doi.org/10.1108/13673271111174320

Renzl, B., 2006, 'Trust in management knowledge sharing: The mediating effects of fear and knowledge documentation', *Omega* 36(2), 206–230.

Saunders, M.N.K., Saunders, M., Lewis, P. & Thornhill, A., 2011, *Research methods for business*, 5th edn., Pearson, London.

Sekaran, U., 2003, *Research methods for business: A skill building approach*, John Wiley & Sons, Inc., New Jersey.

Suppiah, V. & Sandhu, M.S., 2011, 'Organisational culture's influence on tacit knowledge-sharing behaviour', *Journal of Knowledge Management* 15(3), 462–477. http://dx.doi.org/10.1108/13673271111137439

Voelpel, S.C., Von Pierer, H. & Streb, C.K., 2006, 'Mobilizing organizations for innovation and value creation: An integrated model of the mobile company', *Journal of Knowledge Management* 10(6), 5–21.

Annexure 1 starts on the next page →

Annexure 1

Questionnaire

SECTION A

1. Biographical questions

1.1 Are you a(n)

Honours student	Master's student	PHD student
☐	☐	☐

1.2 Are you

<18 years	18–20 years old	21–23 years old
☐	☐	☐

24–26 years old	27–29 years old	>30 years
☐	☐	☐

1.3 Are you a

Full-time student	Part-time student
☐	☐

1.4 Are you permanently employed?

Yes	No
☐	☐

1.5 Are you

Male	Female
☐	☐

SECTION B

2. Internalisation

2.1 After hearing a new idea or concept, I tend to compare it with my experience to help me comprehend the meaning.

Strongly agree	Agree	Neutral	Disagree	Strongly disagree
☐	☐	☐	☐	☐

2.2 I understand better by repeating what was said and by asking 'Is that what you mean?'

Strongly agree	Agree	Neutral	Disagree	Strongly disagree
☐	☐	☐	☐	☐

2.3 I will tell others what I think to make sure my understanding is the same as theirs.

Strongly agree	Agree	Neutral	Disagree	Strongly disagree
☐	☐	☐	☐	☐

2.4 When I have finished saying something, I will ask the other person if it is necessary to repeat what I said, to make sure they understand exactly what I mean.

Strongly agree	Agree	Neutral	Disagree	Strongly disagree
☐	☐	☐	☐	☐

2.5 When communicating with others, I will give them time to think about we discussed.

Strongly agree	Agree	Neutral	Disagree	Strongly disagree
☐	☐	☐	☐	☐

2.6 I understand better by repeating what was said and by asking 'Is that what you mean?'

Strongly agree	Agree	Neutral	Disagree	Strongly disagree
☐	☐	☐	☐	☐

3. Externalisation

3.1 When others can't understand me, I am usually able to give examples to help them understand.

Strongly agree	Agree	Neutral	Disagree	Strongly disagree
☐	☐	☐	☐	☐

3.2 Most of the time, I can transcribe some of the unorganised thoughts into concrete ideas.

Strongly agree	Agree	Neutral	Disagree	Strongly disagree
☐	☐	☐	☐	☐

3.3 I can describe academic or technical terms with conversational language to help communication in a group.

Strongly agree	Agree	Neutral	Disagree	Strongly disagree
☐	☐	☐	☐	☐

3.4 I tend to use comparisons when expressing abstract concepts.

Strongly agree	Agree	Neutral	Disagree	Strongly disagree
☐	☐	☐	☐	☐

3.5 When I try to express abstract concepts, I tend to explain using examples.

Strongly agree	Agree	Neutral	Disagree	Strongly disagree
☐	☐	☐	☐	☐

3.6 I will help others to clearly express what they have in mind, by encouraging them to continue what they are saying.

Strongly agree	Agree	Neutral	Disagree	Strongly disagree
☐	☐	☐	☐	☐

3.7 When others cannot express themselves clearly, I usually help them clarify their points.

Strongly agree	Agree	Neutral	Disagree	Strongly disagree
☐	☐	☐	☐	☐

4. Socialisation

4.1 In academic group discussions, I will actively share my experience with others.

Strongly agree	Agree	Neutral	Disagree	Strongly disagree
☐	☐	☐	☐	☐

4.2 In my academic team, my teammates and I will share life or work experiences with each other.

Strongly agree	Agree	Neutral	Disagree	Strongly disagree
☐	☐	☐	☐	☐

Annexure 1 continues on the next page →

4.3 During group discussion, I try to find out others' opinions, thoughts and other information.

Strongly agree   Agree   Neutral   Disagree   Strongly disagree

4.4 During discussions, I will bring out some concepts, thoughts or ideas.

Strongly agree   Agree   Neutral   Disagree   Strongly disagree

4.5 I often encourage others to express their thoughts.

Strongly agree   Agree   Neutral   Disagree   Strongly disagree

4.6 Before group discussions, I will collect necessary information and show it to the group.

Strongly agree   Agree   Neutral   Disagree   Strongly disagree

4.7 I like to get to know the people with whom I will work before going into a project together.

Strongly agree   Agree   Neutral   Disagree   Strongly disagree

5. Combination

5.1 During a discussion, I tend to organise ideas and make conclusions to facilitate the discussion.

Strongly agree   Agree   Neutral   Disagree   Strongly disagree

5.2 When I come across problems, I tend to use my experience to help solve them.

Strongly agree   Agree   Neutral   Disagree   Strongly disagree

5.3 After every event, I have the habit of organising and summarising what happened.

Strongly agree   Agree   Neutral   Disagree   Strongly disagree

5.4 During discussions, I will organise everyone's thoughts in my mind.

Strongly agree   Agree   Neutral   Disagree   Strongly disagree

5.5 I like to collect new information and make a connection between the new and old knowledge to develop new concepts.

Strongly agree   Agree   Neutral   Disagree   Strongly disagree

5.6 I like to organise ambiguous concepts into a structure.

Strongly agree   Agree   Neutral   Disagree   Strongly disagree

Thank you for your participation.

Source: Developed by primary researcher

15

Knowledge management a competitive edge for law firms in Botswana in the changing business environment

Author:
Madeleine Fombad[1]

Affiliation:
[1]Department of Information Science, University of South Africa, South Africa

Correspondence to:
Madeleine Fombad

Email:
fombamc@unisa.ac.za

Postal address:
798 Thomas Avenue, Eastwood, Arcadia 0083, South Africa

Background: Law firms in Botswana offer a particularly interesting context to explore the effects of transition in the knowledge economy. Acquiring and leveraging knowledge effectively in law firms through knowledge management can result in competitive advantage; yet the adoption of this approach remains in its infancy.

Objectives: This article investigates the factors that will motivate the adoption of knowledge management in law firms in Botswana, and creates an awareness of the potential benefits of knowledge management in these firms.

Method: The article uses both quantitative and qualitative research methods and the survey research design. A survey was performed on all 115 registered law firms and 217 lawyers in Botswana. Interviews were conducted with selected lawyers for more insight.

Results: Several changes in the legal environment have motivated law firms to adopt knowledge management. Furthermore, lawyers appreciate the potential benefits of knowledge management.

Conclusion: With the rise of the knowledge-based economy, coupled with the pressures faced by the legal industry in recent years, law firms in Botswana can no longer afford to rely on the traditional methods of managing knowledge. Knowledge management will, therefore, enhance the cost effectiveness of these firms. Strategic knowledge management certainly helps to prepare law firms in Botswana to be alive to the fact that the systematic harnessing of legal knowledge is no longer a luxury, but an absolute necessity in the knowledge economy. It will also provide an enabling business environment for private sector development and growth and, therefore, facilitate Botswana's drive towards the knowledge-based economy.

Introduction

During the last decade of the 20th century, the global economy witnessed an increasing transition from the traditional resources of land, labour, and capital to the knowledge economy, whereby knowledge is considered as a prime input to production, innovation and economic benefits. Botswana is taking positive strides towards becoming a knowledge-based economy (Bwalya 2010; World Bank 2012). Botswana's drive towards transformation to a knowledge-based economy is envisaged in its 'National Vision 2016' (Presidential Task Group 1997), and the President of Botswana's inaugural speech (Office of the President 2010). One of the seven thematic areas of the 'National Vision 2016' envisages that as an educated and informed nation after 50 years of independence, the knowledge-based economy will contribute to an overall objective of transforming the country into a knowledge society, with research and innovation as the cornerstones of development. In this regard, the government has made sustainable investments in physical and technical infrastructure, businesses, education, research and development to facilitate a knowledge intensive economy. The public and private sectors are making concerted efforts to enhance the drive towards the knowledge economy. Law firms in Botswana, therefore, provide an important context in the private sector to explore the effects of transition into the knowledge economy. In the knowledge economy the production and services are based on knowledge-intensive activities that contribute to accelerating the pace of technical and scientific advancement (Powell & Snellman 2004). Law firms are knowledge-intensive firms, the competitive advantage of which is built on knowledge and how it is used to help clients. A law firm can be described as a business entity that is formed by one or more lawyers to engage in the practice of law and in rendering effective and efficient legal services to clients. Law firms in Botswana are small and they are either sole proprietors or limited liability partnerships. Although the size of these law firms have increased from one to ten lawyers (Fombad 2010; Fombad, Boon & Bothma 2009) to 21 lawyers from 2014 (Harris 2014), the firm size is considered as small. Concerning the size of firms, Mayer-Schoenberger (1995) observes the following:

[S]izes of law firms range widely from sole practitioners [*lawyers practising alone*] to small firms consisting of two to 50 lawyers to midsize firms of 50 to 200 lawyers and to very large professional firms having more than 1000 lawyers. (n.p.)

Lawyers possess professional skills such as legal research, judicial problem-solving and analysis, application of the law to relevant facts, negotiation, drafting, advocacy, interviewing and other general skills such as business management, communication, teamwork, and client relations (Collins 1994; Tjaden 2001).

Although knowledge management has increasingly become a topic of discussion in many competitive law firms (Curve Consulting 2003; Kofoed 2002; Leibowitz 2002; Parson 2002; Rusanow 2003), the empirical studies on the potential benefits and strategic use of knowledge management, amidst the changing legal environment, remain unsung in these firms (Dykema 2014). The studies of Du Plessis (2004, 2011) and Du Plessis and Du Toit (2005) on knowledge management in law firms focused on information and knowledge management in support of legal research in a digital environment. Bopape (2010) examines information technology to support knowledge management and Fombad (2010) suggests strategies for knowledge management in law firms in Botswana; whilst Fombad (2014) examines some lessons for knowledge management in small law firms in Botswana. The findings of this article are based on an update of the author's thesis on knowledge management in law firms in Botswana.

Problem statement

It is becoming apparent that the pressures of the knowledge economy and the changing business environment are compelling law firms to rethink their structures, roles, mission and the manner in which they conduct their business by adopting knowledge management. Nonetheless, strategic knowledge management in law firms in Botswana remains in its initial stages (Fombad 2010, 2014; Fombad *et al*. 2009). This article identifies factors that will motivate the adoption of knowledge management and the potential benefits for law firms, and will also provide guidelines for strategic knowledge management.

Research objective

The article seeks to answer the following questions:

- How is the legal information environment changing?
- What factors are motivating the adoption of knowledge management in law firms in Botswana?
- What are the potential benefits of knowledge management in these firms?

Literature review

This section presents an overview of the concept of knowledge economy, the changes in the legal environment, knowledge management, and the potential benefits of knowledge management to law firms.

The knowledge economy

There is no universal definition of the knowledge economy. Interrelated concepts such as knowledge society, modern society and network capitalism have been used to describe the term. An understanding of the concept of the information economy is important to appreciate its meaning. The information economy is the period after the industrial age during which economic development depended largely on information and the exploitation thereof, an increase in the use of computers, telecommunication, e-governance, e-commerce, online education and universal access to telephones (Martin 1995). The information economy era was characterised by information-intensive organisations, a significant information sector, the social use of information and learning society (Moore 1999). On the other hand, the term 'knowledge economy' was coined from the report of Organisation for Economic Cooperation and Development (OECD) entitled 'The Knowledge-Based Economy' (1996). According to this report, it is an economy characterised by a hierarchy of networks that is fuelled by the rapid rate of change in all aspects of life, including learning. As a consequence, the OECD obliged all sectors of the economy to respond to the demands of this economy by equipping people with the knowledge and necessary skills to survive in this milieu. Pink (2005) observes that the knowledge economy is built on logical, linear, computer-like capabilities of the information economy where information means wealth and power to an economy in which wealth and power are gained by those who have the cognitive and creative capabilities to reframe information into useful knowledge, although information is freely available. Britz *et al*. (2006) summarise the distinct characteristics of a knowledge society as:

access to modern ICTs and the use thereof, the number of scientists in a country, the amount spent on research and development as a percentage of the gross domestic product (GDP), the ability to produce and export, high technology, the number of patents filed in a country, and the number of articles published in highly ranked scholarly journals. (n.p.)

Handzic and Zhou (2005) list the characteristics of a knowledge economy as one that is knowledge centric with visible network effects, rapid and unpredicted changes and innovation. The World Bank identifies the four pillars of development in the knowledge economy as education and training, information infrastructure, economic incentive, an institutional regime, and innovative systems (Chen & Dahlman 2005).

Knowledge economy, therefore, may be referred to as a dematerialised and conceptualised economy driven by affluence and characterised by the use of the following:

- information
- knowledge
- ICTs and distinctive know-how for competitive advantage
- innovation
- learning
- change
- long-term economic growth.

Changes in the legal information environment

Traditionally, the practice of law has been built around law books and print technology. Legal research facilities were centred on the paper-based law library, the precedent bank and the collection of press cuttings (Berring 1997; Suender 2013; Wales Library Resources for Lawyers Project Africa 2001). The situation started changing, albeit gradually with the development of online computer-based research systems like LexisNexis and Weslaw in the 1970s (Katsh 1995). Then, the Internet moved the use of ICTs in law firms beyond the automation of existing practices to innovative concepts and applications such as the intranet, Internet deal rooms, extranet, document and content management, online depositions, real time chat, portals, groupware, expert systems and knowledge management systems (Hopkins & Reynolds 2003; Reach 2006). Nye (1999) predicted that by the year 2025, the Internet would change everything about the practice of law.

As a result of the Internet, the globalisation of business practices has broken down geographical boundaries, leading to an increase in an international collaborative legal practice worldwide (Gottschalk 2014; Wall 1998). Furthermore, there has been an exponential growth in the size of law firms around the world, for example in Botswana the maximum number of lawyers per firm has increased from 11 in 2010 to 21 in 2014. The continuous increase in the number of lawyers and law firms has put pressure on law firms to maintain a competitive edge against one another as far as partners, clients and law graduates are concerned.

The above changes in the legal industry had several consequences, for example information overload has been aggravated. Parson (2002) noted that in the knowledge economy, the explosion of content and the increasing demands for speed in the provision of legal services have ironically led to information anxiety and attention deficit amongst lawyers. Furthermore, clients are becoming computer literate and sophisticated consumers of legal services who expect lawyers to have technologies in place that may enhance their effectiveness (Dubin 2005). In addition, the disintermediation process in law firms has been accelerated (Bradlow 1988; Nye 1999; Susskind 2001). Disintermediation is any activity that does away with an intermediary when rendering services or concluding transactions (Drucker 2000; ESQlawtech 2002). This has given clients the feeling that they are paying for the management skills of lawyers rather than their legal knowledge.

Finally, the competitive business environment has revolutionised the mobility of lawyers. Some are opting for changes to improve on their curriculum vitae and others are in search of greener pastures (Hunter, Beaumont & Lee 2002). There is, therefore, a growing awareness that if measures are not taken, a vast quantity of vital knowledge and expertise would walk out of the door.

Knowledge and knowledge management

Knowledge can take on many different forms and has different meanings to each individual organisation. Closely related concepts such as data and information can easily approximate some form of knowledge. Nonaka and Takeuchi (1995) consider knowledge as a true and justified personal belief that increases an individual's capacity to take action. According to Fahey and Prusak (1998), knowledge is what the knower knows that does not exist independently of a knower, but is rather shaped by one's needs and one's initial stock of knowledge. In this article, knowledge is considered as information combined with experience, context, interpretation, reflection, intuition, creativity plus the ability to use the information to act or innovate. It includes truths, beliefs, perspectives, concepts, judgement, expectations, methodologies and the know-how.

Similar to knowledge, there is still no universally accepted definition of knowledge management. From an information technology perspective Platt (2003) defines knowledge management as accessing, evaluating, managing, organising, filtering and distributing information in a manner that would be useful to end users through a technological platform. From an intellectual capital perspective, Smith (2001) considers knowledge management as an on-going procedural 'bottom-up' process that develops and exploits the tangible assets and intangible knowledge resources of the organisation and shares it across boundaries in the organisation. From a process perspective knowledge management involves activities such as creation, acquisition, identification, storage, sharing and application of knowledge (Gottschalk 2014).

In this article, strategic knowledge management refers to a set of systematic and disciplined actions an organisation can take to obtain the greatest value from the knowledge available. It is the development of an organisational-wide knowledge management capability designed to provide sustainable competitive advantage (Inelcom & K-net 2015). It entails establishing a framework that defines the key elements of knowledge management and their interaction with business strategy, organisational design and the business practice (Gottschalk 2014).

Perceived benefits of knowledge management in law firms

Perceptions of the benefits of knowledge management vary from individual to individual and organisation to organisation. Law firms in Canada, the United States, the United Kingdom and Australia are considering knowledge management as a necessity for meeting emerging client demand for efficiency, accountability, and controlled legal costs (Chester 2002; Nathanson & Levison 2002). Leading United Kingdom law firms have well-developed precedents and know how systems maintained by fulltime professional support lawyers who are senior lawyers and experts in their field (Kay 2002). Several legal researchers (Becerra-Fernandez 1999; Curve Consulting 2003; Gottschalk 2014;

TABLE 1: What would motivate the adoption of knowledge management in your firm? (N = 140).

Variable	1 Strongly agree in %	2 Agree in %	3 Neutral in %	4 Disagree in %	5 Strongly disagree in %
Advanced information communication technologies	74.3	23.6	2.1	-	-
The shift from paper-based to electronic sources of information	67.9	26.4	5.7	-	-
The Internet	65.7[a]	30.0[a]	3.6[a]	0.7[a]	-
Electronic publishing	67.1	27.9	-	-	-
Globalisation of legal services	37.1[a]	28.6[a]	19.3[a]	6.4[a]	3.6[a]
Competition amongst firms	33.6	36.4	25.7	4.3	-
Pressure from clients	20.7	34.3	29.3	15.7	-
Information overload	17.9[a]	23.6[a]	32.9[a]	15.7[a]	-
Loss of key personnel and their knowledge	21.4	32.9	15.7	17.9	12.1
The use of knowledge management tools and practices by other competitors	36.4	52.1	3.6	7.9	-
An increase in the mobility of lawyers	20.7	25.7	26.4	13.6	13.6
The need to identify and to protect strategic knowledge in the firm	50.0	33.6	8.6	6.4	1.4
The desire to promote professional satisfaction	65.0	29.3	5.7	-	-
The desire to support and to encourage a learning culture	63.6	31.4	5.0	-	-
The desire to promote teamwork	65.0	25.7	9.3	-	-
The desire to meet the information and knowledge needs of the lawyer	65.7	30.0	4.3	-	-
Pressure from other professional service firms	25.7	27.9	27.1	14.3	5.0

[a], Percentages that do not add up as a result of non-response.

Kay 2002; Leibowitz 2004; Opp 2004; Whitfield-Jones 1999) have noted that the successful implementation of knowledge management strategy in law firms may result in the following benefits:

- Innovation is sustained and the free flow of ideas is encouraged.
- Learning is enhanced as well as the ability to stay ahead of competition and changes in the legal information environment.
- The quality of knowledge work is improved.
- Individual and group competencies are enhanced.
- It provides opportunities for more effective networking and collaboration.
- Customer service is maintained by streamlining response times.
- Revenue is boosted with the faster arrival of products and services to market.
- Redundancy is eliminated and employee retention rates are enhanced by recognising the value of employees' knowledge and rewarding them for it.
- Operations are streamlined and costs reduced by eliminating redundant or unnecessary processes.

Research methodology

A qualitative and quantitative research method was adopted and open and closed-ended questionnaires and semi-structured interviews were used as instruments. A survey research design was used. The target population was the sampling frame requested and obtained from the Botswana Law Society which consists of a list of registered private law firms; these firms comprised 115 registered law firms in Botswana and a total of 217 lawyers. A census of the total population of 217 was adopted for the questionnaire survey. Interviews were held to complement the census. The researcher adopted the purposive sampling technique and limited the interviews to law firms in Gaborone. Gaborone was deliberately chosen to administer the interviews, because of its accessibility and proximity and the majority

of the lawyers are based in Gaborone. In order to validate the instrument, preliminary interviews were conducted with lawyers. The questionnaire was then critically reviewed to ensure that there is some similarity between the interview questions and those in the questionnaire. The questionnaire was modified and the feedback and suggestions from the promoter taking into account, and the opinions of experts in knowledge management research were sought to evaluate the instrument with regard to comments on language and structure. The Statistical Package for Social Scientists (SPSS) version 15.0 was used for the analysis of the data collected from the close-ended questionnaires. On the other hand, qualitative data were derived from the open-ended questions and the interviews conducted, with 15 lawyers who had been selected from different law firms in Gaborone, were coded using thematic content analyses. About 140 completed questionnaires were returned, which translated to a return rate of 64.5%. The participants were asked to rate the questions on a five point scale of 'strongly agree', 'agree', 'neutral', 'disagree' and 'strongly disagree'.

Data analysis and findings

The frequency distribution of participants, concerning their level of education, revealed that a majority, 116 (83%) have bachelor's degrees and 24 (17.1%) have Master's degrees. Furthermore, amongst other qualifications were executive masters in sports organisations, a post graduate diploma in international law, and a diploma in trial advocacy. With regard to longevity of practice, the length of practice of participants ranges from 1–33 years. The mean number of years of practice is 6 years. With regard to organisational characteristics the following demographics are found:

- 55 participants (39.3%) are sole proprietors
- 49 (35.0%) have 2 lawyers
- 23 (16.4%) have 3 lawyers
- 11 (7.9%) have 4 lawyers
- 1 (0.7%) has 5 lawyers
- 1 (0.7%) has nine lawyers.

TABLE 2: The perceived benefits of knowledge management in law firms in Botswana ($N = 140$).

Variable	1 Strongly agree in %	2 Agree in %	3 Neutral in %	4 Disagree in %	5 Strongly disagree in %
Improve knowledge sharing	60.7	39.3	-	-	-
Improve lawyers efficiency and productivity	63.6	31.4	5.0	-	-
Improve lawyers' relationship vis-à-vis clients and customers	57.1	27.9	15.0	-	-
Prevent duplication in research	60.0	31.4	8.6	-	-
Increase flexibility amongst lawyers	51.4	35.7	7.1	5.7	-
Increase flexibility amongst lawyers	51.4	35.7	7.1	5.7	-
Protect the firm's loss of knowledge	70.0	22.9	7.1	-	-
Result in competitive advantage	52.9	26.4	20.7	-	-
Integrate knowledge within the firm	60.7	31.4	6.4	-	1.4
Improve retention rate of lawyers in the firm	46.4	28.6	20.	50	-
Improve the sharing and transfer of knowledge with partners and strategic alliances	58.6	31.4	10.0	-	-
Enhance economic profitability	60.7	29.3	10.0	-	-

It also emerged from the interviews that the law firms in Botswana remain small with an average of two partners due to the fact that every lawyer wants to become a partner rather than just working as a professional assistant, because partners receive a share of the profit. As a result lawyers constantly leave law firms to start off as sole proprietors or to form small partnerships.

Factors that motivate the adoption of knowledge management in a law firms

Against the background of some of the changes in the legal information environment, this question listed the possible factors that may motivate a firm to adopt knowledge management (Table 1).

In general the responses show that lawyers acknowledged the need for knowledge management in their firms. They acknowledged that the following have triggered the adoption of knowledge management:

- advances in information communication technology (97.9%)
- the Internet (95.7%)
- electronic publishing (95.0%)
- the shift from paper-based to electronic sources (94.3%).

The following are some responses from interviewees about the reasons for adopting knowledge management:

- Lawyers do not stay in one firm; they are moving from firm to firm.
- Lawyers are constantly splitting up in the law firms to start off as sole proprietors or to form partnerships.
- We are under pressure to attract new clientele.
- It will be good to network with other lawyers.
- If only knowledge can be standardised.
- There is a lot of competition out there as to who owns the best knowledge.
- We have to keep up with the changes around us in the international law firms.
- The Internet, computers, observation from other lawyers and networking with other lawyers are a challenge to our firm.

The perceived benefits of knowledge management for the law firms

Various items on perceived benefits of knowledge management are presented in Table 2.

The findings revealed that participants generally recognised the potential benefits of knowledge management. They all agreed (100%) that a good knowledge management attitude would improve knowledge sharing in the firm. Knowledge management attitude is generally reflected in the way a firm accesses and shares its knowledge communication style, trust and teamwork (Forstenlechner 2006; Lambe 2003; Rusanow 2007). These findings contradict the general notion that law firms are noted for their expertise, and secretive, individualistic culture (Lambe 2003; Maiden 2002; Terrett 1998:68). Lawyers further acknowledged that knowledge management would prevent duplication in research, of whom 91.4% agreed. The participants agreed that knowledge management would protect law firms from losing knowledge (92.9%), it would improve the retention rate of lawyers (75.0%) and integrate knowledge within the firm (92.1%). Many lawyers recognised that knowledge management would improve lawyers' relationships with their clients (85.0%). It, therefore, seems that lawyers appreciate the benefits of improving their relationship with their clients (Lim & Klobas 2000). The participants also acknowledged that knowledge management would improve the lawyer's efficiency, productivity (95.0%), and flexibility (87.1%). It is likely that improvement in efficiency and productivity will enhance a lawyer's flexibility, thus resulting in professional satisfaction. These findings confirm the research that knowledge management would expose lawyers with special experience and expertise to work on projects in their area to such an extent that they attain professional excellence, equip themselves with advanced skills and provide exceptional services to clients (Chester 2002; Rodriguez, Garcia & Pizarro 2002; Rusanow 2003, 2007; Wesemann 2006). Timely billing, the ability to respond to the unexpected, the ability to create innovative solutions for blue sky thinking, and the ability to curb legal costs are likely to benefit the client. Law firms in Canada, the United States, the United Kingdom and Australia are considering knowledge management as a necessity for meeting emerging client demand for efficiency, accountability, and controlled legal cost (Chester 2002; Nathanson & Levison 2002; Rusanow 2007; Wesemann 2006).

Most of the participants agreed that knowledge management would enhance economic profitability (90.0%). As a result of the delivery of high quality legal services to satisfied clients, more business will be generated which will result in better economic performance and knowledge management results in the fast delivery of high quality services.

Respondents also agreed that knowledge management will improve the retention rate (75%). Knowledge management initiatives enable firms to attract and retain talented lawyers and also their clients. In situations where lawyers decide to leave the firm, knowledge management provides for a continuity of knowledge. It also helps to capture and effortlessly share senior lawyers' knowledge in the firm. Responses from the 'other' category and the interviews indicated that the perceived benefits of knowledge management in law firms would result in general efficiency, improvement of quality of output, and improvement of the quality of the clients. The following are notable responses from the interviews in this study, with regard to the perceived benefits of knowledge management in law firms in Botswana:

- It is encouraging to know that I can always get what I need within the time frame available for it because currently I spend a lot of time sort of reinventing the wheel.
- It seems to be the trend and an essential function in today's law firm environment.
- As a fairly young legal practitioner, it is heartening to know that with knowledge management in place, there will be somewhere to inquire information about what you do not know because it is presently difficult working without any prior experience and with no one willing to assist you.
- I appreciate its potential to improve the overall efficiency of the firm.
- The thought that it will make my work easy.
- It will improve the quality of clients.
- It will provide the ability to network with other lawyers within and out of the country.

Although lawyers seemingly recognise the potential benefits of knowledge management, these promised benefits remain around the corner because the adoption of knowledge management still remains in its infancy.

Limitations

A major limitation of this paper is that the findings specifically apply to law firms and, therefore, insights into other branches of the legal profession may be lacking that fall under the Judicial Service Commission (e.g. judges, magistrates and court registrars), legal practitioners in the Attorney General's Chambers and, legal academics. Furthermore, it does not examine other professional service firms that render

professional services. Although it is believed that these findings could apply to other branches and professional service firms. Future studies should investigate knowledge management as a competitive edge in the legal profession and in other firms in Botswana that render professional services.

Conclusion and recommendations

This article paints a picture of a profession that is aware of the enormous potential benefits of knowledge management amidst the changes in the legal environment, although the adoption of knowledge management is still in its infancy. In order for law firms in Botswana to sharpen their competitiveness, broaden their influence, and survive in a legal environment characterised by aggressive changes, the approach to knowledge management should be strategically thought out. Centaur Media (2014) posits that knowledge management discourse in law firms has moved from creating and managing internal documents to creating value for the client. On the other hand Winston (2014) argues that knowledge management in law firms has shifted beyond the provision of legal services, to supporting and integrating expanding law firms to cope with information overload, and is now focused on helping attorneys do more with less. It, therefore, stands to reason that strategic knowledge management will entail that law firms in Botswana leverage their knowledge for competitive advantage, build up market trends, and develop business strategies directed at meeting the needs of clients and other lawyers. In rethinking the knowledge management approach in these firms, an understanding and sensitivity to the size, ideals and characteristics of these firms is crucial given that they are predominantly small firms (Fombad 2014). Knowledge management in these firms should be simple and implemented at a rate which is commensurate with their level of resources. Also, issues of cultural resistance are critical (Zeide & Liebowitz 2012). To this end, law firms should create an environment where knowledge, creativity and innovation are valued by facilitating communication amongst people in different locations and from different departments. Law firms should encourage ideas, rewards and success, whilst allowing people to fail and learn from their failures.

Therefore, with the rise of the knowledge-based economy, coupled with the pressures faced by the legal industry in recent years, law firms in Botswana can no longer afford to rely on the traditional methods of managing knowledge, because they need the 'best minds' and the best knowledge in their area of practice. Knowledge management will, therefore, enhance the cost effectiveness of these firms. Although knowledge management is not a quick fix or ready-made panacea, it will certainly help prepare law firms in Botswana to be alive to the fact that the systematic harnessing of legal knowledge is no longer a luxury, but an absolute necessity in the knowledge economy above all, it will provide an enabling business environment to private sector development and growth and, therefore, facilitate

Botswana's drive towards the knowledge-based economy as envisaged in its National Vision 2016.

Acknowledgements
Competing interests

The author declares that she has no financial or personal relationships which may have inappropriately influenced her in writing this article.

References

Becerra-Fernandez, I., 1999, 'Knowledge management today: Changing the corporate culture', in *Proceedings of the 5th International Conference of Decision Science Institute*, July 4–7.

Berring, R., 1997, 'Chaos, cyberspace and tradition: Legal information transmogrified', viewed 04 May 2014, from http://www.law.berkly/edu/journals

Bopape, S., 2010, 'Utilisation of information technology to support information and Knowledge management by lawyers in Polokwane City', *South African Journal of Library and Information Services* 76(2), 129–140.

Bradlow, D., 1988, 'The changing legal environment 1980s and beyond', *ABA Journal* 1, 72–76.

Britz, J., Lor, P., Coetzee, I. & Bester, B., 2006, 'Africa as a knowledge society: A reality check', *The International Information & Library Review* 38, 25–40. http://dx.doi.org/10.1016/j.iilr.2005.12.001

Bwalya, K.J., 2010, 'Botswana's novel approaches for knowledge-based economy facilitation: Issues, policies and contextual framework', *International Journal of Information Communication Technologies and Human Development* 2(1), 59–74. http://dx.doi.org/10.4018/jicthd.2010010104

Centaur Media, 2014, 'How helpful is your KM?', *Lawyer* (*Online Edition*) 9(25).

Chen, D.C. & Dahlman, C.J., 2005, 'The knowledge economy, the KAM methodology and World Bank operations', viewed 17 February 2014, from http://siteresources.worldbank.org

Chester, S., 2002, 'Knowledge management in Canadian law firms', Pacific Legal Technology Conference Vancouver Trade and Technology Centre', viewed 07 June 2014, from www.lawsociety.bc.ca

Collins, H., 1994, 'The place of computer in legal education', *Law Technology Journal* 3(3), viewed 08 August 2014, from http://www.law.warwick.ac

Curve Consulting, 2003, 'Global law firm knowledge management survey report', viewed 09 February 2012, from http://www.curveconsulting.com/pages/

Drucker, P., 2000. 'The new economy and the virtual law firm of the future', viewed 25 August 2012, from http://www.digitallawyer.com/virtual2.html

Du Plessis, T., 2004, 'Information and knowledge management in support of legal research in a digital environment', PhD thesis, Faculty of Arts, University of Rand Afrikaans.

Du Plessis, T., 2011, 'Information and knowledge management at South African law firms', *Potchefstroom Electronic Law Journal* 14(4), 233–258. http://dx.doi.org/10.4314/pelj.v14i4.8

Dubin, M., 2005, 'Creating an environment in the law firms where knowledge management will work', viewed 12 January 2013, from http://www.searchwarp.com

Du Plessis, T. & du Toit, A., 2005, 'Survey of information and knowledge management in South African law firms', *South African Journal of Information Management* 7(1). http://dx.doi.org/10.4102/sajim.v7i1.252

Dykema, E., 2014, 'Knowledge management: Law firm reluctant to reap the rewards', viewed 10 February 2015, from https://caserails.com/blog/knowledge-management-law-firms-reluctant-reap-rewards

ESQlawtech, Ltd., 2002, 'Law office technology transforming the legal profession. The Esqlawtech weekly', viewed 09 June 2012, from http://www.mylawtips.com/officetechnology.html

Fahey, L. & Prusak, L., 1998, 'The Eleven deadliest sins of knowledge management', *California Management Review* 40(3), 265–276. http://dx.doi.org/10.2307/41165954

Fombad, M., 2010, 'Strategies for knowledge management in law firms in Botswana', Ph.D., Dept. of Information Science, University of Pretoria, Pretoria.

Fombad, M., 2014, 'Knowledge management in law firms in Botswana: Some lessons for small law firms', *Journal of Librarianship and Information Science*, viewed 30 May 2014, from http://lis.sagepub.com/content/early/2014/05/28/09610006145364

Fombad, M., Boon, J.A. & Bothma, T.J.D., 2009, 'Strategy for knowledge management in law firms in Botswana', *South African Journal of Information Management* 11(2). http://dx.doi.org/10.4102/sajim.v11i2.405

Forstenlechner, I., 2006, 'Impact of knowledge management on law firm performance: An investigation of causality across cultures', PhD Thesis, School of Industrial and Manufacturing Science, Cranfield University.

Gottschalk, P., 2014, 'Knowledge management strategy in professional service firms', *Advances in Management* 7(3), 16–22.

Handzic, M. & Zhou, A.Z., 2005, 'Knowledge management: An integrative approach', Chandos Publishing, Oxford. http://dx.doi.org/10.1142/5639

Harris, J., 2014, 'Neighbourhood watch', *Lawyer* 28, 14(3), 16–16

Hopkins, R. & Reynolds, P., 2003, 'Redefining privacy and security in the electronic communication age: A lawyers ethical duties in the virtual world of the internet', *The Georgetown Journal of Legal Ethics* 16(4), 675–684.

Hunter, L., Beaumont, P. & Lee, M., 2002, 'Knowledge management practice in Scottish law firms', *Human Resource Management Journal* 12(2), 4–21. http://dx.doi.org/10.1111/j.1748-8583.2002.tb00061.x

Inelcom & K-net, 2015, 'Strategic knowledge management & knowledge', viewed 08 February 2015, from http://www.kbos.net/default.aspx?articleID=10315

Katsh, M., 1995, 'Law in the digital world', viewed 08 May 2013, from http://www.umassp.edu/legal/dw control.html

Kay, S., 2002, 'Benchmarking knowledge management in U.S. and U.K law firms', viewed 11 October 2012, from http://www.llrx.com/features/bench markingkm.html

Kofoed, K., 2002, 'Knowledge management in law firms', MBA Cambridge Business School, University of Cambridge, Cambridge.

Lambe, P., 2003, 'What does knowledge management mean for the law firms', viewed 11 September 2014, from http://www.greenchameleon.com

Leibowitz, W., 2002, 'Knowledge management in the law firm. Wendy Tech Articles', viewed 09 September 2013, from http://www.WendyTech.com

Leibowitz, W., 2004, 'Knowledge management in the law firm. Wendy Tech Articles', viewed 09 September 2013, from http://www.WendyTech.com

Lim, D. & Klobas, J., 2000, 'Knowledge management in small enterprises', *The Electronic Library* 18(6), 420–433. http://dx.doi.org/10.1108/02640470010361178

Maiden, C., 2002, 'The secret life if lawyers reinventing law', viewed 15 January 2013, from http:// www.ask.bm

Moore, N.I., 1999, 'Partners in the information Society', *Library Association Record*, 101(12), 702–703.

Martin, W.J., 1995, *The Global Information Society*, Aslib Gower.

Mayer-Schoenberger, V., 1995, 'Lawyering on the Infohbahn: The European perspective', *Law Technology Journal June* 4(1), 5–95.

Nathanson, A. & Levison, A., 2002, 'Differentiate your firm with knowledge management', *Legal Information Technology*, viewed 5 November 2012, from http://www.brco.com/downloads/articles/

Nonaka, I. & Takeuchi, H., 1995, *The knowledge creating company*, University Press, Oxford.

Nye, A., 1999, 'The lawyer of the future', *Maine Lawyer's Review* 7(12).

Organisation for Economic Cooperation and Development (OECD), 1996, 'The Knowledge-Based Economy', viewed 20 February 2014, from http://www.oecd.org/sti/sci-tech/1913021.pdf

Office of the President, 2010, 'Report on public service customer satisfaction and staff perception surveys', prepared by Economic and Management Consultants. Unpublished.

Opp, K., 2004, 'Commentary: The importance of knowledge management to a firm', viewed 05 May 2013, from http://www.accessmylibrary.com

Parson, M., 2002, 'Uncommon knowledge: The Knowledge management questions for service firms', *Professional Review* 11, 2–3.

Pink, D.H., 2005, 'A whole new mind: moving from the information age to the conceptual age', Penguin, New York.

Platt, N., 2003, 'Knowledge is power: knowledge management remains vital to the firm's success AALL Spectrum', viewed 05 August 2013 from, http://www.llrxcom/features/kmpower.html

Powell, W. & Snellman, K., 2004, 'Thee knowledge economy', *Annual Review of Sociology* 30, 199–220. http://dx.doi.org/10.1146/annurev.soc.29.010202.100037

Presidential Task Group, 1997, *Long-term Vision for Botswana: Towards Prosperity for All*, Government Printer, Gaborone.

Reach, C., 2006, Positioning for power: Technology and the law firm librarian, American Bar Association, viewed 11 June 2012, from http://www.abanet.orgpower.html

Rodriquez, C., Garcia, J. & Pizarro, J., 2002, 'Knowledge management in law firm', *Upgrade* 3(1), 51–54.

Rusanow, G., 2003, Knowledge management is a business imperative, viewed 03 August 2013, from http://www.llrx.com

Rusanow, G., 2007, 'Combining business and practice knowledge management and the law', *Knowledge Management World* 16(1), 12–15.

Smith, E., 2001, 'The role of tacit and explicit knowledge in the workplace', *Journal of Knowledge Management* 5(4), 311–321. http://dx.doi.org/10.1108/13673270110411733

Suender, M., 2013, 'Alternatives to the partnership track', *Law Practice: The Business of Practicing Law* 39(3), 40–43.

Susskind, R., 2001, 'The changing face of private law practice: Part 111. Working notes on deliberations of the committee on research about the future of the legal profession on the current status of the legal profession', viewed 10 September 2012, from http://www.abanet.org

Terret, A., 1998, 'Knowledge management and the law firm', *Journal of Knowledge Management* 2(1), 67–76. http://dx.doi.org/10.1108/EUM0000000004608

Tjaden, T., 2001, *Legal research and writing: Law in a nutshell*, Irwin Law, Toronto.

Wales Library Resources for Lawyers Project Africa, 2001, 'The Bar Human Rights Committee of England and Wales and-The British Council', viewed 10 February 2015, from www.barhumanrights.org.uk/sites/default/files/.../uganda_report.do

Wall, D., 1998, 'Information technology and the shaping of legal practice in the UK', paper presented at the 13th BILETA conference, 27–28 March, viewed 16 December 2012, from http://www.bileta.ac.uk

Wesemann, P., 2006, 'Knowledge management: Is the emperor wearing clothes. Edge International', viewed December 2013, from http://www.edge.ai/Edge International.

Whitfield-Jones, C., 1999, *Business as usual or the end of as we know it*, Managing Partner, London.

Winston, A.M., 2014, 'Law firm knowledge management: A selected annotated bibliography', *Law Library Journal* 2(10), 106.

World Bank, 2012, 'Knowledge economy index, moving towards the knowledge economy', viewed 12 February 2015, from http://botswana.opendataforafrica. org/WBKEI2013/knowledge-economy-index-world-bank-2012

Zeide, E. & Liebowitz, J., 2012, 'Knowledge management in law: A look at cultural resistance', *Legal Information Management* 12(1), 34–38. http://dx.doi. org/10.1017/S1472669612000126

Understanding the use of strategic intelligence as a strategic management tool in the long-term insurance industry in South Africa

Authors:
René Pellissier[1]
J-P. Kruger[1]

Affiliations:
[1]Department of Business Management, University of South Africa, South Africa

Correspondence to:
René Pellissier

Email:
pellir@unisa.ac.za

Postal address:
PO Box 392, UNISA 0003, South Africa

The purpose of this research paper was to explore the extent to which strategic intelligence is utilised within the South African long-term insurance industry and whether it could be used to identify opportunities or threats within the global environment to remain competitive, create greater innovation, and corporate advantage.

The paper obtained the qualitative views and opinions of strategic decision makers, on an executive managerial level within the South African long-term insurance industry, on their organisations use of strategic intelligence. It was found that there are marked differences in the conformity and usage of strategic intelligence and its components between the organisations surveyed, with a measurable difference between large and small organisations. It is, however, generally viewed that the use of a strategic intelligence framework could greatly enhance decision-making.

Data collection for the research undertaken was limited to the 82 long-term insurance companies, which were registered with the South African Financial Services Board. More specifically the focus was on the organisations listed on the Johannesburg Securities Exchange within the Life Assurance sector, within which a final response rate of 36.1% was achieved, including the 100% response rate from the six listed organisations.

By understanding the extent to which strategic intelligence is utilised in the South African long-term insurance industry, and the benefits or problems that are experienced by implementing and using strategic intelligence as an input to the strategic management process we can comprehend the value that strategic intelligence adds in the decision making process. The originality of this work concludes in the identification and utilisation of the most important factors of a strategic intelligence framework that will greatly enhance global corporate decision-making and result in competitive advantage and constant innovation within the South African business environment.

Topic

Strategic intelligence has information as its foundation. This research proposes that, through its ability to absorb sources of information, the synergy of business intelligence, competitive intelligence, and knowledge management combined to form strategic intelligence, will allow organisations to incorporate all of their information and intellectual capital into a single, easily manageable system to meet the intelligence requirements of management's strategic planning and decision-making process.

This research reviews the current understanding and implementation of strategic intelligence systems and processes in the South African long-term insurance industry. This review is performed in order to identify problems experienced and advantages incurred by executive management through the implementation and use of strategic intelligence as an input to the strategic management process. The study further sets out to determine the value of strategic intelligence in the decision-making process. A purposive sampling technique was used to select the six most important organisations in the South African long-term insurance industry. This industry was selected because of its strong focus on information and knowledge, and the agility with which decisions need to be made in order to cope with environmental and technological changes.

We found that most organisations have not embraced any framework for a strategic intelligence system or portal that provide valid strategic intelligence, which could assist in creating competitive advantage and constant innovation. Our research shows that through its ability to absorb sources of information, the synergy of business intelligence, competitive intelligence, and knowledge management combined to form strategic intelligence, will allow organisations to incorporate all of their information and intellectual capital into a single database or system which will meet the intelligence requirements of management.

Research statement

The identification and utilisation of the most important factors of a strategic intelligence framework will greatly enhance global corporate decision-making and result in competitive advantage and constant innovation within the South African business environment.

Methodology

Research is undertaken to increase knowledge, and is based on logical relationships and not just one's personal beliefs. Research involves methods and designs to collect data; arguments as to why results obtained are correct and meaningful, and an explanation of the limitations associated with the research (Leedy & Omrod 2005; Saunders, Lewis & Thornhill 2007).

Research identifies the need to find things out, such as the answers to a number of questions, which suggests a number of purposes for the research (Saunders *et al*. 2007).

The South African business environment comprises many industries and for the purpose of this study the long-term insurance industry was selected. The population was selected as a representative of the greater South African business environment as the organisations in this industry are vulnerable to changes within the macro-environment and micro-environment, are undergoing intense changes within their market and regulatory environment, and their competitive advantage are based on their use of information gathered on these environments.

The primary aim of this research study is to explore the extent to which strategic intelligence is currently utilised within the South African long-term insurance industry and how it can be used to identify opportunities or threats within the global environment to remain competitive, create greater innovation, and corporate advantage.

The following primary research questions were generated from the aforementioned aim:

- What is the extent to which strategic intelligence is utilised within the South African long-term insurance industry?
- How does strategic intelligence form a vital component of strategic management?
- What value does strategic intelligence add to the strategic management process within the South African long-term insurance industry?

Based on the primary research questions listed, the secondary research questions were generated:

- How do South African long-term insurance organisations currently collect and create strategic intelligence?
- What information systems are currently utilised by South African long-term insurance organisations to create strategic intelligence?
- How strategic decisions are made in South African long-term insurance organisations and on what intelligence are these decisions based?
- How South African long-term insurance organisations can best implement strategic intelligence?

A purposive sampling technique was used to select the best cases that would enable the research questions to be answered and result in the research objectives being met. As a homogeneous group, the long-term insurance industry was selected as the target population for the study and the individual organisations approached were identified from the list of valid licenses registered with the Financial Services Board. The unit of analysis was the selected organisations provided by the Financial Services Board. There are 82 long-term insurance companies in South Africa, of which six organisations were listed on the Johannesburg Securities Exchange within the Life Assurance Sector. The listed companies include: Old Mutual Plc., Liberty Group Ltd, Sanlam Ltd, Discovery Holdings Ltd, Clientele Life Ltd, and Metropolitan Holding Ltd.

The selected organisations participated in the research survey and completed the questionnaire. The research goal was therefore met with a 100% response rate. To broaden the scope of the research, the sample size was increased to include all the 82 long-term insurance companies that were registered with the Financial Services Board, which provided an in-depth examination of the use of strategic intelligence within the long-term insurance industry. Within the research results a distinction is made based on the size of the organisation in the South African context with larger organisations having more than 500 employees, whilst smaller organisations have fewer than 500 employees. It is; however, important to stress that the focus of the study was on the larger listed companies, because of their size, turnover, agility and expected efficiencies in this field. The unlisted companies were included to provide a broader range of perspectives into the respective field, and the execution of such in smaller companies. Of these 82, three had closed down before the study was conducted, four organisations confirmed that whilst they did have long-term insurance licences they were not part of the industry, and 14 companies were subsidiaries or divisions of the larger organisations and as such their answers were included with those of the larger organisations. Subtracting these 21 companies from the total sample of 82 left a sample size of 61 organisations. A final response rate of 36.1% was achieved, including the 100% response rate from the six listed organisations.

Strategic intelligence is most often used during the strategic management and strategic decision-making processes which executive and senior management conducts. As a result of the nature of the information being requested, the survey was conducted across the executive managerial level within the sample organisations with a focus on strategic decision makers.

Research data were collected by means of descriptive research, using a (nonprobability) purposive sample of the long-term insurance industry. A large sample was not required for this research because of the focus of this research being on gathering in-depth of information, based on a purposive sample of the long-term insurance industry. A web-based questionnaire was used to collect the data. It is important to note that a comprehensive definition list was included with the questionnaire to enhance the clarity of the terminology used in the survey. The data received from the 22 completed questionnaires were subsequently captured and analysed with the use of the statistical software program SPSS, version 16.0. This software package was used for data coding, data capturing, statistical analysis and internal consistency testing.

The variables from the questionnaire were firstly identified and coded. Secondly, the data was captured into SPSS and cleaned up to assure no anomalies were present. Because a nonprobability sampling technique (purposive sample) was used to select the respondents for the study, no generalisation was possible, and hence no inferential statistical techniques were performed.

In terms of Cross-tabulation Analysis, all variables used in the questionnaire were tabulated against each other, and were individually analysed to identify any relationships. Only variable relationships with scores greater than 7 were used in the analysis (i.e. respondents gave similar Likert scale scores for both variables), as this cut-off was viewed as having the greatest significance. As the sample was not random the significance of the relationship could not be tested by means of the Chi-square test for independence. Furthermore, a correlation matrix was used to simplify the identification of relationships, and analysis focused on relationships that fall into the -1.0 to -0.7 and +0.7 to +1.0 categories, which indicate highly negative or highly positive linear relationships.

In the context of validity in this research study, the questionnaire was tested for face validity, content validity and construct validity. This was performed through a process of pretesting the research instrument by piloting it to a small number of individuals. The comments received from these individuals lead to minor adjustments being made, after which it was distributed to the sample. Furthermore, the internal consistency of the Likert-scale items in each section was measured by means of the Cronbach Alpha Coefficient. The results showed that Cronbach's alpha reliability coefficient was high (above 0.8) for all the sections, meaning that each section shows good internal consistency.

After an introduction to the topic the research results will be analysed according to the structure used in the questionnaire format. The different parts and sections, which comprised the questionnaire, include: strategic management and strategic decision-making, business intelligence, competitive intelligence, knowledge management and strategic intelligence.

Introduction

The world has experienced a radical shift in the basic foundations of how business is conducted. The globalisation of markets and production resulted in national markets being integrated into a single global market trading in global products. The shift has been strengthened through the decline of trade barriers and fundamental developments in communication, information and transportation technologies. Globalisation resulted in greater world output, foreign investment, greater imports and exports and immense competitive pressures both between nations and industries (Hill 2005; Pearce & Robinson 2005).

Advancements in information technology and related developments in communications technology have increased organisations' ability to link global operations into sophisticated information networks. This, in turn, shrinks the time in which information is collected and enables organisations to achieve tight coordination in worldwide operations (Hill 2005; Laudon & Laudon 2007; Pearce & Robinson 2005). External factors influence the organisations' direction, organisational structure and internal processes. These factors that exist in the organisations' remote, industry and operating environments require constant monitoring for the formulation of strategies to optimise the organisations market opportunities and threats to allow them to survive in their competitive environment (Pearce & Robinson 2005).

In the current information age in which knowledge is power, where utilisation of this knowledge adds value to decision-making, organisations employ information to expand and maintain a competitive advantage (Haag, Cummings & Philips 2007). Gathering information and turning this raw data into intelligence through an exercise of human judgement, is a fundamental aspect of business (Murphy 2005). Knowledge and information are vital components in creating wealth for organisations. By utilising information systems in the process of generating knowledge and intelligence, the abundance of available information will allow organisations to generate competitive advantage and constant innovation to survive and prosper in the long term (Laudon & Laudon 2007).

An organisation needs to have knowledge about its business environment (its activities, resources, markets, customers, products, services, and costs) to plan for its current and future success. This knowledge, which could allow for the organisation's successful functioning needs to be disseminated organisation-wide. This results in one of the basic challenges for senior management; how to create a mindset about the present and the future in order to anticipate trends and the directions to be taken (Tham & Kim 2002).

Strategic intelligence

Strategic intelligence can be viewed as what a company needs to know of its business environment to enable it to gain insight into its present processes, anticipate and manage change for the future, design appropriate strategies that will create business value for customers, and improve profitability in current and new markets (Tham & Kim 2002).

Strategic intelligence consists of the aggregation of the various types of intelligentsia, which creates a synergy between business intelligence, competitive intelligence, and knowledge management to provide value-added information and knowledge toward making organisational strategic decisions. Strategic intelligence signifies the creation and transformation of information or knowledge that can be used in high-level decision-making. The emphasis is on how best to position the organisation to deal with future challenges and opportunities to maximise the organisation's success (Liebowitz 2006). Xu and Kaye (2009:12) define strategic intelligence as 'strategically significant information [provided] to senior managers that is scanned, analysed, digested, and is meaningful that could affect senior managers' beliefs, commitments, and actions'.

Strategic intelligence is identified as having the correct information available for the correct people as to allow them to make informed business decisions about the future of their organisations. Without this information, it is believed that it would be difficult for employees to make the correct decisions to achieve and maintain market leadership (Marchand & Hykes 2007). The value of strategic intelligence can therefore be seen through the improvement of the capabilities of managers and workers to learn about potential changes within their business or industry environment without having to redefine intelligence on which previous decisions were based. With the ability to openly share their perceptions, new information and insights whenever and wherever the organisation requires such information will increase the 'intelligence quotient' of all organisational managers (Tham & Kim 2002). Strategic intelligence's interest is less on the present than on the past and on the future, with a time horizon spanning two years in the past and to five to 10 years in the future. By collecting and analysing data from the past, the organisation can evaluate the success (or failure) of its strategies and those of its competitors. This will permit the organisation to better weigh its options for the future (McGonagle & Vella 1999).

The South African long-term insurance industry

Worldwide, the long-term insurance industry has undergone many changes in its working model. These changes are primarily linked to increasing the attractiveness of the industry to consumers. With the advent of technological advances that allow all consumers to shop around for the best products and pricing and the globalisation of markets allowing organisations to compete globally, organisations in this industry are required to stay a step ahead of their competitors by remaining agile and employing information and knowledge for strategic use. Consequently, a number of strategic decisions will have to be made in order to

remain competitive in the foreseeable future. New products, allowing consumers a greater understanding, flexibility and visibility will be required to attract new clients as well as increase market share and remain competitive. However, the utilisation of strategic intelligence during the strategic management process could identify opportunities, and challenges faced. This again, leads to better informed, effective decisions to be made that will assist organisations in gaining greater market share and to compete successfully against local and international competitors.

The modern business environment within the South African long-term insurance market has often been turbulent and volatile. South African organisations are required to engage international and local competitors and customers in a more regulated manner, and despite years of experience in the local environment, even the most successful and established organisations have committed strategic errors in both the local and international markets. An example of this includes a number of local organisations that have faced some difficulty as a result of their offshore subsidiaries having suffered under the financial crisis during the period 2007–2009. This was mainly as a result of a lack of managerial awareness and foresight. Certain organisations have since reviewed their strategies and refocused, or closed down certain divisions. Furthermore, the long-term insurance industry is facing many challenges and changes. For instance, compliance with regulatory requirements, increased competition, the Financial Sector Charter, the International Financial Reporting Standards (IFRS 4), addressing the needs of the low-income market for appropriate products, emerging technologies, inflation and interest rate increases and fluctuations, and, lastly, the Statement of Intent requirements as agreed upon by the Minister of Finance and the Life Offices' Association of South Africa rebuilding public confidence, dealing with issues emanating from the determinations made by the Pension Fund Adjudicator, consumerism and the impact of the global financial market crisis (The Financial Services Board South Africa 2007).

A media release by the Life Offices' Association (Life Offices' Association of South Africa 2008) in February 2008 revealed that South Africa has an insurance gap of more than R10-trillion, by means of life and disability insurance. Whilst the industry has made large gains in the past years, a large insurance deficit is still looming, allowing organisations the opportunity to further increase their market share.

Strategic intelligence has information as its foundation. Information can be collected from both internal and external sources such as: transaction processing, financial or supply chain systems and external databases of customer, product, and supplier information or by further utilising tools such as Michael Porter's Five Forces Model or Value chain analysis to create value by converting data into information. By collecting all this information into a single data warehouse or strategic intelligence repository that combines all the best aspects of strategic intelligence and information systems, a single databank will be created that would align them to provide business with the information and even intelligence it requires (Liebowitz 2006).

This research proposes that, through its ability to absorb sources of information, the synergy of business intelligence, competitive intelligence, and knowledge management combined to form strategic intelligence, will allow organisations to incorporate all of their information and intellectual capital into a single database or system which will meet the intelligence requirements of management. Montgomery and Weinberg (1998) gave an insight into the working or design of a strategic intelligence System, and Liebowitz (2006) and Marchand and Hykes (2007) identified the basis of strategic intelligence. Yet, the researchers are of the opinion that organisations have not yet fully embraced this model for a fully cooperative global internal corporate strategic intelligence system or portal that will incorporate all aspects of strategic intelligence into a single, easily manageable resource for management's strategic planning and decision-making process. This is the subject of this research.

Empirical research results

Strategic management

The first section of the questionnaire was designed to gain an understanding of the extent to which respondents undertake strategic management within the long-term insurance industry. The results suggest that:

- respondents, to a large extent, utilise a formalised strategic management process
- respondents recognise strategic management as a necessary activity for business
- respondents view information as having strategic value
- respondents believe that good strategy hinges on having timely, relevant and high quality information
- respondents attempt to provide their managers with critical and relevant information for strategic decision making; however, smaller organisations that were in greater disagreement do not have the capacity to provide managers with the required information, as larger organisations do
- the majority of respondents believe that they do provide their managers with access to information that provides them a comprehensive and robust perspective on how the organisation is performing, the dynamics at play

in the market place, competitor behaviour, stakeholder perceptions, resource availability, and the implications of trends in these areas for the firm; however, smaller organisations are at a disadvantage to larger organisations.

The results indicate that strategic management is to a large extent utilised within organisations in the long-term insurance industry; however, smaller organisations are at a disadvantage with regards to the provision of information to management.

Business intelligence

The purpose of the second section of the questionnaire was to gain an understanding into the business intelligence activities that are undertaken by the organisations within the long-term insurance industry. Based on the results obtained, the results suggest that:

- respondents collect and utilise business intelligence in decision-making; however, the results distinctly provide evidence that larger organisations make greater use of business intelligence than smaller organisations
- respondents, in general, have business intelligence that is valid, reliable and actionable[1]
- the majority of respondents believed that the availability of business intelligence increased the effectiveness of managerial decision-making
- a greater proportion of organisations did not have a predefined dashboard view of their organisations, than those that did[2]; however, the respondents unanimously agreed that a predefined dashboard view of the organisation is important for managerial decision-making
- a large number of different software applications were used by respondents to gather and generate business intelligence.

The results indicate that business intelligence is to a large extent utilised within organisations in the long-term insurance industry. Further questions exposed that larger organisations make greater use of business intelligence than smaller organisations, and therefore have a much greater competitive advantage as a result of their: access to valid, reliable and actionable business intelligence, predefined dashboard views of their organisations, and software applications used.

....

1. However, a large gap occurred between the results provided by smaller organisations and those of large organisations. Thus, proving that smaller organisations do not have business intelligence that is valid, reliable and actionable.

2. The respondents unanimously agreed that a predefined dashboard view of the organisation is important for managerial decision-making.

TABLE 1: Strategic management sorted by mean scores.

Variable	Question	Mean	SD
Section 1: Strategic management and strategic decision-making			
3.1.3	Our organisational views information as having strategic value.	4.36	0.658
3.1.2	Our organisation recognises strategic management as a necessary activity for business.	4.27	0.703
3.1.4	We believe that good strategy hinges on having timely, relevant and high quality information.	4.23	0.685
3.1.1	We utilise a formalised strategic management process.	3.91	0.811
3.1.5	Our organisation provides its managers with critical and relevant information for strategic decision making.	3.36	0.953
3.1.6	We believe our organisation provides our managers with access to information that provides a comprehensive and robust perspective on how the organisation is performing, the dynamics at play in the market place, competitor behaviour, stakeholder perceptions, resource availability and the implications of trends in these areas for the firm.	3.27	1.032

SD, standard deviation.

TABLE 2: Business intelligence sorted by mean scores.

Variable	Question	Mean	SD
Section 2: Business intelligence			
3.2.5	We believe there is value in having a predefined dashboard view of our organisation.	4.14	0.889
3.2.1	We collect and utilise business intelligence in decision making.	3.50	1.102
3.2.3	The availability of business intelligence has increased the effectiveness of managerial decision making.	3.50	1.102
3.2.2	Our business intelligence is valid, reliable and actionable.	3.36	1.217
3.2.4	We have a predefined dashboard view of our organisation.	2.86	1.424

SD, standard deviation.

Competitive intelligence

The purpose of section three of the questionnaire was to gain an understanding of the competitive intelligence activities that take place within organisations within the long-term insurance industry. The results suggest that:

- larger organisations do have a formal competitive intelligence function, whereas smaller organisations (in general) do not have a formalised competitive intelligence function
- a high number of organisations do make use of competitive intelligence in decision-making even if no formalised function exists for the management of competitive intelligence
- too few organisations have achieved the task of timely creation and distribution of competitive intelligence to management, with larger organisations having greater success in this area
- the vast majority of organisations do utilise external sources of information for market research
- a large number of organisations do evaluate the reliability and accuracy of their sources of information
- large organisations seem to analyse their competitors and have up to date profiles of them, whilst smaller organisations mostly did not
- most organisations are up to date with emerging technologies in their field of business and the benefits or features of these technologies
- organisations are cognisant of new and pending government legislation and legislative trends that impact their organisation
- the most important sources for the collection of competitive intelligence included the analysis of competitor's products (86%), websites (86%), annual reports (77%) and research reports (72%)
- the most common analytical methods or models used within the organisations to generate competitive

intelligence included SWOT analysis and competitor analysis (both with 82%), customer segmentation analysis (72%), industry analysis (64%), and financial analysis and valuation (59%)
- the most popular methods used by organisations to distribute and present intelligence results were email (77%), presentations (72%), and reports (64%)
- very few organisations made use of competitive intelligence software applications.

The results indicate that competitive intelligence activities are more prevalent in a formalised manner in larger organisations in the long-term insurance industry, whilst smaller organisations make much greater use of competitive intelligence on a ad hoc, or when required, basis.

Knowledge management

The purpose of this section of the questionnaire was to gain an understanding of the knowledge management activities that take place within the organisations in the long-term insurance industry. Based on the results obtained, the results suggest that:

- there is strong evidence that organisations believe that knowledge management assists in creating value out of their organisations intangible assets
- organisations view knowledge as a strategic tool
- the majority of organisation's organisational culture is conducive to the sharing of knowledge
- overall, the organisations benefit from the processes created to contribute knowledge
- the majority of organisations did not have a central intelligence repository to which employees were able to contribute or access knowledge
- employees were generally not aware of the benefits of business intelligence and competitive intelligence, which points towards a lack of internal education or marketing

TABLE 3: Competitive intelligence sorted by mean scores.

Variable	Question	Mean	SD
Section 3: Competitive intelligence			
3.3.8	Our organisation is cognisant of new and pending government legislation and legislative trends that impact our organisation.	4.59	0.666
3.3.4	Our organisation utilises external sources of information for market research (research companies).	3.91	1.109
3.3.2	Our organisation makes use of competitive intelligence in decision-making.	3.45	1.101
3.3.7	We are up to date with emerging technologies in our field of business and the benefits/features of these technologies.	3.41	0.959
3.3.5	We evaluate the reliability and accuracy of our sources of information.	3.23	1.110
3.3.6	We analyse our competitors and have up to date profiles of them.	3.23	1.020
3.3.3	Our competitive intelligence is created and distributed to management in a timely fashion.	3.00	1.195
3.3.1	Our organisation has a formal competitive intelligence function (which utilises a standardised competitive intelligence process or framework).	2.59	1.368

SD, standard deviation.

with regards to the benefits of business and competitive intelligence

- a large number of organisations do require their employees to be personally responsible for the transfer and storage of knowledge in their area of speciality
- it seems as though there are a number of organisations that have an environment in which employees do not contribute regular information[3]
- smaller organisations are least likely to have a document management system in place
- most organisations do not have a process in place for the conversion of individually held competence to systems, tools, or templates, do not store intellectual capital, conduct internal knowledge audits or use specific knowledge management software applications but a number made use of in house data stores such as a central file repository on the corporate intranet, Microsoft SharePoint Portal, and in house systems to store and manage knowledge.

The results indicate that the vast majority of organisations in the long-term insurance industry do believe that knowledge management provides value as a strategic tool, and had a culture conducive to knowledge sharing where employees are responsible for contributing knowledge in their specific area of expertise. However, the results show that employees are often not aware of the benefits of their contributions, and that they do not regularly contribute information. The results also showed that most of the organisations lacked internal systems dedicated to the collection and storage of knowledge, which could contribute to the lack of knowledge contributed by employees.

Strategic intelligence

The purpose of this section was to gain an understanding of the strategic intelligence activities that take place within organisations in the long-term insurance industry. Based on the results obtained, the results suggest that:

- strategic intelligence processes are more prevalent in larger organisations

3. This is discouraging as employees are often privy to valuable information, whilst those that do encourage contributions could find themselves with a competitive advantage, whilst and an equal number of organisations do have and do not have facilities available to their employees to enable the sharing of knowledge, with smaller organisations the least likely to have access to the correct technical infrastructure.

- respondents do not, on average, consolidate all their intelligence into a single Intelligence repository
- the majority of respondents do not fuse their business intelligence, competitive intelligence and knowledge management (to create strategic intelligence) for use in decision-making
- respondents believe that strategic intelligence, as a collective, provides better information input to decision makers
- not all intelligence gathered is checked for accuracy
- the majority of respondents did not have a long-term strategic intelligence plan
- strategic intelligence is not used at all levels of decision-making
- a growing proportion of managers use strategic intelligence in their strategic planning and decision-making
- strategic intelligence does assist managers to forge better, fact-based decisions
- strategic intelligence engages managers in the strategy development process
- strategic intelligence assists managers to quantify and qualify strategic choices and articulate strategies
- key decision makers are not always surveyed or interviewed to verify that the intelligence products produced for them satisfy their needs
- strategic intelligence does not form part of the respondents performance appraisal review process
- strategic intelligence can sharpen internal performance monitoring
- strategic intelligence is not a continuous activity in the respondent's organisation
- organisations do not, on average, have dedicated human resources to maintain their Strategic Intelligence function or process
- very few respondents would consider outsourcing their strategic intelligence function
- the respondents linked strategic intelligence requirements to their strategic objectives and their long term goals, believe that the use of strategic intelligence can lead to competitive advantage and innovation, enhances decision-making, plays a critical role in the strategic

TABLE 4: Knowledge management sorted by mean scores.

Variable	Question	Mean	SD
Section 4: Knowledge management			
3.4.2	We view knowledge as a strategic tool.	4.14	0.710
3.4.1	We believe that knowledge management assists in creating value out of our organisations intangible assets.	4.09	0.610
3.4.3	Our organisational culture is conducive to the sharing of knowledge.	3.32	0.995
3.4.4	Our organisation benefits from the processes created to contribute knowledge.	3.18	1.006
3.4.7	Employees are personally responsible for the transfer and storage of knowledge in their area of speciality.	3.18	1.220
3.4.8	Employees regularly report information they have found.	3.09	1.065
3.4.10	Our organisation has a document management system in place.	2.82	1.220
3.4.9	Our organisation has the technical infrastructure to enable knowledge sharing.	2.77	1.307
3.4.12	Our organisation stores intellectual capital.	2.73	1.120
3.4.6	Employees are aware of the benefits of business intelligence and competitive intelligence.	2.64	1.049
3.4.5	Knowledge and intelligence is contributed and accessed by employees by means of a central intelligence repository (which acts as a pool of corporate information).	2.45	1.101
3.4.11	We have a process in place for the conversion of individually held competence to systems, tools, or templates.	2.36	1.177
3.4.13	We conduct an internal knowledge audit (e.g. identify and catalogue what people know, what reports they have, publications).	2.14	1.246

SD, standard deviation.

management process, is most commonly used by the organisations during new product development (95%), when considering competitive advantage (68%), when determining pricing strategies (64%), and when considering market entry strategies (64%)

- strategic intelligence was predominately utilised at a strategic level as an input to decision-making and has its greatest impact at a strategic level
- respondents believed further research should be conducted to identify better methods of implementing strategic intelligence, but that most organisations did not make use of any strategic intelligence software applications or methods and/or models.

The results indicate that the majority of organisations in the long-term insurance industry agree that strategic intelligence is an important component to strategic decision-making. Strategic intelligence can therefore provide their management with better information input that could lead to competitive advantage and innovation. Even so, only a few of the larger organisations have formalised processes or systems in place for the formation and use of strategic intelligence.

Key results

In the previous section, the analysed empirical results of the research survey were discussed in detail. Whilst the results provide interesting findings on their own, the basis of this research is to provide feedback and evidence to answer the research questions based on the research aim. The findings of the empirical results will be discussed per intelligence stream, to provide a detailed understanding of how data and information is collected and transformed into strategic intelligence, in order to answer the research questions.

The results indicate that the intelligence stream, which is most predominantly focused upon, is Business Intelligence, with the majority of respondents collecting Business Intelligence. The results indicate that a number of systems are used to transform the Business Intelligence data into intelligence, which is found to be valid, actionable and reliable. However, a greater proportion of organisations did not transform the data into a predefined dashboard view of their organisations, than those that did, who unanimously agreed that a predefined dashboard view of the organisation is important for managerial decision-making. The results provide evidence that larger organisations make greater use of Business Intelligence than smaller organisations.

How data and information are collected and transformed into strategic intelligence

Data and information are the basic building blocks, which are collected and analysed to form actionable intelligence. Strategic intelligence is comprised of different sources of data, including internal business intelligence, external competitive intelligence, and employee and organisational knowledge, which should be combined to provide the organisational decision makers with accurate intelligence on which to base their decisions.

From a competitive intelligence viewpoint, the results indicate that too few organisations have achieved the task of timely creation and distribution of competitive intelligence to management, with larger organisations having greater success in this area. Furthermore, the majority of organisations utilise external sources of information for market research, with the most important sources for the collection of competitive intelligence including the analysis of competitor's products

TABLE 5: Strategic Intelligence sorted by mean scores.

Variable	Question	Mean	SD
Section 5: Strategic intelligence			
3.5.4	We believe that strategic intelligence, as a collective, provides better information input to decision makers.	3.95	0.785
3.5.20	Strategic intelligence enhances decision-making.	3.95	0.844
3.5.9	We believe strategic intelligence assists managers forge better, fact-based decisions.	3.91	0.750
3.5.21	Strategic intelligence plays a critical role in the strategic management process.	3.82	0.907
3.5.19	The use of strategic intelligence leads to competitive advantage and innovation.	3.77	0.973
3.5.11	Strategic intelligence can assist managers to quantify or qualify strategic choices and articulate strategies.	3.73	1.032
3.5.10	Strategic intelligence engages managers in the strategy development process.	3.64	1.293
3.5.14	Strategic intelligence can sharpen internal performance monitoring.	3.45	1.101
3.5.18	Our strategic intelligence requirements are linked to our strategic objectives and our long term goals.	3.09	1.109
3.5.1	Our organisation has a strategic intelligence process in place.	3.05	1.046
3.5.8	Managers use strategic intelligence in their strategic planning and decision-making.	2.86	1.207
3.5.6	We have a long-term strategic intelligence plan.	2.82	1.296
3.5.7	We use strategic intelligence at all levels of decision-making.	2.73	1.120
3.5.5	All intelligence is checked for accuracy.	2.68	1.249
3.5.3	We fuse our business intelligence, competitive intelligence and knowledge management (to create strategic intelligence) for use in decision-making.	2.50	1.102
3.5.12	Key decision makers are surveyed or interviewed to verify that the intelligence products produced for them satisfy their needs.	2.41	1.098
3.5.17	We would consider outsourcing our Strategic Intelligence function.	2.36	1.002
3.5.2	Our organisation consolidates all our intelligence into a single intelligence repository.	2.27	1.162
3.5.15	Strategic intelligence is a continuous activity in our organisation.	2.23	1.110
3.5.16	Our organisation has dedicated human resources to maintain our strategic intelligence function or process.	2.23	1.193
3.5.13	Strategic intelligence forms part of our performance appraisal review process.	1.68	0.894

SD, standard deviation.

(86%), websites (86%), annual reports (77%) and research reports (72%). The results further suggest that a large number of organisations do evaluate the reliability and accuracy of their sources of information. Although these data sources can be classified as important and useful, the value of them for competitive intelligence purposes can be debated. The majority of them include information on past activities, which, whilst remaining important, give a predominately historical view of the competitors or environment, which is to be analysed. From a competitive intelligence viewpoint, it is always important to have current, up to date, intelligence on your competitor to allow you to anticipate future activities.

After collecting the data, the most commonly used analytical methods or models used within the organisations to generate competitive intelligence included SWOT (i.e. strengths, weaknesses, opportunities, and threats) analysis and competitor analysis (both with 82%), customer segmentation analysis (72%), industry analysis (64%), and financial analysis and valuation (59%). The most popular methods used by organisations to distribute and present intelligence results are email (77%), presentations (72%), and reports (64%).

Based on the results we obtained a discouraging view of how tacit knowledge is collected and transformed into explicit knowledge through a knowledge management transformation process within organisations in the long-term insurance industry emerged. Very few organisations had a process in place for the conversion of individually held tacit competence to explicit systems, tools, or templates. The majority of organisations did not have a central intelligence repository to which employees were able to contribute or access knowledge. An equal number of organisations do have and do not have facilities available to their employees to enable the sharing of knowledge, with smaller organisations the least likely to have access to the correct technical infrastructure. A few larger organisations did; however, have a document management system in place as a central store for documents, very little of it was audited or transformed into Intellectual Capital.

The aforementioned results compare well with the results obtained regarding strategic intelligence. We concluded that the majority of respondents do not fuse their business intelligence, competitive intelligence and knowledge management (to create strategic intelligence) for use in decision-making, and do not, on average, consolidate all their intelligence into a single intelligence repository. Intelligence gathered is often not checked for accuracy, nor do the organisations, on average, have dedicated human resources to maintain their strategic intelligence function or process. The lack of consolidation of strategic intelligence is of particular significance in the context of this research, as the discrepancy between the availability and importance of this intelligence for use in the context of strategic management is of vital importance. Without the correct intelligence available, decision making cannot lead to a competitive advantage over competitors.

It is interesting to note the extent of business intelligence processes and the use thereof, and the prevalence of certain competitive intelligence methods and models over others. This can strongly be related to the popularity of business intelligence in the local technological media, the potential advantages thereof, and the prominence of certain models in the curriculums of tertiary institutions.

The use of information systems to create strategic intelligence

The empirical results suggest that the majority of the respondents did not make use of any specific strategic intelligence information systems, although two respondents did indicate that they made use of internally developed in-house systems created for specific purposes as the need arose. Strategic intelligence is; however, comprised of a number of subcomponents including business intelligence, competitive intelligence and knowledge management, all of which can make use of systems designed exclusively for them.

As part of the survey, respondents were questioned whether individual systems were used. We found that a large number of different software applications were used by respondents to gather and generate business intelligence. Whilst some respondents indicated that they did not make use of any systems, 73% of the respondents did indicate that they used various systems ranging from basic business intelligence portals, in-house business intelligence tools (including the use of SQL databases and excel) based upon the data provided by financial, manufacturing, and marketing systems data, management information systems, and a variety of off the shelf business intelligence packages such as Olikview, Cognos, EG Solutions operational management software, Crystal Reports, RADS (Unisys supported) linked to underlying data warehouse, STD Exergy, Hyperion, Business objects, SAP BI, SPSS Clementine is used for Data Mining and specialist visualisation software. Only 32% of the organisations made use of competitive intelligence Software Applications. This included the use of internally developed systems, the Microsoft suite of products including predominately SharePoint, the electronic storage of documents on servers, and a single respondent indicated their use of a software application named Goldmine. Most organisations do not use specific knowledge management Software applications but a small number made use of in house data stores such as a central file repository on the corporate intranet, Microsoft SharePoint Portal, and in house systems to store and manage knowledge. Further results provided by a single respondent provided detailed information explaining that their operational knowledge, lessons learnt, and technical knowledge are captured in Content Manager, and Microsoft applications. Furthermore, they made use of bodies and structures such as Community of Practice, online learning tools and forums as their Knowledge Management toolkit. Another respondent from a large organisation explained that they did not yet have a centralised approach across their entire organisation; however, individual departments made use of extensive knowledge management practices which were conducted and managed successfully.

The results indicate a resounding bias in the use of Business Intelligence systems, which are used for the management of the organisations internal business environment. It is, however, concerning that few systems are used for the management of information and more critically, intelligence on the organisations external environment. The lack of Knowledge Management systems further indicate that there is a high possibility of losing valuable Intellectual Capital if not captured and stored in centralised systems. Furthermore, the results indicate a huge deficiency in the use of any systems in smaller organisations. Whilst the costs of larger systems is prohibitive, and in instances prove to be highly complex, a number of systems are available for a low cost or in some instances completely free, and can be maintained at a low cost to the organisations.

Based upon these results, it is imperative that organisations should investigate the advantages that systems could provide in influencing the outcomes of both internal and external forces that impact the competitive nature of the organisations. Accordingly, a well-structured and functioning strategic intelligence system should receive urgent attention in organisations within the long-term insurance industry, in order to provide accurate, timely and structured intelligence for use in decision making.

The extent to which strategic intelligence can address the input needs of the strategic decision-making process

From the responses it is clear that the respondents believe that strategic intelligence enhances decision-making. Furthermore, the results showed that strategic intelligence is predominately utilised at a strategic level as an input to decision-making, and that strategic intelligence had the greatest impact at a strategic level. We found that strategic intelligence is most commonly used by the organisations as an input to strategic decisions regarding new product development (95%), when considering competitive advantage (68%), when determining pricing strategies (64%), and when considering market entry strategies (64%). As a result of the nature of strategic intelligence, the intelligence it provides includes intelligence on the organisations internal, external and knowledge environments which can to a large extent address all the input requirements of the strategic decision making process.

The results made it clear that strategic intelligence could to a large extent address the input needs of the strategic decision-making process.

The level of utilisation of strategic intelligence within the South African long-term insurance industry

The empirical results highlight the fact that strategic intelligence processes are more prevalent in larger organisations. This could simply be the result the lack of human and financial resources available to smaller organisations. The results further suggest that most organisations collect and utilise business intelligence in decision making;

however, the results distinctly provide evidence that larger organisations make greater use of business intelligence than smaller organisations. Results further suggest that larger organisations do have a formal competitive intelligence function, whereas smaller organisations, in general did not have a formalised competitive intelligence function. However, results indicate that a high number of organisations do make use of competitive intelligence in decision-making even if no formalised function exists for the management of competitive intelligence. It was found that, with the exception of a few larger organisations, knowledge management is not often utilised and more often constitutes an informal central repository for project and organisational documentation rather than formalised actionable explicit knowledge.

Based upon these results, it seems clear that respondents do believe that strategic intelligence, as a collective, provides better information input to decision makers. Whilst belief is important, reality proved that the majority of respondents did not have a long-term strategic intelligence plan, and that strategic intelligence is not used at all levels of decision-making but that a growing proportion of managers felt its importance and thus started to use strategic intelligence in their strategic planning and decision-making.

How strategic intelligence is used and contributes to the strategic management process within the South African long-term insurance industry

From the empirical results it is apparent that the organisations in the long-term insurance industry do to a large extent, utilise a formalised strategic management process, and therefore recognise strategic management as a necessary activity for business. Furthermore, respondents view information as having strategic value and believe that good strategy hinges on having timely, relevant and high quality information. The results indicate that strategic intelligence is predominately utilised at a strategic level as an input to decision-making, and therefore has the greatest impact at a Strategic level. Respondents further indicated that their strategic intelligence requirements are linked to their strategic objectives and their long term goals.

We found that organisations do attempt to provide their managers with critical and relevant information for strategic decision making; however, smaller organisations that were in greater disagreement do not have the capacity to provide managers with the required information, as larger organisations do. Furthermore, the majority of respondents believe that they do provide their managers with access to information that provides them with a comprehensive and robust perspective on how the organisation is performing, the dynamics at play in the market place, competitor behaviour, stakeholder perceptions, resource availability, and the implications of trends in these areas for the firm. Smaller organisations are; however, at a disadvantage to larger organisations.

The empirical results further showed that organisations do not, on average, have dedicated human resources to maintain their strategic intelligence function or process, and that key decision makers are not always surveyed or interviewed to verify that the intelligence products produced for them satisfy their needs. Strategic intelligence was found to not form part of the respondents' performance appraisal review process and is not a continuous activity in the organisations.

How strategic intelligence adds value to organisations within the South African long-term insurance industry

There are a number of ways in which strategic intelligence can provide value to organisations. The lowest level of value that can be added is in the separate information provided by the components of strategic intelligence, which will now be discussed.

The majority of respondents believed that the availability of business intelligence increased the effectiveness of managerial decision-making, and therefore lead to greater competitive advantage because of their access to valid, reliable and actionable business intelligence, predefined dashboard views of their organisations, and software applications used.

The results indicate the use of competitive intelligence allows the management of organisations to be up to date with emerging technologies in their field of business and the benefits or features of these technologies. Furthermore, it allows organisations to be cognisant of new and pending government legislation and legislative trends that impact their organisation. It was also found that large organisations do in fact analyse their competitors and have up to date profiles of them, whilst smaller organisations mostly did not. Results confirm conclusively that organisations believe that knowledge management assists in creating value out of their organisations intangible assets. Results proved that organisations do view knowledge as a strategic tool, and believe their organisations organisational culture is conducive to the sharing of knowledge and claim to benefit from the processes created to contribute knowledge. A significant amount of organisations require their employees to be personally responsible for the transfer and storage of knowledge in their area of speciality; however, it is clear from the results that there are a number of organisations that have an environment in which employees do not contribute regular information. This is discouraging as employees are often privy to valuable information, whilst those that do encourage contributions could find themselves with a competitive advantage.

The results indicate that the organisations believe that strategic intelligence enhances decision-making and plays a critical role in the strategic management process.

Strategic intelligence therefore provides value by engaging managers in the strategy development process, by assisting management forge better, fact-based decisions, and allows managers to quantify or qualify strategic choices and articulate strategies. This can lead to the sharpening of internal performance monitoring and in conclusion, can lead to competitive advantage and innovation.

Discussion of findings

The research results have shown that there is a clear discrepancy between the theory advocated by dominant researchers in the field of strategic intelligence and its subcomponents. Whilst many of the organisations surveyed indicated their belief that strategic intelligence and its components did in fact provide advantages to their strategic management and strategic decision-making capabilities, very few had the internal capabilities to fully utilise the suggested methods. A number of respondents further indicated that they were not completely aware of the perceived benefits that strategic intelligence could offer, which could imply that not all organisations are aware of research being conducted by academic institutions. A high number of the organisations; however, did indicate their use of strategic management, business intelligence and to an extent competitive intelligence, indicating the greater awareness around these topics in mainstream media.

We were intrigued by the results for the knowledge management and strategic intelligence questions. Whilst the average mean and standard deviation scores remained within a similar range for the questions on strategic management, business intelligence and competitive intelligence, the scores for knowledge management and strategic intelligence decreased to a lower average range. The results for knowledge management and strategic intelligence substantiate the observation made earlier that the theoretical components of the subject matter are agreed with; however, in reality they are often not formally institutionalised within organisations. The reasons for this could be simply the lack of media attention, or case studies to describe their benefits, or simply a lack of resources to sustain them. We further note that there is a difference in the responses of smaller organisations compared to larger organisations. A number of smaller organisations indicated that they did perceive the value that can be provided by the topics discussed in this research; however, these were not of priority to them because of their resource limitations and obvious smaller market scope. On the other hand, a number of larger organisations show higher scores for the variables indicating the greater ability they have in providing resources, for the perceived competitive advantage gain. As a result of the high competition within the long-term insurance industry, it is clear that organisations need to keep informed of any changes that could lead to them gaining an advantage and increased market share.

Lastly, many of the respondents indicated that they would not be prepared to outsource their strategic intelligence functions, whilst the same number of respondents remained neutral to this possibility. A high level of confidentiality could be a reason for this finding; however, the potential remains for a lower cost solution to be developed that could be used in-house to provide the benefits organisations require. This can be further substantiated by the fact that the majority of respondents believed further research should be conducted to identify better methods of implementing strategic intelligence.

Conclusion

Recommendations and future research

Challenges in the global economy, not to mention the challenges faced in the local South African economy, have amplified the necessity for organisations to remain one step ahead of their competitors. Lack of information and knowledge of decisions taken by all role players within the organisations external, and often internal business environments, has led to the weakening and even failure of organisations. Worldwide, the long-term insurance industry has undergone many changes in its working model with changes focused on increasing the attractiveness of the industry to consumers. With the advent of technological advances that allow all consumers to shop around for the best products and pricing, and the globalisation of markets allowing organisations to compete globally, organisations are required to stay a step ahead of their competitors. To achieve this, a number of strategic decisions will need to be made in order for them to remain stable for the foreseeable future. New products, allowing consumers a greater understanding, flexibility and visibility will be required to attract new clients as well as increase market share and remain competitive.

This research proposed that, through its ability to absorb sources of information, the combined synergy of business intelligence, competitive intelligence, and knowledge management that become strategic intelligence, will allow organisations to incorporate all of their information and intellectual capital into a single database or system which will meet the intelligence requirements of management. The results indicate that whilst the surveyed organisations agreed with this proposition, they did not always conform to its suggested methods.

Our initial proposition was that the identification and utilisation of the most important factors of a strategic intelligence framework would greatly enhance global corporate decision-making and result in competitive advantage and constant innovation within the South African business environment. The research results corroborate this. Much of the research proved that, even if just in theory, organisations do believe that a single model or framework could greatly enhance decision-making resulting in competitive advantage and corporate innovation. The purpose of this research was to identify the current use of strategic intelligence in the long-term insurance industry in the South African environment. We found that, whilst larger organisations are aware of, and do make use of certain models and methods that comprise strategic intelligence or its sub-components; no single organisation within the long-term insurance industry makes use of a holistic and comprehensive strategic intelligence model. However, even without the use of such a model, the organisations surveyed are to a large extent still successful in their endeavours.

The research showed that organisations have not yet fully embraced a model for a cooperative global internal corporate strategic intelligence system or portal that will incorporate all aspects of strategic intelligence into a single, easily manageable resource for management's strategic planning and decision-making process, even though it could enhance their ability to withstand the onslaught of global competitors and expand their business into new markets, protect their local market or identify potential merger or acquisition targets, and increase innovation within the organisations. In providing some understanding of the extent in which strategic intelligence is utilised in the South African long-term insurance industry, identifying the benefits or problems experienced by executive management that have not yet been implemented and used strategic intelligence as an input to the strategic management process, we identified the perceived value strategic intelligence in the decision-making process.

By being able to gather and execute strategic intelligence better than their competition, strategic intelligence can be considered an undeniably powerful source of competitive advantage for organisations of all sizes. By managing and utilising strategic intelligence to anticipate changes successfully, allowing organisations to respond to future trends or opportunities will lead to the longevity of those organisations.

Through the in-depth analyses of the use of strategic intelligence as a strategic management tool in the long-term insurance industry, the following recommendations were identified:

- Organisations should place greater emphasis on the development and application of tangible and intangible assets for use in strategic decision-making.
- Organisations should globalise their outlooks and emphasise the sharing of knowledge across borders to withstand changes as a result of the globalisation of markets.
- Organisations should commence with the creation of an intensive and continuous executive learning aptitude, to enhance current strategic decision-making and to empower future leaders about strategic decisions and intentions with regard to their competitive landscape.
- Organisations should focus on educating all employees of the benefits of business intelligence, competitive intelligence, knowledge management and strategic intelligence.
- Organisations should broaden their approach to strategic intelligence gathering and analysis, and the integration of the intelligence into strategic decision-making.
- Organisations should enhance their internal strategic intelligence capabilities through the creation of formalised departments, processes and/or functions.
- Organisations should utilise the methods and tools provided by strategic intelligence to enable internal and external early warning systems.
- Organisations should place more prominence on intelligence-related information for strategic decision makers; however, a greater dispersion across all levels is required.

- Executives who took part in this research understand the key role strategic intelligence can play in achieving competitive advantage and future success, and should therefore continue to find ways to improve their approach to strategic intelligence.

The research study has resulted in the awareness of auxiliary areas which could be further refined through supplementary research. The areas identified are:

- The results of the research have shown that strategic intelligence has a conceptual and empirical support to allow it to function as a strategic management tool, with its own management function, or department. Further research should be conducted to ascertain the feasibility of this.
- The literature survey conducted, with the substantiation by the empirical results have confirmed the perceived benefits of strategic intelligence as a tool in the strategic management process. However, few use the consolidated intelligence provided by strategic intelligence as a strategic management tool. Further research could be conducted into the reasons for this.
- Organisations within the long-term insurance industry show their belief in, but lack of commitment to strategic intelligence as a strategic management tool. Research could be conducted to confirm if this perception is valid only within this industry or prevalent across all South African industries, and why strategic intelligence is not used as a tool.
- Respondents indicated that they believed further research should be conducted to identify better methods of implementing strategic intelligence, human resource skills and capabilities required to conduct and analyse strategic intelligence, and strategic intelligence systems. Further research should be conducted to create a comprehensive, yet simple strategic intelligence model that can easily be implemented and customised to the needs of the individual organisations.
- Further research should be conducted into the use of technology to enable effective information use and delivery. Through the creation of a single technological tool that could be used to consolidate the respective components of strategic intelligence into a single repository or databank, which will meet the intelligence requirements of management.

References

Haag, S., Cummings, M. & Philips, A., 2007, *Management Information Systems for the Information Age*, 6th edn., McGraw-Hill/Irwin, Boston, MA.

Hill, C.W.L., 2005, *International Business: Competing in the Global Marketplace*, 5th edn., McGraw-Hill/Irwin, Boston, MA.

Laudon, K.C. & Laudon, J.P., 2007, *Essentials of Business Information Systems*, 7th edn., Pearson Prentice Hall, Upper Saddle River, NJ.

Leedy, P.D. & Ormrod, J.E., 2005, *Practical Research – Planning and Design*, 8th edn., Prentice Hall, Upper Saddle River, NJ.

Liebowitz, J., 2006, *Strategic Intelligence: Business Intelligence, Competitive Intelligence, and Knowledge Management*, Auerbach Publications, Taylor & Francis Group, Boca Raton, FL. doi:10.1201/9781420013900

Liebowitz, J., 2006, *What they didn't tell you about Knowledge Management*, Scarecrow Press Inc., Lanham, MD.

Life Offices' Association of South Africa, 2008, *LOA study reveals South African life insurance gap of more than R10-trillion*, viewed 10 June 2009, from http://www.loa.co.za

Life Offices' Association of South Africa, 2008, *Consumers spend record R103-billion on life insurance premiums*, viewed 10 June 2009, from http://www.loa.co.za

Marchand, D. & Hykes, A., 2007, 'Leveraging What Your Company Really Knows: A Process View of Strategic Intelligence,' in M. Xu (ed.), *Managing Strategic Intelligence - Techniques and Technologies*, pp. 1–13, Idea Group Inc., University of Portsmouth, UK.

McGonagle, J.J. & Vella, C.M., 1999, *The Internet Age of Competitive Intelligence*, Quorum, Westport, CT.

Montgomery, D.B. & Weinberg, C.B., 1998, 'Toward Strategic Intelligence Systems', *Marketing Management* 6(4), 44–52.

Murphy, C., 2005, *Competitive intelligence: gathering, analysing, and putting it to work*, Gower, Aldershot, Hants, UK.

Pearce, J.A. & Robinson, R.B., 2005, *Strategic Management: Formulation, Implementation and Control*, 9th edn., McGraw-Hill, Boston, MA.

Saunders, M., Lewis, P. & Thornhill, A., 2007, *Research Methods for Business Students*, 4th edn., Prentice Hall, Essex, UK.

Tham, K.D. & Kim, H.M., 2002, 'Towards Strategic Intelligence with Ontology-Based Enterprise Modelling and ABC', proceedings of the IBER Conference, Las Vegas, NV, 21–23 August.

The Financial Services Board South Africa, 2007, *Annual Report*, viewed 10 June 2009, from http://www.fsb.co.za

Xu, M. & Kaye, R., 2009, 'The Nature of Strategic Intelligence: Current Practice and Solutions', in R. Hunter (ed.), *Strategic Information Systems: Concepts, Methodologies, Tools, and Applications* (4 Volumes), pp. 1–19, Information Science Reference, Canada.

17

Enabling information sharing by establishing trust in supply chains

Authors:
Roxanne Piderit[1]
Stephen Flowerday[1]
Rossouw von Solms[2]

Affiliations:
[1]Department of Information Systems, University of Fort Hare, South Africa

[2]School of Information and Communication Technology, Nelson Mandela Metropolitan University, South Africa

Correspondence to:
Roxanne Piderit

Email:
rpiderit@ufh.ac.za

Postal address:
50 Church Street, East London 5201, South Africa

Background: The significant economic importance of the country's automotive industry provided the context for this study. The success of the industry relies on the effectiveness and efficiency of the supply chain, which can be significantly affected by the strength of the supply chain relationships. The role of trust and information sharing in relation to two key theories was considered, namely: organisational information processing theory and game theory. Previous studies have recognised the importance of trust and information sharing in supply chain relationships and considered the effect of trust on information sharing, or the effect of information sharing on trust in a single direction. Thus, the potential cyclical relationship between the two factors has been largely ignored.

Objectives: This paper explored the relationship between trust and information sharing in South African automotive supply chains, and establishes the importance of nurturing a cyclical relationship between these two factors. In addition, the role of information technology (IT) in supporting this relationship was considered. By improving both trust and information sharing, the performance and competitiveness of the supply chain can be improved.

Method: An examination of the effects of a lack of trust in a supply chain relationship, and the consequential lack of information flow, was conducted by means of a case study of an Eastern Cape-based automotive supplier. A case study research method was followed for this study, which made use of multiple data collection methods, including document survey and participant observations. The case selected is an East London based subsidiary of a larger multinational automotive component supplier to both local and international automotive original equipment manufacturers.

Results: The findings led to the conclusion that the way forward for competitive supply chains is to build trust in the supply chain in order to improve information flow, and vice versa. Information technology can be used to nurture this cyclical relationship between trust and information sharing.

Conclusion: It is proposed that simultaneously improving information flow and trust in an interorganisational relationship leads to improved supply chain performance and competitiveness.

Introduction

Globally, governments are recognising the potential impact of automotive manufacturers on an economy and have become dedicated to attracting automakers to their countries and regions. For South Africa, attracting automotive manufacturers and their suppliers to invest in the country has become increasingly important (Barnes & Morris 2008; Fingar 2002). Fingar (2002) discusses the social problems that are rife in South Africa, such as: high unemployment, rampant poverty and the HIV and AIDS epidemic. Significant foreign investment is required to overcome these social problems. In addition, the automotive sector accounts for 7% of South Africa's gross domestic product and provides employment to more than 120 000 workers (Barnes & Morris 2008). Thus, the South African government has made the automotive industry a priority through various policy adjustments (Barnes & Morris 2008; Lorentzen 2006), which are aimed at convincing multinational automotive manufacturers and suppliers to strengthen and deepen their South African operations (Lorentzen 2006). The operations of automotive manufacturers depend on a substantial network of suppliers. As these automotive supply chains can consist of over 300 suppliers, including first-, second- and third-tier suppliers, the cyclical relationship between trust and information sharing in this context, is the focus of this article.

This cyclical trust-information sharing relationship is especially relevant in the automotive industry where manufacturers are under enormous pressure to reduce time to market (TTM), increase flexibility and lower costs in order to be competitive (Pagano & Zagnoli 2001). Fachinelli, Ueltschy and Ueltschy (2007) view trust as a prerequisite for supply chain success. This is substantiated by Covey (2008) who notes that the existence of trust in the supply chain relationship leads to reduced costs and more efficient and effective operations.

Additionally, one needs to consider the role of IT in these interorganisational relationships. Cheng, Lai and Singh (2007) view the use of IT to conduct business transactions, share information and facilitate collaboration as the main determinants of a supply chain's effectiveness. Jharkharia and Shankar (2004) share this view and note that information sharing, supported by IT, is the chief enabler of the effective management of a supply chain. For this reason, there is a global trend toward the IT-enablement of supply chains. The role of IT in the support of a cyclical trust-information sharing relationship is a central concern of this study.

Premkumar, Ramamurthy and Saunders (2005) propose that in order to improve trust in a supply chain relationship, information flow should be enhanced. This can be accomplished by, for example, implementing integrated information systems to improve information flow and reduce uncertainty in the supply chain relationship. At present, information flow is restricted as a result of the competitive nature of the automotive industry. For example, basing decisions on information provided by forecasting systems may lead to the interpretation by supply chain partners that a company intends to compete (Gao & Lee 2005). The result of this perceived threat could be a decreased level of trust in the supply chain relationship.

The economic importance of the South African automotive industry is widely recognised and highlights the significance of this research. This study sets out to explore the cyclical relationship between trust and information sharing in South African automotive supply chains and to consider ways in which efficiency can be improved through the use of the appropriate IT platforms. Following this introduction, the underlying problem is discussed, a brief background to the South African automotive industry is provided and the changing nature of supply chain governance structures is highlighted to provide context. An examination of the role of trust and information sharing in the supply chain context follows, including a discussion of the relevance of the organisational information processing theory and game theory in this context. The cyclical relationship between trust and information sharing is then investigated within the context of an Eastern Cape based automotive supplier. A preliminary solution is provided.

The problem

Ensuring that South Africa continues to be a viable production site for Original Equipment Manufacturers (OEMs) who have invested significantly in the economy is reliant on the local suppliers and supply chain dynamics. This view is supported by Ward (2009:1) from Toyota who states that 'the strength of the supply chain is critical to the success of the automotive industry in general and of Toyota South Africa in particular'. Furthermore, Mangold (2009:1) from Mercedes-Benz notes that 'local suppliers need to improve competitiveness to ensure that local OEMs can compete with their respective international counterparts'. These statements highlight the importance of ensuring that South African automotive supply chains function efficiently through the enhancement of trust between supply chain partners.

Insufficient trust amongst supply chain partners leads to inefficient and ineffective operations in the supply chain, and consequently impacts negatively on the supply chain's competitive advantage (Covey 2008). For this reason, South African automotive supply chains need to have a sufficient level of trust entrenched in the relationships amongst supply chain partners, in order to compete effectively against their global counterparts.

Information sharing can be disrupted through insufficient trust amongst supply chain partners (Fedorowicz & Ghosh 2008). This leads to ineffective and inefficient operations in the supply chain, as insufficient information is available to all supply chain partners in order to make effective decisions. Insufficient information sharing can thus be viewed as detrimental to the supply chain's competitiveness.

Thus, both insufficient trust and insufficient information sharing are viewed as contributing factors to the ineffectiveness and inefficiency of a supply chain's operations, and the resultant negative effect on competitive advantage. Additionally, the cyclical nature of the relationship between trust and information sharing emerges.

The method

A case study research method was followed for this study of the relationship between trust and information sharing in South African automotive supply chains. Kazi & Wolf (2004) point out that a case study can effectively extract examples of both good and bad practice. This is considered appropriate in the context of this research, where an in-depth study of the context is required. Thus, a deeper understanding of the phenomenon under investigation was sought (Cooper & Schindler 2003).

The case itself is a small East London-based subsidiary of a larger multinational automotive component supplier to both local and international automotive OEMs. This case was selected because of the researcher's involvement in the Programme for Industrial Manufacturing Excellence (PRIME), which gave initial access to the organisation. Subsequent involvement with the supplier was, however independent of this programme. This case is considered to be representative of issues faced in similar component suppliers (based on a pilot study conducted at another local supplier and involvement in PRIME). Thus, as pointed out by Cooper and Schindler (2003), the selection of this case can lead to conclusions being drawn about the entire population.

The case study method allows the researcher to make use of various data collection methods to conduct the study. The methods employed were: document survey to provide insight into the organisations current information sharing practices, and participant observations to assess the effectiveness of these information sharing practices and the level of trust evident in supply chain.

As a result of the nature of the case and the data collection techniques chosen, it was not suitable to make use of statistical means of data analysis (Yin 2003). Thus, the data collected was analysed by making use of pattern-matching and logic models as proposed by Yin (2003).

The South African automotive industry

Many multinational automotive OEMs and component suppliers have realised that operations in South Africa can provide an opportunity for competitive advantage (DTI 2005). Relative to the size of the South African market, the automotive sector continues to perform well, and has set the standard for the development of other industries within the country (Africa Research Bulletin 2010), and thus, the Department of Trade and Industry (DTI 2005) believes that national, provincial and local governments should continue to ensure the success of this sector. Despite the economic slump in 2009, the automotive industry has recovered well and vehicle sales have continued to grow and indicate sustainable growth (Africa Research Bulletin 2010).

Besides economic benefits, the automotive sector (which includes both the component suppliers and the assembly operations) is widely viewed as the second biggest employer in South Africa after mining (DTI 2005). Mercedes-Benz South Africa's East London assembly operation is the largest private sector employer in the Eastern Cape and has invested considerably in relieving the socio-economic issues faced by the local community (Mak'Ochieng 2003). The primary challenge the automotive industry faces is the increased exposure to international competition since the introduction of the Motor Industry Development Programme (MIDP) in 1995 (Black 1998).

The MIDP was modelled on a similar attempt in Australia, known as the Automotive Investment and Competitiveness Scheme (Fingar 2002; Franse 2006). This scheme ensured the Australian automotive industry was competitive by awarding import credits to those organisations that performed satisfactorily (Fingar 2002). The structural changes and resultant sheltered atmosphere of the South African automotive industry encouraged automotive OEMs to invest in the country (Franse 2006). The MIDP has since been replaced by the Automotive Investment Scheme (AIS). The AIS is intended to grow and develop the automotive sector through investment in new and replacement automotive models as well as the manufacturing of automotive components (DTI 2010).

Other challenges for the automotive industry include the growth of Asian competitors, limited production capacity, price pressures enforced by multinational partners in order to retain business, soaring oil and raw material prices, skill shortages and a somewhat volatile work force (Ford Motor Company 2005). The influence of Asian manufacturers has resulted in the need to adopt lean principles and 'just-in-time' approaches in order to be competitive which has provided a challenge for the more traditional manufacturers (Burnes & West 2000). These traditional manufacturers also need to ensure that their employees can adapt to these changes (Burnes & West 2000). The Asian manufacturers have managed to reduce costs dramatically and have thus caused concern for the continued viability of South Africa's automotive sector (Franse 2006).

The changing nature of the industry has also required an evolution of the governance structure of supply chains. Peterson (2002) recognises that supply chains have moved beyond the traditional channel master model, where the OEM dominates and specifies the terms of trade across the whole supply chain, to a chain organism model, where there is no dominant organisation and the OEM needs to form strong relationships with the suppliers. Dubey and Jain (2005) conceptualise interorganisational governance as a multidimensional phenomenon that is manifested in structure, processes and contracts. In terms of governance, Dubey and Jain (2005) view a supply chain as either:

- a business network, in which each organisation is autonomous, that collectively addresses problems in the absence of an overarching authority and in which, therefore, there is a need for interorganisational governance; or
- an extended enterprise, in which a local organisation has many stakeholders (including buyers, suppliers, and subcontractors), and thus requires corporate governance to maximise the benefits to the stakeholders.

Decentralising control (as in the business network model described above) allows the supply chain to adapt to unforeseen circumstances, but decentralised decisions often result in suboptimum outcomes at the supply chain level including an increased level of competition between supply chain partners (Gao & Lee 2005). Ryu (2006) considered how a change in the external circumstances of the supply chain affects differing levels of interdependence amongst supply chain participants and found that where the organisations have a low level of interdependence, a change in external circumstances prompts the manufacturers to increase the level of monitoring of their suppliers. However, where the organisations have a high level of interdependence, environmental uncertainty had little or no effect on the level of monitoring (Ryu 2006). Similarly, with the decentralised business network model, a high level of trust, will allow the supply chain to operate efficiently and thus compete effectively in the marketplace.

The role of trust and information sharing in the supply chain

Recent years have seen a shift in the research focus in supply chain management from inter-functional to interorganisational integration and co-ordination (Dubey & Jain 2005). Furthermore, there has been an increased interest in the role of trust in facilitating supply chain partnerships (Sahay 2003). Chu and Fang (2006) acknowledge that insufficient trust amongst supply chain partners leads to inefficient and ineffective performance. Covey (2008) emphasises that a sufficient level of trust in an interorganisational relationship can reduce costs and save time. Thus, trust emerges as an essential element in governing interorganisational relationships in supply chains (Fedorowicz & Ghosh 2008). Additionally, Agarwal and Shankar (2003) view the lack of personal interaction and geographic dispersion of supply chain members to be key elements that hinder the development of trust in these interorganisational relationships. As trust plays an obvious role in efficient supply chains, it is important to investigate it in more detail.

Defining trust

Han, Liu, Sun and Yu (2006) and Smeltzer (1997) acknowledge that although the social sciences have offered definitions and classifications of trust, there is little or no consensus on a definition of trust in a business or supply chain context. It is however acknowledged that a few researchers have made tentative attempts at defining trust (Smeltzer 1997).

Hosmer (1995 in Smeltzer 1997) provides a definition of trust based on organisational theory and philosophy:

> Trust is the expectation by one person, group, or firm of ethically justifiable behaviour – that is, morally correct decisions and actions based upon ethical principles of analysis – on the part of the other person, group or firm in a joint endeavour or economic exchange.
>
> (cited in Smeltzer 1997:41)

McEvily and Tortoriello (2011) conducted a review of organisational literature on trust. Amongst the definitions commonly adopted in organisational literature was that of Rosseau, Burt, Sitkin and Camerer (1998 cited in McEvily & Tortoriello 2011): 'Trust is a psychological state comprising the intention to accept vulnerability based upon positive expectations of the intentions or behaviours of another'.

Ring and VanDe Ven (1994 cited in Smeltzer 1997) provide two additional views of trust. The first is based on confidence or risk in the predictability of the other party's actions, and in this instance parties hedge themselves against uncertain events through guarantees, insurance or law (Smeltzer 1997). The second view is based on confidence in the other party's goodwill, which relies on faith in the integrity of the other party (Smeltzer 1997).

Davis, Mayer and Schoorman (2007:346) concur with Ring and VanDe Ven's first view of trust and define it as the 'willingness to take risk'. As this has been determined to be the most commonly adopted definition of trust in organisational literature (McEvily & Tortoriello 2011), this study has adopted this definition of trust. Based on this definition of trust; the value of trust in supply chain relationships needs to be considered.

The importance of trust in supply chainsThe importance of trust in governing interorganisational relationships can not be ignored. Fedorowicz and Ghosh (2008) explore the key constructs that support the governance of information sharing and material flow coordination in supply chains, which include: trust, bargaining power and contract. Furthermore, it is argued that trust as a governance mechanism plays a crucial role in sharing information amongst business partners (Fedorowicz & Ghosh 2008). In support of this view, Wang and Wei (2007) established that interorganisational governance can create value through information visibility and supply chain flexibility.

To determine the important concepts in supply chain relationships, we conducted a basic content analysis of key articles in the area of supply chain management to identify which concepts are the most prominent in this relationship.

Trust emerges as the dominant concept in this content analysis of research into supply chain relationships, with information sharing as the second most important concept. This suggests the existence of a potentially important relationship between these two concepts.

Determining the level of trust

Several factors have been identified as determinants of the level of trust between supply chain partners, including perceived satisfaction, the reputation of supply chain

TABLE 1: Supply chain concepts (content analysis).

Author	Trust	Information sharing	Bargaining power	Contract	Relational governance	Culture	Decentralised control	Supply chain Performance	Commitment	Uncertainty
Chu & Fang (2006)	X	X	-	-	-	-	-	X	X	-
Dubey & Jain (2005)	-	-	-	-	X	-	-	-	-	-
Fachinelli, Ueltschy & Ueltschy (2007)	X	-	-	-	-	X	-	-	-	-
Fedorowicz & Ghosh (2008)	X	X	X	X	-	-	-	-	-	-
Gao & Lee (2005)	X	-	-	-	-	-	X	-	-	-
Kwon & Suh (2005)	X	X	-	-	-	-	-	-	-	X
Naesens, Pintelon & Taillieu (2007)	X	-	-	-	-	-	-	-	-	-
Ryu (2006)	-	-	-	-	-	-	-	-	-	X
Sahay (2003)	X	X	-	-	-	-	-	-	-	-
Wang & Wei (2007)	-	X	-	-	X	-	-	-	-	-

partners, and the level and quality of communication amongst these supply chain partners (Chu & Fang 2006). Additionally, Kwon and Suh (2005) found that the level of trust amongst supply chain partners is highly reliant on the level of asset investment and information sharing structures. Information sharing, in particular, was found to play a role in reducing uncertainty in the supply chain relationship and thereby improving the level of trust (Kwon & Suh 2005). Furthermore, Naesens, Pintelon and Taillieu (2007) also describe several determinants that affect the level of trust in supply chain relationships, including:

1. the supplier's performance history, which is an indicator of their reliability and competence
2. cumulative interactions, which are a valuable predictor of the supplier's behaviour
3. demonstrations of the supplier's good intentions, which create goodwill trust in the relationship
4. a transference process by which trust is based on other organisations' opinions of the supplier's trustworthiness.

These determinants emphasise the emergence of information sharing as a key factor in building trust in supply chain relationships. The role of IT in support of this trust-information sharing relationship also needs to be considered.

The role of information technology in support of trust and information sharing

With the complicated network of suppliers that make up an automotive supply chain, the management of the multiple relationships is critical to the success of the supply chain (Dubey & Jain 2005). It stands to reason that interorganisational systems will play an important role in maintaining these relationships between the supply chain partners. Various forms of information technology can play a role in reducing the impact of a lack of trust in the supply chain (Gao & Lee 2005), such as forecasting systems. For this reason, the use of information technologies is proposed to overcome these inefficiencies (Gao & Lee 2005).

Cheng et al. (2007) note that merely ensuring technology is used in supply chain management will not ensure that the supply chain is effective and efficient. It is therefore necessary to ensure that the correct IT has been implemented appropriately. Liu (2007) notes that Electronic Data Interchange (EDI), expert systems, communication technologies, database technology and network technology are required in order to ensure coordination of the entire supply chain and enhance the competitiveness of the supply chain as a whole.

Organisational information processing theory

The organisational information processing theory identifies information processing needs and capabilities and the need to obtain optimal performance through a balance of these factors. It views quality information as a requirement in handling uncertainty and improving decision-making. According to Premkumar et al. (2005), organisations have two strategies for dealing with this uncertainty, by either:

- developing buffers, for example inventory buffers to reduce the uncertainty related to demand and supply; or
- enhancing information flow, for example implementing integrated information systems to improve information flow and reduce uncertainty.

Similarly, in supply chains, improving information flow amongst supply chain partners reduces uncertainty in the relationships. This leads to the next subsection where game theory is used to illustrate the importance of information sharing and the concept of trust.

Game theory and trust

Game theory is used to study the choices that are made when costs and benefits are not fixed, but, rather, depend on other players (partners) and the shared information available to the players. According to Flowerday and Von Solms (2006), the amount of information that the various players have about each other is a key determinant of behaviour.

Flowerday and Von Solms (2006) examine the classic example of game theory, known as the prisoner's dilemma, in which two prisoners in separate cells face the dilemma of whether or not to be police informants. Without further communication, the two players need to trust each other. If neither party informs, both receive light sentences because of insufficient evidence. If both inform, both receive heavy sentences. If one party defects, they are set free, whilst the other party is convicted based on the informant's evidence. The dilemma of the scenario, according to Flowerday and Von Solms (2006), highlights the issue of trusting the other player without continuous communication.

Similarly, in a supply chain context, where information is freely shared by all members of the supply chain, the benefits to all members is an increased level of trust in the interorganisational relationship and therefore effective and efficient supply chain operations. If no members of the supply chain reveal information, none can benefit from the improved operations described. If some parties share information, whilst others do not, those that have not shared information can benefit far more than those that have shared information. Thus, the ideal situation would be for supply chain partners to share information freely as this would be to the benefit of the entire supply chain.

According to Lewis (1999), this mutual information sharing is likely to occur if all parties will benefit from the relationship in some way, which makes trust an essential prerequisite for information sharing. Poirier (2003) confirms this view by pointing out that trusting that those who access information will act responsibly and for the good of the entire supply chain, is crucial to the success of the collaboration.

Having defined trust and reviewed the importance of trust in supply chains and how information sharing can support this, the study explored these concepts of information sharing and trust within South African based OEMs and their supply chains.

Evidence of information sharing structures in automotive supply chains

Most automotive OEMs have made some attempt at information sharing with their entire supply chain. These attempts were used to improve efficiency and effectiveness of supply chain relationships and operations. This section details efforts by six of the automotive OEMs with South African-based facilities, namely:

- BMW
- Ford
- General Motors
- Mercedes-Benz
- Toyota
- Volkswagen.

BMW makes use of a web-based document management system that allows easy, secure access to information worldwide (Awazu, Desouza, Jha, Kim & Wecht 2007; Kappe 2001). This is of particular importance in the global setting of multinational automotive suppliers. Furthermore, BMW encourages the use of a 'yellow pages' application to locate experts (Awazu *et al.* 2007; Kappe 2001). This is the most important (and easy to establish) tool for information sharing in multinational automotive supply chains.

Ford's web-based knowledge base is an important tool for dealing with daily problem-solving activities (Jenkins & Tallman 2010; Coughlan & Rukstad 2001). The portals and intranet sites ensure that relationships are formed between the necessary people for problem solving to occur (Rethink IT 2004), as well as allowing information access within the supply chain. This is necessary for globally dispersed employees in a multinational automotive supply chain.

General Motors' efforts include the establishment of centres of excellence in key business areas (Jenkins & Tallman 2010; Coughlan & Rukstad 2001). Even more important is the documentation of lessons that have been learned and discussions of the best practices that is encouraged amongst all the supply chain stakeholders (Coughlan & Rukstad 2001).

Mercedes-Benz's efforts have an interesting history. Initiatives embarked upon include knowledge and information resource mapping, and Communities of Practice (CoPs) that focus on particular situations (Coughlan & Rukstad 2001). Furthermore, the company has identified knowledge areas that require support by the existing CoPs (Jenkins & Tallman 2010; Coughlan & Rukstad 2001). Mercedes-Benz's initiatives hold value for the multinational automotive supplier in terms of bringing geographically dispersed employees and suppliers together to solve problems and ensure the free flow of information within their supply chain.

The success of Toyota's information management initiatives highlights the relevance of information sharing in the automotive sector. These information-sharing practices have allowed Toyota to ensure collaboration and realise significant benefits for the entire supply chain (Liker 2004).

Furthermore, their know-how database allows employees to explore previous problem solving attempts (Liker 2004). This central repository is an important source of information for their entire supply chain network.

Volkswagen has also made use of a web-based knowledge base for query handling (Gregoire & Cohen 2001). Volkswagen's efforts focus on the distribution of the necessary information and solutions to problems throughout the organisation and supply chain (Volkswagen 2007). Similar to BMW, Volkswagen has implemented a 'yellow pages' application, which, together with expert 'rooms' encourages collaboration for problem-solving activities (Volkswagen 2007).

Although this literature points to a free flow of information from the OEM to suppliers, little or no mention is made of information flowing from, or amongst, suppliers. In fact, Toyota appears to be the only automotive manufacturer to have information flowing freely within the supply chain – their continued dominance of the market might be attributed to this (Liker 2004). The case study in the next section provides evidence of poor information sharing within the supply chain.

Case study

In the case study detailed below, no evidence was found of free information flow in the interorganisational relationships in a South African automotive supply chain. The event studied had the potential to shut down operations at the OEM and thus have a ripple effect on the operations of other members of the supply chain. Information gained was not shared with other members in the supply chain, thereby having a negative impact on operations.

Observations relevant to this study centre on one particular instance – the hard drive failure of a production machine that caused production to stop for over a week at the plant under discussion. This resulted in major losses as replacement products had to be shipped in from other manufacturing plants in order to supply the local automotive OEM and prevent incurring further penalties. This issue is typical of problems encountered at this company. If information regarding this failure had been shared with the entire supply chain, all parties could have been able to adjust manufacturing for this period. This was not carried out, as the supplier was concerned that the OEM would source a similar product elsewhere for production and thus jeopardise future contracts between the supplier and OEM.

In order to get the equipment to function correctly, collaboration was required from a number of role players, including, (1) staff at the manufacturers of the machine, (2) the manufacturers and local agents of the industrial computer that runs the machine,(3) subject matter experts at the company's head office in order to install the necessary software (4) and a local IT company to provide technical services.

The effects of a lack of trust can be seen in this supply chain relationship. Had the supplier had a trust relationship with the OEM and other suppliers in the supply chain, information regarding the machine failure and possible production stoppages could have been shared. This would have allowed the OEM, and subsequently the entire supply chain network, to adjust production schedules, for example, by manufacturing a different vehicle that did not make use of the supplier's components. The lack of trust in this supply chain resulted in production shutting down temporarily at the OEM and the supplier incurring the costs of shipping components from an overseas-based partner and penalties associated with halting production at the OEM. Based on this analysis, the next section proposes a way towards a more competitive supply chain. This is then related to the organisational information processing theory and game theory that has been discussed in a previous section.

The way forward for competitive supply chains

As Dubey and Jain (2005) and Peterson (2002) point out, the modern supply chain needs to be collectively competitive. In the chain organism supply chain model mentioned previously (Peterson 2002); the existence of trust in the interorganisational relationship is paramount to the competitiveness of the supply chain.

Where adequate levels of trust exist in the interorganisational relationships, information sharing amongst supply chain partners is maximised. With increased information sharing, transactional costs are reduced and efficiency improved, thereby allowing the supply chain to compete effectively.

At the same time, the more information that is shared, the more trust can be established within the supply chain. Having previously established the role IT has in facilitating information sharing (and thereby enhancing trust), this vital component cannot be ignored. This cyclical relationship between trust and information sharing and the underlying support role of IT is represented in Figure 1.

This view is confirmed by the organisational information processing theory discussed in a previous section, whereby uncertainty in the relationship can be reduced by increasing access to information (Premkumar et al. 2005). This allows the supply chain to improve decision-making and thereby improve operations.

In light of the game theory and the prisoner's dilemma discussed in a previous section, the supplier's choice to cooperate and supply information willingly is directly related to the amount of information available and therefore the level of trust that each of the supply chain partners places in the others. If all supply chain members trust each other, information is shared, and maximum gain for the entire supply chain can be realised in terms of efficiency and effectiveness of operations and competitiveness.

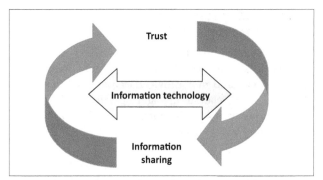

FIGURE 1: The trust-information sharing relationship.

Conclusion

This paper has shown how several works have highlighted the importance of trust in a supply chain and the effects of diminished trust on supply chain operations. All these studies suggest that increasing the level of trust in the interorganisational relationship is required. The relationship between trust and information sharing is important in the context of our research. Several works have highlighted benefits and concerns regarding sharing information amongst supply chain partners, at the same time noting a relationship between trust and information sharing in a singular direction.

This paper considered the relationship between the two concepts (trust and information sharing) and looked at how they influence each other. The use of IT to support this relationship was also established. In order to have a sufficient level of trust in a relationship, a significant level of information sharing is required. Better decision-making can occur if there is sufficient information, and the resultant improved operational performance experienced, results in improved trust in the supply chain partners that have shared the information. Conversely, the sharing of information will only occur if there is a sufficient level of trust amongst supply chain partners. If there is insufficient trust in supply chain partners, there will be unwillingness to share information. Thus, the relationship between trust and information sharing is cyclical – it is not a relationship that occurs in a singular direction as established by the existing literature.

An example of the effects of a lack of trust in a supply chain relationship and the consequential lack of information flow, were provided in a case study of an Eastern Cape based automotive supplier. This led to a proposed way forward for competitive supply chains, in which building trust in the supply chain is essential for improved information flow. This, in turn, leads to improved supply chain performance and competitiveness. Furthermore, this situation leads to improved trust, allowing the supply chain partnership to be mutually beneficial.

References

Agarwal, A. & Shankar, R., 2003, 'On-line trust building in e-enabled supply chains', *Supply Chain Management: An International Journal*, 8(4), 324–334. doi:10.1108/13598540310490080

Awazu, Y., Desouza, K., Jha, S., Kim, J. & Wecht, C., 2007, 'Roles of Information Technology in Distributed and Open Innovation Process' in J. Burke & M. Shaw (eds.), *13th Americas Conference on Information Systems AMCIS 2007 proceedings*, Keystone, USA, August 9–12, 2007, pp. 1–10.

Barnes, J. & Morris, M., 2008, 'Staying alive in the global automotive industry: what can developing economies learn from South Africa about linking into global automotive value chains?', *The European Journal of Development Research* 20(1), 31–55. doi:10.1080/09578810701853157

Black, A., 1998, 'The impact of trade liberalization on the South African automotive industry', paper presented to the TIPS Policy Forum, Gauteng, South Africa, 9–11 September.

Africa Research Bulletin, 2010, 'Economic, Financial and Technical Series', *Company Brief: General* 47(3), pp. 18645–18648, viewed 15 January 2011, from http://onlinelibrary.wiley.com/doi/10.1111/j.1467-6346.2010.03227.x/abstract

Burnes, B. & West, P., 2000, 'Applying organisational learning: Lessons from the automotive industry', *International Journal of Operations and Production Management*, 20(10), 1236–1251. doi:10.1108/01443570010343762

Cheng, T.C.E., Lai, K-H. & Singh, N., 2007, 'Intra-organizational perspectives on IT-enabled supply chains', *Communications of the ACM*, 50(1), 59–65. doi:10.1145/1188913.1188918

Chu, S-Y. & Fang, W-C., 2006, 'Exploring the relationships of trust and commitment in supply chain management', *The Journal of American Academy of Business, Cambridge*, 9(1), 224–228.

Cooper, D.R. & Schindler, P.S., 2003, *Business Research Methods*, 8th edn., McGraw-Hill/Irwin, New York, NY.

Coughlan, P. & Rukstad, M.G., 2001, *DaimlerChrysler Knowledge Management Strategy*, Harvard Business School Publishing, Boston, MA.

Covey, S.M.R., 2008, *The speed of trust: The one thing that changes everything*, Free Press, New York, NY.

Davis, J.H., Mayer, R.C. & Schoorman, F.D., 2007, 'An Integrative Model of Organizational Trust: Past, Present and Future', *Academy of Management* Review, 32(2), 344–354. doi:10.5465/AMR.2007.24348410

Department of Trade and Industry, 2005, *Current Developments in the Automotive Industry 2004*, viewed 15 January 2011, from http://apps.thedti.gov.za/publications/automotiveindustry.pdf

Department of Trade and Industry, 2010,, *Media release: Minister Davies approves Automotive Investment Scheme Guidelines*, viewed 15 January 2011, from http://apps.thedti.gov.za/mediareleases/AIS_media.pdf

Dubey, A. & Jain, K., 2005, 'Supply chain collaboration: A governance perspective', *Supply chain forum: An international journal*, 6(2), 50–57.

Fachinelli, A.C., Ueltschy, L.C. & Ueltschy, M.L., 2007, 'The impact of culture on the generation of trust in global supply chain relationships', *The Marketing Management Journal*, 17(1), 15–26.

Fedorowicz, J. & Ghosh, A., 2008, 'The role of trust in supply chain governance', *Business Process Management Journal*, 14(4), 453–470. doi:10.1108/14637150810888019

Fingar, C. (2002), 'Car wars' in *ifDi magazine*, viewed 02 July 2006, from http://www.fdiintelligence.com/Archive/Car-wars

Flowerday, S. & Von Solms, R., 2006, 'Trust: an Element of Information Security', in S. Fischer-Hubner, K. Rannenberg, L. Yngstrom and S. Lindskog (eds.), *Security and Privacy in Dynamic Environments*, pp. 87–98, IFIP, Springer, USA.

Ford Motor Company (2005), 'Challenges facing the automotive industry' in *Ford Sustainably Report*, viewed 30 March 2006, from http://corporate.ford.com/doc/2004-05_sustainability_report.pdf

Franse, R., 2006, 'The response of an original equipment manufacturer to the motor industry development programme: A case study', MA dissertation, Department of Business Management, Rhodes University.

Gao, J. & Lee, J.D., 2005, 'Trust, information technology, and cooperation in supply chains', *Supply Chain Forum: An international Journal*, 6(2), 82–89.

Gregoire, C. & Cohen, G., 2001, 'Audi Licenses Hyperwave's Collaborative Knowledge Management System', in *Let's see if they use it now: eKnowledge Infrastructure Enables AUDI Employees to Answer Customer...*, viewed 15 January 2011, from http://forums.audiworld.com/showthread.php?t=1815029

Han, Z., Liu, K.J.R., Sun, Y.L. & Yu, W., 2006, 'A Trust Evaluation Framework in Distributed Networks: Vulnerability Analysis and Defense Against Attacks', in E. Monteiro & J.L. Gonzalez (eds.) *IEEE INFOCOM Conference on Computer Communications Proceedings*, Barcelona, Spain, April 23–29, 2006, pp. 1–13.

Jenkins, M. & Tallman, S., 2010, 'The Shifting Geography of Competitive Advantage: Clusters, Networks and Firms', *Journal of Economic Geography*, 10(4) 1–20.

Jharkharia, S. & Shankar, R., 2004, 'IT enablement of supply chains: modeling the enablers', *International Journal of Productivity and Performance Management*, 53(8), 700–712. doi:10.1108/17410400410569116

Kappe, F., 2001, 'Knowledge management: A practical example at BMW', paper presented at the *I-Know 2001*, Graz, Austria, 12–13 July 2001.

Kazi, A.S. & Wolf, P. (eds.), 2004, 'Real-life Knowledge Management: Lessons from the Field', viewed 20 July 2006 from, http://www.knowledgeboard.com/lib/3236.

Kwon, I-W. G. & Suh, T., 2005, 'Trust, commitment and relationships in supply chain management: A path analysis', *Supply chain management: An international Journal*, 10(1), 26–33.

Lewis, J.D., 1999, *Trusted Partners: How Companies Build Mutual Trust and Win Together*, The Free Press, New York, NY.

Liker, J.K., 2004, *The Toyota Way: 14 Management Principles from the World's Greatest Manufacturer*, McGraw-Hill, New York, NY.

Liu, X-F., 2007, 'Study on the application of information technology in supply chain management', *Journal of US-China Public Administration*, 4(1), 72–76.

Lorentzen, J., 2006, *Multinationals on the Periphery: DaimlerChrysler South Africa, Human Capital Upgrading and Regional Economic Development*, Human Sciences Research Council Press, Cape Town.

Mak'Ochieng, A.A., 2003, 'A case study of the strategic nature of DaimlerChrysler South Africa's corporate social investment programmes in the local communities of the Border-Kei region in the Easter Cape province', MA dissertation, Dept. of Business Management, Rhodes University.

Mangold, P., 2009, 'South African Automotive Week: Mercedes-Benz', in *South African Automotive Week*, viewed 27 April 2009, from http://www.saaw.co.za/News/09-04-27/mercedes-benz.aspx.

McEvily, B. & Tortoriello, M., 2011, 'Measuring trust in organisational research: Review and recommendations', *Journal of Trust Research*, 1(1), 23–63. doi:10.1 080/21515581.2011.552424

Naesens, K., Pintelon, L. & Taillieu, T., 2007, 'A framework for implementing and sustaining trust in horizontal partnerships', *Supply chain forum: An international journal* 8(1), 32–44.

Pagano, A. & Zagnoli, P., 2001, '*Modularization, Knowledge Management and Supply Chain Relations: The Trajectory of a European Commercial Vehicle Assembler*', viewed 10 April 2006, from http://citeseerx.ist.psu.edu/viewdoc/download?doi=10.1.1.118.4772&rep=rep1&type=pdf

Peterson, H.C., 2002, 'The "learning" supply chain: Pipeline or pipedream', *American Journal of Agricultural Economics*, 85, (5), 1329–1336. doi:10.1111/1467-8276.00398

Poirier, C.C., 2003, *The Supply Chain Manager's Problem-Solver*, CRC Press, Florida, FL.

Premkumar, G., Ramamurthy, K. & Saunders, C.S., 2005, 'Information processing view of organizations: An exploratory examination of fit in the context', *Journal of Management Information Systems*, 22(1), 257–294.

Rethink IT, 2004, 'The car industry drives forward with knowledge management – Masterclass' in *Rethink IT*, viewed 18 July 2006, from http://findarticles.com/p/articles/mi_m0PAT/is_2004_March/ai_114699548/

Ryu, S., 2006, 'The effect of external and internal environments on interfirm governance', *Journal of business-to-business marketing*, 13(2), 67–89. doi:10.1300/J033v13n02_04

Sahay, B.S., 2003, 'Understanding trust in supply chain relationships', *Industrial management and data systems*, 103(8), 553–563. doi:10.1108/02635570310497602

Smeltzer, L.R., 1997, 'The Meaning and Origin of Trust in Buyer-Supplier Relationships', *International Journal of Purchaising and Materials Management*, Winter,, pp. 40–48.

Volkswagen, 2007, 'Knowledge Management: Knowledge at Volkswagen', viewed 01 September 2007 from http://www.vw-personal.de/www/en/wissen/wissensmanagement.html

Wang, E.T.G. & Wei, H-L., 2007, 'Interorganizational governance value creation: Coordinating for information visibility and flexibility in supply chains', *Decision Sciences*, 38(4), 647–674. doi:10.1111/j.1540-5915.2007.00173.x

Ward, A., 2009, '*South African Automotive Week: Toyota*', viewed 28 April 2009, from http://www.saaw.co.za/News/09-04-28/toyota.aspx.

Yin, R.K., 2003, *Case Study Research: Design and Methods*, 3rd edn, Volume 5, SAGE Publications, California, CA.

18

A tool to increase information-processing capacity for consumer water meter data

Authors:
Heinz E. Jacobs[1]
Kerry A. Fair[2]

Affiliations:
[1]Department of Civil
Engineering, University of
Stellenbosch, South Africa

[2]GLS Software, TechnoPark,
Stellenbosch, South Africa

Correspondence to:
Heinz Jacobs

Email:
hejacobs@sun.ac.za

Postal address:
Private Bag X1, Matieland
7602, South Africa

Background: Water service providers invoice most South African urban consumers for the water they use every month. A secure treasury system generates water invoices at municipalities' financial departments. Information about the water usage of customers initially comes from reading the water meters, usually located in gardens near the front boundaries of properties. Until as recently as 1990, the main purpose of the water meter readings was to generate invoices for water usage. There are various treasury systems for this purpose.

Objective: The objective of this research article was to describe the development of Swift, a locally developed software tool for analysing water meter data from an information management perspective, which engineers in the water field generally use, and to assess critically the influence of Swift on published research and industry. This article focuses on water usage and the challenge of data interchange and extraction as issues that various industries face.

Method: This article presents the first detailed report on Swift. It uses a detailed knowledge review and presents and summarises the findings chronologically.

Results: The water meter data flow path used to be quite simple. The risk of breaches in confidentiality was limited. Technological advances over the years have led to additional knowledge coming from the same water meter readings with subsequent research outputs. However, there are also complicated data flow paths and increased risks. Users have used Swift to analyse more than two million consumers' water meter readings to date. Studies have culminated in 10 peer-reviewed journal articles using the data. Seven of them were in the last five years.

Conclusion: Swift-based data was the basis of various research studies in the past decade. Practical guidelines in the civil engineering fraternity for estimating water use in South Africa have incorporated knowledge from these studies. Developments after 1995 have increased the information processing capacity for water meter data.

Introduction

Background to water information management

Water is a scarce resource, particularly in South Africa. Research in various fields is addressing the need to manage water use and water resources better as well as to ensure the equitable distribution of water to all South Africans. This responsibility usually rests with engineers who face increasing volumes of data from millions of water meter readings gathered over time.

The drive to improve equity of supply and to conserve water in general has led to the neglect of information management. This study has adopted the term 'water information management' (WIM) from Jacobs (2008:4) because it relates to residential water usage and managing related data. The definition of WIM is 'to manage the information pertaining to how and when water is used better.' WIM is a prerequisite for gaining knowledge from water meter data and effective water demand management (WDM). The need for relevant, timely and sufficiently accurate information has increased to a point where it needs advanced software tools and specialised consultants.

Focus of the study

Engineers have used a software package called Swift extensively over the past decade to help them plan water systems (Fair & Compion 2008:49) and, as a spin-off, to assist research into water demand. The Water Research Commission (WRC) compiled the South African National Water Consumption Archive (NWCA), which contains Swift-based data, in 2007. It contains the monthly water usage records of more than two million South African consumers (Van Zyl & Geustyn 2007:3) and probably includes the data of each local reader of this paper. Swift also incorporates functionality for electricity meter data.

What is Swift, where did it start, and how does it function? The only published answers to these questions come from Fair, Loubser, Jacobs & Van der Merwe 2008 (2008:5). These authors provide a very short review of Swift in the description of their research methodology.

The current study is the first to report what one could call 'The Swift story'. Its particular focus is the academic effect that Swift brought about as it pertains to water use.

Scope

The problem of data interchange and management information system (MIS) extraction is a common challenge in industries, as is the method of collecting the data in the first place.

Reports of data analyses from various industries, which are relevant to residential services, include electricity usage (Taylor 1975; Andersson & Damsgaard 1999; Ziramba 2008), sewerage (Butler 1991), petrol and electricity (Houthakker, Verleger& Sheehan 1974), fuel wood (Garbacz 1985a) and fuel oil (Garbacz 1985b). The data these authors analysed, and the methods they used, include consumer perceptions (with spreadsheet-based analyses), study-specific recorded information (through specially installed meters and data loggers) and various methods of extracting data and their subsequent spreadsheet analyses. Some of these studies use elasticity analysis and evaluate how 'susceptible' one parameter is to change in another.

However, the researchers decided it was beyond the scope of this study to cover elasticity analysis and other techniques. The attention of this article is only on residential water usage.

Relevance and motivation

Water meter readings are particularly relevant to a number of people. They include:

- municipal treasurers, who see them as sources of income
- water consumers (like home owners), who receive monthly water invoices from treasurers
- the municipalities' consultants (like financial and technical consultants), who use this information and knowledge for analyses and planning in their respective fields
- academics in the field, who require access to the raw data for further research.

Unfortunately, problems often contaminate the data. They include duplicated records and errors at source. There also seems to be no standard for water meter data in treasury systems. These problems need to be resolved before using the data, or during its extraction. The aims and objectives of enterprise information architecture (EIA) in organisations (Iyamu 2011:5) are particularly relevant to this topic because it includes reducing integration complexity, controlling duplication and replication, validation and correction at source as well as standards for accessing information.

The same information is particularly relevant to organisations like municipalities, consultants and academic institutions.

Galbraith (1977:49) identified five main organisation design strategies in two categories:

- increased information processing capacity
- reduced need for information processing.

The subsequent development of a novel tool (Swift) has increased information processing capacity so that it extends beyond financial systems. Its development and working are the focus of this article. It allows for off-site processing because of restricted access and system performance. Some advanced software tools intended for financial management incorporate components to manage water meter data. However, their focus is on finances.

The researchers spent considerable time reviewing the literature on products similar to Swift. However, they could not identify any peer-reviewed publications on the results from similar products. Swift is a technical tool that focuses on analysing water demand and provides sufficient information for researchers to analyse water usage based on meter readings with certain filters and technical criteria. A substantial review of other work and communication with researchers locally and abroad suggests that researchers usually use Microsoft Excel to achieve the same purpose by importing text-format extracts from treasury data base information (Du Plessis 2012; Fuamba 2012).

Information and data flow

Information managers often use data flow diagrams. They are convenient tools for illustrating how systems process data in terms of various inputs and outputs. One of the elementary components of a data flow diagram is a file or database. A number of municipal databases are relevant to the work presented here and include:

- treasury system data
- town planners' databases with their spatial attributes
- asset registers and infrastructure databases
- technical models of pipe networks to model the flow of water in pipes.

The flow of data between these different databases is often complex and the sensitive nature of the data makes it complicated. Swift provides an interface between data sources and creates the potential to mine information.

Swift as a tool for managing water information

The need for a 'Swift tool'

Water service providers need to optimise their services to consumers by providing sufficient and affordable water. Therefore, the need for accurate information about the system is becoming ever more important. Van Rooyen (2002:2) underlines the importance of using technology to improve the flow of information for management purposes.

The information that technical staff members need is available in municipal treasury databases. They store the readings for every water meter in the system every month, along with land use and other property-related information. The same database contains confidential customer information, including customers' arrears and general account information. Consequently, these databases are vigorously protected against unlawful access. The problem is that treasury systems were not designed to produce the information and statistical reports that the infrastructure managers and engineers need.

This might make a case for integrated systems. However, in the absence of such systems (as is the case locally), there is a dire need from a technical perspective to obtain data from different treasury systems in some specified and predefined format. Van Rooyen (2002:3) noted the need for integrated systems as one of the factors that impede change in typical local treasury departments.

With the current technology, treasury systems data rarely have spatial referencing. In other words, it is not always possible to pinpoint a particular customer on a map – which is exactly what an engineer or planner would like to do. Where it does exist, spatial referencing is never particularly accurate, largely because of mass linking of historical data at some point. Therefore, it is necessary to extract the available information from the databases and use additional manipulation through software designed for this purpose to improve spatial referencing.

Financial systems were also not designed to perform the statistical calculations the various interested parties need. Although the calculations they need to produce the information are theoretically simple, the volume of data that is involved makes it difficult to use spreadsheets. Even in relatively small towns, where there are fewer than 15 000 properties, spreadsheets have become prohibitively inefficient and clumsy because of the large data sets of monthly water meter readings and additional data fields that interested parties need for analyses.

Purpose

The designers of Swift specifically intended it to make water meter data, formerly a closed source of data contained in municipal treasury systems, available to a wider audience such as municipal engineers and their engineering consultants. Later spin-offs would include access for academic use. The intended users were the infrastructure managers who could improve their work, often stipulated in law, to ensure the effective management of water infrastructure.

Swift development and data extraction processes

GLS Software conceived the Swift idea in the early 1990s. The first application occurred when Centurion, a municipality near Pretoria, which is part of the Tshwane Metropolitan Municipality today, needed a water infrastructure master plan update. GLS Consulting Engineers, under the leadership of B.F. Loubser, conducted the project.

At the time the Centurion technical team, comprising the Water Planning Engineer (F. Mouton), the Water Division Manager (L. Lötter) and the City Engineer (A. Lamprecht) were the key role-players. The municipality was using the PROMIS billing system of ICL. The Centurion engineering team became the main instigators of the concept when they insisted on developing an interface to the treasury system. It subsequently engaged GLS Software to develop a tool, which later became known as Swift.

The main aim initially was simply to extract water consumption data for use in hydraulic models of the pipe network in order to plan infrastructure development. This would allow engineers to use accurate estimates of water flows in pipe models instead of estimates based on generalised guidelines for water use.

At the time, the municipality appointed C. Triblehorn, a software programmer, to address the database application and programming. In conjunction with GLS Software, Triblehorn subsequently developed the first-ever interface between the new tool and the treasury system in about 1995. A considerable amount of the original structure and code base remains unchanged, although GLS Software is currently improving it to include better geographical information systems (GIS) integration. Centurion was not alone. Areas like the East Rand (now Ekurhuleni Metropolitan Municipality) also established similar databases and software models (Vorster et al. 1995:2).

In order to access the treasury data at Centurion, ICL had to develop a routine for extracting the water consumption data from the PROMIS billing system whilst maintaining the integrity of the highly sensitive information. Centurion also needed information in addition to the water meter readings. It included meter reading dates, consumers' names, property owners' names, addresses or property codes (to place the users on a map and link the water usage to the closest pipe on the map), land use information, and water tariff codes and property valuations. Suburb allocations were also important because suburbs differed substantially socioeconomically and in water usage.

A detailed technical review of the drivers of water usage, and the subsequent need for particular data fields from the treasury database, is beyond the scope of this article. However, the municipality usually extracts 30 data fields for each water consumer from the treasury database.

Some of the fields extracted from treasury systems for use in Swift, like consumer and owner names, account numbers, property valuations and addresses are sensitive because of identity theft. Identity theft is an increasing local problem (Augustyn 2005:2).

After debating the option of open database connectivity (ODBC) in the conceptual design of Swift, Loubser (2011) recalls that the municipality finally decided to use a snapshot extract as the best method of obtaining the data. The municipality decided that a one-way flow of information from the treasury system was the best option for maintaining the integrity of the treasury system and preventing unwanted access. Loubser (2011) gives a personal account and recalls going to the ICL office with the data specifications, meeting a programmer and walking out of the office a few hours later with a text file of about 30 000 lines. It contained just about all the data he required. For larger and more complex billing systems, the same process can take considerably longer to complete. Extracting the information continues to be an almost insurmountable struggle or very easy, depending on the type of treasury system and the level of co-operation.

Land use and zoning information comes from the most accurate source of data for each municipality. These data sources include the town planning land use and zoning descriptions as well as the land use and zoning codes in the same database. Another source of information is the treasury system billing codes that should be accurate and up to date because municipalities use these codes to generate revenue. Therefore, it was necessary to develop flexible, generic algorithms in Swift to determine the most likely land use and zoning for each stand using a number of ranked data fields.

It soon became clear that municipalities could use Swift to measure water losses by comparing the total water sales from all consumer meters (reported via Swift) to the total volume of water fed into the same region – recorded via a large water meter on the main water supply pipe. Having more than one supply pipe complicates the issue. However, it works in the same way in principle.

Therefore, Swift provided a unique way of enabling engineers to measure the lost water in the system accurately and conveniently. The lost water is simply the difference between the water a municipality supplies to a town and all the water it sells – and records it in the treasury system.

Cross-referencing consumers to model nodes

One of Swift's innovations is 'cross-referencing'. In Swift terminology, this process is 'X-Ref'. Figure 1 illustrates it.

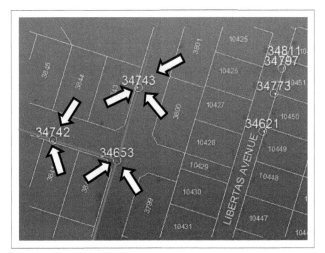

FIGURE 1: Illustration of the Swift cross-referencing process.

From an information management perspective, it is of little use to know how much water a consumer uses without knowing the consumer's spatial whereabouts. In other words, municipalities need to know where the consumer is on a map relative to the water pipes in order to allocate the appropriate volume of water (from Swift) to the correct node in a hydraulic model of the water pipe network. The large yellow arrows show how six properties in the figure 'connect to' the water pipes and nodes: the red lines and yellow circles respectively.

Treasury link

Municipalities obtain Swift databases from their treasury databases. Therefore, Swift has data for every stand and every meter in an area. Fields in the databases contain information about stand-related data like the owner, the consumer, the address, land use, zoning, consumption and tax tariffs of the stand. They also include the value of the stand and any improvements. Information about meters includes the meter readings, the meter serial number and the date of installation.

The researchers adapted the illustration of Swift architecture and related databases, shown in Figure 2, from GLS Software. It shows the interface between treasury, GIS databases, Swift and the planning process. The components include, for example, aspects relevant to the hydraulic network models of the water and sewerage systems. The link is obvious and excluding it from the figure would be an oversight because the water usage Swift derives is a critical input for analysing the water flow in pipes for water (Wadiso software) and sewerage (Sewsan software).

The researchers felt that further discussion of the hydraulic models, plan books, peak flows and master plans were beyond the scope of this article.

Treasurers' data are not open source and one needs a one-way 'dump' of information to obtain the data. After extracting the data from treasury systems and importing them to Swift, the information is available to users in a seamless structured table that they sort, query and save in reports if they need to. It is also possible to view the data and a graphical display of water consumption separately for each user.

Various studies have found that it is important to validate the historical meter records users extract from treasury systems. Users need routines to identify and correct irregularities in the water meter readings. They include sudden drops in readings when municipalities replace a meter, spikes and/or dips in water consumption records and unrealistically high or low readings. Possible causes of these errors include faulty water meters and data capturing errors.

There are also basic methods for checking the integrity of the latest readings against historical meter records. Swift allows users to customise some settings so that users can conduct analyses on any treasury database. For example, a large consumer in one town might not necessarily be a large

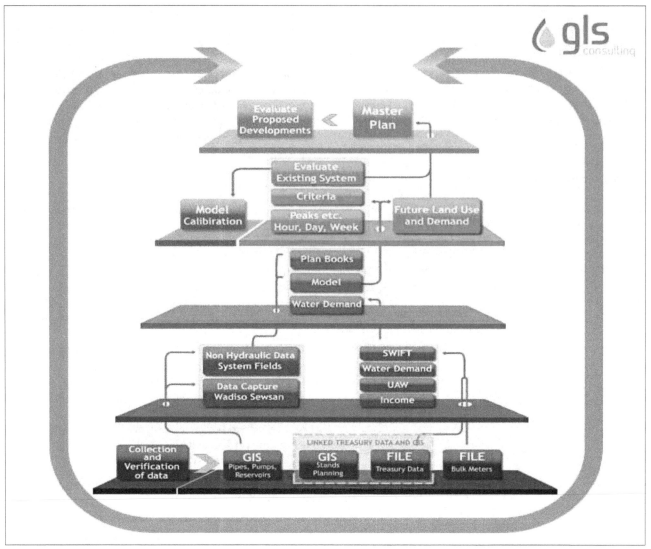

Source: GLS Consulting

FIGURE 2: Illustration of Swift and related management information system architecture.

user in another, larger town. Swift allows users to define the consumption that identifies the large users. Similarly, users can categorise suburbs and land use information into user specific groups so that users can obtain meaningful results from any system.

Currently Swift extract routines integrate with at least 15 different treasury systems, including SAP, Venus and SAMRAS. Swift is in regular use in over 20 municipalities in South Africa and a few locations overseas.

Discussion
From water meter readings to knowledge

The information users obtain from Swift databases is ideal for research into issues relevant to water usage. This is particularly true for civil engineers who need information about water usage to analyse and plan water infrastructure systems, like pipe networks. Therefore, it is not surprising that the WRC funded an extensive research project to compile the NWCA to act as a source for further research (Van Zyl & Geustyn 2007:48).

However, when one considers the chronological publication history of Swift-derived research, it is clear that the first decade of Swift's application drew little academic interest. A review of publications that uses Swift data is the first and only of its kind in academic literature. The chronological list in Table 1 is particularly relevant to the *South African Journal of Information Management* (SAJIM) because each reference reflects a moment in time when users converted basic water meter readings, via a complex system (including Swift), to acquired knowledge that they disseminated in an academic publication. 'Research' implies discovering or verifying information (Oxford English Dictionary 2006).

Chronological review of Swift-based research

In the effort to obtain a better understanding of the origins of Swift data as sources for research outputs, it is necessary to review the related publications and researchers. GLS Software and its sister company GLS Consulting have always maintained strong links with various South African academic institutions, through collaborative research, student mentoring and external reviews. Therefore, it was obvious that research and publications would eventually follow.

All the initial publications had connections with the University of Johannesburg (UJ) in some way. The first notable Swift-based publication in a peer-reviewed journal (Jacobs et al. 2004:2) appeared almost a decade after the first application of Swift. The main author was a doctoral student at UJ at the time.

In an effort to improve the methods for estimating water demand in South Africa, Jacobs et al. (2004) analysed the data, from Swift, of more than 600 000 water meters. Shortly afterwards, another Swift-based publication followed (Van Zyl & Husselman 2006:12). A University of Johannesburg master's student and her promoter were the authors. The authors of these publications were involved in all subsequent academic writings on Swift-derived knowledge, although the research had expanded to include three South African universities by 2011. These are the University of Johannesburg (Griffioen, née Husselman), Stellenbosch University (Jacobs) and the University of Cape Town (Van Zyl).

Table 1 gives a comprehensive chronological list of Swift-based publications. It emphasises the increasing application and relevance of Swift as an academic tool and as a way of managing water meter data.

The National Water Consumption Archive

One can regard the compilation of the National Water Consupmtion Archive (NWCA) in 2007 as the highlight to date in terms of academic outputs that use Swift. Compiling the NWCA was a combined effort between municipalities, whose information it was using, and GLS Software. It developed Swift and needed the water consumption records

to improve service delivery. Various academics also needed the information to gain much-needed knowledge about water consumption in South Africa. The South African WRC funded the research project.

However, problems of confidentiality soon hampered the academic application of the NWCA. In addition, legal problems about the availability of data in the NWCA led to a lack of published work in 2010 and 2011 (see Table 1) compared to the number of publications up to 2009. The right to data in the NWCA currently rests with the WRC, which provides selected fields to interested researchers upon request for the information and requires them to sign a confidentiality clause. The latter is necessary to protect individual water consumers, whose personal information resides in the NWCA. Therefore, potential researchers need to know exactly which data fields they require before the NWCA will release the data. Then, when researchers receive the data, they have to protect it against hackers, who could target the sources that become available afterwards on secure university networks.

Conclusion
Future research needs

Swift has sparked local research into water usage. However, there are research needs that remain. One of the current issues is to maintain the NWCA or to update it regularly (maybe every two years). The NWCA is cumbersome and it needs to reorganise the data fields to make it more user-friendly and to allow researchers to access different classes of data. For example, one could describe each of the fields in the NWCA as general data (open access), personal (available on request) and classified (available after completing the legal forms).

Researchers have presented several approaches to extending the functionality of the NWCA to a web-based tool (Sinske

TABLE 1: Chronological summary of Swift-based research outputs.

Year	Journal or Conference	Type of publication	Citation	Comment regarding research method and outcome
1995	Journal of the South African Institution of Civil Engineering	DOE listed journal; peer reviewed paper	Vorster et al. (2004)	The research was conducted parallel to development of Swift, but insufficient data was available at the time to apply Swift in the research methodology or to report on Swift.
2004	Journal of the South African Institution of Civil Engineering	DOE listed journal; peer reviewed paper	Jacobs et al. (2004)	Swift-derived data was central to the research method in this technical paper. The outcome was a new guideline for estimating domestic water use in SA based on statistical analysis of property size and water use.
2005	Journal of the South African Institution of Civil Engineering	DOE listed journal; peer reviewed paper	Husselman & Van Zyl (2005)	Swift-derived data was central to the research method The outcome extended findings of Jacobs et al. (2004) to include property value
2006	WISA Conference	Reviewed conference paper	Jacobs et al. (2006)	Swift-results used to verify findings from a survey questionnaire on household water use.
2007	Water SA	ISI-listed journal, peer reviewed paper	Jacobs (2007)	Swift applied in novel research to correlate metered household water use and estimated water use based on survey questions.
2007	WRC Report	Peer reviewed research report	Van Zyl & Geustyn (2007)	This was the first funded research based on Swift. Swift was used to compile the SA National Water Consumption Archive (NWCA) comprising over 2 million water consumers' monthly water meter readings.
2008	South African Journal of Information Management	DOE listed journal; peer reviewed paper	Jacobs (2008)	In this first report on WIM in SA, Swift was depicted as part of the schematic flow of water use information.
2008	WISA Conference	Reviewed conference paper	Kriegler & Jacobs (2008)	The first research extending the outcome of Swift-based work to non-domestic water use.
2008	Water SA	ISI-listed journal, peer reviewed paper	Van Zyl et al. (2008)	Swift was used to derive an improved area-based guideline for domestic water use estimation in SA.
2009	CCWI Conference	Reviewed international conference paper	Ilemobade et al. (2009)	Swift was used to derive a probability-based guideline for non-domestic water use.

& Jacobs 2008:1; Van den Berg, Fair & Sinske 2008:209). However, this would require even more complex and rigid ways of preventing identify theft and of addressing confidentiality issues. As long as a decade ago, Van Rooyen (2002:4) reported that the Internet was linking many systems and participants in the market place. This created new benefits, but also new problems or risks. For example, hackers could attempt to access a network in order to steal intellectual property, databases and privileged information and sell the information to crime syndicates (Augustyn 2005:6). These threats impose limitations on the availability of data and restrict research.

Finally, it is necessary to identify and describe ways of improving information management as well as the scope and limitations of using Swift-based data for research. Researchers are currently investigating and developing novel and more advanced software products based on the success of Swift. The current need in industry is to add even more value to the knowledge users gain from Swift to support decisions (like priority lists and query tools for managers) and spatial attributes (like maps). Tools like Google Earth, Google Maps and non-web based geographical information systems hold the key to the next level of increasing information processing capacity.

Acknowledgements

The authors acknowledge Dr B.F. Loubser (GLS Software) for his contribution to this study and for providing the overview of Swift development.

Competing interests

Both authors declare hereby that all efforts were made to be objective in executing and publishing this research. The authors declare that K.A.F. (GLS Software) has a financial relationship(s) which may be perceived by others to have influenced the writing of this paper. The affiliation is noted on the title page.

Authors' contributions

H.E.J. (University of Stellenbosch) was the main author and instigator of this research into the application and effect of Swift on research outputs. K.A.F. (G.L.S. Software) was a director of GLS Software at the time of the project and was responsible for the development of software produced by GLS, including Swift. H.E.J. (University of Stellenbosch) and K.A.F. (GLS Software) contributed equally to the research and this subsequent article. Nonconfidential data and information derived from Swift was kindly made available by GLS at no cost for various research projects at three different South African universities in the past years.

References

Andersson, B. & Damsgaard, N., 1999, 'Residential Electricity Use – Demand Estimations Using Swedish Micro Data', *Proceedings of the 22nd IAEE Annual International Conference*, Vol 2, International Association for Energy Economics Rome, Italy, June 09–12, 1999, pp. 255–264

Augustyn D., 2005, 'Identity theft escalation – You may need to change your life', *South African Journal of Information Management* 7(4), 11 pages, December.

Butler, D., 1991, 'A small-scale study of wastewater discharges from domestic appliances', *Water and Environmental Management Journal* 5, 178–185. http://dx.doi.org/10.1111/j.1747-6593.1991.tb00605.x

Du Plessis, J.A., 2012, email, 10 May, jadup@sun.ac.za

Fair K.A. & Compion J.K., 2008, 'The water distribution system master planning process in South Africa with a focus on metered demand, water loss monitoring, calibration and financial analysis', in J.E. van Zyl, A.A. Ilemobade & H.E. Jacobs (eds.), *Proceedings of the 10th Annual Water Distribution Systems Analysis Conference WDSA2008*, Kruger National Park, South Africa, August 17–20, 2008.

Fair K.A., Loubser B.F., Jacobs H.E. & Van der Merwe J., 2008, 'The Dynamic Master Planning Process – Integrated and continuous updating and planning of sewer systems', *Proceedings of the 11th International Conference on Urban Drainage*, Edinburgh, Scotland, UK, 31 August – 05 September, 2008.

Fuamba, M., 2012, email, 16 April 2012, musandji.fuamba@polymtl.ca

Galbraith J.R., 1977, 'Organization Design', Addison-Wesley, Reading.

Garbacz, C., 1985a, 'Residential Demand for Fuelwood', *Energy Economics* 7(3), 191–193. http://dx.doi.org/10.1016/0140-9883(85)90008-8

Garbacz, C., 1985b, 'Residential Fuel Oil Demand: A Micro-Based National Model', *Applied Economics* 17(4), 669–674. http://dx.doi.org/10.1080/758534697

Houthakker, H.S., Verleger, P.K. & Sheehan, D.P., 1974, 'Dynamic Demand Analyses for Gasoline and Residential Electricity', *American Journal of Agricultural Economics* 56(2), 412–418. http://dx.doi.org/10.2307/1238776

Ilemobade A.A., Van Zyl J.E. & Van Zyl H.J., 2009, 'New guidelines for non-domestic water estimation in South Africa', *Proceedings of Computers and Control in the Water Industry CCWI2009*, September 01–03, 2009, The Edge, University of Sheffield, Sheffield, UK, 7 pages.

Iyamu T., 2011, 'The architecture of information in organisations', *South African Journal of Information Management* 13(1), Art. #419, 9 pages. http://dx.doi.org/10.4102/sajim.v13i1.419

Jacobs H.E., 2008, 'Residential water information management', *South African Journal of Information Management* 10(3), 12 pages.

Jacobs H.E., 2007, 'The first reported correlation between end-use estimates of residential water demand and measured use in South Africa', *Water SA* 33(4), 549–558.

Jacobs H.E., Geustyn L.C. & Loubser B.F., 2006, 'Water – How is it used at home?', *Proceedings of the Water Institute of South Africa Biennial Conference*, Durban, South Africa, May22–25, 2006, viewed n.d., from http://www.ewisa.co.za/literature/

Jacobs H.E., Geustyn L.C., Loubser B.F. & Van Der Merwe B., 2004, 'Estimating residential water demand in Southern Africa', *Journal of the South African Institution of Civil Engineering* 46(4), 2–13.

Loubser B.F., 2011, email, 05 August, erik@gls.co.za

Oxford English Dictionary, 2006, 'Concise Oxford English Dictionary', 11th edn., revised and edited by C. Soanes & A. Stevenson, Oxford University Press, Oxford.

Sinske A.N. & Jacobs H.E., 2008, 'Modelling residential water use with a web-based tool', in P.A. van Brakel (ed.), *Proceedings of 10th Annual Conference on World Wide Web Applications*, September 03–05, 2008, Cape Town, South Africa, Cape Peninsula University of Technology, viewed n.d., from http://www.zaw3.co.za

Taylor, L.D., 1975, 'The demand for electricity: A Survey', *The Bell Journal of Economics* 6 (Spring), 74–110. http://dx.doi.org/10.2307/3003216

Van den Berg T.N., Fair K.A. & Sinske A.N., 2008, 'What are the benefits of universal water metering? Lessons learned at the district of West-Vancouver, British Columbia, Canada', in J.E. van Zyl, A.A. Ilemobade & H.E. Jacobs (eds.), *Proceedings of the 10th Annual Water Distribution Systems Analysis Conference WDSA2008*, Kruger National Park, South Africa, August 17–20, 2008, pp. 209–220.

Van Rooyen J.H., 2002, 'Emerging role of corporate treasury management in cyber space', *South African Journal of Information Management* 4(4), 14 pages, December 2004.

Van Zyl H.J., Ilemobade A.A. & Van Zyl J.E., 2008, 'An improved area-based guideline for domestic water demand estimation in South Africa', *WaterSA* 34(3), 381–392.

Van Zyl J.E. & Geustyn L.C., 2007, 'Development of a National Water Consumption Archive', WRC Report No. 1605/1/07, South African Water Research Commission, Pretoria, South Africa.

Van Zyl J.E. & Husselman M.L., 2006, 'Effect of stand size and income on residential water demand', *Journal of the South African Institution of Civil Engineering* 48(3), 12–16.

Vorster J., Geustyn L.C., Loubser B.F., Tanner A. & Wall K., 1995, 'A strategy and master plan for water supply, storage and distribution in the East Rand region', *Journal of the South African Institution of Civil Engineering* 37(2), 1–5.

Ziramba, E., 2008, 'The demand for residential electricity in South Africa', *Energy Policy* 36(9), 3460–3466. http://dx.doi.org/10.1016/j.enpol.2008.05.026

19

An investigation into e-learning acceptance and gender amongst final year students

Authors:
Willie Chinyamurindi[1]
Herring Shava[1]

Affiliations:
[1]Department of Business Management, University of Fort Hare, South Africa

Correspondence to:
Willie Chinyamurindi

Email:
chinyaz@gmail.com

Postal address:
Private Bag 9083, East London 5200, South Africa

Background: The use of electronic learning (e-learning) systems is gaining popularity especially within a Higher Education (HE) context. However, scholars have identified some factors that affect the utilisation and the acceptance of such systems, one of which is the gender divide, which favours mostly males ahead of females.

Objectives: The objective of this study was to investigate the acceptance of the e-learning system within a South African HE setting, including the influential role of gender in the acceptance of such a system.

Method: Quantitative data was collected through a cross-sectional survey using 113 registered final year students at a South African university who were making use of an e-learning system as part of their teaching delivery. The measuring instrument used was the technology acceptance instrument (TAI) and included measures of computer self-efficacy (CSE), perceived ease of use (PEU), perceived usefulness (PU), and behavioural intention to use (BIU).

Results: The presence of a gender divide was found to exist in this study. Women's ratings of the acceptance of e-learning systems were found to be slightly higher than those of the male respondents. In addition to this, elements of the TAI were found to be related to one another.

Conclusion: The study concludes by arguing that lecturers and facilitators need to pay attention to usage patterns of e-learning systems as they affect how such systems are adopted by their students. Therefore, preceding student acceptance of electronic learning systems should be efforts to address any issues that affect the acceptance and effective utilisation of such systems.

Introduction

Information Communication Technology (ICT) is being incorporated by educational institutions with the aim of aiding the learning process. Most common are those systems that strive to meet the educational needs and goals in the delivering of teaching referred to, in this context, as electronic learning (e-learning) (O'Neill, Singh & O'Donoghue 2004). E-learning systems are those that incorporate the use of technology to aid instructional content or teaching delivery (Moore, Dickson-Deane & Galyen 2011). The advantages of such systems are widely documented. Sun and Zhang (2006) argue that e-learning systems address the constraints of time and distance ultimately allowing students to control their individual learning at their own convenience (Cross 2004). Saadé and Bahli (2005) highlight e-learning systems as using features such as bulletin boards, chat rooms, private email, course content management, quizzes and peer assessment. These bulletin boards not only help to facilitate teaching practice but also to enhance interaction between faculty and its students. According to McNeil, Robin and Miller (2000) all these features create a unique learning experience, given also that sound, video and interactive media can be incorporated.

The focus of this study is on understanding student utilisation of e-learning systems at a rural university in the Eastern Cape Province of South Africa. The rationale for this is motivated by two factors. Firstly, empirical evidence shows that the success of an e-learning system is dependent on its full utilisation. As academics who have been using ICTs such as e-learning in teaching delivery, the authors were interested in ascertaining the usage of such systems from the student's perspective. This can be beneficial in enhancing the student learning experience. Secondly, the authors were interested in the role that gender plays in the utilisation of such e-learning systems. Literature exists in South Africa detailing the existence of gender inequality in various economic and social sectors (Moletsane & Reddy 2008). Such gender inequality has led to calls for research on the acceptance of technology utilisation, especially in the higher education setting (South African Government Communications 1996).

The structure followed in this article is, firstly, to put this research into context. Secondly, the theoretical framework underlying this study is presented leading to the research hypotheses. Thirdly, the research design and methodology section follow. Finally, the results, discussion and a conclusion are presented.

Putting this research into context

The authors of this article are lecturers in the Department of Business Management at a South African university located in the Eastern Cape Province. Their duties entail giving lectures and tutorials for a module called General Management (BEC 322) to a group of 120 final year students. Traditionally, the module has been taught via face-to-face delivery. Owing to personal convictions, it was decided to create new strategies and use tools that improve teaching delivery. The interest was in the use of technology as one of those tools that can potentially aid teaching delivery. This focus fits within the agenda to be found in higher education globally, where the impact of technology on the creation, dissemination, quality, and evaluation of knowledge is deemed important (Rienties, Brouwer & Lygo-Barker 2013).

As part of the evaluation of the module and the subsequent usage of technology in teaching delivery, the interest was on measuring and understanding the acceptance of technology delivery amongst the university's students. Technology acceptance issues have been cited as a cause for resistance based on the perceptions of end-users (Hardgrave & Johnson 2003). Therefore, identifying influential factors on technology acceptance was deemed important and focal for both researchers and practitioners (Hsiao & Yang 2011). For this reason, the authors were interested in identifying and studying the variables that influence technology acceptance in teaching delivery.

Such evaluative feedback would prove useful for two reasons. Firstly, the feedback would help improve future offerings of the module. Secondly, feedback would also form a useful component of a teaching portfolio. A teaching portfolio is viewed as a collection of evidence of descriptions, documents, and examples of what is good teaching (De Rijdt et al. 2006). Such a portfolio has the potential to showcase not only professional capacity but also to serve as an instrument for appraisal, tenure and promotion (Wright, Knight & Pomerleau 1999). In the authors' view, this study offers potential for effective classroom delivery within, and outside, the classroom for both the student and the lecturer.

However, the attention of the authors was shifted towards the role gender plays in the classroom for two reasons. Firstly, was a subjective reflection from one of our female students enrolled in the authors' class. This comment came after using technology in teaching delivery:

> 'Sir, I am from a rural area called Cofimvaba, I have never imagined I would use computer systems like Blackboard so well. Not bad for a girl child, hey Sir'.

This view from this student ignited the interest of the authors into the role gender can play not only with classroom learning but also the utilisation of ICTs such as e-learning. Secondly, literature exists detailing this gendered view not only in society but also in the classroom. For instance, Mahlomaholo (2011) highlighted how the plight of women is at the centre of social transformation in South Africa. This gave birth to the formation of a government department, the Department of Women, Children and Persons with Disability which was set up to deal with issues that affect women, girls and the vulnerable. Despite these efforts, gender inequality is believed to still be prevalent in various sectors and situations in South Africa such as the economy (Hlekiso & Mahlo 2006), corporate sector (Moletsane & Reddy 2008), service delivery (Steyn 2012), training and development (Chinyamurindi & Louw 2010), and within the classroom (Hammond et al. 2007; Mahlomaholo 2011).

This research answers calls for studies that focus on the role of science and technology on the lives of people (Reddy et al. 2013) particularly within education research (Flipsen & van der Weide 2009). Interest is focussed on the acceptance and experience of technology utilisation within a learning context. The interest in studying ICT acceptance and gender together is motivated by calls for research on how ICT can be used to overcome barriers such as inequity for the purpose of redress (Mdlongwa 2012). This article pays attention to a barrier, gender inequity, which characterises not only South African society but also the education landscape (Hammond et al. 2007; Mahlomaholo 2011). The next section explores the theoretical background upon which this research hinges. The focus is on how such inequity affects the utilisation of technology by a sample of students who use ICT as part of their learning experiences.

Theoretical background

An important theoretical consideration specific to the utilisation of technology is the Technology Acceptance Model (Davis 1989; Venkatesh & Davis 2000) referred to hereafter as TAM. This model consists of two beliefs that determine attitudes to adopt a new technology, perceived usefulness and perceived ease of application. The attitude towards adoption depicts the prospective adopter's positive or negative orientation and/or behaviour about adopting a new technology (Venkatesh & Davis 2000). Table 1 outlines the constructs of the TAM including a brief definition based on supporting literature.

The TAM is chosen as a framework to predict and explain human behaviour concerning technology acceptance (Ajzen & Fishbein 1980; Gupta & Jana 2003). The TAM is deemed suitable as a framework for this study given its perceived robustness, from the user's point of view, in predicting individual intentions in relation to technology adoption (Ong & Lai 2006). The thinking here is that human behaviour such as individual beliefs, attitudes, and intentions (Lin, Fofanah & Liang 2011) affect actual ICT use (Chen, Gillenson & Sherrel 2002; Gefen, Karahanna & Straub 2003; Karahanna,

TABLE 1: Elements of the Technology Acceptance Model.

TAM Construct	Definition(s)
Computer self-efficacy (CSE)	An individual's perceptions of his or her ability to use computers in the accomplishment of a task rather than reflecting simple component skills' (Compeau & Higgins 1995).
Perceived usefulness (PU)	This is defined as the degree to which a person believes that using a particular technology would enhance their performance (Davis 1989).
Perceived ease of use (PEU)	This is defined as the degree to which a person believes that using the system would be free of effort (Davis 1989).
Behavioural intention to use (BIU)	This is defined as the predictor of human behaviour to perform a behaviour (Fishbein & Ajzen 1975). From a subjective angle, it is also defined as a person's perception of social pressure regarding the performance of the behaviour (Ajzen & Fishbein 1980).

Straub & Chervany 1999). This thinking gives attention to investigating such behaviour, given its bearing on actual system use and adoption.

The TAM is built around the Theory of Reasoned Action (TRA) (Fishbein & Ajzen 1975), which suggests how individual behaviour is initiated by its behavioural intention to perform a particular task. The result of this is that individual behavioural intention determines one's attitude and subjective norms regarding the behaviour in question (Fishbein & Ajzen 1975). The TRA also posits that intention to act determines behaviour, and causal link is believed to exist between the two (Venkatesh & Davis 2000). The attitude-behavioural intentions relationship, as espoused in constructs of the TAM, assume that all use being equal, intentions to use technology can be formed based upon positive usage of the technology. The PU–BIU relationship assumes this and has been shown to have a positive or negative influence on individual behaviour in organisations (Robinson, Marshall & Stamps 2005). The research therefore seeks to measure perceptions and relationships amongst the constructs of the TAM, with gender as a moderating variable leading to an empirical investigation into relationships between TAM constructs and the moderating role of gender.

For the purpose of this article, ICTs will refer to electronic learning (e-learning) viewed as a learning experience delivered or enabled by electronic technologies, including the Internet, intranets, and extranets (Govindasamy 2002). The e-learning system referred to and adopted in this research refers to a general management course placed on a Learning Management System (LMS) Blackboard. Learning materials such as the learner guide, lecture notes, tutorials, and quizzes were all placed on Blackboard, and each student given equal access. In addition to these, videos, podcasts and audio downloads were placed on the BlackBoard platform. The LMS allowed for collaboration between the students and the lecturer, opportunities to share ideas, tips to solve problems, and explanation of any course-related issues (Schoonenboom 2014). Given this, backdrop the research question set for this study reads:

> How is e-learning acceptance conceptualised within an educational context and to what extent is gender a moderating variable to this (if any) amongst a sample of students?

Literature review
Empirical work using TAM constructs & gender

With reference to relationships amongst TAM constructs, a number of studies in the past three decades support the existence of a relationship (e.g. Agudo-Peregrina, Hernández-Garcia & Pascual-Miguel 2014; Chen et al. 2002; Davis 1989; Malhotra & Galletta 1999; Moon & Kim 2001; Venkatesh & Davis 2000). In summary, empirical studies show CSE to influence PEU (e.g. Grandon, Alshare & Kwun 2005; Jong & Wang 2009; Ong & Lai 2006). In turn, PEU has been found to have a significant effect on PU (e.g. Venkatesh & Davis 2000). Subsequently, a positive relationship has been found to exist between PU and BIU (e.g. Joo & Sang 2013; Lee & Lehto 2013). The thinking here is that a student's confidence in performing specific tasks through the e-learning system coupled by easy access and ease of use of the system will help that student not only navigate through the system but will affect future possible use (Compeau & Higgins 1995; Venkatesh & Davis 2000). Calls have been made for studies on the utility and applicability of the TAM and its constructs, especially within an educational setting (Ong & Lai 2006; Pituch & Lee 2006; Sánchez & Hueros 2010). This study seeks to answer these calls within a South African context.

There appears to be a general consensus of the existence of a gender divide that favours males. In a study by Cherian and Shumba (2011) it was found that males show more positive attitudes towards science than females. Flipsen and van der Weide (2009) suggest that women have fewer options and opportunities to engage in new technologies largely because of their social position. Part of the problem is grounded in traditional ways of thinking that mostly favour males ahead of women (McGregor & Bazi 2001). This thinking implies that the inability to use and access technology in the long run affects not only performance expectancy but also the intention to use technology for learning (Brown & Licker 2003; Pavon & Brown 2010). This research appears to support the existence of gender-based differences in decision-making behaviour as theorised in previous work (e.g. Claes 1999; Feingold 1994).

Previous empirical work has found gender to have a moderating effect when it comes to the acceptance of ICTs (e.g. Chinyamurindi & Louw 2010; Okazaki & Renda dos Santos 2012; Ong & Lai 2006; Srite & Karahanna 2006; Venkatesh et al. 2003). Women in such circumstances have been disadvantaged when it comes to the adoption of technology ahead of their male counterparts. The underlying premise for this finding could be the reason why gender can also exist as a variable that has linkages with socio-economic standing (Lin et al. 2011). The thinking here is that, because of their socio-economic standing in society, women adopt technology differently to men (Sierpe 2005).

A number of studies find women to be disadvantaged when it comes to the adoption and usage of technology. For instance, Agboola (2013) found women to have less confidence than

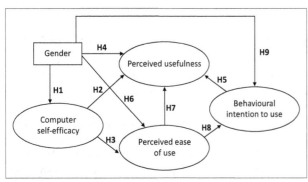

FIGURE 1: Research model.

men in their adoption of technology, although empirical work showed that women spend more time online than men (Pew Internet and American Life Project 2005). Furthermore, women have been found to have higher ratings of anxiety when it comes to using technology (Wild *et al.* 2012). This has often led to the view that ICTs are a male preserve (Nobel 2007; Tahmincioglu 2008) resulting in women having lower ratings with regard to constructs of the TAM (Ong & Lai 2006).

Additionally, research also finds men to rate the usefulness of technology higher than women (Venkatesh & Morris 2000). This could possibly be the reason why women are more anxious about using computers than their male counterparts (Broos 2005). In some instances, this may lead to women showing higher ratings of emotion when it comes to using technology than their male counterparts (Fisk & Stevens 1993). Conversely, women have been found to be motivated more by factors such as process issues (PEU) and the social aspect (subjective norms) than men (Ong & Lai 2006). Based on all these theories the following hypotheses are set for this research:

Hypothesis 1: Men rate CSE higher than women.
Hypothesis 2: CSE influences PU of e-learning indifferently between genders.
Hypothesis 3: CSE influences PEU of e-learning indifferently between genders.
Hypothesis 4: Men rate PU of e-learning higher than women.
Hypothesis 5: PU influences BIU e-learning indifferently between genders.
Hypothesis 6: Men rate PEU of e-learning higher than women.
Hypothesis 7: PEU influences PU of e-learning indifferently between genders.
Hypothesis 8: PEU influences BIU e-learning indifferently between genders.
Hypothesis 9: Men rate BIU e-learning higher than women.

Given the implications of these hypotheses, Figure 1 presents a research model in view of the presented hypotheses:

Research methodology

The authors of this study subscribe to the notion that 'causes' determine the 'outcomes' (Creswell 2014:7). Thus,

in undertaking this study, a post positivist worldview was adopted. Subsequently, this study is of a quantitative design in nature. Quantitative studies seek to explain theories through investigating relationships amongst different study variables. Such variables in quantitative studies are measured through instruments which facilitate the coding of data that in turn leads to statistical data analysis in the form of descriptive and inferential methods (Creswell 2014). This research was carried out following the aforementioned approach.

To gather primary data, researchers made use of a questionnaire. Questionnaires were deemed to be cheap and cost effective allowing for a wider reach. This met our budgetary concerns as researchers. Through a questionnaire, responses are able to be gathered in a standardised manner using already existing measures of the TAM known to be 'well-established, robust, powerful and parsimonious models for predicting user acceptance' (Venkatesh & Davis 2000:186).

Research instrument

The instrument used (18 items) was the TAM which is viewed as the prime tool for testing user acceptance of new technologies (Green 2005) and has been extensively used in various contexts e.g. studying e-government implementation (Lin *et al.* 2011), within healthcare (Pai & Huang 2011), in the South African corporate sector (Chinyamurindi & Louw 2010), and across a wide range of educational settings (Ong & Lai 2006; Pituch & Lee 2006; Sánchez & Hueros 2010). Students were informed that participating in the study was voluntary and ethical consent had to be given through signing an ethical agreement form. A total of 120 students were enrolled for the course, and all the students were given the questionnaire to be part of the research. A total of 113 questionnaires were deemed usable as seven questionnaires had missing data. For taking part in the research, the students all received an incentive (Singer & Bossarte 2006) in the form of 5 marks out of a possible 25 marks for class participation as part of their assessment. The instrument consisted of 18 items on a five-point Likert scale.

Reliability test
Reliability

Merriam (2009) suggests that issues of reliability and validity be addressed when undertaking research as data are collected, analysed and interpreted. Cronbach's alpha coefficient (Cronbach 1951) was used as a test for internal consistency. Santos (1999) argues that the higher the Cronbach value, the more reliable the instrument. He adds that 0.7 is an acceptable reliability coefficient. However, 0.7 has been contested as an acceptable Cronbach value by some statisticians (e.g. Charter 2000; Cortina 1993; Duhachek & Iacobucci 2004; Hakstian & Whalen 1976; Van Zyle, Heinz & Nel 2000). Leontitsis and Pagge (2007:336) thus caution that much of this deadlock is motivated by the 'experience and intuition' of the researcher.

In this study, the Cronbach alpha was calculated for the 18-item questionnaire and found to be 0.74. Since the Cronbach alpha coefficient average for student acceptance of technology was 0.74 and that 0.7 is deemed as an acceptable reliability coefficient, the coefficient for this study suggests that the data gathering instrument had a measure of reliability. Content and face validity was followed in this research. This consisted, amongst others, of a subjective impression of items in the questionnaire. A pilot study was used to pre-test the questionnaire amongst a sample of 25 students not included in the main study. Suggestions and amendments from this process were taken on board with regard to the main study. These included aspects of simplicity and clarity of questions and a detailed suggestion of the need for an introductory section of the questionnaire to help students. The researcher (also lecturer of the BEC 322 module) was present at the time of filling out the questionnaire enabling him to attend to any student concerns that arose out the tests for content and face validity.

Data analysis

Analysis was shared between the authors of this paper and a professional statistician using the Statistical Package for the Social Sciences (SPSS), Version 21. The data analysis was split according to the hypothesis. The first category hypotheses (1, 4, 6, and 9) involved testing ratings of the TAM constructs by gender and were really comparative in nature. Consideration here was given to the need to generate descriptive data in the form of means and standard deviations. A comparison in the means would be able to answer these hypotheses through an exploration of the data. Thereafter, tests of normality of data were considered with reference to the ratio of skewness and kurtosis (Pallant 2010). As a general rule, if the ratio of skewness and kurtosis to their respective standard errors (SE) is not within the range of −1.96 to +1.96, the data are probably not normally distributed (Razali & Wah 2011). Regarding statistical significance, the value was set at a 95% confidence interval level ($p \leq 0.05$).

The second set of hypotheses (2, 3, 5, 6, 7, and 8) were analysed using Multivariate Analysis of Variance (MANOVA). This was carried out with gender (male and female) as independent variable and the mean scores of the scales serving as dependent variables. Tabachnick and Fidell (2007) posit that MANOVA tests are useful for ascertaining whether or not, on a combination of dependent variables, mean differences amongst groups of people are likely to have occurred by chance. These conditions are especially applicable to hypotheses (1, 4, 6, and 9). In addition to tests of statistical difference, tests of effect sizes (Cohen 1988) were used to determine the significance of the relationships of these findings (Steyn 2000).

Results

With regards to descriptive statistics about the data, Table 2 summarises the findings. From the 120 initial questionnaires collected, 113 were deemed usable (94%) with 7 rejected, as

TABLE 2: Biographical characteristics.

Variable	$n = 113$
Gender	
Male	49
Female	64
Computer Knowledge	
Great	24
Good	74
Average	15
Not so Good	-
e-learning Experience	
> 1 year	49
1-2 years	34
< 3 years	30

TABLE 3: Ratings of Technology Acceptance Model Constructs by Gender.

TAM Construct	Men ($n = 49$)		Women ($n = 64$)		
	M	SD	M	SD	Sign.
CSE	2.525	0.589	2.648	0.483	0.226*
PU	1.877	0.582	2.023	0.724	0.252*
PEU	2.086	0.496	2.257	0.496	0.099*
BIU	1.734	0.604	1.835	0.636	0.394*

M, mean, SD, standard deviation; CSE, computer self-efficacy; PU, perceived usefulness; PEU, perceived ease of use; BIU, behavioural intention to use
*, Correlations are significant at $p < 0.05$

TABLE 4: Tests of normality.

Test	CSE	PU	PEU	BIU
n	113	113	113	113
Skewness	0.272	1.255	0.132	0.611
Kurtosis	0.343	3.331	0.004	0.253
Standard error of Kurtosis	0.451	0.451	0.451	0.451

CSE, computer self-efficacy; PU, perceived usefulness; PEU, perceived ease of use; BIU, behavioural intention to use

they were either not filled out correctly or the students did not prefer to be part of the study. A majority of the respondents rated themselves as having good computer knowledge with none of the respondents citing their computer knowledge to be not so good. The majority of the respondents have been using the e-learning system for over a year, as shown in Table 2.

The effects of gender upon CSE, PU, PEU and BIU were examined using mean scores and standard deviations (see Table 3). Significant gender differences were found for CSE, PU, PEU and BIU. These differences indicate that women rated computer self-efficacy, perceived usefulness, perceived ease of use, and behavioural intention to use e-learning slightly higher than men. As a result, Hypothesis 1, Hypothesis 4, Hypothesis 6 and Hypothesis 9 are not supported.

With regards to tests of normality, Table 4 presents the data from the analyses. In the study, the ratios of skewness and kurtosis to their respective standard errors have been calculated and the ratings of CSE and PEU fall within the gazetted range (Razali & Wah 2011) suggesting that the data are approximately normally distributed. However, ratings of BI display evidence of skewness, although the ratings fall within the desired range with regards to kurtosis. PU ratings were ruled not to be normally distributed as the ratios of skewness and kurtosis to their respective standard errors

TABLE 5: Multivariate tests.

Hypotheses	Wilk's Λ	F	P-value	Multivariate η^2
2 (CSE-PU)	0.912	2.110	0.353	0.019
3 (CSE-PEU)	0.964	2.080	0.130	0.036
5 (PU-BIU)	0.986	0.762	0.469	0.014
7 (PEU-PU)	0.973	1.550	0.217	0.027
8 (PEU-BIU)	0.975	1.418	0.247	0.025

CSE, computer self-efficacy; PU, perceived usefulness; PEU, perceived ease of use; BIU, behavioural intention to use
*, Correlations are significant at $p < 0.05$

were calculated and found to be outside the desired and/or gazetted range (Razali & Wah 2011).

The next set of analysis sought to test influences amongst determinants of the TAM by gender. Notably, this included: **CSE – PU**; **CSE – PEU**; **PU – BIU**; **PEU – PU**, and **PEU – BIU**. The aim here was to test if these determinants of the TAM relate indifferently by gender. To achieve this, Multivariate Analysis of Variance (MANOVA) was conducted using an alpha test of 0.05. MANOVA was deemed appropriate here to determine the significance of differences between TAM determinants and gender (Aiken & West 1991). Wilk's Lambda was also used to test whether population mean vectors for all groups were likely to be identical to those of the sample mean vectors for the different groups (Field 2013; Tabachnick & Fidell 2007).

With regard to the relationship between CSE – PU by gender and based on the MANOVA results (Wilks' Lambda = 0.912; F = (2.11) = 1.052; p-value = 0.353 > 0.05), CSE was found to influence PU indifferently between genders thus the null hypothesis (H2) is supported. Table 5 summarises additional MANOVA test results undertaken to test the null hypothesis 3 (CSE – PEU); hypothesis 5 (PU – BIU); hypothesis 7 (PEU – PU) and hypothesis 8 (PEU – BIU) by gender. Overall, results with regard to hypotheses 2, 3, 5, 7, and 8 indicate the absence of a significant effect of gender on TAM constructs namely, CSE, PU, PEU, BIU denoted by the p-value column with all p-values above the significant level of $p = 0.05$.

Discussion, implications, contributions & limitations

The aim of this study was to understand student utilisation of e-learning systems at a rural university in the Eastern Cape Province of South Africa.

The presence of a gender divide was found to exist in this study where women were found to rate other TAM constructs higher than men, thereby contradicting other empirical studies. This finding contradicts previous findings that prescribe gender as a moderating effect (Srite & Karahanna 2006; Venkatesh et al. 2003) as well as a prevailing socio-economic context (Lin et al. 2011) affecting the acceptance of technology and ICTs. Uniquely, this gender divide in relation to ICTs and technology was not found to exist within a South African classroom context and thus further disputes previous studies (e.g. Hammond et al. 2007; Mahlomaholo 2011). Instead, where the gender divide was noted, it was found to

favour females ahead of males (evident in H1, H4, H6, and H9 statistical results). This finding represented a significant move away from previous work that found a gender divide favouring males ahead of females (e.g. Cherian & Shumba 2011; Flipsen & van der Weide 2009; McGregor & Bazi 2001; Ong & Lai 2006).

The study has a number of implications. Firstly, with regard to teaching practice, constructs of TAM can be useful in revealing aspects that need attention concerning e-learning usage. Student confidence in using such systems has a bearing on how the system will be perceived to be of easy access and use. In turn, this affects not only students' continual navigation but also the possible use of such systems such as e-learning (Compeau & Higgins 1995; Venkatesh & Davis 2000). Secondly, our study contributes to the literature by providing insight into individual and psychological factors that influence the adoption and use of technology by testing the TAM empirically. This study also represents a call for studies that examine the utility and applicability of the TAM and its constructs especially within an educational setting (Ong & Lai 2006; Pituch & Lee 2006; Sánchez & Hueros 2010).

This study offers contributions. Firstly, within a South African context it fits within the agenda for studies that cover technology utilisation (Rienties et al. 2013) and gender issues in the classroom (Hammond et al. 2007; Mahlomaholo 2011). Particularly the findings of this work highlight the need to overcome barriers with regards to technology adoption. Addressing these barriers can affect system utilisation and individual optimal use. Secondly, the findings of this study have informed the authors' teaching practice and made them come up with practical interventions to help students with regards to technology adoption. They have started offering tutorials and personalised assistance for students addressing aspects of the TAM constructs. The thinking here is that aspects of the TAM can be a potential cause for resistance based on the perceptions of end-users (Hardgrave & Johnson 2003; Malhotra & Galetta 1999). Based on this, the authors asked for assistance from their Teaching and Learning Centre to offer courses that address basic issues such as computer appreciation skills and how to help students manage their learning using technology. To this end, the current study was a useful window in revealing not only challenges affecting technology adoption but also practical interventions.

Some limitations exist with this work. Firstly, the sample is not generalisable to the entire population of students using technology within a higher education setting. Some factors relating to this can be due to the nature of the parent institution which attracts predominantly black students. Notably, other race groups found within the South African society are not found within the sample, a reason being the demographics at the authors' institution. This skewed sample seriously compromises this study and limits its generalisability. Secondly, though the TAM is viewed as a robust predictor of intention (Ong & Lai 2006) other theoretical frameworks and variables could have been used to add to the predictive power of the TAM. For instance, there is work advocating for the extended TAM (e.g. Cheung & Vogel 2013) incorporating factors such as compatibility (Moore & Benbasat 1991), perceived resource (Mathieson 1991), and sharing (Wasko & Faraj 2005). Although this is a limitation in this study, it can also represent an opportunity for future research.

Future research could take a number of approaches. Firstly, this can include a qualitative investigation into aspects of technology adoption tapping into understanding the experience of technology usage. This can take the form of structured or unstructured interviews into understanding the meaning of behaviours and experiences, such as using technology in a natural flow of a conversation (Patton 2002). This can allow for the triggering of memories, reflection on experiences, elaboration of ideas, and clarification of responses (Rubin & Rubin 2005). Based on this study, an interesting angle to investigate could be the experience of male end-user experience of an e-learning system. This is especially relevant as this study found ratings of TAM constructs to be lower for males than females, a finding that is a stark contrast to previous findings explored in the literature review; a qualitative angle can be useful in understanding this. Secondly, given the status of the authors' university as a previously disadvantaged rural institution it would be interesting to conduct a comparative study using a more affluent urban university. The comparison can be used as a basis to ascertain the influence of university affluence and location towards individual adoption of technology. The outcome of such a study can inform the need to investigate more extraneous variables outside the individual. Finally, as mentioned earlier, more empirical work could include the use of advanced models, with instruments outside the TAM beginning to receive attention (e.g. Cheung & Vogel 2013).

Conclusion

The findings of this study point to the great strides that policies of redress have made in empowering females to adopt technology in the classroom. Notably, female participants in this study rate their usage of technology to be higher than their male counterparts against the TAM constructs when using e-learning. However, the study also paints a picture of the need to not neglect paying attention to males, although previous theorising shows support for their positive usage on TAM constructs.

Acknowledgements

Competing interests

The authors declare that they have no financial or personal relationships which may have inappropriately influenced them in writing this article.

Authors' contributions

Both W.C. (University of Fort Hare) and H.S. (University of Fort Hare) conceptualised the study and collected the data. H.S. conducted the data analysis. Both authors were equally involved in writing up of the article and dealing with comments from the reviewers and the Editorial Board.

References

Agboola, A.K., 2013, 'A study of socio-demographics effects on e-learning adoption among lecturers', *International Journal of Emerging Technology and Advanced Engineering* 3(4), 651–661.

Agudo-Peregrina, Á.F., Hernández-García, Á. & Pascual-Miguel, F.J., 2014, 'Behavioral intention, use behavior and the acceptance of electronic learning systems: Differences between higher education and lifelong learning', *Computers in Human Behavior* 34, 301–314. http://dx.doi.org/10.1016/j.chb.2013.10.035

Aiken, L.S. & West, S.G., 1991, *Multiple regression: Testing and interpreting Interactions*, Sage Publications, Newbury Park.

Ajzen, I. & Fishbein, M., 1980, *Understanding attitudes and predicting social behaviour*, Prentice-Hall, Englewood Cliffs.

Broos, M.A., 2005, 'Gender and information and communication technologies (ICT) anxiety: Male self-assurance and female hesitation', *Cyber Psychology & Behavior* 8(1), 145–166. http://dx.doi.org/10.1089/cpb.2005.8.21

Brown, I. & Licker, P., 2003, 'Exploring differences in Internet adoption and usage between historically advantaged and disadvantaged groups in South Africa', *Journal of Global Information Technology Management* 6(4), 6–26. http://dx.doi.org/10.1080/1097198X.2003.10856358

Charter, R.A., 2000, 'Confidence interval formulas for split-half reliability coefficients', *Psychological Reports* 86, 1168–1170. http://dx.doi.org/10.2466/pr0.2000.86.3c.1168

Chen, L., Gillenson, M.L. & Sherrell, D., 2002, 'Enticing online consumers: An extended technology acceptance perspective', *Information & Management* 39(8), 705–719. http://dx.doi.org/10.1016/S0378-7206(01)00127-6

Cherian, L. & Shumba, A., 2011, 'Sex differences in attitudes toward science among Northern – Sotho speaking learners in South Africa', *Africa Education Review* 8(2), 286–301. http://dx.doi.org/10.1080/18146627.2011.603241

Cheung, R. & Vogel, D., 2013, 'Predicting user acceptance of collaborative technologies: An extension of the technology acceptance model', *Computers & Education* 63, 160–175. http://dx.doi.org/10.1016/j.compedu.2012.12.003

Chinyamurindi, W.T. & Louw, G.J., 2010, 'Gender differences in technology acceptance in selected South African companies: Implications for electronic learning', *South African Journal of Human Resource Management* 8(1), 1–7. http://dx.doi.org/10.4102/sajhrm.v8i1.204

Claes, M.T., 1999, 'Women, men, and management styles', *International Labour Review* 138(4), 431–446. http://dx.doi.org/10.1111/j.1564-913X.1999.tb00396.x

Cohen, J., 1988, *Statistical power analysis for the behavioral sciences*, 2nd edn., Lawrence Erlbaum, New Jersey.

Compeau, D.R. & Higgins, C.A., 1995, 'Computer self-efficacy: Development of a measure and initial test', *MIS Quarterly* 19(2), 189–211. http://dx.doi.org/10.2307/249688

Cortina, J.M., 1993, 'What is coefficient alpha? An examination of theory and application', *Journal of Applied Psychology* 78, 98–104. http://dx.doi.org/10.1037/0021-9010.78.1.98

Creswell, J.W., 2014, *Research design: Qualitative, quantitative, and mixed methods approaches*, 4th edn., SAGE Publications, Inc., Thousand Oaks.

Cronbach, L.J., 1951, 'Coefficient alpha and the internal structure of tests', *Psychometrika* 22(3), 297–334. http://dx.doi.org/10.1007/BF02310555

Cross, J., 2004, 'An informal history of e-learning', *On the Horizon* 12(3), 103–110. http://dx.doi.org/10.1108/10748120410555340

Davis, F., 1989, 'Perceived usefulness, perceived ease of use, and user acceptance of information technology', *MIS Quarterly* 13(3), 318–339. http://dx.doi.org/10.2307/249008

De Rijdt, C., Tiquet, E., Dochy, F. & Devolder, M., 2006, 'Teaching portfolios in higher education and their effects: An explorative study', *Teaching and Teacher Education* 22, 1084–1093. http://dx.doi.org/10.1016/j.tate.2006.07.002

Duhachek, A. & Iacobucci, D., 2004, 'Alpha's standard error (ASE): An accurate and precise confidence interval estimate', *Journal of Applied Psychology* 89, 792–808. http://dx.doi.org/10.1037/0021-9010.89.5.792

Feingold, A., 1994, 'Gender differences in personality: A meta-analysis', *Psychological Bulletin* 116(3), 429–456. http://dx.doi.org/10.1037/0033-2909.116.3.429

Field, A., 2013, *Discovering statistics using IBM SPSS statistics*, 4th edn., Sage, London.

Fishbein, M. & Ajzen, I., 1975, *Belief, attitude, intention, and behavior: An introduction to theory and research*, Addison-Wesley, Reading.

Fisk, S.T. & Stevens, L.E., 1993, 'What's so special about sex? Gender stereotyping & discrimination', in S. Oskamp & M. Costanzo (eds.), *Gender issues in contemporary society*, Sage, Newbury Park.

Flipsen, N.A. & van der Weide, T., 2009, 'Implementing gender issues in ICT', *Africa Education Review* 6(2), 308–323. http://dx.doi.org/10.1080/18146620903274621

Gefen, D., Karahanna, E. & Straub, D.W., 2003, 'Trust and TAM in online shopping: An integrated model', *MIS Quarterly* 27(1), 51–90.

Govindasamy, T., 2002, 'Successful implementation of e-learning: Pedagogical considerations', *Internet and Higher Education* 4, 287–299. http://dx.doi.org/10.1016/S1096-7516(01)00071-9

Grandon, E., Alshare, O. & Kwun, O., 2005, 'Factors influencing student intention to adopt online classes: A cross-cultural study', *Journal of Computing Sciences in Colleges* 20(4), 46–56.

Green, I.F.R., 2005, 'The emancipatory potential of a new information system and its effect on technology acceptance', unpublished PhD thesis, University of Pretoria.

Gupta, M.P. & Jana, D., 2003, 'E-government evaluation: A framework and case study', *Government Information Quarterly* 20, 365–387. http://dx.doi.org/10.1016/j.giq.2003.08.002

Hakstian, A.R. & Whalen, T.E., 1976, 'A K-sample significance test for independent alpha coefficients', *Psychometrika* 41, 219–231. http://dx.doi.org/10.1007/BF02291840

Hammond, C., Linton, D., Smink, J. & Drew, S., 2007, *Dropout risk factors and exemplary programs: A technical report*, National Dropout Prevention Center, Communities in Schools, Inc., Clemson, SC, viewed 20 March 2014, from http://www.dropoutprevention.org/resource/major_reports/communities_in_schools.htm

Hardgrave, B.C. & Johnson, R.A., 2003, 'Toward an information systems development: The case of object-oriented', *IEEE Transactions on Engineering Management* 50(3), 322–336. http://dx.doi.org/10.1109/TEM.2003.817293

Hlekiso, T. & Mahlo, N., 2006, 'Wage trends and inequality in South Africa: A comparative analysis', *South African Reserve Bank: Labour Market Frontiers* 8, 9–16.

Hsiao, C.H. & Yang, C., 2011, 'The intellectual development of the technology acceptance model: A co-citation analysis', *International Journal of Information Management* 31(2), 128–136. http://dx.doi.org/10.1016/j.ijinfomgt.2010.07.003

Jong, D. & Wang, T.S., 2009, 'Student acceptance of web-based learning system', *Proceedings of the 2009 International Symposium on Web Information Systems and Applications (WISA'09)*, pp. 533–553, Nanchang, People's Republic of China.

Joo, J. & Sang, Y., 2013, 'Exploring Koreans' smartphone usage: An integrated model of the technology acceptance model and uses and gratifications theory', *Computers in Human Behavior* 29, 2512–2518. http://dx.doi.org/10.1016/j.chb.2013.06.002

Karahanna, E., Straub, D.W. & Chervany, N.L., 1999, 'Information technology adoption across time: A cross-sectional comparison of pre-adoption and post adoption beliefs', *MS Quarterly* 23(2), 183–213. http://dx.doi.org/10.2307/249751

Lee, D.Y. & Lehto, M.R., 2013, 'User acceptance of YouTube for procedural learning: An extension of the technology acceptance model', *Computers and Education* 61, 193–208. http://dx.doi.org/10.1016/j.compedu.2012.10.001

Leontitsis, A. & Pagge, J., 2007, 'A simulation approach on Cronbach's alpha statistical significance', *Mathematics and Computers in Simulation* 73(5), 336–340. http://dx.doi.org/10.1016/j.matcom.2006.08.001

Lin, F., Fofanah, S.S. & Liang, D., 2011, 'Assessing citizen adoption of e-Government initiatives next term in Gambia: A validation of the technology acceptance model in information systems success', *Government Information Quarterly* 28(2), 271–279. http://dx.doi.org/10.1016/j.giq.2010.09.004

Mahlomaholo, S.M.G., 2011, 'Gender differentials and sustainable learning environments', *South African Journal of Education* 31, 312–321.

Malhotra, Y. & Galletta, D.F., 1999, 'Extending the technology acceptance model to account for social influence: Theoretical bases and empirical validation', in *Proceedings of the 32nd Hawaii International Conference on System Sciences* 1, 1–10, IEEE Computer Society, Washington, DC, Management Review, 14(4), 532–550. http://dx.doi.org/10.1109/hicss.1999.772658

Mathieson, K., 1991, 'Predicting user intentions: Comparing the technology acceptance model with the theory of planned behavior', *Information Systems Research* 2(3), 173–191. http://dx.doi.org/10.1287/isre.2.3.173

McGregor, E. & Bazi, F., 2001, *Gender mainstreaming in science and technology*, viewed 10 January 2014, from https://www.google.co.za/url?sa=t&rct=j&q= &esrc=s&source=web&cd=1&cad=rja&uact=8&ved=0CBwQFjAAahUKEwj_4oqb hd3GAhXI7RQKHTL1CMo&url=http%3A%2F%2Funidadedamullereciencia.xunta. es%2Fsites%2Fdefault%2Ffiles%2Fdocumento%2F2011%2F06%2F154_gender-mainstreaming-science-and-technology-reference-manual-governments-and-other-stakeholders.pdf&ei=EUWmVb-WEMjbU7Lqo9AM&usg=AFQjCNHc02J5gt mDUoSmF8ORqh8AF2yDRw&sig2=iSFOhUbfHCMn8Okk3TRk1g

McNeil, S.G., Robin, B.R. & Miller, R.M., 2000, 'Facilitating interaction, communication and collaboration in online courses', *Computers and Geosciences* 26, 699–708. http://dx.doi.org/10.1016/S0098-3004(99)00106-5

Mdlongwa, T., 2012, 'Information and communication technology (ICT) as a means of enhancing education in schools in South Africa: Challenges, benefits and recommendations', *AISA Policy Brief* 80, 1–7.

Merriam, S.B., 2009, 'Dealing with validity, reliability, and ethics', in S.B. Merriam (ed.), *Qualitative research: A guide to design and implementation*, pp. 209–235, Jossey-Bass, San Francisco.

Moletsane, R. & Reddy, V., 2008, *An assessment of the participation of women in set industry for Department of Science and Technology*, viewed 10 January 2014, from http://www.hsrc.ac.za/research/output/outputDocuments/5505_Moletsane_ Assessmentoftheparticipationofwomen.pdf

Moon, J.W & Kim, Y.G., 2001, 'Extending the TAM for a world-wide-web context', *Information & Management* 38(4), 217–230. http://dx.doi.org/10.1016/S0378-7206(00)00061-6

Moore, G.C. & Benbasat, I., 1991, 'Development of an instrument to measure the perceptions of adopting an information technology innovation', *Information Systems Research* 2(3), 192–222. http://dx.doi.org/10.1287/isre.2.3.192

Moore, J.L., Dickson-Deane, C. & Galyen, K., 2011, 'E-learning, online learning, and distance learning environments: Are they the same?', *The Internet and Higher Education* 14, 129–135. http://dx.doi.org/10.1016/j.iheduc.2010.10.001

Nobel, C., 2007, *Women in technology: A call to action*, InfoWorld, viewed 16 May 2015, from http://www.infoworld.com/d/developer-world/women-in-technology-callaction-919.

Okazaki, S. & Renda dos Santos, L.M., 2012, 'Understanding e-learning adoption in Brazil: Major determinants and gender effects', *The International Review of Research in Open and Distance Learning* 13(4), 91–106.

O'Neill, K., Singh, G. & O'Donoghue, J., 2004, 'Implementing eLearning programmes for higher education: A review of the literature', *Journal of Information Technology* 3, 313–323.

Ong, C.S & Lai, J.Y., 2006, 'Gender differences in perceptions & relationships among dominantsofe-learningacceptance',*ComputersinHumanBehaviour*22(5),816–829. http://dx.doi.org/10.1016/j.chb.2004.03.006

Pai, F.Y. & Huang, K.I., 2011, 'Applying the technology acceptance model to the introduction of healthcare information systems', *Technological Forecasting & Social Change* 78, 650–660. http://dx.doi.org/10.1016/j.techfore.2010.11.007

Pallant, J., 2010, *SPSS survival manual: A step by step guide to data analysis using SPSS*, 4th edn., McGraw-Hill, Maidenhead.

Patton, M.Q., 2002, *Qualitative Research and Evaluation Methods,* Sage, Thousand Oaks.

Pavon, F. & Brown, I., 2010, 'Factors influencing the adoption of the World Wide Web for job-seeking in South Africa', *South African Journal of Information Management* 12(1), Art. #443, 9 pages.

Pew Internet and American Life Project, 2005, *Reports: Demographics*, Author, Washington, DC, viewed 16 May 2015, from http://www.pewinternet.org/PPF/r/171/report_display.asp

Pituch, K.A. & Lee, Y.K., 2006, 'The influence of system characteristics on e-learning use', *Computers and Education* 47, 222–224. http://dx.doi.org/10.1016/j.compedu.2004.10.007

Razali, N.M. & Wah, Y.B., 2011, 'Power comparisons of Shapiro-Wilk, Lillefors and Anderson Darling tests', *Journal of Statistical Modelling and Analytics* 20(1), 21–33.

Reddy, V., Gastrow, M., Juan A. & Roberts, B., 2013, 'Public attitudes to science in South Africa', *South African Journal of Science* 109, 1–8. http://dx.doi.org/10.1590/sajs.2013/1200

Rienties, B., Brouwer, N. & Lygo-Barker, S., 2013, 'The effects of online professional development on higher education teachers' beliefs and intentions towards learning facilitation and technology', *Teaching and Teacher Education* 29, 122–131. http://dx.doi.org/10.1016/j.tate.2012.09.002

Robinson, L., Marshall, G.W. & Stamps, M.B., 2005, 'Sales force use of technology: Antecedents to technology acceptance', *Journal of Business Research* 58(12), 1623–1631. http://dx.doi.org/10.1016/j.jbusres.2004.07.010

Rubin, H.J. & Rubin, I., 2005, *Qualitative interviewing: The art of hearing data,* Sage, Thousand Oaks.

Saadé, R. & Bahli, B., 2005, 'The impact of cognitive absorption on perceived usefulness and perceived ease of use in on-line learning: An extension of the technology acceptance model', *Information and Management* 42, 317–327. http://dx.doi.org/10.1016/j.im.2003.12.013

Sánchez, R.A. & Hueros, 2010, 'Motivational factors that influence the acceptance of Moodle using TAM', *Computers in Human Behavior* 26, 1632–1640. http://dx.doi.org/10.1016/j.chb.2010.06.011

Santos, J., 1999, 'Cronbach's alpha: A tool for assessing the reliability of scales', *Journal of Extension* 37(2), 34–36.

Schoonenboom, J., 2014, 'Using an adapted, task-level technology acceptance model to explain why instructors in higher education intend to use some learning management system tools more than others', *Computers & Education* 71, 247–256. http://dx.doi.org/10.1016/j.compedu.2013.09.016

Sierpe, E., 2005, 'Gender distinctiveness, communicative competence, and the problem of gender judgments in computer-mediated communication', *Computers in Human Behavior* 21(1), 127–145.

Singer, E.E. & Bossarte, R., 2006, 'Incentives for survey participation: When are they coercive?', *American Journal of Preventive Medicine* 31, 411–418. http://dx.doi.org/10.1016/j.amepre.2006.07.013

South African Government Communications, 1996, *White paper on science and technology. South Africa*, viewed 16 May 2015, from http://www.dst.gov.za/publications-policies/legislation/white_papers/Science_Technology_White_Paper.pdf

Srite, M. & Karahanna, E., 2006, 'The role of espoused national cultural values in technology acceptance', *MIS Quarterly* 30(3), 679–704.

Steyn, H.S., 2000, 'Practical significance of the difference in means', *South African Journal of Industrial Psychology* 26(3), 1–3.

Steyn, R., 2012, 'Expanding the suite of measures of gender-based discrimination: Gender differences in ablution facilities in South Africa', *South African Journal Economic Management Sciences* 15(2), 222–234.

Sun, H. & Zhang, P., 2006, 'The role of moderating factors in user technology acceptance', *International Journal of Human Computer Studies* 64, 53–78. http://dx.doi.org/10.1016/j.ijhcs.2005.04.013

Tabachnick, B.G. & Fidell, L.S., 2007, *Using multivariate statistics*, Pearson/Allyn & Bacon, Boston.

Tahmincioglu, M. 2008, *'Your career: Where are the women in tech?'*, viewed 16 May 2015, from http://www.msnbc.msn.com/id/23033748/print/1/displaymode/1098

Van Zyle, J.M., Heinz, N. & Nel, D.G., 2000, 'On the distribution of the maximum likelihood estimator of Cronbach's alpha', *Psychometrika* 65, 271–280. http://dx.doi.org/10.1007/BF02296146

Venkatesh, V. & Davis, F.D., 2000, 'A theoretical extension of the technology acceptance model: Four longitudinal field studies', *Management Science* 46(2), 186–204. http://dx.doi.org/10.1287/mnsc.46.2.186.11926

Venkatesh, V. & Morris, M.G., 2000, 'Why don't men ever stop to ask for directions? Gender, social influence, & their role in technology acceptance & usage behaviour', *MIS Quarterly* 24(1), 115–139. http://dx.doi.org/10.2307/3250981

Venkatesh, V., Morris, M.G., Davis, G.B. & Davis, F.D., 2003, 'User acceptance of information technology: Toward a unified view', *MIS Quarterly* 27(3), 425–478.

Wasko, M.M. & Faraj, S., 2005, 'Why should I share? Examining knowledge contribution in electronic networks of practice', *MIS Quarterly* 29(1), 1–23.

Wild, K.V., Mattek, N., Maxwell, S.A., Dodge, H.H., Jimison, H.B. & Kaye, J.A., 2012, 'Computer related self-efficacy and anxiety in older adults with and without mild cognitive impairment', *Alzheimers Dement* 8(6), 544–522. http://dx.doi.org/10.1016/j.jalz.2011.12.008

Wright, W.A., Knight, P.T. & Pomerleau, N., 1999, 'Portfolio people: Teaching and learning dossiers and innovation in higher education', *Innovative Higher Education,* 24(2), 89–103. http://dx.doi.org/10.1023/B:IHIE.0000008148.71650.e6

20

A knowledge management framework to grow innovation capability maturity

Authors:
Denéle Esterhuizen[1]
Corne Schutte[1]
Adeline du Toit[2]

Affiliations:
[1]Department of Industrial Engineering, University of Stellenbosch, South Africa

[2]Centre for Information and Knowledge Management, University of Johannesburg, South Africa

Correspondence to:
Adeline du Toit

Email:
adutoit@uj.ac.za

Postal address:
PO Box 524, Auckland Park 2006, South Africa

Background: Innovation is a key prerequisite for being organisationally competitive. Therefore, it is imperative that enterprises grow and mature their innovation capability. Knowledge management plays a fundamental role in the ability of enterprises to innovate successfully.

Objectives: There are no formal guidelines for using knowledge management to grow innovation capability maturity. The researchers intended to develop a knowledge management framework that enables innovation capability.

Method: The scope of the research did not allow for the practical implementation of the framework. However, five industry and subject theory experts evaluated the applicability and usability of the framework.

Results: All five experts reported that enterprises could use knowledge management tools and organisational facilitating conditions to allow innovation capability maturity to grow. The importance of the framework is that it gives guidelines for using knowledge management as a vehicle for growing innovation capability maturity.

Conclusion: The framework determines whether enterprises' organisational conditions and knowledge management tools are sufficient to sustain or grow their innovation capability maturity.

Introduction

Innovation is a key prerequisite for achieving organisational competitiveness and long-term wealth in the volatile business environment. Enterprises must be able to innovate, and do so constantly and sustainably, if they are to function competitively (Cavusgil, Calantone & Zhao 2003; Moore 2005; Paap & Katz 2007). The most common way of categorising for innovation is into two high-level categories: product and process innovation (Katz 2007). Neely, Filippini, Forza, Vinelli and Hii (2001) explain that product innovation involves developing and commercialising new tangible products or services. Process innovation involves:

- introducing new, or improving current, manufacturing, distribution and service processes
- any procedures or actions that enterprises introduce to transform resources associated with them.

Du Preez, Schutte, Essmann, Louw and Marais (2009) also emphasise that, with product innovation, all parties involved (the enterprises and their customers) should gain value from the transaction. They also argue that process innovation can relate to high-level managerial processes or to detailed sets of tasks to execute operational processes.

In addition to the product and process innovation categories, Baker (2002) highlights the importance of a third type of innovation: strategy innovation. He argues that product and process innovation alone are no longer adequate, necessitating the introduction of strategy innovation to provide further support. This type of innovation emphasises the importance of long-term views of the contributions of innovation to the competitiveness and success of enterprises. Hamel (2000) confirms this, referring to strategy innovation as business concept innovation (BCI).

BCI involves innovations to a variety of business design variables, including pricing structures, distribution channels and value webs or relationships. With innovation categorised into product, process and strategic innovations, it is necessary to add that a successful innovation is often a combination of the three types of innovations because new strategies can result in new products, which, in turn, require new processes (Du Preez et al. 2009).

Innovation makes it necessary to execute processes. One may show these processes as a life cycle of phases. Du Preez et al. (2009) describe a basic and generic representation of the innovation lifecycle that comprises the phases that follow: invention, feasibility, implementation, operation and disposal. Essmann (2009) points out that learning occurs in activities throughout all the innovation lifecycle phases. At the end of each phase, there are opportunities to learn from the successes and failures of that phase. One may revisit the innovation lifecycle phases in order to execute certain activities again or to refine certain aspects.

There are no known formal guidelines for using knowledge management to grow innovation capability maturity. Consequently, this article investigated how enterprises can use knowledge management tools to advance growth in innovation capability maturity. The question that it will address is whether enterprises can use knowledge management tools and organisational facilitating conditions to enable growth in innovation capability maturity.

Capability maturity models

Innovation capability is the way enterprises can generate innovative outputs. Essmann (2009) points out that enterprises must assess and improve their innovative capability to sustain, repeat and accelerate innovative initiatives. This requirement for assessment and constant improvement takes us directly to the concept of capability maturity models.

Generically, one can see capability maturity models as ways of deciding whether the processes enterprises use, as well as how they use them, characterise mature enterprises (Fairchild 2004). Capability maturity models are sets of structured levels that define how well the activities, practices and processes of enterprises can reliably and sustainably produce the outcomes they want. The two essential goals of capability maturity models are (Essmann 2009):

- to determine the capability maturity of enterprises in terms of a specific domain of practice
- to help to establish and guide improvement that will best suit the enterprises whilst complying with the prescribed best practices of the domain.

These points provide a platform for logical reasoning about the importance of capability maturity models. In order to understand the current position of enterprises compared to their competitors and to enterprises in other industries, it is necessary to establish its capability maturity in terms of a specific domain of practice. In addition, it is important for enterprises to benchmark themselves against the best or against those who are successful in order to determine how much, and in what direction, to improve. Although benchmarking is a recognised practice, it can present problems because most enterprises are reluctant to expose their competitive secrets.

The original Capability Maturity Model® for software (SW-CMM®) is a widely accepted set of guidelines for developing high-performance software enterprises (LeVasseur 2000). Watt Humphrey and colleagues at International Business Machines (IBM) developed the original concept behind SW-CMM® in the early 1980s. He placed the emphasis for improving software development on processes after establishing that the quality of software had a direct relationship with the quality of the processes used to develop it (LeVasseur 2000).

However, the Software Engineering Institute (SEI) of Carnegie Mellon University developed the original SW-CMM® and first published it with the sponsorship of the United States Department of Defence (Cooke-Davies 2004). Most capability maturity models use the initial SW-CMM® of the SEI (Essmann 2009).

More recently, SEI developed Capability Maturity Model Integration® (CMMI®). It is a model consolidated from the bodies of knowledge (or domains of practice) that follow: software development, systems engineering, integrated product and process development and supplier sourcing. Degen-Hientz, Fäustle & Hörmann (2005) describe the CMMI® as a model and industry standard that contains best practices aimed at developing and maintaining products and services throughout their product lifecycles.

The concept of the capability maturity model, or the maturity model, has since spread to many organisational domains of practice. Champlin (2003) confirms this, stating that enterprises have a wide selection of capability maturity models from which to choose, not only between applications, but also within each application. There are capability maturity models for many applications, including software development, information technology (IT) management, project management, data management, business management and knowledge management. The total number of capability maturity models that were available in 2002 already exceeded 120.

Most models have the same basic five-level maturity scale structure. The maturity level descriptions are often similar in the different models.[1] The CMMI® Product Team (2002) defines a maturity level as a 'well-defined evolutionary plateau of process improvement'.

Enterprises do not necessarily start at maturity level 1. One benchmarks them against the capability maturity descriptions of each level and then assigns the appropriate level if they continue to fulfil the requirements the description for that level states. When one assigns a specific level, one also assumes that the enterprises have met the requirements for the previous levels. To reach maturity level 4, for example, enterprises must have continuously fulfilled and institutionalised all the requirements of level 2, level 3 and level 4. Level 1 is the launch pad for successive levels and does not imply that enterprises have met any maturity requirements.

Some recent and/or significant developments in innovation capability maturity models include:

- the Innovation Capability Maturity Model from Indutech (Essmann 2009)
- the Business Innovation Maturity Model from Accelper Consulting (2010)

1. This is possibly because the SW-CMM® is the basis of most other capability maturity models.

- the INPAQT Innovation Capability Maturity Model from INPAQT (2010)
- the Innovation Maturity Model from Tata Consultancy Services Ltd (Narayana 2005)
- the Innovation Maturity Model from OVO (2010)
- the Innovation Maturity Model from PRTM (2007)
- the Innovation Maturity Model from Think For A Change (2009)
- the Innovation Aptitude™ Audit from The Innovation Practice (2007).

Although enterprises use innovation capability maturity models in practice, there is insufficient information to distinguish between them. Furthermore, the theoretical and/or empirical foundations of these innovation capability maturity models are unclear, except for the Innovation Capability Maturity Model of Essmann (2009).

Essmann developed a model that describes a path for improving innovation capability maturity for competitively orientated enterprises. He did this using thorough academic research and practical case studies into the generic and fundamental requirements for organisational innovation capability. He then consolidated these generic and fundamental requirements for organisational innovation capability into his Innovation Capability Maturity Model (ICMM).

A description of the respective *generic* innovation capability maturity levels (with implied intermediate levels between level 1 and level 3 and between level 3 and level 5), as the ICMM specifies, follows. Examples of the innovation capability requirements include:

- **Maturity level 1 - Ad hoc and limited:** The innovation-related practices and procedures are impromptu and limited in their ability to meet the requirements for consistent innovation.
- **Maturity level 3 - Formalisation and predictability**: Enterprises have identified and deployed innovation-related best practices and procedures. This enables them to fulfil the requirements for innovation consistently. This does not imply that they must deploy rigid and stifling structures with which they must comply. Instead, they must use a proactive and planned approach to innovating.
- **Maturity level 5 - Integration, synergy and autonomy:** Once enterprises have achieved formalisation, institutionalising the practices follows – in other words, when activities become natural behaviour. This enables individual autonomy and releasing resources to concentrate on achieving alignment and synergy within and between innovation initiatives and with operational activities.

Essmann (2009) identified 42 essential requirements for organisational innovation capability. He structured these 42 innovation capability requirements within the model. Each has its own *specific* level 1, level 3 and level

5 maturity level scenario descriptions modelled on the *generic* maturity level descriptions:

- developing and conveying innovation strategies and objectives
- championing and encouraging innovation
- involving customers and suppliers in the innovation process
- planning and coordinating the innovation portfolio
- reducing uncertainty and risk
- establishing intellectual property management and sharing policies
- capturing, storing and retrieving data and information.

Role of knowledge management in enabling growth in innovation capability maturity

Gray (2000) states that knowledge management is best understood as the management practices associated with knowledge. Small and Sage (2005/2006) distinguish between two views of knowledge management. One approach focuses on knowledge resources to facilitate access and the reuse of existing explicit knowledge by using almost only information technology tools. The other approach is to treat knowledge management as a multidisciplinary subject that focuses on 'the context and environment for knowledge acquisition, representation, transformation, sharing, and use' (Small and Sage 2005/2006) using behavioural as well as technology management. Du Plessis (2007) argues that knowledge management must align with business strategies to improve enterprises' capability, tempo and effectiveness to deliver products or services through the planned and structured management of the 'creation, sharing, harvesting and leveraging of knowledge as an organizational asset' (Du Plessis 2007).

Davenport and Prusak (2000) point to the benefits of establishing knowledge cultures. They include better corporate alignment and unity, improved innovation through sharing, higher staff morale, increased responsiveness, decreased cycle times, reduced costs and increases in customer satisfaction. Successful knowledge management stimulates the development of creative skills, increases individual commitment, supports employees to outline task objectives systematically in networks that enable them to share knowledge with others and helps employees to determine their resource requirements. It also offers a platform for asking questions and providing innovative solutions (Carneiro 2000). Therefore, the literature provides a strong basis from which to argue that enterprises could use knowledge creation processes when investigating knowledge management guidelines for improving innovation capability maturity (Carneiro 2000; Cavusgil, Calantone & Zhao 2003; Darroch 2005; Du Plessis 2007; Ruggles 1998).

However, the literature on how enterprises can use knowledge management tools and organisational facilitating conditions to enable growth in innovation capability maturity is sparse. At most, it implies that there is a relationship between knowledge management and enterprises' innovation capability maturity. Cavusgil et al (2003) investigated how firms acquire tacit knowledge from partners and how the extent of inter-firm knowledge transfer affects firm innovation capability. Calantone, Cavusgil and Zhao (2002) examined the concept of learning orientation and its effect on firm innovation capability.

Lin (2007) examined the influence of individual factors (enjoyment in helping others and knowledge self-efficacy), organisational factors (top support from managers and organisational rewards) and technology factors (information and communication technology use) on knowledge sharing processes and whether a presence of more of these factors leads to superior organisational innovation capability. This gap in the literature provides the platform for the work this article presents. However, the question of what this implies from a practical point of view remains.

When one evaluates the innovation capability maturity of enterprises, one benchmarks them against the requirements of the maturity level description of each innovation capability and assigns the appropriate level to them. Consequently, when enterprises grow in their innovation capability maturity, one measures them again against the requirements of each maturity level to determine whether their innovation-related activities have improved to such an extent that one can assess them against a higher maturity level description.

However, this does not answer the question of how enterprises can use knowledge creation processes to help them improve their innovation-related activities in order to move from one maturity level description to a higher one.

The answer depends on enterprises' understanding of their key knowledge-related needs when they move to higher maturity levels. If one approaches it from a different angle, enterprises must decide what key knowledge actions (and the key knowledge creation processes) will enable them to move their innovation capability from one maturity level to the next.

In 1994, Nonaka presented two premises that shaped the development of organisational knowledge creation theory:

- one can distinguish tacit and explicit knowledge conceptually along a continuum
- knowledge conversion explains, theoretically and empirically, the interaction between tacit and explicit knowledge.

Nonaka's theory of knowledge creation has 'achieved paradigmatic status since the mid-1990s ... and is highly respected' (Gourlay 2006). Choo and Bontis (2002) described it as 'one of the best known and most influential models in the knowledge strategy literature'. They stated that Nonaka's knowledge creation model 'provides the intellectual scaffolding for a growing number of empirical and theoretical studies in strategic knowledge management'. Gourlay (2006)

points out that the annual increase in the number of citations, as well as the range of categories of journals that have cited this publication, indicate a level of interest that make his research very important.

Nonaka's well-known socialisation, externalisation, combination and internalisation (SECI) model describes how enterprises create knowledge through interactions between explicit and tacit knowledge. Explicit and tacit knowledge grow in both quality and quantity during the process of converting knowledge. The four modes of converting knowledge are socialisation, externalisation, combination and internalisation (Nonaka 1994).

Socialisation is tacit to tacit knowledge transfer. Because tacit knowledge is difficult to formalise and is often time- and space-specific, one acquires and converts tacit knowledge only through shared experience. Socialisation typically occurs when people share the same environment. Examples include traditional apprenticeships (apprentices acquire the tacit knowledge they need through hands-on experience rather than from written manuals or textbooks) and informal social meetings outside of the workplace (creating and sharing worldviews, mental models and mutual trust). It also occurs outside of organisations' boundaries (acquiring and taking advantage of the tacit knowledge embedded in customers or suppliers) (Nonaka 1994).

Externalisation is tacit to explicit knowledge transfer. Knowledge forms when tacit knowledge articulates into explicit knowledge. This allows others to share it and it then becomes the basis of new knowledge. Tacit knowledge becomes explicit through metaphors, analogies, concepts, hypotheses or models.

An example of externalisation is a quality-control cycle that allows employees to make improvements to manufacturing processes by articulating the tacit knowledge of enterprises that they have accumulated over years on the job (Nonaka 1994).

Combination is transferring explicit knowledge to more complex and systematic sets of explicit knowledge. Explicit knowledge accumulates internally in, or externally from, enterprises and then they combine, edit or process it to form new knowledge. They then disseminate it amongst their members. The creative use of computerised communication networks and large-scale databases can then support the processes.

Examples are collecting and contextualising organisation-wide information to form financial reports or breaking down corporate visions into operationalised business or product concepts, where financial reports and operationalised business or product concepts represent new explicit knowledge (Nonaka 1994).

Internalisation is explicit to tacit knowledge transfer, which is similar to 'learning by doing'. Enterprises share the created explicit knowledge and employees convert it into tacit knowledge as they embody it. Enterprises have to actualise explicit knowledge through action and practice.

For example, employees read documents or manuals about their jobs and their enterprises and react to the information. Trainees can internalise the explicit knowledge in the documents to enrich their tacit knowledge bases. Employees can also embody explicit knowledge through simulations or experiments that trigger learning by doing.

A knowledge management framework to grow innovation capability maturity

The aim of the framework (see Figure 1) developed during this study was to investigate organisational support by using business tools to grow innovation capability maturity. The hypothesis was that one could design a knowledge management framework, which would enable growth in innovation capability maturity, by aligning knowledge creation processes to the requirements for moving innovation capability growth from one maturity level to the next.

Consequently, considering the earlier SECI model process descriptions and the descriptions of the generic level of innovation capability maturity detailed earlier, the researchers identified a knowledge-creation path that acts as a key enabler for growth from maturity level 1 to maturity level 5.

This knowledge-growth path is the cornerstone of the search for a knowledge management framework to grow innovation capability maturity. The researchers identified the requirements for knowledge management tools and organisational facilitating conditions, which support the specific knowledge creation processes (that the identified knowledge-creation path highlights), through an extensive literature study. The researchers chose documents based on:

- whether they, directly or indirectly, could provide the requirements for, or the fundamental factors to consider when, managing knowledge
- whether they focused specifically on managing or facilitating the creation of knowledge that occurs during the processes of socialisation, externalisation, combination and internalisation.

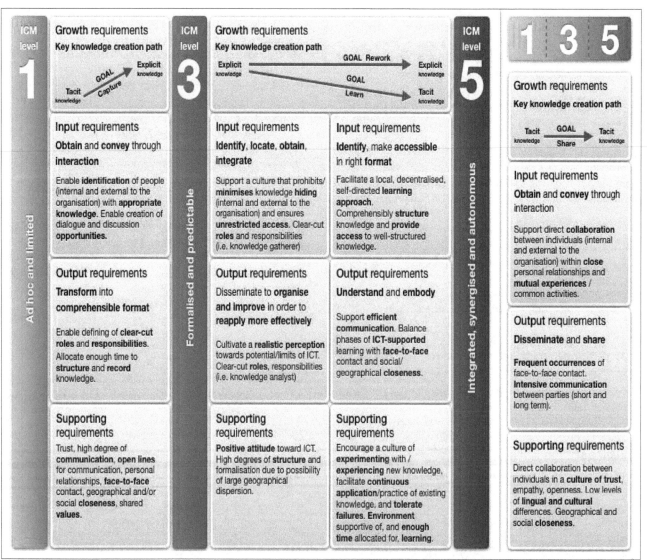

Source: Authors' own data

FIGURE 1: Knowledge management framework to grow innovation capability.

Document selection was also guided by (although not restricted to) author prominence in the field. The result of this investigation was a conceptual framework (see Figure 1) that serves as a guideline for using knowledge management as a vehicle for growing innovation capability maturity.

A descriptive and practical approach to the processes of creating knowledge, especially in order to understand their underlying logic and practical implications, is to see knowledge creation as having an input and output perspective as well as an operational task associated with it (Armistead 1999; Back, Von Krogh, Seufert & Enkel 2005). For example, the process of internalising would have, as an input, explicit knowledge that one has to find, and tacit knowledge, which one has to learn, as an output.

Consequently, the researchers structured the generic requirements for knowledge management tools and the organisational facilitating conditions that support the specific knowledge creation processes (highlighted in the identified knowledge-creation path) into an input, output and supporting perspective for each process of creating knowledge.

Therefore, the structure of the framework comprises three improvement columns that show the key knowledge-creation path:

- one between innovation capability maturity (ICM) level 1 and level 3 (externalisation)
- one between maturity level 3 and level 5 (combination and internalisation)
- the supporting improvement column (socialisation).

Each improvement column contains four main components:

- an innovation capability maturity growth perspective that shows the key knowledge creation processes enterprises need to enable growth in innovation capability maturity
- a knowledge creation input perspective that gives the main knowledge action and the enabling requirements for knowledge management tools to support the input perspective of the specific process of creating knowledge
- a knowledge creation output perspective that gives the main knowledge action and the enabling requirements for knowledge management tools to support the output perspective of the specific process of creating knowledge
- a knowledge creation supporting perspective that gives the elements that are crucial to the success of the specific process(es) for creating knowledge but which relate more to organisational facilitating conditions than only to the input or output aspects of the process of creating knowledge.

The importance of this framework is that it gives guidelines for using knowledge management as a vehicle for growing innovation capability maturity. In practical terms, the framework aims to provide 'as is' and 'to be' reference points for determining whether enterprises' organisational conditions and business tools are sufficient to sustain or grow their innovation capability maturity.

It is important to note that the framework is simply a tool. As with all tools, its success depends on the knowledge, experience and dedication of the person, project team, department or enterprise that is applying it.

The framework provides a reference point for *evaluating* enterprises' organisational conditions and business tools in order to *sustain* innovation capability maturity. If they use the framework, enterprises should be able to answer this question: 'Given our innovation capability maturity level, do our knowledge management-related tools and organisational conditions meet the requirements that will enable us to *fulfil* our innovation-related activity requirements *continuously* for this maturity level?'

The framework provides a reference point for *benchmarking* enterprises' organisational conditions and business tools in order to *grow* their innovation capability maturity. If they use the framework, enterprises should be able to answer this question: Given our innovation capability maturity level, do our knowledge management-related tools and organisational conditions meet the requirements that will enable us to *improve* our innovation-related activity requirements for this maturity level and move from our current maturity level to the next?

Enterprises could obtain these indications of their level of innovation capability maturity formally or informally. A formal indication would entail an assessment of innovation capability maturity – throughout the enterprises, per innovation capability area, per innovation capability requirement or through combinations of them. A less formal indication would mean that enterprises simply benchmark their known innovation-related activities against the generic ICMM maturity level descriptions without going through an official assessment.

Evaluating the framework

Applying the framework practically in real enterprises would prove or disprove the research question, which is whether enterprises can use knowledge management tools and organisational facilitating conditions to enable them to grow their innovation capability maturity.

Unfortunately, this was not possible because one would need anything up to five years or longer to test the framework in practice. Measuring growth in innovation capability maturity takes time, especially when measuring growth through the five maturity phases.

Consequently, the researchers chose five industry and subject theory experts from various fields to evaluate the framework. A limit of the evaluation was that the interviewees could only respond from their own experiences and frames of reference as well as by considering what the researchers presented to them.

The researchers chose a research-evaluation questionnaire and research summary as the ways of facilitating a semi-structured interviewing process as well as for discussing the accuracy, applicability and usability of the framework. The questionnaire contained three background contextualisation questions, five framework-specific questions and a section for comments. The researchers chose the questions to cover all aspects of the framework systematically. Their intention was to create a platform for a comprehensive discussion of the research. The researchers began the evaluation process by sending each expert a 14-page research summary with the framework and the research-evaluation questionnaire electronically.

When they received the documents, the experts could work through the research summary and consider the framework in their own time. The time available to the experts determined how they would respond to the research-evaluation questionnaire. Three preferred to give detailed written answers. This reduced the time they had available for interviews. Two experts preferred to use the evaluation questions as a way of preparing for one-on-one discussions of the research with the authors. The evaluation questions provided a background to these discussions, thereby assuring that all the experts had equal platforms from which to evaluate the research.

The goal of each evaluation differed in the sense that each evaluation aimed to assess a different focus of the research. Even though each expert received the same set of evaluation questions, the three written responses provided unique angles to the questions and highlighted the diverse backgrounds of the experts. Similarly, an emphasis on the discussion of the research aspects relevant to the backgrounds of the experts characterised the two interviews.

Background contextualisation questions

These questions aimed to provide a context for the answers, comments and suggestions the researchers received in response to the framework evaluation. They asked the experts to state their occupations and industries and to explain the extent of their exposure to knowledge management and innovation capability maturity. Table 1 gives an overview of the interviewees' background in the fields of innovation and knowledge management.

Framework-specific questions

These questions aimed to provide a basis for evaluating the accuracy, applicability and usability of the framework systematically.

The first two questions evaluated the accuracy of the identified knowledge-creation path as a key enabler for movement between levels of innovation capability maturity. They asked the experts whether they agreed with the reasoning applied in identifying this knowledge-growth path. Consequently, the questions explored whether this knowledge-growth path accurately addressed the key maturity level description requirements for moving from one maturity level to the next.

The next two questions evaluated the accuracy of the content of the framework and the logic of its structure. They asked the experts whether they agreed with the specific requirements of the knowledge management tools the framework detailed and whether they agreed with the structure of the framework, synthesised to provide an input, output and supporting perspective to each knowledge creation process in the growth path.

The final framework-related evaluation question aimed at determining the applicability and usability of the framework.

Reasoning applied when identifying the knowledge-growth path

All the experts agreed with the reasoning applied when the knowledge-creation path was identified as a key enabler of growth in innovation capability maturity. They also thought that this path accurately addressed the key maturity level description requirements for moving from one maturity level to the next.

However, Expert B remarked that 'I would recommend that you make sure to specify that the growth path that you have identified isn't for the whole organisation; just trying to manage it all.' Expert D agreed completely with the specific knowledge-creation path identified as a key enabler of movement between maturity levels. He was also satisfied that this identified path accurately addressed the key maturity level description requirement for moving from one maturity level to the next. Expert E was unsure what the authors meant by the socialisation process: 'Does it imply that it runs across all CMM levels?'

Agreement with the requirements of the knowledge management tools the framework detailed

Expert A could not find any gaps in the requirements of the specific knowledge management tools and found the

TABLE 1: Interviewees' background in innovation and knowledge management.

Interviewee	Designation	Industry	Exposure to innovation and capability maturity models	Exposure to knowledge management
Expert A	Programme manager	Innovation management consulting	Extensive knowledge of, and experience in, innovation, especially innovation capability maturity	Solid background in knowledge management
Expert B	Lecturer	Academic or strategic consulting	Solid knowledge of innovation but limited formal exposure to capability maturity models	Extensive experience in knowledge management
Expert C	Enterprise architect	Professional services industry	Solid knowledge of capability maturity models	Considerable experience in information management and experience in knowledge management
Expert D	Strategy consultant	Information technology and services industry	Extensive experience in capability maturity models	Limited formal exposure to knowledge management, but practical experience in how it related to the CMMI®
Expert E	General manager	Mobile telecommunication industry	Experience in capability maturity models	Solid background in knowledge management

structure of the framework clear and concise. He added that 'should these activities, tools, methods, etc. be categorised into the framework, it would provide an easy means for referencing the appropriate mechanisms for the task at hand'. Expert B, Expert C and Expert D agreed with the requirements of the tools the framework detailed and the structure of the framework. Expert D commented that 'this framework is very good, I'm 100% with you, and I think it's very valuable.' Expert E questioned whether the authors also intended the use of system tools and technology. She agreed with the structure of the framework, but here the uncertainty about the implication of the socialisation process also surfaced: 'I like the framework – only the socialisation component, exactly where it fits in (across 1 to 5 or for 5 only) as described above is not clear to me.' She suggested that the researchers alter the appearance of the framework to show the socialisation process as a line across all the maturity levels and added that it will improve readers' understanding visually.

Applicability and usability of the framework

Expert A commented that the framework was generic and did not stipulate specific activities, tools or methods but 'should a company go to the effort to select the appropriate tools using the framework and allocate them into the framework, it should be applicable and useful.' He concluded his response by commenting that he would like 'to show appreciation for the seemingly 'simple' framework – it often takes significantly more effort to represent something that is complex in a simple manner while ensuring its accuracy.' Expert B commented:

> 'Don't get me wrong, I think you've got an excellent thing going here; one of the better, more advanced attempts that I've seen, I'm just afraid that you'll make it too complex ....' (Expert B, lecturer, academic or strategic consulting industry)

Expert C gave a positive response from an applicability and usability perspective: 'I think it's very applicable, and on the right level of detail. I find it practical.' However, he recommended that the researchers take care to present the framework so that is understandable:

> 'I think the thing about the framework is contextualisation; it can be difficult to explain to someone who doesn't have the same background and level of knowledge of the subject as you have; where it fits in and how it works.' (Expert C, enterprise architect, professional services industry)

Expert D noted that 'It is definitely usable and valuable within the context of the ICMM, and I think with a little adaptation, it will be valuable to the CMMI community as well.' Expert E responded very positively:

> 'The framework is definitely something that I can personally very easily use in my work environment. I would easily be able to translate it to how I can apply it in our organisation. I went through every block in the framework, asking what the input and output was, and how we can support that, and it was very easy for me to make those links; it works very nicely. What was also very interesting was that it enables you to identify gaps; if you for example say 'identify, locate, obtain and integrate', I can for example go and check that, yes, we can identify, locate

and obtain, but integration is a bit of an issue; so to use it as a bit of a rough analysis.' (Expert E, general manager, mobile telecommunication industry)

To conclude, the researchers can state that they received no criticism during the evaluation process about the ability of the framework to enable growth in innovation capability maturity and that it was unnecessary to change the framework.

One interviewee commented on the visual effect of the framework and its ability to convey the context of its elements. The interviewee was unsure, at first glance, whether the socialisation process ran across all the levels of innovation capability maturity or whether it was only a supporting process at level 5.

No other interviewees had a problem with the visual interpretation of the framework. Therefore, the researchers decided to keep the current framework presentation. It was also possible that the researchers could achieve wider applicability if they refined the framework for use in a CMMI® context, because the CMMI® is the successor to the SW-CMM®, the basis for most maturity models in use.

There are a few differences between the ICMM and CMMI®. They make the framework this document presents not immediately applicable to the CMMI® community. These are that the CMMI® implies that enterprises only need innovation at higher organisational maturity levels. It emerged during the interview process that people who understand the CMMI® very well would still find the framework useful.

All five experts agreed with the statements that follow:

- the reasoning applied when identifying the specific knowledge creation process path as a key enabler of movement between innovation capability maturity levels is logical and sound
- this path addresses the key requirements for growth from one maturity level to the next accurately
- the requirements of the knowledge management tools and the organisational facilitating conditions the framework details for each identified knowledge creation process in the path are accurate.

Interviews with the five subject matter experts support the hypothesis that one can design a knowledge management framework that enables growth in innovation capability maturity by aligning knowledge creation processes to the requirements for moving from one maturity level to the next.

Conclusion

There is a gap in the literature on formal guidelines for using business tools to enable growth in innovation capability maturity. This article introduced innovation capability maturity models and discussed the state of capability maturity. It gave reasons why the ICMM is the foundation for further and related discussions on innovation capability maturity.

The researchers designed a knowledge management framework that enables growth in innovation capability maturity by aligning knowledge creation processes to the requirements for moving from one maturity level to the next. The effect of this framework is that it gives guidelines for using knowledge management as a vehicle for growing innovation capability maturity. The researchers evaluated the ability of the framework to enable growth in innovation capability maturity by using a questionnaire and an interview-based evaluation procedure.

The intention of the framework the article presents is not to be the be-all and end-all solution to enable growth in innovation capability maturity, nor is its intention to provide a step-by-step enterprise-wide knowledge management integration plan. The authors' aim was to investigate organisational support, using business tools, to grow innovation capability maturity. Its unique research contribution lies in that it provides a tangible link between the fields of knowledge management and innovation capability maturity.

A shortcoming of the research is that it did not allow for the practical implementation of the framework. Consequently, five industry and subject experts from various fields evaluated it. The authors received encouraging responses to the practical applicability and usability of the framework from the five interviewees.

The authors suggest that future research should include detailed studies to align the processes for creating knowledge with the requirements for growing innovation capability maturity. Furthermore, the conceptual nature of this research leaves many opportunities for further research into the practical application of the framework because one can only determine the ability of the framework to enable growth in innovation capability maturity via real-world implementation.

Practical implementation would also provide a platform for investigating whether there are gaps in the requirements for knowledge management tools and facilitating conditions and they would indicate the nature of these shortcomings. They could serve as starting points for determining whether future work is necessary to develop an implementation manual and/or an implementation methodology to accompany the framework because the framework is a tool. Its success depends on the knowledge, experience and dedication of the person, project team, department or organisation that will apply it.

This framework is a unique, first conceptual step toward providing knowledge management guidelines to enable growth in innovation capability maturity.

Acknowledgements

Competing interests

The authors declare that they have no financial or personal relationship(s) that may have inappropriately influenced them when they wrote this paper.

Authors' contributions

D.E. (University of Stellenbosch) made the main conceptual contribution and performed all of the research in this study. C.S. (University of Stellenbosch) and A.D.T. (University of Johannesburg) were the co-supervisors. D.E. (University of Stellenbosch) and A.D.T. (University of Johannesburg) wrote the manuscript.

References

Accelper Consulting, 2010, *Business innovation maturity model*, viewed 05 March 2011, from http://accelper.com

Armistead, C., 1999, 'Knowledge management and process performance', *Journal of Knowledge Management* 3(2), 143–157. http://dx.doi.org/10.1108/13673279910275602

Back, A., Von Krogh, G., Seufert, A. & Enkel, E., 2005, *Putting knowledge networks into action: Methodology, development, maintenance*, Springer, Berlin. http://dx.doi.org/10.1007/b138845

Baker, K.A. 2002, 'Management benchmark study, chapter 14: Innovation', viewed 04 May 2011, from http://www.au.af.mil/au/awc/awcgate/doe/benchmark

Calantone, R.J., Cavusgil, S.T. & Zhao, Y. 2002, 'Learning orientation, firm innovation, capability, and firm performance', *Industrial Marketing Management* 31(6), 515–524. http://dx.doi.org/10.1016/S0019-8501(01)00203-6

Carneiro, A., 2000, 'How does knowledge management influence innovation and competitiveness?', *Journal of Knowledge Management* 4(2), 87–98. http://dx.doi.org/10.1108/13673270010372242

Cavusgil, S.T., Calantone, R.J. & Zhao, Y., 2003, 'Tacit knowledge transfer and firm innovation capability', *Journal of Business & Industrial Marketing* 18(1), 6–21. http://dx.doi.org/10.1108/08858620310458615

Champlin, B., 2003, *Toward a comprehensive data management maturity model (DM3)*, viewed 06 May 2011, from http://www.powershow.com/view/1f797-ZDcxZ/Toward_a_Comprehensive_Data_Management_Maturity_Model_DM3_flash_ppt_presentation

Choo, C.W. & Bontis, N., 2002, *The strategic management of intellectual capital and organizational knowledge*, Oxford University Press, New York.

CMMI Product Team, 2002, *Capability maturity model® integration (CMMI®), Version 1.1*, Carnegie-Mellon Software Engineering Institute, Pittsburgh.

Cooke-Davies, T.J., 2004, 'Measurement of organisational maturity: Questions for future research' in *Innovations: Project management research*, Project Management Institute, Newtown Square, PA.

Darroch, J., 2005, 'Knowledge management, innovation and firm performance', *Journal of Knowledge Management* 9(3), 101–115. http://dx.doi.org/10.1108/13673270510602809

Davenport, T.H. & Prusak, L., 2000, *Working knowledge: How organizations manage what they know*, Harvard Business School Press, Boston, MA.

Degen-Hientz, H., Fäustle, M. & Hörmann, K., 2005, 'CMMI – An executive summary', viewed 09 October 2010, from www.kuglermaag.com

Du Plessis, M., 2007, 'The role of knowledge management in innovation', *Journal of Knowledge Management* 11(4), 20–29. http://dx.doi.org/10.1108/13673270710762684

Du Preez, N., Schutte, C., Essmann, H., Louw, L. & Marais, S., 2009, *Enterprise engineering textbook*, University of Stellenbosch, Stellenbosch.

Essmann, H.E., 2009, 'Toward innovation capability maturity', PhD Industrial Engineering Thesis, University of Stellenbosch, Stellenbosch.

Fairchild, A.M., 2004, 'Information technology outsourcing (ITO) governance: An examination of the outsourcing management maturity model', in *37th Hawaii International Conference on System Sciences*, IEEE, Bigh Island, Hawaii, January 05–08, 2004. http://doi.ieeecomputersociety.org/10.1109/HICSS.2004.1265565

Gourlay, S., 2006, 'Conceptualizing knowledge creation: A critique of Nonaka's theory', *Journal of Management Studies* 43(7), 1415–1436. http://dx.doi.org/10.1111/j.1467-6486.2006.00637.x

Gray, P., 2000, *Knowledge management overview, CRITO working paper*, University of California, Irvine, CA.

Hamel, G., 2000, *Leading the revolution*, Harvard Business School Press, Boston, MA.

INPAQT, 2010, 'INPAQT innovation capability maturity model', viewed 12 May 2011, from www.inpaqt.nl

Katz, B., 2007, 'The integration of project management processes with a methodology to manage a radical innovation project', MSc Industrial Engineering Dissertation, University of Stellenbosch, Stellenbosch, South Africa.

LeVasseur, C., 2000, 'Describing the capability maturity model', in *Measure IT*, New York, Gartner.

Lin, H., 2007, 'Knowledge sharing and firm innovation capability: an empirical study', *International Journal of Manpower* 28(3/4), 315–332. http://dx.doi.org/10.1108/01437720710755272

Moore, G.A., 2005, *Dealing with Darwin: How great companies innovate at every phase of their evolution*, Penguin Books, London.

Narayana, M.G.P.L., 2005, A framework approach to measure innovation maturity, in *Proceedings of the Engineering Management Conference,* St John's, Newfoundland, September 11–13.

Neely, A., Filippini, R., Forza, C., Vinelli, A. & Hii, J., 2001, 'A framework for analysing business performance, firm innovation and related contextual factors: Perceptions of managers and policy makers in two European regions', *Integrated Manufacturing Systems* 12(2), 114–124. http://dx.doi.org/10.1108/09576060110384307

Nonaka, I., 1994, 'A dynamic theory of organizational knowledge creation', *Organization Science* 5(1), 14–37. http://dx.doi.org/10.1287/orsc.5.1.14

OVO, 2010, 'Innovation maturity model', viewed 21 January 2011, from http://www.slideshare.net/jdpuva

Paap, J. & Katz, R., 2004, 'Anticipating disruptive innovation', *Research Technology Management* 47(5), 13–22.

PRTM, 2007, 'Innovation maturity model', viewed 04 March 2011 from http://www.innovationtools.com/PDF/Roadmap_PRTM.pdf

Ruggles, R., 1998, 'State of the notion: Knowledge management in practice', *California Management Review* 40(3), 80–89.

Small, C.T. & Sage, A.P., 2005/2006, 'Knowledge management and knowledge sharing: a review', *Information Knowledge Systems Management* 5, 153–169.

The Innovation Practice, 2007, 'Innovation aptitude™ audit', viewed 15 December 2010, from www.theinnovationpractice.com

Think For A Change, 2009, 'Innovation maturity model', viewed 21 February 2011, from http://www.thinkforachange.com

21

The mobile application preferences of undergraduate university students

Author:
Andrea Potgieter[1]

Affiliation:
[1]Department of
Information and Knowledge
Management, University of
Johannesburg, South Africa

Correspondence to:
Andrea Potgieter

Email:
apotgieter@uj.ac.za

Postal address:
PO Box 524, Aucklandpark
2006, South Africa

Background: Smartphones and similar mobile devices have changed the way individuals interact with technology and with each other. The app preferences of smartphone users are vitally important to those seeking to understand the motivation behind app downloads and usage.

Objective: The research problem of this article is centred on the preferences for smartphone apps by the growing market of smartphone users in South Africa. The study includes a demographic profile of the users to establish what attracts this market into downloading smartphone apps.

Methodology: The study employed a mono-method, quantitative methodological framework with an online survey as the data collection instrument. The survey was conducted amongst undergraduate university students in 2013 and repeated again in 2014.

Results: It was found that the 'young adult' demographic, of which the sample of undergraduate university students formed a part, was discerning about which apps they downloaded and that the frequency of downloads occurred less than once a month in most cases. Information and entertainment needs were amongst the top reasons users indicated as motivations for downloading apps.

Conclusion: The study's findings confirmed that the sample had definite preferences regarding which apps the users were downloading, and these preferences depended on the needs that they wished to fulfil. The study also revealed that, even though users were aware of security threats associated with downloading apps, this knowledge did not deter them from continuing to download apps. Future research recommendations also arose from the study, giving direction to prospective studies.

Introduction

Smartphones and similar mobile devices have changed the way individuals interact with technology and with one other. According to Böhmer *et al.* (2011:47), these devices have 'evolved from single-purpose communication devices into dynamic tools that support their users in a wide variety of tasks'. This support is mainly offered through mobile application interfaces (apps) that are designed for specific tasks and downloaded, via an app store, onto the user's smartphone. Based on trends from the literature, it is clear that changes in mobility are continuous and may branch out into many different areas, but for now apps are the main contenders (Lynch 2012; McCarthy 2014).

The effect of mobile connectivity through apps amongst students is also a global phenomenon, as 79% of young adults (ages 18–24) own smartphones, and 70% of these students are using their devices in class to stay connected (Skiba 2014). This article aims at discussing the preferences regarding mobile apps of undergraduate university students, who typically fall within the 'young adult' age group. In addition, it attempts to reveal why the respondents in the study download certain apps by highlighting the respondents' preferences for these mobile apps.

Background to research problem

According to a comprehensive Groupe Speciale Mobile Association (GSMA) study of the socio-economic impact of the mobile industry in sub-Saharan Africa (SSA), over 6% of the region's gross domestic product (GDP) is contributed by mobile operations, which is 'higher than any other comparable region globally' (GSMA 2013). Furthermore, according to the GSMA (2014a) country dashboard, South Africa specifically is 'a Fast Grower market in Southern Africa with four operators and 70.4 million mobile connections'.

The latest GSMA (2014b) Mobile Economy report predicts that SSA is estimated to experience the highest growth of any region with regard to the number of smartphone connections over the next six years. According to the report, there will be 525 million smartphone connections in the region by 2020, and 'for the majority of users, smartphones will be the first device over which to access the Internet and to use new applications and services, as well as to explore digital content'.

It stands to reason that the app preferences of these smartphone users are vitally important to those seeking to understand the motivation behind app downloads and usage, especially when taking into account that 80.2% of South African Internet users use their app-enabled smartphones to access the Internet (Effective Measure 2014). Monica Bannan, vice president of product leadership at Nielsen, agrees that app developers should remain in the know regarding what app users expect:

> As mobile consumption habits evolve, it's imperative that app developers continue to add functionality and robustness to their offerings. Although there does appear to be a limit to the number of apps people are willing to access on a monthly basis, [app users] are spending 31 percent more time than they were last year, proving that it's the content that counts. (Nielsen 2014)

Srivastava (2014), discussing the Nielsen (2014) study, argues that, due to the fact that smartphones have become an integral part of users' lives, 'the selection of specific apps has become more precautionary'. Although the number of app downloads is increasing, users have shown that they prefer to uninstall or delete any apps 'which fail to lure them within a few hours', which leads to new app developers struggling to find new and devoted users (Srivastava 2014). The research problem of this study is centred on the preferences for smartphone apps by the growing market of smartphone users in South Africa. The study includes a demographic profile of the users to establish what attracts this market into downloading smartphone apps.

To highlight these preferences, this study will present findings regarding the app proclivities of 'young adults' (a group of students in this case, the majority of whom were between the age of 18 and 25), as this group of consumers spends the most average hours on their smartphone interacting on apps when compared to other age groups. This age group attributes an average of 5.2 hours daily to smartphone use (Salesforce Marketing Cloud 2014).

The students in this sample typically fell within the 18–25 year age group, with 70% of the 2014 respondents indicating that they fall within the 18–21 year age group and 25% within the 22–25 year age group. This concentration of 'young adult' ages was also prevalent with the 2013 survey, with 73% of those respondents belonging to the 18–21 year age group and 18% within the 22–25 year age group; see Figure 1. It has been established that this age group boasts the most active smartphone and app users, which supported the goal of this research, the search for preferences regarding mobile apps.

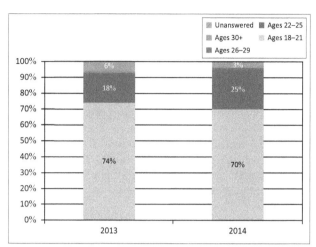

FIGURE 1: Age distribution of samples: 2013 and 2014.

Research methodology

This section constitutes the theoretical perspective of the research, discussing the overall nature of the research activity (Pickard 2013:xviii).

Research design

The research paradigm for this study was quantitative in nature, with a limited number of open-ended questions in the survey, allowing for qualitative interpretation. The philosophical paradigm in which the study was performed was one of positivism, allowing for the creation of broader generalisations based on casual relationships revealed in the data.

The research approach of this study was abductive, where the researcher aimed at generalising from the interactions between the specific and the general. The phenomenon of app choices amongst the sample group was explored in an attempt to identify themes and patterns in order to modify existing theories, or build new theories, about the subject at hand (Saunders, Lewis & Thornhill 2012:144). The researcher employed the use of an online questionnaire to this end.

Research method

The methodological framework prevalent in this study was mono-method quantitative. Although two open-ended questions were present in the survey, the terms that arose from those questions were analysed based on the frequency of each term appearing. The data from these open-ended questions were inducted in a quantitative format, as was the case with the typical Likert-scale questions collected throughout the rest of the questionnaire.

Data collection instrument

The online survey used in the 2014 study was a marginally modified version of the survey implemented by Mashiane and Potgieter in 2013 (Mashiane & Potgieter 2014) for the purpose of comparing results longitudinally. In both 2013 and 2014, the survey was deployed to the sample group through the use of the online university student portal, ULink. This portal offers a survey facility which deploys a survey directly to the relevant users – in this case, undergraduate university students.

The questionnaire consisted of 28 questions, four of which were open-ended questions where respondents could type in the relevant answer. The remaining 24 questions were delivered in a multiple-choice style, giving the respondents the option of choosing the appropriate answer, or a neutral answer ('I don't know' or 'Other') where applicable.

The findings of the 2013 Mashiane and Potgieter (2014) survey were presented at the Pan-Pacific Conference XXXI in Japan in June 2014. The findings of the 2014 survey were presented at the Annual Information and Knowledge Management Conference in South Africa in November 2014. This article will compare and discuss the findings of these two data collection instances.

Survey samples

The sampling technique applied in both data collection instances was one of non-probability convenience sampling, which is appropriate in the quantitative nature of the study's research method (Kumar 2014:242). Saunders *et al.* (2012:176) notes that samples that are selected based on convenience are characteristically easier to access, because these samples are typically familiar to the researcher. Saunders *et al.* (2012:291) also state that, in many instances, samples chosen for convenience seemingly 'meet purposive sample selection criteria that is relevant to the research aim'. Since this study focused on the tendencies of young adults and their preferences regarding app downloads, the sample was both convenient whilst also meeting the purposive criteria of falling within the 'young adult' range.

Using the University of Johannesburg's (UJ) online student portal ULink, the survey was made available to all undergraduate Information Management students at the UJ in June 2013 and again in September 2014. The survey was developed by taking into consideration global trends in mobile app usage surveys. Contemporary surveys were used as guidelines in this endeavour.

In 2013, the survey was made available to 1161 students, the total number of students registered for the subject Information Management on an undergraduate level at the time of the study. A response rate of 62% was achieved with a total of 717 responses successfully captured.

During the 2014 data collection period, September to November, the survey was posted to all undergraduate Information Management students at the UJ. In September 2014, the survey was made available to 1256 undergraduate students, and by 05 November 2014, 522 responses had been captured, amounting to a response rate of 42%.

In both instances, an online survey was selected, since these students access their student portal on a regular basis. The suitability of being able to participate in the survey by using a portal they are familiar with was considered to be an advantage.

Findings

Survey respondents were asked whether they owned an Internet-enabled smartphone. There was a slight increase in the number of respondents as 79% of respondents in 2013 indicated that they owned a smartphone, compared to 84% in 2014. In both instances, this percentage was higher than the smartphone penetration reported for urban dwellers in South Africa, which is 62% (On Device Research 2014).

Subsequently, respondents were asked whether they downloaded apps to their smartphones. This number increased to 77% in 2014, and the increase was to be expected, since apps have been described as 'the single most significant tool driving the mobile economy in South Africa' (World Wide Worx 2013).

In 2013, 44% of respondents indicated that they owned a smartphone with a BlackBerry operating system (OS), and only 13% of respondents owned an Android enabled smartphone. In 2014, BlackBerry was no longer the leader amongst the sample, with only 25% of respondents indicating that they owned a Blackberry device and 37% representing Android; see Figure 2. The loss of market share by BlackBerry had been predicted by Effective Measure (2014); it had also been predicted that the market share would be lost to Samsung (an Android device) and – at least from an OS point of view – is seemingly confirmed in this instance.

When respondents were asked when they searched for an app, the motivation for 2013 and 2014 searches were relatively similar; see Figure 3. A notable difference between the two instances was the most popular reason respondents had pointed out as motivation for searching for an app. In 2013, 48% of respondents indicated that they searched for an app when they 'need information on a brand, its product or its services', whereas the most popular reason in 2014 for

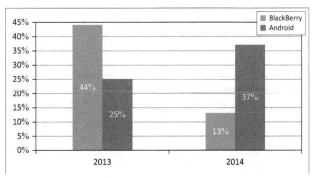

FIGURE 2: Growth of Android adoption from 2013–2014.

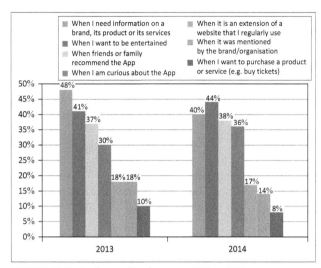

FIGURE 3: Motivation for searching for an app, 2013 vs. 2014.

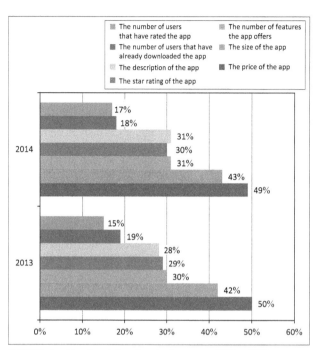

FIGURE 4: Considerations before downloading an app, 2013 vs. 2014.

searching for an app was that respondents 'wanted to be entertained'.

In both 2013 and 2014, the remaining reasons noted for searching for an app were indicated as follows, in descending order of preference:

- When friends or family recommend the app.
- When I am curious about the app.
- When it is an extension of a website that I regularly use.
- When it was mentioned by the brand and/or organisation.
- When I want to purchase a product or service (e.g. buy tickets).

What these findings imply, is that an information need and a need to be entertained are evidently equally important to this sample. The reasons for searching for an app as listed above, are typically less important, but also indicate a hierarchy in the samples' motivations for searching for apps to download. Based on this finding, one could infer that a respondent will most probably search for an app when he or she is bored, or needs information about a product. They will be less likely to do so if an app is an extension of a website that they typically use, or if they want to purchase a product or service.

Respondents were also asked what they considered before downloading an app that they had searched for. Respondents indicated, in both 2013 and 2014, that the price of the app was the most important feature. It must, however, be noted that Pengnate and Delen (2014:7), when controlling for confusing factors such as price, found a strong relationship between 'emotions and the number of an app downloaded', and state that this relationship can hypothetically be described 'by the affect-as-information model and theory of reasoned action'. Therefore, even though the respondents in this sample indicated that price plays a very important role in their selection of an app, they may not be aware of the underlying emotional triggers affecting their choices.

An important secondary consideration was the size of the actual app, possibly implying that device memory is a consideration for this demographic as it influences device performance (Huang *et al.* 2010). Khalid *et al.* (2015:74) confirm this notion by remarking that app users notably complained about 'resource heavy' apps; these apps consumed too much battery life or memory on mobile devices, which caused frustration with regard to performance.

Equally important to one another, but less important overall, was the number of features the app had to offer, the star rating of the app on the app store platform, and the app's description. Pagano and Maalej (2013:132) note a bias in user rating of apps, as users may consider feedback which gives an app a low rating as less helpful than feedback giving an app a higher rating. It becomes evident that feedback which gives an app a better rating is considered more helpful by users, who then rate these positive reviews as more helpful. Taking the partiality of the app rating system into account, it is satisfactory to note that the least consequential of considerations that the respondents in this study took into account before downloading an app were the number of users that have rated the app, and the number of users that have already downloaded the app. This was the case with both the 2013 and the 2014 respondents; see Figure 4.

The issue of security risks was raised with respondents. In 2013, 53% of the respondents indicated a concern regarding security risks when downloading apps, and in 2014, 51% of the respondents indicated a similar concern. The risks associated with downloading mobile apps are real as a MetaIntell study found that 92% of the top 500 downloadable Android apps carry security or privacy risks (Business Wire 2014). Although it is evident that these respondents are aware and concerned about the security risks associated with downloading apps to their phones, it did not deter the majority of respondents from downloading apps regardless of these risks.

Respondents were asked to indicate how many apps they download per month. In 2013, 33% of respondents noted that they do not download apps every month. This percentage remained similar in 2014, when 34% of respondents indicated that they do not download apps on a monthly basis. In 2013 and 2014 respectively, 25% and 22% of respondents indicated that they downloaded at least one app per month; 17% and 16% agreed that they downloaded two to five apps per month. Very few of the respondents downloaded more than five apps per month, with only 5% of respondents in 2013 and 6% in 2014 indicating that they downloaded apps at this rate.

This finding supported the exploration of the research problem of this study, as it was evident that this demographic, although actively using their smartphones according to global standards, were very discerning when downloading apps. The majority of respondents, in both instances, indicated that they do not download apps more than once a month. This suggested that specific criteria were taken into account by these users when they decided to download an app.

The app that most respondents had downloaded at the time of the survey changed from 2013–2014. In 2013, Facebook was a clear favourite with 75% of respondents indicating that they had this app on their smartphone, whereas in 2014, WhatsApp had been installed by 73% of respondents – the highest instance compared to other apps. Unfortunately, many smartphones have Facebook pre-installed at purchase; therefore, it is not a clear indication of whether the respondents had downloaded the app out of their own volition. It does however confirm that this app had not been uninstalled once the device had been personalised by the respondents. Further study of the issue could possibly explore which pre-installed apps remain installed and used on users' phones after purchase.

The fact that WhatsApp was to be found on the majority of the 2014 sample's smartphones was a testament to this app's popularity, as WhatsApp is not typically pre-installed at purchase. The attractiveness of WhatsApp was further confirmed when respondents selected this app as 'the most useful app they had ever downloaded'; 18% of respondents in 2013 and 22% in 2014 sided with WhatsApp in their answers to this open-ended question. The remaining responses were divided, in less frequent instances, between apps such as Facebook, News24 and Opera Mini.

When the question of whether respondents would consider downloading paid-for apps was asked, the response was mostly negative from the 2013 (42%) and the 2014 (46%) sample groups. Considering that 32% of respondents in 2013 and 25% of respondents in 2014 'did not have a

monthly income', and 43% of respondents in 2013 and 28% in 2014 had a monthly income of less that R1000, it was to be expected that paying for apps would not be a priority.

Even though the general attitude seemed to be not to pay for apps, 22% of respondents in 2013 and 17% in 2014 indicated that they had at least one paid-for app installed on their smartphone. The main reasons indicated by respondents that led them to consider paying for an app were 'if the paid-for app appeared to be of a higher quality than a free app that offers the same function' (33% in 2013 and 30% in 2014), or 'if a paid-for app fulfilled a specific need that the respondent considered vital' (28% in both 2013 and 2014).

In 2013, 28% of respondents also indicated that the most they had ever paid for an app had been 'less than R10', whereas 23% indicated the same in 2014. A smaller percentage of respondents in 2013 (18%) and 2014 (19%) confirmed that the most they had ever paid for an app had been 'between R11 and R50'. Even fewer respondents indicated that they had ever paid 'between R51 and R100' for an app, with merely 5% of respondents in 2013 and 4% in 2014. Only 1% of respondents in both 2013 and 2014 indicated that they had ever paid 'more than R100' for an app. This finding can also be linked to the low income bracket of the sample in both 2013 and 2014.

Conclusion and recommendations

This longitudinal study set out to establish the preferences regarding downloading apps of undergraduate university students. Following the analysis of data from two samples, one surveyed in 2013 and the other in 2014, it was found that these groups of 'young adults' were discerning about which apps they download, as the frequency of downloads was relatively low. It was found that less than one app per month was being downloaded by the respondents.

The main motivation for downloading apps was found to be either a need for specific information (in 2013), or a need to be entertained (in 2014). It was also found that the price and size of an app were important considerations when respondents considered downloading an app. The recurring theme of app price was evident, as respondents either had a very small monthly income or no income at all, making the downloading of paid-for apps a non-probability.

On the rare occasions where respondents did download paid-for apps, the motivation had been a perceived higher quality of the paid-for app compared to its free counterparts. In addition to a perceived higher quality of paid-for apps, respondents also indicated that they would choose to purchase one if they considered the paid-for app to be vital to fulfil a specific need. When respondents committed to paying for an app, it was found that most chose an app that cost less than R10 to download.

WhatsApp was found to be a very popular app downloaded by the sample groups. It is suggested that a follow-up study be conducted to establish whether 'popular' apps are apps that had been pre-installed before purchase, as was the case with Facebook. Since respondents indicated that the need to access information and to be entertained were important considerations when downloading apps, it stands to reason that these two popular apps, WhatsApp and Facebook, most likely fulfilled these needs.

The study also showed that app users were aware of the security risks associated with downloading apps to their smartphones, but that these risks were not deterring the download of apps. This is an interesting finding, as it could indicate that these respondents did not regard a threat to their information privacy as a cause for concern; further investigation is needed to explore the issue of security risks in the downloading of apps.

Although some insight was given into the preferences of this demographic with regard to app use, this area of study still poses many unanswered questions, the disregard of risk regarding security when downloading apps being one example. As the use of apps increases, as it has in recent times, these questions need to be explored in order for app developers to create useful products, and also for researchers to gain insight into the interaction of users with their smartphones.

It is further suggested, for future research, to not exclude older generations from research in smartphone and app usage research simply because they have been slower in adopting the technology. For the purpose of this study, the sample explored 'young adults' as this demographic was found to spend the most time interacting using their smartphones. According to Deloitte (2014), however, smartphone penetration by individuals over 55 is on the rise and by 2020 the current gap between this age group and younger demographics will be negligible. A study comparing the differences in app usage amongst all age groups, in South Africa specifically, will offer crucial insight.

Acknowledgements

Competing interests

The authors declare that they have no financial or personal relationships which may have inappropriately influenced them in writing this article.

References

Böhmer, M., Hecht, B., Schöning, J., Krüger, A. & Bauer, B., 2011, 'Falling asleep with Angry Birds, Facebook and Kindle – A large scale study on mobile application usage', *Proceedings of the 13th International Conference on Human Computer Interaction with Mobile Devices and Services*, Stockholm, Sweden, August 30 - September 2, 2011, pp. 47–56.

Business Wire, 2014, *MetaIntell identifies enterprise security risks, privacy risks and data leakage in 92% of top 500 android mobile applications*, viewed 22 January 2014, from http://www.businesswire.com/news/home/20140122006295/en/MetaIntell-Identifies-Enterprise-Security-Risks-Privacy-Risks#.VIcDp9KUcrV

Deloitte, 2014, *The smartphone generation gap: Over-55? There's no app for that*, viewed 26 October 2014, from http://www2.deloitte.com/content/dam/Deloitte/global/Documents/Technology-Media-Telecommunications/gx-tmt-2014prediction-smartphone.pdf

Effective Measure, 2014, *South African mobile report: A survey of desktop user's attitudes and uses of mobile phones*, viewed 26 October 2014, from http://www.effectivemeasure.com/south-african-mobile-report-march-2014

GSMA, 2013, *New GSMA report shows sub-Saharan Africa lea ds the world in mobile growth and impact*, media release, viewed 11 November 2013, from http://www.gsma.com/newsroom/sub-saharan-africa-leads-world/

GSMA, 2014a, *Data » Markets » Africa » South Africa*, viewed 28 October 2014, from https://gsmaintelligence.com/markets/3788/dashboard/

GSMA, 2014b, *The mobile economy: Sub-Saharan Africa 2014*, viewed 28 October 2014, from http://ssa.gsmamobileeconomy.com/

Huang, J., Xu, Q., Tiwana, B., Mao, Z.M., Zhang, M. & Bahl, P., 2010, 'Anatomizing application performance differences on smartphones', *Proceedings of the 8th international conference on mobile systems, applications, and services*, San Francisco, USA, June 15–18, 2010, pp. 165–178.

Khalid, H., Shihab, E., Nagappan, M. & Hassan, A.E., 2015, 'What do mobile app users complain about?', *Software, IEEE* 32(3), 70–77. http://dx.doi.org/10.1109/MS.2014.50

Kumar, R., 2014, *Research methodology: A step by step guide for beginners*, 4th edn., Sage Publishing Ltd., London.

Lynch, W., 2012, *How apps are taking over computing and content*, Web Log Post, viewed 20 November 2012, from http://www.realmdigital.co.za/post/how-apps-are-taking-over-computing-and-content/

Mashiane, S. & Potgieter, A., 2014, 'Enterprise apps: What do consumers really think?', *Proceedings of the Pan-Pacific Conference XXXI*, Osaka, Japan, June 2–5, 2014, pp. 70–72.

McCarthy, N., 2014, 'Mobile app usage by the numbers [infographic]', viewed 29 October 2014, from http://www.forbes.com/sites/niallmccarthy/2014/10/29/mobile-app-usage-by-the-numbers-infographic/

Nielsen, 2014, *Smartphones: So many apps, so much time*, viewed 01 July 2014, from http://www.nielsen.com/us/en/insights/news/2014/smartphones-so-many-apps--so-much-time.html

On Device Research, 2014, *Impact of the mobile Internet in Africa vs UK*, viewed 22 October 2014, from http://www.slideshare.net/OnDevice/impact-of-the-mobile-internet-in-african-lives?redirected_from=save_on_embed

Pagano, D. & Maalej, W., 2013, 'User feedback in the AppStore: An empirical study', *Proceedings of the IEEE 21st International Requirements Engineering Conference (RE)*, Rio de Janeiro, Brazil, July 15–19, 2013, pp. 125–134.

Pengnate, S.F. & Delen, D., 2014, 'Evaluating emotions in mobile application descriptions: Sentiment analysis approach', *Proceedings of the 20th Americas Conference on Information Systems*, Savannah, USA, August 7–9, 2014.

Pickard, A.J., 2013, *Research methods in information*, Facet Publishing, London.

Salesforce Marketing Cloud, 2014, *2014 mobile behavior report*, viewed 26 October 2014, http://www.exacttarget.com/2014-mobile-behavior-report

Saunders, M., Lewis, P. & Thornhill, A., 2012, *Research methods for business students*, Pearson, Essex.

Skiba, D.J., 2014, 'The connected age: Mobile apps and consumer engagement', *Nursing Education Perspectives* 35(3), 199–201. http://dx.doi.org/10.5480/1536-5026-35.3.199

Srivastava, B., 2014, *Mobile app usage to rise, but new apps struggle to find market!*, viewed 17 July 2014, from http://www.dazeinfo.com/2014/07/17/mobile-app-usage-us-2013-catagory-interest-age-group-study/

World Wide Worx, 2013, *The time of the app*, viewed 28 November 2013, from http://www.worldwideworx.com/mobileinternet2014/

22

Knowledge management awareness in a research and development facility: Investigating employee perceptions

Authors:
Andrea Potgieter[1]
Thami Dube[2]
Chris Rensleigh[1]

Affiliations:
[1]Department of
Information and Knowledge
Management, University of
Johannesburg, South Africa

[2]Centre for Information and
Knowledge Management,
University of Johannesburg,
South Africa

Correspondence to:
Andrea Potgieter

Email:
apotgieter@uj.ac.za

Postal address:
PO Box 524, Auckland Park
2006, South Africa

Background: Research and development (R&D) facilities are dependent on knowledge to develop new and improve existing technologies. R&D employees' perceptions of the use and management of knowledge are important as these individuals are the source of the innovation needed to generate and develop new processes and services.

Objectives: This study aimed to understand Sasol R&D employees' perceptions of knowledge management (KM). The study also assessed the attitude of Sasol R&D management towards KM.

Method: The target population for this research included different levels of seniority and education in Sasol R&D. A questionnaire was distributed to a sample of 150 employees in R&D and 50 more who work closely with R&D in support functions.

Results: It was found that the importance of KM is understood by Sasol R&D employees and management. It was established that Sasol R&D management regard KM as important, but that their commitment to KM initiatives is not necessarily evident for employees. A concern highlighted by the study was that employees were not aware of the duties of the identified KM champions within their facility.

Conclusion: It was suggested that Sasol R&D employees should be made aware of the duties of KM champions. It was also established that Sasol R&D management needs to be more visible in their support of KM initiatives. Recommendations based on the findings of the study can assist Sasol R&D, and other facilities attempting to implement a KM strategy, to gain insight into the perceptions of employees and the role management needs to play in the facilitation of this process.

Introduction

Research and development (R&D) facilities are dependent on knowledge to develop new and improve existing technologies. R&D employees' attitude towards the use and management of knowledge is important as these individuals are the source of the innovation needed to generate and develop new processes and services for an organisation. R&D is critical for companies to remain competitive in a modern knowledge and innovation-based economy.

Sasol, a global petrochemical group, was formed in 1950 after the South African government wanted to reduce the country's dependency on foreign oil supply. To achieve this goal, Sasol used Fischer-Tropsch (F-T) technology, which used the gasification of coal to produce hydrocarbon products that included synthetic fuels. Today, the organisation supplies approximately 35% of South Africa's fuel needs. In 1955 the management of Sasol commissioned a laboratory and a testing station with 70 technicians and scientists. In 1957 a formal R&D facility was formed and was named Sasol Technology. Sasol Technology currently employs individuals qualified mostly in various fields of engineering and science; more than 500 postgraduate employees in these fields are employed by the facility.

Knowledge management (KM) strategies result from knowledge workers' awareness of trends in the current business environment, and their responses to those trends (Ndlela & Du Toit 2001:156). The primary objective of this study was to establish Sasol R&D employees' perceptions of KM within the facility.

R&D facilities are commonly used to enhance an organisation's products and services, to ensure a the organisation gains and maintains a competitive edge (Sambamurthy & Subramani 2005). R&D employees are therefore referred to as 'knowledge workers', as they are usually highly educated (Van der Spek & Kingma 2000), implying that their value as employees is tacit. These individuals' level of education, as well as their experience, is important in sustaining innovation, since the primary objective of R&D facilities is to utilise knowledge to develop and improve products and services.

This study aimed to understand Sasol R&D employees' perceptions of KM in the organisation. The study also assessed the attitude of Sasol R&D management towards KM, since the formulation of a KM strategy depends on the ability of management to change the corporate culture into one that creates opportunities for tacit knowledge to be made explicit (Ndlela & Du Toit 2001:156).

The recommendations of this study incorporate the views and opinions of the employees to establish what actions are necessary for the KM strategy that has been adopted to be successful. These recommendations, and key results of the study, were presented at an international conference of KM practitioners and academics in 2012 (Potgieter, Dube & Rensleigh 2012). By assessing whether employees identify and take ownership of the strategy that has been adopted, the facility can identify the needs of its employees and ensure that the maximum level of benefit is gained from this adopted strategy. Recommendations from the results can also assist Sasol R&D management in ensuring that the KM strategy that has been adopted is effective and can deliver positive results for the organisation.

Knowledge management in Sasol research and development

Bishop *et al.* (2008:17) mention that the need organisations have to make better use of their knowledge resources has commanded the adoption of effective KM initiatives as a business solution. Despite the complex nature of knowledge, it is closely related to knowing how to 'get things done' for the benefit of an organisation (Guo & Sheffield 2008). Universally, and specifically in a R&D environment, organisational knowledge is an intangible intellectual asset that: 'plays an important role in the success of any enterprise' (Ndlela & Du Toit 2001:161). This is true in general, but specifically in a technology-driven business environment like Sasol.

In a knowledge-intensive environment such as R&D, for an organisation to remain competitive, it has to have a knowledge advantage (Mrinalini & Nath 2008). Furthermore, knowing how to 'get things done' in an R&D facility is critical because of the nature of the business. Therefore, KM and a subsequent strategy for managing knowledge as a resource can be considered an integral part of the success of a R&D facility. Sasol R&D's criteria for their current KM strategy were based on and benchmarked against internal (within Sasol) and external organisations' best practices (De Wet-Viljoen 2006).

The chosen criteria for the current KM strategy were that it must:

- be better than practices before it
- be proven
- be applicable across Sasol
- be affordable, implementable and sustainable
- add 'obvious and desired' values.

These criteria were a combination of internal and external organisational experiences and recommendations from academic publications. The benchmarking exercise was chosen because it made it easy to compare organisational criteria and simplified the process of making an informed decision. Based on these criteria, and the: 'KM pyramid of excellence' (De Wet-Viljoen 2006), the current KM strategy for Sasol's R&D was developed.

The KM pyramid of excellence currently used by Sasol ensures that all aspects of KM implementation are addressed and that these aspects contribute to the growth of the organisation in the long term. As mentioned, for a KM strategy to be successful within an organisation, there has to be a culture that will promote knowledge sharing; the KM pyramid of excellence emphasises the importance of knowledge transfer to the improvement of knowledge levels within Sasol. After improving knowledge levels, the next step in the KM pyramid of excellence is to create and promote a learning organisation that will lead to the development of competency levels of the employees. According to this reasoning, if the competency of employees is continuously improved, employees may be more motivated to contribute to the knowledge of the organisation.

The ability of an organisation to utilise knowledge to get things done and maintain a competitive advantage is more important for organisations with: 'global ambitions' (Massa & Testa 2009:129). One of the strategies of expanding organisations like Sasol is the formation of joint ventures with local and foreign organisations to enter new markets. The skills and knowledge in the appropriate selection of partners and the management of the alliance can make an important positive contribution to the success of the collaboration (Draulans, De Man & Volberda 2003:155). The successful formation and management of the joint ventures requires that organisations contribute different areas of expertise, both technical and business related. Efficient KM in an R&D facility can give such an organisation a competitive advantage during the formation of these joint ventures.

For an organisation to realise its innovative capacity, it should be able to continuously: 'identify new ways of doing business, develop new technologies and products and enter new markets in new organisational forms' (Teng 2007:119). This is critical in Sasol R&D since innovative ways of doing things and producing new and improving existing products has to be cost effective. The other main objective of a KM strategy is to facilitate effective and efficient knowledge sharing amongst the organisation's employees (Shin 2004:179). If employees share knowledge and experiences, the new and old ideas and procedures can be combined to result in new and improved production processes and products.

Therefore, the feelings and perceptions of employees towards the adopted KM strategy are important in ensuring the success of the initiative and knowledge sharing in the organisation. The perceptions that employees have of the adopted KM strategy can motivate or discourage employees to be creative and innovative. This aspect of KM is especially important in an R&D environment.

Many organisations implement KM strategies on the assumption that competitiveness and efficiency will increase (Schultze & Leidner 2002:219). Researchers and practitioners alike agree that structuring and enlargement of the knowledge base can improve its contribution to the effectiveness of the R&D processes (Lee, Kim & Koh 2009:3662). The availability of knowledge to employees, as was mentioned earlier, can enable employees to be innovative and ensure that the organisation achieves the best from its employees. The current KM strategy adopted within Sasol aims to ensure that the significance of KM is communicated from the low-level employees of the organisation to top management.

Literature review

Research and development facilities: In general and at Sasol

Research and development facilities function as knowledge bases in their organisations, providing a competitive advantage for innovative firms (Jackson, Hitt & Denisi 2003). Successful organisations have the ability to create, disseminate and utilise knowledge efficiently and effectively (Sanghani 2008:7). It can therefore be argued that organisations that have R&D facilities perceive the development of their knowledge base as vitally important in developing and sustaining their competitive advantage. The efficient utilisation of knowledge generated by a R&D facility enables an organisation to develop new and innovative products and processes. This makes R&D the core activity in ensuring an organisation's sustainability of innovation and thus its competitive advantage (Huang 2009).

The main objective of R&D is to develop systems that can enhance productivity and performance within an organisation (Kumaraswamy et al. 2006:681). Organisations, especially organisations with R&D facilities, have to stay abreast of advances in relevant technologies in order to maintain a market leader position. To ensure a leading position, R&D facilities employ specialists, who are employed because of their specialist knowledge in their respective fields, in order to give organisations a competitive advantage (Van der Spek & Kingma 2000:21). R&D facilities require personnel who also have strong academic backgrounds and who are experts in their respective fields of study. Organisations generally employ postgraduates in their R&D facilities, as these individuals have a combination of academic and practical knowledge of the subject being researched (Van der Spek & Kingma 2000:21).

As a strategy to attract and retain these skilled individuals, Sasol encourages and finances its employees to complete master's and doctoral degrees. However, the employee must research topics that are relevant to Sasol's business objectives and which will add value to the organisation's knowledge about the subject. This strategy not only ensures that the employee becomes an expert in the chosen subject; it also ensures that the organisation can maintain a competitive edge in that specific field of research.

As mentioned, Sasol Technology (Sasol's R&D facility) was formed in 1957 and has been pivotal in the establishment of Sasol as the world leader in F-T technology, allowing the organisation to maintain a first-mover advantage and be the spearhead in the chosen market. Sasol has achieved this market leader status through the continuous improvement of current processes and technologies to reduce operational costs, and through collaboration with other industry-related parties. The R&D facility at Sasol has significantly contributed to the continuous improvement of their technologies and processes, as is evident from the various awards and accolades Sasol has received for the contributions it has made in the technology development and engineering field.

Defining knowledge management

According to Foss, Husted and Michailova (2010:456), it is widely accepted that the management of knowledge has become: 'a critical issue for competitive dynamics, international strategy, the building of resources, the boundaries of firms, and many other issues'. In the last decade, knowledge has emerged as a resource that can contribute to an organisation's sustainable competitive advantage (Lopes 2008:7). The existing business environment is fast changing and requires organisations to exploit the knowledge and skills they possess in an efficient way to ensure their survival. Knowledge has become an important factor in creating and maintaining a competitive advantage in this dynamic and turbulent business environment (Davis, Subrahmanian & Westerberg 2005:109).

Knowledge as a resource is scarce and valuable only when it is used (Forcadell & Guadamillas 2002:163). Knowledge should therefore be considered as a strategically important resource (Grant 1996, as quoted in Forcadell & Guadamillas 2002:163). Knowledge management can, in effect, be defined as the management of a highly valuable organisational resource, explaining why: 'making the most from their knowledge has always been organizations' Holy Grail' (Sultan 2013:160).

According to Du Plessis (2008), KM should be viewed as a process for managing an enterprise's intellectual assets, as it is a:

> planned, structured approach to manage the creation, sharing, harvesting and leveraging of knowledge as an organisational asset, to enhance a company's ability, speed and effectiveness in delivering products or services for the benefit of clients, in line with its business strategy. (p. 286)

Dana, Korot and Tovstiga (2005:10) define KM as the management of the integration of organisational information and ideas to generate value for the organisation by facilitating the sharing of knowledge and, through this, promoting continuous organisational learning. Van Bereven (2002) and Robbins (2003) define KM as the process that can be utilised to collect and distribute the collective wisdom within an organisation for the relevant people, to make critical decisions, linking KM strategy to business strategy (López-Nicolás & Meroño-Cerdán 2011:503). KM is also described as a process that can promote and facilitate the sharing of knowledge within an organisation (Singh 2008:5) to assist organisations that want to maintain or achieve a competitive advantage in ensuring that the KM strategies implemented are managed efficiently (Ndlela & Du Toit 2001:155).

The culture within an organisation has to promote knowledge sharing and transfer to ensure a successful KM strategy (Ndlela & Du Toit 2001:160); the increasing relevance of knowledge as a critical organisational resource has encouraged managers to pay greater attention to their organisations' KM strategies (Choi, Poon & Davis 2008:235). Managers are realising the value of KM, since it exposes employees to alternative practices and problem-solving techniques and it can be used to combine 'depth and richness' of experience (Jayawarna and Holt 2009:775).

A successful KM strategy can produce the necessary organisational information required to get the job done better and more efficiently than before (Call 2005:20) and allows improvement of an organisation's learning capability (Forcadell & Guadamillas 2002:162). Finally, KM is strategically important as it can be used as a managerial tool to promote knowledge creation and sharing, which are essential in promoting the innovation process within an organisation (Constantinescu 2009:7) as organisational knowledge plays an important role in the innovation process (López-Nicolás & Merono-Cerdán 2011:502).

Research methodology

A quantitative research methodology was chosen to measure employees' perceptions of KM within Sasol. A survey was distributed to employees of varying years of experience, education levels, races and genders. For the purpose of this research, non-probability convenience sampling was chosen to test if the employees' perceptions of KM are affected by their age, level of education and level of seniority. Convenience sampling was selected to ensure that the sample of the target population represented Sasol R&D employees' perceptions of KM. The target population for this research was 200 employees with varying levels of seniority and education within Sasol R&D, which is based in Sasolburg, South Africa.

The sampling approach aimed to represent all selected categories of employees and to establish whether there are any links that can contribute to shaping the employees' perceptions of KM within Sasol R&D. The questionnaire was distributed to over 150 employees in Sasol R&D and others who work closely with R&D in support functions, but are still part of the Sasol Technology organisation. The questionnaire was web deployed via SurveyMonkey®, an online survey deployment tool. A web-based survey was selected as the targeted population had access to the internet and were computer literate enough to complete the questionnaire without assistance. The completed questionnaires were then captured by STATCON (the Statistical Consultation Services at the University of Johannesburg) for processing and conversion into numerical format for statistical analysis.

Analysis and interpretation of the empirical findings

The sample population

The target population for this research included 200 employees with different levels of seniority and education in Sasol R&D, based in Sasolburg. The sample was chosen to represent all categories of employees and to establish whether there are any criteria that contribute to shaping employees' perceptions of KM within Sasol R&D. The questionnaire was distributed in 2011, to a sample of 150 employees in Sasol R&D and 50 more who work closely with R&D in support functions and are still part of the Sasol Technology organisation.

Table 1 presents some detail of the 54 employees who responded; three employees preferred not to disclose their gender. The total response rate was 36%.

Understanding knowledge management in Sasol research and development

Since the objective of this study was to establish Sasol R&D employees' perceptions of the current KM strategy within Sasol R&D, it was important to establish whether the respondents were familiar with the concept of KM and whether they were familiar with the current KM strategy. Of the respondents, 80% indicated that they were familiar with the concept of KM; only 15% indicated no knowledge of KM or uncertainty relating to KM. Most of the respondents (67%) indicated that they have knowledge of the current KM strategy within Sasol R&D.

Ndlela and Du Toit (2001:164) highlight the assigning of a knowledge leader to any KM initiative as very important. The knowledge leader usually plays the role of a 'knowledge champion' with support from top management. This role: 'should not be made a separate portfolio but the knowledge champion should encourage development of knowledge management qualities in individuals throughout the enterprise'. Jones, Herschel and Moesel (2003:59) mention that knowledge champions: 'work with innovators and opinion leaders to institutionalise and codify new knowledge' in such a way that adds value and renders the knowledge useful and logical within the organisation.

In Sasol R&D, only 23% of the respondents indicated that they understood the duty of the KM champions (the individuals acting as KM catalysts) to a moderate and large extent. The majority of respondents (60%) indicated that they

TABLE 1: A demographic distribution of respondents based on race and gender.

Gender	Number of respondents	% participation of total sample	% participation per gender
Black women	6	11.1	24.0
Black men	5	9.3	18.5
White women	15	27.8	60.0
White men	17	31.5	63.0
Indian women	4	7.4	16.0
Indian men	4	7.4	14.8
Other	3	5.6	-
Total	54	100	-

understood the duties of KM champions to a small or to no extent. This is concerning, since employees take their lead from KM champions and thus a clear understanding of what these KM champions can deliver is crucial.

When respondents were asked whether they perceived KM as important in Sasol R&D, 61% indicated they did perceive KM as important in this facility; however, 52% indicated that they were not familiar with Sasol R&D's KM strategy. This confirms that, even though Sasol R&D employees recognised that KM was an important asset to Sasol R&D, a large number of employees were not familiar with the strategy to ensure the effective management of knowledge.

The perceived value of knowledge management

Respondents were asked whether they thought KM can give an organisation a competitive advantage; 72% of respondents agreed that KM can give an organisation a competitive advantage. Employees also saw the value of KM to individual employees: 24% and 46% of respondents indicated that KM can improve the contribution of individual employees to a 'large extent' and 'moderate extent', respectively. The positive perceptions illustrated by these results bode well for Sasol R&D, as KM should be a voluntary activity: 'the value proposition should be sold to them so that they can see the benefit of knowledge management' (Du Plessis 2008:289).

Furthermore, according to 44% of respondents, KM has improved the innovation of Sasol R&D employees and 35% of respondents indicated that the current KM strategy has improved knowledge transfer amongst Sasol R&D employees in general. It should be noted that the time frame of employment for respondents ranged from one year, to 23 years. This indicates general perceptions by Sasol R&D employees that KM in fact adds value to the organisation.

The R&D facility of an innovative organisation embodies the knowledge-based capability of the organisation that wants to maintain and sustain competitive advantage (Jackson, Hitt & Denisi 2003). An innovative organisation is continuously learning and improving the employees' capabilities and skills to ensure that the competitive advantage of the organisation is sustained. Most of the respondents (80%) agreed that KM is the foundation of a learning organisation whilst 72% indicated that KM can help the organisation's competitive advantage. The majority of respondents (70%) indicated that KM can improve knowledge sharing within Sasol R&D. The overall perception that is reflected by employees' responses is that KM is a valuable strategy to have within Sasol R&D because it can improve the employees output and, therefore, the organisations' competitive advantage and profitability.

Management and the knowledge management strategy

In order for a KM initiative, such as developing and implementing a KM strategy, to be successful, top-level support is crucial; without this level of support, a KM initiative will never work (Bishop *et al.* 2008:23). Du Plessis (2008:288) highlights the importance of the involvement of organisational management in KM initiatives by stating that management support of KM initiatives: 'creates trust and respect amongst other members of staff, which makes it easier for staff to participate'. The active support of KM initiative by management also creates: 'a feeling of integrity in the organisation and recognition for the knowledge they share' (Du Plessis, 2008:288).

It was evident from the results that a significant number of respondents (41%) were of the opinion that management took KM initiatives within Sasol R&D seriously. However, 41% of the respondents were of the opinion that management promotes a KM culture to a 'small' or to 'no extent'; only 24% of the respondents indicated that management promoted a KM culture to 'a moderate extent'. This is concerning, since the organisational culture sets the tone of knowledge sharing and ultimately KM within the organisation.

Almost half (48%) of the respondents, also indicated that they are of the opinion that the Sasol R&D KM strategy does not reach employees. This illustrates the disconnect that employees feel towards the current KM strategy, indicating that they do not feel part of the initiative. Further reiterating this conclusion, more than half of the respondents (56%) were of the opinion that management only involves employees in Sasol R&D KM initiatives to a 'small extent' or to 'no extent'. Based on these findings, it can be argued that the concern is not necessarily that Sasol R&D management does not regard KM as important, but that their commitment to these initiatives are not relayed to the employees and therefore are not significantly evident in the organisational culture that Sasol R&D management promotes.

Conclusion

It was established that R&D facilities are dependent on knowledge to develop systems that can enhance productivity and performance within an organisation and to develop new and improve existing technologies. It was also established that the perceptions that R&D employees have regarding the use and management of knowledge is important since KM should be a voluntary activity. The importance of knowledge within R&D facilities and the perceptions that R&D employees have of how this knowledge is managed is therefore clear.

This study specifically aimed to establish the perceptions that Sasol R&D employees have of KM in their organisation. The study also assessed the manner in which Sasol R&D management is perceived to interact with knowledge, mainly through the implementation of a KM strategy. In general, it was discovered that Sasol R&D employees have a positive perceptions of the value that KM can add to their organisation, both on a strategic and an individual level.

A concern highlighted by the study was that Sasol R&D employees were not aware of the duties of the identified KM champions within their facility, which could potentially lead to knowledge gaps or a lack of knowledge sharing. As mentioned, this finding is concerning, since employees take their lead from KM champions and thus a clear understanding of what these KM champions can deliver is crucial.

As far as Sasol R&D management's perceived contribution to creating a KM culture is concerned, it was established that Sasol R&D management regard KM as important, but that their commitment to the KM initiatives is not necessarily evident to employees. This lack of apparent support is the reason for the lack of a knowledge sharing organisational culture, which Sasol R&D management essentially promotes.

In conclusion, it can be noted that the importance of KM is understood by Sasol R&D employees and management alike. Sasol R&D employees need to be made aware of the duties of KM champions in order to take advantage of the services relating to KM that these individuals can offer. Finally, Sasol R&D management needs to be more visible in its support of the facility's KM initiatives, specifically all processes relating to the KM strategy. Management should also actively involve Sasol R&D employees in the development of a KM strategy and subsequently the revision of such a strategy after implementation. Once this has been achieved, the benefits drawn from the KM strategy can aid Sasol R&D in enhancing productivity and performance within the facility and it can support employees in developing innovative new technologies whilst continuously improving those that already exist.

Acknowledgements

Competing interests

The authors declare that they have no financial or personal relationship(s) that may have inappropriately influenced them in writing this article.

Authors' contributions

T.D. (University of Johannesburg) conducted this study at Sasol towards the completion of his dissertation for the MCom in Business Management degree. C.R. (University of Johannesburg) and A.P. (University of Johannesburg) acted as supervisor and co-supervisor respectively.

References

Bishop, J., Bouchlaghem, D., Glass, J. & Matsumoto, I., 2008, 'Ensuring the effectiveness of a knowledge management initiative', *Journal of Knowledge Management* 12(4), 16–29. http://dx.doi.org/10.1108/13673270810884228

Call, D., 2005, 'Knowledge management – not rocket science', *Journal of Knowledge Management* 9(2), 19–30. http://dx.doi.org/10.1108/13673270510590191

Choi, B., Poon, S.K. & Davis, J.G., 2008, 'Effects of knowledge management strategy on organizational performance: A complementary theory-based approach', *Omega The International Journal of Management Science* 36(4), 235–251. http://dx.doi.org/10.1016/j.omega.2006.12.003

Constantinescu, M., 2009, 'Knowledge management: Focus on innovation and labour productivity in a knowledge-based economy', *The Icfai University Journal of Knowledge Management* VII(1), 7–33.

Dana, L., Korot, L. & Tovstiga, G., 2005, 'A cross-national comparison of knowledge management practices', *International Journal of Manpower* 26(1), 10–22. http://dx.doi.org/10.1108/01437720510587244

Davis, J., Subrahmanian, E. & Westerberg, A.W., 2005, 'The "global" and "local" in knowledge management', *Journal of Knowledge Management* 9(1), 101–112. http://dx.doi.org/10.1108/13673270510582992

De Wet-Viljoen, S., 2006, *Internal benchmarking best practices identified*, Sasol Technology, Johannesburg.

Draulans, J., De Man, A.P. & Volberda, H.W., 2003, 'Building alliance capability management techniques for superior alliance performance', *Long Range Planning* 36(2), 155–166. http://dx.doi.org/10.1016/S0024-6301(02)00173-5

Du Plessis, M., 2008, 'What bars organisations from managing knowledge successfully?', *International Journal of Information Management* 28(4), 285–292. http://dx.doi.org/10.1016/j.ijinfomgt.2008.02.006

Forcadell, F.J. & Guadamillas, F., 2002, 'A case study on the implementation of a knowledge management strategy oriented to innovation', *Knowledge and Process Management* 9(3), 162–171. http://dx.doi.org/10.1002/kpm.143

Foss, N.J., Husted, K. & Michailova, S., 2010, 'Governing knowledge sharing in organizations: Levels of analysis, governance mechanisms, and research directions', *Journal of Management Studies* 47(3), 455–482. http://dx.doi.org/10.1111/j.1467-6486.2009.00870.x

Guo, Z. & Sheffield, J., 2008, 'A paradigmatic and methodological examination of knowledge management research: 2000 to 2004', *Decision Support Systems* 44(3), 673–688. http://dx.doi.org/10.1016/j.dss.2007.09.006

Huang, C., 2009, 'Knowledge sharing and group cohesiveness on performance: An empirical study of technology R&D teams in Taiwan', *Technovation* 29(11), 768–797. http://dx.doi.org/10.1016/j.technovation.2009.04.003

Jackson, S.E., Hitt. M.A. & Denisi. A.S., 2003, *Managing knowledge for sustained competitive advantage: Designing strategies for effective human resources management*, HB Printing, USA.

Jayawarna, D. & Holt, R., 2009, 'Knowledge and quality management: An R&D perspective', *Technovation* 29(11), 775–785. http://dx.doi.org/10.1016/j.technovation.2009.04.004

Jones, N.B., Herschel, R.T. & Moesel, D.D., 2003, 'Using "knowledge champions" to facilitate knowledge management', *Journal of Knowledge Management* 7(1), 49–63. http://dx.doi.org/10.1108/13673270310463617

Kumaraswamy, M.M., Palaneeswaran, E., Rahman, M.M., Ugwu, O.O., & Ng, S.T., 2006, 'Synergising R&D initiatives for e-enhancing management support systems', *Automation in Construction* 15(6), 681–692. http://dx.doi.org/10.1016/j.autcon.2005.10.001

Lee, H.J., Kim, J.W. & Koh, J., 2009, 'A contingent approach on knowledge portal design for R&D teams: Relative importance of knowledge portal functionalities', *Expert Systems with Applications* 36(2), 3662–3670. http://dx.doi.org/10.1016/j.eswa.2008.02.061

Lopes, I.T., 2008, 'Towards an electronic knowledge management culture', *The Icfai University Journal of Knowledge Management* 6(4), 7–28.

López-Nicolás, C. & Meroño-Cerdán, A.L., 2011, 'Strategic knowledge management, innovation and performance', *International Journal of Information Management* 31(6), 502–509. http://dx.doi.org/10.1016/j.ijinfomgt.2011.02.003

Massa, S. & Testa, S., 2009, 'A knowledge management approach to organizational competitive advantage: Evidence from the food sector', *European Management Journal* 27(2), 129–141. http://dx.doi.org/10.1016/j.emj.2008.06.005

Mrinalini, N. & Nath, P., 2008, 'Knowledge management in research and technology organizations in a globalized era', *Perspectives on Global Development and Technology* 7(1), 37–54. http://dx.doi.org/10.1163/156914907X253206

Ndlela, L.T. & Du Toit, A.S.A., 2001, 'Establishing a knowledge management programme for competitive advantage in an enterprise', *International Journal of Information Management* 21(2), 151–165. http://dx.doi.org/10.1016/S0268-4012(01)00007-X

Potgieter, A., Dube, T.I. & Rensleigh, C.W., 2012, 'The perception and practice of knowledge management in a research and development facility', *The 8th International Conference on Knowledge Management Proceedings*, Johannesburg, South Africa, September 4–6, 2012, pp. 198–203.

Robbins, S.P., 2003, *Organizational Behaviour*, 10th edn., Prentice-Hall, Upper Saddle River.

Sambamurthy, V. & Subramani, M., 2005, 'Special issue on information technologies and knowledge management', *MIS Quarterly* 29(2), 193–195.

Sanghani, P., 2008, 'Does organization size matter for starting knowledge management program?', *The Icfai University Journal of Knowledge Management* 6(1), 7–20.

Schultze, U. & Leidner, D.E., 2002, 'Studying knowledge management in information systems research: discourses and theoretical assumptions', *MIS Quarterly* 26(3), 213–242. http://dx.doi.org/10.2307/4132331

Shin, M., 2004, 'A framework for evaluating economics of knowledge management systems', *Information and Management* 42(1), 179–196. http://dx.doi.org/10.1016/j.im.2003.06.006

Singh, S.J., 2008, 'Role of leadership in knowledge management: A study', *Journal of Knowledge Management* 12(4), 3–15. http://dx.doi.org/10.1108/13673270810884219

Sultan, N., 2013, 'Knowledge management in the age of cloud computing and Web 2.0: Experiencing the power of disruptive innovations', *International Journal of Information Management* 33(5), 160–165. http://dx.doi.org/10.1016/j.ijinfomgt.2013.05.010

Teng, B., 2007, 'Managing intellectual property in R&D alliances', *International Journal of Technology Management* 38(1), 160–177. http://dx.doi.org/10.1504/IJTM.2007.012434

Van Beveren, J., 2002, 'A model of knowledge acquisition that refocuses knowledge', *Journal of Knowledge Management* 6(1), 18–23. http://dx.doi.org/10.1108/13673270210417655

Van der Spek, R. & Kingma, J., 2000, 'Achieving successful knowledge management initiatives', in J. Reeves (ed.), *Liberating knowledge*, pp. 20–30, Caspian, London.

23

The impact of shared domain knowledge on strategic information systems planning and alignment

Authors:
Simla Maharaj[1]
Irwin Brown[1]

Affiliations:
[1]Department of Information Systems, University of Cape Town, South Africa

Correspondence to:
Irwin Brown

Email:
irwin.brown@uct.ac.za

Postal address:
Private Bag, Rondebosch 7701, South Africa

Background: Lack of alignment or harmony between information technology (IT) and business imperatives continues to plague organisations despite decades of research. Strategic information systems planning (SISP) is the process of coordinating the relationship between IT and the business in order to steer alignment. Shared domain knowledge (SDK) is a factor that is posited as important for improving both SISP and alignment, which is theorised to be the main outcome of SISP.

Objectives: The aim of this article is to examine the impact of SDK on SISP and alignment.

Method: Data were gathered from management consultants in a large, global IT organisation, through the use of a structured questionnaire, and analysed.

Results: It was shown that SDK positively influences SISP characteristics and the alignment outcome. Specifically, it was found that high levels of rationality in SISP positively influenced the intellectual dimension of alignment, whilst IT manager participation in business planning influenced the social dimension of alignment. SDK was found to have a bearing on all of the SISP characteristics measured (i.e. rationality, adaptation, business planning-SISP integration and IT manager participation in business planning). SDK was also found to positively impact both the intellectual and social dimensions of alignment.

Conclusion: The implications of the findings are that fostering a knowledge sharing environment in organisations will help improve alignment, as well as the formal processes designed to steer alignment such as SISP.

Introduction

Strategic information systems planning (SISP) has been established as a core activity in the governance and management of information technology (IT) in organisations (Bechor *et al.* 2010; Hayward 2013). SISP is carried out in organisations primarily as a means to improve the level of alignment between IT and business strategies and objectives (Karanja & Patel 2012). Both SISP and business-IT alignment have been consistently ranked as key issues amongst IT managers globally, which highlights the importance of research into these phenomena (Luftman *et al.* 2013). SISP can be seen as the *process* by which alignment is achieved and is variously referred to as information systems strategic planning (ISSP), information systems (IS) strategy development or formation (i.e. formulation and implementation) and IS strategising (Peppard, Galliers & Thorogood 2014). Business-IT alignment has been theorised to be a key *outcome* of SISP (Lederer & Salmela 1996; Osman, El Beltagi & Hardaker 2013; Yang, Pita & Singh 2014). Business-IT alignment, when viewed as an outcome of SISP, is defined as the state in which IT and business plans and strategies are coherently interrelated, as well as the degree to which there is congruence of vision between business and IT executives on business and IT strategy (Reich & Benbasat 2000; Silvius 2013).

Shared domain knowledge (SDK) between business and IT executives is known to enhance efficiency and effectiveness of strategic IT management processes such as SISP (Ranganathan & Sethi 2002). There is evidence too that SDK has a direct impact on business-IT alignment, that is, there is not only an indirect impact through SISP (Preston & Karahanna 2009). The purpose of this research is hence to interrogate the various direct and indirect relationships between SDK, SISP and business-IT alignment in order to gain a better understanding of the dynamics between these important factors (Leonard & Seddon 2012). The research question posed is: *What is the impact of shared domain knowledge on strategic information systems planning and its effectiveness, as measured by alignment?*

In the next section the key concepts underpinning the study will be elucidated, after which the research model is established. The methodology by which data were collected and analysed is then outlined after which the results are presented. Discussion and implications of the results follow, then the article is concluded.

Conceptual background

Shared domain knowledge, strategic information systems planning characteristics and *business-IT alignment* and their interrelationships are the focus of attention in this study, so each will be discussed logically in turn.

Shared domain knowledge (SDK)

SDK is defined as the ability of IT and business executives to mutually understand the key processes in the domains of business and IT respectively and to be able to mutually contribute and participate meaningfully in the activities of each domain (Chan, Sabherwal & Thatcher 2006). Related concepts that have received attention in literature include shared knowledge and knowledge sharing (Kearns & Lederer 2003; Pai 2005; Preston & Karahanna 2009; Reich & Benbasat 2000). Shared knowledge is described as 'an understanding and appreciation among IT and line managers for the technologies and processes that affect their mutual performance' (Reich & Benbasat 2000), whilst Pai (2005) describes knowledge sharing as 'a set of behaviours that involve the exchange of information or assistance to others'. Implicit in our definition of SDK are the elements of shared knowledge and knowledge sharing; hence, literature related to the latter two concepts has relevance to discussions of SDK too (Preston & Karahanna 2009). A strong environment and culture of knowledge sharing is argued to be conducive to effective strategising (Teubner 2013). Kearns and Lederer (2003) examined how knowledge sharing (represented by the transfer of knowledge between CIO and CEO) assists in generating competitive advantage. SDK and knowledge sharing have been shown to be key considerations in achieving alignment between business and IT objectives (Chan *et al.* 2006; Pai 2005; Preston & Karahanna 2009; Reich & Benbasat 2000; Tan & Gallupe 2006). Ranganathan and Sethi (2002) examined the impact of SDK on rationality in strategic IT decisions and found a strong and positive influence. Whilst issues such as competitive advantage, alignment and rationality in decision-making are associated with SISP, there have been few studies that explicitly link SDK to SISP; hence, there still remains a research gap on how these phenomena interrelate. The next section discusses key characteristics associated with SISP.

Strategic information systems planning (SISP) and its characteristics

Improving SISP has persisted as a key issue for IT executives for several decades now (Luftman *et al.* 2013); hence, research on this phenomenon remains relevant to pursue. SISP is defined as a strategic endeavour that involves identification of a prioritised portfolio of IT applications for an enterprise, together with the necessary infrastructure, resources, organisational structure and change management considerations necessary for implementation (Baker 1995 as cited by Brown 2004; Teubner 2013). This definition for SISP has persisted for over two decades, which demonstrates that SISP is an enduring activity for IT management in a dynamic and rapidly evolving field.

Whilst there are a large number of methodologies to choose from when carrying out SISP, common to most are several key phases and activities. These methodology-independent phases include strategic awareness (preparing for the SISP process), situational analysis (analysing the external and internal business and IS environment), strategy conception (conceiving and evaluating alternative scenarios), strategy formulation (selecting a strategy) and implementation planning (Mirchandani & Lederer 2014; Newkirk & Lederer 2006).

It has been found that success of SISP varies depending on the characteristics of the SISP approach being used in an organisation (Grover & Segars 2005; Osman *et al.* 2013; Silvius & Stoop 2013). Key SISP characteristics include the levels of rationality, adaptation and integration with business planning (Segars & Grover 1999; Teo & King 1997). SISP approaches exhibiting high levels of rationality, adaptation and integration have been found to be the most successful, especially in the context of a volatile environment (Grovers & Segars 2005). The typical measure of SISP success is the extent of business-IT alignment achieved (Sylvius 2013).

Rationality in SISP is recognised by comprehensiveness in decision-making, a top-down flow of decision-making, a focus on control and a high degree of formalisation (Chen *et al.* 2010; Segars & Grover 1999). Adaptation is evidenced by frequent meetings to consider and revise plans and broad participation of stakeholders (Segars & Grover 1999). Business planning-IS planning (BP-ISP) integration varies from having no integration at one extreme to a fully integrated process at the other extreme. Table 1 provides detailed definitions of these elements.

An aspect that is related to BP-ISP integration, but deserves separate consideration in the context of SISP is the level of IT manager participation in business planning (Kearns & Lederer 2003). Whilst organisations may have mechanisms and structures for BP-ISP integration, the level of IT manager participation in business planning may still vary. For example, an IT manager may be present at business planning sessions, but if not fully part of the proceedings, and if their voice is not taken in to account, then participation and involvement of IT managers will still be low (Cordoba 2009).

Strategic information systems planning (SISP) effectiveness – Alignment

SISP effectiveness has been defined as the extent to which key planning objectives have been fulfilled (Premkumar & King 1994). Key objectives of SISP include alignment between business and IT objectives, analysis of the business and IT environment, improved cooperation between stakeholders to ensure plan implementation and

TABLE 1: Strategic information systems planning process — Characteristics.

Characteristic	Definition
Comprehensiveness	The extent to which an organisation attempts to be exhaustive or inclusive in making and integrating decisions
Flow	The locus of authority or devolution of responsibilities for strategic planning (top-down, bottom-up, interactive)
Focus	The balance between creativity and control orientations inherent within the strategic planning system
Formalisation	The existence of structures, techniques, written procedures and policies that guide the planning process
Frequency	The frequency of planning activities or cycles and, relatedly, the frequency of evaluation and revision of strategic choices (occasional vs continuous)
Participation	The breadth of involvement in strategic planning (narrow vs wide)
BP-ISP integration	The level of integration between business planning and SISP (business-led, IT-led, reciprocal, full integration or proactive) (Reich & Benbasat 2000; Teo & King 1997)
IT manager participation in business planning	IT manager attendance, participation and involvement in business planning (Kearns & Sabherwal 2007)

Sources: Grover, V. & Segars, A.H., 2005, 'An empirical evaluation of stages of strategic information systems planning: Patterns of process design and effectiveness', *Information & Management* 42, 761–779. http://dx.doi.org/10.1016/j.im.2004.08.002; Teo, T. & King, W., 1997, 'Integration between business planning and information systems planning: An evolutionary contingency perspective', *Journal of Management Information Systems* 14(1), 185–214.

improvements in organisational capability to carry out SISP (Segars & Grover 1999; Yang *et al.* 2014). From amongst these objectives, alignment has been persistently noted as the key objective of SISP (Chen *et al.* 2010; Karanja & Patel 2012; Silvius 2013).

The concept of alignment is broad and multi-faceted (Chan & Reich 2007). Alignment can be viewed as a process or an outcome (Karpovsky & Galliers 2015). The perspective adopted in this study is that it is the outcome of SISP. When viewed as an outcome of SISP, key dimensions of alignment have been identified as the intellectual and social dimension (Reich & Benbasat 2000). The intellectual dimension is defined as the state in which a set of high-quality interrelated business plans and IT plans exist (Reich & Benbasat 1996). The social dimension refers to the state in which IT and business executives understand and are committed to the business and IT mission, objectives and plans (Reich & Benbasat 2000). Reich and Benbasat (2000) further distinguish between short-term social alignment – the degree of mutual understanding between business and IT executives of business and IT objectives – and long-term alignment – the congruence of shared vision between business and IT executives. Few studies have considered both the intellectual and social dimensions in one study, due to a lack of conceptual clarity around these dimensions and their measurement (Chan & Reich 2007; Schlosser, Wagner & Coltman 2012).

Hypothesis development

Drawing from the literature on SDK, SISP and alignment, a set of hypotheses to be tested were derived. These will be discussed in turn.

BP-ISP integration and alignment

Reich and Benbasat (2000) demonstrated a positive relationship between BP-ISP integration and the social dimension of alignment. BP-ISP integration is also expected to have an impact on the intellectual dimension of alignment. For example Brown (2004) suggests that greater BP-ISP integration yields a more useful and comprehensive IS plan, signalling high levels of intellectual alignment. Hence the following hypotheses are supported:

H1: BP-ISP integration positively influences the social dimension of alignment

H2: BP-ISP integration positively influences the intellectual dimension of alignment

SISP rational-adaptation and alignment

Grover and Segars (2005) demonstrate that a process characterised by high levels of both rationality and adaptation is associated with successful SISP. Success was measured in their study by assessing, amongst other elements, alignment. The measure of alignment they used included items relating to both the intellectual and social dimensions, hence supporting the following hypotheses:

H3: Rationality in SISP positively influences the social dimension of alignment

H4: Rationality in SISP positively influences the intellectual dimension of alignment

H5: Adaptation in SISP positively influences the social dimension of alignment

H6: Adaptation in SISP positively influences the intellectual dimension of alignment

IT manager participation in business planning and alignment

IT manager participation in business planning has been shown to lead to positive outcomes such as achieving alignment (Chi *et al.* 2005; Kearns & Lederer 2003; Kearns & Sabherwal 2007). There needs to be caution against paying lip service to the concept of participation (Cordoba 2009), for example inviting the IT manager to be part of business planning activities, but not taking on board their suggestions and input:

H7: IT manager participation in business planning positively influences the social dimension of alignment

H8: IT manager participation in business planning positively influences the intellectual dimension of alignment

Shared domain knowledge and SISP characteristics

The benefits of SDK for IT strategic management have been well reported. Ranganathan and Sethi (2002) demonstrate its positive impact on rationality in strategic IT decision-making. Rationality was operationalised by dimensions of comprehensiveness and formalisation, attributes noticeable in a rational SISP process (Segars & Grover 1999). SDK has been associated with IT manager participation in business planning and business manager participation in SISP (Kearns & Sabherwal 2007; Reich & Benbasat 2000); a characteristic of SISP adaptation is business participation in SISP (Grover & Segars 2005). SDK has also been associated with BP-ISP integration (Kearns & Sabherwal 2007; Reich & Benbasat 2000). Hence, the following hypotheses are supported:

H9: Shared domain knowledge positively influences rationality in SISP

H10: Shared domain knowledge positively influences adaptation in SISP

H11: Shared domain knowledge positively influences BP-ISP integration

H12: Shared domain knowledge positively influences IT manager participation in business planning

Shared domain knowledge and alignment

A lack of shared knowledge between business and IT is argued to be one of the key challenges to achieving alignment (Chan & Reich 2007). Chan *et al.* (2006) demonstrate the effect of SDK on the intellectual dimension of alignment, whilst Reich and Benbasat (2000) and Preston and Karahanna (2009) demonstrate this impact on the social dimension of alignment in the long term and short term respectively. Hypotheses supported are:

H13: Shared domain knowledge positively influences the social dimension of alignment

H14: Shared domain knowledge positively influences the intellectual dimension of alignment

The conceptual model illustrating these 14 hypotheses is illustrated in Figure 1.

Research methodology

The research methodology followed a positivist, quantitative, hypothetico-deductive approach. Further details on the research instrument, the data collection process and the data analysis procedure are provided in this section.

Development of the measures for research constructs

The measures used in this study were based on validated instruments from relevant studies (Cohen & Toleman 2006; Kearns & Lederer 2003; Kearns & Sabherwal 2007; Ranganathan & Sethi 2002; Reich & Benbasat 2000; Segars & Grover 1999; Teo & King 1997). These measures and their sources are illustrated in Appendix 1. A seven-point Likert scale ranging from 1 for 'strongly disagree' to 7 for 'strongly agree' was employed in the questionnaire for all items except BP-ISP integration, which employed a typology of integration modes as per Teo and King (1997).

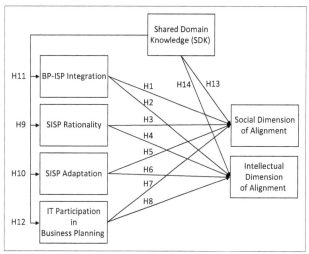

FIGURE 1: Conceptual model.

SDK was measured using the Ranganathan and Sethi (2002) instrument supplemented by measures from Kearns and Sabherwal (2007). SISP rationality was operationalised in this study by the dimensions of comprehensiveness and formalisation as in Ranganathan and Sethi (2002). The measurement scales for comprehensiveness and formalisation were adapted from instruments developed by Segars and Grover (1999). For the higher order characteristic of SISP adaptation, dimensions of participation and frequency were used, again using measures developed by Segars and Grover (1999). IT manager participation in business planning was measured with the instrument developed by Kearns and Sabherwal (2007).

For BP-ISP integration the measure by Teo and King (1997) was used, which provided a typology of integration varying from administrative (little or no integration) to sequential (SISP follows business planning) to reciprocal (SISP and business planning are mutually interacting) to full integration (no separate SISP and business planning). Reich and Benbasat (2000) also identified proactive integration (SISP precedes business planning) as a type of integration, so this mode was also added to the measure. Respondents were asked to select which description most closely fitted the BP-ISP integration level in the organisation they were involved with.

The research questions used for measuring the social dimension of alignment construct were adapted from an instrument from a study by Cohen and Toleman (2006). This instrument included both short-term and long-term alignment measures. For measuring the intellectual dimension of alignment measures were adapted from an instrument by Kearns and Lederer (2003).

Data collection
Sampling

The target population for this study consisted of consultants from a large, global IT organisation who were based at companies that had conducted SISP in the last 10 years. These consultants had participated in SISP at the specific company in which they were based. Most studies in SISP rely on the views of the IT executive to represent the organisation, whilst a few also include the business executive. The views of external consultants are not often represented in SISP research. The advantage of obtaining a consultant perspective is that it may offer a perhaps less biased view of SISP in organisations than that of IT or business executives. Random sampling was used so that each population member had an equal chance of being selected. Three-hundred consultants from the large global IT organisation were asked to respond to the questionnaire.

Pilot testing

The questionnaire was first pre-tested by three academics with experience in this area of research. Wording of questions (such as tenses) was amended as a result. A pilot test was thereafter conducted with five IT consultants, three of whom were from the large, global IT organisation with two others from other organisations. Based on the feedback, some questions were reworded and some questions were removed as the respondents felt that they were repetitive. Generally, the questionnaire was well understood with positive feedback, for example that the instructions were clear and the length of the questionnaire was adequate. The changes that were suggested in the feedback were made accordingly and the final questionnaire was posted on a website to be used for data collection.

Data collection procedure

The online questionnaire was hosted on a general survey website and all consultants in the sample were sent an email which included the link to the questionnaire. Confidentiality of responses was assured and respondents were asked to provide their contact details in the survey if they wished to receive a copy of the findings of this study. Email reminders were sent every two weeks for one month to ensure that the maximum number of consultants answered the questionnaire. The responses to the questionnaire were saved to the website's database and downloads of the responses were available at all times.

Response rate

Three-hundred consultants from one large, global IT organisation were targeted for this survey and on closure of the online survey, a total of 175 consultants had responded to the survey. On analysis of the responses, it was found that 59 questionnaires were answered completely, representing a 19.7% response rate. Although low, this was deemed an acceptable response rate for this type of survey, as it is widely acknowledged that surveys targeting senior level managers and professionals suffer from low response rates. Other SISP survey-based studies have had similar response rates (e.g. Cohen 2008; Mirchandani & Lederer 2014).

Data analysis procedure

The first part of the data analysis process was to conduct basic descriptive statistics on the questionnaire responses.

Frequency tables based on the demographic data in the responses were developed. The next part of the data analysis was the execution of a factor analysis exercise to validate the items and to identify if there were any structures in the relationships between items. The Cronbach's alpha coefficient for the final set of research items was thereafter applied to test reliability. Finally the hypotheses developed in this study were tested using multiple linear regression.

Data analysis and results
Demographic profile

The demographic profile of the respondents is illustrated in the tables below. Table 2 reveals that 72% of the sample had senior executive experience and 74% had more than 10 years of IS experience. Approximately 90% of the respondents had up to 15 years of SISP experience with about 9% of the respondents having more than 15 years of SISP experience.

Diverse industries were represented in the sample. Manufacturing and finance had the most responses – about 32% and 31% of the sample respectively (Table 3). The transport, engineering, service, government, retail, communications and IT industries had less than 10% responses each, but together they accounted for about 35% of the responses. Other descriptive data revealed that most organisations were large in terms of annual revenue. About

TABLE 2: Level of experience of respondents.

Item	f	%
Level of management experience		
Junior	5	8.6
Middle	10	17.2
Senior	42	72.4
Number of years of IS experience		
<5	7	12.1
5–10	7	12.1
10–15	17	29.3
15–20	15	25.9
>20	11	19.0
Number of years of SISP experience		
<5	20	34.5
5–10	25	43.1
10–15	7	12.1
15–20	4	6.9
>20	1	1.7

TABLE 3: Industry in which SISP was conducted.

Industry	f	%
Manufacturing	19	32.8
Communications	5	8.6
Finance	18	31.0
Retail	1	1.7
IT	3	5.2
Government	4	6.9
Transport	3	5.2
Engineering	1	1.7
Service	3	5.2

f, frequency

38% had revenues in excess of USD 500 million and only 9% had revenues of less than USD 5 million.

Construct and discriminant validity

The questionnaire was derived from previously validated instruments, so confirmatory factor analysis (CFA) was used to assess construct and discriminant validity (Tan & Teo 2000). Commonly applied decision rules were used, including using a minimum eigenvalue of 1 as a cut-off value for extraction, deleting items with factor loadings of less than 0.5 on all factors, or greater than 0.5 on two or more factors, using varimax rotation and so on (Tan & Teo 2000). Through progressive refinement, a set of validated constructs emerged.

Appendix 2 shows the factor loadings achieved after elimination of items. SDK loaded on two factors – one related to business knowledge of IS (SDK_BUS) and the other related to IS knowledge of business (SDK_IS). Together these two sub-factors made up SDK. Also loading as distinct factors were SISP rationality (RATIONAL) and SISP adaptation (ADAPT). It was expected that rationality would have two sub-factors – comprehensiveness and formalisation – but these two loaded together as a single factor of rationality (RATIONAL), which was nevertheless consistent with their common underlying meaning. Adaptation too was expected to have two factors – participation and frequency – but once again it loaded as a single factor (ADAPT), which was again consistent with the commonality in meaning. IT manager participation in business planning (ISBP) loaded as a separate factor, as expected.

Amongst the alignment factors two major dimensions were expected – the social dimension of alignment and intellectual dimension of alignment. The social dimension had two separate sub-factors – long-term alignment (SOC_LT ALIGN) and short-term alignment (SOC_STALIGN). The intellectual dimension of alignment also had two sub-factors – IS plan-business plan alignment (INT_ISPBPALIGN) and business plan-IS plan alignment (INT_BPISPALIGN). The refined constructs thus exhibited adequate construct and discriminant validity.

Instrument reliability

In order to assess reliability of the refined instrument, the Cronbach's alpha was calculated for each construct (Tan & Teo 2000). Reliability is indicated if the Cronbach's alpha is greater than 0.7. The lowest Cronbach's alpha was 0.76, thus demonstrating that all measures exhibited reliability (see Appendix 2).

Items means and standard deviations

Table 4 shows that the mean for SDK is close to 5, which reveals that respondents on average agreed that IT and business executives had the ability to understand and were able to participate in the others' key processes and to respect

TABLE 4: Descriptive statistics.

Item	M	SD
Shared domain knowledge (SDK)	4.9	0.97
SISP rationality (RATIONAL)	4.4	1.13
SISP adaptation (ADAPT)	4.9	1.19
IT manager participation business planning (ISBP)	4.3	1.53
Social dimension of alignment	4.5	1.23
Intellectual dimension of alignment	4.5	1.23

M, mean; SD, standard deviation

each other's unique contribution and challenges. The mean scores for SISP rationality (RATIONAL) and IT manager participation in business planning (ISBP) were about 4, implying respondents were on average neutral with respect to the extent to which their organisations exhibited a high degree of rationality and participation in business planning. SISP adaptation (ADAPT), social alignment and intellectual alignment had means that were closer to 5. This reveals that respondents on average agreed that there was a high degree of SISP adaptation. They also agreed on average that there was a state within the respective companies where business and IT executives understood and were committed to the business and IT mission, objectives and plans, and they agreed on average that there was a close linkage between the IS strategy and business strategy.

BP-ISP integration types

In terms of BP-ISP integration, just over 48% of organisations exhibited sequential integration, which means that a sequential relationship existed between business planning and SISP, with IS plans primarily focused on providing support for business plans. About 19% of the companies exhibited administrative integration, which represents a weak relationship between business planning and SISP. About 16% of the companies exhibited reciprocal integration, representing a reciprocal and interdependent relationship between business planning and SISP, in which SISP plays a role in both supporting and influencing business plans. About 12% of the sample claimed there was full BP-ISP integration with little distinction between business planning processes and SISP processes. Only 5% of the sample showed proactive BP-ISP integration in which IS objectives precede the formulation of business objectives and are used as input to their development. Hence, all BP-ISP integration types were present, demonstrating the diversity of the sample.

Multiple linear regression

Multiple linear regression was used to test the 14 hypotheses formulated in this study. The dependent variables against which the independent variables were regressed were the social dimension of alignment, intellectual dimension of alignment and the SISP characteristics (rationality, adaptation, BP-ISP integration and IT manager participation in business planning). The common dependent variable was SDK. The results of the multiple linear regression are illustrated in Table 5 together with the associated hypotheses. p-values that were less than or equal to 0.05 were considered significant.

TABLE 5: Results of multiple linear regression.

Dependent item	Hypothesis	Independent item	Beta	p-level
Social dimension of alignment	H1	BP-ISP integration	−0.04	0.624
	H3	Rationality	0.15	0.124
	H5	Adaptation	0.07	0.550
	H7	*IT manager participation in business planning*	*0.55*	*0.000*
	H13	*SDK*	*0.25*	*0.022*
Intellectual dimension of alignment	H2	BP-ISP integration	0.05	0.620
	H4	*Rationality*	*0.26*	*0.026*
	H6	Adaptation	0.05	0.726
	H7	IT manager participation in business planning	0.21	0.091
SISP characteristics	*H14*	*SDK*	*0.38*	*0.006*
Rationality	*H9*	*SDK*	*0.41*	*0.001*
Adaptation	*H10*	*SDK*	*0.68*	*0.000*
BP-ISP integration	*H11*	*SDK*	*0.52*	*0.000*
IT manager participation in business planning	*H12*	*SDK*	*0.65*	*0.000*

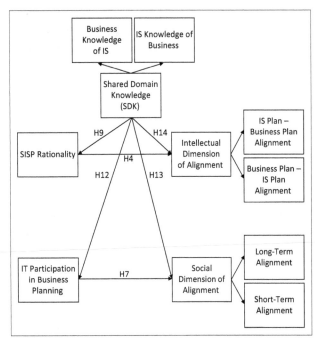

FIGURE 2: Refined conceptual model.

It was noticeable that all hypotheses concerning the impact of SDK (H9 to H14) were supported, meaning that SDK had an impact on all SISP characteristics (rationality, adaptation, BP-ISP integration and IT manager participation in business planning), as well SISP effectiveness (social dimension of alignment and intellectual dimension of alignment). In terms of the influence of SISP characteristics on alignment, the social dimension of alignment was impacted by IT manager participation in business planning only (H7) and not by rationality, adaptation or BP-ISP integration. The intellectual dimension of alignment was impacted by rationality only (H4) and not adaptation, BP-ISP integration or IT manager participation in business planning.

The results in Table 5 lead to the refined conceptual model, as shown in Figure 2. SISP adaptation and BP-ISP integration were only weakly associated with the alignment dimensions and so were removed from the model. The factor analysis revealed a two-factor structure for shared domain knowledge (business

knowledge of IS and IS knowledge of business), intellectual dimension of alignment (IS plan-business plan alignment and business plan-IS plan alignment) and the social dimension of alignment (long-term and short-term alignment).

Discussion and implications
SISP characteristics and alignment

The social and intellectual dimensions of alignment respectively were used as a measure of SISP effectiveness. The impact of the SISP characteristics of rationality, adaptation, BP-ISP integration and IT manager participation in business planning were tested. It was found that there was support only for IT manager participation in business planning positively influencing the social dimension of alignment. The positive influence arises because IT manager participation in business planning involves IT executives regularly attending business meetings, participating in setting business goals and objectives and being involved early in the meetings for major projects. All of these actions ultimately contribute to the social dimension of alignment: the shared vision of business and IS executives on the role of IS in the organisation and the mutual understanding of each other's domains. This finding is in keeping with the results of Kearns and Sabherwal (2006). The lack of influence of rationality, BP-ISP integration and adaptation would suggest that formalised SISP procedures, structural mechanisms for BP-ISP integration, business executive participation in SISP sessions and frequent SISP meetings are less useful for achieving social alignment. Business executives would likely not have time to attend too many SISP sessions, so a better strategy is for the IT manager to go to the business planning meetings and there make contributions for the strategic use of IT in organisations.

In terms of the influence of the aforementioned SISP characteristics on the intellectual dimension of alignment, there was only support for SISP rationality positively influencing intellectual alignment. So, a high level of comprehensiveness, formalised procedures and documentation of outputs in SISP ensures that the documented IS plan reflects the business mission and goals and supports the business strategies. In a like manner, it ensures that the business plan can refer to the

IS plan and that it utilises the strategic capability of IS and contains reasonable expectations of IS. The lack of influence of adaptation, BP-ISP integration and IT manager participation in business planning perhaps indicates that for achieving alignment on the intellectual level, the best strategy is a highly rational SISP process that follows a formal methodology and procedure and yields a comprehensive well-documented IS plan, with links and references to business plans and strategies.

In all, these findings yield interesting insights into the role of SISP in achieving alignment and how the different characteristics affect alignment. Segars and Grover (1999) show through cluster analysis that a SISP process characterised by rationality and adaptation is associated with SISP effectiveness (alignment, analysis, cooperation and capability improvement respectively). Their study never tests the relationships between the separate SISP characteristics and the separate dimensions of SISP effectiveness. This study makes a contribution by empirically testing the relationships between specific SISP characteristics and alignment and reveals that the rationality dimension of SISP is important for intellectual alignment, whilst for social alignment, the IT manager participation in business planning might be more important than a formal SISP process.

SDK and SISP characteristics

The SISP characteristics of rationality, adaptation, BP-ISP integration and IT manager participation in business planning have been shown to be important, not only to alignment, but also to other measures of SISP effectiveness such as analysis, cooperation, capability improvement, IS function performance, IS contribution to business performance and improved business performance itself (Kearns & Sabherwal 2007; Premkumar & King 1994; Segars & Grover 1999). Hence, it is important that ways of enhancing these characteristics are found. SDK was found to positively influence all of the aforementioned characteristics. Hence, improving SDK (i.e. IS knowledge of business and business knowledge of IS) provides for an important strategy for improving SISP in organisations.

SDK and SISP effectiveness – Alignment

With the overall SISP effectiveness being measured by the social dimension of alignment and the intellectual dimension of alignment, SDK was tested against both and it was found that there was support for SDK positively influencing both the social and intellectual dimensions of alignment. The findings suggest that achieving social alignment may not require a detailed formalised SISP process. Rather, through improving SDK in an organisation, a shared vision and shared understanding between business and IS executives can be achieved. Coupled with IT manager participation in business planning, which itself is strengthened by SDK, the social dimension of alignment can be strongly realised.

For achieving intellectual alignment a rational SISP process is still needed, but even in this case, SDK will be of complementary value both to improving levels of rationality and directly to improving the intellectual dimension of alignment.

Summary

In summary, the findings suggest that organisations should focus on creating a knowledge sharing environment between business and IT and seek for ways to strengthen IS knowledge of business and business knowledge of IS. In this way SISP characteristics and outcomes such as alignment will be improved.

Limitations and future research

The target population of this study consisted of consultants from one large, global IT organisation, based at various customer sites around the world, who participated or observed the SISP in the company where they were based. Even though the responses were based on various types of organisation from various industries, including responses from consultants only could be a limitation of this study. Bias could result from these consultants possibly having a deeper knowledge of IS, which could have resulted in them responding to the questionnaire from an IS perspective. A suggestion for further research could be to test the research model that was developed in this study by including various roles from business and IT in the target population. A further limitation is the small number of completed questionnaires on which the conclusions of this study were based. Even though there were 175 responses, only 59 of the 175 were complete. Future research could try to elicit a higher response rate in order to test if all the hypotheses in this study still hold true with more response data.

Conclusion

The objective of this study was to investigate the impact of SDK on SISP and its effectiveness, as measured by alignment. The research model included the examination of how SDK impacted the SISP process dimensions (rationality, adaptation, BP-ISP integration and IT manager participation in business planning), how the SISP process dimensions (rationality, adaptation, BP-ISP integration and IT manager participation in business planning) impacted SISP effectiveness (measured by social and intellectual alignment) and lastly how SDK impacted SISP effectiveness (i.e. alignment). Few, if any, studies have investigated all these facets in a single study.

On a methodological level, the study has contributed by demonstrating the validity and reliability of measures for investigating SISP characteristics, alignment and SDK, these being taken from disparate sources. The study reveals a two-factor structure for SDK (business knowledge of IS and IS knowledge of business), the intellectual dimension of alignment (IS plan-business plan alignment and vice versa) and the social dimension of alignment (long-term and short-term alignment respectively), in keeping with the conceptualisation of these constructs.

The study makes a theoretical contribution by revealing the impact of SISP on two dimensions of alignment – the social and intellectual respectively. In so doing it is shown that a formal, comprehensive rational SISP process is the key driver of the intellectual dimension of alignment, whilst the social dimension of alignment is more likely achievable by the IT manager participating in business planning rather than vice versa (i.e. business executives participating in SISP). Shared domain knowledge between business and IT executives positively influences both SISP and the dimensions of alignment.

These findings are of practical benefit, as three actions for organisations to implement can be garnered, these being: (1) improve rationality of SISP processes as a means to improving the intellectual dimension of alignment; (2) involve IT managers strategically in business planning to improve the social dimension of alignment; (3) establish a knowledge sharing culture and implement mechanisms to build shared domain knowledge in the organisation. Implementing these initiatives will improve both SISP and the aforementioned facets of alignment.

Acknowledgements

Competing interests

The authors declare that they have no financial or personal relationships that may have inappropriately influenced them in writing this article.

Authors' contributions

S.M. (University of Cape Town) conducted the overall study whilst registered as a student at the University of Cape Town. I.B. (University of Cape Town) supervised the study and contributed to writing the article.

References

Bechor, T., Neumann, S., Zviran, M. & Glezer, C., 2010, 'A contingency model for estimating success of strategic information systems planning', *Information & Management* 47(1), 17–29. http://dx.doi.org/10.1016/j.im.2009.09.004

Brown, I.T.J., 2004, 'Testing and extending theory in strategic information systems planning through literature analysis', *Information Resources Management Journal* 17(4), 19–47. http://dx.doi.org/10.4018/irmj.2004100102

Chan, Y.E. & Reich, B.H., 2007, 'IT alignment: What have we learned?', *Journal of Information Technology* 22(4), 297–315. http://dx.doi.org/10.1057/palgrave.jit.2000109

Chan, Y.E., Sabherwal, R. & Thatcher, J.B., 2006, 'Antecedents and outcomes of strategic IS alignment: An empirical investigation', *IEEE Transactions on Engineering Management* 53(1), 27–47. http://dx.doi.org/10.1109/TEM.2005.861804

Chen, D.Q., Mocker, M., Preston, D.S. & Teubner, A., 2010, 'Information systems strategy: Reconceptualization, measurement, and implications', *MIS Quarterly* 34(2), 233–259.

Chi, L., Jones, K.G., Lederer, A.L., Li, P., Newkirk, H.E. & Sethi, V., 2005, 'Environmental assessment in strategic information systems planning', *International Journal of Information Management* 25(3), 253–269. http://dx.doi.org/10.1016/j.ijinfomgt.2004.12.004

Cohen, J.F., 2008, 'Contextual determinants and performance implications of information systems strategy planning within South African firms', *Information & Management*, 45(8), 547–555. http://dx.doi.org/10.1016/j.im.2008.09.001

Cohen, J.F. & Toleman, M., 2006, 'The IS–business relationship and its implications for performance: An empirical study of South African and Australian organisations', *International Journal of Information Management* 26, 457–468. http://dx.doi.org/10.1016/j.ijinfomgt.2006.06.002

Cordoba, J.R., 2009, 'Critical reflection in planning information systems: A contribution from critical systems thinking', *Information Systems Journal* 19(2), 123–147. http://dx.doi.org/10.1111/j.1365-2575.2007.00284.x

Grover, V. & Segars, A.H., 2005, 'An empirical evaluation of stages of strategic information systems planning: Patterns of process design and effectiveness', *Information & Management* 42, 761–779. http://dx.doi.org/10.1016/j.im.2004.08.002

Hayward, J., 2013, 'Vision and strategic information systems planning in the UK HE Sector', *Proceedings of the UK Academy for Information Systems Conference 2013*, Paper 13, viewed from http://aisel.aisnet.org/ukais2013/13

Karanja, E. & Patel, S.C., 2012, 'A review of research trends in strategic information systems planning', *International Journal of Business Information Systems* 10(2), 151–177. http://dx.doi.org/10.1504/IJBIS.2012.047145

Karpovsky, A. & Galliers, R.D., 2015, 'Aligning in practice: From current cases to a new agenda', *Journal of Information Technology* 30, 136–160. http://dx.doi.org/10.1057/jit.2014.34

Kearns, G.S. & Lederer, A.L., 2003, 'A resource-based view of IT strategic alignment: How knowledge sharing creates competitive advantage', *Decision Sciences* 34(1), 1–29. http://dx.doi.org/10.1111/1540-5915.02289

Kearns, G.S. & Sabherwal, R., 2006, 'Strategic alignment between business and information technology: A knowledge-based view of behaviours, outcomes, and consequences', *Journal of Management Information Systems* 23(3), 129–162. http://dx.doi.org/10.2753/MIS0742-1222230306

Kearns, G.S. & Sabherwal, R., 2007, 'Antecedents and consequences of information systems planning integration', *IEEE Transactions on Engineering Management* 54(4), 628–643. http://dx.doi.org/10.1109/TEM.2007.906848

Lederer, A.L. & Salmela, H., 1996, 'Toward a theory of strategic information systems planning', *Journal of Strategic Information Systems* 5(3), 237–253. http://dx.doi.org/10.1016/S0963-8687(96)80005-9

Leonard, J. & Seddon, P., 2012, 'A meta-model of alignment', *Communications of the Association for Information Systems* 31(11), 230–259.

Luftman, J., Zadeh, H.S., Derksen, B., Santana, M., Rigoni, E.H. & Huang, Z.D., 2013, 'Key information technology and management issues 2012–2013: An international study', *Journal of Information Technology* 28(4), 354–366. http://dx.doi.org/10.1057/jit.2013.22

Mirchandani, D.A. & Lederer, A.L., 2014, 'Autonomy and procedural justice in strategic systems planning', *Information Systems Journal* 24(1), 29–59. http://dx.doi.org/10.1111/j.1365-2575.2012.00419.x

Newkirk, H.E. & Lederer, A.L., 2006, 'The effectiveness of strategic information systems planning under environmental uncertainty', *Information & Management* 43(4), 481–501. http://dx.doi.org/10.1016/j.im.2005.12.001

Osman, E., El Beltagi, I.M. & Hardaker, G., 2013, 'The impact of leadership orientation on strategic information systems planning processes, with an application to Libyan organizations', *Information Technology for Development* November, 1–27. http://dx.doi.org/10.1080/02681102.2013.856283

Pai, J.-C., 2005, 'An empirical study of the relationship between knowledge sharing and IS/IT strategic planning (ISSP)', *Management Decision* 44(1), 105–122. http://dx.doi.org/10.1108/00251740610641490

Peppard, J., Galliers, R.D. & Thorogood, A., 2014, 'Information systems strategy as practice: Micro strategy and strategizing for IS', *Journal of Strategic Information Systems* 23(1), 1–10. http://dx.doi.org/10.1016/j.jsis.2014.01.002

Premkumar, G. & King, W.R., 1994, 'Organisational characteristics and information systems planning: An empirical study', *Information Systems Research* 5, 75–109. http://dx.doi.org/10.1287/isre.5.2.75

Preston, D.M. & Karahanna, E., 2009, 'Antecedents of IS strategic alignment: A nomological network', *Information Systems Research* 20(2), 159–179. http://dx.doi.org/10.1287/isre.1070.0159

Ranganathan, C. & Sethi, V., 2002, 'Rationality in strategic information technology decisions: The impact of shared domain knowledge and IT unit structure', *Decision Sciences* 33(1), 59–86. http://dx.doi.org/10.1111/j.1540-5915.2002.tb01636.x

Reich, B.H. & Benbasat, I., 1996, 'Measuring the linkage between business and information technology objectives', *MIS Quarterly* 20, 453–468. http://dx.doi.org/10.2307/249542

Reich, B.H. & Benbasat, I., 2000, 'Factors that influence the social dimension of alignment between business and IT objectives', *MIS Quarterly* 24(1), 81–113. http://dx.doi.org/10.2307/3250980

Schlosser, F., Wagner, H.T. & Coltman, T., 2012, 'Reconsidering the dimensions of business-IT alignment', *Proceedings of the 45th Hawaii International Conference on System Science*, 5053–5061. http://dx.doi.org/10.1109/hicss.2012.497

Segars, A. & Grover, V., 1999, 'Profiles of strategic information systems planning', *Information Systems Research* 10(3), 199–232. http://dx.doi.org/10.1287/isre.10.3.199

Silvius, A.J., 2013, *Business and IT alignment in context*, PhD thesis, Utrecht University, The Netherlands.

Silvius, A.J. & Stoop, J., 2013, 'The relationship between the process of strategic information systems planning and its success: An explorative study', *Proceedings of the 46th Hawaii International Conference on Systems Sciences*, 4495–4501. http://dx.doi.org/10.1109/hicss.2013.536

Tan, F.B. & Gallupe, B., 2006, 'Aligning business and information systems thinking: A cognitive approach', *IEEE Transactions on Engineering Management* 53(2), 223–237. http://dx.doi.org/10.1109/TEM.2006.872243

Tan, M. & Teo, T.S.H, 2000, 'Factors influencing the adoption of internet banking', *Journal of the Association of Information Systems* 1(5), 1–44.

Teo, T. & King, W., 1997, 'Integration between business planning and information systems planning: An evolutionary contingency perspective', *Journal of Management Information Systems* 14(1), 185–214.

Teubner, R.A., 2013, 'Information systems strategy', *Business & Information Systems Engineering* 5(4), 243–257. http://dx.doi.org/10.1007/s12599-013-0279-z

Yang, J., Pita, Z. & Singh, M., 2014, 'Measurement of determinants for enhancing strategic information systems planning (SISP) success and dynamic capabilities in South Korea', *Proceedings of the 25th Australasian Conference on Information Systems*, 8–10 December, Auckland, New Zealand.

Appendix starts on the next page →

Appendix

APPENDIX 1: Item measures.

Item	Variable	Source
Shared domain knowledge measure		
Business knowledge		
SDK1	Business executives recognised the potential of IS as a competitive weapon.	Ranganathan and Sethi (2002)
SDK2	Business executives recognised IS as a tool to increase productivity.	Ranganathan and Sethi (2002)
SDK3	Business executives were highly knowledgeable about the firm's information technology assets and opportunities.	Kearns and Sabherwa (2007)
SDK4	Business executives agreed that information technology could have important intangible benefits that should be funded.	Kearns and Sabherwal (2007)
IS knowledge		
SDK5	IS executives were highly knowledgeable about business operations of the firm.	Ranganathan and Sethi (2002)
SDK6	IS executives were highly knowledgeable about business strategies of the firm.	Ranganathan and Sethi (2002)
SISP rationality measure		
Comprehensiveness		
COMP1	The company attempted to be exhaustive in gathering information relevant for SISP.	Segars and Grover (1999)
COMP2	Before a decision was made, each possible course of action was thoroughly evaluated.	Segars and Grover (1999)
COMP3	The company attempted to determine optimal courses of action from identified alternatives.	Segars and Grover (1999)
COMP4	There was little trial-and-error in the SISP process.	Segars and Grover (1999)
COMP5	Decisions were delayed until they were sure that all alternatives were evaluated.	Segars and Grover (1999)
Formalisation		
FORM1	Policies and procedures greatly influenced the process of SISP within the firm.	Segars and Grover (1999)
FORM2	Formalised planning techniques in the SISP process were utilised.*	Segars and Grover (1999)
FORM3	The process for strategic planning was very structured.	Segars and Grover (1999)
FORM4	Written guidelines to structure strategic IS planning existed in the organisation.*	Segars and Grover (1999)
FORM5	The process and outputs of strategic IS planning were formally documented.	Segars and Grover (1999)
SISP adaptation measure		
Participation		
PART1	Business executives were actively involved in strategic IS planning.	Segars and Grover (1999)
PART2	A variety of functional area managers participated in the process of IS planning.	Segars and Grover (1999)
PART3	The process for strategic IS planning included numerous participants.	Segars and Grover (1999)
PART4	Strategic IS planning was a relatively isolated organisational activity (R).*	Segars and Grover (1999)
PART5	The level of participation in SISP by diverse interests of the organisation was high.*	Segars and Grover (1999)
Frequency		
FREQ1	Conformance to strategic plans were constantly evaluated and reviewed.*	Segars and Grover (1999)
FREQ2	Strategic plans were frequently adjusted to better adapt them to changing conditions.	Segars and Grover (1999)
FREQ3	Strategic IS planning was a continuous process.	Segars and Grover (1999)
FREQ4	Formal planning for information systems was undertaken as the need arose.	Segars and Grover (1999)
FREQ5	Face-to-face meetings to discuss strategic planning issues were frequently scheduled.	Segars and Grover (1999)
BP-ISP integration measure		
AI	**Administrative integration:** In this type of integration, there is a weak relationship between business planning (BP) and information systems planning (ISP). Generally there is little significant effort to use information technology (e.g. computers, telecommunications) to support business plans.	Teo and King (1997)
SI	**Sequential integration:** In this type of integration, a sequential relationship exists between business planning (BP) and information systems planning (ISP). BP provides direction for ISP. ISP primarily focuses on providing support for business plans.	Teo and King (1997)
RI	**Reciprocal integration:** In this type of integration, there is a reciprocal and interdependent relationship between business planning (BP) and information systems planning (ISP). ISP plays both a role in supporting and influencing business plans.	Teo and King (1997)
FI	**Full integration:** In this type of integration, there is little distinction between the business planning (BP) process and the Information systems planning (ISP) process. Business and information systems strategies are developed concurrently in the same integrated planning process.	Teo and King (1997)
PI	**Proactive:** IS objectives precede the formulation of business objectives and are used as input to their development. IS is considered significant in changing the basis of competition.	Reich and Benbasat (2000)
IT manager participation in business planning		
ISBP1	IS executives regularly attended business meetings.	Kearns and Sabherwal (2006)
ISBP2	IS executives participated in setting business goals and strategies.	Kearns and Sabherwal (2006)
ISBP3	IS executives were involved early in the meetings for major projects.	Kearns and Sabherwal (2006)
Social dimension of alignment measure		
Long-term alignment		
SOC_LT_AL1	Business and IS executives shared a common vision for the long-term role of IS within the organisation.	Cohen and Toleman (2006)
SOC_LT_AL2	Business and IS executives agreed on priorities for the organisational use of IS.	Cohen and Toleman (2006)
SOC_LT_AL3	Business and IS executives agreed on the key IS management issues affecting the organisation.	Cohen and Toleman (2006)

*, Dropped items.

Appendix 1 continues on the next page →

APPENDIX 1 (Continues...): Item measures.

Item	Variable	Source
Social dimension of alignment measure†		
Short-term alignment		
IS understands business		
SOC_ST_AL_IS_BUS1	IS executives had a good level of understanding of strategic business plans.	Cohen and Toleman (2006)
SOC_ST_AL_IS_BUS2	IS executives had a good level of understanding of the work environment of the business.*	Cohen and Toleman (2006)
Business understands IS		
SOC_ST_AL_BUS_IS1	Business executives had a good level of understanding of the work environment of the IS function.*	Cohen and Toleman (2006)
SOC_ST_AL_IS_BUS2	Business executives had a good level of understanding of strategic IS plans.	Cohen and Toleman (2006)
Intellectual dimension of alignment		
IS plan-business plan alignment		
INT_AL1	The IS plan reflected the business plan mission.	Kearns and Lederer (2003)
INT_AL2	The IS plan reflected the business plan goals.	Kearns and Lederer (2003)
INT_AL3	The IS plan supported the business strategies.	Kearns and Lederer (2003)
INT_AL4	The IS plan recognised external business environment factors.	Kearns and Lederer (2003)
INT_AL5	The IS plan reflected the business plan resource constraints.	Kearns and Lederer (2003)
Business plan-IS plan alignment		
INT_AL6	The business plan referred to the IS plan.	Kearns and Lederer (2003)
INT_AL7	The business plan referred to specific IS applications.*	Kearns and Lederer (2003)
INT_AL8	The business plan referred to specific information technologies.*	Kearns and Lederer (2003)
INT_AL9	The business plan utilised the strategic capability of IS.	Kearns and Lederer (2003)
INT_AL10	The business plan contained reasonable expectations of IS.	Kearns and Lederer (2003)

*, Dropped items.
†, Data continues from previous column.

APPENDIX 2: Cronbach's alpha and factor analysis.

Items	ADAPT	RATIONAL	SDK_BUS	ISBP	SDK_IS
Cronbach's alpha	0.88	0.91	0.84	0.94	0.91
SDK1	0.43	0.10	0.71	0.19	0.04
SDK2	0.24	−0.11	0.64	0.35	0.02
SDK3	0.11	0.25	0.70	0.27	0.23
SDK4	0.03	−0.05	0.80	0.06	−0.08
SDK5	0.23	0.04	0.17	0.31	0.79
SDK6	0.26	0.10	0.04	0.20	0.79
COMP1	−0.12	0.73	0.44	−0.07	0.16
COMP2	0.26	0.80	0.18	0.09	−0.01
COMP3	0.35	0.68	0.15	0.00	0.20
COMP4	0.03	0.57	0.16	0.32	−0.06
COMP5	−0.01	0.77	−0.06	0.18	−0.04
FORM1	−0.02	0.79	−0.08	0.15	−0.07
FORM3	0.26	0.74	−0.03	0.16	0.23
FORM5	0.38	0.71	0.13	0.17	0.23
PART1	0.62	0.19	0.24	0.43	0.24
PART2	0.72	0.06	0.30	0.17	0.38
PART3	0.82	0.06	0.00	0.12	−0.04
FREQ2	0.51	0.47	0.01	0.26	0.20
FREQ3	0.59	0.38	0.23	0.24	0.11
FREQ4	0.60	0.50	0.04	0.21	0.26
FREQ5	0.59	0.19	0.34	0.06	0.10
ISBP1	0.26	0.22	0.29	0.77	0.15
ISBP2	0.25	0.31	0.16	0.81	0.20
ISBP3	0.19	0.16	0.16	0.81	0.17
Explained variance	4.08	6.02	4.20	4.86	2.75
Proportional total	0.11	0.16	0.11	0.13	0.07

Items	INT_ISPBPALIGN	INT_BPISPALIGN	SOC_STALIGN	SOC_LTALIGN
Cronbach's alpha	0.93	0.92	0.76	0.92
SOC_LT_AL1	0.20	0.36	0.45	0.54
SOC_LT_AL2	0.22	0.12	0.39	0.78
SOC_LT_AL3	0.25	−0.02	0.39	0.63
SOC_ST_AL_IS_BUS1	0.38	0.15	0.65	0.21
SOC_ST_AL_BUS_IS2	0.14	0.33	0.72	0.35
INT_AL1	0.80	0.22	0.19	0.28
INT_AL2	0.78	0.27	0.21	0.24
INT_AL3	0.72	0.19	0.36	0.20
INT_AL4	0.80	0.01	0.12	−0.19
INT_AL5	0.85	0.15	0.04	0.14
INT_AL6	0.26	0.58	0.19	0.22
INT_AL9	0.19	0.55	0.36	−0.03
INT_AL10	0.32	0.54	0.32	0.07
Explained Variance	4.36	4.20	4.86	2.42
Proportional total	0.12	0.11	0.13	0.07

24

Use of social media platforms for improving academic performance at Further Education and Training colleges

Authors:
Godwin P. Dzvapatsva[1]
Zoran Mitrovic[1]
Anthony D. Dietrich[1]

Affiliation:
[1]Department of Information Systems, University of the Western Cape, South Africa

Correspondence to:
Godwin Dzvapatsva

Email:
gpdzvapatsva@yahoo.com

Postal address:
2 Gabriel Road, Plumstead 7800, Cape Town, South Africa

Background: The National Certificate Vocational (NC[V]) curriculum offered by Further Education and Training (FET) colleges was introduced in 2007 to address the skills shortage in South Africa. Information Technology (IT) lecturers encountered a number of challenges in delivering lessons throughout the course, which affected the academic performance of learners. The biggest challenges identified were the lack of adequate contact hours for the course and inconsistency in the way in which final examination papers were set.

Objectives: The aim of the project was to investigate the use of: (1) a knowledge portal for verifying the quality of assessments by lecturers and (2) social media to increase contact time with FET college students in an attempt to improve their academic performance.

Method: The NC(V) level 3 student test scores for 2011 were compared to those of 2012. In addition to the test scores, students also received a questionnaire so as to determine their perceptions on social media usage. Lecturers also received a questionnaire on their perception of the knowledge portal.

Results: The data collected from seven lecturers and 38 students indicated a 35% (from 30% – 65%) improvement in academic performance after the introduction of the interventions, that is social media and a knowledge portal; an indication of the importance of electronic media in enhancing learning.

Conclusion: The research offered FET lecturers an additional method for learning and teaching in that they could use the knowledge portal to set up quality assessments for the students and social media to increase contact learning time.

Introduction

The skills shortage in South Africa has seen the government making frantic efforts to address the problem through Further Education and Training (FET) colleges. One such initiative was the National Certificate Vocational (NC[V]) curriculum, which was introduced in 2007. The target population for the NC(V) curriculum is learners who passed Grade 9. As reflected by the low pass rate of 2011 and preceding years, this curriculum is however proving to be challenging to most of the students. It remains the task of the lecturer to come up with innovative ways to ensure that students perform well. This study suggests the use of social media (SM) by students and a knowledge portal (KP) for assessments by lecturers to improve academic efficiency. The two suggested solutions, SM and a KP, have been found in separate studies to be vital in the sharing of knowledge between students and lecturers (Dietrich, Whyte & Mitrovic 2011; Dzvapatsva 2013; Koles & Nagy 2012). All the knowledge generated from previous lecturers and other sources, for example departmental sample papers, is stored and transferred to other lecturers through the KP for assessments. The students are encouraged to use the Facebook (FB) group created by lecturers to increase contact time outside normal learning time.

It is presumed that most of the senior staff at the FET colleges grasp the need to share knowledge with the junior staff so as to increase or enhance learning; thus, they 'are eager to introduce knowledge management paradigms' (Bock & Kim 2002). From the literature (Koles & Nagy 2012) it appears that SM platforms have a remarkable effect on learning.

The use of electronic platforms, especially SM, for the purpose of knowledge sharing amongst FET students has been criticised by various researchers (Hamid, Chang & Kurnia 2009; Sarachan & Reinson 2011). A random sample of lecturers at a South African FET college indicated that most of the students from non-IT departments were against the idea of using electronic platforms, especially SM, for the purpose of knowledge dissemination amongst students and lecturers. These lecturers argued that electronic platforms like FB are disruptive and destructive. However, other researchers (Kabilan, Ahmad & Abidin 2010) found the opposite to be true. They argued that SM platforms like FB could bring positive results in academic performance, if well administered. This is why the authors of this article decided to use FB to increase the contact time required for the subject by the students and the KP for knowledge sharing amongst lecturers. It was the view of these researchers (Dzvapatsva 2013; Dietrich *et al.* 2011) that NC(V) was heavily congested in terms of the time needed for the subject and students were left with not enough time to study or to do research whilst at the college (Leung 2002). Owing to the geographical distance, students could be contacted via SM platforms, like FB, which could accessed by most students from any location.

Apart from the students, the lecturers do not have enough time to do research or examine the subject content from previous lecturers or fellow subject experts. The KP seems to be the best electronic source which lecturers can use as reference for work done by previous and current subject experts. At the same time, FB seems to offer an alternative in capturing students' attention outside the classroom to review what they have learnt or will learn in the following lecture.

Background

The NC(V) programme was introduced to FET colleges in 2007 in an effort to redress the skills imbalance in South Africa. All learners who wanted to proceed with their studies along a chosen career path, for example Information Technology (IT), Business Administration, Engineering, Marketing or Tourism, could opt for the NC(V) programme. The NC(V) programme draws its students from Grade 9–12. The entry qualification is a pass in Grade 9, or the student must be older than 16 years. It runs for a period of three years, thus level 2 to level 4. Each year is an exit point. At each level a student is expected to successfully complete seven subjects, which comprise four core subjects, two fundamental ones, and one elective. Most students, however, struggle to pass all seven subjects so as to be promoted to the next level. The promotional policy allows students with a pass in five subjects to proceed to the next level. Lecturers have to work extremely hard and implement measures to improve students' performance so that FET colleges remain economically viable; these measures include the use of electronic platforms. In the event that a student is promoted to the next level whilst requiring one or two subjects for the previous level, he or she will have to do seven subjects of the present level and two extra subjects, which becomes stressful for the student. In view of the aforementioned, lecturers had to design means to assist students and to improve academic efficiency at each level, hence the introduction of electronic platforms. At the South African FET colleges used for this study, the SM platform, Facebook, has been used to contact learners outside the normal teaching time to increase contact hours for the Programming component, which has been

identified as one of the challenging subjects. The lecturers also used a portal for the setting up of assessments, subject notes, tests, and worked-out solutions. This has presumably been suggested to assist in drastically reducing the bottleneck and directly improve the throughput rate of students at FET colleges, which ultimately will contribute towards overall academic fulfilment (Dzvapatsva 2013). Studies by researchers, including Kabilan *et al.* (2010), has shown the positive use of SM for academic improvement, ultimately improving the throughput rate. In parallel, researchers like Rajalakshmi and WahidiBanu (2009) identified the KP application as a possible solution to academic inefficiency.

Literature review

It should be noted that whilst the traditional medium of face-to-face interaction offers numerous advantages for teaching and learning, it is controlled by time and space. In that respect it becomes crucial to embrace new technologies to supplement the current traditional ones in the teaching and learning of college and university students. With electronic media, the world becomes the classroom, available 24/7, and not confined to Mondays to Fridays.

According to Kaplan and Haenlein (2010), SM is defined as 'a group of Internet-based applications that build on the ideological and technological foundations of Web 2.0, and that allow the creation and exchange of User Generated Content'. The two main aspects discussed here are media research and social processes. Each medium used by the lecturer differs in its degree of effectiveness, depending on whether it is visual, acoustic or physical (Short, Williams & Christie 1976). Taking this into consideration, the current generation of students are more visual, hence the use of FB. It should also be considered that these students are a product of Outcome Based Education (OBE), which requires them to demonstrate the skills and subject content that they are expected to learn, regardless of whether they are comfortable with the medium used. Students prefer a medium which increases self-disclosure and self-presentation, thereby increasing social influence. The more a medium reduces ambiguity and uncertainty, the more it is accepted by communicating students (Daft & Lengel 1986).

Generally, SM encompasses the following:

- social networking sites (SNS), such as Facebook, Twitter, MySpace and LinkedIn
- media sharing sites, such as YouTube, Flickr and Tumbler
- wikis and blogs
- syndication of content through Rich Site Summary (RSS) feeds
- republishing tools (Gikas & Grant 2013).

According to Greenhow (2011, cited in Gikas & Grand 2013), SM 'tools in learning promotes a more student-centred course'. SM allows learners to network and work in partnership with each other and instructors.

Barczyk and Duncan (2011) identified elements that shape how Web 2.0 tools can be used meaningfully. Without structure, SM can negatively impact student learning. According to Barczyk and Duncan (2011), SM is used for educational purposes by lecturers at colleges and universities for learning and teaching. Studies by Barczyk and Duncan (2011) also indicated that more than half of the surveyed professors used tools such as videos, blogs, podcasts, video casts, and wikis in their classes. In his framework of SM, Kietzmann *et al.* (2011) identified seven building blocks for its functionality and usage: identity, conversation, sharing, presence, relationship, reputation and groups (Rosmalab & Rosmalab 2012). The diagram in Figure 1 illustrates the SM functionality framework.

SM is not new in the learning and teaching sector, but it is still not widely accepted. It is important to note that if, and only if, the medium is used for educational purposes and following set regulations by students to supplement the existing medium, a positive result will be obtained within the FET sector (Dzvapatsva 2013). Dzvapatsva (2013) states that students with certain personality types, who might have proved to be difficult to engage, can benefit more from the use of electronic media.

For example, 'shy students' proved to have benefited more online than they had done through face-to-face interaction with the lecturer (Dzvapatsva 2013). However, the electronic medium should be used to supplement the already existing methods or mediums, and should not be a complete replacement. SM helps learners to collaborate and interact with each other, which are key aspects in higher education. Furthermore, SM facilitates informal learning (Ebner *et al.* 2010). Informal learning is described

as contextualised, unorganised, but intentional (Gikas & Grant 2013). Mobile computing, which is an extension of electronic learning through mobile devices, can be used to do research, investigate, collect information and collaborate with other students through social networking sites (SNS). The information gathered will be used to supplement formal learning (Gikas & Grand 2013). Electronic platforms like SM and a KP allow students to access study material and communicate with classmates and instructors, no matter where they are (Gikas & Grand 2013). In addition, electronic platforms allow students to classify, control and evaluate existing knowledge, and successfully put together and communicate this as new knowledge.

Within the higher education sector, especially at FET colleges in South Africa, an information technology subject is found in most courses, either as Life Orientation (LO) or as Office Data Processing (ODP). These subjects focus on familiarising students with technology. Furthermore, they developing the academic skills required to locate specialised information, as well as for managing data, conducting online research, creating and managing documents and internet usage software. Lecturers in the field of Information Communication and Technology (ICT) should be aware of the fact that electronic technologies have transformed learning styles as most students would been using SM, for example FB, Twitter and Whatsapp, for a few years already, mainly by means of electronic devices, and lately, mobile devices.

Social media challenges within the FET sector

E-learning platforms like SM and KPs offer many advantages when compared to the traditional chalk-and-board methods. Some of the possible advantages, as noted by Cantoni, Cellario and Porta (2004), include:

- less expensive to deliver and faster
- provides consistent content, unlike in traditional methods where different lecturers can teach the same content differently
- it works from anywhere and anytime (virtual classroom)
- it can improve retention through varying types of content through videos and interaction
- it provides immediate feedback, especially if mobile devices are being used
- students are not afraid to make mistakes online so they can take risks and that alone can have a lasting positive effect (n.p.).

E-learning platforms are different from classroom-based learning; hence they require accurate development, monitoring and management. Electronic platforms, such as portals, require real subject experts to generate new skills in content and to verify the existing knowledge. It requires lecturers to be cognitively sensitive and well-sequenced. It also requires the explicit selection of instructional design to make learning experiences effective and long-lasting (Cantoni *et al.* 2004). Cantoni *et al.* (2004:336) state that electronic platforms may be 'intimidating, confusing or

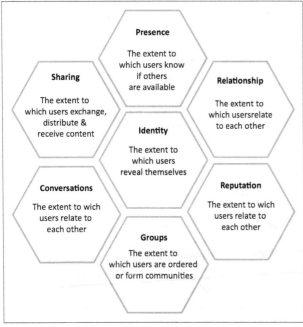

Source: Adapted from Kietzmann, J.H., Hermkens, K., McCarthy, I.P. & Silvestre, B.S., 2011, 'Social media? Get serious! Understanding the functional building blocks of social media', *Business Horizons* 54, 241–251

FIGURE 1: Social media functionality framework.

simply frustrating, lacking part of the informal social interaction and face-to-face contact of traditional classroom training'. This has been pointed out by some college lecturers who refused to use SM, citing them as disruptive. Another major concern is privacy issues, when platforms like FB are considered, which store an individual's details forever.

Because electronic learning platforms are free and can be used at liberty, they require self-discipline and more responsibility from students, which might be a challenge considering the type of students enrolled at FET colleges. Most of the students have social, economic and behavioural difficulties (SEBD).

Knowledge portals in higher education

Portal applications offer institutions a planned means of increasing their competitive advantage by encouraging innovation and research activities, which might lead to a greater success rate in grant acquisition, as well as growth in terms of prestige (Rajalakshmi & WahidiBanu 2009). According to Nonaka and Takeuchi (1995), knowledge creation comprises the utilisation of existing knowledge that is new to a group (tacit) or to an individual. The process becomes comprehensive when the collected knowledge is stored and can be retrieved in future for use by a group or an individual. A KP in this case offers the best option in capturing, sharing and transferring the knowledge; the knowledge acquired is of limited value if not captured, stored and shared. The ultimate goal for the organisation will be knowledge retention, which a KP offers.

Research methodology

The research unfolded as a dual process. Action research was used in both phases. The first phase investigated how the use of FB could improve the quality and quantity of passes for core subjects. Two NC(V) classes with 45 students doing Computer Programming (CP) as a subject were used for the research. FB was used to contact the students doing CP outside normal teaching time. Lecturers created two FB groups and invited students randomly to use the platform. The one group used FB with lecturer facilitation and they formed the control group (Group A), whilst the other group (Group B) used FB without lecturer facilitation.

The second phase of this study focused on improving lecturer efficiency through the quality of assessments and the study or lecturer notes prepared by former and current lecturers, approved by the programme manager based on the assessment guideline document. Before the implementation of SM and the KP, students struggled during the final examinations owing to the lack of exposure to subject experts outside the college. This phase aimed to assess whether or not the application of the KP would assist in improving the performance of students. The sample assessments which lecturers used from the KP would assist in boosting the students' year mark and prepare them for the final summative examination. The KP was made public so that all lecturers could use it. They only needed to create an account and register on the local intranet server which

hosted the portal. Further, a check on academic efficiency (if any) needed to be tabled and explanations given on whether the pass rates were in relation to portal usage or non-usage.

The subject moderators, in most cases post level two lecturers, would score each lecturer for moderation of the papers. A high score is regarded as full compliance to quality, which is necessary for the students to prepare for their summative tests. The KP served as a central location or repository of resource materials needed by each subject lecturer in respective subject areas. The moderation result, classified according to Department of Education grading, is shown in Table 1.

At the end of the year, the results of the lecturers who used the KP portal were compared to those who did not use the portal; thus, those of 2011 and preceding years. The intent was to use these scores as a baseline to measure variation (either positive or negative) after the implementation of the KP.

The portal prototype was adapted and extended to cater for lecturer interaction whilst on campus. Lecturer interaction was however limited to the campus, although they could access the portal offline. Availability of the KP offline meant that lecturers could familiarise themselves with the set of questions that the students could expect at the end of the year and the expected answers. Also, lecturers could streamline the study material to ensure that the material offered a good match to the national examinations at the end of the year. The KP would be updated on a regular basis to ensure that new trends in the IT sector were addressed. Rau, Gao and Wu (2008) found that students were motivated and enthusiastic to learn once they managed to master assessments set on the KP.

Implementation

The researchers intended to collect data from 45 students, but seven students dropped out of college along the way. Eventually, 38 questionnaire responses were collected. Data was also collected from the seven lecturers on their use of the KP. Descriptive statistics was used in the form of frequencies, averages and percentages to illustrate the results from the collected data.

Data collection for the research was twofold:

1. **Responses from questionnaires distributed to students using SM:** Two NC(V) level three classes were used for this study. The combined classes were given a baseline test before the introduction of SM. At a later stage, students were randomly split into two separate (virtual) classes for the purpose of this study. One group (Group A) used SM with lecturer facilitation; the other group

TABLE 1: Department of Education moderation gradings.

Category	Scores (%)
Strongly valid	90–100
Valid	80–89
Acceptable	70–79
Average	60–69
Sub-standard	Below 60

(Group B) did not have lecturer facilitation. This random split was done to avoid possible bias. A FB group was created for use by Group A, whilst Group B studied with use of SM but without lecturer monitoring. This study aimed to determine how the increase in contact time through SM would assist the students in improving their performance. At the end of the term, a questionnaire was distributed to the remaining 38 students, and an analysis was done. Also, test scores for the subject were compared for the two groups.

2. **Responses from lecturers and those students who used the KP:** The KP used for the research was designed using open source software (PHP, MySQL and CSS) and hosted on the college's internal web server after seeking permission from the campus manager/principal. Lecturers were able to access it from any computer laboratory at the college and in their offices. All lecturers from the IT Department were asked to familiarise themselves with the portal and the information collected which was used for their assessment moderation. The results obtained from the moderation exercise were compared to those before the use of the KP.

Findings

Increase in contact time

From Group A (with FB use), 83% (n = 15) indicated that FB helped to increase their contact time. Group B had six respondents who shared the same sentiments, which is 67.7% of the total number of respondents (the combined group). From the two groups it could be observed that the students generally agreed that FB could be useful for increasing contact time with the learning material, their peers, and the lecturers or subject experts.

Role of FB in learning computer programming

In Group A, 94.4% (A = 11; SA = 6; totalling 17 students) of the students stated that SM could be used to study CP. In Group B, 23% (n = 3) of the students were of the opinion that FB could be used to study CP, whilst 69.2% (n = 9) of the students from this group were neutral on SM usage in this regard. From these findings it is clear that more students, even those who did not use SM, agreed on the potential of SM to increase the contact time needed for practical subjects like CP. Ten students (55.6%) indicated that SM had positively changed their attitude towards studying CP and seven (38.9%) stated that FB increased their involvement towards studying the subject. Lesser percentages were obtained from Group B, namely 23.1% (n = 4) and 15.4% (n = 3) respectively. More importantly, the number of students who were satisfied by the responses they received on the FB platform, 67% (n = 12), was significant when compared to the 15.4% (n = 2) from Group B, with 53.8% offering a neutral response, and 30.8% (n = 4) stating that the responses from their fellow students were not satisfactory, nor reliable.

It is important to note here that the research was conducted in two phases. The one phase attempted to determine

whether or not the use of a SM application would improve the contact time necessary for increasing performance, whilst the second phase concentrated on the quality of assessments within the NC(V) component of the Department of ICT at the FET college. All seven lecturers teaching ICT subjects used the KP for their assessments. Assessment quality is currently reflected 'as a moderation percentage obtained after the subject moderator has scrutinised both lecturer and student portfolios of evidence' (Dietrich et al. 2011). Table 2 represents the moderation scores supplied by the respondents for each of the listed subjects before the application of the KP.

The KP prototype was launched after the first term moderation. All staff members were introduced to the KP and a training session was conducted during a staff development meeting. All lecturers were encouraged to comment freely through email as they interacted with the portal. For the lecturers, the portal included samples of lesson plans and explained how each lesson outcome is achieved when planning. Typical formative assessments included on the KP could be used by both lecturers and students to assess the content. The portal also provided a central store from which lecturers could access important subject content.

Table 3 illustrates average moderation scores for each of the subjects after three rounds of moderation.

It is clear from the results of the survey that the participants of the study had a positive experience with the KP prototype. Table 4 further highlights the positive variation of moderation scores achieved after the introduction of the portal.

As the results show, almost all the subjects, except Hardware and Software, showed an improvement in moderation results. However, it must be noted that even though Electronics showed an improvement of +/-10%, this is still regarded as below expected or outside the Valid Assessment range. The expected/valid assessment should score an average of between 80% and 89% during moderation. Introduction to Systems Development and Data Communication achieved average scores of above 90%.

Apart from initial technical difficulties experienced during the first phase roll-out of the portal, there were few challenges of any significance. This is partly due to the fact that interaction was at first restricted mainly to lecturers to determine whether or not it would affect the validity of their assessment instruments. However, when interaction

TABLE 2: The moderation scores before the knowledge portal introduction.

Category	Scores (%)
Introduction to Information Systems	70–79
Introduction to Systems Development	70–79
Electronics	60–69
Systems Analysis L3	60–69
Hardware and Software	80–89
Principles of Computer Programming	70–79
Systems Analysis L4	70–79
Computer Programming	70–79
Data Communication and Networking	80–89

TABLE 3: The moderation scores after the knowledge portal introduction.

Moderation scores	0%–59%	60%–69%	70%–79%	80%–89%	90%–100%
Introduction to Information Systems	-	-	-	x	-
Introduction to Systems Development	-	-	-	-	x
Electronics	-	-	x	-	-
Systems Analysis level 3	-	-	-	x	-
Hardware and Software	-	-	-	x	-
Principles of Computer Programming	-	-	-	x	-
Systems Analysis level 4	-	-	-	x	-
Computer Programming	-	-	-	x	-
Data Communication and Networking	-	-	-	-	x

TABLE 4: The comparison of the moderation scores before and after the knowledge portal introduction.

Moderation scores	Before knowledge portal introduction					After knowledge portal introduction				
	0%–59%	60%–69%	70%–79%	80%–89%	90%–100%	0%–59%	60%–69%	70%–79%	80%–89%	90%–100%
Introduction to Information Systems	-	-	x	-	-	-	-	-	x	-
Introduction to Systems Development	-	-	x	-	-	-	-	-	-	x
Electronics	-	x	-	-	-	-	-	x	-	-
Systems Analysis level 3	-	x	-	-	-	-	-	-	x	-
Hardware and Software	-	-	-	x	-	-	-	-	x	-
Principles of Computer Programming	-	-	x	-	-	-	-	-	x	-
Systems Analysis level 4	-	-	x	-	-	-	-	-	x	-
Computer Programming	-	-	x	-	-	-	-	-	x	-
Data Communication and Networking	-	-	-	x	-	-	-	-	-	x

was extended to include students, some problems (mainly involving IT infrastructure) occurred that were not as easy to avoid. Bandwidth was the biggest challenge, which the IT support technicians said was as a result of abuse by some students. There was also an increase in network activity as most students realised the importance of the KP. The other challenge which had to be addressed was access everywhere on the campus, apart from the computer laboratories. Despite these factors, there was a remarkable improvement in the throughput rate from six students graduating in 2011 to 18 students in 2012.

Conclusion

The research confirms and expands on previous research (Dietrich *et al.* 2011; Koles & Nagy 2012; Dzvapatsva 2013; Rau *et al.* 2008) on the potential of electronic platforms (SM and KP) to increase the performance of FET learners in South Africa. As stated by Gikas and Grand (2013), educators need to make use of emerging technology to teach the so-called Net Generation of students. In fact, Rosmalab and Rosmalab (2012) show that using diverse SM tools together to perform various tasks is more likely to increase individual knowledge acquisition. Learning through electronic platforms like SM and a KP indicates that valuable learning relies not only on social relations and association, but also on personal expression and information aggregation. Having seen the potential of SM and a KP, it should be emphasised that policies on these platforms need to be followed to obtain the best results from students, as they can be a problem if not well monitored (Cantoni *et al.* 2004:336).

This article assists in providing a glimpse into the countless ways in which electronic platforms might be used to provide

the support needed for collaboration, networking and information sharing within FET institutions. Furthermore, this research will contribute towards a better understanding of how electronic platforms (i.e. SM and a KP) can be used in FET colleges in South Africa. This research confirms that the created KP was valuable not only as a knowledge repository, but also to support other processes. These processes include administrative issues and team building amongst staff members. The researchers hope that future research on the topic will build on, extend, test and complement the results which have been presented in this article.

Limitations of the study

The research only focused on FB, without comparing it to other mediums. However, the data collected provides a good platform for future research as it shows the current trends in learning and teaching.

Final thoughts

Consistent with social media trends in general, ICT educators have a responsibility towards themselves (i.e. continuing professional development, joint research, academic or scholarly communication, publishing and producing peer reviewed articles), their students (improving their pass rates and empowering them to have more control over their own education), and the general public. Although SM and other electronic learning platforms offer opportunities, there is an increased need for training on how to use these technologies to improve and augment teaching and learning to support FET students and lecturers, with the ultimate objective of improving pass rates. However, if there are no clear policies on usage, the platforms can be abused by students.

Acknowledgements

Competing interests

The authors declare that they have no financial or personal relationship(s) that may have inappropriately influenced them in writing this article.

Authors' contributions

G.P.D. (University of the Western Cape) and A.J.D. (University of the Western Cape) conducted the research and drafted the article, whilst Z.M. (University of the Western Cape) mentored and contributed significantly to the finalisation of the article.

References

Bock, G.W. & Kim, Y.G., 2002, 'Breaking the myths of rewards: An exploratory study of attitudes about knowledge sharing', *Information Resource Management Journal* 15(2), 14–21. http://dx.doi.org/10.4018/irmj.2002040102

Barczyk, C.C. & Duncan, D.G., 2011, 'Social networking media as a tool for teaching business administration courses', *International Journal of Humanities and Social Science* 1(17).

Cantoni, V., Cellario, M. & Porta, M., 2004, 'Perspectives and challenges in e-learning: Towards natural interaction paradigms', *Journal of Visual Languages and Computing* 15, 333–345. http://dx.doi.org/10.1016/j.jvlc.2003.10.002

Daft, R.L. & Lengel, R.H., 1986, 'Organizational information requirements, media richness and structural design', *Management Science* 32(5), 554–571. http://dx.doi.org/10.1287/mnsc.32.5.554

Dzvapatsva, G.P., 2013, 'The use of social media as a means of improving the quantity and quality of the pass rate in computer programming at FET colleges in the Western Cape', Masters dissertation, University of the Western Cape.

Dietrich, A., Whyte, G. & Mitrovic, Z., 2011, 'E-learning at FET colleges: The application of a knowledge portal within the ICT Department of the College of Cape Town', *The ResNes Conference 2011*, East London, South Africa.

Ebner, M., Lienhardt, C., Rohs, M. & Meyer, I., 2010, 'Microblogs in Higher Education – A chance to facilitate informal and process-oriented learning?', *Computers & Education* 55(1), 92–100. http://dx.doi.org/10.1016/j.compedu.2009.12.006

Hamid, S., Chang, S. & Kurnia, S., 2009, 'Identifying the use of online social networking in higher education', *ASCILITE 2009 conference*, December 2009, pp. 6–9.

Kabilan, K.M., Ahmad, N. & Abidin, M.J.Z., 2010, 'Facebook: An online environment for learning of English in institutions of higher education?' *Internet and Higher Education* 13, 179–187. http://dx.doi.org/10.1016/j.iheduc.2010.07.003

Kaplan, A.M. & Haenlein, M., 2010, 'Users of the world, unite! The challenges and opportunities of social media', *Business Horizons* 53(1), 59–68. http://dx.doi.org/10.1016/j.bushor.2009.09.003

Kietzmann, J.H., Hermkens, K., McCarthy, I.P. & Silvestre, B.S., 2011, 'Social media? Get serious! Understanding the functional building blocks of social media', *Business Horizons* 54, 241–251. http://dx.doi.org/10.1016/j.bushor.2011.01.005

Koles, B. & Nagy, P., 2012, 'Facebook usage patterns and school attitudes', *Multicultural Education & Technology Journal* 6(1), 4-17. http://dx.doi.org/10.1108/17504971211216283

Gikas, J. & Grant, M.M., 2013, 'Mobile computing devices in higher education: Student perspectives on learning with cellphones, smart phones and social media', *Internet and Higher Education* 19, 18–26.

Leung, C.F., 2002, 'Promoting an active learning environment within a congested curriculum', *International Conference on Engineering Education Proceedings*, Manchester, United Kingdom.

Nonaka, I. & Takeuchi, H., 1995, *The knowledge-creating company*, Oxford University Press, New York.

Rajalakshmi, S. & WahidiBanu, D., 2009, 'Developing an education web portal for knowledge sharing and capturing', *International Journal of Engineering and Technology* 1(3). http://dx.doi.org/10.7763/IJET.2009.V1.43

Rau, P.P., Gao, Q. & Wu, L., 2008, 'Using mobile communication technology in high school education: Motivation, pressure, and learning performance', *Computers & Education* 50, 1–22. http://dx.doi.org/10.1016/j.compedu.2006.03.008

Rosmalab, F. & Rosmalab, D., 2012, 'Study of social networking usage in higher education environment', *3rd International Conference on e-Learning ICEL 2011*, 23–24 November 2011, Bandung, Indonesia, *Procedia - Social and Behavioral Sciences* 67, 156–166.

Sarachan, J. & Reinson, K.F., 2011, 'Public issues, private concerns: Social media and course management systems in higher education', *Cutting-edge Technologies in Higher Education* 1, 227–244. http://dx.doi.org/10.1108/S2044-9968(2011)0000001014

Short, J.W., Williams, E.E. & Christie, B., 1976, *The social psychology of telecommunications*, John Wiley, London.

25

Innovation capability of managers in Nigerian large-scale manufacturing companies

Authors:
Sunday O. Popoola[1]
Olaronke O. Fagbola[2]

Affiliations:
[1]Department of Library, Archival and Information Studies, University of Ibadan, Nigeria

[2]Ibadan Study Centre Library, National Open University of Nigeria, Nigeria

Correspondence to:
Olaronke Fagbola

Email:
olaronke65@hotmail.com

Postal address:
PO Box 14294, University of Ibadan Post Office, Ibadan, Oyo State, Nigeria

Background: Manufacturing companies in Nigeria operate in a turbulent business environment and managers therein need quality information to operate with keen market competition. Information seeking behavior and use as well as knowledge sharing are critical ingredients to enhance innovation capability of managers in business organisations like manufacturing companies for survival.

Objectives: This study examines the contributions of information-seeking behaviour, information utilation and knowledge sharing to the prediction of the innovation capability of managers in large-scale manufacturing companies in Nigeria with special reference to the food, beverages and tobacco companies.

Method: A total enumeration technique was used to administer copies of a questionnaire to a population of 400 managers in 12 food, beverages and tobacco companies that are listed on the Nigerian Stock Exchange. Of these, 357 responded. The response rate achieved was 89.3%.

Results: The study found that there were significant multiple relationships between information-seeking behaviour, information utilisation, knowledge sharing and the innovation capability of the respondents. It was also found that information-seeking behaviour, information utilisation and knowledge sharing jointly and individually predict the innovation capability of the respondents. In addition, information-seeking behaviour contributed 22.18%, information utilisation contributed 44.12%, and knowledge sharing contributed 40.88% to the prediction of innovation capability of managers in food, beverages and tobacco companies in Nigeria. The study equally found that, apart from the traditional ways of sharing knowledge in organisations, social media technology such as Facebook and Twitter, amongst others, are new ways of sharing knowledge in large-scale manufacturing companies in Nigeria.

Conclusion: The study recommends that managers in these companies should be encouraged to seek for more information, make more intensive use of information and share knowledge in order to improve their innovation capability.

Introduction

Creativity and innovation is at the heart of modern businesses like manufacturing companies in Nigeria. Programmes of organisational innovation are typically tightly linked to organisational goals and objectives, to the business plan and to competitive positioning in the market. Davila, Epstein and Shelton (2006) noted that companies cannot grow through cost reduction and re-engineering alone without innovation. Innovation is the key element in providing aggressive top-line growth and in increasing bottom-line results. It is about introducing change into a relatively stable system (Marshall 2013). Many businesses embrace innovation with the primary goal of driving growth and consequently, improving shareholders' value, and making maximum profit. In general, manufacturing companies tend to spend a significant amount of their profits on innovation programmes, that is, making radical changes to their established products, processes and services.

Innovation is a new idea applied to initiating or improving a product, process or service. The concept of innovation encompasses new production-process technologies, new structures or administrative systems and new plans or programmes pertaining to organisational members. It is concerned with the work required to make an idea viable (Marshall 2013; Tidd 2001). In the organisational context, innovation may be linked to performance and growth through improvements in efficiency, effectiveness, productivity, quality of service and product, competitive positioning, market share and so on. Hesselbein, Goldsmith and Sommerville (2002) defined innovation as change that creates a new dimension of performance. Innovation is the new process, method, business model, partnership and route to a market (Sloane 2012). For the purpose of this study, innovation capability is defined as the successful exploitation of new ideals by the managers in any organisation, particularly manufacturing companies, to bring about radical or incremental changes to products, services and processes.

Information and knowledge are the basic ingredients needed by managers in organisations to bring about innovation. Information is data that has been processed into a form that is meaningful to the recipient or user and is of perceived value in current or future decisions. Information can also be seen as any communication or representation of knowledge such as facts, data, ideas, messages, opinions or images in any medium or form, including textual, numerical, graphic, cartographic, narrative or audio-visual forms. Information is a meaningful message transmitted from source to receivers or users. Information is an asset like the human resources, financial resources, material, machines and energy necessary for the efficient and effective management of business operations in order to produce high-quality products and services.

What is more, managers in businesses like manufacturing companies need and seek all forms of information such as legal, technical, commercial, political, economic, social, geographical, demographic and cultural information in order to improve their creative and innovative capabilities. Information-seeking success occurs in an organisation when a manager or an employee obtains the right information in the right format at the right place at the right time to the right extent at the right level and to the right amount with the least effort.

Krikelas (1983) stated that information-seeking begins when someone perceives that the current state of knowledge is less than that needed to deal with some issue or problem and that the process ends when the perception no longer exists. The need for creativity and innovation may put much pressure on the managers in businesses like manufacturing companies to seek and use information and knowledge. Baldwin and Rice (1997) reiterated that knowledge workers, including managers, continually search for new information. They monitor, store and disseminate company and industry-related information. Their information-seeking behaviour may be influenced by their environment.

However, Zamani and Pezeshki (2005) averred that information behaviour is a broad term encompassing the ways in which individuals articulate their information needs and in which they seek, evaluate, select and use information. Information-seeking behaviour may be defined as all methods and ways by which an individual employed to search for, gain access to and retrieve needed information from various sources for use. Houtari and Wilson (2001) reported that the executive managers in both academic and business institutions in United Kingdom and Finland most often used meetings and personal contact to obtain internal and external information at the level of the company, but they used telecommunications (phone and fax) to get hold of external information at the level of marketing and sales. For the purpose of this study, the utilisation of information is defined as the correct application of messages, facts, opinions, signs, symbols, images, sounds, ideas, signals and processed data by the managers in order to bring about desired results from problems at hand, leading to innovation in an organisation.

Human knowledge is a critical factor in the production of goods and services in any organisation. Knowledge is obtained when an individual or manager uses information to resolve problems at hand or is better informed concerning a random event or phenomenon of which he or she has a gap in knowledge or understanding. Knowledge exists in people's minds. In the 'resource-based' view of the firm, knowledge is considered to be the most important strategic resource (Conner & Prahaad 1996). Many organisations have recognised that knowledge is a valuable intangible resource that holds the key to competitive advantage (Kang, Chen & Fang 2010).

Organisational creativity and innovation may be improved when managers and employees share knowledge. Knowledge sharing means that individuals mutually adjust their beliefs and actions through more or less intense interactions (Krough 2002). Knowledge sharing occurs in an organisation when the human elements therein are willing to share or transfer or distribute insights, experiences, preferences, lessons learned and effective practices amongst themselves. Business performance may be enhanced when knowledge is created, transferred and used for the common good of all categories of employees. Knowledge sharing may also be seen as the active process or act of communicating one's personal intellectual capital willingly to others and others freely receiving it. It is designed to transform individual knowledge into organisational knowledge (Adamovic, Potgieter & Mearns 2012). The process of knowledge sharing in businesses is cyclical in nature, and modern organisation culture is synonymous with knowledge sharing processes (Adamovic *et al.* 2012).

In the last few years, manufacturing companies survived economically in spite of poor economic policies by the government in Nigeria. Their survival could be seen in terms of continued existence, quality products produced, increased sales and profits and improved production processes. In addition, their strong capital base, coupled with better corporate governance through the use of creativity and innovation programmes, could have made it possible for them to be listed on the Nigerian stock exchange (Popoola 2012).

In the minds of the researchers, the pertinent question which requires further investigation is: What is the innovation capability of organisations in Nigeria with regard to the information-seeking behaviour, information utilisation and knowledge sharing of their managers. Besides this, literature concerning the link between information-seeking behaviour and its utilisation for organisational innovation is scarce. It is in the light of this that the present study investigates the relationship between innovation capability and the information-seeking behaviour, information utilisation and knowledge sharing amongst managers in large-scale manufacturing companies in Nigeria with special reference to food, beverages and tobacco companies.

Purpose of the study

The main purpose of this study is to examine the contribution of information-seeking, information utilisation and knowledge sharing to the prediction of innovation capability of managers in large-scale manufacturing companies in Nigeria.

Research hypotheses

The following hypotheses were formulated and tested at α = 0.05 level of significance to guide the study:

1. There is no significant multiple relationship amongst the information-seeking behaviour, information utilisation, knowledge sharing and innovation capability of the respondents.
2. Information-seeking behaviour, information utilisation and knowledge sharing will not significantly predict innovation capability of the respondents.

Literature review

Information is a construct with different meanings and interpretations, and as such, each author defines it from their own perspective. Information may be viewed as data that have been processed, organised and presented in a form which is comprehended to have significance and meaning to the recipient. Information can also be defined as ideas, opinions, messages, facts, images, sounds, codes, symbols, signs, signals, voices, computer programmes (software), databases, processed data or the like, obtained from published and unpublished sources. This information is capable of improving the knowledge state of a user concerning a random event or phenomenon. Therefore, information becomes knowledge when a user of information bridges the gap that exists in his or her understanding of a particular event or subject (Popoola 2006).

Houtari and Wilson (2001) defined human information behaviour as the totality of behaviour (active or passive) in which people engage to gain access to, organise and use information. Thus, it will comprise not only pro-active steps to gain access but also the passive reception of information, which then, or later, turns out to be of use (Wilson 1999). Information-seeking behaviour which results from the recognition of some need (Wilson 1997) is defined by Krikelas (1983) as any activity of an individual that is undertaken to identify a message that satisfies a perceived need. Chew (1994) suggests that, when an individual is driven to seek information as a result of 'needing to know', three modes of questioning behaviour are exhibited: questions to discover what is happening (orientation), questions to check that the person is on the right track (re-orientation) and questions to form an opinion or solve a problem (construction). Information-seeking behaviour may be defined as the purposive searching for information as a consequence of a need to satisfy some goal (Wilson 2000). For the purpose of this study, information-seeking behaviour may be viewed as all manners and ways by which managers in large-scale manufacturing companies identify, access and retrieve their needed information from the available sources in order to improve their innovation capability.

However, previous studies revealed that the personality (Heinstrom 2003), discipline (Ocholla 1999), task performance (Bystrom 2000), work performance (Popoola 2002), users' psychological characteristics (Wilson 2000) and individual characteristics (Allen & Kim 2001) influenced the information-seeking behaviour of users. Before the relevant information is obtained, the searchers must overcome possible obstacles, which are sometimes psychological in nature. They must experience the situation as rewarding enough, and they themselves must be competent enough to actually take the final decision to seek for their needed information (Wilson 1981; Wilson & Walsh 1996). Emotional aspects like feelings of frustration, impatience, information overload, resistance to new information and computer aversion may form barriers to the process to look for information (Nahl 2001). The feeling of uncertainty, often expressed as anxiety or worry, is strongly exhibited at the beginning of a search process when the users become aware of their lack of knowledge about the topic (Kuhlthau 1993). It must be noted that the cognitive ability of a manager in a business like a manufacturing company may influence his or her capacity to seek for needed information and use it for improved innovation capability. Motivation and interest influence the way in which information is used and critically evaluated (Limberg 1998). The more a manager is interested in and motivated to improve organisational creativity and innovation, the more likely it is that he or she will seek for more information.

Nevertheless, within the context of this study, the utilisation of information may be defined as the correct or suitable application of news, facts, messages, ideas, opinions, codes, symbols, signals, signs, images, sounds, voices, computer programmes (software), databases and processed data obtained from published and unpublished sources. The information is capable of improving the innovation capability of managers in manufacturing companies. Managers in businesses obtain their needed information from a wide range of formal sources such as libraries, record offices, online databases, Internet, textbooks, journals and trade literature as well as from informal sources like colleagues or subordinate staff. Blandin and Brown (1977) examined the relationship between perceived environmental uncertainty and the information search behaviour of top-level managers in four electronics firms and four wood-product firms in America. They found significant positive correlations between the level of perceived uncertainty and their reliance on external information sources, their use of informal information sources, their frequency of use of all information sources and the amount of time allocated to environmentally related information gathering.

Kotter (1982) reported that successful general managers in nine corporations in various industries in cities across the United States seek information aggressively, often by asking critical questions that provide useful answers for setting agendas. They rely more on information from discussions with individuals than on books, magazines or reports. Jones and McLeod (1986) explored the use of information sources by senior managers in the four decisional roles and reported that information from subordinates was frequently obtained and valued highly. White (1986) studied managers' information needs and use in manufacturing organisations in Britain and found that no correlation exist between the managers' functional roles (production, sales, marketing, finance or personnel) and their information needs. Further, marketing and sales managers, who are typically considered to be externally oriented, were found to use large amounts of internally produced data. Indeed, managers in manufacturing companies may demand and use information for equipment maintenance, financial planning, product development and marketing.

Popoola (2003) established that managers in oil companies in Nigeria sourced their needed information mostly from colleagues, subordinate staff, customers, government publications, newspapers and magazines, radio or television and internal reports. Information about competitors is merely one piece of all the relevant information that managers in organisations need when acquiring information from their business environment. They equally need, acquire and use information relating to the success of competitors' products in the market and the whole environment, including economic, legal, cultural and demographic background (Hermel 2001; Revelli 2000). Miller (2001) averred that business information could better be acquired from direct contact with customers, printed information documents and electronic information services. The specific information which executive managers and directors need and use to formulate business strategic plans and improve productivity in business organisations may include financial data, stock-market information, monetary and fiscal policies by government, mergers and acquisition of firms, technological information, business ownership and shareholders and advertising costs as well as information on financial crime. Benczur (2005) found that the acquisition and use of information in Western European companies to monitor their business environment so as to determine the course of action improved their sales volume. In actual fact, information and knowledge are very important resources that industrial firms need in order to foster creativity and innovation in their workforce. Input to an organisation come in the form of information resources and knowledge. Innovative organisations are active in reconfiguring new information resources and securing new knowledge. Information resources must be effectively managed, and knowledge must be shared to a great extent before organisations could enhance the creativity and innovation base of their workers. Luecke and Katz (2003) reiterated that innovation is generally understood as the introduction of a new thing or method, but innovation actually is the embodiment, combination or synthesis of knowledge in original, relevant and valued new products, processes or services.

Kim and Mauborgne (1999) claimed that organisations that have sustained high growth and profits follow a strategy of value innovation. A strategy of value innovation will allow an organisation to break out of a competitive imitative trap and make competitors irrelevant. Adamovic et al. (2012) remarked that organisations that share knowledge will gain improved innovation capability and hence sustain competitive advantage. O'Sullivan (2002) identified poor knowledge management, poor communication and a lack of access to relevant information, amongst others, as common causes of failure within the innovation process in most organisations. Knowledge is often defined as internalised information (Ingwersen 1992) and understood as a blend of explicit and tacit information (Nonaka 1994). This means that there are several kinds of knowledge at different levels of the organisation.

Knowledge lies in human minds and exists only if there is a human mind to do the knowing (Widen-Wulff & Suomi 2007). Liebowitz (1999) believed that knowledge management is the process of knowledge identification, acquisition, saving, sharing, application and selling. According to Kathiravelu, Mansor and Kenny (2013), knowledge management can be described as the processes taken by firms to produce, maintain and share knowledge. Ajiferuke (2003) remarked that knowledge management involves the management of explicit knowledge, that is, knowledge that has been codified in documents, databases, webpages, et cetera and the provision of an enabling environment for the development, nurturing, utilisation and sharing of employees' tacit knowledge, that is, know-how, skills or expertise. The execution of an appropriate knowledge management programme in a business has the potential of improving customer services, continually improving business processes, quickly bringing new products to markets and bringing innovative new ideas to commercialisation (Heisig & Vorbeck 2001).

Knowledge sharing is an important component of knowledge management. It is the procedure undertaken by people whenever an idea is to be exchanged. This can take the form of discussion, document exchange or face-to-face interaction so that new knowledge can be formed (Kathiravelu et al. 2013). With the advent of new technology, knowledge sharing has taken on new dimensions, hence the submission of Adamovic et al. (2012) that social media technology which are digital in nature (Facebook, Twitter, Wiki, blog) can assist the process of sharing knowledge in organisations because they allow easy and instant communication. The efficient and effective sharing and use of information and knowledge in organisations may foster creativity and innovation in employees. Knowledge sharing means that individuals mutually adjust their beliefs and actions through more or less intense interactions (Krough 2002). Knowledge sharing is the willingness of employees within an organisation to voluntarily donate their tacit knowledge or know-how, skills or expertise to others whilst others are happily collecting and applying the knowledge to solve creative and innovative problems. Liao, Fei and Chen (2007) reported that knowledge sharing and absorptive capacity has a significant correlation with the innovation capability amongst employees in Taiwan's knowledge-intensive industries. The systematic sharing of knowledge is assuming a larger role in all kinds of organisations around the world (Luen & Al-Hawamdeh 2001; World Bank 1998). Morrow (2001) averred that the potential benefits of knowledge management abound and range from improving productivity, decision-making, customer service and innovation in an organisation. Be that as it may, the knowledge sharing which is an integral part of knowledge management has a tendency of bringing about improved work performance, creativity and innovation amongst employees in an organisation. Strategies for knowledge sharing in organisations include face-to-face interaction, discussion and document exchange. Lately knowledge sharing in organisations is also done via corporate intranets such as wikis, blogs, Facebook and Twitter. Social media technology provides the conduit and means for people to share knowledge, insights and experience (Bradley & McDonald 2011).

However, innovation capability may be viewed as the ability of employees, particularly managers, to successfully exploit new ideas in order to bring about radical changes or improvements in methods, services and products in an organisation. Innovation is a critical activity for businesses that want to achieve competitive advantage and make super profits in dynamic markets. Organisational and strategic leadership research posits that strategic leaders or top managers heavily influence the organisation's capabilities by establishing an organisational culture, motivating and enabling managers and employees and building capacity for change and innovation (Daft 2001; Yukl 1999). The adoption of innovation involves the initiation of novel ideas that can successfully be executed to solve organisational problems. Novel ideas and solutions require knowledge and expertise (Mumford 2000). Education might provide individuals with specific knowledge needed for task performance and novel problem solving (Lee, Wong & Chong 2005). Since the newness of innovation creates a sense of uncertainty, the managers' greater ability to gain information to reduce that uncertainty would facilitate the adoption of innovation (Rogers 1995). Arguably, information dissemination, information utilisation and knowledge sharing as well as level of education may influence the innovation capability of managers in an organisation.

Research methodology

An ex-post-facto descriptive research design was adopted for the study. This is because the independent variables (information-seeking behaviour, information utilisation and knowledge sharing) were not under the direct control of the researchers, and their manifestations having already occurred or because they are inherently not easy to manipulate. The relationship amongst the independent variables and dependent variable (innovation capability) was examined. The study population comprised of 400 managers in 12 food, beverage and tobacco companies quoted on the Nigeria Stock Exchange as at April 2008. The total

enumeration technique was used to cover all 400 managers in the manufacturing companies studied. A set of tools was used for data collection, namely questionnaire-tagged information-seeking behaviour, information utilisation and the knowledge sharing and innovation capability of managers (ISBIUKSICM).

The questionnaire was divided into five main sections. Section-A deals with the demographic information of the respondents, for example gender, age, marital status, job tenure, job status, department of work and highest educational qualification. Section B contains 20 items that deals with the information-seeking behaviour of the respondents. The typical examples of the items are as follows:

- Most often, I seek the needed information from work mates and professional colleagues.
- When I experience an information overload in my workplace, I adopt the filtering method to obtain relevant information.
- I regularly browse through the Internet using known search engines to seek and obtain information.

The items were measured on a 4-point Likert Scale, namely very true of me = 4, true of me = 3, occasionally true of me = 2 and not true of me = 1. It has a reliability coefficient of $\alpha = 0.83$, using the Cronbach-Alpha method.

Section-C deals with the information utilisation of the respondents, that is, their utilisation of information sources and specific types of information utilised by the respondents. It was measured on a 4-point Likert Scale using the following response format: very highly utilised = 4, highly utilised = 3, occasionally utilised = 2, not utilised = 1. It has a reliability coefficient of $\alpha = 0.74$, using the Cronbach-Alpha method, which is a method for determining the content validity of a measuring instrument used for data collection. Section D deals with knowledge sharing by the respondents. It has 10 items developed by Liao et al. (2007). The typical examples of the items are as follows:

- I often share with my colleagues the new working skills that I learn.
- Sharing knowledge with my colleagues is regarded as something normal in my company.
- Our company staff often exchanges knowledge of working skills and information.

The items were measured on a 5-point Likert Scale: totally agree = 5, agree = 4, neutral = 3, disagree = 2, totally disagree = 1. It has a reliability coefficient of $\alpha = 0.87$, using the Cronbach-Alpha method.

Section-E deals with innovation and management and consists of 18 items as developed by Liao et al. (2007). The typical examples of the items are as follows:

- Our company often develops new products and services well accepted by the market.
- The new manufacturing process or operation procedure employed by our company arouses imitation from competitors.

- Our company emphasizes innovative and creative capability when recruiting staff.

The items were measured on a 5-point Likert Scale: totally agree = 5, agree = 4, neutral = 3, disagree = 2, totally disagree = 1. It has reliability coefficients for product innovation (α = 0.93), process innovation (α = 0.90), and management innovation (α = 0.92). The overall reliability coefficient for the innovation capability scale is α = 0.93, using Cronbach-Alpha method.

The printed copies of the questionnaire were administered to 400 managers in the studied companies through physical contact with the help of five research assistants who were post-graduate students in the Department of Library, Archival and Information Studies, University of Ibadan, Ibadan, Nigeria. The census method was used to cover all 400 managers in large-scale manufacturing companies in Nigeria. Of the 400 managers, 357 responded, giving a response rate of 89.3%. The questionnaire administration and response rate are shown in Table 1. The data that were collected were analysed using simple-correlation and multiple-regression analysis with the aid of Statistical Package for Social Sciences (SPSS). A simple-correlation analysis was performed using Pearson's product-moment correlation method on the data collected from the field, namely information-seeking behaviour, information utilisation, knowledge sharing and innovation capability of the respondents. The independent variables are information-seeking behaviour, information utilisation and knowledge sharing whilst the dependent variable is innovation capability. Data on innovation capability were run on the independent variables using a multiple-regression analysis whilst Pearson's product-moment correlation method was used to correlate data on each of the independent variables on innovation capability of the respondents.

Findings

The gender distribution of the respondents showed that 255 (71.4%) were males whilst 102 (28.6%) were females.

This means that more males were recruited into the managerial positions in the food, beverage and tobacco companies in Nigeria. The age distribution of the respondents ranged

between 23 and 49 years with mean age = 32.8 (SD = 4.8) years. Of the 357 respondents, 158 (44.3%) were single whilst the remaining 199 (55.7%) were married. The distribution of the respondents' highest educational qualification revealed that 185 (51.8%) had a bachelor degree, 97 (27.2%) had a post-graduate diploma, and 75 (21.0%) had master's degree in business-oriented disciplines. The job tenure of the respondents ranged between 8 and 32 years with the mean = 19.8 (SD = 6.4) years.

The result of the study (Table 2) revealed that the very highly utilised information sources by the respondents were customers = 3.99 (SD = 0.125), colleagues = 3.98 (SD = 0.128), trade literature = 3.96 (SD = 0.126), Internet or online databases = 3.95 (SD = 0.124), newspapers or magazines = 3.94 (SD = 0.121), company files = 3.93 (SD = 0.129), textbooks or journals = 3.92 (SD = 0.123) and government publications = 3.90 (SD = 0.127). The company library was never used = 1.44 (SD = 0.028).

From Table 3, the mean and standard deviation scores of the major types of information utilised by the respondents were prices of goods and services = 4.99 (SD = 0.128), labour matters = 4.97 (SD = 0.212), tax laws = 4.97 (SD = 0.216), investment opportunities = 4.96 (SD = 0.214), energy availability and costs = 4.96 (SD = 0.213), financial data = 4.94 (SD = 0.212), technological = 4.93 (SD = 0.218) and crime rate = 4.91 (SD = 0.210).

It is shown in Table 4 that the major modes of knowledge sharing by the respondents in large-scale manufacturing companies in Nigeria are staff meetings (100.0%), personal contact (100.0%), the telephone (99.4%), email (98.6%), work progress reports (98.0%), social media (Facebook, Twitter, Wikis, etc., 67.2%), blogs (56.0%), et cetera. However, instant messaging (29.4%) and newsgroups (5.6%) were amongst the least-used modes of knowledge sharing by managers in large-scale manufacturing companies in Nigeria.

Table 5 presents a summary of the test for a significant relationship between information-seeking behaviour, information utilisation, knowledge sharing and innovation capability of the respondents.

TABLE 1: Questionnaire administration and response rate.

Company	Population	Number responded	Response rate (%)
7-up Bottling Company, PLC	65	54	83.1
Big Treat, PLC	20	20	100.0
Cadbury Nigeria, PLC	45	40	88.9
Dangote Flour Mills, PLC	20	20	100.0
Dangote Sugar Refinery, PLC	22	18	81.0
Ferdinand Oil Mill, PLC	15	15	100.0
Flour Mills Nigeria, PLC	18	18	100.0
National Salt Company Nigeria PLC	22	20	90.9
Nestle Nigeria, PLC	25	22	88.0
Nigeria Bottling Company, PLC	75	65	86.7
UTC Nigeria, PLC	45	40	88.9
Nigeria Flour Mills, PLC	28	25	89.3
Total	**400**	**357**	**89.3**

PLC, Public limited company

TABLE 2: Mean and standard deviation score of information utilisation (sources) of the respondents.

Information sources	$\bar{x}$	SD
Customers	3.99	0.125
Colleagues	3.98	0.128
Trade literature	3.96	0.126
Internet/online databases	3.95	0.124
Newspapers/magazines	3.94	0.121
Company files	3.93	0.129
Textbooks/journals	3.92	0.123
Government publications	3.90	0.127
Company library	1.44	0.028

$\bar{x}$, mean; SD, standard deviation.

TABLE 3: Mean and standard deviation score of types of information utilised by the respondents.

Information types	$\bar{x}$	SD
Prices of goods and services	4.99	0.128
Labour matters	4.97	0.212
Tax laws	4.97	0.216
Investment opportunities	4.96	0.214
Energy availability and costs	4.96	0.213
Financial data	4.94	0.212
Technological	4.93	0.218
Crime rate	4.91	0.210

$\bar{x}$, mean; SD, standard deviation.

TABLE 4: Distribution of respondents by modes of knowledge sharing in large-scale manufacturing companies in Nigeria (N = 357).

Modes of knowledge sharing	Yes		No	
	n	%	n	%
Email	352	98.6	5	1.40
Teleconferencing	250	70.0	107	30.0
Instant messaging	105	29.4	252	70.6
Telephone	355	99.4	2	0.06
Work progress report	350	98.0	7	2.0
Staff meeting	357	100.0	-	-
Blogs	200	56.0	157	44.0
Discussion groups	100	28.0	257	72.0
News group	20	5.60	337	94.9
Personal contact	357	100.0	-	-
Social media (Facebook, blog, Twitter, Wiki's)	240	67.2	117	32.8

TABLE 5: Summary of test of significant relationship amongst information-seeking behaviour, information utilisation, knowledge sharing and innovation capability of the respondents.

Variables	$\bar{x}$	SD	IC(r)	Significant P
Information-seeking behaviour (ISB)	22.56	4.42	0.554	0.036
Information utilisation (IU)	24.68	4.68	0.642	0.025
Knowledge sharing (KS)	28.42	5.34	0.586	0.021
Innovation capability (IC)	30.24	5.43	1.000	−

$\bar{x}$, mean; SD, standard deviation; IC, innovation capability; r, correlation coefficient.

The mean and standard deviation scores of information-seeking behaviour of the respondents are = 22.56 (SD = 4.42) whilst the mean and standard deviation scores of their innovation capability are = 30.24 (SD = 5.43). Therefore, there is a significant relationship between information-seeking behaviour and innovation capability of the respondents (r = 0.554; $p < 0.05$). Also, the mean and standard deviation scores of information utilisation of the respondents are = 24.68 (SD = 4.68) whilst the mean and standard deviation scores of their innovation capability are = 30.2 (SD = 5.43). Thus, there is a significant relationship between the information utilisation and innovation capability of the respondents

(r = 0.642; $p < 0.05$). The mean and standard deviation scores of the knowledge sharing of the respondents are = 28.42 (SD = 5.34) whilst the mean and standard deviation scores of their innovation capability are = 30.24 (SD = 5.43). It is therefore established that there is a significant relationship between knowledge sharing and innovation capability of the respondents (r = 0.586; $p < 0.05$).

Table 6 shows the summary of a multiple-regression analysis of information-seeking behaviour, information utilisation and knowledge sharing on innovation capability of the respondents.

TABLE 6: Summary of multiple-regression analysis of information-seeking behaviour, information utilisation and knowledge sharing on innovation capability of the respondents.

Source of Variation	df	SS	MS	F-ratio	Significant P
Due to Regression	3	1923.66	641.22	-	-
Due to Error	353	10108.42	28.64	-	-
Total	356	12032.08	669.86	22.39	0.028

Note: Adjusted R^2 = 0.3914; Adjusted R = 0.6256; Standard Error of Estimate (SEE) = 5.35 df, degrees of freedom; SS, sum of squares; MS, mean square.

TABLE 7: Summary of test of significance of independent variables to the prediction of innovation capability of the respondents.

Variables	df	REq. Coeff (B)	SE (B)	Betain	T	Significant P
Constant	353	0.1806	0.1246	-	1.45	0.082
Information-seeking behaviour (ISB)	353	0.2141	0.0448	0.2218	4.78	0.036*
Information utilisation (IU)	353	0.4222	0.0681	0.4412	6.20	0.028*
Knowledge sharing (KS)	353	0.3316	0.0652	0.4088	5.09	0.042*

*, significant at α = 0.05
df, degrees of freedom; REq. Coeff(B), coefficient of regression model; SE(B), standard error of Betain; Betain, relative contribution value; T, student's t-statistic.

The test of hypothesis one revealed that there is a significant multiple relationship amongst information-seeking behaviour, information utilisation, knowledge sharing and innovation capability of the respondents (R = 0.6256; $p < 0.05$).

More so, the test of hypothesis two shows that information-seeking behaviour, information utilisation and knowledge sharing, when taken together, significantly predict the innovation capability of the respondents ($F(3; 353) = 22.39$; $p < 0.05$). Further, a post-hoc test reveals that each of the independent variables, that is, information-seeking behaviour ($B = 0.2141$; $df = 353$; $T = 4.78$; $p < 0.05$), information utilisation ($B = 0.4222$; $df = 353$; $T = 6.20$; $p < 0.05$) and knowledge sharing ($B = 0.3316$; $df = 353$; $T = 5.09$; $p < 0.05$) significantly predict the innovation capability of the respondents. This could not have happened due to chance because going by the adjusted R^2 value of 0.3914, one can argue that about 39.14% of the total variance in innovation capability of managers in the large-scale manufacturing companies in Nigeria is explained by a linear combination of their information-seeking behaviour, information utilisation and knowledge sharing.

This can mathematically be expressed thus IC = 0.2141ISB + 0.4222IU + 0.3316KS. Furthermore, going by the values of Betain, one can therefore submit that information-seeking behaviour contributed 22.18%, information utilisation contributed 44.12% and knowledge sharing contributed 40.88% to the prediction of innovation capability of the respondents.

Discussion of findings

Managers in business organisations function in the world of information. They also operate within an information-rich environment where different information sources are available to them to acquire their needed information for improving their creativity and innovation capability. This study found that customers, colleagues, reports, trade literature, Internet or online databases, newspapers or magazines, company files, textbooks or journals and government publications were very highly utilised information sources by the managers of food, beverages and tobacco companies in Nigeria.

Similarly, (Choo 1994; O'Connell & Zimmerman 1979; Olatunji 1994; Stabell 1978) reported that managers in manufacturing companies most frequently utilised customers, colleagues, online information services, newspapers or magazines, broadcast media (radio and television), reports, company files, trade literature and government publications. It is very surprising to find that the respondents never made use of the information resources and services in their company library. Lester and Waters (1989) support this finding by reporting that managers in large United Kingdom companies considered traditional sources, such as libraries, as too tedious and frustrating to use. They are also sceptical about the value of information-brokering services.

This study further revealed that the major types of information utilised by the managers in food, beverage and tobacco companies in Nigeria were prices of goods and services, labour matters, tax laws, investment opportunities, energy availability and costs, financial data, technological information and crime rate. Adebisi (2006) remarked that most managers in Nigerian manufacturing companies made use of price data, tax laws, monetary policies, export and import data, exchange rates, labour matters and scientific and technical matters in producing value-added goods. The study of large South Korean firms by Goshal and Kim (1986) concluded that managers required and made use of information about the immediate business environment, that is competitors, existing technologies, product markets, general social, economic and political matters. Similarly, Revelli (2000) and Hermel (2001) remarked that managers in organisations need, acquire and use information relating to the success of competitors' products in the market and the whole environment, including the economic, legal, cultural and demographic background.

Nevertheless, this study also found that information-seeking behaviour, information utilisation and knowledge sharing had a significant multiple relationships with the innovation capability of the managers in food, beverages and tobacco companies in Nigeria. Bawden (1986) posited that information utilisation may affect the creativity and innovation of users. Access and the ability for contact and information exchange with external organisational systems as well as good information-seeking behaviour by the working force are essential for innovation in an organisation (Fennel 1984; Kimberly 1978). The process to adopt innovation in organisations has been divided into a variety of phases, namely awareness, initiation, selection, adoption, implementation and routinisation (Klein & Sorra 1996). It must be noted that information-seeking behaviour, information utilisation and knowledge sharing are essential ingredients at every stage of the innovation process in an organisation. Liao *et al.* (2007) found that knowledge sharing has a positive influence on the innovation capability amongst employees of Taiwan's knowledge-intensive industries.

However, the most critical finding of this study is that information-seeking behaviour, information utilisation and knowledge sharing significantly predicts the innovation capability of managers in food, beverages and tobacco companies in Nigeria. This does not occur by a mere chance because about 39.14% of the total variance in innovation capability of managers in food and beverages and tobacco companies in Nigeria can be attributed to a linear combination of their information-seeking behaviour, information utilisation and knowledge sharing. In addition, information-seeking behaviour contributed 22.18%, information utilisation contributed 44.12% and knowledge sharing contributed 40.88% to the prediction of the innovation capability of the respondents. Arguably, information utilisation can be regarded as the greatest contributor to the prediction of innovation capability of managers in food, beverages and tobacco companies in Nigeria.

Conclusion and recommendation

Innovation is the spinal cord of the modern competing organisational environment. Also in the fiercely and keen competitive 21st century market place, innovative ability is essential for company survival. Successful innovative firms therefore cultivate creative ideals that add value to their produced goods and services. Information and knowledge has been accepted widely as the corporate assets that businesses must exploit in order to improve their business performance. Information availability, accessibility and utilisation as well as knowledge creation, transfer, sharing and use are critical factors that are considered necessary for facilitating organisational creativity and innovation in the business world. How well the workforce, particularly the managers in organisations, has been able to meet their information and knowledge requirements will determine the extent of their creative and innovative capabilities. This study therefore established that information-seeking behaviour, information utilisation and knowledge sharing jointly and individually predict the innovation capability of the managers in food, beverages and tobacco companies in Nigeria and that information utilisation is the most potent contributor to the prediction of the innovation capability of the respondents. Based on the major findings of this study, it is therefore recommended that managers in the studied

companies be encouraged to make more intensive use of information in order to improve their innovation capability. Management should provide a conducive environment for knowledge sharing amongst the managers to improve their innovation capability. They should be encouraged to seek for accurate, reliable and complete information so as to enhance their innovation capability. The management of the companies should provide education and training on creativity and innovation to their workforce, particularly managers. Library staff should also provide information literacy programmes in order to stimulate the level of demand and use of their information resources and services amongst the managers in the studied companies.

Acknowledgements
Competing interests

The authors declare that they have no financial or personal relationship(s) that may have inappropriately influenced them in writing this article

Authors' contributions

S.O.P. (University of Ibadan) contributed by means of Conceptualising the study; background to the study; literature review; design and validity of the measuring instrument (Questionnaire); and the data analysis and interpretations. O.O.F. (National Open University of Nigeria) contributed to this article through the literature review; field administration/data collection; data editing; abstract.

References

Adamovic, D., Potgieter, A. & Mearns, M., 2012, 'Knowledge sharing through social media: Investigating trends and technologies in a global marketing and advertising research', *South African Journal of Information Management* (14)1, Art. #514, 7 pages. http://dx.doi.org/10.4102/sajim.v14i1.514

Adebisi, M.O., 2006, 'Role of information management and information use in business performance of manufacturing firms', *Journal of Organizational Development* 18(2), 140–151.

Ajiferuke, I., 2003, 'Role of information professionals in knowledge management programmes: Empirical evidence from Canada', *Informing Science June*, 329–339.

Allen, B.L. & Kim, K.S., 2001, 'Person and context in information seeking: Interaction between cognitive and task variables', *New Review of Information Behaviour Research* 2, 1–16.

Baldwin, N.S. & Rice, R.E., 1997, 'Information-seeking behaviour of securities analysts: Individual and institutional influences, information sources and channels, and outcomes', *Journal of the American Society for Information Science* 48(8), 674–693. http://dx.doi.org/10.1002/(SICI)1097-4571(199708)48:8%3C674::AID-ASI2%3E3.0.CO;2-P

Bawden, D., 1986, 'Information systems and the stimulation of creativity', *Journal of Information Science* 12(4), 203–216. http://dx.doi.org/10.1177/016555158601200501

Benczur, D., 2005, 'Environmental scanning: How developed is information acquisition in Western European companies?', *Information Research* 11(1), 1–18.

Blandin, J.S. & Brown, W.B., 1977, 'Uncertainty and management's search for information', *Institute of Electrical and Electronics Engineers, Transaction on Engineering Management* 24(4), 14–19.

Bradley, A.J. & McDonald, M.P., 2011, *Social media versus knowledge management*, HBR Blog Network, viewed 20 July 2013, from http://blogs.hbr.org/2011/10/social-media-versus-knowledge

Bystrom, K., 2000, 'The effects of task complexity on the relationship between information types acquired and information source used', *New Review of Information Behaviour Research* 1, 85–101.

Chew, F., 1994, 'The relationship of information needs to issue relevance and media use', *Journalism Quarterly* 71, 676–688. http://dx.doi.org/10.1177/107769909407100318

Choo, C.W., 1994, 'Perception and use of information sources by chief executives in environmental scanning', *Library and Information Science Research* (16)1, 23–40. http://dx.doi.org/10.1016/0740-8188(94)90040-X

Conner, K.R. & Prahaad, C.K., 1996, 'A resource based theory of the firm: Knowledge versus opportunism', *Organization Science* 7, 477–501. http://dx.doi.org/10.1287/orsc.7.5.477

Daft, R.L., 2001, *'Organization theory and design*, South-western, Cincinnati.

Davila, T., Epstein, M.J. & Shelton, R., 2006, *Making innovation work: How to manage it, measure it, and profit from it*, Wharton School Publishing, Upper Saddle River.

Fennel, M.L., 1984, 'Synergy, influence and information in the adoption of administrative innovations', *Academy of Management Journal* 27(2), 113–129. http://dx.doi.org/10.2307/255960

Goshal, S. & Kim, S.K., 1986, 'Building effective intelligence systems for competitive advantage', *Sloan Management Review* 28(1), 49–58.

Heinstrom, J., 2003, 'Five personality dimensions and their influence on information behaviour', *Information Research* 9(1), 1–23.

Heisig, P. & Vorbeck, J., 2001, 'Bench marking survey results', in K. Martins, P. Heisig & J. Vorbeck (eds.), *Knowledge management: Best practices in Europe*, pp. 97–123, Springer-Verlag, Berlin. http://dx.doi.org/10.1007/978-3-662-04466-7_6

Hermel, L., 2001, *Maitriser et pratiquer la veille strateique*, Afnor, Paris.

Hesselbein, F., Goldsmith, M. & Sommerville, I., 2002, *Leading for innovation: And organizing for results*, Jossey-Bass, London.

Houtari, M. & Wilson, T.D., 2001, 'Determining organizational information needs: The critical success factors approach', *Information Research* 6(3), 1–15.

Ingwersen, P., 1992, *Information retrieval and interaction*, Tyler, London.

Jones, J.W. & McLeod, R., 1986, 'The structure of executive information systems: An exploratory analysis', *Decision Sciences* 17(2), 220–249. http://dx.doi.org/10.1111/j.1540-5915.1986.tb00223.x

Kang, Y., Chen, G., Ko, C. & Fang, C., 2010, 'The exploratory study of on-line knowledge sharing by applying wiki collaboration system', *Scientific Research* 2, 243–248. http://dx.doi.org/10.4236/ib.2010.23031

Kathiravelu, S.R., Mansor, N.N.A. & Kenny, K., 2013, 'Factors influencing knowledge sharing behaviour (KSB) among employees of public services in Malaysia', *International Journal of Academic Research in Economics and Management Sciences* 2(3), 107–119.

Kim, W.C. & Mauborgne, R., 1999, 'Strategy, value, innovation and the knowledge economy', *Sloan Management Review Spring*, 41–54.

Kimberly, J.R., 1978, 'Hospital innovation adoption: The role of integration into external information environments', *Journal of Health and Social Behaviour* 19(2), 361–373. http://dx.doi.org/10.2307/2136583

Klein, K.J. & Sorra, J.S., 1996, 'The challenge of innovation implementation', *Academy of Management Review* 21, 1055–1080. http://dx.doi.org/10.2307/259164

Kotter, J.P., 1982, 'What effective general managers really do', *Harvard Business Review* 60(6), 156–167.

Krikelas, J., 1983, 'Information seeking behaviour: Patterns and concepts', *Drexel Library Quarterly* 19, 5–20.

Krough, G., 2002, 'The communal resource and information systems', *Journal of Strategic Information Systems* 11, 85–107. http://dx.doi.org/10.1016/S0963-8687(02)00006-9

Kuhlthau, C.C., 1993, *Seeking meaning: A process approach to Library and Information Services*, Ablex, Norwood.

Lee, S.H., Wong, P.K. & Chong, C.L., 2005, 'Human and social capital explanations for R and D outcome', *Institute of Electrical and Electronics Engineers, Transactions on Engineering Management* 52, 59–68. http://dx.doi.org/10.1109/TEM.2004.839955

Lester, R. & Waters, J., 1989, 'Environmental scanning and business strategy, London: British Library, Research and Developmental Department', *Library and Information Research Report* 75, 1–148.

Liao, S., Fei, W. & Chen, C., 2007, 'Knowledge sharing, absorptive capacity, and innovation capability: An empirical study of Taiwan's knowledge-intensive industries', *Journal of Information Science* 33(3), 340–359. http://dx.doi.org/10.1177/0165551506070739

Liebowitz, J., 1999, 'Key ingredients to the success of an organization's knowledge management strategy', *Knowledge and Process Management* 6(1), 37–40. http://dx.doi.org/10.1002/(SICI)1099-1441(199903)6:1%3C37::AID-KPM40%3E3.0.CO;2-M

Limberg, L., 1998, *Att Soka information for all lara*, Gothenburg, Valfrid.

Luecke, R. & Katz, R., 2003, Managing creativity and innovation, Harvard Business School Press, Boston.

Luen, T.W. & Al-Hawamdeh, S., 2001, 'Knowledge management in the public sector: Principles and practice in police work', *Journal of Information Science* 27, 311–318. http://dx.doi.org/10.1177/016555150102700502

Marshall, D., 2013, 'There's a critical difference between creativity and innovation', viewed 15 July 2013, from http://www.businessinsider.com/difference-between-creativity-and-innovation-2013-4

Miller, M.A., 2001, 'Influence of business information sources' utilization on workers' productivity', *Journal of Corporate Banking Management* 10(2), 58–64.

Morrow, N.M., 2001, 'Knowledge management: An introduction', *Annual Review of Information Science and Technology* 35, 381–422.

Mumford, M.D., 2000, 'Managing creative people: Strategies and tactics for innovation', *Human Resources Management Review* 10(2), 313–355. http://dx.doi.org/10.1016/S1053-4822(99)00043-1

Nahl, D., 2001, 'A conceptual framework for explaining information behaviour', *Studies in Media and Information Literacy Education* 1(2), 1–12. http://dx.doi.org/10.3138/sim.1.2.001

Nonaka, I., 1994, 'A dynamic theory of organizational knowledge creation', *Organizational Science* 5(1), 44–55. http://dx.doi.org/10.1287/orsc.5.1.14

Ocholla, D., 1999, 'Insights into information-seeking and communicating behaviour of academics', *International Information and Library Review* 31(3), 111–143. http://dx.doi.org/10.1006/iilr.2000.0116

O'Connell, J.J. & Zimmerman, J.W., 1979, 'Scanning the international environment', *California Management Review* 22(2), 15–23. http://dx.doi.org/10.2307/41165317

Olatunji, O.A., 1994, 'Availability and utilization of information sources and services in Cadbury Nigeria PLC, Lagos', MLS dissertation, Department of Library, Archival and Information Studies, University of Ibadan, Ibadan.

O'Sullivan, D., 2002, 'Framework for managing development in the networked organizations', *Journal of Computers in Industry* 47(1), 77–78. http://dx.doi.org/10.1016/S0166-3615(01)00135-X

Popoola, S.O., 2002, 'Information-seeking behaviour and use as correlates of perceived work performance of corporate Insurance managers in Nigeria', *Ife Behavioural Research* 4(1), 14–34.

Popoola, S.O., 2003, 'Environmental scanning for strategic advantage of managers in oil companies in Nigeria', *Nigeria Libraries* 37(1), 42–56.

Popoola, S.O., 2006, 'Information accessibility and utilization as factors influencing decision-making of managers in commercial banks in Nigeria', *Library Herald* 44(2), 89–110.

Popoola, S.O., 2012, 'Information utilization capacity and organizational development in Nigeria', paper presented at a Training workshop on Information for Industrial Development, organized by Economic Management Group at Eko Hotel, Lagos, Nigeria, 10–12 October.

Revelli, C., 2000, *Intelligence strategique sur Internet*, Dunod, Paris.

Rogers, E.M., 1995, *Diffusion of innovation*, Free Press, New York.

Sloane, P., 2012, 'What's the difference between creativity and innovation?', viewed 25 July2013, from http://www.innovationexcellence.com/blog/2012/08/04/whats-the-difference-between-creativity-and -innovation/

Stabell, C., 1978, 'Integrative complexity of information environment perception and information use: An empirical investigation', *Organizational Behaviour and Human Performance* 22 (1), 116–142. http://dx.doi.org/10.1016/0030-5073(78)90009-0

Tidd, J., 2001, 'Innovation management in context: Environment, organization and performance', *International Journal of Management Review* 3(3), 169–183. http://dx.doi.org/10.1111/1468-2370.00062

White, D.A. 1986, 'Information use and needs in manufacturing organizations: Organizational factors in information behaviour', *International Journal of Information Management* 6(3), 157–170. http://dx.doi.org/10.1016/0268-4012(86)90003-4

Widen-Wulff, G. & Suomi, R., 2007, 'Utilization of information resources for business success: The knowledge sharing model', *Information Resources Management Journal* 20(1), 46–67. http://dx.doi.org/10.4018/irmj.2007010104

Wilson, T.D., 1981, 'On user studies and information needs', *Journal of Documentation* 37(1), 3–15. http://dx.doi.org/10.1108/eb026702

Wilson, T.D., 1997, 'Information behaviour: An inter-disciplinary perspective', *Information Processing and Management* 33(4), 551–572. http://dx.doi.org/10.1016/S0306-4573(97)00028-9

Wilson, T.D., 1999, 'Models in information behaviour research', *Journal of Documentation* 55(4), 249–270. http://dx.doi.org/10.1108/EUM0000000007145

Wilson, T.D., 2000, 'Human information behaviour', *Information Sciences* 3(2), 49–55.

Wilson, T.D. & Walsh, C., 1996, *Information behaviour: An inter-disciplinary perspective*, British Library Research and Information Centre, London.

World Bank, 1998, 'Knowledge for development', World Development report, no. 21, viewed 10 March 1999, from http://www.worldbank.org/wdr/wdr98/index.htm

Yukl, G., 1999, 'An evaluative essay on current conceptions of effective leadership', *European Journal of Work and Organizational Psychology* 8(2), 33–48. http://dx.doi.org/10.1080/135943299398429

Zamani, N. & Pezeshki-Rad, G., 2005, 'Information-seeking behaviour of Iranian extension managers and specialists', *Information Research* 10(3), 1–10.

Permissions

All chapters in this book were first published in SAJIM, by AOSIS Publishing; hereby published with permission under the Creative Commons Attribution License or equivalent. Every chapter published in this book has been scrutinized by our experts. Their significance has been extensively debated. The topics covered herein carry significant findings which will fuel the growth of the discipline. They may even be implemented as practical applications or may be referred to as a beginning point for another development.

The contributors of this book come from diverse backgrounds, making this book a truly international effort. This book will bring forth new frontiers with its revolutionizing research information and detailed analysis of the nascent developments around the world.

We would like to thank all the contributing authors for lending their expertise to make the book truly unique. They have played a crucial role in the development of this book. Without their invaluable contributions this book wouldn't have been possible. They have made vital efforts to compile up to date information on the varied aspects of this subject to make this book a valuable addition to the collection of many professionals and students.

This book was conceptualized with the vision of imparting up-to-date information and advanced data in this field. To ensure the same, a matchless editorial board was set up. Every individual on the board went through rigorous rounds of assessment to prove their worth. After which they invested a large part of their time researching and compiling the most relevant data for our readers.

The editorial board has been involved in producing this book since its inception. They have spent rigorous hours researching and exploring the diverse topics which have resulted in the successful publishing of this book. They have passed on their knowledge of decades through this book. To expedite this challenging task, the publisher supported the team at every step. A small team of assistant editors was also appointed to further simplify the editing procedure and attain best results for the readers.

Apart from the editorial board, the designing team has also invested a significant amount of their time in understanding the subject and creating the most relevant covers. They scrutinized every image to scout for the most suitable representation of the subject and create an appropriate cover for the book.

The publishing team has been an ardent support to the editorial, designing and production team. Their endless efforts to recruit the best for this project, has resulted in the accomplishment of this book. They are a veteran in the field of academics and their pool of knowledge is as vast as their experience in printing. Their expertise and guidance has proved useful at every step. Their uncompromising quality standards have made this book an exceptional effort. Their encouragement from time to time has been an inspiration for everyone.

The publisher and the editorial board hope that this book will prove to be a valuable piece of knowledge for researchers, students, practitioners and scholars across the globe.

List of Contributors

Tiko Iyamu
Department of Informatics, Tshwane University of Technology, South Africa

Graham Wright
Faculty of Health Sciences, Walter Sisulu University, South Africa

Lizette de Jager, Albertus A.K. Buitendag and Jacobus S. van der Walt
Department of Computer Science, Tshwane University of Technology, South Africa

Elmarie Papageorgiou
School of Accountancy, University of the Witwatersrand, South Africa

Herman de Bruyn
Department of Business Management, University of Johannesburg, South Africa

Eugene B. Visser
Purple Cow Communications, Cape Town, South Africa

Melius Weideman
Website Attributes Research Centre, Cape Peninsula University of Technology, South Africa

Luyanda Dube
Department of Information Science, University of South Africa, South Africa

Patrick Ngulube
Department of Interdisciplinary Research and Postgraduate Studies, University of South Africa, South Africa

Lionel Dawson and Jean-Paul Van Belle
Department of Information Systems, University of Cape Town, South Africa

Mark Tomlinson and Jackie Stewart
Department of Psychology, University of Stellenbosch, South Africa

Mary Jane Rotheram-Borus and Dallas Swendeman
Global Center for Children and Families, University of California, United States of America

Tanya Doherty and Petrida Ijumba
Systems Research Unit, Medical Research Council, South Africa

Alexander C. Tsai
Robert Wood Johnson Health and Society Scholars Program, Harvard University, United States of America
Center for Global Health, Massachusetts General Hospital, United States of America

Ingrid le Roux
Philani Nutrition and Development Project, Cape Town, South Africa

Debra Jackson
School of Public Health, University of the Western Cape, South Africa

Andi Friedman
Clyral, Durban, South Africa

Mark Colvin
Maromi Health Research, South Africa

Mickey Chopra
UNICEF, New York, United States of America

Tendani J. Lavhengwa and Jacobus S. van der Walt
Department of Informatics, Tshwane University of Technology, South Africa

Eve M. Lavhengwa
Audit Services, Department of Minerals Resources, South Africa

Avain Mannie and Chris M. Adendorff
Department of Business and Economics Science, Nelson Mandela Metropolitan University, Port Elizabeth, South Africa

Herman J. van Niekerk
Department of Business and Economics Science, Nelson Mandela Metropolitan University, Port Elizabeth, South Africa
Suritec, Cape Town, South Africa

Lameshnee Chetty and Martie Mearns
Centre for Information and Knowledge Management, University of Johannesburg, South Africa

Joel Arthur and Chris Rensleigh
Department of Information and Knowledge Management, University of Johannesburg, South Africa

Peter L. Mkhize
School of Computing, University of South Africa, South Africa

Kreeson Naicker and Karunagaran Naidoo
School of Management, Information Technology & Governance, University of KwaZulu-Natal, South Africa

Krishna K. Govender
School of Management, Information Technology & Governance, University of KwaZulu-Natal, South Africa
Regenesys Business School, Johannesburg, South Africa

Madeleine Fombad
Department of Information Science, University of South Africa, South Africa

René Pellissier and J-P. Kruger
Department of Business Management, University of South Africa, South Africa

Roxanne Piderit and Stephen Flowerday
Department of Information Systems, University of Fort Hare, South Africa

Rossouw von Solms
School of Information and Communication Technology, Nelson Mandela Metropolitan University, South Africa

Heinz E. Jacobs
Department of Civil Engineering, University of Stellenbosch, South Africa

Kerry A. Fair
GLS Software, TechnoPark, Stellenbosch, South Africa

Willie Chinyamurindi and Herring Shava
Department of Business Management, University of Fort Hare, South Africa

Denéle Esterhuizen and Corne Schutte
Department of Industrial Engineering, University of Stellenbosch, South Africa

Adeline du Toit
Centre for Information and Knowledge Management, University of Johannesburg, South Africa

Andrea Potgieter
Department of Information and Knowledge Management, University of Johannesburg, South Africa

Andrea Potgieter and Chris Rensleigh
Department of Information and Knowledge Management, University of Johannesburg, South Africa

Thami Dube
Centre for Information and Knowledge Management, University of Johannesburg, South Africa

Simla Maharaj and Irwin Brown
Department of Information Systems, University of Cape Town, South Africa

Godwin P. Dzvapatsva, Zoran Mitrovic and Anthony D. Dietrich
Department of Information Systems, University of the Western Cape, South Africa

Sunday O. Popoola
Department of Library, Archival and Information Studies, University of Ibadan, Nigeria

Olaronke O. Fagbola
Ibadan Study Centre Library, National Open University of Nigeria, Nigeria

Index

Printed in the USA
CPSIA information can be obtained
at www.ICGtesting.com
JSHW052024301024
72690JS00004B/153

9 781632 406156